THE HISTORY OF ENGLAND

VOLUME I

MACMILLAN AND CO., Limited
LONDON · BOMBAY · CALCUTTA
MELBOURNE

THE MACMILLAN COMPANY
NEW YORK · BOSTON · CHICAGO
DALLAS · SAN FRANCISCO

THE MACMILLAN CO. OF CANADA, Ltd.
TORONTO

Lord Macaulay

from a daguerreotype in the possession
of the Rt. Hon. Sir George Trevelyan O.M.

Emery Walker Ph.sc

THE HISTORY OF ENGLAND

FROM THE ACCESSION OF JAMES THE SECOND

BY

LORD MACAULAY

EDITED BY

CHARLES HARDING FIRTH, M.A.

REGIUS PROFESSOR OF MODERN HISTORY IN THE
UNIVERSITY OF OXFORD

IN SIX VOLUMES

Volume I

MACMILLAN AND CO., LIMITED
ST. MARTIN'S STREET, LONDON

1913

COPYRIGHT

PREFACE

It seems surprising that no illustrated edition of Macaulay's History of England has hitherto been issued. It is true that each of the six volumes of the Albany edition contains a portrait as its frontispiece, but no attempt has yet been made to supply a full pictorial accompaniment to Macaulay's narrative. A detailed account of a few eventful years naturally offers ample opportunities to the illustrator, and there are few authors who more constantly refer, either directly or indirectly, to engravings and pictures in order to elucidate their descriptions of persons and places.

A statement of the sources from which the illustrations have been derived and the principles upon which they have been selected will not be out of place. The first object was to obtain portraits of the actors in the drama. "In all my poor historical investigations," wrote Carlyle, "it has been, and always is, one of the most primary wants to procure a bodily likeness of the personage enquired after ; a good portrait, if such exists ; failing that, even an indifferent if sincere one. In short, *any* representation, made by a faithful human creature, of that face and figure, which he saw with his eyes, and which I can never see with mine, is now valuable to me."

These volumes therefore contain, side by side with the portraits of the kings and statesmen who played leading parts on the stage, representations of the minor characters who passed for a moment across it. In the case of important personages several portraits are usually given, in order to show them at different times in their career, or as they appeared to the eyes of different observers. Sometimes rude engravings have been included, either because they represent the popular conception of a great man, or because no other portrait could be procured. The historical rather than the artistic merits of an illustration have often determined the choice.

Of Macaulay himself four portraits are given. The earliest in date is that by John Partridge, presented by Viscount Knutsford to the National Portrait Gallery in 1910. It was probably a study for the figure of Macaulay in the " Meeting of the Royal Fine Arts Commission at Gwydyr House in the year 1846," which was also painted by Partridge. This too is in the National Portrait Gallery, but owing to its condition is no longer exhibited. Next in order of time is the sketch by Richard Doyle—a single figure taken from a caricature entitled " Unhappy Ghosts wandering on the banks of the Styx." It represents eight politicians who had failed to obtain seats at the general election of 1847, waiting for Charon's boat, and Macaulay is at the head of the file. This is number 891 in the collection of Political Sketches by H. B. Allowing for the exaggerations of a caricaturist the features of the profile in Doyle's sketch are very like those of the head in the bronze medallion of Macaulay, modelled by Marochetti in 1848, and purchased by the National Portrait Gallery in 1877. In the same year that institution also acquired a painting by Sir Francis Grant, which was presented to it by Sir William Stirling Maxwell. One cannot accept it as a good likeness, the features are lacking in character, and there is no strength in the face. It is the original study for a portrait painted for Speaker Denison about 1854.[1]

Besides these pictures there are several photographs. One by Claudet, said to have been taken about 1857, is engraved as the frontispiece to Macaulay's " Life and Letters." It is a half length representing Macaulay seated, with his hands crossed, leaning on a stick—a favourite attitude of his in conversation.

Another is reproduced as the frontispiece to this edition. It is a daguerrotype in the possession of Sir George Trevelyan, taken about 1855, and remarkable for its realistic truth and psychological interest.

---

[1] There are also (1) a portrait by S. W. Reynolds, painted and engraved in 1833; (2) a crayon portrait by G. Richmond, described in Macaulay's Diary under February 19, 1850, as one with which he was contented ; (3) a portrait by E. U. Eddis, painted about 1850; (4) a drawing by E. M. Ward, representing Macaulay in his study in the Albany ; (5) a posthumous portrait by James Archer in the possession of the Reform Club ; (6) a statue by Woolner in the ante-chapel of Trinity College.

LORD MACAULAY

From the painting by J. Partridge in the National Portrait Gallery

He was good enough to give me a copy, and to allow it to be reproduced here. " My desire is," writes Sir George, " that the world should see him as he was—dress, face, and gesture. It is by far the best portrait of the man, homely, shrewd, above all kindly—the uncle who gave me £20 in tips my last year at Harrow—and with a look of absolutely unconscious power and ability."

There is a bluff, honest look about the face, which is very attractive. Carlyle, as several acrid references in his Diary show, was not at first very friendly to Macaulay. " A squat, thickset, low-browed, short, little, grizzled man of fifty " he once termed him. But later he recognised the mingled homeliness and honesty of his character. " I said to myself, yon Macaulay's an honest fellow made out of oatmeal."

Thirty-eight of the coloured portraits of sovereigns and statesmen contained in this book, and over fifty of the portraits in black and white have been derived from the National Portrait Gallery. Macaulay was one of the thirteen original trustees appointed in December, 1856, when that institution was founded, though he was not able to attend more than one meeting of the Board. It is fitting that so many of the illustrations of his History should come from that source. The National Portrait Gallery of Scotland, the Glasgow Exhibition of 1911, the Hampton Court and Dulwich Galleries, the Bodleian Gallery and other public collections of pictures have supplied other illustrations. Many private owners also have been good enough to allow pictures in their possession to be reproduced, as the list at the conclusion of this introduction shows.

Lely, Kneller, Wissing, Dahl and other foreign portrait painters who worked in England are copiously represented, while English painters such as Riley, Mrs. Beale, Wright, and Richardson, have also contributed their share. There is one difficulty, however, which besets everyone who attempts to deal with English portraits, and it is not easy to overcome. There are many portraits whose authorship is far from certain : pictures are attributed by experts at one time to one artist and then to another. These new attributions are not always based on documentary evidence : often they depend on considerations of style and technique, which are largely matters of opinion rather than fact. It has seemed best, with this caution, to follow throughout the last editions of the catalogues of the public collections in which particular paintings are

LORD MACAULAY

From a caricature published by Richard Doyle in 1847

to be found, or to accept in the case of pictures in the possession of private persons the traditional attributions.

In the case of engraved portraits there is less room for doubt. Two of the artists who have supplied illustrations for these volumes, namely, David Logan and Robert White, frequently drew from the life the portraits which they subsequently engraved. Some of White's sketches have been preserved. One of these, a drawing in Indian ink, touched in red chalk, representing Simon Patrick, Bishop of Ely, is reproduced in colours in Volume IV. of this book. It is derived from the Sutherland Collection in the Bodleian Library.[1] Alexander Hendras Sutherland, who died in 1820, devoted himself to collecting illustrations for Clarendon's History of the Rebellion and Burnet's History of his Own Time, and in 1837 Mrs. Sutherland presented the collection to the Bodleian Library. The six volumes of the folio editions of the histories mentioned are inlaid and bound, forming sixty-one elephant folio volumes containing 19,224 portraits, views, and other illustrations. There are, for instance, 552 portraits of Charles II., 276 of James II., 175 of Mary, and 431 of William III. Of the 431 portraits of William III., no less than 363 are separate plates. But the collection is valuable not only from the number of the portraits, but for the excellence of many of the examples selected. It contains original drawings as well as engravings : for instance, the views of Glencoe and Killiecrankie reproduced in Chapters XIII. and XVIII. were both sketched by G. F. Robson for the purpose of illustrating Burnet's History, and there are water-colour sketches by Thomas Athow, G. Shepherd, S. Harding, and G. P. Harding, of many other places and of various portraits in private collections which did not happen to have been engraved when Mr. Sutherland was making his collection. The sketch of Maratti's portrait of the Earl of Sunderland, given in Chapter VII., and that of Sir Ralph Delaval, will serve as examples.

Another characteristic of the Sutherland Collection is the number of French, Dutch, German, and Italian engraved portraits and historical prints. The engravers of Amsterdam, to gratify the curiosity of their countrymen about public affairs, produced prints representing most of the political events which occurred in various parts of Europe as well

---

[1] A full account of the Sutherland Collection is given in Dr. W. D. Macray's Annals of the Bodleian, ed. 1890. p. 331.

as portraits of the politicians and soldiers whose names were familiar to the public.   One such series of prints, produced at Amsterdam under the title of "Engelants Schouwtoneel" or "Le Théatre d'Angleterre," has supplied representations of scenes such as the capture of Argyle,

LORD MACAULAY

From a bronze medallion by Baron Marochetti in the National Portrait Gallery

the Seven Bishops going to the Tower, and the Flight of James II. Schoonebeek's prints being destined for popular consumption are rather coarsely executed.   At Paris in the Cabinet des Estampes many French prints of a similar nature are preserved which are better specimens of engraving.   From this source are derived the pictures representing scenes

such as the Reception of James II. by Louis XIV., Louis XIV. in the
Trenches before Namur, and the signature of the Treaty of Ryswick.

One branch of the graphic arts which flourished more in Holland
than in any other country was the art of caricature.   It needed a free
soil for its growth.   The Dutch satirists of the latter part of the seventeenth century aimed their shafts against Louis XIV. and the Papacy
as the great enemies of political and religious freedom.   In this war
James II., as the ally of the King of France and the tool of the Jesuits,
was continually attacked.   Of these designs, many of which were
engraved by Romeyn de Hooghe, the British Museum possesses a
considerable number.   Generally they are allegorical in their nature,
full of obscure allusions and hidden meanings.   The Dutch caricaturist
did not seek to draw the likeness of a real person and make him
ridiculous by exaggerating his traits and his characteristics : he drew a
conventional figure with emblematic attributes representing the moral
and intellectual qualities of the person meant, and crowded as many of
these figures into his design as he could find room to insert.   Even
for contemporaries it was necessary to add a lengthy commentary
at the foot of the print in order to explain its meaning.   Hence in
reproducing these and other caricatures to illustrate the narrative of
Macaulay, it has seemed desirable for the benefit of modern readers to
add a reference to the catalogue of Satirical Prints in the British Museum.

The English caricatures of the period are simpler and ruder than
the Dutch.   Their meaning is generally unmistakeable.   Devices such
as the Scots holding the nose of Charles II. to a grindstone, or William
holding the Pope's nose to a grindstone, explain themselves.   Even the
more ambitious English caricatures have the same qualities of bluntness
and intelligibility.   Occasionally an English caricaturist borrowed something from a Dutch design or put English verses below a foreign print ;
but political caricature in England was in the main a coarse and vigorous
native growth.   Social caricature, which did not really begin till the
eighteenth century, was more influenced by foreign art, at all events at
first.

A more continuous commentary on the political events of the later
part of the seventeenth century is supplied by the medals produced in
England, France, and Holland.   Besides giving glorified likenesses of
the sovereigns in whose honour they were struck, they afford realistic

representations of minor personages. If Louis XIV. is made to look like a Greek god and William III. like a Roman emperor, Monck, Clarendon, Sancroft, and others are more truthfully and naturally drawn. Some scenes too, such as the burning of the catholic chapels in London and the perils of William III. in his voyage to Holland, are better represented in the clear-cut reliefs on medals than in contemporary engravings of the same incidents. Many of the medals are satirical. French medals exulting over the repeated defeats of William III. in Flanders represent him as a drum, with the motto, " Mon sort est d'être battu." A Dutch medal contrasts the figure of Louis XIV. "tyrannus debilis" with that of William III. "liberator florens." One medal often answers another. The French medal on the battle of Beachy Head shows in the distance the flying ships of England and Holland, while in the foreground Louis XIV. like Neptune drives his team of sea horses triumphantly over the waves ; beneath is the legend, " Illi imperium pelagi." The English medal on La Hogue has a background of burning ships; in front a figure with a trident, rising from the waters, knocks Louis XIV. from his car into the sea, with the words " Imperium pelagi nobis."

The Dutch satirical medals were, as every historian tells us, one of the grievances of Charles II. and Louis XIV. against the republic. They are collected and described in G. van Loon's " Histoire Métallique des Pays-Bas" and similar works. The Academy of Medals and Inscriptions founded by Louis XIV. published in 1702 a collection of " Médailles sur les principaux événements du règne de Louis le Grand," in which all his triumphs are depicted. Older English histories, such as the illustrated edition of Rapin and Walter Harris's Life of William III., contain many sheets of engraved coins and medals, but the most useful modern collection is the series of photographic reproductions entitled " Medallic Illustrations of the History of Great Britain and Ireland," published by the British Museum.

Maps and plans are another necessary supplement to a detailed history of any period. Wherever possible, the plans of places given in these pages are reproductions of contemporary engravings. Those of sieges and battles in Ireland are nearly all derived from George Story's " Impartial History of the Wars of Ireland, illustrated with sculptures describing the most important places of action," which was published in 1693. Others are added from Walter Harris's Life of William III.

published in 1749. The plan of Beachy Head is from a contemporary broadside, that of Sedgmoor from a drawing in the Pepys Collection. Sometimes a particular plan has been inserted because it is referred to by Macaulay in his notes; for instance, the plan of Belfast in 1685, and that of Covent Garden. Of the larger maps several have been specially made for this edition by Mr. Emery Walker: those of Argyle's expedition in 1685 and of Dundee's marches in 1689 are based on the maps given in Dr. C. Wilcock's Life of Argyle and Professor C. S. Terry's Life of Dundee.

The views of places and buildings which are given here come from a variety of sources. In Macaulay's description of the condition of England at the time when James II. ascended the throne he mentions more than once "the drawings of English Landscapes made for the Grand Duke Cosmo" as representing certain characteristics of English scenery and illustrating certain facts in the history of English agriculture. Cosmo III. visited England in 1669; his travels through England were published in 1821 and contain 39 views copied from sketches made at the time, four of which are reproduced in this edition, Wenzel Hollar's engravings represent London and its buildings about the middle of the 17th century and during the early part of the reign of Charles II., David Loggan's views of the colleges of Oxford and Cambridge were issued one in 1675 and the other in 1690. John Kip's bird's-eye views of various palaces and mansions belong to the period of Queen Anne or George I.; the first volume of his Britannia Illustrata appeared in 1707. The two brothers Samuel and Nathaniel Buck drew and engraved their "prospects" of cities, abbeys, and castles between 1711 and 1753; they were collected and republished in 1774 under the title of "Buck's Antiquities or Venerable Remains." Nor should Sutton Nicholls be omitted, who engraved between 1720 and 1730 a large number of views of buildings in London, including Southampton Square, the church of St. Mary le Bow, Newcastle House, and many others to which Macaulay makes special reference. Views of cities and castles in Scotland in William the Third's time are supplied by John Slezer's Theatrum Scotiae, which was published in 1693. Unluckily there is no similar collection of views of Ireland for the same period.

There remain to be mentioned three other classes of illustrations

which help to elucidate the text : broadsides, ballads, and autographs.
Of the broadsides some, such as the advertisement of the flying coach
from Oxford to London, or the description of the Prince of Orange's
entry into Exeter, are inserted because Macaulay specially mentions
them amongst the authorities in his footnotes.   Others, such as " Good
news for the Church of England " or " The Manner of Curing the
King's Evil," have been selected for reproduction because they support
or further develop the historian's arguments on some particular question.
They represent also a class of evidence, neglected by most historians, to
which Macaulay paid special attention.   Like the ballads they furnish
indications of public opinion and public feeling, which the newspapers,
few as yet and more easily controlled by the government, did not
so adequately express.   Macaulay was thoroughly familiar with the
ballads and political poems printed during the reigns of James II.
and William III.   He knew very well the collection of lampoons
and satires published under the title of " Poems on Affairs of State."
He had searched the Roxburghe Ballads and the Bagford Ballads—
since reprinted by the Ballad Society, but then only available in their
original broadside form in the British Museum.   Above all he had
carefully studied the great collection brought together by Mr. Pepys,
during the enforced leisure which he enjoyed after the Revolution had
removed him from the secretaryship of the Admiralty.   This collection
of ballads, now in the Pepys Library at Magdalene College, Cambridge,
is the least known of all the great collections, and was consulted
by Macaulay more than any of the others.   The majority of the
ballads employed to illustrate this edition of his History come from
that source, which the liberality of the Master and Fellows of
Magdalene College permitted me freely to utilise.   The rude verses in
which the poets of the streets mourned for Mary or for William,
rejoiced for the taking off of Chimney Money, celebrated the exploits
of popular highwaymen, or complained of high taxes and low wages,
had a special interest for Macaulay because he sought to realise the
character and ideas of the common people.   " A great part of their
history," he said, " is to be learnt only from ballads."

On the other hand the facsimiles of autograph letters here
reproduced supplement the portraits of the kings and statesmen
who appear in Macaulay's pages, and possibly the student of character

may find indications of it in their handwriting as well as in their faces. But it is necessary to remember that the letters are all reproduced on a smaller scale than the originals, and that the style is on the whole a more certain index to the man than the formation of the words. The documents reproduced are derived mainly from the British Museum, though a few come from the Record Office or the Bodleian Library. Some, such as the letters of Monmouth and Marlborough, illustrate mainly the character of the writer ; others, such as the order which forced Lord Torrington to fight the battle of Beachy Head, the page taken from the invitation to William III., and William III.'s intended speech when he thought of throwing up the government of England, illustrate a particular political crisis treated at length by Macaulay.

A few words in conclusion on the text of this edition of the History. Macaulay's work was published in three instalments. Volumes one and two, which contained ten chapters and ended with the offer of the crown to William and Mary on 13th February, 1689, were published in December, 1848. Volumes three and four, containing chapters eleven to twenty-two, and carrying the story down to the close of the war with France in 1697, were published in December, 1855. In 1857 Macaulay carefully revised these twenty-two chapters, adding some notes in which he admitted certain errors which had been pointed out, and defended certain statements which had been controverted. He also made some small verbal alterations and silently corrected a few inaccuracies. " I have no more corrections to make at present," he wrote to Mr. Longman in 1858. " I am inclined to hope that the book will be as nearly faultless, as to typographical execution, as any work of equal extent that is to be found in the world."

The third instalment of the History, consisting of chapters twenty-three to twenty-five, was not published till more than a year after Macaulay's death. As a consecutive narrative it ends with the prorogation of Parliament on April 11, 1700. Then follow two fragments. The larger one deals with the last three months of the year 1701, relates the death of James II., and breaks off in the middle of the general election which took place at the end of the year. The smaller fragment describes the illness and the death of William III., who died on March 8, 1702. This smaller fragment was deciphered by Lady Trevelyan from the rough sketch left by Macaulay; the rest of the three concluding chapters were fairly transcribed and revised for publication by the author himself. The fifth volume of the History appeared in March, 1861, under the editorship of Lady Trevelyan.

Macaulay's method of composing his History has been described in detail by Sir George Trevelyan. " As soon as he had got into his head all the information relating to any particular episode in his History he would sit down and write off the whole story at a headlong pace; sketching in the outlines under the general and audacious impulse of a first conception; and securing in black and white each idea, and epithet, and turn of phrase, as it flowed straight from his busy brain to his rapid fingers. His manuscript, at this stage, to the eyes of anyone but himself, appeared to consist of column after column of dashes and flourishes, in which a straight line, with a half-formed letter at each end, and another in the middle, did duty for a word. It was from amidst a chaos of such hieroglyphics that Lady Trevelyan, after her brother's death, deciphered that account of the last days of William which fitly closes the History. As soon as Macaulay had finished his rough draft he began to fill it in at the rate of six sides of foolscap every morning, written in so large a hand and with such a multitude of erasures, that the whole six pages were, on an average, compressed into two pages of print. This portion he called his task, and he was never quite easy unless he completed it daily."

A reduced facsimile of one of these foolscap pages, now in the possession of Sir George Trevelyan, is given by his kind permission on page 3 of this volume. It is part of a passage in the twenty-third chapter, where, in the course of a description of the Earl of Portland's embassy to Paris in 1698, Macaulay introduces a dialogue between Portland and his secretary Prior in order to illustrate the character of the two men. Another page of the manuscript of the History is preserved in the British Museum; it is a passage in the twenty-fifth chapter, where Macaulay mentions Sir Hans Sloane as " the founder of the magnificent Museum which is one of the glories of our country."

The notes to this edition of Macaulay's History include all those which he added when he revised the text of his work in 1857. It has not been thought desirable to add any new references or any comments.

Many years ago Mr. Gladstone, in a review of Sir George Trevelyan's Life of Macaulay, expressed the hope that the day would come when a critical edition of the History would be published, in which the author's statements would be examined and tested, his bias corrected, and his errors pointed out. There are errors it is certain ; during the last fifty years so much new material on the history of the period has been published, and so many new sources have become accessible, that there is room for a critical study of Macaulay's History, and some need for one. But an illustrated edition of a British classic is not the proper place for a critical commentary, and it has seemed best to reserve any critical observations for a separate publication. The task of illustrating the History necessitated a close scrutiny of Macaulay's pages, and while it made some defects and omissions more apparent, it has increased, not diminished, my admiration for what Macaulay succeeded in doing. Instead, therefore, of any general criticism, I have prefixed to the History this account of the sources from which the illustrations come, partly as an explanation of the principles adopted in their choice, partly in order to assist other students of the period who wish to pursue the subject further. It has not always proved possible to obtain the portraits or views required, and sometimes practical considerations of size and form prevented the inclusion of particular illustrations. In so large a piece of work, too, mistakes are inevitable, whatever trouble an editor may take to avoid them. For such mistakes I apologise before-hand to my critics, and it remains only to thank my helpers.

My thanks are specially due to the Librarian and Curators of the Bodleian for the large use they have permitted me to make of the Sutherland Collection and of the portraits under their control, and to Mr. Horace Hart for the care devoted to photographing portraits and engravings. I am very grateful to the Master and Fellows of Magdalene College, Cambridge, and in particular to Mr. Stephen Gaselee, their Librarian, for the liberality with which I have been allowed to consult and utilise the various collections of Mr. Pepys. Mr. C. J. Holmes, the Director of the National Portrait Gallery, and Mr. J. D. Milner have given me ungrudging assistance, and the reference collection under their charge has been of the greatest possible use. Two ladies, my secretary, Miss D. K. Broster, and Mrs. R. L. Poole, the compiler of the Catalogue of Oxford Portraits, have given me great help.

To Mr. Emery Walker my obligations are still greater. He has not only taken special care in the production of the illustrations, but has placed his extensive knowledge of portraits and topographical prints unreservedly at my service, besides giving me practical advice of the greatest value throughout the enterprise.

I desire also to thank the following persons for kindly granting permission to photograph portraits in their possession : His Grace the Duke of Bedford, K.G., for Rachel, Lady Russell ; His Grace the Duke of Buccleuch, for John, Duke of Marlborough ; the Earl of Crawford, for Colin, third Earl of Balcarres ; His Grace the Duke of Devonshire, for George Savile, Marquis of Halifax ; Viscount Dillon, for Queen Elizabeth ; the Earl of Sandwich, for the Duchess of Mazarin ; the Earl of Strathmore, for Viscount Dundee ; Mrs Alfred Waterhouse, for William Penn ; the Committee of the Scottish Exhibition at Glasgow, and the following owners of pictures there exhibited : His Grace the Duke of Atholl, for the first Duke of Atholl ; Macleod of Macleod, for the first Marquis of Atholl ; the Earl of Mar and Kellie, for the Earl of Angus ; Mrs. Nisbet Hamilton Ogilvy, for Lord Belhaven ; the Earl of Stair, for the first Earl of Stair ; the University of Glasgow, for John Arbuthnot ; Captain Murray Dunlop, for William Carstairs. For the photographs of historical pottery I am indebted to Dr. J. W. L. Glaisher.

Several publishers have kindly placed at my service plates which are their property—namely, Messrs. George Bell & Sons, Messrs. Archibald Constable & Co., Messrs. James MacLehose & Sons, and Mr. Martin Secker. While thanking them here collectively, my obligations to each individually are acknowledged in the list of illustrations.

C. H. FIRTH.

CONTENTS OF THE FIRST VOLUME

CHAPTER I

b

CHAPTER II

CONTENTS

CONTENTS

CHAPTER IV

CONTENTS

LIST OF ILLUSTRATIONS

LIST OF ILLUSTRATIONS

LIST OF ILLUSTRATIONS xxxiii

LIST OF ILLUSTRATIONS

FULL PAGE PLATES IN COLOUR

HISTORY OF ENGLAND

CHAPTER I

I PURPOSE to write the history of England from the accession of King James the Second down to a time which is within the memory of men still living. I shall recount the errors which, in a few months, alienated a loyal gentry and priesthood from the House of Stuart. I shall trace the course of that revolution which terminated the long struggle between our sovereigns and their parliaments, and bound up together the rights of the people and the title of the reigning dynasty. I shall relate how the new settlement was, during many troubled years, successfully defended against foreign and domestic enemies; how, under that settlement, the authority of law and the security of property were found to be compatible with a liberty of discussion and of individual action never before known; how, from the auspicious union of order and freedom, sprang a prosperity of which the annals of human affairs had furnished no example; how our country, from a state of ignominious vassalage, rapidly rose to the place of umpire among European powers; how her opulence and her martial glory grew together; how, by wise and resolute good faith, was gradually established a public credit fruitful of marvels which to the statesmen of any former age would have seemed incredible; how a gigantic commerce gave birth to a maritime power, compared with which every other maritime power, ancient or modern, sinks into insignificance; how Scotland, after ages of enmity, was at length united to England, not merely by legal bonds, but by indissoluble ties of interest and affection; how, in America, the British colonies rapidly became far mightier and wealthier than the realms which Cortes and Pizarro had added to the dominions of Charles the Fifth; how in Asia, British adventurers founded an empire not less splendid and more durable than that of Alexander.

Nor will it be less my duty faithfully to record disasters mingled with triumphs, and great national crimes and follies far more humiliating than any disaster. It will be seen that even what we justly account our chief blessings were not without alloy. It will be seen that the system which effectually secured our liberties against the encroachments of kingly power gave birth to a new class of abuses from which absolute monarchies are exempt. It will be seen that, in consequence partly of unwise interference, and partly of unwise neglect, the increase of wealth and the extension of trade produced, together with immense good, some evils from which poor and rude societies are free. It will be seen how, in two important dependencies of the crown, wrong was followed by just retribution; how imprudence and obstinacy broke the ties which bound the North American colonies to the parent state; how Ireland, cursed by the domination of race over race, and of religion over religion, remained indeed a member of the empire, but a withered and distorted member, adding no strength to the body politic, and reproachfully pointed at by all who feared or envied the greatness of England.

Yet, unless I greatly deceive myself, the general effect of this chequered narrative will be to excite thankfulness in all religious minds, and hope in the breasts of all patriots. For the history of our country during the last hundred and sixty years is eminently the history of physical, of moral, and of intellectual improvement. Those who compare the age on which their lot has fallen with a golden age which exists only in their imagination may talk of degeneracy and decay: but no man who is correctly informed as to the past will be disposed to take a morose or desponding view of the present.

I should very imperfectly execute the task which I have undertaken if I were merely to treat of battles and sieges, of the rise and fall of administrations, of intrigues in the palace, and of debates in the parliament. It will be my endeavour to relate the history of the people as well as the history of the government, to trace the progress of useful and ornamental arts, to describe the rise of religious sects and the changes of literary taste, to portray the manners of successive generations, and not to pass by with neglect even the revolutions which have taken place in dress, furniture, repasts, and public amusements. I shall cheerfully bear the reproach of having descended below the dignity of history, if I can succeed in placing before the English of the nineteenth century a true picture of the life of their ancestors.

The events which I propose to relate form only a single act of a great and eventful drama extending through ages, and must be very imperfectly understood unless the plot of the preceding acts be well known. I shall therefore introduce my narrative by a slight sketch of the history of our country from the earliest times. I shall pass very rapidly over many centuries: but I shall dwell at some length on the

...let, and, being himself a man of orthodox opinions and regular life, he was not disposed to give his confidence to one whom he supposed to be an evil jester. Prior, with much address, and perhaps with the help of a little hypocrisy, completely removed this unfavourable impression. He talked on serious subjects seriously, quoted the New Testament apposite[ly], vindicated Hammond from the charge of Popery, and, by way of a decisive blow, gave the definition of a true Church from the ~~Thirty~~ nineteenth Article. Portland stared at him. "I am glad, Mr Prior, to find you so good a Christian. I was afraid that you were an Atheist." "An Atheist, my good Lord!" cried Prior "What could lead your lordship to entertain such a suspicion?" ~~...~~ "Why," ~~said~~ Portland, "I knew that you were a poet; and I took it for granted that you did not believe in a God." "My Lord," said the wit, "you do us poets the greatest injustice. Of all people we are the farthest from Atheism. The Atheists do not even ~~believe~~ worship the true God; and we are always invoking and hymning false Gods whom everybody else...

vicissitudes of that contest which the administration of King James the Second brought to a decisive crisis.[1]

Nothing in the early existence of Britain indicated the greatness which she was destined to attain. Her inhabitants, when first they became known to the Tyrian mariners, were little superior to the natives of the Sandwich Islands. She was subjugated by the Roman arms; but she received only a faint tincture of Roman arts and letters. Of the western provinces which obeyed the Cæsars she was the last that was conquered, and the first that was flung away. No magnificent remains of Latian porches and aqueducts are to be found in Britain. No writer of British birth is reckoned among the masters of Latian poetry and eloquence. It is not probable that the islanders were at any time generally familiar with the tongue of their Italian rulers. From the Atlantic to the vicinity of the Rhine the Latin has, during many centuries, been predominant. It drove out the Celtic; it was not driven out by the Teutonic; and it is at this day the basis of the French, Spanish, and Portuguese languages. In our island the Latin appears never to have superseded the old Gaelic speech, and could not stand its ground against the German.

Britain under the Romans

The scanty and superficial civilisation which the Britons had derived from their southern masters was effaced by the calamities of the fifth century. In the continental kingdoms into which the Roman empire was then dissolved, the conquerors learned much from the conquered race. In Britain the conquered race became as barbarous as the conquerors.

All the chiefs who founded Teutonic dynasties in the continental provinces of the Roman empire, Alaric, Theodoric, Clovis, Alboin, were zealous Christians. The followers of Ida and Cerdic, on the other hand, brought to their settlements in Britain all the superstitions of the Elbe. While the German princes who reigned at Paris, Toledo, Arles, and Ravenna listened with reverence to the instructions of bishops, adored the relics of martyrs, and took part eagerly in disputes touching the Nicene theology, the rulers of Wessex and Mercia were still performing savage rites in the temples of Thor and Woden.

Britain under the Saxons

The continental kingdoms which had risen on the ruins of the Western Empire kept up some intercourse with those eastern provinces where the ancient civilisation, though slowly fading away under the influence of misgovernment, might still astonish and instruct barbarians,

---

[1] In this, and in the next chapter, I have very seldom thought it necessary to cite authorities: for, in these chapters, I have not detailed events minutely, or used recondite materials; and the facts which I mention are for the most part such that a person tolerably well read in English history, if not already apprised of them, will at least know where to look for evidence of them. In the subsequent chapters I shall carefully indicate the sources of my information.

where the court still exhibited the splendour of Diocletian and Constantine, where the public buildings were still adorned with the sculptures of Polycletus and the paintings of Apelles, and where laborious pedants, themselves destitute of taste, sense, and spirit, could still read and interpret the masterpieces of Sophocles, of Demosthenes, and of Plato. From this communion Britain was cut off. Her shores were, to the polished race which dwelt by the Bosporus, objects of a mysterious horror, such as that with which the Ionians of the age of Homer had regarded the Straits of Scylla and the city of the Læstrygonian cannibals. There was one province of our island in which, as Procopius had been told, the ground was covered with serpents, and the air was such that no man could inhale it and live. To this desolate region the spirits of the departed were ferried over from the land of the Franks at midnight. A strange race of fishermen performed the ghastly office. The speech of the dead was distinctly heard by the boatmen : their weight made the keel sink deep in the water ; but their forms were invisible to mortal eye. Such were the marvels which an able historian, the contemporary of Belisarius, of Simplicius, and of Tribonian, gravely related in the rich and polite Constantinople, touching the country in which the founder of Constantinople had assumed the imperial purple. Concerning all the other provinces of the Western Empire we have continuous information. It is only in Britain that an age of fable completely separates two ages of truth. Odoacer and Totila, Euric and Thrasimund, Clovis, Fredegunda, and Brunechild, are historical men and women. But Hengist and Horsa, Vortigern and Rowena, Arthur and Mordred are mythical persons, whose very existence may be questioned, and whose adventures must be classed with those of Hercules and Romulus.

At length the darkness begins to break ; and the country which had been lost to view as Britain reappears as England. The conversion of the Saxon colonists to Christianity was the first **Conversion** of a long series of salutary revolutions. It is true that the **of the** **Saxons to** Church had been deeply corrupted both by that superstition **Christianity** and by that philosophy against which she had long contended, and over which she had at last triumphed. She had given a too easy admission to doctrines borrowed from the ancient schools, and to rites borrowed from the ancient temples. Roman policy and Gothic ignorance, Grecian ingenuity and Syrian asceticism, had contributed to deprave her. Yet she retained enough of the sublime theology and benevolent morality of her earlier days to elevate many intellects, and to purify many hearts. Some things also which at a later period were justly regarded as among her chief blemishes were, in the seventh century, and long afterwards, among her chief merits. That the sacerdotal order should encroach on the functions of the civil magistrate would, in our time, be a great evil. But that which in an age of good government is an evil may, in an age of grossly bad government, be a blessing. It is better that mankind should be governed by wise laws well administered, and by an enlightened public opinion, than by priestcraft : but it is better that men should be governed by priestcraft than by brute violence, by such a prelate as Dunstan than by such a warrior as Penda. A society sunk in ignorance, and ruled by mere physical force, has great reason to rejoice when a class, of which the influence is intellectual and moral, rises to ascendency. Such a class will doubtless abuse its power : but mental power, even when abused, is still a nobler and better power than that which consists merely in corporeal strength. We read in our Saxon chronicles of tyrants, who, when at the height of greatness, were smitten with remorse, who abhorred the pleasures and dignities which they had purchased by guilt, who abdicated their crowns, and who sought to atone for their offences by cruel penances and incessant prayers. These stories have drawn forth bitter expressions of contempt from some writers who, while they boasted of liberality, were in truth as narrow-minded as any monk of the dark ages, and whose habit was to apply to all events in the history of the world the standard received in the Parisian society of the eighteenth century. Yet surely a system which, however deformed by superstition, introduced strong moral restraints into communities previously governed only by vigour of muscle and by audacity of spirit, a system which taught the fiercest and mightiest ruler that he was, like his meanest bondman, a responsible being, might have seemed to deserve a more respectful mention from philosophers and philanthropists.

The same observations will apply to the contempt with which, in the last century, it was fashionable to speak of the pilgrimages, the sanctuaries, the crusades, and the monastic institutions of the middle ages. In times when men were scarcely ever induced to travel by liberal curiosity, or by the pursuit of gain, it was better that the rude inhabitant of the North should visit Italy and the East as a pilgrim, than that he should never see anything but those squalid cabins and uncleared woods amidst which he was born. In times when life and when female honour were exposed to daily risk from tyrants and marauders, it was better that the precinct of a shrine should be regarded with an irrational awe, than that there should be no refuge inaccessible to cruelty and licentiousness. In times when statesmen were incapable of forming extensive political combinations, it was better that the Christian nations should be roused and united for the recovery of the Holy Sepulchre, than that they should, one by one, be overwhelmed by the Mahometan power. Whatever reproach may, at a later period, have been justly thrown on the indolence and luxury of religious orders, it was surely good that, in an age of ignorance and violence, there should be quiet cloisters and gardens, in which the arts of peace could be safely cultivated, in which gentle and contemplative natures could find an asylum, in which one brother could employ himself in transcribing the Æneid of Virgil, and another in meditating the Analytics of Aristotle, in which he who had a genius for art might illuminate a martyrology or carve a crucifix, and in which he who had a turn for natural philosophy might make experiments on the properties of plants and minerals. Had not such retreats been scattered here and there, among the huts of a miserable peasantry, and the castles of a ferocious aristocracy, European society would have consisted merely of beasts of burden and beasts of prey. The Church has many times been compared by divines to the ark of which we read in the Book of Genesis : but never was the resemblance more perfect than during that evil time when she alone rode, amidst darkness and tempest, on the deluge beneath which all the great works of ancient power and wisdom lay entombed, bearing within her that feeble germ from which a second and more glorious civilisation was to spring.

Even the spiritual supremacy arrogated by the Pope was, in the dark ages, productive of far more good than evil. Its effect was to unite the nations of Western Europe in one great commonwealth. What the Olympian chariot course and the Pythian oracle were to all the Greek cities, from Trebizond to Marseilles, Rome and her Bishop were to all Christians of the Latin communion, from Calabria to the Hebrides. Thus grew up sentiments of enlarged benevolence. Races separated from each other by seas and mountains acknowledged a fraternal tie and a common code of public law. Even in war, the cruelty of the conqueror was not seldom mitigated by the recollection that he and his vanquished enemies were all members of one great federation.

Into this federation our Saxon ancestors were now admitted. A regular communication was opened between our shores and that part of Europe in which the traces of ancient power and policy were yet discernible. Many noble monuments which have since been destroyed or defaced still retained their pristine magnificence ; and travellers, to whom Livy and Sallust were unintelligible, might gain from the Roman aqueducts and temples some faint notion of Roman history. The dome of Agrippa, still glittering with bronze, the mausoleum of Adrian, not yet deprived of its columns and statues, the Flavian amphitheatre, not yet degraded into a quarry, told to the rude English pilgrims some part of the story of that great civilised world which had passed away. The islanders returned, with awe deeply impressed on their half opened

minds, and told the wondering inhabitants of the hovels of London and
York that, near the grave of Saint Peter, a mighty race, now extinct,
had piled up buildings which would never be dissolved till the
judgment day.   Learning followed in the train of Christianity.   The
poetry and eloquence of the Augustan age was assiduously studied in
Mercian and Northumbrian monasteries.   The names of Bede and
Alcuin were justly celebrated throughout Europe.   Such was the state
of our country when, in the ninth century, began the last great migra-
tion of the northern barbarians.

During many years Denmark and Scandinavia continued to pour
forth innumerable pirates, distinguished by strength, by valour, by
Danish   merciless ferocity, and by hatred of the Christian name.   No
invasions   country suffered so much from these invaders as England.
Her coast lay near to the ports whence they sailed ; nor was any shire
so far distant from the sea as to be secure from attack.   The same
atrocities which had attended the victory of the Saxon over the Celt
were now, after the lapse of ages, suffered by the Saxon at the hand of
the Dane.   Civilisation, just as it began to rise, was met by this blow,
and sank down once more.   Large colonies of adventurers from the
Baltic established themselves on the eastern shores of our island, spread
gradually westward, and, supported by constant reinforcements from
beyond the sea, aspired to the dominion of the whole realm.   The
struggle between the two fierce Teutonic breeds lasted through six
generations.   Each was alternately paramount.   Cruel massacres followed by cruel retribution, provinces wasted, convents plundered, and
cities rased to the ground, make up the greater part of the history of
those evil days.   At length the North ceased to send forth a constant
stream of fresh depredators ; and from that time the mutual aversion
of the races began to subside.   Intermarriage became frequent.   The
Danes learned the religion of the Saxons ; and thus one cause of
deadly animosity was removed.   The Danish and Saxon tongues, both
dialects of one widespread language, were blended together.   But the
distinction between the two nations was by no means effaced, when an
event took place which prostrated both, in common slavery and
degradation, at the feet of a third people.

The Normans were then the foremost race of Christendom.   Their
valour and ferocity had made them conspicuous among the rovers
The   whom Scandinavia had sent forth to ravish Western Europe.
Normans   Their sails were long the terror of both coasts of the Channel.
Their arms were repeatedly carried far into the heart of the Carlo-
vingian empire, and were victorious under the walls of Maestricht and
Paris.   At length one of the feeble heirs of Charlemagne ceded to the
strangers a fertile province, watered by a noble river, and contiguous to

the sea which was their favourite element. In that province they founded a mighty state, which gradually extended its influence over the neighbouring principalities of Britanny and Maine. Without laying aside that dauntless valour which had been the terror of every land from the Elbe to the Pyrenees, the Normans rapidly acquired all, and more than all, the knowledge and refinement which they found in the country where they settled. Their courage secured their territory against foreign invasion. They established internal order, such as had long been unknown in the Frank empire. They embraced Christianity ; and with Christianity they learned a great part of what the clergy had to teach. They abandoned their native speech, and adopted the French tongue, in which the Latin was the predominant element. They speedily raised their new language to a dignity and importance which it had never before possessed. They found it a barbarous jargon ; they fixed it in writing ; and they employed it in legislation, in poetry, and in romance. They renounced that brutal intemperance to which all the other branches of the great German family were too much inclined. The polite luxury of the Norman presented a striking contrast to the coarse voracity and drunkenness of his Saxon and Danish neighbours. He loved to display his magnificence, not in huge piles of food and hogsheads of strong drink, but in large and stately edifices, rich armour, gallant horses, choice falcons, well ordered tournaments, banquets delicate rather than abundant, and wines remarkable rather for their exquisite flavour than for their intoxicating power. That chivalrous spirit, which has exercised so powerful an influence on the politics, morals, and manners of all the European nations, was found in the highest exaltation among the Norman nobles. Those nobles were distinguished by their graceful bearing and insinuating address. They were distinguished also by their skill in negotiation, and by a natural eloquence which they assiduously cultivated. It was the boast of one of their historians that the Norman gentlemen were orators from the cradle. But their chief fame was derived from their military exploits. Every country, from the Atlantic Ocean to the Dead Sea, witnessed the prodigies of their discipline and valour. One Norman knight, at the head of a handful of warriors, scattered the Celts of Connaught. Another founded the monarchy of the Two Sicilies, and saw the emperors both of the East and of the West fly before his arms. A third, the Ulysses of the first crusade, was invested by his fellow soldiers with the sovereignty of Antioch ; and a fourth, the Tancred whose name lives in the great poem of Tasso, was celebrated through Christendom as the bravest and most generous of the deliverers of the Holy Sepulchre.

The vicinity of so remarkable a people early began to produce an effect on the public mind of England. Before the Conquest, English princes received their education in Normandy. English sees and English estates were bestowed on Normans. The French of Normandy was familiarly spoken in the palace of Westminster. The court of Rouen seems to have been to the court of Edward the Confessor what the court of Versailles long afterwards was to the court of Charles the Second.

The battle of Hastings, and the events which followed it, not only placed a Duke of Normandy on the English throne, but gave up the **The Norman Conquest** whole population of England to the tyranny of the Norman race. The subjugation of a nation by a nation has seldom, even in Asia, been more complete. The country was portioned out among the captains of the invaders. Strong military institutions, closely connected with the institution of property, enabled the foreign conquerors to oppress the children of the soil. A cruel penal code, cruelly enforced, guarded the privileges, and even the sports, of the alien tyrants. Yet the subject race, though beaten down and trodden under foot, still made its sting felt. Some bold men, the favourite heroes of our oldest ballads, betook themselves to the woods, and there, in defiance of curfew laws and forest laws, waged a predatory war against their oppressors. Assassination was an event of daily occurrence. Many Normans suddenly disappeared leaving no trace. The corpses of many were found bearing the marks of violence. Death by torture was denounced against the murderers, and strict search was made for them, but generally in vain; for the whole nation was in a conspiracy to screen them. It was at length thought necessary to lay a heavy fine on every Hundred in which a person of French extraction should be found slain; and this regulation was followed up by another regulation, providing that every person who was found slain should be supposed to be a Frenchman, unless he were proved to be a Saxon.

During the century and a half which followed the Conquest, there is, to speak strictly, no English history. The French Kings of England rose, indeed, to an eminence which was the wonder and dread of all neighbouring nations. They conquered Ireland. They received the homage of Scotland. By their valour, by their policy, by their fortunate matrimonial alliances, they became far more powerful on the Continent than their liege lords the Kings of France. Asia, as well as Europe, was dazzled by the power and glory of our tyrants. Arabian chroniclers recorded with unwilling admiration the fall of Acre, the defence of Joppa, and the victorious march to Ascalon; and Arabian mothers long awed their infants to silence with the name of the lionhearted Plantagenet. At one time it seemed that the line of Hugh Capet was about to end as the Merovingian and Carlovingian lines had ended, and that a single great monarchy would spread from the Orkneys to the Pyrenees. So strong an association is established in most minds between the greatness of a sovereign and the greatness of the nation which he rules, that almost every historian of England has expatiated with a sentiment of exultation on the power and splendour of her foreign masters, and has lamented the decay of that power and splendour as a calamity to our country. This is, in truth, as absurd as it would be in a Haytian negro of our time to dwell with national pride on the greatness of Lewis the Fourteenth, and to speak of Blenheim and Ramilies with patriotic regret and shame. The Conqueror and his descendants to the fourth generation were not Englishmen : most of them were born in France : they spent the greater part of their lives in France : their ordinary speech was French : almost every high office in their gift was filled by a Frenchman : every acquisition which they made on the Continent estranged them more and more from the population of our island. One of the ablest among them indeed attempted to win the hearts of his English subjects by espousing an English princess. But, by many of his barons, this marriage was regarded as a marriage between a white planter and a quadroon girl would now be regarded in Virginia. In history he is known by the honourable surname of Beauclerc ; but, in his own time, his own countrymen called him by a Saxon nickname, in contemptuous allusion to his Saxon connection.

Had the Plantagenets, as at one time seemed likely, succeeded in uniting all France under their government, it is probable that England would never have had an independent existence. Her princes, her lords, her prelates, would have been men differing in race and language from the artisans and the tillers of the earth. The revenues of her great proprietors would have been spent in festivities and diversions on the banks of the Seine. The noble language of Milton and Burke would have remained a rustic dialect, without a literature, a fixed grammar, or a fixed orthography, and would have been contemptuously abandoned to the use of boors. No man of English extraction would have risen to eminence, except by becoming in speech and habits a Frenchman.

England owes her escape from such calamities to an event which her historians have generally represented as disastrous. Her interest was so directly opposed to the interest of her rulers that **Separation of England and Normandy** she had no hope but in their errors and misfortunes. The talents and even the virtues of her first six French Kings were a curse to her. The follies and vices of the seventh were her salvation. Had John inherited the great qualities of his father, of Henry Beauclerc, or of the Conqueror, nay, had he even possessed the martial courage of Stephen or of Richard, and had the King of France at the same time been as incapable as all the other successors of Hugh Capet had been, the House of Plantagenet must have risen to unrivalled ascendency in Europe. But, just at this conjuncture, France, for the first time since the death of Charlemagne, was governed by a prince of great firmness and ability. On the other hand England, which, since the battle of Hastings, had been ruled generally by wise statesmen, always by brave soldiers, fell under the dominion of a trifler and a coward. From that moment her prospects brightened. John was driven from Normandy. The Norman nobles were compelled to make their election between the island and the continent. Shut up by the sea with the people whom they had hitherto oppressed and despised, they gradually came to regard England as their country, and the English as their countrymen. The two races, so long hostile, soon found that they had common interests and common enemies. Both were alike aggrieved by the tyranny of a bad king. Both were alike indignant at the favour shown by the court to the natives of Poitou and Aquitaine. The greatgrandsons of those who had fought under William and the greatgrandsons of those who had fought under Harold began to draw near to each other in friendship ; and the first pledge of their reconciliation was the Great Charter, won by their united exertions, and framed for their common benefit.

Here commences the history of the English nation. The history of the preceding events is the history of wrongs inflicted and sustained by **Amalga-** various tribes, which indeed all dwelt on English ground, but **mation of** which regarded each other with aversion such as has scarcely **races** ever existed between communities separated by physical barriers. For even the mutual animosity of countries at war with each other is languid when compared with the animosity of nations which, morally separated, are yet locally intermingled. In no country has the enmity of race been carried farther than in England. In no country has that enmity been more completely effaced. The stages of the process by which the hostile elements were melted down into one homogeneous mass are not accurately known to us. But it is certain that, when John became King, the distinction between Saxons and Normans was strongly marked, and that before the end of the reign of his grandson it had almost disappeared. In the time of Richard the First, the ordinary imprecation of a Norman gentleman was " May I become an Englishman ! " His ordinary form of indignant denial was " Do you take me for an Englishman ? " The descendant of such a gentleman a hundred years later was proud of the English name.

The sources of the noblest rivers which spread fertility over continents, and bear richly laden fleets to the sea, are to be sought in wild and barren mountain tracts, incorrectly laid down in maps, and rarely explored by travellers. To such a tract the history of our country during the thirteenth century may not unaptly be compared. Sterile and obscure as is that portion of our annals, it is there that we must seek for the origin of our freedom, our prosperity, and our glory. Then it was that the great English people was formed, that the national character began to exhibit those peculiarities which it has ever since retained, and that our fathers became emphatically islanders, islanders not merely in geographical position, but in their politics, their feelings, and their manners. Then first appeared with distinctness that constitution which has ever since, through all changes, preserved its identity; that constitution of which all the other free constitutions in the world are copies, and which, in spite of some defects, deserves to be regarded as the best under which any great society has ever yet existed during many ages. Then it was that the House of Commons, the archetype of all the representative assemblies which now meet, either in the old or in the new world, held its first sittings. Then it was that the common law rose to the dignity of a science, and rapidly became a not unworthy rival of the imperial jurisprudence. Then it was that the courage of those sailors who manned the rude barks of the Cinque Ports first made the flag of England terrible on the seas. Then it was that the most ancient colleges which still exist at both the great national seats of learning were founded. Then was formed that language, less musical indeed than the languages of the south, but in force, in richness, in aptitude for all the highest purposes of the poet, the philosopher, and the orator, inferior to the tongue of Greece alone. Then too appeared the first faint dawn of that noble literature, the most splendid and the most durable of the many glories of England.

Early in the fourteenth century the amalgamation of the races was all but complete; and it was soon made manifest, by signs not to be mistaken, that a people inferior to none existing in the world had been formed by the mixture of three branches of the great Teutonic family with each other, and with the aboriginal Britons. There was, indeed, scarcely any thing in common between the England to which John had been chased by Philip Augustus, and the England from which the armies of Edward the Third went forth to conquer France.

A period of more than a hundred years followed, during which the chief object of the English was to establish, by force of arms, a great empire on the Continent. The claim of Edward to the inheri- **English** tance occupied by the House of Valois was a claim in which **conquests on the** it might seem that his subjects were little interested. But the **Continent** passion for conquest spread fast from the prince to the people. The war differed widely from the wars which the Plantagenets of the twelfth century had waged against the descendants of Hugh Capet. For the success of Henry the Second, or of Richard the First, would have made England a province of France. The effect of the successes of Edward the Third and Henry the Fifth was to make France, for a time, a province of England. The disdain with which, in the twelfth century, the conquerors from the Continent had regarded the islanders, was now retorted by the islanders on the people of the Continent. Every yeoman from Kent to Northumberland valued himself as one of a race born for victory and dominion, and looked down with scorn on the nation before which his ancestors had trembled. Even those knights of Gascony and Guienne who had fought gallantly under the Black Prince were regarded by the English as men of an inferior breed, and were contemptuously excluded from honourable and lucrative commands. In no long time our ancestors altogether lost sight of the original ground of quarrel. They began to consider the crown of France as a mere appendage to the crown of England ; and when, in violation of the ordinary law of succession, they transferred the crown of England to the House of Lancaster, they seem to have thought that the right of Richard the Second to the crown of France passed, as of course, to that house. The zeal and vigour which they displayed present a remarkable contrast to the torpor of the French, who were far more deeply interested in the event of the struggle. The most splendid victories recorded in the history of the middle ages were gained at this time, against great odds, by the English armies. Victories indeed they were of which a nation may justly be proud ; for they are to be attributed to the moral superiority of the victors, a superiority which was most striking in the lowest ranks. The knights of England found worthy rivals in the knights of France. Chandos encountered an equal foe in Du Guesclin. But France had no infantry that dared to face the English bows and bills. A French King was brought prisoner to London. An English King was crowned at Paris. The banner of Saint George was carried far beyond the Pyrenees and the Alps. On the south of the Ebro the English won a great battle, which for a time decided the fate of Leon and Castile ; and the English Companies obtained a terrible preeminence among the bands of warriors who let out their weapons for hire to the princes and commonwealths of Italy.

Nor were the arts of peace neglected by our fathers during that stirring period. While France was wasted by war, till she at length found in her own desolation a miserable defence against invaders, the English gathered in their harvests, adorned their cities, pleaded, traded, and studied in security. Many of our noblest architectural monuments belong to that age. Then rose the fair chapels of New College and of Saint George, the nave of Winchester and the choir of York, the spire of Salisbury and the majestic towers of Lincoln. A copious and forcible language, formed by an infusion of French into German, was now the

HENRY V

From the painting in the National Portrait Gallery. Artist unknown

common property of the aristocracy and of the people. Nor was it long before genius began to apply that admirable machine to worthy purposes. While English warriors, leaving behind them the devastated provinces of France, entered Valladolid in triumph, and spread terror to the gates of Florence, English poets depicted in vivid tints all the wide variety of human manners and fortunes, and English thinkers aspired to know, or dared to doubt, where bigots had been content to wonder and to believe. The same age which produced the Black Prince and Derby, Chandos and Hawkwood, produced also Geoffrey Chaucer and John Wycliffe.

In so splendid and imperial a manner did the English people, properly so called, first take place among the nations of the world. Yet while we contemplate with pleasure the high and commanding qualities which our forefathers displayed, we cannot but admit that the end which they pursued was an end condemned both by humanity and by enlightened policy, and that the reverses which compelled them, after a long and bloody struggle, to relinquish the hope of establishing a great continental empire, were really blessings in the guise of disasters. The spirit of the French was at last aroused : they began to oppose a vigorous national resistance to the foreign conquerors ; and from that time the skill of the English captains and the courage of the English soldiers were, happily for mankind, exerted in vain. After many desperate struggles, and with many bitter regrets, our ancestors gave up the contest. Since that age no British government has ever seriously and steadily pursued the design of making great conquests on the Continent. The people, indeed, continued to cherish with pride the recollection of Cressy, of Poitiers, and of Agincourt. Even after the lapse of many years it was easy to fire their blood and to draw forth their sub- sidies by promising them an expedition for the conquest of France. But happily the energies of our country have been directed to better objects ; and she now occupies in the history of mankind a place far more glorious than if she had, as at one time seemed not improbable, acquired by the sword an ascendency similar to that which formerly belonged to the Roman republic.

Cooped up once more within the limits of the island, the warlike people employed in civil strife those arms which had been the terror of **Wars of the Roses** Europe. The means of profuse expenditure had long been drawn by the English barons from the oppressed provinces of France. That source of supply was gone : but the ostentatious and luxurious habits which prosperity had engendered still remained ; and the great lords, unable to gratify their tastes by plundering the French, were eager to plunder each other. The realm to which they were now confined would not, in the phrase of Comines, the most judicious

HENRY VII

From the painting in the National Portrait Gallery. Artist unknown

observer of that time, suffice for them all.   Two aristocratical factions,
headed by two branches of the royal family, engaged in a long and
fierce struggle for supremacy.   As the animosity of those factions did
not really arise from the dispute about the succession, it lasted long
after all ground of dispute about the succession was removed.   The
party of the Red Rose survived the last prince who claimed the crown
in right of Henry the Fourth.   The party of the White Rose survived
the marriage of Richmond and Elizabeth.   Left without chiefs who
had any decent show of right, the adherents of Lancaster rallied round
a line of bastards, and the adherents of York set up a succession of
impostors.   When, at length, many aspiring nobles had perished on
the field of battle or by the hands of the executioner, when many
illustrious houses had disappeared for ever from history, when those
great families which remained had been exhausted and sobered by
calamities, it was universally acknowledged that the claims of all the
contending Plantagenets were united in the house of Tudor.

Meanwhile a change was proceeding infinitely more momentous
than the acquisition or loss of any province, than the rise or
fall of any dynasty.   Slavery and the evils by which slavery
is everywhere accompanied were fast disappearing.

**Extinc-
tion of
villenage**

It is remarkable that the two greatest and most salutary social
revolutions which have taken place in England, that revolution which,
in the thirteenth century, put an end to the tyranny of nation over
nation, and that revolution which, a few generations later, put an end
to the property of man in man, were silently and imperceptibly effected.
They struck contemporary observers with no surprise, and have received
from historians a very scanty measure of attention.   They were brought
about neither by legislative regulation nor by physical force.   Moral
causes noiselessly effaced first the distinction between Norman and
Saxon, and then the distinction between master and slave.   None can
venture to fix the precise moment at which either distinction ceased.
Some faint traces of the old Norman feeling might perhaps have been
found late in the fourteenth century.   Some faint traces of the institution of villenage were detected by the curious so late as the days of the
Stuarts ; nor has that institution ever, to this hour, been abolished by
statute.

It would be most unjust not to acknowledge that the chief agent
in these two great deliverances was religion ; and it may perhaps be
doubted whether a purer religion might not have been found
a less efficient agent.   The benevolent spirit of the Christian
morality is undoubtedly adverse to distinctions of caste.
But to the Church of Rome such distinctions are peculiarly
odious ; for they are incompatible with other distinctions which are

**Beneficial
operation of
the Roman
Catholic
religion**

ELIZABETH OF YORK

From the painting in the National Portrait Gallery. Artist unknown

essential to her system. She ascribes to every priest a mysterious dignity which entitles him to the reverence of every layman ; and she does not consider any man as disqualified, by reason of his nation or of his family, for the priesthood. Her doctrines respecting the sacerdotal character, however erroneous they may be, have repeatedly mitigated some of the worst evils which can afflict society. That superstition cannot be regarded as unmixedly noxious which, in regions cursed by the tyranny of race over race, creates an aristocracy altogether independent of race, inverts the relation between the oppressor and the oppressed, and compels the hereditary master to kneel before the spiritual tribunal of the hereditary bondman. To this day, in some countries where negro slavery exists, Popery appears in advantageous contrast to other forms of Christianity. It is notorious that the antipathy between the European and African races is by no means so strong at Rio Janeiro as at Washington. In our own country this peculiarity of the Roman Catholic system produced, during the middle ages, many salutary effects. It is true that, shortly after the battle of Hastings, Saxon prelates and abbots were violently deposed, and that ecclesiastical adventurers from the Continent were intruded by hundreds into lucrative benefices. Yet even then pious divines of Norman blood raised their voices against such a violation of the constitution of the Church, refused to accept mitres from the hands of William, and charged him, on the peril of his soul, not to forget that the vanquished islanders were his fellow Christians. The first protector whom the English found among the dominant caste was Archbishop Anselm. At a time when the English name was a reproach, and when all the civil and military dignities of the kingdom were supposed to belong exclusively to the countrymen of the Conqueror, the despised race learned, with transports of delight, that one of themselves, Nicholas Breakspear, had been elevated to the papal throne, and had held out his foot to be kissed by ambassadors sprung from the noblest houses of Normandy. It was a national as well as a religious feeling that drew great multitudes to the shrine of Becket, whom they regarded as the enemy of their enemies. Whether he was a Norman or a Saxon may be doubted : but there is no doubt that he perished by Norman hands, and that the Saxons cherished his memory with peculiar tenderness and veneration, and, in their popular poetry, represented him as one of their own race. A successor of Becket was foremost among the refractory magnates who obtained that charter which secured the privileges both of the Norman barons and of the Saxon yeomanry. How great a part the Roman Catholic ecclesiastics subsequently had in the abolition of villenage we learn from the unexceptional testimony of Sir Thomas Smith, one of the ablest Protestant counsellors of Elizabeth.

When the dying slaveholder asked for the last sacraments, his spiritual attendants regularly adjured him, as he loved his soul, to emancipate his brethren for whom Christ had died.   So successfully had the Church used her formidable machinery that, before the Reformation came, she had enfranchised almost all the bondmen in the kingdom except her own, who, to do her justice, seem to have been very tenderly treated.

There can be no doubt that, when these two great revolutions had been effected, our forefathers were by far the best governed people in Europe.   During three hundred years the social system had been in a constant course of improvement.   Under the first Plantagenets there had been barons able to bid defiance to the sovereign, and peasants degraded to the level of the swine and oxen which they tended.   The exorbitant power of the baron had been gradually reduced.   The condition of the peasant had been gradually elevated.   Between the aristocracy and the working people had sprung up a middle class, agricultural and commercial.   There was still, it may be, more inequality than is favourable to the happiness and virtue of our species: but no man was altogether above the restraints of law ; and no man was altogether below its protection.

That the political institutions of England were, at this early period, regarded by the English with pride and affection, and by the most enlightened men of neighbouring nations with admiration and envy, is proved by the clearest evidence.   But touching the nature of those institutions there has been much dishonest and acrimonious controversy.

The historical literature of England has indeed suffered grievously from a circumstance which has not a little contributed to her prosperity. The change, great as it is, which her polity has undergone during the last six centuries, has been the effect of gradual development, not of demolition and reconstruction.   The present constitution of our country is, to the constitution under which she flourished five hundred years ago, what the tree is to the sapling, what the man is to the boy.   The alteration has been great.   Yet there never was a moment at which the chief part of what existed was not old.   A polity thus formed must abound in anomalies. But for the evils arising from mere anomalies we have ample compensation.   Other societies possess written constitutions more symmetrical. But no other society has yet succeeded in uniting revolution with prescription, progress with stability, the energy of youth with the majesty of immemorial antiquity.

This great blessing, however, has its drawbacks : and one of those drawbacks is that every source of information as to our early history

The early English polity often misrepresented

has been poisoned by party spirit. As there is no country where statesmen have been so much under the influence of the past, so there is no country where historians have been so much under the influence of the present. Between these two things, indeed, there is a natural connection. Where history is regarded merely as a picture of life and manners, or as a collection of experiments from which general maxims of civil wisdom may be drawn, a writer lies under no very pressing temptation to misrepresent transactions of ancient date. But where history is regarded as a repository of titledeeds, on which the rights of governments and nations depend, the motive to falsification becomes almost irresistible. A Frenchman is not now impelled by any strong interest either to exaggerate or to underrate the power of the Kings of the house of Valois. The privileges of the States General, of the States of Britanny, of the States of Burgundy, are to him matters of as little practical importance as the constitution of the Jewish Sanhedrim or of the Amphictyonic Council. The gulph of a great revolution completely separates the new from the old system. No such chasm divides the existence of the English nation into two distinct parts. Our laws and customs have never been lost in general and irreparable ruin. With us the precedents of the middle ages are still valid precedents, and are still cited, on the gravest occasions, by the most eminent statesmen. For example, when King George the Third was attacked by the malady which made him incapable of performing his regal functions, and when the most distinguished lawyers and politicians differed widely as to the course which ought, in such circumstances, to be pursued, the Houses of Parliament would not proceed to discuss any plan of regency till all the precedents which were to be found in our annals, from the earliest times, had been collected and arranged. Committees were appointed to examine the ancient records of the realm. The first case reported was that of the year 1217 : much importance was attached to the cases of 1326, of 1377, and of 1422 : but the case which was justly considered as most in point was that of 1455. Thus in our country the dearest interests of parties have frequently been staked on the results of the researches of antiquaries. The inevitable consequence was that our antiquaries conducted their researches in the spirit of partisans.

It is therefore not surprising that those who have written concerning the limits of prerogative and liberty in the old polity of England should generally have shown the temper, not of judges, but of angry and uncandid advocates. For they were discussing, not a speculative matter, but a matter which had a direct and practical connection with the most momentous and exciting disputes of their own day. From the commencement of the long contest between the Parliament and the Stuarts down to the time when the pretensions of the Stuarts ceased to be formidable, few questions were practically more important than the question whether the administration of that family had or had not been in accordance with the ancient constitution of the kingdom. This question could be decided only by reference to the records of preceding reigns. Bracton and Fleta, the Mirror of Justice and the Rolls of Parliament, were ransacked to find pretexts for the excesses of the Star Chamber on one side, and of the High Court of Justice on the other. During a long course of years every Whig historian was anxious to prove that the old English government was all but republican, every Tory historian to prove that it was all but despotic.

With such feelings, both parties looked into the chronicles of the middle ages. Both readily found what they sought ; and both obsti-nately refused to see anything but what they sought. The champions of the Stuarts could easily point out instances of oppression exercised on the subject. The defenders of the Roundheads could as easily produce instances of determined and successful resistance offered to the Crown. The Tories quoted, from ancient writings, expressions almost as servile as were heard from the pulpit of Mainwaring. The Whigs discovered expressions as bold and severe as any that resounded from the judg-ment seat of Bradshaw. One set of writers adduced numerous instances in which Kings had extorted money without the authority of Parlia-ment. Another set cited cases in which the Parliament had assumed to itself the power of inflicting punishment on Kings. Those who saw only one half of the evidence would have concluded that the Planta-genets were as absolute as the Sultans of Turkey : those who saw only the other half would have concluded that the Plantagenets had as little real power as the Doges of Venice ; and both conclusions would have been equally remote from the truth.

The old English government was one of a class of limited monarchies which sprang up in Western Europe during the middle ages, and which, notwithstanding many diversities, bore to **Nature of** one another a strong family likeness. That there should **the limited** **monarchies** have been such a likeness is not strange. The countries in **of the** which those monarchies arose had been provinces of the same **middle ages** great civilised empire, and had been overrun and conquered, about the same time, by tribes of the same rude and warlike nation. They were members of the same great coalition against Islam. They were in com-munion with the same superb and ambitious Church. Their polity naturally took the same form. They had institutions derived partly from imperial Rome, partly from papal Rome, partly from the old Germany. All had Kings ; and in all the kingly office became by degrees strictly hereditary. All had nobles bearing titles which had originally indicated military rank. The dignity of knighthood, the rules of heraldry, were common to all. All had richly endowed ecclesiastical establishments, municipal corporations enjoying large franchises, and senates whose consent was necessary to the validity of some public acts.

Of these kindred constitutions the English was, from an early period, justly reputed the best. The prerogatives of the sovereign were **Prerogatives of the early English Kings** undoubtedly extensive. The spirit of religion and the spirit of chivalry concurred to exalt his dignity. The sacred oil had been poured on his head. It was no disparagement to the bravest and noblest knights to kneel at his feet. His person was inviolable. He alone was entitled to convoke the Estates of the realm : he could at his pleasure dismiss them ; and his assent was necessary to all their legislative acts. He was the chief of the executive administration, the sole organ of communication with foreign powers, the captain of the military and naval forces of the state, the fountain of justice, of mercy, and of honour. He had large powers for the regulation of trade. It was by him that money was coined, that weights and measures were fixed, that marts and havens were appointed. His ecclesiastical patronage was immense. His hereditary revenues, economically administered, sufficed to meet the ordinary charges of government. His own domains were of vast extent. He was also feudal lord paramount of the whole soil of his kingdom, and, in that capacity, possessed many lucrative and many formidable rights, which enabled him to annoy and depress those who thwarted him, and to enrich and aggrandise, without any cost to himself, those who enjoyed his favour.

But his power, though ample, was limited by three great constitutional principles, so ancient that none can say when they **Limitations of the prerogative** began to exist, so potent that their natural development, continued through many generations, has produced the order of things under which we now live.

First, the King could not legislate without the consent of his Parliament. Secondly, he could impose no tax without the consent of his Parliament. Thirdly, he was bound to conduct the executive administration according to the laws of the land, and, if he broke those laws, his advisers and his agents were responsible.

No candid Tory will deny that these principles had, five hundred years ago, acquired the authority of fundamental rules. On the other hand, no candid Whig will affirm that they were, till a later period, cleared from all ambiguity, or followed out to all their consequences. A constitution of the middle ages was not, like a constitution of the eighteenth or nineteenth century, created entire by a single act, and fully set forth in a single document. It is only in a refined and speculative age that a polity is constructed on system. In rude societies the progress of government resembles the progress of language and of versification. Rude societies have language, and often copious and energetic language : but they have no scientific grammar, no definitions of nouns and verbs, no names for declensions, moods, tenses, and voices. Rude societies have versification, and often versification of great power and sweetness : but they have no metrical canons ; and the minstrel whose numbers, regulated solely by his ear, are the delight of his audience, would himself be unable to say of how many dactyls and trochees each of his lines consists. As eloquence exists before syntax, and song before prosody, so government may exist in a high degree of excellence long before the limits of legislative, executive, and judicial power have been traced with precision.

It was thus in our country. The line which bounded the royal prerogative, though in general sufficiently clear, had not everywhere been drawn with accuracy and distinctness. There was, therefore, near the border some debatable ground on which incursions and reprisals continued to take place, till, after ages of strife, plain and durable landmarks were at length set up. It may be instructive to note in what way, and to what extent, our ancient sovereigns were in the habit of violating the three great principles by which the liberties of the nation were protected.

No English King has ever laid claim to the general legislative power. The most violent and imperious Plantagenet never fancied himself competent to enact, without the consent of his great council, that a jury should consist of ten persons instead of twelve, that a widow's dower should be a fourth part instead of a third, that perjury should be a felony, or that the custom of gavelkind should be introduced into Yorkshire.[1] But the King had the power of pardoning offenders ; and there is one point at which the power of pardoning and the power of legislating seem to fade into each other, and may easily, at least in a simple age, be confounded. A penal statute is virtually annulled if the penalties which it imposes are regularly remitted as often as they are incurred. The sovereign was undoubtedly competent to remit penalties without limit. He was therefore competent to annul virtually a penal statute. It might seem that there could be no serious objection to his doing formally what he might do virtually. Thus, with the help of subtle and courtly lawyers, grew up, on the doubtful frontier which separates executive from legislative functions, that great anomaly known as the dispensing power.

That the King could not impose taxes without the consent of Parliament is admitted to have been, from time immemorial, a fundamental law of England. It was among the articles which John was compelled

[1] This is excellently put by Mr. Hallam in the first chapter of his Constitutional History.

by the Barons to sign. Edward the First ventured to break through the rule : but, able, powerful, and popular as he was, he encountered an opposition to which he found it expedient to yield. He covenanted accordingly in express terms, for himself and his heirs, that they would never again levy any aid without the assent and goodwill of the Estates of the realm. His powerful and victorious grandson attempted to violate this solemn compact : but the attempt was strenuously withstood. At length the Plantagenets gave up the point in despair : but, though they ceased to infringe the law openly, they occasionally contrived, by evading it, to procure an extraordinary supply for a temporary purpose. They were interdicted from taxing ; but they claimed the right of begging and borrowing. They therefore sometimes begged in a tone not easily to be distinguished from that of command, and sometimes borrowed with small thought of repaying. But the fact that they thought it necessary to disguise their exactions under the names of benevolences and loans sufficiently proves that the authority of the great constitutional rule was universally recognised.

The principle that the King of England was bound to conduct the administration according to law, and that, if he did anything against law, his advisers and agents were answerable, was established at a very early period, as the severe judgments pronounced and executed on many royal favourites sufficiently prove. It is, however, certain that the rights of individuals were often violated by the Plantagenets, and that the injured parties were often unable to obtain redress. According to law no Englishman could be arrested or detained in confinement merely by the mandate of the sovereign. In fact, persons obnoxious to the government were frequently imprisoned without any other authority than a royal order. According to law, torture, the disgrace of the Roman jurisprudence, could not, in any circumstances, be inflicted on an English subject. Nevertheless, during the troubles of the fifteenth century, a rack was introduced into the Tower, and was occasionally used under the plea of political necessity. But it would be a great error to infer from such irregularities that the English monarchs were, either in theory or in practice, absolute. We live in a highly civilised society, through which intelligence is so rapidly diffused by means of the press and of the post office that any gross act of oppression committed in any part of our island is, in a few hours, discussed by millions. If the sovereign were now to immure a subject in defiance of the writ of Habeas Corpus, or to put a conspirator to the torture, the whole nation would be instantly electrified by the news. In the middle ages the state of society was widely different. Rarely and with great difficulty did the wrongs of individuals come to the knowledge of the public. A man might be illegally confined during many months in the castle of Carlisle or Norwich ; and no whisper of the transaction might reach London. It is highly probable that the rack had been many years in use before the great majority of the nation had the least suspicion that it was ever employed. Nor were our ancestors by any means so much alive as we are to the importance of maintaining great general rules. We have been taught by long experience that we cannot without danger suffer any breach of the constitution to pass unnoticed. It is therefore now universally held that a government which unnecessarily exceeds its powers ought to be visited with severe parliamentary censure, and that a government which, under the pressure of a great exigency, and with pure intentions, has exceeded its powers, ought without delay to apply to Parliament for an act of indemnity. But such were not the feelings of the Englishmen of the fourteenth and fifteenth centuries. They were little disposed to contend for a principle merely as a principle, or to cry out against an irregularity which was not also felt to be a grievance. As long as the general spirit of the administration was mild and popular, they were willing to allow some latitude to their sovereign. If, for ends generally acknowledged to be good, he exerted a vigour beyond the law, they not only forgave, but applauded him, and, while they enjoyed security and prosperity under his rule, were but too ready to believe that whoever had incurred his displeasure had deserved it. But to this indulgence there was a limit ; nor was that King wise who presumed far on the forbearance of the English people. They might sometimes allow him to overstep the constitutional line : but they also claimed the privilege of overstepping that line themselves, whenever his encroachments were so serious as to excite alarm. If, not content with occasionally oppressing individuals, he dared to oppress great masses, his subjects promptly appealed to the laws, and, that appeal failing, appealed as promptly to the God of battles.

Our forefathers might indeed safely tolerate a king in a few excesses ; for they had in reserve a check which soon brought the fiercest and proudest king to reason, the check of physical force. It is difficult for an Englishman of the nineteenth century to imagine to himself the facility and rapidity with which, four hundred years ago, this check was applied. The people have long unlearned the use of arms. The art of war has been carried to a perfection unknown to former ages ; and the knowledge of that art is confined to a particular class. A hundred thousand soldiers, well disciplined and commanded, will keep down ten millions of ploughmen and artisans. A few regiments of household troops are sufficient to overawe all the discontented spirits of a large capital. In the meantime the effect of the constant progress of wealth has been to make insurrection far more terrible to thinking men than maladministration.

Resistance an ordinary check on tyranny in the middle ages

Immense sums have been expended on works which, if a rebellion broke out, might perish in a few hours. The mass of movable wealth collected in the shops and warehouses of London alone exceeds five-hundredfold that which the whole island contained in the days of the Plantagenets ; and, if the government were subverted by physical force, all this movable wealth would be exposed to imminent risk of spolia-tion and destruction. Still greater would be the risk to public credit, on which thousands of families directly depend for subsistence, and with which the credit of the whole commercial world is inseparably connected. It is no exaggeration to say that a civil war of a week on English ground would now produce disasters which would be felt from the Hoangho to the Missouri, and of which the traces would be discernible at the distance of a century. In such a state of society resistance must be regarded as a cure more desperate than almost any malady which can afflict the state. In the middle ages, on the contrary, resistance was an ordinary remedy for political distempers, a remedy which was always at hand, and which, though doubtless sharp at the moment, produced no deep or lasting ill effects. If a popular chief raised his standard in a popular cause, an irregular army could be assembled in a day. Regular army there was none. Every man had a slight tincture of soldiership, and scarcely any man more than a slight tincture. The national wealth consisted chiefly in flocks and herds, in the harvest of the year, and in the simple buildings inhabited by the people. All the furniture, the stock of shops, the machinery which could be found in the realm was of less value than the property which some single parishes now contain. Manufactures were rude ; credit was almost unknown. Society, therefore, recovered from the shock as soon as the actual conflict was over. The calamities of civil war were confined to the slaughter on the field of battle, and to a few subsequent executions and confiscations. In a week the peasant was driving his team and the esquire flying his hawks over the field of Towton or of Bosworth, as if no extraordinary event had interrupted the regular course of human life.

More than a hundred and sixty years have now elapsed since the English people have by force subverted a government. During the hundred and sixty years which preceded the union of the Roses, nine Kings reigned in England. Six of these nine Kings were deposed. Five lost their lives as well as their crowns. It is evident, therefore, that any comparison between our ancient and our modern polity must lead to most erroneous conclusions, unless large allowance be made for the effect of that restraint which resistance and the fear of resistance constantly imposed on the Plantagenets. As our ancestors had against tyranny a most important security which we want, they might safely

HENRY VI

From the painting in the National Portrait Gallery. Artist unknown

dispense with some securities to which we justly attach the highest importance. As we cannot, without the risk of evils from which the imagination recoils, employ physical force as a check on misgovernment, it is evidently our wisdom to keep all the constitutional checks on misgovernment in the highest state of efficiency, to watch with jealousy the first beginnings of encroachment, and never to suffer irregularities, even when harmless in themselves, to pass unchallenged, lest they acquire the force of precedents. Four hundred years ago such minute vigilance might well seem unnecessary. A nation of hardy archers and spearmen might, with small risk to its liberties, connive at some illegal acts on the part of a prince whose general administration was good, and whose throne was not defended by a single company of regular soldiers.

Under this system, rude as it may appear when compared with those elaborate constitutions of which the last seventy years have been fruitful, the English long enjoyed a large measure of freedom and happiness. Though, during the feeble reign of Henry the Sixth, the state was torn, first by factions, and at length by civil war; though Edward the Fourth was a prince of dissolute and imperious character; though Richard the Third has generally been represented as a monster of depravity; though the exactions of Henry the Seventh caused great repining; it is certain that our ancestors, under those Kings, were far better governed than the Belgians under Philip, surnamed the Good, or the French under that Lewis who was styled the Father of his people. Even while the wars of the Roses were actually raging, our country appears to have been in a happier condition than the neighbouring realms during years of profound peace. Comines was one of the most enlightened statesmen of his time. He had seen all the richest and most highly civilised parts of the Continent. He had lived in the opulent towns of Flanders, the Manchesters and Liverpools of the fifteenth century. He had visited Florence, recently adorned by the magnificence of Lorenzo, and Venice, not yet humbled by the confederates of Cambray. This eminent man deliberately pronounced England to be the best governed country of which he had any knowledge. Her constitution he emphatically designated as a just and holy thing, which, while it protected the people, really strengthened the hands of a prince who respected it. In no other country, he said, were men so effectually secured from wrong. The calamities produced by our intestine wars seemed to him to be confined to the nobles and the fighting men, and to leave no traces such as he had been accustomed to see elsewhere, no ruined dwellings, no depopulated cities.

It was not only by the efficiency of the restraints imposed on the royal prerogative that England was advantageously distinguished

EDWARD IV

From the painting in the possession of the Society of Antiquaries.   Artist unknown

from most of the neighbouring countries.   A peculiarity equally important, though less noticed, was the relation in which the nobility stood

here to the commonalty.   There was a strong hereditary
aristocracy: but it was of all hereditary aristocracies the
least insolent and exclusive.   It had none of the invidious
character of a caste.   It was constantly receiving members
from the people, and constantly sending down members to mingle with
the people.   Any gentleman might become a peer.   The younger son
of a peer was but a gentleman.   Grandsons of peers yielded precedence
to newly made knights.   The dignity of knighthood was not beyond
the reach of any man who could by diligence and thrift realise a good
estate, or who could attract notice by his valour in a battle or a siege.
It was regarded as no disparagement for the daughter of a Duke, nay
of a royal Duke, to espouse a distinguished commoner.   Thus, Sir John
Howard married the daughter of Thomas Mowbray Duke of Norfolk.
Sir Richard Pole married the Countess of Salisbury, daughter of George
Duke of Clarence.   Good blood was indeed held in high respect : but
between good blood and the privileges of peerage there was, most
fortunately for our country no necessary connection.   Pedigrees as long,
and scutcheons as old, were to be found out of the House of Lords as
in it.   There were new men who bore the highest titles.   There were
untitled men well known to be descended from knights who had broken
the Saxon ranks at Hastings, and scaled the walls of Jerusalem.   There
were Bohuns, Mowbrays, De Veres, nay, kinsmen of the House of Plantagenet, with no higher addition than that of Esquire, and with no civil
privileges beyond those enjoyed by every farmer and shopkeeper.   There
was therefore here no line like that which in some other countries divided
the patrician from the plebeian.   The yeoman was not inclined to murmur
at dignities to which his own children might rise.   The grandee was not
inclined to insult a class into which his own children must descend.

After the wars of York and Lancaster, the links which connected
the nobility and the commonalty became closer and more numerous
than ever.   The extent of the destruction which had fallen on the old
aristocracy may be inferred from a single circumstance.   In the year
1451 Henry the Sixth summoned fifty-three temporal Lords to parliament.   The temporal Lords summoned by Henry the Seventh to the
parliament of 1485 were only twenty-nine, and of these several had
recently been elevated to the peerage.   During the following century the
ranks of the nobility were largely recruited from among the gentry.
The constitution of the House of Commons tended greatly to promote
the salutary intermixture of classes.   The knight of the shire was the
connecting link between the baron and the shopkeeper.   On the same
benches on which sate the goldsmiths, drapers, and grocers, who had

RICHARD III

From the painting in the National Portrait Gallery. Artist unknown

been returned to parliament by the commercial towns, sate also members who, in any other country, would have been called noblemen, hereditary lords of manors, entitled to hold courts and to bear coat armour, and able to trace back an honourable descent through many generations. Some of them were younger sons and brothers of lords. Others could boast of even royal blood. At length the eldest son of an Earl of Bedford, called in courtesy by the second title of his father, offered himself as candidate for a seat in the House of Commons, and his example was followed by others. Seated in that house, the heirs of the great peers naturally became as zealous for its privileges as any of the humble burgesses with whom they were mingled. Thus our democracy was, from an early period, the most aristocratic, and our aristocracy the most democratic in the world ; a peculiarity which has lasted down to the present day, and which has produced many important moral and political effects.

The government of Henry the Seventh, of his son, and of his grandchildren was, on the whole, more arbitrary than that of the Plantagenets. Personal character may in some degree explain the difference ; for courage and force of will were common to all the men and women of the House of Tudor. They exercised their power during a period of a hundred and twenty years, always with vigour, often with violence, sometimes with cruelty. They, in imitation of the dynasty which had preceded them, occasionally invaded the rights of the subject, occasionally exacted taxes under the name of loans and gifts, and occasionally dispensed with penal statutes : nay, though they never presumed to enact any permanent law by their own authority, they occasionally took upon themselves, when Parliament was not sitting, to meet temporary exigencies by temporary edicts. It was, however, impossible for the Tudors to carry oppression beyond a certain point : for they had no armed force, and they were surrounded by an armed people. Their palace was guarded by a few domestics, whom the array of a single shire, or of a single ward of London, could with ease have overpowered. These haughty princes were therefore under a restraint stronger than any which mere law can impose, under a restraint which did not, indeed, prevent them from sometimes treating an individual in an arbitrary and even in a barbarous manner, but which effectually secured the nation against general and long continued oppression. They might safely be tyrants within the precinct of the court : but it was necessary for them to watch with constant anxiety the temper of the country. Henry the Eighth, for example, encountered no opposition when he wished to send Buckingham and Surrey, Anne Boleyn and Lady Salisbury, to the scaffold. But when, without the consent of Parliament, he demanded of his subjects a contribution

Government of the Tudors

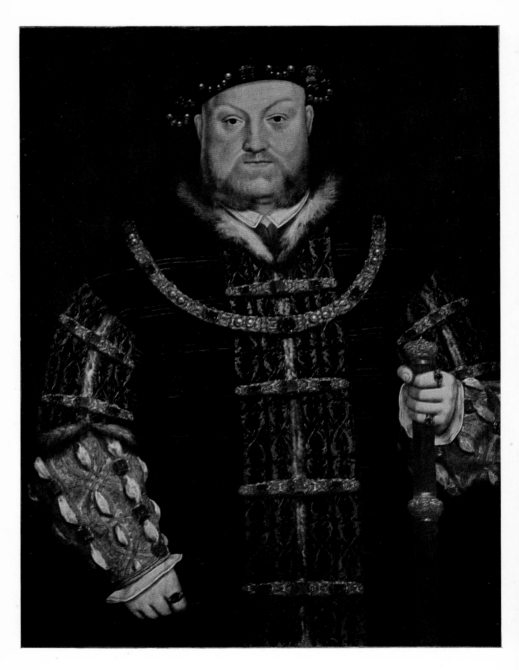

HENRY VIII., 1491-1547.

From the painting attributed to Luke Hornebolt, in the National Portrait Gallery.

amounting to one sixth of their goods, he soon found it necessary to retract. The cry of hundreds of thousands was that they were English and not French, freemen and not slaves. In Kent the royal commissioners fled for their lives. In Suffolk four thousand men appeared in arms. The King's lieutenants in that county vainly exerted themselves to raise an army. Those who did not join in the insurrection declared that they would not fight against their brethren in such a quarrel. Henry, proud and selfwilled as he was, shrank, not without reason, from a conflict with the roused spirit of the nation. He had before his eyes the fate of his predecessors who had perished at Berkeley and Pomfret. He not only cancelled his illegal commissions ; he not only granted a general pardon to all the malecontents ; but he publicly and solemnly apologised for his infraction of the laws.

His conduct, on this occasion, well illustrates the whole policy of his house. The temper of the princes of that line was hot, and their spirit high : but they understood the character of the nation which they governed, and never once, like some of their predecessors, and some of their successors, carried obstinacy to a fatal point. The discretion of the Tudors was such, that their power, though it was often resisted, was never subverted. The reign of every one of them was disturbed by formidable discontents : but the government was always able either to sooth the mutineers, or to conquer and punish them. Sometimes, by timely concessions, it succeeded in averting civil hostilities ; but in general it stood firm, and called for help on the nation. The nation obeyed the call, rallied round the sovereign, and enabled him to quell the disaffected minority.

Thus, from the age of Henry the Third to the age of Elizabeth, England grew and flourished under a polity which contained the germ of our present institutions, and which, though not very exactly defined, or very exactly observed, was yet effectually prevented from degenerating into despotism, by the awe in which the governors stood of the spirit and strength of the governed.

But such a polity is suited only to a particular stage in the progress of society. The same causes which produce a division of labour in the peaceful arts must at length make war a distinct science and a distinct trade. A time arrives when the use of arms begins to occupy the entire attention of a separate class. It soon appears that peasants and burghers, however brave, are unable to stand their ground against veteran soldiers, whose whole life is a preparation for the day of battle, whose nerves have been braced by long familiarity with danger, and whose movements have all the precision of clockwork. It is found that the defence of nations can no longer be safely entrusted to warriors taken from the plough or the loom for a campaign of forty days. If any state forms a great regular army, the bordering states must imitate the example, or must submit to a foreign yoke. But, where a great regular army exists, limited monarchy, such as it was in the middle ages, can exist no longer. The sovereign is at once emancipated from what had been the chief restraint on his power ; and he inevitably becomes absolute, unless he is subjected to checks such as would be superfluous in a society where all are soldiers occasionally, and none permanently.

With the danger came also the means of escape. In the monarchies of the middle ages the power of the sword belonged to the prince ; but the power of the purse belonged to the nation ; and the progress of civilisation, as it made the sword of the prince more and more formidable to the nation, made the purse of the nation more and more necessary to the prince. His hereditary revenues would no longer suffice, even for the expenses of civil government. It was utterly impossible that, without a regular and extensive system of taxation, he could keep in constant efficiency a great body of disciplined troops. The policy which the parliamentary assemblies of Europe ought to have adopted was to take their stand firmly on their constitutional right to give or withhold money, and resolutely to refuse funds for the support of armies, till ample securities had been provided against despotism.

Limited monarchies of the middle ages generally turned into absolute monarchies

This wise policy was followed in our country alone. In the neighbouring kingdoms great military establishments were formed ; no new safeguards for public liberty were devised ; and the consequence was, that the old parliamentary institutions everywhere ceased to exist. In France, where they had always been feeble, they languished, and at length died of mere weakness. In Spain, where they had been as strong as in any part of Europe, they struggled fiercely for life, but struggled too late. The mechanics of Toledo and Valladolid vainly defended the privileges of the Castilian Cortes against the veteran battalions of Charles the Fifth. As vainly, in the next generation, did the citizens of Saragossa stand up against Philip the Second, for the old constitution of Aragon. One after another, the great national councils of the continental monarchies, councils once scarcely less proud and powerful than those which sate at Westminster, sank into utter insignificance. If they met, they met merely as our Convocation now meets, to go through some venerable forms.

In England events took a different course. This singular felicity she owed chiefly to her insular situation. Before the end of the fifteenth century great military establishments were indispensable to the dignity, and even to the safety, of the French and Castilian monarchies. If either of those two powers had disarmed, it would soon have been compelled to submit to the dictation

The English monarchy a singular exception

of the other. But England, protected by the sea against invasion, and rarely engaged in warlike operations on the Continent, was not, as yet, under the necessity of employing regular troops. The sixteenth century, the seventeenth century, found her still without a standing army. At the commencement of the seventeenth century political science had made considerable progress. The fate of the Spanish Cortes and of the French States General had given solemn warning to our Parliaments ; and our Parliaments, fully aware of the nature and magnitude of the danger, adopted, in good time, a system of tactics which, after a contest protracted through three generations, was at length successful.

Almost every writer who has treated of that contest has been desirous to show that his own party was the party which was struggling to preserve the old constitution unaltered. The truth however is that the old constitution could not be preserved unaltered. A law, beyond the control of human wisdom, had decreed that there should no longer be governments of that peculiar class which, in the fourteenth and fifteenth centuries, had been common throughout Europe. The question, therefore, was not whether our polity should undergo a change, but what the nature of the change should be. The introduction of a new and mighty force had disturbed the old equilibrium, and had turned one limited monarchy after another into an absolute monarchy. What had happened elsewhere would assuredly have happened here, unless the balance had been redressed by a great transfer of power from the crown to the parliament. Our princes were about to have at their command means of coercion such as no Plantagenet or Tudor had ever possessed. They must inevitably have become despots, unless they had been, at the same time, placed under restraints to which no Plantagenet or Tudor had ever been subject.

It seems certain, therefore, that, had none but political causes been at work, the seventeenth century would not have passed away without a fierce conflict between our Kings and their Parliaments. But other causes of perhaps greater potency contributed to produce the same effect. While the government of the Tudors **The Reformation and its effects** was in its highest vigour an event took place which has coloured the destinies of all Christian nations, and in an especial manner the destinies of England. Twice during the middle ages the mind of Europe had risen up against the domination of Rome. The first insurrection broke out in the south of France. The energy of Innocent the Third, the zeal of the young orders of Francis and Dominic, and the ferocity of the Crusaders whom the priesthood let loose on an unwarlike population, crushed the Albigensian churches. The second reformation had its origin in England, and spread to Bohemia. The Council of Constance, by removing some ecclesiastical disorders which had given scandal to

Christendom, and the princes of Europe, by unsparingly using fire and sword against the heretics, succeeded in arresting and turning back the movement. Nor is this much to be lamented. The sympathies of a Protestant, it is true, will naturally be on the side of the Albigensians and of the Lollards. Yet an enlightened and temperate Protestant will perhaps be disposed to doubt whether the success, either of the Albigensians or of the Lollards, would, on the whole, have promoted the happiness and virtue of mankind. Corrupt as the Church of Rome was, there is reason to believe that, if that Church had been overthrown in the twelfth or even in the fourteenth century, the vacant space would have been occupied by some system more corrupt still. There was then, through the greater part of Europe, very little knowledge ; and that little was confined to the clergy. Not one man in five hundred could have spelled his way through a psalm. Books were few and costly. The art of printing was unknown. Copies of the Bible, inferior in beauty and clearness to those which every cottager may now command, sold for prices which many priests could not afford to give. It was obviously impossible that the laity should search the Scriptures for themselves. It is probable therefore, that, as soon as they had put off one spiritual yoke, they would have put on another, and that the power lately exercised by the clergy of the Church of Rome would have passed to a far worse class of teachers. The sixteenth century was comparatively a time of light. Yet even in the sixteenth century a considerable number of those who quitted the old religion followed the first confident and plausible guide who offered himself, and were soon led into errors far more serious than those which they had renounced. Thus Matthias and Kniperdoling, apostles of lust, robbery, and murder, were able for a time to rule great cities. In a darker age such false prophets might have founded empires ; and Christianity might have been distorted into a cruel and licentious superstition, more noxious, not only than Popery, but even than Islamism.

About a hundred years after the rising of the Council of Constance, that great change emphatically called the Reformation began. The fulness of time was now come. The clergy were no longer the sole or the chief depositories of knowledge. The invention of printing had furnished the assailants of the Church with a mighty weapon which had been wanting to their predecessors. The study of the ancient writers, the rapid development of the powers of the modern languages, the unprecedented activity which was displayed in every department of literature, the political state of Europe, the vices of the Roman court, the exactions of the Roman chancery, the jealousy with which the wealth and privileges of the clergy were naturally regarded by laymen, the jealousy with which the Italian ascendency was naturally regarded by men born on our side of the Alps, all these things gave to the teachers of the new theology an advantage which they perfectly understood how to use.

Those who hold that the influence of the Church of Rome in the dark ages was, on the whole, beneficial to mankind may yet with perfect consistency regard the Reformation as an inestimable blessing. The

THE PRESENTATION OF THE BIBLE TO HENRY VIII

From an illustration to Foxe's Acts and Monuments

leading strings, which preserve and uphold the infant, would impede the fullgrown man. And so the very means by which the human mind is, in one stage of its progress, supported and propelled, may, in another stage, be mere hindrances. There is a season in the life both of an individual and of a society, at which submission and faith, such as at a later period would be justly called servility and credulity, are useful qualities. The child who teachably and undoubtingly listens to the instructions of his elders is likely to improve rapidly. But the man who should receive with childlike docility every assertion and dogma uttered by another man no wiser than himself would become contemptible. It is the same with communities. The childhood of the European nations was passed under the tutelage of the clergy. The ascendency of the sacerdotal order was long the ascendency which naturally and properly belongs to intellectual superiority. The priests, with all their faults, were by far the wisest portion of society. It was, therefore, on the whole, good that they should be respected and obeyed. The encroachments of the ecclesiastical power on the province of the civil power produced much more happiness than misery, while the ecclesiastical power was in the hands of the only class that had studied history, philosophy, and public law, and while the civil power was in the hands of savage chiefs, who could not read their own grants and edicts. But a change took place. Knowledge gradually spread among laymen. At the commencement of the sixteenth century many of them were in every intellectual attainment fully equal to the most enlightened of their spiritual pastors. Thenceforward that dominion, which, during the dark ages, had been, in spite of many abuses, a legitimate and salutary guardianship, became an unjust and noxious tyranny.

From the time when the barbarians overran the Western Empire to the time of the revival of letters, the influence of the Church of Rome had been generally favourable to science, to civilisation, and to good government. But, during the last three centuries, to stunt the growth of the human mind has been her chief object. Throughout Christendom, whatever advance has been made in knowledge, in freedom, in wealth, and in the arts of life, has been made in spite of her, and has everywhere been in inverse proportion to her power. The loveliest and most fertile provinces of Europe have, under her rule, been sunk in poverty, in political servitude, and in intellectual torpor, while Protestant countries, once proverbial for sterility and barbarism, have been turned by skill and industry into gardens, and can boast of a long list of heroes and statesmen, philosophers and poets. Whoever, knowing what Italy and Scotland naturally are, and what, four hundred years ago, they actually were, shall now compare the country round Rome with the country round Edinburgh, will be able to form some judgment as to the tendency of Papal domination. The descent of Spain, once the first among monarchies, to the lowest depths of degradation, the elevation of Holland, in spite of many natural disadvantages, to a position such as no commonwealth so small has ever reached, teach the same lesson. Whoever passes in Germany from a Roman Catholic to a Protestant principality, in Switzerland from a Roman Catholic to a Protestant canton, in Ireland from a Roman Catholic to a Protestant county, finds that he has passed from a lower to a higher grade of civilisation. On the other side of the Atlantic the same law prevails. The Protestants of the United States have left far behind them the Roman Catholics of Mexico, Peru, and Brazil. The Roman Catholics of Lower Canada remain inert, while the whole continent round them is in a ferment with Protestant activity and enterprise. The French have doubtless shown an energy and an intelligence which, even when misdirected, have justly entitled them to be called a great people. But this apparent exception, when examined, will be found to confirm the rule ; for in no country that is called Roman Catholic has the Roman Catholic Church, during several generations, possessed so little authority as in France. The literature of France is justly held in high esteem throughout the world. But if we deduct from that literature all that belongs to four parties which have been, on different grounds, in rebellion against the Papal domination, all that belongs to the Protestants, all that belongs to the assertors of the Gallican liberties, all that belongs to the Jansenists, and all that belongs to the philosophers, how much will be left ?

It is difficult to say whether England owes more to the Roman Catholic religion or to the Reformation. For the amalgamation of races and for the abolition of villenage, she is chiefly indebted to the influence which the priesthood in the middle ages exercised over the laity. For political and intellectual freedom, and for all the blessings which political and intellectual freedom have brought in their train, she is chiefly indebted to the great rebellion of the laity against the priesthood.

The struggle between the old and the new theology in our country was long, and the event sometimes seemed doubtful. There were two extreme parties, prepared to act with violence or to suffer with stubborn resolution. Between them lay, during a considerable time, a middle party, which blended, very illogically, but by no means unnaturally, lessons learned in the nursery with the sermons of the modern evangelists, and, while clinging with fondness to old observances, yet detested abuses with which those observances were closely connected. Men in such a frame of mind were willing to obey, almost with thankfulness, the dictation of an able ruler who spared them the trouble of judging for themselves, and, raising a firm and commanding voice above the uproar of controversy, told them how to worship and what to believe. It is not strange, therefore, that the Tudors should have been able to exercise a great influence on ecclesiastical affairs ; nor is it strange that their influence should, for the most part, have been exercised with a view to their own interest.

Henry the Eighth attempted to constitute an Anglican Church differing from the Roman Catholic Church on the point of the supremacy, and on that point alone. His success in this attempt was extraordinary. The force of his character, the singularly favourable situation in which he stood with respect to foreign powers, the immense wealth which the spoliation of the abbeys placed at his disposal, and the support of that class which still halted between two opinions, enabled him to bid defiance to both the extreme parties, to burn as heretics those who avowed the tenets of the Reformers, and to hang as traitors those who owned the authority of the Pope. But Henry's system died with him. Had his life been prolonged, he would have found it difficult to maintain a position assailed with equal fury by all who were zealous either for the new or for the old opinions. The ministers who held the royal prerogatives in trust for his infant son could not venture to persist in so hazardous a policy ; nor could Elizabeth venture to return to it. It was necessary to make a choice. The government must either submit to Rome, or must obtain the aid of the Protestants. The government and the Protestants had only one thing in common, hatred of the Papal power. The English Reformers were eager to go as far as their brethren on the Continent. They unanimously condemned as Antichristian numerous dogmas and practices to which Henry had stubbornly adhered, and which Elizabeth reluctantly abandoned. Many felt a strong repugnance even to things indifferent which had formed part of the polity or ritual of the mystical Babylon. Thus Bishop Hooper, who died manfully at Gloucester for his religion, long refused to wear the episcopal vestments. Bishop Ridley, a martyr of still greater renown, pulled down the ancient altars of his diocese, and ordered the Eucharist to be administered in the middle of churches, at tables which the Papists irreverently termed oyster boards. Bishop Jewel pronounced the clerical garb to be a stage dress, a fool's coat, a relique of the Amorites, and promised that he would spare no labour to extirpate such degrading absurdities. Archbishop Grindal long hesitated about accepting a mitre from dislike of what he regarded as the mummery of consecration. Bishop Parkhurst uttered a fervent prayer that the Church of England would propose to herself the Church of Zurich as the absolute pattern of a Christian community. Bishop Ponet was of opinion that the word Bishop should be abandoned to the Papists, and that the chief officers of the purified church should be called Superintendents. When it is considered that none of these prelates belonged to the extreme section of the Protestant party, it cannot be doubted that, if the general sense of that party had been followed, the work of reform would have been carried on as unsparingly in England as in Scotland.

EDWARD VI

From the painting in the National Portrait Gallery. School of Holbein

But, as the government needed the support of the Protestants, so
the Protestants needed the protection of the government.
Much was therefore given up on both sides : an union was
effected ; and the fruit of that union was the Church of
England.

To the peculiarities of this great institution, and to the strong
passions which it has called forth in the minds both of friends and of
enemies, are to be attributed many of the most important events which
have, since the Reformation, taken place in our country ; nor can the
secular history of England be at all understood by us, unless we study
it in constant connection with the history of her ecclesiastical polity.

The man who took the chief part in settling the conditions of the
alliance which produced the Anglican Church was Archbishop Cranmer.
He was the representative of both the parties which, at that time, needed
each other's assistance.   He was at once a divine and a courtier.   In
his character of divine he was perfectly ready to go as far in the way of
change as any Swiss or Scottish Reformer.   In his character of courtier
he was desirous to preserve that organisation which had, during many
ages, admirably served the purposes of the Bishops of Rome, and might
be expected now to serve equally well the purposes of the English Kings
and of their ministers.   His temper and his understanding eminently
fitted him to act as mediator.   Saintly in his professions, unscrupulous
in his dealings, zealous for nothing, bold in speculation, a coward and a
timeserver in action, a placable enemy and a lukewarm friend, he was
in every way qualified to arrange the terms of the coalition between the
religious and the worldly enemies of Popery.

To this day the constitution, the doctrines, and the services of the
Church, retain the visible marks of the compromise from which she
sprang.   She occupies a middle position between the Churches
of Rome and Geneva.   Her doctrinal confessions and discourses, composed by Protestants, set forth principles of theology in
which Calvin or Knox would have found scarcely a word to disapprove.
Her prayers and thanksgivings, derived from the ancient Breviaries, are
very generally such that Cardinal Fisher or Cardinal Pole might have
heartily joined in them.   A controversialist who puts an Arminian sense
on her Articles and Homilies will be pronounced by candid men to be
as unreasonable as a controversialist who denies that the doctrine of
baptismal regeneration can be discovered in her Liturgy.

The Church of Rome held that episcopacy was of divine institution,
and that certain supernatural graces of a high order had been transmitted
by the imposition of hands through fifty generations, from the Eleven
who received their commission on the Galilean mount, to the bishops
who met at Trent.   A large body of Protestants, on the other hand,

ARCHBISHOP CRANMER

From the painting by G. Fliccius in the National Portrait Gallery regarded prelacy as positively unlawful, and persuaded themselves that they found a very different form of ecclesiastical government prescribed in Scripture. The founders of the Anglican Church took a middle course. They retained episcopacy; but they did not declare it to be an institution essential to the welfare of a Christian society, or to the efficacy of the sacraments. Cranmer, indeed, on one important occasion, plainly avowed his conviction that, in the primitive times, there was no distinction between bishops and priests, and that the laying on of hands was altogether superfluous.

Among the Presbyterians, the conduct of public worship is, to a great extent, left to the minister. Their prayers, therefore, are not exactly the same in any two assemblies on the same day, or on any two days in the same assembly. In one parish they are fervent, eloquent, and full of meaning. In the next parish they may be languid or absurd. The priests of the Roman Catholic Church, on the other hand, have, during many generations, daily chaunted the same ancient confessions, supplications, and thanksgivings, in India and Lithuania, in Ireland and Peru. The service, being in a dead language, is intelligible only to the learned; and the great majority of the congregation may be said to assist as spectators rather than as auditors. Here, again, the Church of England took a middle course. She copied the Roman Catholic forms of prayer, but translated them into the vulgar tongue, and invited the illiterate multitude to join its voice to that of the minister.

In every part of her system the same policy may be traced. Utterly rejecting the doctrine of transubstantiation, and condemning as idolatrous all adoration paid to the sacramental bread and wine, she yet, to the disgust of the Puritan, required her children to receive the memorials of divine love, meekly kneeling upon their knees. Discarding many rich vestments which surrounded the altars of the ancient faith, she yet retained, to the horror of weak minds, a robe of white linen, typical of the purity which belonged to her as the mystical spouse of Christ. Discarding a crowd of pantomimic gestures which, in the Roman Catholic worship, are substituted for intelligible words, she yet shocked many rigid Protestants by marking the infant just sprinkled from the font with the sign of the cross. The Roman Catholic addressed his prayers to a multitude of Saints, among whom were numbered many men of doubtful, and some of hateful, character. The Puritan refused the addition of Saint even to the apostle of the Gentiles, and to the disciple whom Jesus loved. The Church of England, though she asked for the intercession of no created being, still set apart days for the commemoration of some who had done and suffered great things for the faith. She retained confirmation and ordination as edifying rites; but she degraded them from the rank of sacraments. Shrift was no part of her system. Yet she gently invited the dying penitent to confess his sins to a divine, and empowered her ministers to sooth the departing soul by an absolution which breathes the very spirit of the old religion. In general it may be said that she appeals more to the understanding, and less to the senses and the imagination, than the Church of Rome, and that she appeals less to the understanding, and more to the senses and imagination, than the Protestant Churches of Scotland, France, and Switzerland.

Nothing, however, so strongly distinguished the Church of England from other Churches as the relation in which she stood to the monarchy. The King was her head. The limits of the authority which he possessed, as such, were not traced, and indeed have never yet been traced, with precision. The laws which declared him supreme in ecclesiastical matters were drawn rudely and in general terms. If, for the purpose of ascertaining the sense of those laws, we examine the books and lives of those who founded the English Church, our perplexity will be increased. For the founders of the English Church wrote and acted in an age of violent intellectual fermentation, and of constant action and reaction. They therefore often contradicted each other, and sometimes contradicted themselves. That the King was, under Christ, sole head of the Church, was a doctrine which they all with one voice affirmed: but those words had very different significations in different mouths, and in the same mouth at different conjunctures. Sometimes an authority which would have satisfied Hildebrand was ascribed to the sovereign : then it dwindled down to an authority little more than that which had been claimed by many ancient English princes who had been in constant communion with the Church of Rome. What Henry and his favourite counsellors meant, at one time, by the supremacy, was certainly nothing less than the whole power of the keys. The King was to be the Pope of his kingdom, the vicar of God, the expositor of Catholic verity, the channel of sacramental graces. He arrogated to himself the right of deciding dogmatically what was ortho-dox doctrine and what was heresy, of drawing up and imposing confes-sions of faith, and of giving religious instruction to his people. He proclaimed that all jurisdiction, spiritual as well as temporal, was derived from him alone, and that it was in his power to confer episcopal autho-rity, and to take it away. He actually ordered his seal to be put to commissions by which bishops were appointed, who were to exercise their functions as his deputies, and during his pleasure. According to this system, as expounded by Cranmer, the King was the spiritual as well as the temporal chief of the nation. In both capacities His High-ness must have lieutenants. As he appointed civil officers to keep his seal, to collect his revenues, and to dispense justice in his name, so he appointed divines of various ranks to preach the gospel, and to

Relation in which she stood to the crown

administer the sacraments.   It was unnecessary that there should be
any imposition of hands. The King,—such was the opinion of Cranmer
given in the plainest words,—might, in virtue of authority derived from
God, make a priest ; and the priest so made needed no ordination whatever.   These opinions the Archbishop, in spite of the opposition of less
courtly divines, followed out to every legitimate consequence.   He held
that his own spiritual functions, like the secular functions of the Chancellor and Treasurer, were at once determined by a demise of the crown.
When Henry died, therefore, the Primate and his suffragans took out
fresh commissions, empowering them to ordain and to govern the Church
till the new sovereign should think fit to order otherwise.   When it was
objected that a power to bind and to loose, altogether distinct from
temporal power, had been given by our Lord to his apostles, some theologians of this school replied that the power to bind and to loose had
descended, not to the clergy, but to the whole body of Christian men,
and ought to be exercised by the chief magistrate as the representative
of the society.   When it was objected that Saint Paul had spoken of
certain persons whom the Holy Ghost had made overseers and shepherds of the faithful, it was answered that King Henry was the very
overseer, the very shepherd, whom the Holy Ghost had appointed, and
to whom the expressions of Saint Paul applied.[1]

These high pretensions gave scandal to Protestants as well as to
Catholics ; and the scandal was greatly increased when the supremacy,
which Mary had resigned back to the Pope, was again annexed to the
crown, on the accession of Elizabeth.   It seemed monstrous that a
woman should be the chief bishop of a Church in which an apostle had
forbidden her even to let her voice be heard.   The Queen, therefore,
found it necessary expressly to disclaim that sacerdotal character which
her father had assumed, and which, according to Cranmer, had been
inseparably joined, by divine ordinance, to the regal function.   When the
Anglican confession of faith was revised in her reign, the supremacy was
explained in a manner somewhat different from that which had been
fashionable at the court of Henry.   Cranmer had declared, in emphatic
terms, that God had immediately committed to Christian princes the
whole cure of all their subjects, as well concerning the administration
of God's word for the cure of souls, as concerning the administration of
things political.[2]   The thirty-seventh article of religion, framed under
Elizabeth, declares, in terms as emphatic, that the ministering of God's
word does not belong to princes.   The Queen, however, still had over

---

[1] See a very curious paper which Strype believed to be in Gardiner's handwriting. Ecclesiastical Memorials, Book I. Chap. xvii.

[2] These are Cranmer's own words. See the Appendix to Burnet's History of the Reformation,
Part I. Book III. No. 21. Question 9.

the Church a visitatorial power of vast and undefined extent.   She was entrusted by Parliament with the office of restraining and punishing heresy and every sort of ecclesiastical abuse, and was permitted to delegate her authority to commissioners.   The Bishops were little more than her ministers.   Rather than grant to the civil magistrate the absolute power of nominating spiritual pastors, the Church of Rome, in the eleventh century, set all Europe on fire.   Rather than grant to the civil magistrate the absolute power of nominating spiritual pastors, the ministers of the Church of Scotland, in our own time, resigned their livings by hundreds.   The Church of England had no such scruples.   By the royal authority alone her prelates were appointed.   By the royal authority alone her Convocations were summoned, regulated, prorogued, and dissolved.   Without the royal sanction her canons had no force.   One of the articles of her faith was that without the royal consent no ecclesiastical council could lawfully assemble.   From all her judicatures an appeal lay, in the last resort, to the sovereign, even when the question was whether an opinion ought to be accounted heretical, or whether the administration of a sacrament had been valid.   Nor did the Church grudge this extensive power to our princes.   By them she had been called into existence, nursed through a feeble infancy, guarded from Papists on one side and from Puritans on the other, protected against Parliaments which bore her no good will, and avenged on literary assailants whom she found it hard to answer.   Thus gratitude, hope, fear, common attachments, common enmities, bound her to the throne.   All her traditions, all her tastes, were monarchical.   Loyalty became a point of professional honour among her clergy, the peculiar badge which distinguished them at once from Calvinists and from Papists.   Both the Calvinists and the Papists, widely as they differed in other respects, regarded with extreme jealousy all encroachments of the temporal power on the domain of the spiritual power.   Both Calvinists and Papists maintained that subjects might justifiably draw the sword against ungodly rulers.   In France Calvinists resisted Charles the Ninth: Papists resisted Henry the Fourth : both Papists and Calvinists resisted Henry the Third.   In Scotland Calvinists led Mary captive.   On the north of the Trent Papists took arms against the English throne.   The Church of England meantime condemned both Calvinists and Papists, and loudly boasted that no duty was more constantly or earnestly inculcated by her than that of submission to princes.

The advantages which the crown derived from this close alliance with the Established Church were great ; but they were not without serious drawbacks.   The compromise arranged by Cranmer had from the first been considered by a large body of Protestants as a scheme for serving two masters, as an attempt to unite the worship of the Lord

H.E. I   D

with the worship of Baal. In the days of Edward the Sixth the scruples of this party had repeatedly thrown great difficulties in the way of the government. When Elizabeth came to the throne, those difficulties were much increased. Violence naturally engenders violence. The spirit of Protestantism was therefore far fiercer and more intolerant after **The** the cruelties of Mary than before them. Many persons who **Puritans** were warmly attached to the new opinions had, during the evil days, taken refuge in Switzerland and Germany. They had been hospitably received by their brethren in the faith, had sate at the feet of the great doctors of Strasburg, Zurich, and Geneva, and had been, during some years, accustomed to a more simple worship, and to a more democratical form of church government, than England had yet seen. These men returned to their country, convinced that the reform which had been effected under King Edward had been far less searching and extensive than the interests of pure religion required. But it was in vain that they attempted to obtain any concession from Elizabeth. Indeed her system, wherever it differed from her brother's, seemed to them to differ for the worse. They were little disposed to submit, in matters of faith, to any human authority. They had recently, in reliance on their own interpretation of Scripture, risen up against a Church strong in immemorial antiquity and catholic consent. It was by no common exertion of intellectual energy that they had thrown off the yoke of that gorgeous and imperial superstition; and it was vain to expect that, immediately after such an emancipation, they would patiently submit to a new spiritual tyranny. Long accustomed, when the priest lifted up the host, to bow down with their faces to the earth, as before a present God, they had learned to treat the mass as an idolatrous mummery. Long accustomed to regard the Pope as the successor of the chief of the apostles, as the bearer of the keys of earth and heaven, they had learned to regard him as the Beast, the Antichrist, the Man of Sin. It was not to be expected that they would immediately transfer to an upstart authority the homage which they had withdrawn from the Vatican; that they would submit their private judgment to the authority of a Church founded on private judgment alone; that they would be afraid to dissent from teachers who themselves dissented from what had lately been the universal faith of western Christendom. It is easy to conceive the indignation which must have been felt by bold and inquisitive spirits, glorying in newly acquired freedom, when an institution younger by many years than themselves, an institution which had, under their own eyes, gradually received its form from the passions and interests of a court, began to mimic the lofty style of Rome.

Since these men could not be convinced, it was determined that they should be persecuted. Persecution produced its natural effect on

MARY TUDOR

From the painting by Johannes Corvus in the National Portrait Gallery them. It found them a sect : it made them a faction. To their hatred of the Church was now added hatred of the Crown. The two senti-

Their republican spirit ments were intermingled ; and each embittered the other. The opinions of the Puritan concerning the relation of ruler and subject were widely different from those which were inculcated in the Homilies. His favourite divines had, both by precept and by example, encouraged resistance to tyrants and persecutors. His fellow Calvinists in France, in Holland, and in Scotland, were in arms against idolatrous and cruel princes. His notions, too, respecting the government of the state took a tinge from his notions respecting the government of the Church. Some of the sarcasms which were popularly thrown on episcopacy might, without much difficulty, be turned against royalty ; and many of the arguments which were used to prove that spiritual power was best lodged in a synod seemed to lead to the conclusion that temporal power was best lodged in a parliament.

Thus, as the priest of the Established Church was, from interest, from principle, and from passion, zealous for the royal prerogatives, the Puritan was, from interest, from principle, and from passion, hostile to them. The power of the discontented sectaries was great. They were found in every rank ; but they were strongest among the mercantile classes in the towns, and among the small proprietors in the country. Early in the reign of Elizabeth they began to return a majority of the

No systematic parliamentary opposition offered to the government of Elizabeth House of Commons. And doubtless, had our ancestors been then at liberty to fix their attention entirely on domestic questions, the strife between the Crown and the Parliament would instantly have commenced. But that was no season for internal dissensions. It might, indeed, well be doubted whether the firmest union among all the orders of the state could avert the common danger by which all were threatened. Roman Catholic Europe and reformed Europe were struggling for death or life. France, divided against herself, had, for a time, ceased to be of any account in Christendom. The English government was at the head of the Protestant interest, and, while persecuting Presbyterians at home, extended a powerful protection to Presbyterian Churches abroad. At the head of the opposite party was the mightiest prince of the age, a prince who ruled Spain, Portugal, Italy, the Netherlands, the East and the West Indies, whose armies repeatedly marched to Paris, and whose fleets kept the coasts of Devonshire and Sussex in alarm. It long seemed probable that Englishmen would have to fight desperately on English ground for their religion and independence. Nor were they ever for a moment free from apprehensions of some great treason at home. For in that age it had become a point of conscience and of honour with many men of generous natures to sacrifice their country to their religion. A succession of dark plots, formed by Roman Catholics against the life of the Queen and the existence of the nation, kept society in constant alarm. Whatever might be the faults of Elizabeth, it was plain that, to speak humanly, the fate of the realm and of all reformed Churches was staked on the security of her person and on the success of her administration. To strengthen her hands was, therefore, the first duty of a patriot and a Protestant ; and that duty was well performed. The Puritans, even in the depths of the prisons to which she had sent them, prayed, and with no simulated fervour, that she might be kept from the dagger of the assassin, that rebellion might be put down under her feet, and that her arms might be victorious by sea and land. One of the most stubborn of the stubborn sect, immediately after his hand had been lopped off for an offence into which he had been hurried by his intemperate zeal, waved his hat with the hand which was still left him, and shouted " God save the Queen ! " The sentiment with which these men regarded her has descended to their posterity. The Noncon-formists, rigorously as she treated them, have, as a body, always venerated her memory.[1]

During the greater part of her reign, therefore, the Puritans in the House of Commons, though sometimes mutinous, felt no disposition to array themselves in systematic opposition to the government. But, when the defeat of the Armada, the successful resistance of the United Provinces to the Spanish power, the firm establishment of Henry the Fourth on the throne of France, and the death of Philip the Second, had secured the State and the Church against all danger from abroad, an obstinate struggle, destined to last during several generations, instantly began at home.

It was in the Parliament of 1601 that the opposition which had, during forty years, been silently gathering and husbanding strength, fought its first great battle and won its first victory. The ground was well chosen. The English sovereigns had always been entrusted with the supreme direction of commercial police. It was their undoubted prerogative to regulate coin, weights, and measures, and to appoint fairs, markets, and ports. The line which bounded their authority over trade had, as usual, been but loosely drawn. They therefore, as usual, encroached on the province which

Question of the monopolies

---

[1] The Puritan historian, Neal, after censuring the cruelty with which she treated the sect to which he belonged, concludes thus : " However, notwithstanding all these blemishes, Queen Elizabeth stands upon record as a wise and politic princess, for delivering her kingdom from the difficulties in which it was involved at her accession, for preserving the Protestant reformation against the potent attempts of the Pope, the Emperor, and King of Spain abroad, and the Queen of Scots and her Popish subjects at home. . . . She was the glory of the age in which she lived, and will be the admiration of posterity."—History of the Puritans, Part I. Chap. viii

rightfully belonged to the legislature. The encroachment was, as usual, patiently borne, till it became serious. But at length the Queen took upon herself to grant patents of monopoly by scores. There was scarcely a family in the realm which did not feel itself aggrieved by the oppression and extortion which this abuse naturally caused. Iron, oil, vinegar, coal, saltpetre, lead, starch, yarn, skins, leather, glass, could be bought only at exorbitant prices. The House of Commons met in an angry and determined mood. It was in vain that a courtly minority blamed the Speaker for suffering the acts of the Queen's Highness to be called in question. The language of the discontented party was high and menacing, and was echoed by the voice of the whole nation. The coach of the chief minister of the crown was surrounded by an indignant populace, who cursed the monopolies, and exclaimed that the prerogative should not be suffered to touch the old liberties of England. There seemed for a moment to be some danger that the long and glorious reign of Elizabeth would have a shameful and disastrous end. She, however, with admirable judgment and temper, declined the contest, put herself at the head of the reforming party, redressed the grievance, thanked the Commons, in touching and dignified language, for their tender care of the general weal, brought back to herself the hearts of the people, and left to her successors a memorable example of the way in which it behoves a ruler to deal with public movements which he has not the means of resisting.

In the year 1603 the great Queen died. That year is, on many accounts, one of the most important epochs in our history. It was then **Scotland and Ireland become parts of the same empire with England** that both Scotland and Ireland became parts of the same empire with England. Both Scotland and Ireland, indeed, had been subjugated by the Plantagenets; but neither country had been patient under the yoke. Scotland had, with heroic energy, vindicated her independence, had, from the time of Robert Bruce, been a separate kingdom, and was now joined to the southern part of the island in a manner which rather gratified than wounded her national pride. Ireland had never, since the days of Henry the Second, been able to expel the foreign invaders; but she had struggled against them long and fiercely. During the fourteenth and fifteenth centuries the English power in that island was constantly declining, and, in the days of Henry the Seventh, sank to the lowest point. The Irish dominions of that prince consisted only of the counties of Dublin and Louth, of some parts of Meath and Kildare, and of a few seaports scattered along the coast. A large portion even of Leinster was not yet divided into counties. Munster, Ulster, and Connaught were ruled by petty sovereigns, partly Celts, and partly degenerate Normans, who had forgotten their origin and had adopted the Celtic

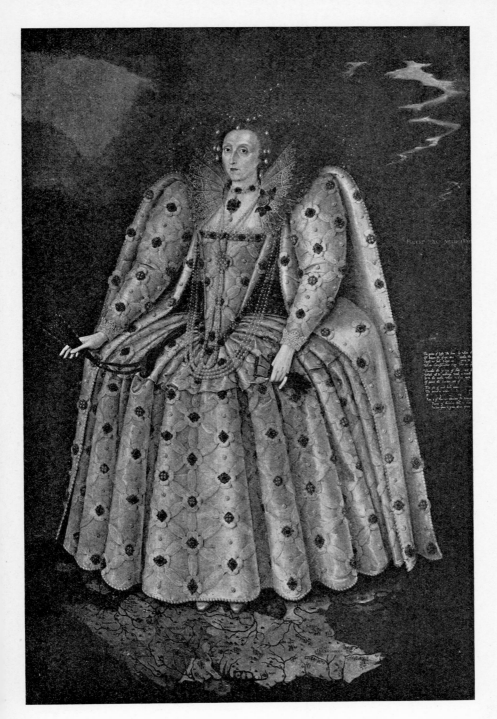

QUEEN ELIZABETH

From a portrait in the possession of Viscount Dillon

language and manners. But, during the sixteenth century, the English power had made great progress. The half savage chieftains who reigned beyond the pale had submitted one after another to the lieutenants of the Tudors. At length, a few weeks before the death of Elizabeth, the conquest, which had been begun more than four hundred years before by Strongbow, was completed by Mountjoy. Scarcely had James the First mounted the English throne when the last O'Donnel and O'Neil who have held the rank of independent princes kissed his hand at White-hall. Thenceforward his writs ran and his judges held assizes in every part of Ireland ; and the English law superseded the customs which had prevailed among the aboriginal tribes.

In extent Scotland and Ireland were nearly equal to each other, and were together nearly equal to England, but were much less thickly peopled than England, and were very far behind England in wealth and civilisation. Scotland had been kept back by the sterility of her soil ; and, in the midst of light, the thick darkness of the middle ages still rested on Ireland.

The population of Scotland, with the exception of the Celtic tribes which were thinly scattered over the Hebrides and over the mountainous parts of the northern shires, was of the same blood with the population of England, and spoke a tongue which did not differ from the purest English more than the dialects of Somersetshire and Lancashire differed from each other. In Ireland, on the contrary, the population, with the exception of the small English colony near the coast, was Celtic, and still kept the Celtic speech and manners.

In natural courage and intelligence both the nations which now became connected with England ranked high. In perseverance, in self-command, in forethought, in all the virtues which conduce to success in life, the Scots have never been surpassed. The Irish, on the other hand, were distinguished by qualities which tend to make men interesting rather than prosperous. They were an ardent and impetuous race, easily moved to tears or to laughter, to fury or to love. Alone among the nations of northern Europe they had the susceptibility, the vivacity, the natural turn for acting and rhetoric, which are indigenous on the shores of the Mediterranean Sea. In mental cultivation Scotland had an in-disputable superiority. Though that kingdom was then the poorest in Christendom, it already vied in every branch of learning with the most favoured countries. Scotsmen, whose dwellings and whose food were as wretched as those of the Icelanders of our time, wrote Latin verse with more than the delicacy of Vida, and made discoveries in science which would have added to the renown of Galileo. Ireland could boast of no Buchanan or Napier. The genius, with which her aboriginal inhabitants were largely endowed, showed itself as yet only in ballads which, wild and rugged as they were, seemed to the judging eye of Spenser to contain a portion of the pure gold of poetry.

Scotland, in becoming part of the British monarchy, preserved her dignity. Having, during many generations, courageously withstood the English arms, she was now joined to her stronger neighbour on the most honourable terms. She gave a King instead of receiving one. She retained her own constitution and laws. Her tribunals and parliaments remained entirely independent of the tribunals and parliaments which sate at Westminster. The administration of Scotland was in Scottish hands; for no Englishman had any motive to emigrate northward, and to contend with the shrewdest and most pertinacious of all races for what was to be scraped together in the poorest of all treasuries. Nevertheless Scotland by no means escaped the fate ordained for every country which is connected, but not incorporated, with another country of greater resources. Though in name an independent kingdom, she was, during more than a century, really treated, in many respects, as a subject province.

Ireland was undisguisedly governed as a dependency won by the sword. Her rude national institutions had perished. The English colonists submitted to the dictation of the mother country, without whose support they could not exist, and indemnified themselves by trampling on the people among whom they had settled. The parliaments which met at Dublin could pass no law which had not been previously approved by the English Privy Council. The authority of the English legislature extended over Ireland. The executive administration was entrusted to men taken either from England or from the English pale, and, in either case, regarded as foreigners, and even as enemies, by the Celtic population.

But the circumstance which, more than any other, has made Ireland to differ from Scotland remains to be noticed. Scotland was Protestant. In no part of Europe had the movement of the popular mind against the Roman Catholic Church been so rapid and violent. The Reformers had vanquished, deposed, and imprisoned their idolatrous sovereign. They would not endure even such a compromise as had been effected in England. They had established the Calvinistic doctrine, discipline, and worship; and they made little distinction between Popery and Prelacy, between the Mass and the Book of Common Prayer. Unfortunately for Scotland, the prince whom she sent to govern a fairer inheritance had been so much annoyed by the pertinacity with which her theologians had asserted against him the privileges of the synod and the pulpit that he hated the ecclesiastical polity to which she was fondly attached as much as it was in his effeminate nature to hate anything, and had no sooner mounted the English throne than he began to show an intolerant zeal for the government and ritual of the English Church.

The Irish were the only people of northern Europe who had remained true to the old religion. This is to be partly ascribed to the circumstance that they were some centuries behind their neighbours in knowledge. But other causes had cooperated. The Reformation had been a national as well as a moral revolt. It had been, not only an insurrection of the laity against the clergy, but also an insurrection of all the branches of the great German race against an alien domination. It is a most significant circumstance that no large society of which the tongue is not Teutonic has ever turned Protestant, and that, wherever a language derived from that of ancient Rome is spoken, the religion of modern Rome to this day prevails. The patriotism of the Irish had taken a peculiar direction. The object of their animosity was not Rome, but England ; and they had especial reason to abhor those English sovereigns who had been the chiefs of the great schism, Henry the Eighth and Elizabeth. During the vain struggle which two generations of Milesian princes maintained against the Tudors, religious enthusiasm and national enthusiasm became inseparably blended in the minds of the vanquished race. The new feud of Protestant and Papist inflamed the old feud of Saxon and Celt. The English conquerors, meanwhile, neglected all legitimate means of conversion. No care was taken to provide the vanquished nation with instructors capable of making themselves understood. No translation of the Bible was put forth in the Irish language. The government contented itself with setting up a vast hierarchy of Protestant archbishops, bishops, and rectors, who did nothing, and who, for doing nothing, were paid out of the spoils of a Church loved and revered by the great body of the people.

There was much in the state both of Scotland and of Ireland which might well excite the painful apprehensions of a farsighted statesman. As yet, however, there was the appearance of tranquillity. For the first time all the British isles were peaceably united under one sceptre.

It should seem that the weight of England among European nations ought, from this epoch, to have greatly increased. The territory which her new King governed was, in extent, nearly double that which Elizabeth had inherited. His empire was the most complete within itself and the most secure from attack that was to be found in the world. The Plantagenets and Tudors had been repeatedly under the necessity of defending themselves against Scotland while they were engaged in continental war. The long conflict in Ireland had been a severe and perpetual drain on their resources. Yet even under such disadvantages those sovereigns had been highly considered throughout Christendom. It might, therefore, not unreasonably be expected that England, Scot-

land, and Ireland combined would form a state second to none that
then existed.

All such expectations were strangely disappointed. On the day of
the accession of James the First England descended from the rank
which she had hitherto held, and began to be regarded as a   Diminution
power hardly of the second order. During many years the   of the im-
great British monarchy, under four successive princes of the   portance of
England
House of Stuart, was scarcely a more important member of   after the
accession of
the European system than the little kingdom of Scotland had   James I
previously been. This, however, is little to be regretted. Of James the
First, as of John, it may be said that, if his administration had been
able and splendid, it would probably have been fatal to our country,
and that we owe more to his weakness and meanness than to the wisdom and courage of much better sovereigns. He came to the throne
at a critical moment. The time was fast approaching when either the
King must become absolute, or the Parliament must control the whole
executive administration. Had James been, like Henry the Fourth,
like Maurice of Nassau, or like Gustavus Adolphus, a valiant, active,
and politic ruler, had he put himself at the head of the Protestants of
Europe, had he gained great victories over Tilly and Spinola, had
he adorned Westminster with the spoils of Bavarian monasteries and
Flemish cathedrals, had he hung Austrian and Castilian banners in
Saint Paul's, and had he found himself, after great achievements, at
the head of fifty thousand troops, brave, well disciplined, and devotedly
attached to his person, the English Parliament would soon have been
nothing more than a name. Happily he was not a man to play such a
part. He began his administration by putting an end to the war which
had raged during many years between England and Spain ; and from
that time he shunned hostilities with a caution which was proof against
the insults of his neighbours and the clamours of his subjects. Not till
the last year of his life could the influence of his son, his favourite, his
Parliament, and his people combined, induce him to strike one feeble
blow in defence of his family and of his religion. It was well for those
whom he governed that he in this matter disregarded their wishes. The
effect of his pacific policy was that, in his time, no regular troops were
needed, and that, while France, Spain, Italy, Belgium, and Germany
swarmed with mercenary soldiers, the defence of our island was still
confided to the militia.

As the King had no standing army, and did not even attempt to
form one, it would have been wise in him to avoid any conflict with his
people. But such was his indiscretion that, while he altogether neglected
the means which alone could make him really absolute, he constantly
put forward, in the most offensive form, claims of which none of his

predecessors had ever dreamed.   It was at this time that those strange theories which Filmer afterwards formed into a system, and which be-

Doctrine of divine right came the badge of the most violent class of Tories and high churchmen, first emerged into notice.   It was gravely maintained that the Supreme Being regarded hereditary monarchy, as opposed to other forms of government, with peculiar favour ; that the rule of succession in order of primogeniture was a divine institution, anterior to the Christian, and even to the Mosaic dispensation ; that no human power, not even that of the whole legislature, no length of adverse possession, though it extended to ten centuries, could deprive a legitimate prince of his rights ; that the authority of such a prince was necessarily always despotic ; that the laws, by which, in England and in other countries, the prerogative was limited, were to be regarded merely as concessions which the sovereign had freely made and might at his pleasure resume ; and that any treaty which a king might conclude with his people was merely a declaration of his present intentions, and not a contract of which the performance could be demanded.   It is evident that this theory, though intended to strengthen the foundations of government, altogether unsettles them.   Does the divine and immutable law of primogeniture admit females, or exclude them ?   On either supposition half the sovereigns of Europe must be usurpers, reigning in defiance of the law of God, and liable to be dispossessed by the rightful heirs.   The doctrine that kingly government is peculiarly favoured by Heaven receives no countenance from the Old Testament ; for in the Old Testament we read that the chosen people were blamed and punished for desiring a king, and that they were afterwards commanded to withdraw their allegiance from him.   Their whole history, far from countenancing the notion that succession in order of primogeniture is of divine institution, would rather seem to indicate that younger brothers are under the especial protection of heaven.   Isaac was not the eldest son of Abraham, nor Jacob of Isaac, nor Judah of Jacob, nor David of Jesse, nor Solomon of David.   Nor does the system of Filmer receive any countenance from those passages of the New Testament which describe government as an ordinance of God : for the government under which the writers of the New Testament lived was not a hereditary monarchy. The Roman Emperors were republican magistrates, named by the senate. None of them pretended to rule by right of birth ; and, in fact, both Tiberius, to whom Christ commanded that tribute should be given, and Nero, whom Paul directed the Romans to obey, were, according to the patriarchal theory of government, usurpers.   In the middle ages the doctrine of indefeasible hereditary right would have been regarded as heretical : for it was altogether incompatible with the high pretensions of the Church of Rome.   It was a doctrine unknown to the founders of

JAMES I

From the painting by P. Van Somer in the National Portrait Gallery the Church of England. The Homily on Wilful Rebellion had strongly, and indeed too strongly, inculcated submission to constituted authority, but had made no distinction between hereditary and elective monarchies, or between monarchies and republics. Indeed most of the predecessors of James would, from personal motives, have regarded the patriarchal theory of government with aversion. William Rufus, Henry the First, Stephen, John, Henry the Fourth, Henry the Fifth, Henry the Sixth, Richard the Third, and Henry the Seventh, had all reigned in defiance of the strict rule of descent. A grave doubt hung over the legitimacy both of Mary and of Elizabeth. It was impossible that both Catharine of Aragon and Anne Boleyn could have been lawfully married to Henry the Eighth; and the highest authority in the realm had pronounced that neither was so. The Tudors, far from considering the law of succession as a divine and unchangeable institution, were constantly tampering with it. Henry the Eighth obtained an act of parliament, giving him power to leave the crown by will, and actually made a will to the prejudice of the royal family of Scotland. Edward the Sixth, unauthorised by Parliament, assumed a similar power, with the full approbation of the most eminent Reformers. Elizabeth, conscious that her own title was open to grave objection, and unwilling to admit even a reversionary right in her rival and enemy the Queen of Scots, induced the Parliament to pass a law, enacting that whoever should deny the competency of the reigning sovereign, with the assent of the Estates of the realm, to alter the succession, should suffer death as a traitor. But the situation of James was widely different from that of Elizabeth. Far inferior to her in abilities and in popularity, regarded by the English as an alien, and excluded from the throne by the testament of Henry the Eighth, the King of Scots was yet the undoubted heir of William the Conqueror and of Egbert. He had, therefore, an obvious interest in inculcating the superstitious notion that birth confers rights anterior to law, and unalterable by law. It was a notion, moreover, well suited to his intellect and temper. It soon found many advocates among those who aspired to his favour, and made rapid progress among the clergy of the Established Church.

Thus, at the very moment at which a republican spirit began to manifest itself strongly in the Parliament and in the country, the claims of the monarch took a monstrous form which would have disgusted the proudest and most arbitrary of those who had preceded him on the throne.

James was always boasting of his skill in what he called kingcraft; and yet it is hardly possible even to imagine a course more directly opposed to all the rules of kingcraft than that which he followed. The policy of wise rulers has always been to disguise strong acts under popular forms. It was thus that Augustus and Napoleon established absolute monarchies, while the public regarded them merely as eminent citizens invested with temporary magistracies. The policy of James was the direct reverse of theirs. He enraged and alarmed his Parliament by constantly telling them that they held their privileges merely during his pleasure, and that they had no more business to inquire what he might lawfully do than what the Deity might lawfully do. Yet he quailed before them, abandoned minister after minister to their vengeance, and suffered them to tease him into acts directly opposed to his strongest inclinations. Thus the indignation excited by his claims and the scorn excited by his concessions went on growing together. By his fondness for worthless minions, and by the sanction which he gave to their tyranny and rapacity, he kept discontent constantly alive. His cowardice, his childishness, his pedantry, his ungainly person and manners, his provincial accent, made him an object of derision. Even in his virtues and accomplishments there was something eminently unkingly. Throughout the whole course of his reign, all the venerable associations by which the throne had long been fenced were gradually losing their strength. During two hundred years all the sovereigns who had ruled England, with the single exception of the unfortunate Henry the Sixth, had been strongminded, highspirited, courageous, and of princely bearing. Almost all had possessed abilities above the ordinary level. It was no light thing that, on the very eve of the decisive struggle between our Kings and their Parliaments, royalty should be exhibited to the world stammering, slobbering, shedding unmanly tears, trembling at a drawn sword, and talking in the style alternately of a buffoon and of a pedagogue.

In the meantime the religious dissensions, by which, from the days of Edward the Sixth, the Protestant body had been distracted, had become more formidable than ever. The interval which had separated the first generation of Puritans from Cranmer and Jewel was small indeed when compared with the interval which separated the third generation of Puritans from Laud and Hammond. While the recollection of Mary's cruelties *The separation between the Church and the Puritans becomes wider* was still fresh, while the power of the Roman Catholic party still inspired apprehension, while Spain still retained ascendency and aspired to universal dominion, all the reformed sects knew that they had a strong common interest and a deadly common enemy. The animosity which they felt towards each other was languid when compared with the animosity which they all felt towards Rome. Conformists and Nonconformists had heartily joined in enacting penal laws of extreme severity against the Papists. But when more than half a century of undisturbed possession had given confidence to the Established Church, when nine tenths of the nation had become heartily Protestant, when England was at peace with all the world, when there was no danger that Popery would be forced by foreign arms on the nation, when the last confessors who had stood before Bonner had passed away, a change took place in the feeling of the Anglican clergy. Their hostility to the Roman Catholic doctrine and discipline was considerably mitigated. Their dislike of the Puritans, on the other hand, increased daily. The controversies which had from the beginning divided the Protestant party took such a form as made reconciliation hopeless ; and new controversies of still greater importance were added to the old subjects of dispute.

The founders of the Anglican Church had retained episcopacy as an ancient, a decent, and a convenient ecclesiastical polity, but had not declared that form of church government to be of divine institution. We have already seen how low an estimate Cranmer had formed of the office of a Bishop. In the reign of Elizabeth, Jewel, Cooper, Whitgift, and other eminent doctors defended prelacy, as innocent, as useful, as what the state might lawfully establish, as what, when established by the state, was entitled to the respect of every citizen. But they never denied that a Christian community without a Bishop might be a pure Church.[1] On the contrary, they regarded the Protestants of the Continent as of the same household of faith with themselves. Englishmen in England were indeed bound to acknowledge the authority of the Bishop, as they were bound to acknowledge the authority of the Sheriff and of the Coroner : but the obligation was purely local. An English churchman, nay even an English prelate, if he went to Holland, conformed without scruple to the established religion of Holland. Abroad the ambassadors of Elizabeth and James went in state to the very worship which Elizabeth and James persecuted at home, and carefully abstained from decorating their private chapels after the Anglican

---

[1] On this subject, Bishop Cooper's language is remarkably clear and strong. He maintains, in his Answer to Martin Marprelate, printed in 1589, that no form of church government is divinely ordained ; that Protestant communities, in establishing different forms, have only made a legitimate use of their Christian liberty ; and that episcopacy is peculiarly suited to England, because the English constitution is monarchical. "All those Churches," says the Bishop, " in which the Gospell, in these daies, after great darknesse, was first renewed, and the learned men whom God sent to instruct them, I doubt not but have been directed by the Spirite of God to retaine this liberty, that, in external government and other outward orders, they might choose such as they thought in wisedome and godlinesse to be most convenient for the state of their countrey and disposition of their people. Why then should this liberty that other countreys have used under anie colour be wrested from us ? I think it therefore great presumption and boldnesse that some of our nation, and those, whatever they may think of themselves, not of the greatest wisedome and skill, should take upon them to controlle the whole realme, and to binde both prince and people in respect of conscience to alter the present state, and tie themselves to a certain platforme devised by some of our neighbours, which, in the judgment of many wise and godly persons, is most unfit for the state of a Kingdome."

fashion, lest scandal should be given to weaker brethren. An instrument is still extant by which the Primate of all England, in the year

THE SYNOD OF DORT

From a Dutch engraving in the Sutherland Collection in the Bodleian Library

1582, authorised a Scotch minister, ordained, according to the laudable
forms of the Scotch Church, by the Synod of East Lothian, to preach
and administer the sacraments in any part of the province of Canter-

bury.[1] In the year 1603, the Convocation solemnly recognised the Church of Scotland, a Church in which episcopal control and episcopal ordination were then unknown, as a branch of the Holy Catholic Church of Christ.[2] It was even held that Presbyterian ministers were entitled to place and voice in œcumenical councils. When the States General of the United Provinces convoked at Dort a synod of doctors not episcopally ordained, an English Bishop and an English Dean, commissioned by the head of the English Church, sate with those doctors, preached to them, and voted with them on the gravest questions of theology.[3] Nay, many English benefices were held by divines who had been admitted to the ministry in the Calvinistic form used on the Continent ; nor was reordination by a Bishop in such cases then thought necessary, or even lawful.[4]

But a new race of divines was already rising in the Church of England. In their view the episcopal office was essential to the welfare of a Christian society and to the efficacy of the most solemn ordinances of religion. To that office belonged certain high and sacred privileges, which no human power could give or take away. A Church might as well be without the doctrine of the Trinity, or the doctrine of the Incarnation, as without the apostolical orders ; and the Church of Rome, which, in the midst of all her corruptions, had retained the apostolical orders, was nearer to primitive purity than those reformed societies which had rashly set up, in opposition to the divine model, a system invented by men.

In the days of Edward the Sixth and of Elizabeth, the defenders of the Anglican ritual had generally contented themselves with saying that it might be used without sin, and that, therefore, none but a perverse and undutiful subject would refuse to use it when enjoined to do so by the magistrate. Now, however, that rising party which claimed for the polity of the Church a celestial origin began to ascribe to her services a new dignity and importance. It was hinted that, if the established worship had any fault, that fault was extreme simplicity, and that the

---

[1] Strype's Life of Grindal, Appendix to Book II. No. xvii.　　　[2] Canon 55. of 1603.

[3] Joseph Hall, then dean of Worcester, and afterwards bishop of Norwich, was one of the commissioners. In his life of himself, he says : " My unworthiness was named for one of the assistants of that honourable, grave, and reverend meeting." To high churchmen this humility will seem not a little out of place.

[4] It was by the Act of Uniformity, passed after the Restoration, that persons not episcopally ordained were, for the first time, made incapable of holding benefices. No man was more zealous for this law than Clarendon. Yet he says ; " This was new : for there had been many, and at present there were some, who possessed benefices with cure of souls and other ecclesiastical promotions, who had never received orders but in France or Holland ; and these men must now receive new ordination, which had been always held unlawful in the Church, or by this act of parliament must be deprived of their livelihood which they enjoyed in the most flourishing and peaceable time of the Church."

Reformers had, in the heat of their quarrel with Rome, abolished many ancient ceremonies which might with advantage have been retained. Days and places were again held in mysterious veneration. Some practices which had long been disused, and which were commonly regarded as superstitious mummeries, were revived. Paintings and carvings, which had escaped the fury of the first generation of Protestants, became the objects of a respect such as to many seemed idolatrous.

No part of the system of the old Church had been more detested by the Reformers than the honour paid to celibacy. They held that the doctrine of Rome on this subject had been prophetically condemned by the apostle Paul, as a doctrine of devils ; and they dwelt much on the crimes and scandals which seemed to prove the justice of this awful denunciation. Luther had evinced his own opinion in the clearest manner, by espousing a nun. Some of the most illustrious bishops and priests who had died by fire during the reign of Mary had left wives and children. Now, however, it began to be rumoured that the old monastic spirit had reappeared in the Church of England ; that there was in high quarters a prejudice against married priests ; that even laymen, who called themselves Protestants, had made resolutions of celibacy which almost amounted to vows ; nay, that a minister of the established religion had set up a nunnery, in which the psalms were chaunted at midnight, by a company of virgins dedicated to God.[1]

Nor was this all. A class of questions, as to which the founders of the Anglican Church and the first generation of Puritans had differed little or not at all, began to furnish matter for fierce disputes. The controversies which had divided the Protestant body in its infancy had related almost exclusively to Church government and to ceremonies. There had been no serious quarrel between the contending parties on points of metaphysical theology. The doctrines held by the chiefs of the hierarchy touching original sin, faith, grace, predestination, and election, were those which are popularly called Calvinistic. Towards the close of Elizabeth's reign her favourite prelate, Archbishop Whitgift, drew up, in concert with the Bishop of London and other theologians, the celebrated instrument known by the name of the Lambeth Articles. In that instrument the most startling of the Calvinistic doctrines are affirmed with a distinctness which would shock many who, in our age, are reputed Calvinists. One clergyman, who took the opposite side, and spoke harshly of Calvin, was arraigned for his presumption by the University of Cambridge, and escaped punishment only by expressing his firm belief in the tenets of reprobation and final perseverance, and

---

[1] Peckard's Life of Ferrar ; The Arminian Nunnery, or a Brief Description of the late erected monastical Place called the Arminian Nunnery, at Little Gidding in Huntingdonshire, 1641.

his sorrow for the offence which he had given to pious men by reflecting on the great French reformer. The school of divinity of which Hooker was the chief occupies a middle place between the school of Cranmer and the school of Laud ; and Hooker has, in modern times, been claimed by the Arminians as an ally. Yet Hooker pronounced Calvin to have been a man superior in wisdom to any other divine that France had produced, a man to whom thousands were indebted for the knowledge of divine truth, but who was himself indebted to God alone. When the Arminian controversy arose in Holland, the English government and the English Church lent strong support to the Calvinistic party ; nor is the English name altogether free from the stain which has been left on that party by the imprisonment of Grotius and the judicial murder of Barneveldt.

But, even before the meeting of the Dutch synod, that part of the Anglican clergy which was peculiarly hostile to the Calvinistic Church government and to the Calvinistic worship had begun to regard with dislike the Calvinistic metaphysics ; and this feeling was very naturally strengthened by the gross injustice, insolence, and cruelty of the party which was prevalent at Dort. The Arminian doctrine, a doctrine less austerely logical than that of the early Reformers, but more agreeable to the popular notions of the divine justice and benevolence, spread fast and wide. The infection soon reached the court. Opinions which, at the time of the accession of James, no clergyman could have avowed without imminent risk of being stripped of his gown, were now the best title to preferment. A divine of that age, who was asked by a simple country gentleman what the Arminians held, answered, with as much truth as wit, that they held all the best bishoprics and deaneries in England.

While the majority of the Anglican clergy quitted, in one direction, the position which they had originally occupied, the majority of the Puritan body departed, in a direction diametrically opposite, from the principles and practices of their fathers. The persecution which the separatists had undergone had been severe enough to irritate, but not severe enough to destroy. They had been, not tamed into submission, but baited into savageness and stubbornness. After the fashion of oppressed sects, they mistook their own vindictive feelings for emotions of piety, encouraged in themselves by reading and meditation a disposition to brood over their wrongs, and, when they had worked themselves up into hating their enemies, imagined that they were only hating the enemies of heaven. In the New Testament there was little indeed which, even when perverted by the most disingenuous exposition, could seem to countenance the indulgence of malevolent passions. But the Old Testament contained the history of a race selected by God to be witnesses of his unity and ministers of his vengeance, and specially

RICHARD HOOKER

From the painting in the National Portrait Gallery. Artist unknown

commanded by him to do many things which, if done without his special command, would have been atrocious crimes. In such a history it was not difficult for fierce and gloomy spirits to find much that might be distorted to suit their wishes. The extreme Puritans therefore began to feel for the Old Testament a preference, which, perhaps, they did not distinctly avow even to themselves; but which showed itself in all their sentiments and habits. They paid to the Hebrew language a respect which they refused to that tongue in which the discourses of Jesus and the epistles of Paul have come down to us. They baptized their children by the names, not of Christian saints, but of Hebrew patriarchs and warriors. In defiance of the express and reiterated declarations of Luther and Calvin, they turned the weekly festival by which the Church had, from the primitive times, commemorated the resurrection of her Lord, into a Jewish Sabbath. They sought for principles of jurisprudence in the Mosaic law, and for precedents to guide their ordinary conduct in the books of Judges and Kings. Their thoughts and discourse ran much on acts which were assuredly not recorded as examples for our imitation. The prophet who hewed in pieces a captive king, the rebel general who gave the blood of a queen to the dogs, the matron who, in defiance of plighted faith, and of the laws of eastern hospitality, drove the nail into the brain of the fugitive ally who had just fed at her board, and who was sleeping under the shadow of her tent, were proposed as models to Christians suffering under the tyranny of princes and prelates. Morals and manners were subjected to a code resembling that of the synagogue, when the synagogue was in its worst state. The dress, the deportment, the language, the studies, the amusements of the rigid sect were regulated on principles not unlike those of the Pharisees who, proud of their washed hands and broad phylacteries, taunted the Redeemer as a sabbath-breaker and a winebibber. It was a sin to hang garlands on a Maypole, to drink a friend's health, to fly a hawk, to hunt a stag, to play at chess, to wear lovelocks, to put starch into a ruff, to touch the virginals, to read the Fairy Queen. Rules such as these, rules which would have appeared insupportable to the free and joyous spirit of Luther, and contemptible to the serene and philosophical intellect of Zwingle, threw over all life a more than monastic gloom. The learning and eloquence by which the great Reformers had been eminently distinguished, and to which they had been, in no small measure, indebted for their success, were regarded by the new school of Protestants with suspicion, if not with aversion. Some precisians had scruples about teaching the Latin grammar, because the names of Mars, Bacchus, and Apollo occurred in it. The fine arts were all but proscribed. The solemn peal of the organ was superstitious. The light music of Ben Jonson's masques was dissolute. Half the fine paintings in England were idolatrous, and the

CHARLES I., 1600-1649.

From the painting by Daniel Mytens, in the National Portrait Gallery.

other half indecent.   The extreme Puritan was at once known from other men by his gait, his garb, his lank hair, the sour solemnity of his face, the upturned white of his eyes, the nasal twang with which he spoke, and, above all, by his peculiar dialect.   He employed, on every occasion, the imagery and style of Scripture.   Hebraisms violently introduced into the English language, and metaphors borrowed from the boldest lyric poetry of a remote age and country, and applied to the common concerns of English life, were the most striking peculiarities of this cant, which moved, not without cause, the derision both of Prelatists and libertines.

Thus the political and religious schism which had originated in the sixteenth century was, during the first quarter of the seventeenth century, constantly widening.   Theories tending to Turkish despotism were in fashion at Whitehall.   Theories tending to republicanism were in favour with a large portion of the House of Commons.   The violent Prelatists who were, to a man, zealous for prerogative, and the violent Puritans who were, to a man, zealous for the privileges of Parliament, regarded each other with animosity more intense than that which, in the preceding generation, had existed between Catholics and Protestants.

While the minds of men were in this state, the country, after a peace of many years, at length engaged in a war which required strenuous exertions.   This war hastened the approach of the great constitutional crisis.   It was necessary that the King should have a large military force.   He could not have such a force without money.   He could not legally raise money without the consent of Parliament.   It followed, therefore, that he either must administer the government in conformity with the sense of the House of Commons, or must venture on such a violation of the fundamental laws of the land as had been unknown during several centuries.   The Plantagenets and the Tudors had, it is true, occasionally supplied a deficiency in their revenue by a benevolence or a forced loan: but these expedients were always of a temporary nature. To meet the regular charge of a long war by regular taxation, imposed without the consent of the Estates of the realm, was a course which Henry the Eighth himself would not have dared to take.   It seemed, therefore, that the decisive hour was approaching, and that the English Parliament would soon either share the fate of the senates of the Continent, or obtain supreme ascendency in the state.

Just at this conjuncture James died.   Charles the First succeeded to the throne.   He had received from nature a far better understanding, a far stronger will, and a far keener and firmer temper than **Accession** his father's.   He had inherited his father's political theories, **and character** and was much more disposed than his father to carry them **Charles I** into practice.   He was, like his father, a zealous episcopalian.   He was, moreover, what his father had never been, a zealous Arminian, and, though no Papist, liked a Papist much better than a Puritan. It would be unjust to deny that Charles had some of the qualities of a good, and even of a great prince. He wrote and spoke, not, like his father, with the exactness of a professor, but after the fashion of intelligent and well educated gentlemen. His taste in literature and art was excellent, his manner dignified, though not gracious, his domestic life without blemish. Faithlessness was the chief cause of his disasters, and is the chief stain on his memory. He was, in truth, impelled by an incurable propensity to dark and crooked ways. It may seem strange that his conscience, which, on occasions of little moment, was sufficiently sensitive, should never have reproached him with this great vice. But there is reason to believe that he was perfidious, not only from constitution and from habit, but also on principle. He seems to have learned from the theologians whom he most esteemed that between him and his subjects there could be nothing of the nature of mutual contract ; that he could not, even if he would, divest himself of his despotic authority ; and that, in every promise which he made, there was an implied reservation that such promise might be broken in case of necessity, and that of the necessity he was the sole judge.

And now began that hazardous game on which were staked the destinies of the English people. It was played on the side of the House of Commons with keenness, but with admirable dexterity, coolness, and perseverance. Great statesmen who looked far behind them and far before them were at the head of that assembly. They were resolved to place the King in such a situation that he must either conduct the administration in conformity with the wishes of his Parliament, or make outrageous attacks on the most sacred principles of the constitution. They accordingly doled out supplies to him very sparingly. He found that he must govern either in harmony with the House of Commons, or in defiance of all law. His choice was soon made. He dissolved his first Parliament, and levied taxes by his own authority. He convoked a second Parliament, and found it more intractable than the first. He again resorted to the expedient of dissolution, raised fresh taxes without any show of legal right, and threw the chiefs of the opposition into prison. At the same time a new grievance, which the peculiar feelings and habits of the English nation made insupportably painful, and which seemed to all discerning men to be of fearful augury, excited general discontent and alarm. Companies of soldiers were billeted on the people; and martial law was, in some places, substituted for the ancient jurisprudence of the realm.

The King called a third Parliament, and soon perceived that the opposition was stronger and fiercer than ever. He now determined on a change of tactics. Instead of opposing an inflexible resistance to the

Tactics of the opposition in the House of Commons

SIR JOHN ELIOT

From the engraving by F. Holl in Forster's Life of Eliot

demands of the Commons, he, after much altercation and many evasions, agreed to a compromise which, if he had faithfully adhered to it, would have averted a long series of calamities. The Parliament granted an ample supply. The King ratified, in the most solemn manner, that **Petition of Right** celebrated law, which is known by the name of the Petition of Right, and which is the second Great Charter of the liberties of England. By ratifying that law he bound himself never again to raise money without the consent of the Houses, never again to imprison any person, except in due course of law, and never again to subject his people to the jurisdiction of courts martial.

The day on which the royal sanction was, after many delays, solemnly given to this great Act, was a day of joy and hope. The Commons, who crowded the bar of the House of Lords, broke forth into loud acclamations as soon as the clerk had pronounced the ancient form of words by which our princes have, during many ages, signified their assent to the wishes of the Estates of the realm. Those acclamations were reechoed by the voice of the capital and of the nation ; but within three weeks it became manifest that Charles had no intention of observing the compact into which he had entered. The supply given by the representatives of the nation was collected. The promise by which that supply had been obtained was broken. A violent contest followed. The Parliament was dissolved with every mark of royal displeasure. Some of the most distinguished members were imprisoned ; and one of them, Sir John Eliot, after years of suffering, died in confinement.

Charles, however, could not venture to raise, by his own authority, taxes sufficient for carrying on war. He accordingly hastened to make peace with his neighbours, and thenceforth gave his whole mind to British politics.

Now commenced a new era. Many English Kings had occasionally committed unconstitutional acts : but none had ever systematically attempted to make himself a despot, and to reduce the Parliament to a nullity. Such was the end which Charles distinctly proposed to himself. From March 1629 to April 1640, the Houses were not convoked. Never in our history had there been an interval of eleven years between Parliament and Parliament. Only once had there been an interval of even half that length. This fact alone is sufficient to refute those who represent Charles as having merely trodden in the footsteps of the Plantagenets and Tudors.

It is proved, by the testimony of the King's most strenuous supporters, that, during this part of his reign, the provisions of the Petition **Petition of Right violated** of Right were violated by him, not occasionally, but constantly, and on system ; that a large part of the revenue was raised without any legal authority ; and that persons obnoxious

The Right Honourable Sr THOMAS WENTWORTH Bar^t Earl of STRAFFORDE,
Viscount Wentworth Baron Wentworth of Wentworth Woodhouse, Newmarch, Oversley and Raby,
Lord Lieutenant of the Kingdom of IRELAND, and Lord President of the North of England,
of his Majesty's most Honourable Privy Council and Knight of the most Noble Order of ye Garter.
And Sr Philip Mainwaring Secretary of State.

STRAFFORD AND HIS SECRETARY

From the engraving by Vertue after the painting by Sir A. Van Dyck to the government languished for years in prison, without being ever called upon to plead before any tribunal.

For these things history must hold the King himself chiefly responsible. From the time of his third Parliament he was his own prime minister. Several persons, however, whose temper and talents were suited to his purposes, were at the head of different departments of the administration.

Thomas Wentworth, successively created Lord Wentworth and Earl of Strafford, a man of great abilities, eloquence, and courage, but of a Character cruel and imperious nature, was the counsellor most trusted and designs in political and military affairs. He had been one of the most of Went- distinguished members of the opposition, and felt towards worth those whom he had deserted that peculiar malignity which has, in all ages, been characteristic of apostates. He perfectly understood the feelings, the resources, and the policy of the party to which he had lately belonged, and had formed a vast and deeply meditated scheme which very nearly confounded even the able tactics of the statesmen by whom the House of Commons had been directed. To this scheme, in his confidential correspondence, he gave the expressive name of Thorough. His object was to do in England all, and more than all, that Richelieu was doing in France ; to make Charles a monarch as absolute as any on the Continent ; to put the estates and the personal liberty of the whole people at the disposal of the crown ; to deprive the courts of law of all independent authority, even in ordinary questions of civil right between man and man ; and to punish with merciless rigour all who murmured at the acts of the government, or who applied, even in the most decent and regular manner, to any tribunal for relief against those acts.[1]

This was his end ; and he distinctly saw in what manner alone this end could be attained. There was, in truth, about all his notions a clearness, a coherence, a precision, which, if he had not been pursuing an object pernicious to his country and to his kind, would have justly entitled him to high admiration. He saw that there was one instrument, and only one, by which his vast and daring projects could be carried into execution. That instrument was a standing army. To the forming of such an army, therefore, he directed all the energy of his strong mind. In Ireland, where he was viceroy, he actually succeeded in establishing a military despotism, not only over the aboriginal popu-

[1] The correspondence of Wentworth seems to me fully to bear out what I have said in the text. To transcribe all the passages which have led me to the conclusion at which I have arrived, would be impossible ; nor would it be easy to make a better selection than has already been made by Mr. Hallam. I may, however, direct the attention of the reader particularly to the very able paper which Wentworth drew up respecting the affairs of the Palatinate. The date is March 31. 1637.

lation, but also over the English colonists, and was able to boast that, in that island, the King was as absolute as any prince in the whole world could be.[1]

The ecclesiastical administration was, in the meantime, principally directed by William Laud, Archbishop of Canterbury. Of all the prelates of the Anglican Church, Laud had departed farthest from the principles of the Reformation, and had drawn nearest to Rome. His theology was more remote than even that of the Dutch Arminians from the theology of the Calvinists. His passion for ceremonies, his reverence for holidays, vigils, and sacred places, his ill concealed dislike of the marriage of ecclesiastics, the ardent and not altogether disinterested zeal with which he asserted the claims of the clergy to the reverence of the laity, would have made him an object of aversion to the Puritans, even if he had used only legal and gentle means for the attainment of his ends. But his understanding was narrow ; and his commerce with the world had been small. He was by nature rash, irritable, quick to feel for his own dignity, slow to sympathise with the sufferings of others, and prone to the error, common in superstitious men, of mistaking his own peevish and malignant moods for emotions of pious zeal. Under his direction every corner of the realm was subjected to a constant and minute inspection. Every little congregation of separatists was tracked out and broken up. Even the devotions of private families could not escape the vigilance of his spies. Such fear did his rigour inspire that the deadly hatred of the Church, which festered in innumerable bosoms, was generally disguised under an outward show of conformity. On the very eve of troubles, fatal to himself and to his order, the Bishops of several extensive dioceses were able to report to him that not a single dissenter was to be found within their jurisdiction.[2]

Character of Laud

The tribunals afforded no protection to the subject against the civil and ecclesiastical tyranny of that period. The judges of the common law, holding their situations during the pleasure of the King, were scandalously obsequious. Yet, obsequious as they were, they were less ready and less efficient instruments of arbitrary power than a class of courts, the memory of which is still, after the lapse of more than two centuries, held in deep abhorrence by the nation. Foremost among these courts in power and in infamy were the Star Chamber and the High Commission, the former a political, the latter a religious inquisition. Neither was a part of the old constitution of England. The Star Chamber had been remodelled, and the High Commission created, by the Tudors. The power which these boards had possessed before the accession of Charles had been extensive and

Star Chamber and High Commission

---

[1] These are Wentworth's own words. See his letter to Laud, dated Dec. 16. 1634.
[2] See his report to Charles for the year 1639.

formidable, but had been small indeed when compared with that which they now usurped. Guided chiefly by the violent spirit of the primate, and freed from the control of Parliament, they displayed a rapacity, a violence, a malignant energy, which had been unknown to any former age. The government was able through their instrumentality, to fine, imprison, pillory, and mutilate without restraint. A separate council which sate at York, under the presidency of Wentworth, was armed, in defiance of law, by a pure act of prerogative, with almost boundless power over the northern counties. All these tribunals insulted and defied the authority of Westminster Hall, and daily committed excesses which the most distinguished Royalists have warmly condemned. We are informed by Clarendon that there was hardly a man of note in the realm who had not personal experience of the harshness and greediness of the Star Chamber, that the High Commission had so conducted itself that it had scarce a friend left in the kingdom, and that the tyranny of the Council of York had made the Great Charter a dead letter on the north of the Trent.

The government of England was now, in all points but one, as despotic as that of France. But that one point was all important. There was still no standing army. There was, therefore, no security that the whole fabric of tyranny might not be subverted in a single day; and, if taxes were imposed by the royal authority for the support of an army, it was probable that there would be an immediate and irresistible explosion. This was the difficulty which more than any other perplexed Wentworth. The Lord Keeper Finch, in concert with other lawyers who were employed by the government, recommended an expedient, which was eagerly adopted. The ancient princes of England, as they called on the inhabitants of the counties near Scotland to arm and array themselves for the defence of the border, had sometimes called on the maritime counties to furnish ships for the defence of the coast. **Shipmoney** In the room of ships money had sometimes been accepted. This old practice it was now determined, after a long interval, not only to revive but to extend. Former princes had raised shipmoney only in time of war : it was now exacted in a time of profound peace. Former princes, even in the most perilous wars, had raised shipmoney only along the coasts : it was now exacted from the inland shires. Former princes had raised shipmoney only for the maritime defence of the country : it was now exacted, by the admission of the Royalists themselves, with the object, not of maintaining a navy, but of furnishing the King with supplies which might be increased at his discretion to any amount, and expended at his discretion for any purpose.

The whole nation was alarmed and incensed. John Hampden, an opulent and well born gentleman of Buckinghamshire, highly considered

ARCHBISHOP LAUD

From the painting in the National Portrait Gallery after Sir A. Van Dyck in his own neighbourhood, but as yet little known to the kingdom generally, had the courage to step forward, to confront the whole power of the government, and take on himself the cost and the risk of disputing the prerogative to which the King laid claim. The case was argued before the judges in the Exchequer Chamber. So strong were the arguments against the pretensions of the crown that, dependent and servile as the judges were, the majority against Hampden was the smallest possible. Still there was a majority. The interpreters of the law had pronounced that one great and productive tax might be imposed by the royal authority. Wentworth justly observed that it was impossible to vindicate their judgment except by reasons directly leading to a conclusion which they had not ventured to draw. If money might legally be raised without the consent of Parliament for the support of a fleet, it was not easy to deny that money might, without consent of Parliament, be legally raised for the support of an army.

The decision of the judges increased the irritation of the people. A century earlier, irritation less serious would have produced a general rising. But discontent did not now so readily as in an earlier age take the form of rebellion. The nation had been long steadily advancing in wealth and in civilisation. Since the great northern Earls took up arms against Elizabeth seventy years had elapsed; and during those seventy years there had been no civil war. Never, during the whole existence of the English nation, had so long a period passed without intestine hostilities. Men had become accustomed to the pursuits of peaceful industry, and, exasperated as they were, hesitated long before they drew the sword.

This was the conjuncture at which the liberties of the nation were in the greatest peril. The opponents of the government began to despair of the destiny of their country; and many looked to the American wilderness as the only asylum in which they could enjoy civil and spiritual freedom. There a few resolute Puritans, who, in the cause of their religion, feared neither the rage of the ocean nor the hardships of uncivilised life, neither the fangs of savage beasts nor the tomahawks of more savage men, had built, amidst the primeval forest, villages which are now great and opulent cities, but which have, through every change, retained some trace of the character derived from their founders. The government regarded these infant colonies with aversion, and attempted violently to stop the stream of emigration, but could not prevent the population of New England from being largely recruited by stouthearted and Godfearing men from every part of the old England. And now Wentworth exulted in the near prospect of Thorough. A few years might probably suffice for the execution of his great design. If strict economy were observed, if all collision with foreign powers were care-

JOHN HAMPDEN

From the painting by R. Walker in the National Portrait Gallery fully avoided, the debts of the crown would be cleared off : there would be funds available for the support of a large military force ; and that force would soon break the refractory spirit of the nation.

At this crisis an act of insane bigotry suddenly changed the whole face of public affairs. Had the King been wise, he would have pursued

Resistance to the Liturgy in Scotland a cautious and soothing policy towards Scotland till he was master in the South. For Scotland was of all his kingdoms that in which there was the greatest risk that a spark might produce a flame, and that a flame might become a conflagration. Constitutional opposition, indeed, such as he had encountered at Westminster, he had not to apprehend at Edinburgh. The Parliament of his northern kingdom was a very different body from that which bore the same name in England. It was ill constituted : it was little considered ; and it had never imposed any serious restraint on any of his predecessors. The three Estates sate in one house. The commissioners of the burghs were considered merely as retainers of the great nobles. No act could be introduced till it had been approved by the Lords of Articles, a committee which was really, though not in form, nominated by the crown. But, though the Scottish Parliament was obsequious, the Scottish people had always been singularly turbulent and ungovernable. They had butchered their first James in his bedchamber : they had repeatedly arrayed themselves in arms against James the Second : they had slain James the Third on the field of battle : their disobedience had broken the heart of James the Fifth : they had deposed and imprisoned Mary : they had led her son captive ; and their temper was still as intractable as ever. Their habits were rude and martial. All along the southern border, and all along the line between the highlands and the lowlands raged an incessant predatory war. In every part of the country men were accustomed to redress their wrongs by the strong hand. Whatever loyalty the nation had anciently felt to the Stuarts had cooled during their long absence. The supreme influence over the public mind was divided between two classes of malecontents, the lords of the soil and the preachers ; lords animated by the same spirit which had often impelled the old Douglasses to withstand the royal house, and preachers who had inherited the republican opinions and the unconquerable spirit of Knox. Both the national and religious feelings of the population had been wounded. All orders of men complained that their country, that country which had, with so much glory, defended her independence against the ablest and bravest Plantagenets, had, through the instrumentality of her native princes, become in effect, though not in name, a province of England. In no part of Europe had the Calvinistic doctrine and discipline taken so strong a hold on the public mind. The Church of Rome was regarded by the great body of the people with a hatred which might justly be called ferocious; and the Church of England, which seemed to be every day becoming more and more like the Church of Rome, was an object of scarcely less aversion.

The government had long wished to extend the Anglican system over the whole island, and had already, with this view, made several changes highly distasteful to every Presbyterian. One innovation, however, the most hazardous of all, because it was directly cognisable by the senses of the common people, had not yet been attempted. The public worship of God was still conducted in the manner acceptable to the nation. Now, however, Charles and Laud determined to force on the Scots the English liturgy, or rather a liturgy which, wherever it differed from that of England, differed, in the judgment of all rigid Protestants, for the worse.

To this step, taken in the mere wantonness of tyranny, and in criminal ignorance or more criminal contempt of public feeling, our country owes her freedom. The first performance of the foreign ceremonies produced a riot. The riot rapidly became a revolution. Ambition, patriotism, fanaticism, were mingled in one headlong torrent. The whole nation was in arms. The power of England was indeed, as appeared some years later, sufficient to coerce Scotland : but a large part of the English people sympathised with the religious feelings of the insurgents ; and many Englishmen who had no scruple about antiphonies and genuflexions, altars and surplices, saw with pleasure the progress of a rebellion which seemed likely to confound the arbitrary projects of the court, and to make the calling of a Parliament necessary.

For the senseless freak which had produced these effects Wentworth is not responsible.[1] It had, in fact, thrown all his plans into confusion. To counsel submission, however, was not in his nature. An attempt was made to put down the insurrection by the sword : but the King's military means and military talents were unequal to the task. A Parliament called and dissolved To impose fresh taxes on England in defiance of law would, at this conjuncture, have been madness. No resource was left but a Parliament ; and in the spring of 1640 a Parliament was convoked.

The nation had been put into good humour by the prospect of seeing constitutional government restored, and grievances redressed. The new House of Commons was more temperate and more respectful to the throne than any which had sate since the death of Elizabeth. The moderation of this assembly has been highly extolled by the most distinguished Royalists, and seems to have caused no small vexation and disappointment to the chiefs of the opposition : but it was the uniform practice of Charles, a practice equally impolitic and ungenerous, to refuse

[1] See his letter to the Earl of Northumberland, dated July 30. 1638.

My very good Lord,

What euer my occasions or hast be, itt must not depriue me the happines of still putting your L^p in remembrance, of this seruantt of yours, who will euer be the readiest to receaue, and the most carefull to fullfill your commaundes in the whole world. Heare J am the whilst in exceeaue labour, to gett a little before hande with my busineße if posibly J maybe soe happy, being to deale with a Generation, that haue the pointes of ther weapon turned wholly to ther owne priuates, but wee edge att all for the publike, heare they are as dull, as sharpe and eager to cutt out for themselues in the other. J see itt is a maxime amongst them, to keepe the Depuÿe as ignorantt as poßibly they can, that soe allbeit not in place, yet he may be subordinate to them in knowledge, wch J take to be the true reason, that not any one of them hetherto hath made me any proposition att all for the bettering of his Ma.^tyes seruice, J am purposed on the other side to open my eyes as wide as J can, and dispaire not in time to be able to sounde the depthe, they conceit soe much to reserue from me. J finde all the reuenew heare reduced to fee farmes and noe poßible meanes consequently to aduance itt, and in the meane time greate matters expected indeed imposibilities from me in Englande, wch is a wofull condition of a seruantt to dwell under the preßure of expectation, and be lefft or afforded noe meanes to discharadge himself,

from vnder the burthen of itt. J beseech your Lop lett me in this as J haue
dun in many things els finde your fauour and be pleased to take me we
faire into your care, as to weede out this growing inconveniences forth of our
maisters minde, incase you at any time finde itt to shoote up wth
him; ther is not many that haue the meanes to doe it for me, nor
many the particulars wherein you may oblige me more then in this,
J shall be sure to doe the vttermost that lies in me, for J haue a harte
can willingly sacrifise all that euer J haue for his Maty (if J doe not
deceaue my self) wth a chearfullnes and faithe extraordinary, only
J am fearefull that whilst imposibilities are expected at my hands
the best J can doe, should not be accepted, nay imputed into me as a
crime. My lo. J will detaine you noe longer farther then to
beseeche you to be confident J must euer inuiolably approue my
self

Dublin this 27th of August.
1633.

yor Lops.
most humble and most faithfull
seruant

Wentworth

all compliance with the desires of his people, till those desires were expressed in a menacing tone. As soon as the Commons showed a disposition to take into consideration the grievances under which the country had suffered during eleven years, the King dissolved the Parliament with every mark of displeasure.

Between the dissolution of this shortlived assembly and the meeting of that ever memorable body known by the name of the Long Parliament, intervened a few months, during which the yoke was pressed down more severely than ever on the nation, while the spirit of the nation rose up more angrily than ever against the yoke. Members of the House of Commons were questioned by the Privy Council touching their parliamentary conduct, and thrown into prison for refusing to reply. Ship-money was levied with increased rigour. The Lord Mayor and the Sheriffs of London were threatened with imprisonment for remissness in collecting the payments. Soldiers were enlisted by force. Money for their support was exacted from their counties. Torture, which had always been illegal, and which had recently been declared illegal even by the servile judges of that age, was inflicted for the last time in England in the month of May 1640.

Everything now depended on the event of the King's military operations against the Scots. Among his troops there was little of that feeling which separates professional soldiers from the mass of a nation, and attaches them to their leaders. His army, composed for the most part of recruits, who regretted the plough from which they had been violently taken, and who were imbued with the religious and political sentiments then prevalent throughout the country, was more formidable to himself than to the enemy. The Scots, encouraged by the heads of the English opposition, and feebly resisted by the English forces, marched across the Tweed and the Tyne, and encamped on the borders of Yorkshire. And now the murmurs of discontent swelled into an uproar by which all spirits save one were overawed. But the voice of Strafford was still for Thorough; and he, even in this extremity, showed a nature so cruel and despotic, that his own pikemen were ready to tear him in pieces.

There was yet one last expedient which, as the King flattered himself, might save him from the misery of facing another House of Commons. To the House of Lords he was less averse. The Bishops were devoted to him; and, though the temporal peers were generally dissatisfied with his administration, they were, as a class, so deeply interested in the maintenance of order, and in the stability of ancient institutions, that they were not likely to call for extensive reforms. Departing from the uninterrupted practice of centuries, he called a Great Council consisting of Lords alone. But the Lords were too prudent to assume the unconstitutional functions with which he wished to invest them. Without money, without credit, without authority even in his own camp, he yielded to the pressure of necessity. The Houses were convoked; and the elections proved that, since the spring, the distrust and hatred with which the government was regarded had made fearful progress.

In November 1640 met that renowned Parliament which, in spite of many errors and disasters, is justly entitled to the reverence and gratitude of all who, in any part of the world, enjoy the **The Long** blessings of constitutional government.   **Parliament**

During the year which followed, no very important division of opinion appeared in the Houses. The civil and ecclesiastical administration had, through a period of near twelve years, been so oppressive and so unconstitutional that even those classes of which the inclinations are generally on the side of order and authority were eager to promote popular reforms, and to bring the instruments of tyranny to justice. It was enacted that no interval of more than three years should ever elapse between Parliament and Parliament, and that, if writs under the Great Seal were not issued at the proper time, the returning officers should, without such writs, call the constituent bodies together for the choice of representatives. The Star Chamber, the High Commission, the Council of York were swept away. Men who, after suffering cruel mutilations, had been confined in remote dungeons, regained their liberty. On the chief ministers of the crown the vengeance of the nation was unsparingly wreaked. The Lord Keeper, the Primate, the Lord Lieutenant were impeached. Finch saved himself by flight. Laud was flung into the Tower. Strafford was put to death by act of attainder. On the day on which this act passed, the King gave his assent to a law by which he bound himself not to adjourn, prorogue, or dissolve the existing Parliament without its own consent.

After ten months of assiduous toil, the Houses, in September 1641, adjourned for a short vacation; and the King visited Scotland. He with difficulty pacified that kingdom by consenting, not only to relinquish his plans of ecclesiastical reform, but even to pass, with a very bad grace, an act declaring that episcopacy was contrary to the word of God.

The recess of the English Parliament lasted six weeks. The day on which the Houses met again is one of the most remarkable epochs in our history. From that day dates the corporate existence **First appear-** of the two great parties which have ever since alternately **ance of the** governed the country. In one sense, indeed, the distinction **two great** which then became obvious had always existed, and always **English** must exist. For it has its origin in diversities of temper, of under- **parties** standing, and of interest, which are found in all societies, and which will be found till the human mind ceases to be drawn in opposite directions by the charm of habit and by the charm of novelty. Not only in politics, but in literature, in art, in science, in surgery and mechanics, in navigation and agriculture, nay, even in mathematics, we find this distinction.   Everywhere there is a class of men who cling with fondness to whatever is ancient, and who, even when convinced by overpowering reasons that innovation would be beneficial, consent to it with many misgivings and forebodings.   We find also everywhere another class of men, sanguine in hope, bold in speculation, always pressing forward, quick to discern the imperfections of whatever exists, disposed to think lightly of the risks and inconveniences which attend improvements, and disposed to give every change credit for being an improvement.   In the sentiments of both classes there is something to approve.   But of both the best specimens will be found not far from the common frontier. The extreme section of one class consists of bigoted dotards : the extreme section of the other consists of shallow and reckless empirics.

There can be no doubt that in our very first Parliaments might have been discerned a body of members anxious to preserve, and a body eager to reform.   But, while the sessions of the legislature were short, these bodies did not take definite and permanent forms, array themselves under recognised leaders, or assume distinguishing names, badges, and war cries.   During the first months of the Long Parliament, the indignation excited by many years of lawless oppression was so strong and general that the House of Commons acted as one man.   Abuse after abuse disappeared without a struggle.   If a small minority of the representative body wished to retain the Star Chamber and the High Commission, that minority, overawed by the enthusiasm and by the numerical superiority of the reformers, contented itself with secretly regretting institutions which could not, with any hope of success, be openly defended.   At a later period the Royalists found it convenient to antedate the separation between themselves and their opponents, and to attribute the Act which restrained the King from dissolving or proroguing the Parliament, the Triennial Act, the impeachment of the ministers, and the attainder of Strafford, to the faction which afterwards made war on the King.   But no artifice could be more disingenuous. Every one of those strong measures was actively promoted by the men who were afterwards foremost among the Cavaliers.   No republican spoke of the long misgovernment of Charles more severely than Colepepper.   The most remarkable speech in favour of the Triennial Bill was made by Digby.   The impeachment of the Lord Keeper was moved by Falkland.   The demand that the Lord Lieutenant should be kept close prisoner was made at the bar of the Lords by Hyde.   Not till the law attainting Strafford was proposed did the signs of serious disunion become visible.   Even against that law, a law which nothing but extreme necessity could justify, only about sixty members of the House of Commons voted. It is certain that Hyde was not in the minority, and that Falkland not only voted with the majority, but spoke strongly for the bill. Even the few who entertained a scruple about inflicting death by a retrospective enactment thought it necessary to express the utmost abhorrence of Strafford's character and administration.

But under this apparent concord a great schism was latent; and when, in October 1641, the Parliament reassembled after a short recess, two hostile parties, essentially the same with those which, under different names, have ever since contended, and are still contending, for the direction of public affairs, appeared confronting each other. During some years they were designated as Cavaliers and Roundheads. They were subsequently called Tories and Whigs; nor does it seem that these appellations are likely soon to become obsolete.

It would not be difficult to compose a lampoon or a panegyric on either of these renowned factions. For no man not utterly destitute of judgment and candour will deny that there are many deep stains on the fame of the party to which he belongs, or that the party to which he is opposed may justly boast of many illustrious names, of many heroic actions, and of many great services rendered to the state. The truth is that, though both parties have often seriously erred, England could have spared neither. If, in her institutions, freedom and order, the advantages arising from innovation and the advantages arising from prescription, have been combined to an extent elsewhere unknown, we may attribute this happy peculiarity to the strenuous conflicts and alternate victories of two rival confederacies of statesmen, a confederacy zealous for authority and antiquity, and a confederacy zealous for liberty and progress.

It ought to be remembered that the difference between the two great sections of English politicians has always been a difference rather of degree than of principle. There were certain limits on the right and on the left, which were very rarely overstepped. A few enthusiasts on one side were ready to lay all our laws and franchises at the feet of our Kings. A few enthusiasts on the other side were bent on pursuing, through endless civil troubles, their darling phantom of a republic. But the great majority of those who fought for the crown were averse to despotism; and the great majority of the champions of popular rights were averse to anarchy. Twice, in the course of the seventeenth century, the two parties suspended their dissensions, and united their strength in a common cause. Their first coalition restored hereditary monarchy. Their second coalition rescued constitutional freedom.

It is also to be noted that these two parties have never been the whole nation, nay, that they have never, taken together, made up a majority of the nation. Between them has always been a great mass,

which has not steadfastly adhered to either, which has sometimes remained inertly neutral, and which has sometimes oscillated to and fro.
That mass has more than once passed in a few years from one extreme
to the other, and back again.   Sometimes it has changed sides, merely
because it was tired of supporting the same men, sometimes because it
was dismayed by its own excesses, sometimes because it had expected
impossibilities, and had been disappointed.   But, whenever it has leaned
with its whole weight in either direction, that weight has, for the time,
been irresistible.

When the rival parties first appeared in a distinct form, they seemed
to be not unequally matched.   On the side of the government was a
large majority of the nobles, and of those opulent and well descended
gentlemen to whom nothing was wanting of nobility but the name.
These, with the dependents whose support they could command, were
no small power in the state.   On the same side were the great body of
the clergy, both the Universities, and all those laymen who were strongly
attached to episcopal government and to the Anglican ritual.   These
respectable classes found themselves in the company of some allies much
less decorous than themselves.   The Puritan austerity drove to the King's
faction all who made pleasure their business, who affected gallantry,
splendour of dress, or taste in the lighter arts.   With these went all who
live by amusing the leisure of others, from the painter and the comic poet,
down to the ropedancer and the Merry Andrew.   For these artists well
knew that they might thrive under a superb and luxurious despotism,
but must starve under the rigid rule of the precisians.   In the same
interest were the Roman Catholics to a man.   The Queen, a daughter
of France, was of their own faith.   Her husband was known to be strongly
attached to her, and not a little in awe of her.   Though undoubtedly a
Protestant on conviction, he regarded the professors of the old religion
with no ill will, and would gladly have granted them a much larger
toleration than he was disposed to concede to the Presbyterians.   If the
opposition obtained the mastery, it was probable that the sanguinary
laws enacted against Papists, in the reign of Elizabeth, would be severely
enforced.   The Roman Catholics were therefore induced by the strongest
motives to espouse the cause of the court.   They in general acted with
a caution which brought on them the reproach of cowardice and luke-
warmness : but it is probable that, in maintaining great reserve, they
consulted the King's interest as well as their own.   It was not for his
service that they should be conspicuous among his friends.

The main strength of the opposition lay among the small freeholders
in the country, and among the merchants and shopkeepers of the towns.
But these were headed by a formidable minority of the aristocracy, a
minority which included the rich and powerful Earls of Northumberland,

QUEEN HENRIETTA MARIA

From the painting attributed to Jan Van Belcamp in the National Portrait Gallery

Bedford, Warwick, Stamford, and Essex, and several other Lords of great wealth and influence. In the same ranks was found the whole body of Protestant Nonconformists, and most of those members of the Established Church who still adhered to the Calvinistic opinions which, forty years before, had been generally held by the prelates and clergy. The municipal corporations took, with few exceptions, the same side. In the House of Commons the opposition preponderated, but not very decidedly.

Neither party wanted strong arguments for the course which it was disposed to take. The reasonings of the most enlightened Royalists may be summed up thus :—" It is true that great abuses have existed ; but they have been redressed. It is true that precious rights have been invaded ; but they have been vindicated and surrounded with new securities. The sittings of the Estates of the realm have been, in defiance of all precedent and of the spirit of the constitution, intermitted during eleven years ; but it has now been provided that henceforth three years shall never elapse without a Parliament. The Star Chamber, the High Commission, the Council of York, oppressed and plundered us ; but those hateful courts have now ceased to exist. The Lord Lieutenant aimed at establishing military despotism ; but he has answered for his treason with his head. The Primate tainted our worship with Popish rites, and punished our scruples with Popish cruelty ; but he is awaiting in the Tower the judgment of his peers. The Lord Keeper sanctioned a plan by which the property of every man in England was placed at the mercy of the Crown ; but he has been disgraced, ruined, and compelled to take refuge in a foreign land. The ministers of tyranny have expiated their crimes. The victims of tyranny have been compensated for their sufferings. It would therefore be most unwise to persevere further in that course which was justifiable and necessary when we first met, after a long interval, and found the whole administration one mass of abuses. It is time to take heed that we do not so pursue our victory over despotism as to run into anarchy. It was not in our power to overturn the bad institutions which lately afflicted our country, without shocks which have loosened the foundations of government. Now that those institutions have fallen we must hasten to prop the edifice which it was lately our duty to batter. Henceforth it will be our wisdom to look with jealousy on schemes of innovation, and to guard from encroachment all the prerogatives with which the law has, for the public good, armed the sovereign."

Such were the views of those men of whom the excellent Falkland may be regarded as the leader. It was contended on the other side with not less force, by men of not less ability and virtue, that the safety which the liberties of the English people enjoyed was rather apparent than real, and that the arbitrary projects of the court would be resumed as soon as the vigilance of the Commons was relaxed.   True it was,—such was the reasoning of Pym, of Hollis, and of Hampden,—that many good laws had been passed : but, if good laws had been sufficient to restrain the King, his subjects would have had little reason ever to complain of his administration.   The recent statutes were surely not of more authority than the Great Charter or the Petition of Right.   Yet neither the Great Charter, hallowed by the veneration of four centuries, nor the Petition of Right, sanctioned, after mature reflection, and for valuable consideration, by Charles himself, had been found effectual for the protection of the people.   If once the check of fear were withdrawn, if once the spirit of opposition were suffered to slumber, all the securities for English freedom resolved themselves into a single one, the royal word ; and it had been proved by a long and severe experience that the royal word could not be trusted.

The two parties were still regarding each other with cautious hostility, and had not yet measured their strength, when news arrived which inflamed the passions and confirmed the opinions of both.   The *The Irish* great chieftains of Ulster, who, at the time of the accession of *Rebellion* James, had, after a long struggle, submitted to the royal authority, had not long brooked the humiliation of dependence.   They had conspired against the English government, and had been attainted of treason. Their immense domains had been forfeited to the crown, and had soon been peopled by thousands of English and Scotch emigrants.   The new settlers were, in civilisation and intelligence, far superior to the native population, and sometimes abused their superiority.   The animosity produced by difference of race was increased by difference of religion. Under the iron rule of Wentworth, scarcely a murmur was heard : but, when that strong pressure was withdrawn, when Scotland had set the example of successful resistance, when England was distracted by internal quarrels, the smothered rage of the Irish broke forth into acts of fearful violence.   On a sudden, the aboriginal population rose on the colonists. A war, to which national and theological hatred gave a character of peculiar ferocity, desolated Ulster, and spread to the neighbouring provinces.   The castle of Dublin was scarcely thought secure.   Every post brought to London exaggerated accounts of outrages which, without any exaggeration, were sufficient to move pity and horror.   These evil tidings roused to the height the zeal of both the great parties which were marshalled against each other at Westminster.   The Royalists maintained that it was the first duty of every good Englishman and Protestant, at such a crisis, to strengthen the hands of the sovereign.   To the opposition it seemed that there were now stronger reasons than ever for thwarting and restraining him.   That the commonwealth was in danger was undoubtedly a good reason for giving large powers to a trustworthy magistrate : but it was a good reason for taking away powers from a magistrate who was at heart a public enemy. To raise a great army had always been the King's first object. A great army must now be raised. It was to be feared that, unless some new securities were devised, the forces levied for the reduction of Ireland would be employed against the liberties of England. Nor was this all. A horrible suspicion, unjust indeed, but not altogether unnatural, had arisen in many minds. The Queen was an avowed Roman Catholic : the King was not regarded by the Puritans, whom he had mercilessly persecuted, as a sincere Protestant ; and so notorious was his duplicity, that there was no treachery of which his subjects might not, with some show of reason, believe him capable. It was soon whispered that the rebellion of the Roman Catholics of Ulster was part of a vast work of darkness which had been planned at Whitehall.

After some weeks of prelude, the first great parliamentary conflict between the parties, which have ever since contended, and are still con-
The remonstrance tending, for the government of the nation, took place on the twenty-second of November 1641. It was moved by the opposition, that the House of Commons should present to the King a remonstrance, enumerating the faults of his administration from the time of his accession, and expressing the distrust with which his policy was still regarded by his people. That assembly, which a few months before had been unanimous in calling for the reform of abuses, was now divided into two fierce and eager factions of nearly equal strength. After a hot debate of many hours, the remonstrance was carried by only eleven votes.

The result of this struggle was highly favourable to the conservative party. It could not be doubted that only some great indiscretion could prevent them from shortly obtaining the predominance in the Lower House. The Upper House was already their own. Nothing was wanting to insure their success, but that the King should, in all his conduct, show respect for the laws and scrupulous good faith towards his subjects.

His first measures promised well. He had, it seemed, at last discovered that an entire change of system was necessary, and had wisely made up his mind to what could no longer be avoided. He declared his determination to govern in harmony with the Commons, and, for that end, to call to his councils men in whose talents and character the Commons might place confidence. Nor was the selection ill made. Falkland, Hyde, and Colepepper, all three distinguished by the part which they had taken in reforming abuses and in punishing evil ministers, were invited to become the confidential advisers of the Crown, and were solemnly assured by Charles that he would take no step in any way affecting the Lower House of Parliament without their privity.

Had he kept this promise, it cannot be doubted that the reaction which was already in progress would very soon have become quite as strong as the most respectable Royalists would have desired. Already the violent members of the opposition had begun to despair of the fortunes of their party, to tremble for their own safety, and to talk of selling their estates and emigrating to America. That the fair prospects which had begun to open before the King were suddenly overcast, that his life was darkened by adversity, and at length shortened by violence, is to be attributed to his own faithlessness and contempt of law.

REDUCED FACSIMILE OF THE KING'S ORDER FOR THE IMPEACHMENT
OF THE FIVE MEMBERS

The truth seems to be that he detested both the parties into which the House of Commons was divided : nor is this strange ; for in both those parties the love of liberty and the love of order were mingled, though in different proportions. The advisers whom necessity had compelled him to call round him were by no means men after his own heart. They had joined in condemning his tyranny, in abridging his power, and in punishing his instruments. They were now indeed prepared to defend in a strictly legal way his strictly legal prerogative ; but they would have recoiled with horror from the thought of reviving Wentworth's projects of Thorough. They were, therefore, in the King's opinion, traitors, who differed only in the degree of their seditious malignity from Pym and Hampden.

He accordingly, a few days after he had promised the chiefs of the constitutional Royalists that no step of importance should be taken with-

Impeach-
ment of
the five
members

out their knowledge, formed a resolution the most momentous of his whole life, carefully concealed that resolution from them, and executed it in a manner which overwhelmed them with shame and dismay. He sent the Attorney General to impeach Pym, Hollis, Hampden, and other members of the House of Commons of high treason at the bar of the House of Lords. Not content with this flagrant violation of the Great Charter and of the uninterrupted practice of centuries, he went in person, accompanied by armed men, to seize the leaders of the opposition within the walls of Parliament.

The attempt failed. The accused members had left the House a short time before Charles entered it. A sudden and violent revulsion of feeling, both in the Parliament and in the country, followed. The most favourable view that has ever been taken of the King's conduct on this occasion by his most partial advocates is that he had weakly suffered himself to be hurried into a gross indiscretion by the evil counsels of his wife and of his courtiers. But the general voice loudly charged him with far deeper guilt. At the very moment at which his subjects, after a long estrangement produced by his maladministration, were returning to him with feelings of confidence and affection, he had aimed a deadly blow at all their dearest rights, at the privileges of Parliament, at the very principle of trial by jury. He had shown that he considered opposition to his arbitrary designs as a crime to be expiated only by blood. He had broken faith, not only with his Great Council and with his people, but with his own adherents. He had done what, but for an unforeseen accident, would probably have produced a bloody conflict round the Speaker's chair. Those who had the chief sway in the Lower House now felt that not only their power and popularity, but their lands and their necks, were staked on the event of the struggle in which they were engaged. The flagging zeal of the party opposed to the court revived in an instant. During the night which followed the outrage the whole city of London was in arms. In a few hours the roads leading to the capital were covered with multitudes of yeomen spurring hard to Westminster with the badges of the parliamentary cause in their hats. In the House of Commons the opposition became at once irresistible, and carried, by more than two votes to one, resolutions of unprecedented violence. Strong bodies of the trainbands, regularly relieved, mounted guard round Westminster Hall. The gates of the King's palace were daily besieged by a furious multitude whose taunts and execrations were heard even in the presence chamber, and who could scarcely be kept out of the royal apartments by the gentlemen of the household. Had Charles remained much longer in his stormy capital, it is probable that the Commons would have found a plea for making him, under outward forms of respect, a state prisoner.

He quitted London, never to return till the day of a terrible and memorable reckoning had arrived. A negotiation began which occupied many months. Accusations and recriminations passed back-   Departure ward and forward between the contending parties. All   of Charles from accommodation had become impossible. The sure punish-   London ment which waits on habitual perfidy had at length overtaken the King. It was to no purpose that he now pawned his royal word, and invoked heaven to witness the sincerity of his professions. The distrust with which his adversaries regarded him was not to be removed by oaths or treaties. They were convinced that they could be safe only when he was utterly helpless. Their demand, therefore, was, that he should surrender, not only those prerogatives which he had usurped in violation of ancient laws and of his own recent promises, but also other prerogatives which the English Kings had always possessed, and continue to possess at the present day. No minister must be appointed, no peer created, without the consent of the Houses. Above all, the sovereign must resign that supreme military authority which, from time beyond all memory, had appertained to the regal office.

That Charles would comply with such demands while he had any means of resistance was not to be expected. Yet it will be difficult to show that the Houses could safely have exacted less. They were truly in a most embarrassing position. The great majority of the nation was firmly attached to hereditary monarchy. Those who held republican opinions were as yet few, and did not venture to speak out. It was therefore impossible to abolish kingly government. Yet it was plain that no confidence could be placed in the King. It would have been absurd in those who knew, by recent proof, that he was bent on destroying them, to content themselves with presenting to him another Petition of Right, and receiving from him fresh promises similar to those which he had repeatedly made and broken. Nothing but the want of an army had prevented him from entirely subverting the old constitution of the realm. It was now necessary to levy a great regular army for the conquest of Ireland ; and it would therefore have been mere insanity to leave him in possession of that plenitude of military authority which his ancestors had enjoyed.

When a country is in the situation in which England then was, when the kingly office is regarded with love and veneration, but the person who fills that office is hated and distrusted, it should seem that the course which ought to be taken is obvious. The dignity of the office should be preserved : the person should be discarded. Thus our ancestors acted in 1399 and in 1689. Had there been, in 1642, any man occupying a position similar to that which Henry of Lancaster occupied at the time of the deposition of Richard the Second, and which William of Orange occupied at the time of the deposition of James the Second, it is probable that the Houses would have changed the dynasty, and would have made no formal change in the constitution. The new King, called to the throne by their choice, and dependent on their support, would have been under the necessity of governing in conformity with their wishes and opinions. But there was no prince of the blood royal in the parliamentary party ; and, though that party contained many men of high rank, and many men of eminent ability, there was none who towered so conspicuously above the rest that he could be proposed as a candidate for the crown. As there was to be a King, and as no new King could be found, it was necessary to leave the regal title to Charles. Only one course, therefore, was left : and that was to disjoin the regal title from the regal prerogatives.

The change which the Houses proposed to make in our institutions, though it seems exorbitant, when distinctly set forth and digested into articles of capitulation, really amounts to little more than the change which, in the next generation, was effected by the Revolution. It is true that, at the Revolution, the sovereign was not deprived by law of the power of naming his ministers: but it is equally true that, since the Revolution, no minister has been able to retain office six months in opposition to the sense of the House of Commons. It is true that the sovereign still possesses the power of creating peers, and the more important power of the sword : but it is equally true that in the exercise of these powers the sovereign has, ever since the Revolution, been guided by advisers who possess the confidence of the representatives of the nation. In fact, the leaders of the Roundhead party in 1642, and the statesmen who, about half a century later, effected the Revolution, had exactly the same object in view. That object was to terminate the contest between the Crown and the Parliament, by giving to the Parliament a supreme control over the executive administration. The statesmen of the Revolution effected this indirectly by changing the dynasty. The Roundheads of 1642, being unable to change the dynasty, were compelled to take a direct course towards their end.

We cannot, however, wonder that the demands of the opposition, importing as they did a complete and formal transfer to the Parliament of powers which had always belonged to the Crown, should have shocked that great party of which the characteristics are respect for constituted authority and dread of violent innovation. That party had recently been in hopes of obtaining by peaceable means the ascendency in the

House of Commons; but every such hope had been blighted. The duplicity of Charles had made his old enemies irreconcileable, had driven back into the ranks of the disaffected a crowd of moderate men who were in the very act of coming over to his side, and had so cruelly mortified his best friends that they had for a time stood aloof in silent shame and resentment. Now, however, the constitutional Royalists were forced to make their choice between two dangers; and they thought it their duty rather to rally round a prince whose past conduct they condemned, and whose word inspired them with little confidence, than to suffer the regal office to be degraded, and the polity of the realm to be entirely remodelled. With such feelings, many men whose virtues and abilities would have done honour to any cause ranged themselves on the side of the King.

In August 1642 the sword was at length drawn; and soon, in almost every shire of the kingdom, two hostile factions appeared in arms against each other. It is not easy to say which of the contending parties was at first the more formidable. The Houses commanded London and the counties round London, the fleet, the navigation of the Thames, and most of the large towns and seaports. They had at their disposal almost all the military stores of the kingdom, and were able to raise duties, both on goods imported from foreign countries, and on some important products of domestic industry. The King was ill provided with artillery and ammunition. The taxes which he laid on the rural districts occupied by his troops produced, it is probable, a sum far less than that which the Parliament drew from the city of London alone. He relied, indeed, chiefly, for pecuniary aid, on the munificence of his opulent adherents. Many of these mortgaged their land, pawned their jewels, and broke up their silver chargers and christening bowls, in order to assist him. But experience has fully proved that the voluntary liberality of individuals, even in times of the greatest excitement, is a poor financial resource when compared with severe and methodical taxation, which presses on the willing and unwilling alike.

Charles, however, had one advantage, which, if he had used it well, would have more than compensated for the want of stores and money, and which, notwithstanding his mismanagement, gave him, during some months, a superiority in the war. His troops at first fought much better than those of the Parliament. Both armies, it is true, were almost entirely composed of men who had never seen a field of battle. Nevertheless, the difference was great. The parliamentary ranks were filled with hirelings whom want and idleness had induced to enlist. Hampden's regiment was regarded as one of the best; and even Hampden's regiment was described by Cromwell as a mere rabble of

tapsters and serving men out of place.   The royal army, on the other
hand, consisted in great part of gentlemen, high spirited, ardent, accustomed to consider dishonour as more terrible than death, accustomed to
fencing, to the use of fire arms, to bold riding, and to manly and perilous
sport, which has been well called the image of war.   Such gentlemen,
mounted on their favourite horses, and commanding little bands, composed of their younger brothers, grooms, gamekeepers, and huntsmen,
were, from the very first day on which they took the field, qualified to
play their part with credit in a skirmish.   The steadiness, the prompt
obedience, the mechanical precision of movement, which are characteristic of the regular soldier, these gallant volunteers never attained.
But they were at first opposed to enemies as undisciplined as themselves,
and far less active, athletic, and daring.   For a time, therefore, the
Cavaliers were successful in almost every encounter.

The Houses had also been unfortunate in the choice of a general.
The rank and wealth of the Earl of Essex made him one of the most
important members of the parliamentary party.   He had borne arms on
the Continent with credit, and, when the war began, had as high a
military reputation as any man in the country.   But it soon appeared
that he was unfit for the post of Commander in Chief.   He had little
energy and no originality.   The methodical tactics which he had learned
in the war of the Palatinate did not save him from the disgrace of being
surprised and baffled by such a Captain as Rupert, who could claim no
higher fame than that of an enterprising partisan.

Nor were the officers who held the chief commissions under Essex
qualified to supply what was wanting in him.   For this, indeed, the
Houses are scarcely to be blamed.   In a country which had not, within
the memory of the oldest person living, made war on a great scale by
land, generals of tried skill and valour were not to be found.   It was
necessary, therefore, in the first instance, to trust untried men ; and the
preference was naturally given to men distinguished either by their
station, or by the abilities which they had displayed in Parliament.   In
scarcely a single instance, however, was the selection fortunate.   Neither
the grandees nor the orators proved good soldiers.   The Earl of Stamford, one of the greatest nobles of England, was routed by the Royalists
at Stratton.   Nathaniel Fiennes, inferior to none of his contemporaries
in talents for civil business, disgraced himself by the pusillanimous surrender of Bristol.   Indeed, of all the statesmen who at this juncture
accepted high military commands, Hampden alone appears to have
carried into the camp the capacity and strength of mind which had
made him eminent in politics.

When the war had lasted a year, the advantage was decidedly with
the Royalists.   They were victorious, both in the western and in the

northern counties. They had wrested Bristol, the second city in the kingdom, from the Parliament. They had won several battles, and had not sustained a single serious or ignominious defeat. Among the Roundheads adversity had begun to produce dissension and discontent. The Parliament was kept in alarm, sometimes by plots, and sometimes by riots. It was thought necessary to fortify London against the royal army, and to hang some disaffected citizens at their own doors. Several of the most distinguished peers who had hitherto remained at Westminster fled to the court at Oxford; nor can it be doubted that, if the operations of the Cavaliers had, at this season, been directed by a sagacious and powerful mind, Charles would soon have marched in triumph to Whitehall.

Successes of the Royalists

But the King suffered the auspicious moment to pass away; and it never returned. In August 1643 he sate down before the city of Gloucester. That city was defended by the inhabitants and by the garrison, with a determination such as had not, since the commencement of the war, been shown by the adherents of the Parliament. The emulation of London was excited. The trainbands of the City volunteered to march wherever their services might be required. A great force was speedily collected, and began to move westward. The siege of Gloucester was raised: the Royalists in every part of the kingdom were disheartened: the spirit of the parliamentary party revived; and the apostate Lords, who had lately fled from Westminster to Oxford, hastened back from Oxford to Westminster.

And now a new and alarming class of symptoms began to appear in the distempered body politic. There had been, from the first, in the parliamentary party, some men whose minds were set on objects from which the majority of that party would have shrunk with horror. These men were, in religion, Independents. They conceived that every Christian congregation had, under Christ, supreme jurisdiction in things spiritual; that appeals to provincial and national synods were scarcely less unscriptural than appeals to the Court of Arches, or to the Vatican; and that Popery, Prelacy, and Presbyterianism were merely three forms of one great apostasy. In politics the Independents were, to use the phrase of their time, root and branch men, or, to use the kindred phrase of our own time, radicals. Not content with limiting the power of the monarch, they were desirous to erect a commonwealth on the ruins of the old English polity. At first they had been inconsiderable, both in numbers and in weight; but before the war had lasted two years they became, not indeed the largest, but the most powerful faction in the country. Some of the old parliamentary leaders had been removed by death; and others had forfeited the public confidence. Pym had been borne, with princely honours, to

Rise of the Independents

a grave among the Plantagenets.   Hampden had fallen, as became him, while vainly endeavouring, by his heroic example, to inspire his followers with courage to face the fiery cavalry of Rupert.   Bedford had been untrue to the cause.   Northumberland was known to be lukewarm. Essex and his lieutenants had shown little vigour and ability in the conduct of military operations.   At such a conjuncture it was that the Independent party, ardent, resolute, and uncompromising, began to raise its head, both in the camp and in the House of Commons.

The soul of that party was Oliver Cromwell.   Bred to peaceful occupations, he had, at more than forty years of age, accepted a com-
Oliver   mission in the parliamentary army.   No sooner had he be-
Cromwell   come a soldier than he discerned, with the keen glance of genius, what Essex and men like Essex, with all their experience, were unable to perceive.   He saw precisely where the strength of the Royalists lay, and by what means alone that strength could be overpowered.   He saw that it was necessary to reconstruct the army of the Parliament. He saw also that there were abundant and excellent materials for the purpose, materials less showy, indeed, but more solid, than those of which the gallant squadrons of the King were composed.   It was necessary to look for recruits who were not mere mercenaries, for recruits of decent station and grave character, fearing God and zealous for public liberty. With such men he filled his own regiment, and, while he subjected them to a discipline more rigid than had ever before been known in England, he administered to their intellectual and moral nature stimulants of fearful potency.

The events of the year 1644 fully proved the superiority of his abilities.   In the south, where Essex held the command, the parliamentary forces underwent a succession of shameful disasters ; but in the north the victory of Marston Moor fully compensated for all that had been lost elsewhere.   That victory was not a more serious blow to the Royalists than to the party which had hitherto been dominant at Westminster ; for it was notorious that the day, disgracefully lost by the Presbyterians, had been retrieved by the energy of Cromwell, and by the steady valour of the warriors whom he had trained.

These events produced the Selfdenying Ordinance and the new model of the army.   Under decorous pretexts, and with every mark of respect,
Selfdenying   Essex and most of those who had held high posts under him
Ordinance   were removed ; and the conduct of the war was intrusted to very different hands.   Fairfax, a brave soldier, but of mean understanding and irresolute temper, was the nominal Lord General of the forces ; but Cromwell was their real head.

Cromwell made haste to organise the whole army on the same principles on which he had organised his own regiment.   As soon as this

OLIVER CROMWELL, 1599-1658.
From the painting by Robert Walker, in the National Portrait Gallery.

process was complete, the event of the war was decided. The Cavaliers had now to encounter natural courage equal to their own, enthusiasm stronger than their own, and discipline such as was utterly wanting to them. It soon became a proverb that the soldiers of Fairfax and Cromwell were men of a different breed from the soldiers of Essex. At Naseby took place the first great encounter between the Royalists and the remodelled army of the Houses. The victory of the Roundheads was complete and decisive. It was followed by other triumphs in rapid succession. In a few months the authority of the Parliament was fully established over the whole kingdom. Charles fled to the Scots, and was by them, in a manner which did not much exalt their national character, delivered up to his English subjects.

Victory of the Parliament

While the event of the war was still doubtful, the Houses had put the Primate to death, had interdicted, within the sphere of their authority, the use of the Liturgy, and had required all men to subscribe that renowned instrument known by the name of the Solemn League and Covenant. Covenanting work, as it was called, went on fast. Hundreds of thousands affixed their names to the rolls, and, with hands lifted up towards heaven, swore to endeavour, without respect of persons, the extirpation of Popery and Prelacy, heresy and schism, and to bring to public trial and condign punishment all who should hinder the reformation of religion. When the struggle was over, the work of innovation and revenge was pushed on with increased ardour. The ecclesiastical polity of the kingdom was remodelled. Most of the old clergy were ejected from their benefices. Fines, often of ruinous amount, were laid on the Royalists, already impoverished by large aids furnished to the King. Many estates were confiscated. Many proscribed Cavaliers found it expedient to purchase, at an enormous cost, the protection of eminent members of the victorious party. Large domains, belonging to the crown, to the bishops, and to the chapters, were seized, and either granted away or put up to auction. In consequence of these spoliations, a great part of the soil of England was at once offered for sale. As money was scarce, as the market was glutted, as the title was insecure, and as the awe inspired by powerful bidders prevented free competition, the prices were often merely nominal. Thus many old and honourable families disappeared and were heard of no more ; and many new men rose rapidly to affluence.

But, while the Houses were employing their authority thus, it suddenly passed out of their hands. It had been obtained by calling into existence a power which could not be controlled. In the summer of 1647, about twelve months after the last fortress of the Cavaliers had submitted to the Parliament, the Parliament was compelled to submit to its own soldiers.

Thirteen years followed, during which England was, under various
names and forms, really governed by the sword. Never before
that time, or since that time, was the civil power in our country
subjected to military dictation.

The army which now became supreme in the state was an army very
different from any that has since been seen among us. At present the
pay of the common soldier is not such as can seduce any but the humblest
class of English labourers from their calling. A barrier almost impass-
able separates him from the commissioned officer. The great majority
of those who rise high in the service rise by purchase. So numerous
and extensive are the remote dependencies of England, that every man
who enlists in the line must expect to pass many years in exile, and
some years in climates unfavourable to the health and vigour of the
European race. The army of the Long Parliament was raised for home
service. The pay of the private soldier was much above the wages earned
by the great body of the people; and, if he distinguished himself by
intelligence and courage, he might hope to attain high commands. The
ranks were accordingly composed of persons superior in station and
education to the multitude. These persons, sober, moral, diligent, and
accustomed to reflect, had been induced to take up arms, not by the
pressure of want, not by the love of novelty and license, not by the arts
of recruiting officers, but by religious and political zeal, mingled with
the desire of distinction and promotion. The boast of the soldiers, as
we find it recorded in their solemn resolutions, was that they had not
been forced into the service, nor had enlisted chiefly for the sake of lucre,
that they were no janissaries, but freeborn Englishmen, who had, of their
own accord, put their lives in jeopardy for the liberties and religion of
England, and whose right and duty it was to watch over the welfare
of the nation which they had saved.

A force thus composed might, without injury to its efficiency, be
indulged in some liberties which, if allowed to any other troops, would
have proved subversive of all discipline. In general, soldiers who
should form themselves into political clubs, elect delegates, and pass
resolutions on high questions of state, would soon break loose from all
control, would cease to form an army, and would become the worst and
most dangerous of mobs. Nor would it be safe, in our time, to tolerate
in any regiment religious meetings, at which a corporal versed in
Scripture should lead the devotions of his less gifted colonel, and
admonish a backsliding major. But such was the intelligence, the
gravity, and the selfcommand of the warriors whom Cromwell had
trained, that in their camp a political organisation and a religious
organisation could exist without destroying military organisation. The
same men, who, off duty, were noted as demagogues and field preachers,

Sr being Comanded by you to this
servise, I thinke my selfe bound to ac-
quaint you with the good hand of God
towards you, and vs, wee marched yesterday
after the Kinge whoe went before vs
from Hauentree to Hauersbrow, and quartered about six miles from him, this day
wee marched towards him, Hee drew out
to meete vs, both Armies engaged, wee
after 3. howres fight, very doubtfull
att last routed his Armie, killed and
tooke about 5000. very many officers
but of what quallityo wee yett know
not, wee tooke alsoe about 200. carriages
all hee had, and all his gunns, beinge
12. in number, whereof 2 were Demi
canon, 2 demie Culueringes, and (I
thinke) the rest Sacres, wee pursued
enimie from three miles short of Ha
to nine beyond, euen to sight of Leic
whether the Kinge fled. Sr this is none
other but the hand of God, and to him
aloane belongs the Glorie, wherein none is
and to share with him. The Generall
serued you with all faythfullnesse, in
honor, and the best comendations I can
giue him is, that I ... say Her ...

attributes all to God, and would rather perish then assume to him selfe,
which is an honest and thriueinge way, and yett as much for braueery may
be giuen to him in this action as to a man. Honest men serued you faythfully
in this action. Sr they are trustye, I beseech you in the name of God not to
discorage them: I that haue had aboundant cause for this to beleeue the hand of his,
in all that was done, in it, Hee that venters his life for the libertye of his
countrey, I wish hee trust God for the libertye of his consience, and you
for the libertye hee fights for, in this hee rests whoe is

Your most humble seruant
Oliver Cromwell

Haruey 14th 1645.
Hauersbrow.

REDUCED FACSIMILE OF CROMWELL'S LETTER TO THE SPEAKER OF THE
HOUSE OF COMMONS ON THE BATTLE OF NASEBY

British Museum

were distinguished by steadiness, by the spirit of order, and by prompt obedience on watch, on drill, and on the field of battle.

In war this strange force was irresistible. The stubborn courage characteristic of the English people was, by the system of Cromwell, at once regulated and stimulated. Other leaders have maintained order as strict. Other leaders have inspired their followers with zeal as ardent. But in his camp alone the most rigid discipline was found in company with the fiercest enthusiasm. His troops moved to victory with the precision of machines, while burning with the wildest fanaticism of Crusaders. From the time when the army was remodelled to the time when it was disbanded, it never found, either in the British islands or on the Continent, an enemy who could stand its onset. In England, Scotland, Ireland, Flanders, the Puritan warriors, often surrounded by difficulties, sometimes contending against threefold odds, not only never failed to conquer, but never failed to destroy and break in pieces whatever force was opposed to them. They at length came to regard the day of battle as a day of certain triumph, and marched against the most renowned battalions of Europe with disdainful confidence. Turenne was startled by the shout of stern exultation with which his English allies advanced to the combat, and expressed the delight of a true soldier, when he learned that it was ever the fashion of Cromwell's pikemen to rejoice greatly when they beheld the enemy; and the banished Cavaliers felt an emotion of national pride, when they saw a brigade of their countrymen, outnumbered by foes and abandoned by friends, drive before it in headlong rout the finest infantry of Spain, and force a passage into a counterscrap which had just been pronounced impregnable by the ablest of the Marshals of France.

But that which chiefly distinguished the army of Cromwell from other armies was the austere morality and the fear of God which pervaded all ranks. It is acknowledged by the most zealous Royalists that, in that singular camp, no oath was heard, no drunkenness or gambling was seen, and that, during the long dominion of the soldiery, the property of the peaceable citizen and the honour of woman were held sacred. If outrages were committed, they were outrages of a very different kind from those of which a victorious army is generally guilty. No servant girl complained of the rough gallantry of the redcoats. Not an ounce of plate was taken from the shops of the goldsmiths. But a Pelagian sermon, or a window on which the Virgin and Child were painted, produced in the Puritan ranks an excitement which it required the utmost exertions of the officers to quell. One of Cromwell's chief difficulties was to restrain his musketeers and dragoons from invading by main force the pulpits of ministers whose discourses, to use the language of that time, were not savoury; and too many of our cathedrals still bear the marks of the hatred with which those stern spirits regarded every vestige of Popery.

To keep down the English people was no light task even for that army. No sooner was the first pressure of military tyranny felt, than the nation, unbroken to such servitude, began to struggle fiercely. Insurrections broke out even in those counties which, during the recent war, had been the most submissive to the Parliament. Indeed, the Parliament itself abhorred its old defenders more than its old enemies, and was desirous to come to terms of accommodation with Charles at the expense of the troops. In Scotland, at the same time, a coalition was formed between the Royalists and a large body of Presbyterians who regarded the doctrines of the Independents with detestation. At length the storm burst. There were risings in Norfolk, Suffolk, Essex, Kent, Wales. The fleet in the Thames suddenly hoisted the royal colours, stood out to sea, and menaced the southern coast. A great Scottish force crossed the frontier and advanced into Lancashire. It might well be suspected that these movements were contemplated with secret complacency by a majority both of the Lords and of the Commons.

Risings against the military government suppressed

But the yoke of the army was not to be so shaken off. While Fairfax suppressed the risings in the neighbourhood of the capital, Oliver routed the Welsh insurgents, and, leaving their castles in ruins, marched against the Scots. His troops were few, when compared with the invaders ; but he was little in the habit of counting his enemies. The Scottish army was utterly destroyed. A change in the Scottish government followed. An administration, hostile to the King, was formed at Edinburgh ; and Cromwell, more than ever the darling of his soldiers, returned in triumph to London.

And now a design, to which, at the commencement of the civil war, no man would have dared to allude, and which was not less inconsistent with the Solemn League and Covenant than with the old law of England, began to take a distinct form. The austere warriors who ruled the nation had, during some months, meditated a fearful vengeance on the captive King. When and how the scheme originated ; whether it spread from the general to the ranks, or from the ranks to the general ; whether it is to be ascribed to policy using fanaticism as a tool, or to fanaticism bearing down policy with headlong impulse, are questions which, even at this day, cannot be answered with perfect confidence. It seems, however, on the whole, probable that he who seemed to lead was really forced to follow, and that, on this occasion, as on another great occasion a few years later, he sacrificed his own judgment and his own inclinations to the wishes of the army. For the power which he had called into existence

Proceedings against the King

was a power which even he could not always control; and, that he
might ordinarily command, it was necessary that he should sometimes
obey.   He publicly protested that he was no mover in the matter, that
the first steps had been taken without his privity, that he could not
advise the Parliament to strike the blow, but that he submitted his own
feelings to the force of circumstances which seemed to him to indicate
the purposes of Providence.   It has been the fashion to consider these
professions as instances of the hypocrisy which is vulgarly imputed to
him.   But even those who pronounce him a hypocrite will scarcely
venture to call him a fool.   They are therefore bound to show that he
had some purpose to serve by secretly stimulating the army to take that
course which he did not venture openly to recommend.   It would be
absurd to suppose that he, who was never by his respectable enemies
represented as wantonly cruel or implacably vindictive, would have taken
the most important step of his life under the influence of mere malevolence.   He was far too wise a man not to know, when he consented to
shed that august blood, that he was doing a deed which was inexpiable,
and which would move the grief and horror, not only of the Royalists,
but of nine tenths of those who had stood by the Parliament.   Whatever visions may have deluded others, he was assuredly dreaming neither
of a republic on the antique pattern, nor of the millennial reign of the
saints.   If he already aspired to be himself the founder of a new
dynasty, it was plain that Charles the First was a less formidable com-
petitor than Charles the Second would be.   At the moment of the death
of Charles the First the loyalty of every Cavalier would be transferred,
unimpaired, to Charles the Second.   Charles the First was a captive :
Charles the Second would be at liberty.   Charles the First was an object
of suspicion and dislike to a large proportion of those who yet shuddered
at the thought of slaying him : Charles the Second would excite all the
interest which belongs to distressed youth and innocence.   It is impossible to believe that considerations so obvious, and so important, escaped
the most profound politician of that age.   The truth is that Cromwell
had, at one time, meant to mediate between the throne and the Parliament, and to reorganise the distracted State by the power of the sword,
under the sanction of the royal name.   In this design he persisted till
he was compelled to abandon it by the refractory temper of the soldiers,
and by the incurable duplicity of the King.   A party in the camp
began to clamour for the head of the traitor, who was for treating with
Agag.   Conspiracies were formed.   Threats of impeachment were loudly
uttered.   A mutiny broke out, which all the vigour and resolution of
Oliver could hardly quell.   And though, by a judicious mixture of
severity and kindness, he succeeded in restoring order, he saw that it
would be in the highest degree difficult and perilous to contend against

the rage of warriors, who regarded the fallen tyrant as their foe, and as the foe of their God. At the same time it became more evident than ever that the King could not be trusted. The vices of Charles had grown upon him. They were, indeed, vices which difficulties and perplexities generally bring out in the strongest light. Cunning is the natural defence of the weak. A prince therefore, who is habitually a deceiver when at the height of power, is not likely to learn frankness in the midst of embarrassments and distresses. Charles was not only a most unscrupulous but a most unlucky dissembler. There never was a politician to whom so many frauds and falsehoods were brought home by undeniable evidence. He publicly recognised the Houses at Westminster as a legal Parliament, and, at the same time, made a private minute in council declaring the recognition null. He publicly disclaimed all thought of calling in foreign aid against his people : he privately solicited aid from France, from Denmark, and from Loraine. He publicly denied that he employed Papists : at the same time he privately sent to his generals directions to employ every Papist that would serve. He publicly took the sacrament at Oxford, as a pledge that he never would even connive at Popery : he privately assured his wife, that he intended to tolerate Popery in England ; and he authorised Lord Glamorgan to promise that Popery should be established in Ireland. Then he attempted to clear himself at his agent's expense. Glamorgan received, in the royal handwriting, reprimands intended to be read by others, and eulogies which were to be seen only by himself. To such an extent, indeed, had insincerity now tainted the King's whole nature, that his most devoted friends could not refrain from complaining to each other, with bitter grief and shame, of his crooked politics. His defeats, they said, gave them less pain than his intrigues. Since he had been a prisoner, there was no section of the victorious party which had not been the object both of his flatteries and of his machinations : but never was he more unfortunate than when he attempted at once to cajole and to undermine Cromwell.

Cromwell had to determine whether he would put to hazard the attachment of his party, the attachment of his army, his own greatness, nay his own life, in an attempt, which would probably have been vain, to save a prince whom no engagement could bind. With many struggles and misgivings, and probably not without many prayers, the decision was made. Charles was left to his fate. The military saints resolved that, in defiance of the old laws of the realm, and of the almost universal sentiment of the nation, the King should expiate his crimes with his blood. He for a time expected a death like that of his unhappy predecessors, Edward the Second and Richard the Second. But he was in no danger of such treason. Those who had him in their gripe were not

midnight stabbers. What they did they did in order that it might be a
spectacle to heaven and earth, and that it might be held in everlasting
remembrance. They enjoyed keenly the very scandal which they gave.
That the ancient constitution and the public opinion of England were
directly opposed to regicide made regicide seem strangely fascinating to
a party bent on effecting a complete political and social revolution. In
order to accomplish their purpose, it was necessary that they should first
break in pieces every part of the machinery of the government ; and
this necessity was rather agreeable than painful to them. The Commons
passed a vote tending to accommodation with the King. The soldiers
excluded the majority by force. The Lords unanimously rejected the
proposition that the King should be brought to trial. Their house was
instantly closed. No court, known to the law, would take on itself the
office of judging the fountain of justice. A revolutionary tribunal was
His execu-   created. That tribunal pronounced Charles a tyrant, a traitor,
tion   a murderer, and a public enemy ; and his head was severed
from his shoulders, before thousands of spectators, in front of the banqueting hall of his own palace.

In no long time it became manifest that those political and religious
zealots, to whom this deed is to be ascribed, had committed, not only a
crime, but an error. They had given to a prince, hitherto known to his
people chiefly by his faults, an opportunity of displaying, on a great
theatre, before the eyes of all nations and all ages, some qualities which
irresistibly call forth the admiration and love of mankind, the high spirit
of a gallant gentleman, the patience and meekness of a penitent Christian.
Nay, they had so contrived their revenge that the very man whose life
had been a series of attacks on the liberties of England now seemed to
die a martyr in the cause of those liberties. No demagogue ever produced such an impression on the public mind as the captive King, who,
retaining in that extremity all his regal dignity, and confronting death
with dauntless courage, gave utterance to the feelings of his oppressed
people, manfully refused to plead before a court unknown to the law,
appealed from military violence to the principles of the constitution,
asked by what right the House of Commons had been purged of its
most respectable members and the House of Lords deprived of its legislative functions, and told his weeping hearers that he was defending, not
only his own cause, but theirs. His long misgovernment, his innumerable perfidies, were forgotten. His memory was, in the minds of the
great majority of his subjects, associated with those free institutions
which he had, during many years, laboured to destroy : for those free
institutions had perished with him, and, amidst the mournful silence of
a community kept down by arms, had been defended by his voice alone.
From that day began a reaction in favour of monarchy and of the exiled

The following text appears within the engraving:

Clarior è tenebris

IMMOTA TRIUMPHANS

GLORIA

Speck

CRESCIT SUB PONDERE VIRTVS

Aſperam, at Levem

Gratia

Christi Tracto

IN VERBO TVO SPES MEA

Splendidam, & Gravem

Mundi Calco

Guil: Marshall delineae et Sculpsit.

The Explanation of the EMBLEME.

Ponderibus *genus omne mali, probriſg, gravatus,*
(Viceſq, ferenda ferens, Palma ut Depreſsa, *reſurgo.*

Ac, velut undarum Fluctûs Ventiſq, *furorem*
Irati Populi Rupes immota *repello.*
Clarior è tenebris, *cœleſtis Stella, coruſco.*
(Victor et æternùm—felici pace triumpho.

Auro Fulgentem *rutilo gemmiſq, micantem,*
At curis Gravidam *ſpernendo* calco Coronam.

Spinoſam, *at ferri facilem, quo* Spes mea, Christi
Auxilio, Nobis *non eſt* tractare moleſtum.

Æternam, *fixis* fidei, *ſempèrq,—*beatam
In Cœlos oculis Specto, Nobiſq, *paratam.*

Quod Vanum *eſt, ſperno; quod* Christi Gratia *præbet*
Amplecti studium eſt. Virtutis Gloria *merces.*

To X͡Ρ ὀδὲν ἠδίκησε τὴν πόλιν, ὀὲ τὸ Κάππα.

Though clogg'd with weights of miſeries
Palm-like Depreſs'd, I higher rise.

And as th'unmoved Rock out-brave's
The boiſtrous Windes and rageing waves:
So triumph I. And shine more bright
In sad Affliction's Darkſom night.

That Splendid, but yet toilſom Crown
Regardleſsly I trample down.

With joie I take this Crown of thorn,
Though ſharp, yet eaſie to be born.

That heav'nlie Crown, already mine,
I View with eies of Faith divine.

I ſlight vain things; and do embrace
Glorie, the juſt reward of Grace.

G.D.

EMBLEMATIC PRINT OF CHARLES I PREFIXED TO EIKON BASILIKE

house, a reaction which never ceased till the throne had again been set up in all its old dignity.

At first, however, the slayers of the King seemed to have derived new energy from that sacrament of blood by which they had bound themselves closely together, and separated themselves for ever from the great body of their countrymen. England was declared a commonwealth. The House of Commons, reduced to a small number of members, was nominally the supreme power in the state. In fact, the army and its great chief governed everything. Oliver had made his choice. He had kept the hearts of his soldiers, and had broken with almost every other class of his fellow citizens. Beyond the limits of his camps and fortresses he could scarcely be said to have a party. Those elements of force which, when the civil war broke out, had appeared arrayed against each other, were combined against him ; all the Cavaliers, the great majority of the Roundheads, the Anglican Church, the Presbyterian Church, the Roman Catholic Church, England, Scotland, Ireland. Yet such was his genius and resolution that he was able to overpower and crush everything that crossed his path, to make himself more absolute master of his country than any of her legitimate Kings had been, and to make his country more dreaded and respected than she had been during many generations under the rule of her legitimate Kings.

England had already ceased to struggle. But the two other kingdoms which had been governed by the Stuarts were hostile to the new republic. The Independent party was equally odious to the Roman Catholics of Ireland and to the Presbyterians of Scotland. Both those countries, lately in rebellion against Charles the First, now acknowledged the authority of Charles the Second.

But everything yielded to the vigour and ability of Cromwell. In a few months he subjugated Ireland, as Ireland had never been subjugated during the five centuries of slaughter which had elapsed since the landing of the first Norman settlers. He resolved to put an end to that conflict of races and religions which had so long distracted the island, by making the English and Protestant population decidedly predominant. For this end he gave the rein to the fierce enthusiasm of his followers, waged war resembling that which Israel waged on the Canaanites, smote the idolaters with the edge of the sword, so that great cities were left without inhabitants, drove many thousands to the Continent, shipped off many thousands to the West Indies, and supplied the void thus made by pouring in numerous colonists, of Saxon blood, and of Calvinistic faith. Strange to say, under that iron rule, the conquered country began to wear an outward face of prosperity. Districts, which had recently been as wild as those where the first white settlers of Connecticut were contending with the red men,

Subjugation of Ireland and Scotland

DIEV ET MON DROIT.

The Second Charles. Heire of y Royall Martyr,
who for Religion and his Subiects Charter
spent the best Blood y uniust Sword ere dyde.
since the rude Souldier pierced our Saviours side.
who such a Father hadst, art such a Son
redeeme thy people and assume thy Owne.   J. C.

Guil Faithorne sculp:

CHARLES II

From an engraving by Faithorne published during his exile

were in a few years transformed into the likeness of Kent and Norfolk. New buildings, roads, and plantations were everywhere seen. The rent of estates rose fast ; and soon the English landowners began to complain that they were met in every market by the products of Ireland, and to clamour for protecting laws.

From Ireland the victorious chief, who was now in name, as he had long been in reality, Lord General of the armies of the Commonwealth, turned to Scotland. The young King was there. He had consented to profess himself a Presbyterian, and to subscribe the Covenant ; and, in return for these concessions, the austere Puritans who bore sway at Edinburgh had permitted him to assume the crown, and to hold, under their inspection and control, a solemn and melancholy court. This mock royalty was of short duration. In two great battles Cromwell annihilated the military force of Scotland. Charles fled for his life, and, with extreme difficulty, escaped the fate of his father. The ancient kingdom of the Stuarts was reduced, for the first time, to profound submission. Of that independence, so manfully defended against the mightiest and ablest of the Plantagenets, no vestige was left. The English Parliament made laws for Scotland. English judges held assizes in Scotland. Even that stubborn Church, which has held its own against so many governments, scarce dared to utter an audible murmur.

Thus far there had been at least the semblance of harmony between the warriors who had subjugated Ireland and Scotland and the politicians **Expulsion of the Long Parliament** who sate at Westminster : but the alliance which had been cemented by danger was dissolved by victory. The Parliament forgot that it was but the creature of the army. The army was less disposed than ever to submit to the dictation of the Parliament. Indeed the few members who made up what was contemptuously called the Rump of the House of Commons had no more claim than the military chiefs to be esteemed the representatives of the nation. The dispute was soon brought to a decisive issue. Cromwell filled the House with armed men. The Speaker was pulled out of his chair, the mace taken from the table, the room cleared, and the door locked. The nation, which loved neither of the contending parties, but which was forced, in its own despite, to respect the capacity and resolution of the General, looked on with patience, if not with complacency.

King, Lords, and Commons, had now in turn been vanquished and destroyed ; and Cromwell seemed to be left the sole heir of the powers of all three. Yet were certain limitations still imposed on him by the very army to which he owed his immense authority. That singular body of men was, for the most part, composed of zealous republicans. In the act of enslaving their country, they had deceived themselves into the belief that they were emancipating her. The book which they most venerated furnished them with a precedent which was frequently in their mouths. It was true that the ignorant and ungrateful nation murmured against its deliverers. Even so had another chosen nation murmured against the leader who brought it, by painful and dreary paths, from the house of bondage to the land flowing with milk and honey. Yet had that leader rescued his brethren in spite of themselves ; nor had he shrunk from making terrible examples of those who contemned the proffered freedom, and pined for the fleshpots, the taskmasters, and the idolatries of Egypt. The object of the warlike saints who surrounded Cromwell was the settlement of a free and pious commonwealth. For that end they were ready to employ, without scruple, any means, however violent and lawless. It was not impossible, therefore, to establish by their aid a dictatorship such as no King had ever exercised : but it was probable that their aid would be at once withdrawn from a ruler who, even under strict constitutional restraints, should venture to assume the kingly name and dignity.

The sentiments of Cromwell were widely different. He was not what he had been ; nor would it be just to consider the change which his views had undergone as the effect merely of selfish ambition. He had, when he came up to the Long Parliament, brought with him from his rural retreat little knowledge of books, no experience of great affairs, and a temper galled by the long tyranny of the government and of the hierarchy. He had, during the thirteen years which followed, gone through a political education of no common kind. He had been a chief actor in a succession of revolutions. He had been long the soul, and at last the head, of a party. He had commanded armies, won battles, negotiated treaties, subdued, pacified, and regulated kingdoms. It would have been strange indeed if his notions had been still the same as in the days when his mind was principally occupied by his fields and his religion, and when the greatest events which diversified the course of his life were a cattle fair or a prayer meeting at Huntingdon. He saw that some schemes of innovation for which he had once been zealous, whether good or bad in themselves, were opposed to the general feeling of the country, and that, if he persevered in those schemes, he had nothing before him but constant troubles, which must be suppressed by the constant use of the sword. He therefore wished to restore, in all essentials, that ancient constitution which the majority of the people had always loved, and for which they now pined. The course afterwards taken by Monk was not open to Cromwell. The memory of one terrible day separated the great regicide for ever from the House of Stuart. What remained was that he should mount the ancient English throne, and reign according to the ancient English polity. If he could effect this, he might hope that the wounds of the lacerated State would heal fast. Great numbers of honest and quiet men would speedily rally round him. Those Royalists whose attachment was rather to institutions than to persons, to the kingly office than to King Charles the First or King Charles the Second, would soon kiss the hand of King Oliver. The peers, who now remained sullenly at their country houses, and refused to take any part in public affairs, would, when summoned to their House by the writ of a King in possession, gladly resume their ancient functions. Northumberland and Bedford, Manchester and Pembroke, would be proud to bear the crown and the spurs, the sceptre and the globe, before the restorer of aristocracy. A sentiment of loyalty would gradually bind the people to the new dynasty ; and, on the decease of the founder of that dynasty, the royal dignity might descend with general acquiescence to his posterity.

The ablest Royalists were of opinion that these views were correct, and that, if Cromwell had been permitted to follow his own judgment, the exiled line would never have been restored. But his plan was directly opposed to the feelings of the only class which he dared not offend. The name of King was hateful to the soldiers. Some of them were indeed unwilling to see the administration in the hands of any single person. The great majority, however, were disposed to support their general, as elective first magistrate of a commonwealth, against all factions which might resist his authority : but they would not consent that he should assume the regal title, or that the dignity, which was the just reward of his personal merit, should be declared hereditary in his family. All that was left to him was to give to the new republic a constitution as like the constitution of the old monarchy as the army would bear. That his elevation to power might not seem to be merely his own act, he convoked a council, composed partly of persons on whose support he could depend, and partly of persons whose opposition he might safely defy. This assembly, which he called a Parliament, and which the populace nicknamed, from one of the most conspicuous members, Barebone's Parliament, after exposing itself during a short time to the public contempt, surrendered back to the General the powers which it had received from him, and left him at liberty to frame a plan of government.

His plan bore, from the first, a considerable resemblance to the old English constitution : but, in a few years, he thought it safe to proceed **The Protec-** further, and to restore almost every part of the ancient system **torate of** under new names and forms. The title of King was not re- **Oliver** **Cromwell** vived : but the kingly prerogatives were intrusted to a Lord High Protector. The sovereign was called not His Majesty, but His Highness. He was not crowned and anointed in Westminster Abbey, but was solemnly enthroned, girt with a sword of state, clad in a robe of purple, and presented with a rich Bible, in Westminster Hall. His office was not declared hereditary : but he was permitted to name his successor ; and none could doubt that he would name his son.

A House of Commons was a necessary part of the new polity.   In constituting this body, the Protector showed a wisdom and a public spirit which were not duly appreciated by his contemporaries.   The vices of the old representative system, though by no means so serious as they afterwards became, had already been remarked by farsighted men. Cromwell reformed that system on the same principles on which Mr. Pitt, a hundred and thirty years later, attempted to reform it, and on

The Portraiture of Mr Praise God Barebone

MR. PRAISEGOD BAREBONE

From a contemporary broadside

which it was at length reformed in our own times.   Small boroughs were disfranchised even more unsparingly than in 1832; and the number of county members was greatly increased.   Very few unrepresented towns had yet grown into importance.   Of those towns the most considerable were Manchester, Leeds, and Halifax.   Representatives were given to all three.   An addition was made to the number of the members for the capital.   The elective franchise was placed on such a footing that every man of substance, whether possessed of freehold estates in land or not, had a vote for the county in which he resided.   A few Scotchmen and a few of the English colonists settled in Ireland were summoned to the assembly which was to legislate, at Westminster, for every part of the British isles.

To create a House of Lords was a less easy task. Democracy does not require the support of prescription. Monarchy has often stood without that support. But a patrician order is the work of time. Oliver found already existing a nobility, opulent, highly considered, and as popular with the commonalty as any nobility has ever been. Had he, as King of England, commanded the peers to meet him in Parliament according to the old usage of the realm, many of them would undoubtedly have obeyed the call. This he could not do ; and it was to no purpose that he offered to the chiefs of illustrious families seats in his new senate. They conceived that they could not accept a nomination to an upstart assembly without renouncing their birthright and betraying their order. The Protector was, therefore, under the necessity of filling his Upper House with new men who, during the late stirring times, had made themselves conspicuous. This was the least happy of his contrivances, and displeased all parties. The Levellers were angry with him for instituting a privileged class. The multitude, which felt respect and fondness for the great historical names of the land, laughed without restraint at a House of Lords, in which lucky draymen and shoemakers were seated, to which few of the old nobles were invited, and from which almost all those old nobles who were invited turned disdainfully away.

How Oliver's Parliaments were constituted, however, was practically of little moment : for he possessed the means of conducting the administration without their support, and in defiance of their opposition. His wish seems to have been to govern constitutionally, and to substitute the empire of the laws for that of the sword. But he soon found that, hated as he was, both by Royalists and Presbyterians, he could be safe only by being absolute. The first House of Commons which the people elected by his command, questioned his authority, and was dissolved without having passed a single act. His second House of Commons, though it recognised him as Protector, and would gladly have made him King, obstinately refused to acknowledge his new Lords. He had no course left but to dissolve the Parliament. " God," he exclaimed, at parting, " be judge between you and me ! "

Yet was the energy of the Protector's administration in nowise relaxed by these dissensions. Those soldiers who would not suffer him to assume the kingly title stood by him when he ventured on acts of power, as high as any English King has ever attempted. The government, therefore, though in form a republic, was in truth a despotism, moderated only by the wisdom, the sobriety, and the magnanimity of the despot. The country was divided into military districts. Those districts were placed under the command of Major Generals. Every

WITHAL

Ik wist het blinde graauw van 't Hol-ziek Engeland,
Door Loosheid tegens 't Huis van Stuart op te ruyen:
Nu buigt den Breedenraad voor myn gestrengen hand:
Des zal my Londen haast op 's Konings zeetel kruyen.

DUTCH CARICATURE REPRESENTING CROMWELL WITH CROWN AND SCEPTRE

From a broadside in the possession of the editor

insurrectionary movement was promptly put down and punished. The fear inspired by the power of the sword, in so strong, steady, and expert a hand, quelled the spirit both of Cavaliers and Levellers. The loyal gentry declared that they were still as ready as ever to risk their lives for the old government and the old dynasty, if there were the slightest hope of success : but to rush, at the head of their serving men and tenants, on the pikes of brigades victorious in a hundred battles and sieges, would be a frantic waste of innocent and honourable blood. Both Royalists and Republicans, having no hope in open resistance, began to revolve dark schemes of assassination : but the Protector's intelligence was good : his vigilance was unremitting ; and, whenever he moved beyond the walls of his palace, the drawn swords and cuirasses of his trusty bodyguards encompassed him thick on every side.

Had he been a cruel, licentious, and rapacious prince, the nation might have found courage in despair, and might have made a convulsive effort to free itself from military domination. But the grievances which the country suffered, though such as excited serious discontent, were by no means such as impel great masses of men to stake their lives, their fortunes, and the welfare of their families against fearful odds. The taxation, though heavier than it had been under the Stuarts, was not heavy when compared with that of the neighbouring states and with the resources of England. Property was secure. Even the Cavalier, who refrained from giving disturbance to the new settlement, enjoyed in peace whatever the civil troubles had left him. The laws were violated only in cases where the safety of the Protector's person and government was concerned. Justice was administered between man and man with an exactness and purity not before known. Under no English government since the Reformation, had there been so little religious persecution. The unfortunate Roman Catholics, indeed, were held to be scarcely within the pale of Christian charity. But the clergy of the fallen Anglican Church were suffered to celebrate their worship on condition that they would abstain from preaching about politics. Even the Jews, whose public worship had, ever since the thirteenth century, been interdicted, were, in spite of the strong opposition of jealous traders and fanatical theologians, permitted to build a synagogue in London.

The Protector's foreign policy at the same time extorted the ungracious approbation of those who most detested him. The Cavaliers could scarcely refrain from wishing that one who had done so much to raise the fame of the nation had been a legitimate King ; and the Republicans were forced to own that the tyrant suffered none but himself to wrong his country, and that, if he had robbed her of liberty, he had at least given her glory in exchange. After half a century during which England had been of scarcely more weight in European politics than Venice or Saxony, she at once became the most formidable power in the world, dictated terms of peace to the United Provinces, avenged

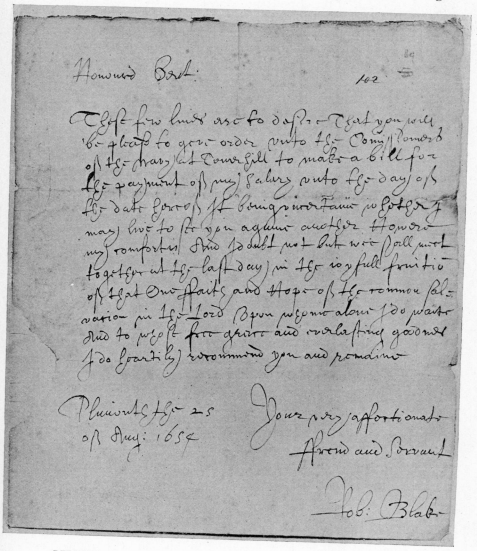

REDUCED FACSIMILE OF A LETTER FROM ROBERT BLAKE TO THE
COMMISSIONERS OF THE ADMIRALTY

British Museum

the common injuries of Christendom on the pirates of Barbary, vanquished the Spaniards by land and sea, seized one of the finest West Indian islands, and acquired on the Flemish coast a fortress which consoled the national pride for the loss of Calais. She was supreme on the ocean. She was the head of the Protestant interest. All the reformed Churches scattered over Roman Catholic kingdoms acknowledged Cromwell as their guardian. The Huguenots of Languedoc, the shepherds who, in the hamlets of the Alps, professed a Protestantism older than that of Augsburg, were secured from oppression by the mere terror of his great name. The Pope himself was forced to preach humanity and moderation to Popish princes. For a voice which seldom threatened in vain had declared that, unless favour were shown to the people of God, the English guns should be heard in the Castle of Saint Angelo. In truth, there was nothing which Cromwell had, for his own sake and that of his family, so much reason to desire as a general religious war in Europe. In such a war he must have been the captain of the Protestant armies. The heart of England would have been with him. His victories would have been hailed with an unanimous enthusiasm unknown in the country since the rout of the Armada, and would have effaced the stain which one act, condemned by the general voice of the nation, has left on his splendid fame. Unhappily for him he had no opportunity of displaying his admirable military talents, except against the inhabitants of the British isles.

While he lived his power stood firm, an object of mingled aversion, admiration, and dread to his subjects. Few indeed loved his government; but those who hated it most hated it less than they feared it. Had it been a worse government, it might perhaps have been overthrown in spite of all its strength. Had it been a weaker government, it would certainly have been overthrown in spite of all its merits. But it had moderation enough to abstain from those oppressions which drive men mad; and it had a force and energy which none but men driven mad by oppression would venture to encounter.

It has often been affirmed, but with little reason, that Oliver died at a time fortunate for his renown, and that, if his life had been prolonged, it would probably have closed amidst disgraces and disasters. It is certain that he was, to the last, honoured by his soldiers, obeyed by the whole population of the British islands, and dreaded by all foreign powers, that he was laid among the ancient sovereigns of England with funeral pomp such as London had never before seen, and that he was succeeded by his son Richard as quietly as any King had ever been succeeded by any Prince of Wales.

During five months, the administration of Richard Cromwell went on so tranquilly and regularly that all Europe believed him to be firmly established on the chair of state. In truth his situation was in some respects much more advantageous than that of his father. The young

Oliver succeeded by Richard

man had made no enemy. His hands were unstained by civil blood. The Cavaliers themselves allowed him to be an honest, goodnatured gentleman. The Presbyterian party, powerful both in numbers and in wealth, had been at deadly feud with the late Protector, but was disposed to regard the present Protector with favour. That party had always been desirous to see the old civil polity of the realm restored with some clearer definitions and some stronger safeguards for public liberty, but had many reasons for dreading the restoration of the old family. Richard was the very man for politicians of this description. His humanity, ingenuousness, and modesty, the mediocrity of his abilities, and the docility with which he submitted to the guidance of persons wiser than himself, admirably qualified him to be the head of a limited monarchy.

For a time it seemed highly probable that he would, under the direction of able advisers, effect what his father had attempted in vain. A Parliament was called, and the writs were directed after the old fashion. The small boroughs which had recently been disfranchised regained their lost privilege : Manchester, Leeds, and Halifax ceased to return members ; and the county of York was again limited to two knights. It may seem strange to a generation which has been excited almost to madness by the question of Parliamentary reform that great shires and towns should have submitted with patience, and even with complacency, to this change : but though speculative men might, even in that age, discern the vices of the old representative system, and predict that those vices would, sooner or later, produce serious practical evil, the practical evil had not yet been felt. Oliver's representative system, on the other hand, though constructed on sound principles, was not popular. Both the events in which it originated, and the effects which it had produced, prejudiced men against it. It had sprung from military violence. It had been fruitful of nothing but disputes. The whole nation was sick of government by the sword, and pined for government by the law. The restoration, therefore, even of anomalies and abuses, which were in strict conformity with the law, and which had been destroyed by the sword, gave general satisfaction.

Among the Commons there was a strong opposition, consisting partly of avowed Republicans, and partly of concealed Royalists : but a large and steady majority appeared to be favourable to the plan of reviving the old civil constitution under a new dynasty. Richard was solemnly recognised as first magistrate. The Commons not only consented to transact business with Oliver's Lords, but passed a vote acknowledging the right of those nobles who had, in the late troubles, taken the side of public liberty, to sit in the Upper House of Parliament without any new creation.

Thus far the statesmen by whose advice Richard acted had been successful. Almost all the parts of the government were now constituted as they had been constituted at the commencement of the civil war. Had the Protector and the Parliament been suffered to proceed undisturbed, there can be little doubt that an order of things similar to that which was afterwards established under the House of Hanover would have been established under the House of Cromwell. But there was in the state a power more than sufficient to deal with Protector and Parliament together. Over the soldiers Richard had no authority except that which he derived from the great name which he had inherited. He had never led them to victory. He had never even borne arms. All his tastes and habits were pacific. Nor were his opinions and feelings on religious subjects approved by the military saints. That he was a good man he evinced by proofs more satisfactory than deep groans or long sermons, by humility and suavity when he was at the height of human greatness, and by cheerful resignation under cruel wrongs and misfortunes : but the cant then common in every guardroom gave him a disgust which he had not always the prudence to conceal. The officers who had the principal influence among the troops stationed near London were not his friends. They were men distinguished by valour and conduct in the field, but destitute of the wisdom and civil courage which had been conspicuous in their deceased leader. Some of them were honest, but fanatical, Independents and Republicans. Of this class Fleetwood was the representative. Others were impatient to be what Oliver had been. His rapid elevation, his prosperity and glory, his inauguration in the Hall, and his gorgeous obsequies in the Abbey, had inflamed their imagination. They were as well born as he, and as well educated : they could not understand why they were not as worthy to wear the purple robe, and to wield the sword of state ; and they pursued the objects of their wild ambition, not, like him, with patience, vigilance, sagacity, and determination, but with the restlessness and irresolution characteristic of aspiring mediocrity. Among these feeble copies of a great original the most conspicuous was Lambert.

On the very day of Richard's accession the officers began to conspire against their new master. The good understanding which existed between him and his Parliament hastened the crisis. Alarm and resentment spread through the camp. Both the religious and the professional feelings of the army were deeply wounded. It seemed that the Independents were to be subjected to the Presbyterians, and that the men of the sword were to be subjected to the men of the gown. A coalition was formed between the military malecontents and the republican minority of the House of Commons. It may well be doubted whether Richard could have triumphed over that

Fall of Richard and revival of the Long Parliament

coalition, even if he had inherited his father's clear judgment and iron courage. It is certain that simplicity and meekness like his were not

MAJOR GENERAL LAMBERT

From a mezzotint by Francis Place

the qualities which the conjuncture required. He fell ingloriously, and without a struggle. He was used by the army as an instrument for the purpose of dissolving the Parliament, and was then contemptuously thrown aside. The officers gratified their republican allies by declaring that the expulsion of the Rump had been illegal, and by inviting that assembly to resume its functions. The old Speaker and a quorum of the old members came together, and were proclaimed, amidst the scarcely stifled derision and execration of the whole nation, the supreme power in the commonwealth. It was at the same time expressly declared that there should be no first magistrate, and no House of Lords.

But this state of things could not last. On the day on which the Long Parliament revived, revived also its old quarrel with the army. Second ex- Again the Rump forgot that it owed its existence to the pulsion of the Long pleasure of the soldiers, and began to treat them as subjects. Parliament Again the doors of the House of Commons were closed by military violence; and a provisional government, named by the officers, assumed the direction of affairs.

Meanwhile the sense of great evils, and the strong apprehension of still greater evils close at hand, had at length produced an alliance between the Cavaliers and the Presbyterians. Some Presbyterians had, indeed, been disposed to such an alliance even before the death of Charles the First : but it was not till after the fall of Richard Cromwell that the whole party became eager for the restoration of the royal house. There was no longer any reasonable hope that the old constitution could be reestablished under a new dynasty. One choice only was left, the Stuarts or the army. The banished family had committed great faults ; but it had dearly expiated those faults, and had undergone a long, and, it might be hoped, a salutary training in the school of adversity. It was probable that Charles the Second would take warning by the fate of Charles the First. But, be this as it might, the dangers which threatened the country were such that, in order to avert them, some opinions might well be compromised, and some risks might well be incurred. It seemed but too likely that England would fall under the most odious and degrading of all kinds of government, under a government uniting all the evils of despotism to all the evils of anarchy. Anything was preferable to the yoke of a succession of incapable and inglorious tyrants, raised to power, like the Deys of Barbary, by military revolutions recurring at short intervals. Lambert seemed likely to be the first of these rulers ; but within a year Lambert might give place to Desborough, and Desborough to Harrison. As often as the truncheon was transferred from one feeble hand to another, the nation would be pillaged for the purpose of bestowing a fresh donative on the troops. If the Presbyterians obstinately stood aloof from the Royalists, the state was lost ; and men might well doubt whether, by the combined exertions of Presbyterians and Royalists, it could be saved. For the dread of that invincible army was on all the inhabitants of the island ; and the Cavaliers, taught by a hundred

GEORGE MONCK, DUKE OF ALBEMARLE, K.G., 1608-1670.

From the painting by Sir Peter Lely, in the National Portrait Gallery.

disastrous fields how little numbers can effect against discipline, were even more completely cowed than the Roundheads.

While the soldiers remained united, all the plots and risings of the malecontents were ineffectual. But a few days after the second expulsion of the Rump, came tidings which gladdened the hearts of all who were attached either to monarchy or to liberty. That mighty force which had, during many years, acted as one man, and which, while so acting, had been found irresistible, was at length divided against itself. The army of Scotland had done good service to the Commonwealth, and was in the highest state of efficiency. It had borne no part in the late revolutions, and had seen them with indignation resembling the indignation which the Roman legions posted on the Danube and the Euphrates felt, when they learned that the empire had been put up to sale by the Prætorian Guards. It was intolerable that certain regiments should, merely because they happened to be quartered near Westminster, take on themselves to make and unmake several governments in the course of half a year. If it were fit that the state should be regulated by the soldiers, those soldiers who upheld the English ascendency on the north of the Tweed were as well entitled to a voice as those who garrisoned the Tower of London. There appears to have been less fanaticism among the troops stationed in Scotland than in any other part of the army; and their general, George Monk, was himself the very opposite of a zealot. He had, at the commencement of the civil war, borne arms for the King, had been made prisoner by the Roundheads, had then accepted a commission from the Parliament, and, with very slender pretensions to saintship, had raised himself to high commands by his courage and professional skill. He had been an useful servant to both the Protectors, had quietly acquiesced when the officers at Westminster pulled down Richard and restored the Long Parliament, and would perhaps have acquiesced as quietly in the second expulsion of the Long Parliament, if the provisional government had abstained from giving him cause of offence and apprehension. For his nature was cautious and somewhat sluggish; nor was he at all disposed to hazard sure and moderate advantages for the chance of obtaining even the most splendid success. He seems to have been impelled to attack the new rulers of the Commonwealth less by the hope that, if he overthrew them, he should become great, than by the fear that, if he submitted to them, he should not even be secure. Whatever were his motives, he declared himself the champion of the oppressed civil power, refused to acknowledge the usurped authority of the provisional government, and, at the head of seven thousand veterans, marched into England.

This step was the signal for a general explosion. The people every-

The army of Scotland marches into England

where refused to pay taxes. The apprentices of the City assembled by thousands and clamoured for a free Parliament. The fleet sailed up the Thames, and declared against the tyranny of the soldiers. The soldiers, no longer under the control of one commanding mind, separated into factions. Every regiment, afraid lest it should be left alone a mark for the vengeance of the oppressed nation, hastened to make a separate peace. Lambert, who had hastened northward to encounter the army of Scotland, was abandoned by his troops, and became a prisoner. During thirteen years the civil power had, in every conflict, been compelled to yield to the military power. The military power now humbled itself before the civil power. The Rump, generally hated and despised, but still the only body in the country which had any show of legal authority, returned again to the house from which it had been twice ignominiously expelled.

In the mean time Monk was advancing towards London. Wherever he came, the gentry flocked round him, imploring him to use his power for the purpose of restoring peace and liberty to the distracted nation. The General, coldblooded, taciturn, zealous for no polity and for no religion, maintained an impenetrable reserve. What were at this time his plans, and whether he had any plan, may well be doubted. His great object, apparently, was to keep himself, as long as possible, free to choose between several lines of action. Such, indeed, is commonly the policy of men who are, like him, distinguished rather by wariness than by farsightedness. It was probably not till he had been some days in the capital that he had made up his mind. The cry of the whole people was for a free Parliament ; and there could be no doubt that a Parliament really free would instantly restore the exiled family. The Rump and the soldiers were still hostile to the House of Stuart. But the Rump was universally detested and despised. The power of the soldiers was indeed still formidable, but had been greatly diminished by discord. They had no head. They had recently been, in many parts of the country, arrayed against each other. On the very day before Monk reached London, there was a fight in the Strand between the cavalry and the infantry. An united army had long kept down a divided nation ; but the nation was now united, and the army was divided.

Monk declares for a free Parliament   During a short time, the dissimulation or irresolution of Monk kept all parties in a state of painful suspense. At length he broke silence, and declared for a free Parliament.

As soon as his declaration was known, the whole nation was wild with delight. Wherever he appeared thousands thronged round him, shouting and blessing his name. The bells of all England rang joyously : the gutters ran with ale ; and, night after night, the sky five miles round London was reddened by innumerable bonfires. Those Presbyterian members of the House of Commons who had many years before been expelled by the army, returned to their seats, and were hailed with acclamations by great multitudes, which filled Westminster Hall and Palace Yard. The Independent leaders no longer dared to show their faces in the streets, and were scarcely safe within their own dwellings. Temporary provision was made for the government : writs were issued for a general election ; and then that memorable Parliament, which had, in the course of twenty eventful years, experienced every variety of fortune, which had triumphed over its sovereign, which had been enslaved and degraded by its servants, which had been twice ejected and twice restored, solemnly decreed its own dissolution.

The result of the elections was such as might have been expected from the temper of the nation. The new House of Commons **General** consisted, with few exceptions, of persons friendly to the royal **election of** family. The Presbyterians formed the majority. **1660**

That there would be a restoration now seemed almost certain ; but whether there would be a peaceable restoration was matter of painful doubt. The soldiers were in a gloomy and savage mood. They hated the title of King. They hated the name of Stuart. They hated Presbyterianism much, and Prelacy more. They saw with bitter indignation that the close of their long domination was approaching, and that a life of inglorious toil and penury was before them. They attributed their ill fortune to the weakness of some generals, and to the treason of others. One hour of their beloved Oliver might even now restore the glory which had departed. Betrayed, disunited, and left without any chief in whom they could confide, they were yet to be dreaded. It was no light thing to encounter the rage and despair of fifty thousand fighting men, whose backs no enemy had ever seen. Monk, and those with whom he acted, were well aware that the crisis was most perilous. They employed every art to sooth and to divide the discontented warriors. At the same time vigorous preparation was made for a conflict. The army of Scotland, now quartered in London, was kept in good humour by bribes, praises, and promises. The wealthy citizens grudged nothing to a red coat, and were indeed so liberal of their best wine, that warlike saints were sometimes seen in a condition not very honourable either to their religious or to their military character. Some refractory regiments Monk ventured to disband. In the meantime the greatest exertions were made by the provisional government, with the strenuous aid of the whole body of the gentry and magistracy, to organise the militia. In every county the trainbands were held ready to march ; and this force cannot be estimated at less than a hundred and twenty thousand men. In Hyde Park twenty thousand citizens, well armed and accoutred, passed in review, and showed a spirit which justified the hope that, in case of need, they would fight

REDUCED FACSIMILE OF A LETTER FROM CHARLES II TO HIS SISTER
DESCRIBING HIS RECEPTION IN ENGLAND

British Museum

manfully for their shops and firesides. The fleet was heartily with the nation. It was a stirring time, a time of anxiety, yet of hope. The prevailing opinion was that England would be delivered, but not without a desperate and bloody struggle, and that the class which had so long ruled by the sword would perish by the sword.

Happily the dangers of a conflict were averted. There was indeed one moment of extreme peril. Lambert escaped from his confinement, and called his comrades to arms. The flame of civil war was actually rekindled ; but by prompt and vigorous exertion it was trodden out before it had time to spread. The luckless imitator of Cromwell was

MEDAL STRUCK TO CELEBRATE THE RESTORATION OF CHARLES II

again a prisoner. The failure of his enterprise damped the spirit of the soldiers ; and they sullenly resigned themselves to their fate.

The new Parliament, which, having been called without the royal writ, is more accurately described as a Convention, met at Westminster. The Lords repaired to the hall, from which they had, during more than eleven years, been excluded by force. Both Houses instantly invited the King to return to his country. He was proclaimed with pomp never before known. A gallant fleet convoyed him from Holland to the coast of Kent. When he landed, the cliffs of Dover were covered by thousands of gazers, among whom scarcely one could be found who was not weeping with delight. The journey to London was a continued triumph. The whole road from Rochester was bordered by booths and tents, and looked like an interminable fair. Everywhere flags were flying, bells and music sounding, wine and ale flowing in rivers to the health of him whose return was the return of peace, of law, and of freedom. But in the midst of the general joy, one spot presented a dark and threatening aspect. On Blackheath the army was drawn up to welcome the sovereign. He smiled, bowed, and extended his hand graciously to the lips of the colonels and majors. But all his courtesy was vain. The countenances of the soldiers were sad and lowering ; and, had they given way to their feelings, the festive pageant of which they reluctantly made a part would have had a mournful and bloody end. But there was no concert among them. Discord and defection had left them no confidence in their chiefs or in each other. The whole array of the City of London was under arms. Numerous companies of militia had assembled from various parts of the realm, under the command of loyal noblemen and gentlemen, to welcome the King. That great day closed in peace ; and the restored wanderer reposed safe in the palace of his ancestors.

CHAPTER II

THE history of England, during the seventeenth century, is the history of the transformation of a limited monarchy, constituted after the fashion of the middle ages, into a limited monarchy suited to that more advanced state of society in which the public charges can no longer be borne by the estates of the crown, and in which the public defence can no longer be intrusted to a feudal militia. We have seen that the politicians who were at the head of the Long Parliament made, in 1642, a great effort to accomplish this change by transferring, directly and formally, to the Estates of the realm the choice of ministers, the command of the army, and the superintendence of the whole executive administration. This scheme was, perhaps, the best that could then be contrived : but it was completely disconcerted by the course which the civil war took. The Houses triumphed, it is true ; but not till after such a struggle as made it necessary for them to call into existence a power which they could not control, and which soon began to domineer over all orders and all parties. During a few years, the evils inseparable from military government were, in some degree, mitigated by the wisdom and magnanimity of the great man who held the supreme command. But, when the sword, which he had wielded, with energy indeed, but with energy always guided by good sense and generally tempered by good nature, had passed to captains who possessed neither his abilities nor his virtues, it seemed too probable that order and liberty would perish in one ignominious ruin.

Conduct of those who restored the House of Stuart unjustly censured

That ruin was happily averted. It has been too much the practice of writers zealous for freedom to represent the Restoration as a disastrous event, and to condemn the folly or baseness of that Convention which recalled the royal family without exacting new securities against maladministration. Those who hold this language do not comprehend the real nature of the crisis which followed the deposition of Richard Cromwell. England was in imminent danger of falling under the tyranny of a succession of small men raised up and pulled down by military

caprice. To deliver the country from the domination of the soldiers
was the first object of every enlightened patriot : but it was an object
which, while the soldiers were united, the most sanguine could scarcely
expect to attain. On a sudden a gleam of hope appeared. General
was opposed to general, army to army. On the use which might be
made of one auspicious moment depended the future destiny of the
nation. Our ancestors used that moment well. They forgot old
injuries, waved petty scruples, adjourned to a more convenient season
all dispute about the reforms which our institutions needed, and stood
together, Cavaliers and Roundheads, Episcopalians and Presbyterians, in
firm union, for the old laws of the land against military despotism. The
exact partition of power among King, Lords, and Commons, might
well be postponed till it had been decided whether England should be
governed by King, Lords, and Commons, or by cuirassiers and pikemen.
Had the statesmen of the Convention taken a different course, had they
held long debates on the principles of government, had they drawn up
a new constitution and sent it to Charles, had conferences been opened,
had couriers been passing and repassing during some weeks between
Westminster and the Netherlands, with projects and counterprojects,
replies by Hyde and rejoinders by Prynne, the coalition on which the
public safety depended would have been dissolved : the Presbyterians
and Royalists would certainly have quarrelled : the military factions
might possibly have been reconciled ; and the misjudging friends of
liberty might long have regretted, under a rule worse than that of the
worst Stuart, the golden opportunity which had been suffered to escape.

The old civil polity was, therefore, by the general consent of both
the great parties, reestablished. It was again exactly what it had been

Abolition of
tenures by
knight
service

when Charles the First, eighteen years before, withdrew from
his capital. All those acts of the Long Parliament which had
received the royal assent were admitted to be still in full
force. One fresh concession, a concession in which the Cavaliers were even
more deeply interested than the Roundheads, was easily obtained from
the restored King. The military tenure of land had been originally
created as a means of national defence. But in the course of ages whatever was useful in the institution had disappeared ; and nothing was left
but ceremonies and grievances. A landed proprietor who held an estate
under the crown by knight service,—and it was thus that most of the
soil of England was held,—had to pay a large fine on coming to his
property. He could not alienate one acre without purchasing a license.
When he died, if his domains descended to an infant, the sovereign was
guardian, and was not only entitled to great part of the rents during the
minority, but could require the ward, under heavy penalties, to marry
any person of suitable rank. The chief bait which attracted a needy

sycophant to the court was the hope of obtaining, as the reward of servility and flattery, a royal letter to an heiress. These abuses had perished with the monarchy. That they should not revive with it was

MEDALS COMMEMORATING THE DUKE OF ALBEMARLE,
THE MARRIAGE OF CHARLES II. TO CATHERINE OF BRAGANZA,
AND THE EARL OF CLARENDON

the wish of every landed gentleman in the kingdom. They were, there-fore, solemnly abolished by statute; and no relic of the ancient tenures in chivalry was suffered to remain, except those honorary services which are still, at a coronation, rendered to the person of the sovereign by some lords of manors.

The troops were now to be disbanded. Fifty thousand men, accustomed to the profession of arms, were at once thrown on the world : and **Disbanding of the army** experience seemed to warrant the belief that this change would produce much misery and crime, that the discharged veterans would be seen begging in every street, or that they would be driven by hunger to pillage. But no such result followed. In a few months there remained not a trace indicating that the most formidable army in the world had just been absorbed into the mass of the community. The Royalists themselves confessed that, in every department of honest industry, the discarded warriors prospered beyond other men, that none was charged with any theft or robbery, that none was heard to ask an alms, and that, if a baker, a mason, or a waggoner attracted notice by his diligence and sobriety, he was in all probability one of Oliver's old soldiers.

The military tyranny had passed away ; but it had left deep and enduring traces in the public mind. The name of standing army was long held in abhorrence : and it is remarkable that this feeling was even stronger among the Cavaliers than among the Roundheads. It ought to be considered as a most fortunate circumstance that, when our country was, for the first and last time, ruled by the sword, the sword was in the hands, not of her legitimate princes, but of those rebels who slew the King and demolished the Church. Had a prince, with a title as good as that of Charles, commanded an army as good as that of Cromwell, there would have been little hope indeed for the liberties of England. Happily that instrument by which alone the monarchy could be made absolute became an object of peculiar horror and disgust to the monarchical party, and long continued to be inseparably associated in the imagination of Royalists and Prelatists with regicide and field preaching. A century after the death of Cromwell, the Tories still continued to clamour against every augmentation of the regular soldiery, and to sound the praise of a national militia. So late as the year 1786, a minister who enjoyed no common measure of their confidence found it impossible to overcome their aversion to his scheme of fortifying the coast : nor did they ever look with entire complacency on the standing army, till the French Revolution gave a new direction to their apprehensions.

The coalition which had restored the King terminated with the **Disputes between the Roundheads and Cavaliers renewed** danger from which it had sprung ; and two hostile parties again appeared ready for conflict. Both indeed were agreed as to the propriety of inflicting punishment on some unhappy men who were, at that moment, objects of almost universal hatred. Cromwell was no more ; and those who had fled before him were forced to content themselves with the miserable satisfaction of digging up, hanging, quartering, and burning the remains of the greatest prince that has ever ruled England. Other objects of vengeance, few

OLIVERUS CROMWELL, REX INDEPENDENTIUM, ANGLIAE TYRANNUS

Number 1002 in the British Museum Catalogue of Satirical Prints

indeed, yet too many, were found among the republican chiefs. Soon, however, the conquerors, glutted with the blood of the regicides, turned against each other. The Roundheads, while admitting the virtues of the late King, and while condemning the sentence passed upon him by an illegal tribunal, yet maintained that his administration had been, in many things, unconstitutional, and that the Houses had taken arms against him from good motives and on strong grounds. The monarchy, these politicians conceived, had no worse enemy than the flatterer who exalted the prerogative above the law, who condemned all opposition to regal encroachments, and who reviled, not only Cromwell and Harrison, but Pym and Hampden, as traitors. If the King wished for a quiet and prosperous reign, he must confide in those who, though they had drawn the sword in defence of the invaded privileges of Parliament, had yet exposed themselves to the rage of the soldiers in order to save his father, and had taken the chief part in bringing back the royal family.

The feeling of the Cavaliers was widely different. During eighteen years they had, through all vicissitudes, been faithful to the Crown. Having shared the distress of their prince, were they not to share his triumph? Was no distinction to be made between them and the disloyal subject who had fought against his rightful sovereign, who had adhered to Richard Cromwell, and who had never concurred in the restoration of the Stuarts, till it appeared that nothing else could save the nation from the tyranny of the army? Grant that such a man had, by his recent services, fairly earned his pardon. Yet were his services, rendered at the eleventh hour, to be put in comparison with the toils and sufferings of those who had borne the burden and heat of the day? Was he to be ranked with men who had no need of the royal clemency, with men who had, in every part of their lives, merited the royal gratitude? Above all, was he to be suffered to retain a fortune raised out of the substance of the ruined defenders of the throne? Was it not enough that his head and his patrimonial estate, a hundred times forfeited to justice, were secure, and that he shared, with the rest of the nation, in the blessings of that mild government of which he had long been the foe? Was it necessary that he should be rewarded for his treason at the expense of men whose only crime was the fidelity with which they had observed their oath of allegiance? And what interest had the King in gorging his old enemies with prey torn from his old friends? What confidence could be placed in men who had opposed their sovereign, made war on him, imprisoned him, and who, even now, instead of hanging down their heads in shame and contrition, vindicated all that they had done, and seemed to think that they had given an illustrious proof of loyalty by just stopping short of regicide? It was true that they had lately assisted to set up the throne : but it was not less true that they had previously pulled it down, and that they still avowed principles which might impel them to pull it down again. Undoubtedly it might be fit that marks of royal approbation should be bestowed on some converts who had been eminently useful : but policy, as well as justice and gratitude, enjoined the King to give the highest place in his regard to those who, from first to last, through good and evil, had stood by his house. On these grounds the Cavaliers very naturally demanded indemnity for all that they had suffered, and preference in the distribution of the favours of the Crown. Some violent members of the party went further, and clamoured for large categories of proscription.

The political feud was, as usual, exasperated by a religious feud. The King found the Church in a singular state. A short time before the commencement of the civil war, his father had given a Religious reluctant assent to a bill, strongly supported by Falkland, dissension which deprived the Bishops of their seats in the House of Lords : but Episcopacy and the Liturgy had never been abolished by law. The Long Parliament, however, had passed ordinances which had made a complete revolution in Church government and in public worship. The new system was, in principle, scarcely less Erastian than that which it displaced. The Houses, guided chiefly by the counsels of the accomplished Selden, had determined to keep the spiritual power strictly subordinate to the temporal power. They had refused to declare that any form of ecclesiastical polity was of divine origin ; and they had provided that, from all the Church courts, an appeal should lie in the last resort to Parliament. With this highly important reservation, it had been resolved to set up in England a hierarchy closely resembling that which now exists in Scotland. The authority of councils, rising one above another in regular gradation, was substituted for the authority of Bishops and Archbishops. The Liturgy gave place to the Presbyterian Directory. But scarcely had the new regulations been framed, when the Independents rose to supreme influence in the state. The Independents had no disposition to enforce the ordinances touching classical, provincial, and national synods. Those ordinances, therefore, were never carried into full execution. The Presbyterian system was fully established nowhere but in Middlesex and Lancashire. In the other fifty counties, almost every parish seems to have been unconnected with the neighbouring parishes. In some districts, indeed, the ministers formed themselves into voluntary associations, for the purpose of mutual help and counsel; but these associations had no coercive power. The patrons of livings, being now checked by neither Bishop nor Presbytery, would have been at liberty to confide the cure of souls to the most scandalous of mankind, but for the arbitrary intervention of Oliver. He established, by his own authority, a board of commissioners, called Triers. Most of these persons were Independent divines ; but a few Presbyterian ministers and a few laymen had seats. The certificate of the Triers stood in the place both of institution and of induction ; and without such a certificate no person could hold a benefice. This was undoubtedly one of the most despotic acts ever done by any English ruler. Yet, as it was generally felt that, without some such precaution, the country would be overrun by ignorant and drunken reprobates, bearing the name and receiving the pay of ministers, some highly respectable persons, who were not in general friendly to Cromwell, allowed that, on this occasion, he had been a public benefactor. The presentees whom the Triers had approved took possession of the rectories, cultivated the glebe lands, collected the tithes, prayed without book or surplice, and administered the Eucharist to communicants seated at long tables.

Thus the ecclesiastical polity of the realm was in inextricable confusion. Episcopacy was the form of government prescribed by the old law which was still unrepealed. The form of government prescribed by parliamentary ordinance was Presbyterian. But neither the old law nor the parliamentary ordinance was practically in force. The Church actually established may be described as an irregular body made up of a few Presbyteries and many Independent congregations, which were all held down and held together by the authority of the government.

Of those who had been active in bringing back the King, many were zealous for Synods and for the Directory, and many were desirous to terminate by a compromise the religious dissensions which had long agitated England. Between the bigoted followers of Laud and the bigoted followers of Knox there could be neither peace nor truce : but it did not seem impossible to effect an accommodation between the moderate Episcopalians of the school of Usher and the moderate Presbyterians of the school of Baxter. The moderate Episcopalians would admit that a Bishop might lawfully be assisted by a council. The moderate Presbyterians would not deny that each provincial assembly might lawfully have a permanent president, and that this president might lawfully be called a Bishop. There might be a revised Liturgy which should not exclude extemporaneous prayer, a baptismal service in which the sign of the cross might be used or omitted at discretion, a communion service at which the faithful might sit if their consciences forbade them to kneel. But to no such plan could the great body of the Cavaliers listen with patience. The religious members of that party were conscientiously attached to the whole system of their Church. She had been dear to their murdered King. She had consoled them in defeat and penury. Her service, so often whispered in an inner chamber during the season of trial, had such a charm for them that they were unwilling to part with a single response. Other Royalists, who made little pretence to piety, yet loved the episcopal Church because she was the foe of their foes. They valued a prayer or a ceremony, not on account of the comfort which it conveyed to themselves, but on account of the vexation which it gave to the Roundheads, and were so far from being disposed to purchase union by concession that they objected to concession chiefly because it tended to produce union.

Such feelings, though blamable, were natural and not wholly inexcusable. The Puritans had undoubtedly, in the day of their power, given cruel provocation. They ought to have learned, if from nothing else, yet from their own discontents, from their own struggles, from their own victory, from the fall of that proud hierarchy by which they had been so heavily oppressed, that, in England, **Unpopularity of the Puritans**

THE COMMITTEE

A Caricature against the Covenanters. Number 1080 in the British Museum Catalogue of Satirical Prints

and in the seventeenth century, it was not in the power of the civil magistrate to drill the minds of men into conformity with his own system of theology. They proved, however, as intolerant and as meddling as ever Laud had been. They interdicted under heavy penalties the use of the Book of Common Prayer, not only in churches, but even in private houses. It was a crime in a child to read by the bedside of a sick parent one of those beautiful collects which had soothed the griefs of forty generations of Christians. Severe punishments were denounced against such as should presume to blame the Calvinistic mode of worship. Clergymen of respectable character were not only ejected from their benefices by thousands, but were frequently exposed to the outrages of a fanatical rabble. Churches and sepulchres, fine works of art and curious remains of antiquity, were brutally defaced. The Parliament resolved that all pictures in the royal collection which contained representations of Jesus or of the Virgin Mother should be burned. Sculpture fared as ill as painting. Nymphs and Graces, the work of Ionian chisels, were delivered over to Puritan stonemasons to be made decent. Against the lighter vices the ruling faction waged war with a zeal little tempered by humanity or by common sense. Sharp laws were passed against betting. It was enacted that adultery should be punished with death. The illicit intercourse of the sexes, even where neither violence nor seduction was imputed, where no public scandal was given, where no conjugal right was violated, was made a misdemeanour. Public amusements, from the masques which were exhibited at the mansions of the great down to the wrestling matches and grinning matches on village greens, were vigorously attacked. One ordinance directed that all the Maypoles in England should forthwith be hewn down. Another proscribed all theatrical diversions. The playhouses were to be dismantled, the spectators fined, the actors whipped at the cart's tail. Ropedancing, puppetshows, bowls, horse-racing, were regarded with no friendly eye. But bearbaiting, then a favourite diversion of high and low, was the abomination which most strongly stirred the wrath of the austere sectaries. It is to be remarked that their antipathy to this sport had nothing in common with the feeling which has, in our own time, induced the legislature to interfere for the purpose of protecting beasts against the wanton cruelty of men. The Puritan hated bearbaiting, not because it gave pain to the bear, but because it gave pleasure to the spectators. Indeed, he generally contrived to enjoy the double pleasure of tormenting both spectators and bear.[1]

---

[1] How little compassion for the bear had to do with the matter is sufficiently proved by the following extract from a paper entitled A perfect Diurnal of some Passages of Parliament, and from other Parts of the Kingdom, from Monday July 24th, to Monday July 31st, 1643. "Upon the queen's coming from Holland, she brought with her, besides a company of savage-like ruffians, a company of savage bears, to what purpose you may judge by the sequel. Those bears were left about Newark, and were brought into country towns constantly on the Lord's day to be baited, such is the religion those here related would settle amongst us ; and, if any went about to hinder or but speak against their damnable profanations, they were presently noted as Round-heads and Puritans, and sure to be plundered for it. But some of Colonel Cromwell's forces coming by accident into Uppingham town, in Rutland, on the Lord's day, found these bears playing there in the usual manner, and, in the height of their sport, caused them to be seized upon, tied to a tree and shot." This was by no means a solitary instance. Colonel Pride, when Sheriff of Surrey, ordered the beasts in the bear garden of Southwark to be killed. He is repre-sented by a loyal satirist as defending the act thus :—"The first thing that is upon my spirits is the killing of the bears, for which the people hate me, and call me all the names in the rainbow. But did not David kill a bear ? Did not the Lord Deputy Ireton kill a bear ? Did not another lord of ours kill five bears ?"—Last Speech and Dying Words of Thomas Pride.

Perhaps no single circumstance more strongly illustrates the temper of the precisians than their conduct respecting Christmas day. Christmas had been, from time immemorial, the season of joy and domestic affection, the season when families assembled, when children came home from school, when quarrels were made up, when carols were heard in every street, when every house was decorated with evergreens, and every table was loaded with good cheer. At that season all hearts not utterly destitute of kindness were enlarged and softened. At that season the poor were admitted to partake largely of the overflowings of the wealth of the rich, whose bounty was peculiarly acceptable on account of the shortness of the days and of the severity of the weather. At that season the interval between landlord and tenant, master and servant, was less marked than through the rest of the year. Where there is much enjoyment there will be some excess : yet, on the whole, the spirit in which the holiday was kept was not unworthy of a Christian festival. The Long Parliament gave orders, in 1644, that the twenty-fifth of December should be strictly observed as a fast, and that all men should pass it in humbly bemoaning the great national sin which they and their fathers had so often committed on that day by romping under the mistletoe, eating boar's head, and drinking ale flavoured with roasted apples. No public act of that time seems to have irritated the common people more. On the next anniversary of the festival formidable riots broke out in many places. The constables were resisted, the magistrates insulted, the houses of noted zealots attacked, and the proscribed service of the day openly read in the churches.

Such was the spirit of the extreme Puritans, both Presbyterian and Independent. Oliver, indeed, was little disposed to be either a persecutor or a meddler. But Oliver, the head of a party, and consequently, to a great extent, the slave of a party, could not govern altogether according to his own inclinations. Even under his administration many magistrates, within their own jurisdiction, made themselves as odious as Sir Hudibras, interfered with all the pleasures of the neighbourhood, dispersed festive meetings, and put fiddlers in the stocks. Still more formidable was the zeal of the soldiers. In every village where they appeared there was an end of dancing, bellringing, and hockey. In London they several times interrupted theatrical performances at which the Protector had the judgment and good nature to connive.

With the fear and hatred inspired by such a tyranny contempt was largely mingled. The peculiarities of the Puritan, his look, his dress, his dialect, his strange scruples, had been, ever since the time of Elizabeth, favourite subjects with mockers. But these peculiarities appeared far more grotesque in a faction which ruled a great empire than in obscure and persecuted congregations. The cant, which had moved laughter when it was heard on the stage from Tribulation Wholesome and Zeal-of-the-Land Busy, was still more laughable when it proceeded from the lips of Generals and Councillors of State.   It is also to be noticed that during the civil troubles several sects had sprung into existence, whose eccentricities surpassed anything that had before been seen in England. A mad tailor, named Lodowick Muggleton, wandered from pothouse to pothouse, tippling ale, and denouncing eternal torments against those who refused to believe, on his testimony, that the Supreme Being was only six feet high, and that the sun was just four miles from the earth.[1] George Fox had raised a tempest of derision by proclaiming that it was a violation of Christian sincerity to designate a single person by a plural pronoun, and that it was an idolatrous homage to Janus and Woden to talk about January and Wednesday.   His doctrine, a few years later, was embraced by some eminent men, and rose greatly in the public estimation.   But at the time of the Restoration the Quakers were popularly regarded as the most despicable of fanatics.   By the Puritans they were treated with severity here, and were persecuted to the death in New England.   Nevertheless the public, which seldom makes nice distinctions, often confounded the Puritan with the Quaker.   Both were schismatics.   Both hated episcopacy and the Liturgy.   Both had what seemed extravagant whimsies about dress, diversions, and postures. Widely as the two differed in opinion, they were popularly classed together as canting schismatics ; and whatever was ridiculous or odious in either increased the scorn and aversion which the multitude felt for both.

Before the civil wars, even those who most disliked the opinions and manners of the Puritan were forced to admit that his moral conduct was generally, in essentials, blameless ; but this praise was now no longer bestowed, and, unfortunately, was no longer deserved.   The general fate of sects is to obtain a high reputation for sanctity while they are oppressed, and to lose it as soon as they become powerful : and the reason is obvious.   It is seldom that a man enrolls himself in a pro-scribed body from any but conscientious motives.   Such a body, there-fore, is composed, with scarcely an exception, of sincere persons.   The most rigid discipline that can be enforced within a religious society is a very feeble instrument of purification, when compared with a little sharp persecution from without.   We may be certain that very few persons, not seriously impressed by religious convictions, applied for baptism while Diocletian was vexing the Church, or joined themselves to Pro-testant congregations at the risk of being burned by Bonner.   But, when a sect becomes powerful, when its favour is the road to riches and dignities, worldly and ambitious men crowd into it, talk its language,

[1] See Penn's New Witnesses proved Old Heretics, and Muggleton's works, *passim*.

conform strictly to its ritual, mimic its peculiarities, and frequently go beyond its honest members in all the outward indications of zeal. No discernment, no watchfulness, on the part of ecclesiastical rulers, can prevent the intrusion of such false brethren. The tares and the wheat must grow together. Soon the world begins to find out that the godly are not better than other men, and argues, with some justice, that, if not better, they must be much worse. In no long time all those signs which were formerly regarded as characteristic of a saint are regarded as characteristic of a knave.

Thus it was with the English Nonconformists. They had been oppressed ; and oppression had kept them a pure body. They then became supreme in the state. No man could hope to rise to eminence and command but by their favour. Their favour was to be gained only by exchanging with them the signs and passwords of spiritual fraternity. One of the first resolutions adopted by Barebone's Parliament, the most intensely Puritanical of all our political assemblies, was that no person should be admitted into the public service till the House should be satisfied of his real godliness. What were then considered as the signs of real godliness, the sadcoloured dress, the sour look, the straight hair, the nasal whine, the speech interspersed with quaint texts, the Sunday, gloomy as a Pharisaical Sabbath, were easily imitated by men to whom all religions were the same. The sincere Puritans soon found themselves lost in a multitude, not merely of men of the world, but of the very worst sort of men of the world. For the most notorious libertine who had fought under the royal standard might justly be thought virtuous when compared with some of those who, while they talked about sweet experiences and comfortable scriptures, lived in the constant practice of fraud, rapacity, and secret debauchery. The people, with a rashness which we may justly lament, but at which we cannot wonder, formed their estimate of the whole body from these hypocrites. The theology, the manners, the dialect of the Puritan were thus associated in the public mind with the darkest and meanest vices. As soon as the Restoration had made it safe to avow enmity to the party which had so long been predominant, a general outcry against Puritanism rose from every corner of the kingdom, and was often swollen by the voices of those very dissemblers whose villany had brought disgrace on the Puritan name.

Thus the two great parties, which, after a long contest, had for a moment concurred in restoring monarchy, were, both in politics and in religion, again opposed to each other. The great body of the nation leaned to the Royalists. The crimes of Strafford and Laud, the excesses of the Star Chamber and of the High Commission, the great services which the Long Parliament had, during the first year of its existence, rendered to the state, had faded from the minds of men.   The execution of Charles the First, the sullen tyranny of the Rump, the violence of the army, were remembered with loathing ; and the multitude was inclined to hold all who withstood the late King responsible for his death and for the subsequent disasters.

The House of Commons, having been elected while the Presbyterians were dominant, by no means represented the general sense of the people.   Most of the members, while execrating Cromwell and Bradshaw, reverenced the memory of Essex and of Pym.   One sturdy Cavalier, who ventured to declare that all who had drawn the sword against Charles the First were as much traitors as those who had cut off his head, was called to order, placed at the bar, and reprimanded by the Speaker.   The general wish of the House undoubtedly was to settle the ecclesiastical disputes in a manner satisfactory to the moderate Puritans. But to such a settlement both the court and the nation were averse.

The restored King was at this time more loved by the people than any of his predecessors had ever been.   The calamities of his house, the heroic death of his father, his own long sufferings and romantic adventures, made him an object of tender interest.   His return had delivered the country from an intolerable bondage.   Recalled by the voice of both the contending factions, he was in a position which enabled him to arbitrate between them ; and in some respects he was well qualified for the task.   He had received from nature excellent parts and a happy temper.   His education had been such as might have been expected to develope his understanding, and to form him to the practice of every public and private virtue.   He had passed through all varieties of fortune, and had seen both sides of human nature.   He had, while very young, been driven forth from a palace to a life of exile, penury, and danger.   He had, at the age when the mind and body are in their highest perfection, and when the first effervescence of boyish passions should have subsided, been recalled from his wanderings to wear a crown.   He had been taught by bitter experience how much baseness, perfidy, and ingratitude may lie hid under the obsequious demeanour of courtiers.   He had found, on the other hand, in the huts of the poorest, true nobility of soul.   When wealth was offered to any who would betray him, when death was denounced against all who should shelter him, cottagers and serving men had kept his secret truly, and had kissed his hand under his mean disguises with as much reverence as if he had been seated on his ancestral throne.   From such a school it might have been expected that a young man who wanted neither abilities nor amiable qualities would have come forth a great and good King.   Charles came forth from that school with social habits, with polite and engaging manners, and with some talent for lively con-

Character of Charles II

versation, addicted beyond measure to sensual indulgence, fond of sauntering and of frivolous amusements, incapable of selfdenial and of exertion, without faith in human virtue or in human attachment, without desire of renown, and without sensibility to reproach. According to him, every person was to be bought : but some people haggled more about their price than others ; and when this haggling was very obstinate and very skilful it was called by some fine name. The chief trick by which clever men kept up the price of their abilities was called integrity. The chief trick by which handsome women kept up the price of their beauty was called modesty. The love of God, the love of country, the love of family, the love of friends, were phrases of the same sort, delicate and convenient synonymes for the love of self. Thinking thus of mankind, Charles naturally cared very little what they thought of him. Honour and shame were scarcely more to him than light and darkness to the blind. His contempt of flattery has been highly commended, but seems, when viewed in connection with the rest of his character, to deserve no commendation. It is possible to be below flattery as well as above it. One who trusts nobody will not trust sycophants. One who does not value real glory will not value its counterfeit.

It is creditable to Charles's temper that, ill as he thought of his species, he never became a misanthrope. He saw little in men but what was hateful. Yet he did not hate them. Nay, he was so far humane that it was highly disagreeable to him to see their sufferings or to hear their complaints. This however is a sort of humanity which, though amiable and laudable in a private man whose power to help or hurt is bounded by a narrow circle, has in princes often been rather a vice than a virtue. More than one well disposed ruler has given up whole provinces to rapine and oppression, merely from a wish to see none but happy faces round his own board and in his own walks. No man is fit to govern great societies who hesitates about disobliging the few who have access to him, for the sake of the many whom he will never see. The facility of Charles was such as has perhaps never been found in any man of equal sense. He was a slave without being a dupe. Worthless men and women, to the very bottom of whose hearts he saw, and whom he knew to be destitute of affection for him and undeserving of his confidence, could easily wheedle him out of titles, places, domains, state secrets and pardons. He bestowed much ; yet he neither enjoyed the pleasure nor acquired the fame of beneficence. He never gave spontaneously ; but it was painful to him to refuse. The consequence was that his bounty generally went, not to those who deserved it best, nor even to those whom he liked best, but to the most shameless and importunate suitor who could obtain an audience.

CHARLES II

From a mezzotint by Sherwin

CATHERINE OF BRAGANZA

From a mezzotint by Sherwin

The motives which governed the political conduct of Charles the Second differed widely from those by which his predecessor and his successor were actuated.   He was not a man to be imposed upon by the patriarchal theory of government and the doctrine of divine right. He was utterly without ambition.   He detested business, and would sooner have abdicated his crown than have undergone the trouble of really directing the administration.   Such was his aversion to toil, and such his ignorance of affairs, that the very clerks who attended him when he sate in council could not refrain from sneering at his frivolous remarks, and at his childish impatience.   Neither gratitude nor revenge had any share in determining his course ; for never was there a mind on which both services and injuries left such faint and transitory impressions.   He wished merely to be a King such as Lewis the Fifteenth of France afterwards was ; a King who could draw without limit on the treasury for the gratification of his private tastes, who could hire with wealth and honours persons capable of assisting him to kill the time, and who, even when the state was brought by maladministration to the depths of humiliation and to the brink of ruin, could still exclude unwelcome truth from the purlieus of his own seraglio, and refuse to see and hear whatever might disturb his luxurious repose.   For these ends, and for these ends alone, he wished to obtain arbitrary power, if it could be obtained without risk or trouble.   In the religious disputes which divided his Protestant subjects his conscience was not at all interested. For his opinions oscillated in contented suspense between infidelity and Popery.   But, though his conscience was neutral in the quarrel between the Episcopalians and the Presbyterians, his taste was by no means so. His favourite vices were precisely those to which the Puritans were least indulgent.   He could not get through one day without the help of diversions which the Puritans regarded as sinful.   As a man eminently well bred, and keenly sensible of the ridiculous, he was moved to contemptuous mirth by the Puritan oddities.   He had indeed some reason to dislike the rigid sect.   He had, at the age when the passions are most impetuous and when levity is most pardonable, spent some months in Scotland, a King in name, but in fact a state prisoner in the hands of austere Presbyterians.   Not content with requiring him to conform to their worship and to subscribe their Covenant, they had watched all his motions, and lectured him on all his youthful follies.   He had been compelled to give reluctant attendance at endless prayers and sermons, and might think himself fortunate when he was not insolently reminded from the pulpit of his own frailties, of his father's tyranny, and of his mother's idolatry.   Indeed he had been so miserable during this part of his life that the defeat which made him again a wanderer might be regarded as a deliverance rather than as a calamity.   Under the influence of such feelings as these Charles was desirous to depress the party which had resisted his father.

The King's brother, James Duke of York, took the same side. Though a libertine, James was diligent, methodical, and fond of authority and business. His understanding was singularly slow and narrow, and his temper obstinate, harsh, and unforgiving. That such a prince should have looked with no good will on the free institutions of England, and on the party which was peculiarly zealous for those institutions, can excite no surprise. As yet

Characters of the Duke of York and Earl of Clarendon

THE SCOTS HOLDING THEIR YOUNG KING'S NOSE TO THE GRINDSTONE

Number 812 in the British Museum Catalogue of Satirical Prints

the Duke professed himself a member of the Anglican Church : but he had already shown inclinations which had seriously alarmed good Protestants.

The person on whom devolved at this time the greatest part of the labour of governing was Edward Hyde, Chancellor of the realm, who was soon created Earl of Clarendon. The respect which we justly feel for Clarendon as a writer must not blind us to the faults which he committed as a statesman. Some of those faults, however, are explained and excused by the unfortunate position in which he stood. He had, during the first year of the Long Parliament, been honourably distinguished among the senators who laboured to redress the grievances of the nation. One of the most odious of those grievances, the Council of York, had been removed in consequence chiefly of his exertions. When the great schism took place, when the reforming party and the conservative party first appeared marshalled against each other, he, with many wise and good men, took the conservative side. He thenceforward followed the fortunes of the court, enjoyed as large a share of the confidence of Charles the First as the reserved nature and tortuous policy of that prince allowed to any minister, and subsequently shared the exile and directed the political conduct of Charles the Second. At the Restoration Hyde became chief minister. In a few months it was announced that he was closely related by affinity to the royal house. His daughter had become, by a secret marriage, Duchess of York. His grandchildren might perhaps wear the crown. He was raised by this illustrious connection over the heads of the old nobility of the land, and was for a time supposed to be allpowerful. In some respects he was well fitted for his great place. No man wrote abler state papers. No man spoke with more weight and dignity in Council and in Parliament. No man was better acquainted with general maxims of statecraft. No man observed the varieties of character with a more discriminating eye. It must be added that he had a strong sense of moral and religious obligation, a sincere reverence for the laws of his country, and a conscientious regard for the honour and interest of the Crown. But his temper was sour, arrogant, and impatient of opposition. Above all, he had been long an exile; and this circumstance alone would have completely disqualified him for the supreme direction of affairs. It is scarcely possible that a politician, who has been compelled by civil troubles, to go into banishment, and to pass many of the best years of his life abroad, can be fit, on the day on which he returns to his native land, to be at the head of the government. Clarendon was no exception to this rule. He had left England with a mind heated by a fierce conflict which had ended in the downfall of his party and of his own fortunes. From 1646 to 1660 he had lived beyond sea, looking on all that passed at home from a great distance, and through a false medium. His notions of public affairs were necessarily derived from the reports of plotters, many of whom were ruined and desperate men. Events naturally seemed to him auspicious, not in proportion as they increased the prosperity and glory of the nation, but in proportion as they tended to hasten the hour of his own return. His wish, a wish which he has not disguised, was that, till his countrymen brought back the old line, they might never enjoy quiet or freedom. At length he returned; and,

IACOBVS EBORACENSIS ET ALBANIÆ DVX, COMES VLTONIÆ &c.

JAMES, DUKE OF YORK

From a mezzotint by Blooteling, after Sir P. Lely

without having a single week to look about him, to mix with society, to note the changes which fourteen eventful years had produced in the national character and feelings, he was at once set to rule the state.   In such circumstances, a minister of the greatest tact and docility would probably have fallen into serious errors.   But tact and docility made no part of the character of Clarendon.   To him England was still the England of his youth ; and he sternly frowned down every theory and every practice which had sprung up during his own exile.   Though he was far from meditating any attack on the ancient and undoubted power of the House of Commons, he saw with extreme uneasiness the growth of that power.   The royal prerogative, for which he had long suffered, and by which he had at length been raised to wealth and dignity, was sacred in his eyes.   The Roundheads he regarded both with political and with personal aversion.   To the Anglican Church he had always been strongly attached, and had repeatedly, where her interests were concerned, separated himself with regret from his dearest friends.   His zeal for Episcopacy and for the Book of Common Prayer was now more ardent than ever, and was mingled with a vindictive hatred of the Puritans, which did him little honour either as a statesman or as a Christian.

While the House of Commons which had recalled the royal family was sitting, it was impossible to effect the reestablishment of the old ecclesiastical system.   Not only were the intentions of the court strictly concealed, but assurances which quieted the minds of the moderate Presbyterians were given by the King in the most solemn manner.   He had promised, before his restoration, that he would grant liberty of conscience to his subjects.   He now repeated that promise, and added a promise to use his best endeavours for the purpose of effecting a compromise between the contending sects.   He wished, he said, to see the spiritual jurisdiction divided between bishops and synods.   The Liturgy should be revised by a body of learned divines, one half of whom should be Presbyterians.   The questions respecting the surplice, the posture at the Eucharist, and the sign of the cross in baptism, should be settled in a way which would set tender consciences at ease.   When the King had thus laid asleep the vigilance of those whom he most feared, he dissolved the Parliament.   He had already given his assent to an act by which an amnesty was granted, with few exceptions, to all who, during the late troubles, had been guilty of political offences.   He had also obtained from the Commons a grant for life of taxes, the annual produce of which was estimated at twelve hundred thousand pounds.   The actual income, indeed, during some years, amounted to little more than a million : but this sum, together with the hereditary revenue of the crown, was then sufficient to defray the expenses of the government in

Honoratissimus Illustrissimusqȝ Dominus D. EDOARDUS HIDE. Eques Auratus, CLARENDONIÆ Comes, Comburiæ Vicecomis, Baro HIDE de Hindon, Summus Angliæ, nec non almæ Oxoniensis Academiæ Cancellarius, ac sacræ Maⁱⁱ regiæ à secretioribus Concilijs.

EDWARD HYDE, EARL OF CLARENDON

From an engraving by D. Loggan

time of peace.   Nothing was allowed for a standing army.   The nation was sick of the very name ; and the least mention of such a force would have incensed and alarmed all parties.

Early in 1661 took place a general election.   The people were mad with loyal enthusiasm.   The capital was excited by preparations for the most splendid coronation that had ever been known. The result was that a body of representatives was returned, such as England had never yet seen.   A large proportion of the successful candidates were men who had fought for the Crown and the Church, and whose minds had been exasperated by many injuries and insults suffered at the hands of the Roundheads.   When the members met, the passions which animated each individually acquired new strength from sympathy.   The House of Commons was, during some years, more zealous for royalty than the King, more zealous for episcopacy than the Bishops.   Charles and Clarendon were almost terrified at the completeness of their own success.   They found themselves in a situation not unlike that in which Lewis the Eighteenth and the Duke of Richelieu were placed while the Chamber of 1815 was sitting.   Even if the King had been desirous to fulfil the promises which he had made to the Presbyterians, it would have been out of his power to do so.   It was indeed only by the strong exertion of his influence that he could prevent the victorious Cavaliers from rescinding the act of indemnity, and retaliating without mercy all that they had suffered.

The Commons began by resolving that every member should, on pain of expulsion, take the sacrament according to the form prescribed by the old Liturgy, and that the Covenant should be burned by the hangman in Palace Yard.   An act was passed, which not only acknowledged the power of the sword to be solely in the King, but declared that in no extremity whatever could the two Houses be justified in withstanding him by force.   Another act was passed which required every officer of a corporation to receive the Eucharist according to the rites of the Church of England, and to swear that he held resistance to the King's authority to be in all cases unlawful. A few hotheaded men wished to bring in a bill, which should at once annul all the statutes passed by the Long Parliament, and should restore the Star Chamber and the High Commission ; but the reaction, violent as it was, did not proceed quite to this length.   It still continued to be the law that a Parliament should be held every three years : but the stringent clauses which directed the returning officers to proceed to election at the proper time, even without the royal writ, were repealed. The Bishops were restored to their seats in the Upper House.   The old ecclesiastical polity and the old Liturgy were revived without any

General election of 1661

Violence of the Cavaliers in the new Parliament

modification which had any tendency to conciliate even the most reasonable Presbyterians. Episcopal ordination was now, for the first time, made an indispensable qualification for church preferment. About two thousand ministers of religion, whose conscience did not suffer them to conform, were driven from their benefices in one day. The dominant party exultingly reminded the sufferers that the Long Parliament, when at the height of power, had turned out a still greater number of Royalist divines. The reproach was but too well founded : but the Long Parliament had at least allowed to the divines whom it ejected a provision sufficient to keep them from starving ; and this example the Cavaliers, intoxicated with animosity, had not the justice and humanity to follow.

Then came penal statutes against Nonconformists, statutes for which precedents might too easily be found in the Puritan legislation, but to which the King could not give his assent without a breach of promises publicly made, in the most important crisis of his life, to those on whom his fate depended. The Presbyterians, in extreme distress and terror, fled to the foot of the throne, and pleaded their recent services and the royal faith solemnly and repeatedly plighted. The King wavered. He could not deny his own hand and seal. He could not but be conscious that he owed much to the petitioners. He was little in the habit of resisting importunate solicitation. His temper was not that of a persecutor. He disliked the Puritans indeed ; but in him dislike was a languid feeling, very little resembling the energetic hatred which had burned in the heart of Laud. He was, moreover, partial to the Roman Catholic religion ; and he knew that it would be impossible to grant liberty of worship to the professors of that religion without extending the same indulgence to Protestant dissenters. He therefore made a feeble attempt to restrain the intolerant zeal of the House of Commons ; but that House was under the influence of far deeper convictions and far stronger passions than his own. After a faint struggle he yielded, and passed, with the show of alacrity, a series of odious acts against the separatists. It was made a crime to attend a dissenting place of worship. A single justice of the peace might convict without a jury, and might, for the third offence, pass sentence of transportation beyond sea for seven years. With refined cruelty it was provided that the offender should not be transported to New England, where he was likely to find sympathising friends. If he returned to his own country before the expiration of his term of exile, he was liable to capital punishment. A new and most unreasonable test was imposed on divines who had been deprived of their benefices for nonconformity ; and all who refused to take that test were prohibited from coming within five miles of any town which was governed by a corporation, of any town which was represented in Parliament, or of any town where

Persecution of the Puritans

they had themselves resided as ministers. The magistrates, by whom these rigorous statutes were to be enforced, were in general men inflamed by party spirit and by the remembrance of wrongs suffered in the time of the Commonwealth. The gaols were therefore soon crowded with dissenters ; and, among the sufferers, were some of whose genius and virtue any Christian society might well be proud.

The Church of England was not ungrateful for the protection which she received from the government. From the first day of her existence, she had been attached to monarchy. But, during the quarter of a century which followed the Restoration, her zeal for royal authority and hereditary right passed all bounds. She had suffered with the House of Stuart. She had been restored with that House. She was connected with it by common interests, friendships, and enmities. It seemed impossible that a day could ever come when the ties which bound her to the children of her august martyr would be sundered, and when the loyalty in which she gloried would cease to be a pleasing and profitable duty. She accordingly magnified in fulsome phrase that prerogative which was constantly employed to defend and to aggrandise her, and reprobated, much at her ease, the depravity of those whom oppression, from which she was exempt, had goaded to rebellion. Her favourite theme was the doctrine of nonresistance. That doctrine she taught without any qualification, and followed out to all its extreme consequences. Her disciples were never weary of repeating that in no conceivable case, not even if England were cursed with a King resembling Busiris or Phalaris, with a King who, in defiance of law, and without the pretence of justice, should daily doom hundreds of innocent victims to torture and death, would all the Estates of the realm united be justified in withstanding his tyranny by physical force. Happily the principles of human nature afford abundant security that such theories will never be more than theories. The day of trial came ; and the very men who had most loudly and most sincerely professed this extravagant loyalty were, in every county of England, arrayed in arms against the throne.

Property all over the kingdom was now again changing hands. The national sales, not having been confirmed by Act of Parliament, were regarded by the tribunals as nullities. The bishops, the deans, the chapters, the Royalist nobility and gentry, reentered on their confiscated estates, and ejected even purchasers who had given fair prices. The losses which the Cavaliers had sustained during the ascendency of their opponents were thus in part repaired ; but in part only. All actions for mesne profits were effectually barred by the general amnesty; and the numerous Royalists, who, in order to discharge fines imposed by the Long Parliament, or in order to purchase the favour of powerful

THOMAS WRIOTHESLEY, FOURTH EARL OF SOUTHAMPTON

From the painting in the National Portrait Gallery, after Sir P. Lely

Roundheads, had sold land for much less than the real value, were not relieved from the legal consequences of their own acts.

While these changes were in progress, a change still more important took place in the morals and manners of the community. Those passions and tastes which, under the rule of the Puritans, had been sternly repressed, and, if gratified at all, had been gratified by stealth, broke forth with ungovernable violence as soon as the check was withdrawn. Men flew to frivolous amusements and to criminal pleasures with the greediness which long and enforced abstinence naturally produces. Little restraint was imposed by public opinion. For the nation, nauseated with cant, suspicious of all pretensions to sanctity, and still smarting from the recent tyranny of rulers austere in life and powerful in prayer, looked for a time with complacency on the softer and gayer vices. Still less restraint was imposed by the government. Indeed there was no excess which was not encouraged by the ostentatious profligacy of the King and of his favourite courtiers. A few counsellors of Charles the First, who were now no longer young, retained the decorous gravity which had been thirty years before in fashion at Whitehall. Such were Clarendon himself, and his friends, Thomas Wriothesley, Earl of Southampton, Lord Treasurer, and James Butler, Duke of Ormond, who, having through many vicissitudes struggled gallantly for the royal cause in Ireland, now governed that kingdom as Lord Lieutenant. But neither the memory of the services of these men, nor their great power in the state, could protect them from the sarcasms which modish vice loves to dart at obsolete virtue. The praise of politeness and vivacity could now scarcely be obtained except by some violation of decorum. Talents great and various assisted to spread the contagion. Ethical philosophy had recently taken a form well suited to please a generation equally devoted to monarchy and to vice. Thomas Hobbes had, in language more precise and luminous than has ever been employed by any other metaphysical writer, maintained that the will of the prince was the standard of right and wrong, and that every subject ought to be ready to profess Popery, Mahometanism, or Paganism, at the royal command. Thousands who were incompetent to appreciate what was really valuable in his speculations, eagerly welcomed a theory which, while it exalted the kingly office, relaxed the obligations of morality, and degraded religion into a mere affair of state. Hobbism soon became an almost essential part of the character of the fine gentleman. All the lighter kinds of literature were deeply tainted by the prevailing licentiousness. Poetry stooped to be the pandar of every low desire. Ridicule, instead of putting guilt and error to the blush, turned her formidable shafts against innocence and truth. The restored Church contended indeed against the prevailing immorality,

Change in the morals of the community

THOMAS HOBBES

From the painting by J. M. Wright, in the National Portrait Gallery but contended feebly, and with half a heart.   It was necessary to the decorum of her character that she should admonish her erring children : but her admonitions were given in a somewhat perfunctory manner. Her attention was elsewhere engaged.   Her whole soul was in the work of crushing the Puritans, and of teaching her disciples to give unto Cæsar the things which were Cæsar's.   She had been pillaged and oppressed by the party which preached an austere morality.   She had been restored to opulence and honour by libertines.   Little as the men of mirth and fashion were disposed to shape their lives according to her precepts, they were yet ready to fight knee deep in blood for her cathedrals and palaces, for every line of her rubric and every thread of her vestments.   If the debauched Cavalier haunted brothels and gambling houses, he at least avoided conventicles.   If he never spoke without uttering ribaldry and blasphemy, he made some amends by his eagerness to send Baxter and Howe to gaol for preaching and praying. Thus the clergy, for a time, made war on schism with so much vigour that they had little leisure to make war on vice.   The ribaldry of Etherege and Wycherley was, in the presence and under the special sanction of the head of the Church, publicly recited by female lips in female ears, while the author of the Pilgrim's Progress languished in a dungeon for the crime of proclaiming the gospel to the poor.   It is an unquestionable and a most instructive fact that the years during which the political power of the Anglican hierarchy was in the zenith were precisely the years during which national virtue was at the lowest point.

Scarcely any rank or profession escaped the infection of the prevailing immorality ; but those persons who made politics their business **Profligacy of** were perhaps the most corrupt part of the corrupt society. **politicians**   For they were exposed, not only to the same noxious influences which affected the nation generally, but also to a taint of a peculiar and of a most malignant kind.   Their character had been formed amidst frequent and violent revolutions and counterrevolutions. In the course of a few years they had seen the ecclesiastical and civil polity of their country repeatedly changed.   They had seen an Episcopal Church persecuting Puritans, a Puritan Church persecuting Episcopalians, and an Episcopal Church persecuting Puritans again.   They had seen hereditary monarchy abolished and restored.   They had seen the Long Parliament thrice supreme in the state, and thrice dissolved amidst the curses and laughter of millions.   They had seen a new dynasty rapidly rising to the height of power and glory, and then on a sudden hurled down from the chair of state without a struggle.   They had seen a new representative system devised, tried, and abandoned.   They had seen a new House of Lords created and scattered.   They had seen great masses of property violently transferred from Cavaliers to Round-

THE FRONTISPIECE TO LEVIATHAN

heads, and from Roundheads back to Cavaliers. During these events no man could be a stirring and thriving politician who was not prepared to change with every change of fortune. It was only in retirement that any person could long keep the character either of a steady Royalist or of a steady Republican. One who, in such an age, is determined to attain civil greatness must renounce all thought of consistency. Instead of affecting immutability in the midst of endless mutation, he must be always on the watch for the indications of a coming reaction. He must seize the exact moment for deserting a falling cause. Having gone all lengths with a faction while it was uppermost, he must suddenly extricate himself from it when its difficulties begin, must assail it, must persecute it, must enter on a new career of power and prosperity in company with new associates. His situation naturally developes in him to the highest degree a peculiar class of abilities and a peculiar class of vices. He becomes quick of observation and fertile of resource. He catches without effort the tone of any sect or party with which he chances to mingle. He discerns the signs of the times with a sagacity which to the multitude appears miraculous, with a sagacity resembling that with which a veteran police officer pursues the faintest indications of crime, or with which a Mohawk warrior follows a track through the woods. But we shall seldom find, in a statesman so trained, integrity, constancy, any of the virtues of the noble family of Truth. He has no faith in any doctrine, no zeal for any cause. He has seen so many old institutions swept away, that he has no reverence for prescription. He has seen so many new institutions, from which much had been expected, produce mere disappointment, that he has no hope of improvement. He sneers alike at those who are anxious to preserve and at those who are eager to reform. There is nothing in the state which he could not, without a scruple or a blush, join in defending or in destroying. Fidelity to opinions and to friends seems to him mere dulness and wrongheadedness. Politics he regards, not as a science of which the object is the happiness of mankind, but as an exciting game of mixed chance and skill, at which a dexterous and lucky player may win an estate, a coronet, perhaps a crown, and at which one rash move may lead to the loss of fortune and of life. Ambition, which, in good times, and in good minds, is half a virtue, now, disjoined from every elevated and philanthropic sentiment, becomes a selfish cupidity scarcely less ignoble than avarice. Among those politicians who, from the Restoration to the accession of the House of Hanover, were at the head of the great parties in the state, very few can be named whose reputation is not stained by what, in our age, would be called gross perfidy and corruption. It is scarcely an exaggeration to say that the most unprincipled public men who have taken part in affairs within our memory would, if tried by the standard which was in fashion during the latter part of the seventeenth century, deserve to be regarded as scrupulous and disinterested.

While these political, religious, and moral changes were taking place in England, the royal authority had been without difficulty reestablished in every other part of the British islands. In Scotland the **State of** restoration of the Stuarts had been hailed with delight; **Scotland** for it was regarded as the restoration of national independence. And true it was that the yoke which Cromwell had imposed was, in appearance, taken away, that the Scottish Estates again met in their old hall at Edinburgh, and that the Senators of the College of Justice again administered the Scottish law according to the old forms. Yet was the independence of the little kingdom necessarily rather nominal than real: for, as long as the King had England on his side, he had nothing to apprehend from disaffection in his other dominions. He was now in such a situation that he could renew the attempt which had proved destructive to his father without any danger of his father's fate. Charles the First had tried to force his own religion by his regal power on the Scots at a moment when both his religion and his regal power were unpopular in England; and he had not only failed, but had raised troubles which had ultimately cost him his crown and his head. Times had now changed: England was zealous for monarchy and prelacy; and therefore the scheme which had formerly been in the highest degree imprudent might be resumed with little risk to the throne. The government resolved to set up a prelatical church in Scotland. The design was disapproved by every Scotchman whose judgment was entitled to respect. Some Scottish statesmen who were zealous for the King's prerogative had been bred Presbyterians. Though little troubled with scruples, they retained a preference for the religion of their childhood; and they well knew how strong a hold that religion had on the hearts of their countrymen. They remonstrated strongly: but, when they found that they remonstrated in vain, they had not virtue enough to persist in an opposition which would have given offence to their master; and several of them stooped to the wickedness and baseness of persecuting what in their consciences they believed to be the purest form of Christianity. The Scottish Parliament was so constituted that it had scarcely ever offered any serious opposition even to Kings much weaker than Charles then was. Episcopacy, therefore, was established by law. As to the form of worship, a large discretion was left to the clergy. In some churches the English Liturgy was used. In others, the ministers selected from that Liturgy such prayers and thanksgivings as were likely to be least offensive to the people. But in general the doxology was sung at the close of public worship; and the Apostles' Creed was recited when baptism was administered. By the great body of the Scottish nation the new Church was detested both as superstitious and as foreign ; as tainted with the corruptions of Rome, and as a mark of the predominance of England.   There was, however, no general insurrection.   The country was not what it had been twenty-two years before.   Disastrous war and alien domination had tamed the spirit of the people.   The aristocracy, which was held in great honour by the middle class and by the populace, had put itself at the head of the movement against Charles the First, but proved obsequious to Charles the Second.   From the English Puritans no aid was now to be expected. They were a feeble party, proscribed both by law and by public opinion. The bulk of the Scottish nation, therefore, sullenly submitted, and, with many misgivings of conscience, attended the ministrations of the Episcopal clergy, or of Presbyterian divines who had consented to accept from the government a half toleration, known by the name of the Indulgence.   But there were, particularly in the western lowlands, many fierce and resolute men, who held that the obligation to observe the Covenant was paramount to the obligation to obey the magistrate. These people, in defiance of the law, persisted in meeting to worship God after their own fashion.   The Indulgence they regarded, not as a partial reparation of the wrongs inflicted by the State on the Church, but as a new wrong, the more odious because it was disguised under the appearance of a benefit.   Persecution, they said, could only kill the body ; but the black Indulgence was deadly to the soul.   Driven from the towns, they assembled on heaths and mountains.   Attacked by the civil power, they without scruple repelled force by force.   At every conventicle they mustered in arms.   They repeatedly broke out into open rebellion.   They were easily defeated, and mercilessly punished : but neither defeat nor punishment could subdue their spirit.   Hunted down like wild beasts, tortured till their bones were beaten flat, imprisoned by hundreds, hanged by scores, exposed at one time to the license of soldiers from England, abandoned at another time to the mercy of troops of marauders from the Highlands, they still stood at bay in a mood so savage that the boldest and mightiest oppressor could not but dread the audacity of their despair.

Such was, during the reign of Charles the Second, the state of Scotland.   Ireland was not less distracted.   In that island existed feuds, **State of Ireland** compared with which the hottest animosities of English politicians were lukewarm.   The enmity between the Irish Cavaliers and the Irish Roundheads was almost forgotten in the fiercer enmity which raged between the English and the Celtic races.   The interval between the Episcopalian and the Presbyterian seemed to vanish, when compared with the interval which separated both from the Papist. During the late civil troubles the greater part of the Irish soil had been transferred from the vanquished nation to the victors. To the favour of the Crown few either of the old or of the new occupants had any pretensions. The despoilers and the despoiled had, for the most part, been rebels alike. The government was soon perplexed and wearied by the conflicting claims and mutual accusations of the two incensed factions. Those colonists among whom Cromwell had portioned out the conquered territory, and whose descendants are still called Crom-

THE DUKE AND DUCHESS OF LAUDERDALE

From a mezzotint by R. Williams, after the portrait by Sir P. Lely

wellians, asserted that the aboriginal inhabitants were deadly enemies of the English nation under every dynasty, and of the Protestant religion in every form. They described and exaggerated the atrocities which had disgraced the insurrection of Ulster: they urged the King to follow up with resolution the policy of the Protector; and they were not ashamed to hint that there would never be peace in Ireland till the old Irish race should be extirpated. The Roman Catholics extenuated their offence as they best might, and expatiated in piteous language on the severity of their punishment, which, in truth, had not been lenient. They implored Charles not to confound the innocent with the guilty, and reminded him that many of the guilty had atoned for their fault by returning to their allegiance, and by defending his rights against the murderers of his father. The court, sick of the importunities of two parties, neither of which it had any reason to love, at length relieved itself from trouble by dictating a compromise. That system, cruel, but most complete and energetic, by which Oliver had proposed to make the island thoroughly English, was abandoned. The Cromwellians were induced to relinquish a third part of their acquisitions. The land thus surrendered was capriciously divided among claimants whom the government chose to favour. But great numbers who protested that they were innocent of all disloyalty, and some persons who boasted that their loyalty had been signally displayed, obtained neither restitution nor compensation, and filled France and Spain with outcries against the injustice and ingratitude of the House of Stuart.

Meantime the government had, even in England, ceased to be popular. The Royalists had begun to quarrel with the court and with each other; and the party which had been vanquished, trampled down, and, as it seemed, annihilated, but which had still retained a strong principle of life, again raised its head, and renewed the interminable war.

The government become unpopular in England

Had the administration been faultless, the enthusiasm with which the return of the King and the termination of the military tyranny had been hailed could not have been permanent. For it is the law of our nature that such fits of excitement shall always be followed by remissions. The manner in which the court abused its victory made the remission speedy and complete. Every moderate man was shocked by the insolence, cruelty, and perfidy with which the Nonconformists were treated. The penal laws had effectually purged the oppressed party of those insincere members whose vices had disgraced it, and had made it again an honest and pious body of men. The Puritan, a conqueror, a ruler, a persecutor, a sequestrator, had been detested. The Puritan, betrayed and evil entreated, deserted by all the timeservers who, in his prosperity, had claimed brotherhood with him, hunted from his home, forbidden under severe penalties to pray or receive the sacrament according to his conscience, yet still firm in his resolution to obey God rather than man, was, in spite of some unpleasing recollections, an object of pity and respect to well constituted minds. These feelings became stronger when it was noised abroad that the court was not disposed to treat Papists with the same rigour which had been shown to Presbyterians. A vague suspicion that the King and the Duke were not sincere Protestants sprang up and gathered strength. Many persons too who had been disgusted by the austerity and hypocrisy of the Saints of the Commonwealth began to be still more disgusted by the open profligacy of the court and of the Cavaliers, and were disposed to

GENERAL THOMAS DALYELL

From a mezzotint by C. Turner, after an engraving by Vandrebanc

doubt whether the sullen preciseness of Praise God Barebone might not be preferable to the outrageous profaneness and licentiousness of the Buckinghams and Sedleys. Even immoral men, who were not utterly destitute of sense and public spirit, complained that the government treated the most serious matters as trifles, and made trifles its serious business. A King might be pardoned for amusing his leisure with wine, wit, and beauty. But it was intolerable that he should sink into a mere lounger and voluptuary, that the gravest affairs of state should be neglected, and that the public service should be starved and the finances deranged in order that harlots and parasites might grow rich.

A large body of Royalists joined in these complaints, and added many sharp reflections on the King's ingratitude. His whole revenue, indeed, would not have sufficed to reward them all in proportion to their own consciousness of desert. For to every distressed gentleman who had fought under Rupert or Derby his own services seemed eminently meritorious, and his own sufferings eminently severe. Every one had flattered himself that, whatever became of the rest, he should be largely recompensed for all that he had lost during the civil troubles, and that the restoration of the monarchy would be followed by the restoration of his own dilapidated fortunes. None of these expectants could restrain his indignation, when he found that he was as poor under the King as he had been under the Rump or the Protector. The negligence and extravagance of the court excited the bitter indignation of these loyal veterans. They justly said that one half of what His Majesty squandered on concubines and buffoons would gladden the hearts of hundreds of old Cavaliers who, after cutting down their oaks and melting their plate to help his father, now wandered about in threadbare suits, and did not know where to turn for a meal.

At the same time a sudden fall of rents took place. The income of every landed proprietor was diminished by five shillings in the pound. The cry of agricultural distress rose from every shire in the kingdom; and for that distress the government was, as usual, held accountable. The gentry, compelled to retrench their expenses for a period, saw with indignation the increasing splendour and profusion of Whitehall, and were immovably fixed in the belief that the money which ought to have supported their households had, by some inexplicable process, gone to the favourites of the King.

The minds of men were now in such a temper that every public act excited discontent. Charles had taken to wife Catharine Princess of Portugal. The marriage was generally disliked; and the murmurs became loud when it appeared that the King was not likely to have any legitimate posterity. Dunkirk, won by Oliver from Spain, was sold to Lewis the Fourteenth, King of France. This bargain excited general indignation. Englishmen were already beginning to observe with uneasiness the progress of the French power, and to regard the House of Bourbon with the same feeling with which their grandfathers had regarded the House of Austria. Was it wise, men asked, at such a time, to make any addition to the strength of a monarchy already too formidable? Dunkirk was, moreover, prized by the people, not merely

GEORGE VILLIERS, SECOND DUKE OF BUCKINGHAM

From a mezzotint by I. Beckett, after the painting by Verelst

as a place of arms, and as a key to the Low Countries, but also as a trophy of English valour. It was to the subjects of Charles what Calais had been to an earlier generation, and what the rock of Gibraltar, so manfully defended, through disastrous and perilous years, against the fleets and armies of a mighty coalition, is to ourselves. The plea of economy might have had some weight, if it had been urged by an economical government. But it was notorious that the charges of Dunkirk fell far short of the sums which were wasted at court in vice and folly. It seemed insupportable that a sovereign, profuse beyond example in all that regarded his own pleasures, should be niggardly in all that regarded the safety and honour of the state.

The public discontent was heightened, when it was found that, while Dunkirk was abandoned on the plea of economy, the fortress of Tangier, which was part of the dower of Queen Catharine, was repaired and kept up at an enormous charge. That place was associated with no recollections gratifying to the national pride : it could in no way promote the national interests : it involved us in inglorious, unprofitable, and interminable wars with tribes of half savage Mussulmans ; and it was situated in a climate singularly unfavourable to the health and vigour of the English race.

But the murmurs excited by these errors were faint, when compared with the clamours which soon broke forth. The government engaged **War with** in war with the United Provinces. The House of Commons **the Dutch** readily voted sums unexampled in our history, sums exceeding those which had supported the fleets and armies of Cromwell at the time when his power was the terror of all the world. But such was the extravagance, dishonesty, and incapacity of those who had succeeded to his authority, that this liberality proved worse than useless. The sycophants of the court, ill qualified to contend against the great men who then directed the arms of Holland, against such a statesman as De Witt, and such a commander as De Ruyter, made fortunes rapidly, while the sailors mutinied from very hunger, while the dockyards were unguarded, while the ships were leaky and without rigging. It was at length determined to abandon all schemes of offensive war ; and it soon appeared that even a defensive war was a task too hard for that administration. The Dutch fleet sailed up the Thames, and burned the ships of war which lay at Chatham. It was said that, on the very day of that great humiliation, the King feasted with the ladies of his seraglio, and amused himself with hunting a moth about the supper room. Then, at length, tardy justice was done to the memory of Oliver. Everywhere men magnified his valour, genius, and patriotism. Everywhere it was remembered how, when he ruled, all foreign powers had trembled at the name of England, how the States General, now so haughty, had crouched at his feet, and how, when it was known that he was no more, Amsterdam was lighted up as for a great deliverance, and children ran along the canals, shouting for joy that the Devil was dead. Even Royalists exclaimed that the state could be saved only by calling the old soldiers of the Commonwealth to arms. Soon the capital began to feel the miseries of a blockade. Fuel was scarcely to be procured. Tilbury Fort, the place where Elizabeth had, with manly spirit, hurled

ADMIRAL DE RUYTER

From a mezzotint by Blooteling, after the painting by Lievens

foul scorn at Parma and Spain, was insulted by the invaders. The roar of foreign guns was heard, for the first and last time, by the citizens of London. In the Council it was seriously proposed that, if the enemy advanced, the Tower should be abandoned. Great multitudes of people assembled in the streets crying out that England was bought and sold. The houses and carriages of the ministers were attacked by the populace; and it seemed likely that the government would have to deal at once with an invasion and with an insurrection. The extreme danger, it is true, soon passed by. A treaty was concluded, very different from the treaties which Oliver had been in the habit of signing ; and the nation was once more at peace, but was in a mood scarcely less fierce and sullen than in the days of shipmoney.

The discontent engendered by maladministration was heightened by calamities which the best administration could not have averted. While the ignominious war with Holland was raging, London suffered two great disasters, such as never, in so short a space of time, befell one city. A pestilence, surpassing in horror any that during three centuries had visited the island, swept away, in six months, more than a hundred thousand human beings. And scarcely had the dead cart ceased to go its rounds, when a fire, such as had not been known in Europe since the conflagration of Rome under Nero, laid in ruins the whole city, from the Tower to the Temple, and from the river to the purlieus of Smithfield.

Had there been a general election while the nation was smarting under so many disgraces and misfortunes, it is probable that the Round-heads would have regained ascendency in the state. But the Parliament was still the Cavalier Parliament, chosen in the transport of loyalty which had followed the Restoration. Nevertheless it soon became evident that no English legislature, however loyal, would now consent to be merely what the legislature had been under the Tudors. From the death of Elizabeth to the eve of the civil war, the Puritans, who predominated in the representative body, had been constantly, by a dexterous use of the power of the purse, encroaching on the province of the executive government. The gentlemen who, after the Restoration, filled the Lower House, though they abhorred the Puritan name, were well pleased to inherit the fruit of the Puritan policy. They were indeed most willing to employ the power which they possessed in the state for the purpose of making their King mighty and honoured, both at home and abroad : but with the power itself they were resolved not to part. The great English revolution of the seventeenth century, that is to say, the transfer of the supreme control of the executive administration from the crown to the House of Commons, was, through the whole long existence of this Parliament, proceeding noiselessly, but rapidly and steadily. Charles, kept poor by his follies and vices, wanted money. The Commons alone could legally grant him money. They could not be prevented from putting their own

Opposition in the House of Commons

price on their grants.　The price which they put on their grants was this, that they should be allowed to interfere with every one of the King's prerogatives, to wring from him his consent to laws which he disliked, to break up cabinets, to dictate the course of foreign policy, and even to direct the administration of war.　To the royal office, and the royal person, they loudly and sincerely professed the strongest attachment. But to Clarendon they owed no allegiance ; and they fell on **Fall of** him as furiously as their predecessors had fallen on Strafford. **Clarendon** The minister's virtues and vices alike contributed to his ruin.　He was the ostensible head of the administration, and was therefore held responsible even for those acts which he had strongly, but vainly, opposed in Council.　He was regarded by the Puritans, and by all who pitied them, as an implacable bigot, a second Laud, with much more than Laud's understanding.　He had on all occasions maintained that the Act of Indemnity ought to be strictly observed ; and this part of his conduct, though highly honourable to him, made him hateful to all those Royalists who wished to repair their ruined fortunes by suing the Roundheads for damages and mesne profits.　The Presbyterians of Scotland attributed to him the downfall of their Church.　The Papists of Ireland attributed to him the loss of their lands.　As father of the Duchess of York, he had an obvious motive for wishing that there might be a barren Queen ; and he was therefore suspected of having purposely recommended one.　The sale of Dunkirk was justly imputed to him.　For the war with Holland, he was, with less justice, held accountable.　His hot temper, his arrogant deportment, the indelicate eagerness with which he grasped at riches, the ostentation with which he squandered them, his picture gallery, filled with masterpieces of Vandyke which had once been the property of ruined Cavaliers, his palace, which reared its long and stately front right opposite to the humbler residence of our Kings, drew on him much deserved, and some undeserved, censure.　When the Dutch fleet was in the Thames, it was against the Chancellor that the rage of the populace was chiefly directed. His windows were broken ; the trees of his garden were cut down ; and a gibbet was set up before his door.　But nowhere was he more detested than in the House of Commons.　He was unable to perceive that the time was fast approaching when that House, if it continued to exist at all, must be supreme in the state, when the management of that House would be the most important department of politics, and when, without the help of men possessing the ear of that House, it would be impossible to carry on the government.　He obstinately persisted in considering the Parliament as a body in no respect differing from the Parliament which had been sitting when, forty years before, he first began to study law at the Temple.　He did not wish to deprive the legislature of those

VIEW OF THE MONUMENT

With Caricatures illustrating the Popish Plot

In pursuance of an Order of the Comittee for City Landes
J doe heerwith offer the severall designes which some monthes
since J shewed His Ma:tie for his approbation, who was then pleased
to thinke a large Ball of metall gilt would be most agreeable,
in regard it would giue an Ornament to the Town, at a very
great distance; not that His Ma:tie disliked a Statue; and if
any proposall of this sort be more acceptable to the City J
shall most readily represent the same to His Ma:tie

I cannot but comend a Large Statue as carrying much
dignitie with it, & that w:ch would bee more valewable in the
Eyes of Forreiners & strangers. It hath been proposed to
cast such a one in Brasse of 12 foot high for 1000:l.b.
J hope (if it be allowed) wee may find those who will cast
a figure. for that mony of 15 foot high, w:ch will suit the
greatnesse of the pillar & is (as J take it) the largest at this
day extant; and this would undoubtedly bee the noblest
finishing that can be found answerable to soe goodly a worke
in all mens Judgements.

A Ball of Copper 9 foot Diameter cast in severall peeces
with the flames & gilt may well be don with the Iron worke
& fixing for 350:l.b. and this will be most acceptable of any
thing inferior to a Statue, by reason of the good appearance
at distance; and because one may goe up into it; & upon
occasion use it for fireworkes.

A Phænix was at first thought of; & is the ornament
in the wooden modell of the pillar, w:ch J caused to be made
before it was begun; but upon second thoughtes J rejected it
because it will be costly, not easily understood at that Hight,
and worse understood at a distance; & lastly dangerous by reason
of the sayle. the spread winges will carry in the winde.

The Belcony must be made of substantiall well forged worke
there being noe need at that distance of filed worke, and
J suppose (for J cannot exactly guesse the weight) it may be
well performed & fixed according to a good designe for fourscore &
ten poundes including painting. All w:ch is humbly submitted to your
consideration.
Chr: Wren

July 28:th
1675

REDUCED FACSIMILE OF WREN'S REPORT ON THE MONUMENT

From the original in the British Museum

powers which were inherent in it by the old constitution of the realm :
but the new development of those powers, though a development
natural, inevitable, and to be prevented only by utterly destroying the
powers themselves, disgusted and alarmed him.   Nothing would have
induced him to put the great seal to a writ for raising shipmoney, or to
give his voice in Council for committing a member of Parliament to the
Tower, on account of words spoken in debate : but, when the Commons
began to inquire in what manner the money voted for the war had been
wasted, and to examine into the maladministration of the navy, he
flamed with indignation.   Such inquiry, according to him, was out of
their province.   He admitted that the House was a most loyal assembly,
that it had done good service to the crown, and that its intentions were
excellent.   But, both in public and in the closet, he, on every occasion,
expressed his concern that gentlemen so sincerely attached to monarchy
should unadvisedly encroach on the prerogative of the monarch.   Widely
as they differed in spirit from the members of the Long Parliament, they
yet, he said, imitated that Parliament in meddling with matters which
lay beyond the sphere of the Estates of the realm, and which were
subject to the authority of the crown alone.   The country, he maintained, would never be well governed till the knights of shires and the
burgesses were content to be what their predecessors had been in the
days of Elizabeth.   All the plans which men more observant than himself of the signs of that time proposed, for the purpose of maintaining a
good understanding between the Court and the Commons, he disdainfully rejected as crude projects, inconsistent with the old polity of
England.   Towards the young orators, who were rising to distinction
and authority in the Lower House, his deportment was ungracious : and
he succeeded in making them, with scarcely an exception, his deadly
enemies.   Indeed one of his most serious faults was an inordinate contempt for youth : and this contempt was the more unjustifiable, because
his own experience in English politics was by no means proportioned
to his age.   For so great a part of his life had been passed abroad that
he knew less of that world in which he found himself on his return than
many who might have been his sons.

For these reasons he was disliked by the Commons.   For very
different reasons he was equally disliked by the Court.   His morals as
well as his politics were those of an earlier generation.   Even when he
was a young law student, living much with men of wit and pleasure, his
natural gravity and his religious principles had to a great extent preserved him from the contagion of fashionable debauchery ; and he was
by no means likely, in advanced years and in declining health, to turn
libertine.   On the vices of the young and gay he looked with an
aversion almost as bitter and contemptuous as that which he felt for the

theological errors of the sectaries. He missed no opportunity of showing his scorn of the mimics, revellers, and courtesans who crowded the

ANNE HYDE, DUCHESS OF YORK

From the painting by Sir P. Lely in the National Portrait Gallery

palace; and the admonitions which he addressed to the King himself were very sharp, and, what Charles disliked still more, very long. Scarcely any voice was raised in favour of a minister loaded with the double odium of faults which roused the fury of the people, and of virtues which annoyed and importuned the sovereign. Southampton was no more. Ormond performed the duties of friendship manfully and faithfully, but in vain. The Chancellor fell with a great ruin. The seal was taken from him : the Commons impeached him : his head was not safe : he fled from the country : an act was passed which doomed him to perpetual exile ; and those who had assailed and undermined him began to struggle for the fragments of his power.

The sacrifice of Clarendon in some degree took off the edge of the public appetite for revenge. Yet was the anger excited by the profusion and negligence of the government, and by the miscarriages of the late war, by no means extinguished. The counsellors of Charles, with the fate of the Chancellor before their eyes, were anxious for their own safety. They accordingly advised their master to soothe the irritation which prevailed both in the Parliament and throughout the country, and for that end, to take a step which has no parallel in the history of the House of Stuart, and which was worthy of the prudence and magnanimity of Oliver.

We have now reached a point at which the history of the great English revolution begins to be complicated with the history of foreign politics. The power of Spain had, during many years, been declining. She still, it is true, held in Europe the Milanese and the two Sicilies, Belgium, and Franche Comté. In America her dominions still spread, on both sides of the equator, far beyond the limits of the torrid zone. But this great body had been smitten with palsy, and was not only incapable of giving molestation to other states, but could not, without assistance, repel aggression. France was now, beyond all doubt, the greatest power in Europe. Her resources have, since those days, absolutely increased, but have not increased so fast as the resources of England. It must also be remembered that, a hundred and eighty years ago, the empire of Russia, now a monarchy of the first class, was as entirely out of the system of European politics as Abyssinia or Siam, that the House of Brandenburg was then hardly more powerful than the House of Saxony, and that the republic of the United States had not then begun to exist. The weight of France, therefore, though still very considerable, has relatively diminished. Her territory was not in the days of Lewis the Fourteenth quite so extensive as at present : but it was large, compact, fertile, well placed both for attack and for defence, situated in a happy climate, and inhabited by a brave, active, and ingenious people. The state implicitly obeyed the direction of a single mind. The great fiefs which, three hundred years before, had been, in all but name, independent principalities, had been annexed to the crown. Only a few old

State of European politics, and ascendency of France

CLARENDON HOUSE, ST. JAMES'S

From an engraving by John Dunstall

men could remember the last meeting of the States General. The resistance which the Huguenots, the nobles, and the parliaments had offered to the kingly power, had been put down by the two great Cardinals who had ruled the nation during forty years. The government was now a despotism, but, at least in its dealings with the upper classes, a mild and generous despotism, tempered by courteous manners and chivalrous sentiments. The means at the disposal of the sovereign were, for that age, truly formidable. His revenue, raised, it is true, by a severe and unequal taxation which pressed heavily on the cultivators of the soil, far exceeded that of any other potentate. His army, excellently disciplined, and commanded by the greatest generals then living, already consisted of more than a hundred and twenty thousand men. Such an array of regular troops had not been seen in Europe since the downfall of the Roman empire. Of maritime powers France was not the first. But, though she had rivals on the sea, she had not yet a superior. Such was her strength during the last forty years of the seventeenth century, that no enemy could singly withstand her, and that two great coalitions, in which half Christendom was united against her, failed of success.

The personal qualities of the French King added to the respect inspired by the power and importance of his kingdom. No sovereign has ever represented the majesty of a great state with more dignity and grace. He was his own prime minister, and performed the duties of a prime minister with an ability and an industry which could not be reasonably expected from one who had in infancy succeeded to a crown, and who had been surrounded by flatterers before he could speak. He had shown, in an eminent degree, two talents invaluable to a prince, the talent of choosing his servants well, and the talent of appropriating to himself the chief part of the credit of their acts. In his dealings with foreign powers he had some generosity, but no justice. To unhappy allies who threw themselves at his feet, and had no hope but in his compassion, he extended his protection with a romantic disinterestedness, which seemed better suited to a knight errant than to a statesman. But he broke through the most sacred ties of public faith without scruple or shame, whenever they interfered with his interest, or with what he called his glory. His perfidy and violence, however, excited less enmity than the insolence with which he constantly reminded his neighbours of his own greatness and of their littleness. He did not at this time profess the austere devotion which, at a later period, gave to his court the aspect of a monastery. On the contrary, he was as licentious, though by no means as frivolous and indolent, as his brother of England. But he was a sincere Roman Catholic; and both his conscience and his vanity

Character of Lewis XIV.

impelled him to use his power for the defence and propagation of the true faith, after the example of his renowned predecessors, Clovis, Charlemagne, and Saint Lewis.

LEWIS XIV

From an engraving by Grignon, after a painting by P. Mignard

Our ancestors naturally looked with serious alarm on the growing power of France. This feeling, in itself perfectly reasonable, was mingled with other feelings less praiseworthy. France was our old enemy. It was against France that the most glorious battles recorded in our annals had been fought. The conquest of France had been twice effected by the Plantagenets. The loss of France had been long remembered as a great national disaster. The title of King of France was still borne by our sovereigns. The lilies of France still appeared, mingled with our own lions, on the shield of the House of Stuart. In the sixteenth century the dread inspired by Spain had suspended the animosity of which France had anciently been the object. But the dread inspired by Spain had given place to contemptuous compassion ; and France was again regarded as our national foe. The sale of Dunkirk to France had been the most generally unpopular act of the restored King. Attachment to France had been prominent among the crimes imputed by the Commons to Clarendon. Even in trifles the public feeling showed itself. When a brawl took place in the streets of West-minster between the retinues of the French and Spanish embassies, the populace, though forcibly prevented from interfering, had given un-equivocal proofs that the old antipathy to France was not extinct.

France and Spain were now engaged in a more serious contest. One of the chief objects of the policy of Lewis throughout his life was to extend his dominions towards the Rhine. For this end he had engaged in war with Spain, and he was now in the full career of con-quest. The United Provinces saw with anxiety the progress of his arms. That renowned federation had reached the height of power, prosperity, and glory. The Batavian territory, conquered from the waves and defended against them by human art, was in extent little superior to the principality of Wales. But all that narrow space was a busy and populous hive, in which new wealth was every day created, and in which vast masses of old wealth were hoarded. The aspect of Holland, the rich cultivation, the innumerable canals, the ever whirling mills, the endless fleets of barges, the quick succession of great towns, the ports bristling with thousands of masts, the large and stately man-sions, the trim villas, the richly furnished apartments, the picture galleries, the summer houses, the tulip beds, produced on English tra-vellers in that age an effect similar to the effect which the first sight of England now produces on a Norwegian or a Canadian. The States General had been compelled to humble themselves before Cromwell. But after the Restoration they had taken their revenge, had waged war with success against Charles, and had concluded peace on honourable terms. Rich, however, as the Republic was, and highly considered in Europe, she was no match for the power of Lewis. She apprehended, not without good cause, that his kingdom might soon be extended to her frontiers ; and she might well dread the immediate vicinity of a

VIEW OF DUNKIRK IN 1712. From an engraving in the Sutherland Collection monarch so great, so ambitious, and so unscrupulous.   Yet it was not easy to devise any expedient which might avert the danger.   The Dutch alone could not turn the scale against France.   On the side of the Rhine no help was to be expected.   Several German princes had been gained by Lewis ; and the Emperor himself was embarrassed by the discontents of Hungary.   England was separated from the United Provinces by the recollection of cruel injuries recently inflicted and endured ; and her policy had, since the Restoration, been so devoid of wisdom and spirit, that it was scarcely possible to expect from her any valuable assistance.

But the fate of Clarendon and the growing ill humour of the Parliament determined the advisers of Charles to adopt on a sudden a policy which amazed and delighted the nation.

The English resident at Brussels, Sir William Temple, one of the most expert diplomatists and most pleasing writers of that age, had The Triple   already represented to his court that it was both desirable and Alliance   practicable to enter into engagements with the States General for the purpose of checking the progress of France.   For a time his suggestions had been slighted; but it was now thought expedient to act on them.   He was commissioned to negotiate with the States General. He proceeded to the Hague, and soon came to an understanding with John De Witt, then the chief minister of Holland.   Sweden, small as her resources were, had, forty years before, been raised by the genius of Gustavus Adolphus to a high rank among European powers, and had not yet descended to her natural position.   She was induced to join on this occasion with England and the States.   Thus was formed that coalition known as the Triple Alliance.   Lewis showed signs of vexation and resentment, but did not think it politic to draw on himself the hostility of such a confederacy in addition to that of Spain.   He consented, therefore, to relinquish a large part of the territory which his armies had occupied.   Peace was restored to Europe ; and the English government, lately an object of general contempt, was, during a few months, regarded by foreign powers with respect scarcely less than that which the Protector had inspired.

At home the Triple Alliance was popular in the highest degree. It gratified alike national animosity and national pride.   It put a limit to the encroachments of a powerful and ambitious neighbour.   It bound the leading Protestant states together in close union.   Cavaliers and Roundheads rejoiced in common : but the joy of the Roundhead was even greater than that of the Cavalier.   For England had now allied herself strictly with a country republican in government and Presbyterian in religion, against a country ruled by an arbitrary prince and attached to the Roman Catholic Church.   The House of Commons loudly applauded the treaty; and some uncourtly grumblers described it as the only good thing that had been done since the King came in.

The King, however, cared little for the approbation of his Parliament or of his people. The Triple Alliance he regarded merely as a temporary

JOHN DE WITT

From a mezzotint by Blooteling, after the portrait by J. de Bane

expedient for quieting discontents which had seemed likely to become serious. The independence, the safety, the dignity of the nation **The Country** over which he presided were nothing to him. He had begun **Party** to find constitutional restraints galling. Already had been formed in the Parliament a strong connection known by the name of the Country Party. That party included all the public men who leaned towards Puritanism and Republicanism, and many who, though attached to the Church and to hereditary monarchy, had been driven into opposition by dread of Popery, by dread of France, and by disgust at the extravagance, dissoluteness, and faithlessness of the court. The power of this band of politicians was constantly growing. Every year some of those members who had been returned to Parliament during the loyal excitement of 1661 had dropped off; and the vacant seats had generally been filled by persons less tractable. Charles did not think himself a King while an assembly of subjects could call for his accounts before paying his debts, and could insist on knowing which of his mistresses or boon companions had intercepted the money destined for the equipping and manning of the fleet. Though not very studious of fame, he was galled by the taunts which were sometimes uttered in the discussions of the Commons, and on one occasion attempted to restrain the freedom of speech by disgraceful means. Sir John Coventry, a country gentleman, had, in debate, sneered at the profligacy of the court. In any former reign he would probably have been called before the Privy Council and committed to the Tower. A different course was now taken. A gang of bullies was secretly sent to slit the nose of the offender. This ignoble revenge, instead of quelling the spirit of opposition, raised such a tempest that the King was compelled to submit to the cruel humiliation of passing an act which attainted the instruments of his revenge, and which took from him the power of pardoning them.

But, impatient as he was of constitutional restraints, how was he to emancipate himself from them? He could make himself despotic only by the help of a great standing army; and such an army was not in existence. His revenues did indeed enable him to keep up some regular troops: but those troops, though numerous enough to excite great jealousy and apprehension in the House of Commons and in the country, were scarcely numerous enough to protect Whitehall and the Tower against a rising of the mob of London. Such risings were, indeed, to be dreaded; for it was calculated that in the capital and its suburbs dwelt not less than twenty thousand of Oliver's old soldiers.

Since the King was bent on emancipating himself from the control of Parliament, and since, in such an enterprise, he could not hope for effectual aid at home, it followed that he must look for aid abroad. The power and wealth of the King of France might be equal to the arduous task of establishing absolute monarchy in England. Such an ally would undoubtedly expect substantial proofs of gratitude for such a service. Charles must descend to the rank of a great vassal, and must make peace and war according to the directions

Connection between Charles II. and France

HENRIETTA, DUCHESS OF ORLEANS

From the painting by P. Mignard in the National Portrait Gallery of the government which protected him.   His relation to Lewis would closely resemble that in which the Rajah of Nagpore and the King of Oude now stand to the British government.   Those princes are bound to aid the East India Company in all hostilities, defensive and offensive, and to have no diplomatic relations but such as the East India Company shall sanction.   The Company in return guarantees them against insurrection.   As long as they faithfully discharge their obligations to the paramount power, they are permitted to dispose of large revenues, to fill their palaces with beautiful women, to besot themselves in the company of their favourite revellers, and to oppress with impunity any subject who may incur their displeasure.[1]   Such a life would be insupportable to a man of high spirit and of powerful understanding.   But to Charles, sensual, indolent, unequal to any strong intellectual exertion, and destitute alike of all patriotism and of all sense of personal dignity, the prospect had nothing unpleasing.

That the Duke of York should have concurred in the design of degrading that crown which it was probable that he would himself one day wear may seem more extraordinary.   For his nature was haughty and imperious ; and, indeed, he continued to the very last to show, by occasional starts and struggles, his impatience of the French yoke.   But he was almost as much debased by superstition as his brother by indolence and vice.   James was now a Roman Catholic.   Religious bigotry had become the dominant sentiment of his narrow and stubborn mind, and had so mingled itself with his love of rule, that the two passions could hardly be distinguished from each other.   It seemed highly improbable that, without foreign aid, he would be able to obtain ascendency, or even toleration, for his own faith : and he was in a temper to see nothing humiliating in any step which might promote the interests of the true Church.

A negotiation was opened which lasted during several months.   The chief agent between the English and French courts was the beautiful, graceful, and intelligent Henrietta, Duchess of Orleans, sister of Charles, sister in law of Lewis, and a favourite with both.   The King of England offered to declare himself a Roman Catholic, to dissolve the Triple Alliance, and to join with France against Holland, if France would engage to lend him such military and pecuniary aid as might make him independent of his Parliament.   Lewis at first affected to receive these propositions coolly, and at length agreed to them with the air of a man who is conferring a great favour : but in truth, the course which he had resolved to take was one by which he might gain and could not lose.

It seems certain that he never seriously thought of establishing despotism and Popery in England by force of arms.   He must have

---

[1] I am happy to say, that, since this passage was written, the territories both of the Rajah of Nagpore and of the King of Oude have been added to the British Dominions. (1857.)

been aware that such an enterprise would be in the highest degree arduous and hazardous, that it would task to the utmost all the energies of France during many years, and that it would be alto- Views of Lewis with respect to England gether incompatible with more promising schemes of aggran- disement, which were dear to his heart. He would indeed willingly have acquired the merit and the glory of doing a great service on reasonable terms to the Church of which he was a member. But he was little disposed to imitate his ancestors who, in the twelfth and thirteenth centuries, had led the flower of French chivalry to die in Syria and Egypt ; and he well knew that a crusade against Protestantism in Great Britain would not be less perilous than the expeditions in which the armies of Lewis the Seventh and of Lewis the Ninth had perished. He had no motive for wishing the Stuarts to be absolute. He did not regard the English constitution with feelings at all resembling those which have in later times induced princes to make war on the free institutions of neighbouring nations. At present a great party zealous for popular government has ramifications in every civilised country. Any important advantage gained anywhere by that party is almost certain to be the signal for general commotion. It is not wonderful that governments threatened by a common danger should combine for the purpose of mutual insurance. But in the seventeenth century no such danger existed. Between the public mind of England and the public mind of France, there was a great gulph. Our institutions and our factions were as little understood at Paris as at Constantinople. It may be doubted whether any one of the forty members of the French Academy had an English volume in his library, or knew Shakspeare, Jonson, or Spenser, even by name. A few Huguenots, who had inherited the mutinous spirit of their ancestors, might perhaps have a fellow feeling with their brethren in the faith, the English Roundheads : but the Huguenots had ceased to be formidable. The French, as a people, attached to the Church of Rome, and proud of the greatness of their King and of their own loyalty, looked on our struggles against Popery and arbitrary power, not only without admiration or sympathy, but with strong disapprobation and disgust. It would therefore be a great error to ascribe the conduct of Lewis to apprehensions at all resembling those which, in our age, induced the Holy Alliance to interfere in the internal troubles of Naples and Spain.

Nevertheless, the propositions made by the court of Whitehall were most welcome to him. He already meditated gigantic designs, which were destined to keep Europe in constant fermentation during more than forty years. He wished to humble the United Provinces, and to annex Belgium, Franche Comté, and Loraine to his dominions. Nor was this all. The King of Spain was a sickly child. It was likely that he would

THE CHATEAU OF VERSAILLES

VERSAILLES FROM THE COURTYARD OF THE CHATEAU

From an engraving in the Sutherland Collection

die without issue.   His eldest sister was Queen of France.   A day
would almost certainly come, and might come very soon, when the House
of Bourbon might lay claim to that vast empire on which the sun never
set.   The union of two great monarchies under one head would doubtless
be opposed by a continental coalition.   But for any continental coalition
France singlehanded was a match.   England could turn the scale.   On
the course which, in such a crisis, England might pursue, the destinies
of the world would depend; and it was notorious that the English
Parliament and nation were strongly attached to the policy which had
dictated the Triple Alliance.   Nothing, therefore, could be more gratifying to Lewis than to learn that the princes of the House of Stuart
needed his help, and were willing to purchase that help by unbounded
subserviency.   He determined to profit by the opportunity, and laid
down for himself a plan to which, without deviation, he adhered, till the
Revolution of 1688 disconcerted all his politics.   He professed himself
desirous to promote the designs of the English court.   He promised
large aid.   He from time to time doled out such aid as might serve to
keep hope alive, and as he could without risk or inconvenience spare.
In this way, at an expense very much less than that which he incurred
in building and decorating Versailles or Marli, he succeeded in making
England, during nearly twenty years, almost as insignificant a member
of the political system of Europe as the republic of San Marino.

His object was not to destroy our constitution, but to keep the
various elements of which it was composed in a perpetual state of conflict, and to set irreconcilable enmity between those who had the power
of the purse and those who had the power of the sword.   With this
view he bribed and stimulated both parties in turn, pensioned at once the
ministers of the crown and the chiefs of the opposition, encouraged the
court to withstand the seditious encroachments of the Parliament, and conveyed to the Parliament intimations of the arbitrary designs of the court.

One of the devices to which he resorted for the purpose of obtaining
an ascendency in the English counsels deserves especial notice.   Charles,
though incapable of love in the highest sense of the word, was the slave
of any woman whose person excited his desires, and whose airs and
prattle amused his leisure.   Indeed a husband would be justly derided
who should bear from a wife of exalted rank and spotless virtue half
the insolence which the King of England bore from concubines who,
while they owed everything to his bounty, caressed his courtiers almost
before his face.   He had patiently endured the termagant passions of
Barbara Palmer and the pert vivacity of Eleanor Gwynn.   Lewis
thought that the most useful envoy who could be sent to London, would
be a handsome, licentious, and crafty Frenchwoman.   Such a woman
was Louisa, a lady of the House of Querouaille, whom our rude ancestors

LOUISE RENÉE DE QUÉROUAILLE, DUCHESS OF PORTSMOUTH, 1647-1734.

From the painting by P. Mignard, in the National Portrait Gallery.

called Madam Carwell. She was soon triumphant over all her rivals, was created Duchess of Portsmouth, was loaded with wealth, and obtained a dominion which ended only with the life of Charles.

The most important conditions of the alliance between the crowns were digested into a secret treaty which was signed at Dover **Treaty of** in May 1670, just ten years after the day on which Charles **Dover** had landed at that very port amidst the acclamations and joyful tears of a too confiding people.

By this treaty Charles bound himself to make public profession of the Roman Catholic religion, to join his arms to those of Lewis for the purpose of destroying the power of the United Provinces, and to employ the whole strength of England, by land and sea, in support of the rights of the House of Bourbon to the vast monarchy of Spain. Lewis, on the other hand, engaged to pay a large subsidy, and promised that, if any insurrection should break out in England, he would send an army at his own charge to support his ally.

This compact was made with gloomy auspices. Six weeks after it had been signed and sealed, the charming princess, whose influence over her brother and brother in law had been so pernicious to her country, was no more. Her death gave rise to horrible suspicions which, for a moment, seemed likely to interrupt the newly formed friendship between the Houses of Stuart and Bourbon : but in a short time fresh assurances of undiminished good will were exchanged between the confederates.

The Duke of York, too dull to apprehend danger, or too fanatical to care about it, was impatient to see the article touching the Roman Catholic religion carried into immediate execution : but Lewis had the wisdom to perceive that, if this course were taken, there would be such an explosion in England as would probably frustrate those parts of the plan which he had most at heart. It was therefore determined that Charles should still call himself a Protestant, and should still, at high festivals, receive the sacrament according to the ritual of the Church of England. His more scrupulous brother ceased to appear in the royal chapel.

About this time died the Duchess of York, daughter of the banished Earl of Clarendon. She had been, during some years, a concealed Roman Catholic. She left two daughters, Mary and Anne, afterwards successively Queens of Great Britain. They were bred Protestants by the positive command of the King, who knew that it would be vain for him to profess himself a member of the Church of England, if children who seemed likely to inherit his throne were, by his permission, brought up as members of the Church of Rome.

The principal servants of the crown at this time were men whose names have justly acquired an unenviable notoriety. We must take heed, however, that we do not load their memory with infamy which of right belongs to their master.   For the treaty of Dover the King himself is chiefly answerable.   He held conferences on it with the French agents : he wrote many letters concerning it with his own hand : he was the person who first suggested the most disgraceful articles which it contained ; and he carefully concealed some of those articles from the majority of his Cabinet.

Few things in our history are more curious than the origin and growth of the power now possessed by the Cabinet.   From an early

Nature of the English Cabinet period the Kings of England had been assisted by a Privy Council to which the law assigned many important functions and duties.   During several centuries this body deliberated on the gravest and most delicate affairs.   But by degrees its character changed.   It became too large for despatch and secrecy.   The rank of Privy Councillor was often bestowed as an honorary distinction on persons to whom nothing was confided, and whose opinion was never asked.   The sovereign, on the most important occasions, resorted for advice to a small knot of leading ministers.   The advantages and disadvantages of this course were early pointed out by Bacon, with his usual judgment and sagacity : but it was not till after the Restoration that the interior council began to attract general notice.   During many years old fashioned politicians continued to regard the Cabinet as an unconstitutional and dangerous board.   Nevertheless, it constantly became more and more important.   It at length drew to itself the chief executive power, and has now been regarded, during several generations, as an essential part of our polity.   Yet, strange to say, it still continues to be altogether unknown to the law : the names of the noblemen and gentlemen who compose it are never officially announced to the public : no record is kept of its meetings and resolutions ; nor has its existence ever been recognised by any Act of Parliament.

During some years the word Cabal was popularly used as synonymous with Cabinet.   But it happened by a whimsical coincidence that,

The Cabal in 1671, the Cabinet consisted of five persons the initial letters of whose names made up the word Cabal ; Clifford, Arlington, Buckingham, Ashley, and Lauderdale.   These ministers were therefore emphatically called the Cabal ; and they soon made that appellation so infamous that it has never since their time been used except as a term of reproach.

Sir Thomas Clifford was a Commissioner of the Treasury, and had greatly distinguished himself in the House of Commons.   Of the members of the Cabal he was the most respectable.   For, with a fiery and imperious temper, he had a strong though a lamentably perverted sense of duty and honour.

Henry Bennet, Lord Arlington, then Secretary of State, had, since he came to manhood, resided principally on the Continent, and had learned that cosmopolitan indifference to constitutions and religions

THOMAS CLIFFORD, FIRST BARON CLIFFORD OF CHUDLEIGH

From the painting by Sir P. Lely in the National Portrait Gallery

which is often observable in persons whose life has been passed in vagrant diplomacy. If there was any form of government which he liked, it was that of France. If there was any Church for which he felt a preference, it was that of Rome. He had some talent for conversation, and some talent also for transacting the ordinary business of office. He had learned, during a life passed in travelling and negotiating, the art of accommodating his language and deportment to the society in which he found himself. His vivacity in the closet amused the King : his gravity in debates and conferences imposed on the public ; and he had succeeded in attaching to himself, partly by services and partly by hopes, a considerable number of personal retainers.

Buckingham, Ashley, and Lauderdale were men in whom the immorality which was epidemic among the politicians of that age appeared in its most malignant type, but variously modified by great diversities of temper and understanding. Buckingham was a sated man of pleasure, who had turned to ambition as to a pastime. As he had tried to amuse himself with architecture and music, with writing farces and with seeking for the philosopher's stone, so he now tried to amuse himself with a secret negotiation and a Dutch war. He had already, rather from fickleness and love of novelty than from any deep design, been faithless to every party. At one time he had ranked among the Cavaliers. At another time warrants had been out against him for maintaining a treasonable correspondence with the remains of the Republican party in the city. He was now again a courtier, and was eager to win the favour of the King by services from which the most illustrious of those who had fought and suffered for the royal house would have recoiled with horror.

Ashley, with a far stronger head, and with a far fiercer and more earnest ambition, had been equally versatile. But Ashley's versatility was the effect, not of levity, but of deliberate selfishness. He had served and betrayed a succession of governments. But he had timed all his treacheries so well that, through all revolutions, his fortunes had constantly been rising. The multitude, struck with admiration by a prosperity which, while everything else was constantly changing, remained unchangeable, attributed to him a prescience almost miraculous, and likened him to the Hebrew statesman of whom it is written that his counsel was as if a man had inquired of the oracle of God.

Lauderdale, loud and coarse both in mirth and anger, was perhaps, under the outward show of boisterous frankness, the most dishonest man in the whole Cabal. He had made himself conspicuous among the Scotch insurgents in 1638 by his zeal for the Covenant. He was accused of having been deeply concerned in the sale of Charles the First to the English Parliament, and was therefore, in the estimation of good Cavaliers, a traitor, if possible, of a worse description than those who had sate in the High Court of Justice. He often talked with noisy jocularity of the days when he was a canter and a rebel. He was

HENRY BENNETT, EARL OF ARLINGTON

From an engraving by Houbraken, after the portrait by Sir P. Lely now the chief instrument employed by the court in the work of forcing episcopacy on his reluctant countrymen ; nor did he in that cause shrink from the unsparing use of the sword, the halter, and the boot. Yet those who knew him knew that thirty years had made no change in his real sentiments, that he still hated the memory of Charles the First, and that he still preferred the Presbyterian form of church government to every other.

Unscrupulous as Buckingham, Ashley, and Lauderdale were, it was not thought safe to intrust to them the King's intention of declaring himself a Roman Catholic. A false treaty, in which the article concerning religion was omitted, was shown to them. The names and seals of Clifford and Arlington are affixed to the genuine treaty. Both these statesmen had a partiality for the old Church, a partiality which the brave and vehement Clifford in no long time manfully avowed, but which the colder and meaner Arlington concealed, till the near approach of death scared him into sincerity. The three other cabinet ministers, however, were not men to be easily kept in the dark, and probably suspected more than was distinctly avowed to them. They were certainly privy to all the political engagements contracted with France, and were not ashamed to receive large gratifications from Lewis.

The first object of Charles was to obtain from the Commons supplies which might be employed in executing the secret treaty. The Cabal, holding power at a time when our government was in a state of transition, united in itself two different kinds of vices belonging to two different ages and to two different systems. As those five evil counsellors were among the last English statesmen who seriously thought of destroying the Parliament, so they were the first English statesmen who attempted extensively to corrupt it. We find in their policy at once the latest trace of the Thorough of Strafford, and the earliest trace of that methodical bribery which was afterwards practised by Walpole. They soon perceived, however, that, though the House of Commons was chiefly composed of Cavaliers, and though places and French gold had been lavished on the members, there was no chance that even the least odious parts of the scheme arranged at Dover would be supported by a majority. It was necessary to have recourse to fraud. The King accordingly professed great zeal for the principles of the Triple Alliance, and pretended that, in order to hold the ambition of France in check, it would be necessary to augment the fleet. The Commons fell into the snare, and voted a grant of eight hundred thousand pounds. The Parliament was instantly prorogued ; and the court, thus emancipated from control, proceeded to the execution of the great design.

The financial difficulties however were serious. A war with Holland could be carried on only at enormous cost. The ordinary revenue was not more than sufficient to support the government in time of peace. The eight hundred thousand pounds out of which the Commons had just been tricked would not defray the naval and military charge of a single year of hostilities. After the terrible lesson given by the Long Parliament, even the Cabal did not venture to recommend benevolences or shipmoney. In this perplexity Ashley and Clifford proposed a flagitious breach of public faith. The goldsmiths of London were then not only dealers in the precious metals, but also bankers, and were in the habit of advancing large sums of money to the government. In return for these advances they received assignments on the revenue, and were repaid with interest as the taxes came in. About thirteen hundred thousand pounds had been in this way intrusted to the honour of the state. On a sudden it was announced that it was not convenient to pay the principal, and that the lenders must content themselves with interest. They were consequently unable to meet their own engagements. The Exchange was in an uproar : several great mercantile houses broke ; and dismay and distress spread through all society. Meanwhile rapid strides were made towards despotism. Proclamations, dispensing with Acts of Parliament, or enjoining what only Parliament could lawfully enjoin, appeared in rapid succession. Of these edicts the most important was the Declaration of Indulgence. By this instrument the penal laws against Roman Catholics were set aside ; and, that the real object of the measure might not be perceived, the laws against Protestant Nonconformists were also suspended.

Shutting of the Exchequer

A few days after the appearance of the Declaration of Indulgence, war was proclaimed against the United Provinces. By sea the Dutch maintained the struggle with honour ; but on land they were at first borne down by irresistible force. A great French army passed the Rhine. Fortress after fortress opened its gates. Three of the seven provinces of the federation were occupied by the invaders. The fires of the hostile camp were seen from the top of the Stadthouse of Amsterdam. The Republic, thus fiercely assailed from without, was torn at the same time by internal dissensions. The government was in the hands of a close oligarchy of powerful burghers. There were numerous selfelected Town Councils, each of which exercised, within its own sphere, many of the rights of sovereignty. These councils sent delegates to the Provincial States, and the Provincial States again sent delegates to the States General. A hereditary first magistrate was no essential part of this polity. Nevertheless one family, singularly fertile of great men, had gradually obtained a large and somewhat indefinite authority. William, first of the name, Prince of Orange Nassau, and Stadtholder of Holland, had headed the memorable insurrection against Spain. His son Maurice had been

War with the United Provinces, and their extreme danger

GVILHELMVS D.G. PRINCEPS AVRIACVS, COMES NASSAVIÆ etc. MDCXLIII.

WILLIAM II, PRINCE OF ORANGE

From a mezzotint by L. von Siegen, after a painting by Honthorst

AVGVSTA MARIA CAROLI M·B·REG·FILIA GVILHELMI PRINC·AVR·SPONSA

MARY, DAUGHTER OF CHARLES I, AND WIFE OF WILLIAM II, PRINCE OF ORANGE

From a mezzotint by L. von Siegen, after a painting by Honthorst

Captain General and first minister of the States, had, by eminent abilities and public services, and by some treacherous and cruel actions, raised himself to almost kingly power, and had bequeathed a great part of that power to his family. The influence of the Stadtholders was an object of extreme jealousy to the municipal oligarchy. But the army, and that great body of citizens which was excluded from all share in the government, looked on the Burgomasters and Deputies with a dislike resembling the dislike with which the legions and the common people of Rome regarded the Senate, and were as zealous for the House of Orange as the legions and the common people of Rome for the House of Cæsar. The Stadtholder commanded the forces of the commonwealth, disposed of all military commands, had a large share of the civil patronage, and was surrounded by pomp almost regal.

Prince William the Second had been strongly opposed by the oligarchical party. His life had terminated in the year 1650, amidst great civil troubles. He died childless : the adherents of his house were left for a short time without a head ; and the powers which he had exercised were divided among the Town Councils, the Provincial States, and the States General.

But, a few days after William's death, his widow, Mary, daughter of Charles the First, King of Great Britain, gave birth to a son, destined to raise the glory and authority of the House of Nassau to the highest point, to save the United Provinces from slavery, to curb the power of France, and to establish the English constitution on a lasting foundation.

This Prince, named William Henry, was from his birth an object of serious apprehension to the party now supreme in Holland, and of loyal attachment to the old friends of his line. He enjoyed high

William, Prince of Orange consideration as the possessor of a splendid fortune, as the chief of one of the most illustrious houses in Europe, as a Magnate of the German empire, as a prince of the blood royal of England, and, above all, as the descendant of the founders of Batavian liberty. But the high office which had once been considered as hereditary in his family, remained in abeyance ; and the intention of the aristocratical party was that there should never be another Stadtholder. The want of a first magistrate was, to a great extent, supplied by the Grand Pensionary of the Province of Holland, John de Witt, whose abilities, firmness, and integrity had raised him to unrivalled authority in the councils of the municipal oligarchy.

The French invasion produced a complete change. The suffering and terrified people raged fiercely against the government. In their madness they attacked the bravest captains and the ablest statesmen of the distressed commonwealth. De Ruyter was insulted by the rabble. De Witt was torn in pieces before the gate of the palace of the States

THE MURDER OF JOHN AND CORNELIUS DE WITT

From a contemporary broadside in the Sutherland Collection

General at the Hague. The Prince of Orange, who had no share in the guilt of the murder, but who, on this occasion, as on another lamentable occasion twenty years later, extended to crimes perpetrated in his cause an indulgence which has left a stain on his glory, became chief of the government without a rival. Young as he was, his ardent and unconquerable spirit, though disguised by a cold and sullen manner, soon roused the courage of his dismayed countrymen. It was in vain that both his uncle and the French King attempted by splendid offers to seduce him from the cause of the Republic. To the States General he spoke a high and inspiriting language. He even ventured to suggest a scheme which has an aspect of antique heroism, and which, if it had been accomplished, would have been the noblest subject for epic song that is to be found in the whole compass of modern history. He told the deputies that, even if their natal soil and the marvels with which human industry had covered it were buried under the ocean, all was not lost. The Hollanders might survive Holland. Liberty and pure religion, driven by tyrants and bigots from Europe, might take refuge in the farthest isles of Asia. The shipping in the ports of the republic would suffice to carry two hundred thousand emigrants to the Indian Archipelago. There the Dutch commonwealth might commence a new and more glorious existence, and might rear, under the Southern Cross, amidst the sugar canes and nutmeg trees, the Exchange of a wealthier Amsterdam, and the schools of a more learned Leyden. The national spirit swelled and rose high. The terms offered by the allies were firmly rejected. The dykes were opened. The whole country was turned into one great lake, from which the cities, with their ramparts and steeples, rose like islands. The invaders were forced to save themselves from destruction by a precipitate retreat. Lewis, who, though he sometimes thought it necessary to appear at the head of his troops, greatly preferred a palace to a camp, had already returned to enjoy the adulation of poets and the smiles of ladies in the newly planted alleys of Versailles.

And now the tide turned fast. The event of the maritime war had been doubtful : by land the United Provinces had obtained a respite ; and a respite, though short, was of infinite importance. Alarmed by the vast designs of Lewis, both the branches of the great House of Austria sprang to arms. Spain and Holland, divided by the memory of ancient wrongs and humiliations, were reconciled by the nearness of the common danger. From every part of Germany troops poured towards the Rhine. The English government had already expended all the funds which had been obtained by pillaging the public creditor. No loan could be expected from the City. An attempt to raise taxes by the royal authority would have at once produced a rebellion ; and

Lewis, who had now to maintain a contest against half Europe, was in no condition to furnish the means of coercing the people of England. It was necessary to convoke the Parliament.

In the spring of 1673, therefore, the Houses reassembled after a recess of near two years. Clifford, now a peer and Lord Treasurer, and Ashley, now Earl of Shaftesbury and Lord Chancellor, were the persons on whom the King principally relied as Parliamentary managers. The Country Party instantly began to attack the policy of the Cabal. The attack was made, not in the way of storm, but by slow and scientific approaches. The Commons at first held out hopes that they would give support to the King's foreign policy, but insisted that he should purchase that support by abandoning his whole system of domestic policy. Their chief object was to obtain the revocation of the Declaration of Indulgence. Of all the many unpopular steps taken by the government the most unpopular was the publishing of this Declaration. The most opposite sentiments had been shocked by an act so liberal, done in a manner so despotic. All the enemies of religious freedom, and all the friends of civil freedom, found themselves on the same side; and these two classes made up nineteen twentieths of the nation. The zealous Churchman exclaimed against the favour which had been shown both to the Papist and to the Puritan. The Puritan, though he might rejoice in the suspension of the persecution by which he had been harassed, felt little gratitude for a toleration which he was to share with Antichrist. And all Englishmen who valued liberty and law, saw with uneasiness the deep inroad which the prerogative had made into the province of the legislature.

Meeting of the Parliament

Declaration of Indulgence

It must in candour be admitted that the constitutional question was then not quite free from obscurity. Our ancient Kings had undoubtedly claimed and exercised the right of suspending the operation of penal laws. The tribunals had recognised that right. Parliaments had suffered it to pass unchallenged. That some such right was inherent in the crown, few even of the Country Party ventured, in the face of precedent and authority, to deny. Yet it was clear that, if this prerogative were without limit, the English government could scarcely be distinguished from a pure despotism. That there was a limit was fully admitted by the King and his ministers. Whether the Declaration of Indulgence lay within or without the limit was the question; and neither party could succeed in tracing any line which would bear examination. Some opponents of the government complained that the Declaration suspended not less than forty statutes. But why not forty as well as one? There was an orator who gave it as his opinion that the King might constitutionally dispense with bad laws, but not with good laws. The absurdity of such a distinction it is needless to expose. The doctrine which seems to have been generally received in the House of Commons was, that the dispensing power was confined to secular matters, and did not extend to laws enacted for the security of the established religion. Yet, as the King was supreme head of the Church, it should seem that, if he possessed the dispensing power at all, he might well possess that power where the Church was concerned. When the courtiers on the other side attempted to point out the bounds of this prerogative, they were not more successful than the opposition had been.

The truth is that the dispensing power was a great anomaly in politics. It was utterly inconsistent in theory with the principles of mixed government : but it had grown up in times when people troubled themselves little about theories.[1]   It had not been very grossly abused in practice. It had therefore been tolerated, and had gradually acquired a kind of prescription. At length it was employed, after a long interval, in an enlightened age, and at an important conjuncture, to an extent never before known, and for a purpose generally abhorred. It was instantly subjected to a severe scrutiny. Men did not, indeed, at first, venture to pronounce it altogether unconstitutional. But they began to perceive that it was at direct variance with the spirit of the constitution, and would, if left unchecked, turn the English government from a limited into an absolute monarchy.

Under the influence of such apprehensions, the Commons denied the King's right to dispense, not indeed with all penal statutes, but with **It is cancelled, and the Test Act passed** penal statutes in matters ecclesiastical, and gave him plainly to understand that, unless he renounced that right, they would grant no supply for the Dutch war.   He, for a moment, showed some inclination to put everything to hazard : but he was strongly advised by Lewis to submit to necessity, and to wait for better times, when the French armies, now employed in an arduous struggle on the Continent, might be available for the purpose of suppressing discontent in England.   In the Cabal itself the signs of disunion and treachery began to appear.   Shaftesbury, with his proverbial sagacity, saw that a violent reaction was at hand, and that all things were tending towards a crisis resembling that of 1640.   He was determined that such a crisis should not find him in the situation of Strafford.   He therefore turned suddenly round, and acknowledged, in the House of Lords, that the Declaration was illegal.   The King, thus deserted by his ally and by his Chancellor, yielded, cancelled the Declaration, and solemnly promised that it should never be drawn into precedent.

[1] The most sensible thing said in the House of Commons, on this subject, came from Sir William Coventry :—" Our ancestors never did draw a line to circumscribe prerogative and liberty."

ANTHONY ASHLEY COOPER, FIRST EARL OF SHAFTESBURY

From the painting by John Greenhill in the National Portrait Gallery

Even this concession was insufficient. The Commons, not content with having forced their sovereign to annul the Indulgence, next extorted his unwilling assent to a celebrated law, which continued in force down to the reign of George the Fourth. This law, known as the Test Act, provided that all persons holding any office, civil or military, should take the oath of supremacy, should subscribe a declaration against transubstantiation, and should publicly receive the sacrament according to the rites of the Church of England. The preamble expressed hostility only to the Papists : but the enacting clauses were scarcely more unfavourable to the Papists than to the rigid Puritans. The Puritans, however, terrified at the evident leaning of the court towards Popery, and encouraged by some churchmen to hope that, as soon as the Roman Catholics should have been effectually disarmed, relief would be extended to Protestant Nonconformists, made little opposition ; nor could the King, who was in extreme want of money, venture to withhold his sanction. The act was passed ; and the Duke of York was consequently under the necessity of resigning the great place of Lord High Admiral.

Hitherto the Commons had not declared against the Dutch war. But, when the King had, in return for money cautiously doled out, The Cabal relinquished his whole plan of domestic policy, they fell dissolved impetuously on his foreign policy. They requested him to dismiss Buckingham and Lauderdale from his councils for ever, and appointed a committee to consider the propriety of impeaching Arlington. In a short time the Cabal was no more. Clifford, who, alone of the five, had any claim to be regarded as an honest man, refused to take the new test, laid down his white staff, and retired to his country seat. Arlington quitted the post of Secretary of State for a quiet and dignified employment in the Royal household. Shaftesbury and Buckingham made their peace with the opposition, and appeared at the head of the stormy democracy of the city. Lauderdale, however, still continued to be minister for Scotch affairs, with which the English Parliament could not interfere.

And now the Commons urged the King to make peace with Holland, and expressly declared that no more supplies should be granted for the war, unless it should appear that the enemy obstinately refused to consent to reasonable terms. Charles found it necessary to postpone to a more convenient season all thought of executing the treaty of Peace with Dover, and to cajole the nation by pretending to return to the United the policy of the Triple Alliance. Temple, who, during the Provinces ascendency of the Cabal, had lived in seclusion among his books and flower beds, was called forth from his hermitage. By his instrumentality a separate peace was concluded with the United Provinces

THOMAS OSBORNE.
Earl of Danby, Lord high
Treasurer of England.

P. Lely Pinxit.   A.Blooteling Fec: et Ex:

SIR THOMAS OSBORNE, AFTERWARDS EARL OF DANBY

From an engraving by Blooteling, after the portrait by Sir P. Lely and he again became ambassador at the Hague, where his presence was regarded as a sure pledge for the sincerity of his court.

The chief direction of affairs was now intrusted to Sir Thomas Osborne, a Yorkshire baronet, who had, in the House of Commons, shown eminent talents for business and debate.   Osborne became Lord Treasurer, and was soon created Earl of Danby.

Administration of Danby

He was not a man whose character, if tried by any high standard of morality, would appear to merit approbation.   He was greedy of wealth and honours, corrupt himself, and a corrupter of others. The Cabal had bequeathed to him the art of bribing Parliaments, an art still rude, and giving little promise of the rare perfection to which it was brought in the following century.   He improved greatly on the plan of the first inventors.   They had merely purchased orators : but every man who had a vote, might sell himself to Danby.   Yet the new minister must not be confounded with the negotiators of Dover.   He was not without the feelings of an Englishman and a Protestant ; nor did he, in his solicitude for his own interests, ever wholly forget the interests of his country and of his religion.   He was desirous, indeed, to exalt the prerogative : but the means by which he proposed to exalt it were widely different from those which had been contemplated by Arlington and Clifford.   The thought of establishing arbitrary power, by calling in the aid of foreign arms, and by reducing the kingdom to the rank of a dependent principality, never entered into his mind.   His plan was to rally round the monarchy those classes which had been the firm allies of the monarchy during the troubles of the preceding generation, and which had been disgusted by the recent crimes and errors of the court. With the help of the old Cavalier interest, of the nobles, of the country gentlemen, of the clergy, and of the Universities, it might, he conceived, be possible to make Charles, not indeed an absolute sovereign, but a sovereign scarcely less powerful than Elizabeth had been.

Prompted by these feelings, Danby formed the design of securing to the Cavalier party the exclusive possession of all political power, both executive and legislative.   In the year 1675, accordingly, a bill was offered to the Lords which provided that no person should hold any office, or should sit in either House of Parliament, without first declaring on oath that he considered resistance to the kingly power as in all cases criminal, and that he would never endeavour to alter the government either in Church or State.   During several weeks the debates, divisions, and protests caused by this proposition kept the country in a state of excitement.   The opposition in the House of Lords, headed by two members of the Cabal who were desirous to make their peace with the nation, Buckingham and Shaftesbury, was beyond all precedent vehement and pertinacious, and at length proved successful.   The bill was not indeed rejected, but was retarded, mutilated, and at length suffered to drop.

So arbitrary and so exclusive was Danby's scheme of domestic policy. His opinions touching foreign policy did him more honour. They were in truth directly opposed to those of the Cabal, and differed little from those of the Country Party. He bitterly lamented the degraded situation to which England was reduced, and declared, with more energy than politeness, that his dearest wish was to cudgel the French into a proper respect for her. So little did he disguise his feelings that, at a great banquet where the most illustrious dignitaries of the State and of the Church were assembled, he not very decorously filled his glass to the confusion of all who were against a war with

MEDAL CELEBRATING THE MARRIAGE OF WILLIAM AND MARY

France. He would indeed most gladly have seen his country united with the powers which were then combined against Lewis, and was for that end bent on placing Temple, the author of the Triple Alliance, at the head of the department which directed foreign affairs. But the power of the prime minister was limited. In his most confidential letters he complained that the infatuation of his master prevented England from taking her proper place among European nations. Charles was insatiably greedy of French gold: he had by no means relinquished the hope that he might, at some future day, be able to establish absolute monarchy by the help of the French arms; and for both reasons he wished to maintain a good understanding with the court of Versailles.

Thus the sovereign leaned towards one system of foreign politics, and the minister towards a system diametrically opposite. Neither the sovereign nor the minister, indeed, was of a temper to pursue any object with undeviating constancy. Each occasionally yielded to the importunity of the other ; and their jarring inclinations and mutual concessions gave to the whole administration a strangely capricious character. Charles sometimes, from levity and indolence, suffered Danby to take steps which Lewis resented as mortal injuries. Danby, on the other hand, rather than relinquish his great place, sometimes stooped to compliances which caused him bitter pain and shame. The King was brought to consent to a marriage between the Lady Mary, eldest daughter and presumptive heiress of the Duke of York, and William of Orange, the deadly enemy of France, and the hereditary champion of the Reformation. Nay, the brave Earl of Ossory, son of Ormond, was sent to assist the Dutch with some British troops, who, on the most bloody day of the whole war, signally vindicated the national reputation for stubborn courage. The Treasurer, on the other hand, was induced, not only to connive at some scandalous pecuniary transactions which took place between his master and the court of Versailles, but to become, unwillingly indeed and ungraciously, an agent in those transactions.

Meanwhile, the Country Party was driven by two strong feelings in two opposite directions. The popular leaders were afraid of the greatness of Lewis, who was not only making head against the whole strength of the continental alliance, but was even gaining ground. Yet they were afraid to entrust their own King with the means of curbing France, lest those means should be used to destroy the liberties of England. The conflict between these apprehensions, both of which were perfectly legitimate, made the policy of the Opposition seem as eccentric and fickle as that of the Court. The Commons called for a war with France, 'till the King, pressed by Danby to comply with their wish, seemed disposed to yield, and began to raise an army. But, as soon as they saw that the recruiting had commenced, their dread of Lewis gave place to a nearer dread. They began to fear that the new levies might be employed on a service in which Charles took much more interest than in the defence of Flanders. They therefore refused supplies, and clamoured for disbanding as loudly as they had just before clamoured for arming. Those historians who have severely reprehended this inconsistency do not appear to have made sufficient allowance for the embarrassing situation of subjects who have reason to believe that their prince is conspiring with a foreign and hostile power against their liberties. To refuse him military resources is to leave the state defenceless. Yet to give him military resources may be only to arm him against the state. In such circumstances vacillation cannot be considered as a proof of dishonesty or even of weakness.

Embarrassing situation of the Country Party

These jealousies were studiously fomented by the French King. He had long kept England passive by promising to support the throne against the Parliament. He now, alarmed at finding that the patriotic counsels of Danby seemed likely to prevail in the closet, began to inflame the Parliament against the throne. Between Lewis and the Country Party there was one thing, and one only in common, profound distrust of Charles. Could the Country Party have been certain that their sovereign meant only to

DUTCH CARICATURE REPRESENTING CHARLES II AND LEWIS XIV

Number 1055 in the British Museum Catalogue of Satirical Prints

make war on France, they would have been eager to support him. Could Lewis have been certain that the new levies were intended only to make war on the constitution of England, he would have made no attempt to stop them. But the unsteadiness and faithlessness of Charles were such that the French government and the English opposition, agreeing in nothing else, agreed in disbelieving his protestations, and were equally desirous to keep him poor and without an army. Communications were opened between Barillon, the Ambassador of Lewis, and those English politicians who had always professed, and who indeed sincerely felt, the greatest dread and dislike of the French

ascendency.   The most upright member of the Country Party, William
Lord Russell, son of the Earl of Bedford, did not scruple to concert
with a foreign mission schemes for embarrassing his own sovereign.
This was the whole extent of Russell's offence.   His principles and his
fortune alike raised him above all temptations of a sordid kind : but
there is too much reason to believe that some of his associates were less
scrupulous.   It would be unjust to impute to them the extreme wickedness of taking bribes to injure their country.   On the contrary, they
meant to serve her : but it is impossible to deny that they were mean
and indelicate enough to let a foreign prince pay them for serving her.
Among those who cannot be acquitted of this degrading charge was one
man who is popularly considered as the personification of public spirit,
and who, in spite of some great moral and intellectual faults, has a just
claim to be called a hero, a philosopher, and a patriot.   It is impossible
to see without pain such a name in the list of the pensioners of France.
Yet it is some consolation to reflect that, in our time, a public man
would be thought lost to all sense of duty and of shame, who should
not spurn from him a temptation which conquered the virtue and the
pride of Algernon Sidney.

The effect of these intrigues was that England, though she occasionally took a menacing attitude, remained inactive till the continental
Peace of   war, having lasted near seven years, was terminated by the
Nimeguen   treaty of Nimeguen.   The United Provinces, which in 1672
had seemed to be on the verge of utter ruin, obtained honourable and
advantageous terms.   This narrow escape was generally ascribed to the
ability and courage of the young Stadtholder.   His fame was great
throughout Europe, and especially among the English, who regarded
him as one of their own princes, and rejoiced to see him the husband of
their future Queen.   France retained many important towns in the Low
Countries and the great province of Franche Comté.   Almost the whole
loss was borne by the decaying monarchy of Spain.

A few months after the termination of hostilities on the Continent
came a great crisis in English politics.   Towards such a crisis things
Violent dis- had been tending during eighteen years.   The whole stock of
contents in popularity, great as it was, with which the King had com-
England   menced his administration, had long been expended.   To
loyal enthusiasm had succeeded profound disaffection.   The public mind
had now measured back again the space over which it had passed
between 1640 and 1660, and was once more in the state in which it
had been when the Long Parliament met.

The prevailing discontent was compounded of many feelings.   One
of these was wounded national pride.   That generation had seen
England, during a few years, allied on equal terms with France,

victorious over Holland and Spain, the mistress of the sea, the terror of Rome, the head of the Protestant interest. Her resources had not diminished ; and it might have been expected that she would have been at least as highly considered in Europe under a legitimate King, strong in the affection and willing obedience of his subjects, as she had been under an usurper whose utmost vigilance and energy were required to keep down a mutinous people. Yet she had, in consequence of the imbecility and meanness of her rulers, sunk so low that any German or Italian principality which brought five thousand men into the field was a more important member of the commonwealth of nations.

With the sense of national humiliation was mingled anxiety for civil liberty. Rumours, indistinct indeed, but perhaps the more alarming by reason of their indistinctness, imputed to the court a deliberate design against all the constitutional rights of Englishmen. It had even been whispered that this design was to be carried into effect by the intervention of foreign arms. The thought of such intervention made the blood, even of the Cavaliers, boil in their veins. Some who had always professed the doctrine of nonresistance in its full extent were now heard to mutter that there was one limitation to that doctrine. If a foreign force were brought over to coerce the nation, they would not answer for their own patience.

But neither national pride nor anxiety for public liberty had so great an influence on the popular mind as hatred of the Roman Catholic religion. That hatred had become one of the ruling passions of the community, and was as strong in the ignorant and profane as in those who were Protestants from conviction. The cruelties of Mary's reign, cruelties which even in the most accurate and sober narrative excite just detestation, and which were neither accurately nor soberly related in the popular martyrologies, the conspiracies against Elizabeth, and above all the Gunpowder Plot, had left in the minds of the vulgar a deep and bitter feeling which was kept up by annual commemorations, prayers, bonfires, and processions. It should be added that those classes which were peculiarly distinguished by attachment to the throne, the clergy and the landed gentry, had peculiar reasons for regarding the Church of Rome with aversion. The clergy trembled for their benefices ; the landed gentry for their abbeys and great tithes. While the memory of the reign of the Saints was still recent, hatred of Popery had in some degree given place to hatred of Puritanism : but, during the eighteen years which had elapsed since the Restoration, the hatred of Puritanism had abated, and the hatred of Popery had increased. The stipulations of the treaty of Dover were accurately known to very few : but some hints had got abroad. The general impression was that a great blow was about to be aimed at the Protestant religion. The King was suspected by many of a leaning towards Rome. His brother and heir presumptive was known to be a bigoted Roman Catholic. The first Duchess of York had died a Roman Catholic. James had then, in defiance of the remonstrances of the House of Commons, taken to wife the Princess Mary of Modena, another Roman Catholic. If there should be sons by this marriage, there was reason to fear that they might be bred Roman Catholics, and that a long succession of princes, hostile to the established faith, might sit on the English throne. The constitution had recently been violated for the purpose of protecting the Roman Catholics from the penal laws. The ally by whom the policy of England had, during many years, been chiefly governed was not only a Roman Catholic, but a persecutor of the reformed Churches. Under such circumstances it is not strange that the common people should have been inclined to apprehend a return of the times of her whom they called Bloody Mary.

Thus the nation was in such a temper that the smallest spark might raise a flame. At this conjuncture fire was set in two places at once to the vast mass of combustible matter ; and in a moment the whole was in a blaze.

The French court, which knew Danby to be its mortal enemy, artfully contrived to ruin him by making him pass for its friend. Lewis, **Fall of Danby** by the instrumentality of Ralph Montague, a faithless and shameless man who had resided in France as minister from England, laid before the House of Commons proofs that the Treasurer had been concerned in an application made by the court of Whitehall to the court of Versailles for a sum of money. This discovery produced its natural effect. The Treasurer was, in truth, exposed to the vengeance of Parliament, not on account of his delinquencies, but on account of his merits ; not because he had been an accomplice in a criminal transaction, but because he had been a most unwilling and unserviceable accomplice. But of the circumstances, which have, in the judgment of posterity, greatly extenuated his fault, his contemporaries were ignorant. In their view he was the broker who had sold England to France. It seemed clear that his greatness was at an end, and doubtful whether his head could be saved.

Yet was the ferment excited by this discovery slight, when compared with the commotion which arose when it was noised abroad that a **The Popish plot** great Popish plot had been detected. One Titus Oates, a clergyman of the Church of England, had, by his disorderly life and heterodox doctrine, drawn on himself the censure of his spiritual superiors, had been compelled to quit his benefice, and had ever since led an infamous and vagrant life. He had once professed himself a Roman Catholic, and had passed some time on the Continent in English colleges of the order of Jesus. In those seminaries he had heard much wild talk about the best means of bringing England back to the true Church. From hints thus furnished he constructed a hideous romance,

RALPH MONTAGUE, AFTERWARDS DUKE OF MONTAGUE

From a mezzotint in the Sutherland Collection

resembling rather the dream of a sick man than any transaction which ever took place in the real world. The Pope, he said, had entrusted the government of England to the Jesuits. The Jesuits had, by commissions under the seal of their society, appointed Roman Catholic clergymen, noblemen, and gentlemen, to all the highest offices in Church and State.

The Papists had burned down London once.   They had tried to burn it down again.   They were at that moment planning a scheme for setting fire to all the shipping in the Thames.   They were to rise at a signal and massacre all their Protestant neighbours.   A French army was at the same time to land in Ireland.   All the leading statesmen and divines of England were to be murdered.   Three or four schemes had been formed for assassinating the King.   He was to be stabbed.   He was to be poisoned in his medicine.   He was to be shot with silver bullets.   The public mind was so sore and excitable that these lies readily found credit with the vulgar ; and two events which speedily took place led even some reflecting men to suspect that the tale, though evidently distorted and exaggerated, might have some foundation.

Edward Coleman, a very busy, and not very honest, Roman Catholic intriguer, had been among the persons accused.   Search was made for his papers.   It was found that he had just destroyed the greater part of them.   But a few which had escaped contained some passages such as, to minds strongly prepossessed, might seem to confirm the evidence of Oates.   Those passages indeed, when candidly construed, appear to express little more than the hopes which the posture of affairs, the predilections of Charles, the still stronger predilections of James, and the relations existing between the French and English courts, might naturally excite in the mind of a Roman Catholic strongly attached to the interests of his Church.   But the country was not then inclined to construe the letters of Papists candidly ; and it was urged, with some show of reason, that, if papers which had been passed over as unimportant were filled with matter so suspicious, some great mystery of iniquity must have been contained in those documents which had been carefully committed to the flames.

A few days later it was known that Sir Edmund Berry Godfrey, an eminent justice of the peace who had taken the depositions of Oates against Coleman, had disappeared.   Search was made ; and Godfrey's corpse was found in a field near London.   It was clear that he had died by violence.   It was equally clear that he had not been set upon by robbers.   His fate is to this day a secret.   Some think that he perished by his own hand ; some, that he was slain by a private enemy.   The most improbable supposition is that he was murdered by the party hostile to the court, in order to give colour to the story of the plot.   The most probable supposition seems, on the whole, to be that some hotheaded Roman Catholic, driven to frenzy by the lies of Oates and by the insults of the multitude, and not nicely distinguishing between the perjured accuser and the innocent magistrate, had taken a revenge of which the history of persecuted sects furnishes but too many examples.   If this were so, the assassin must have afterwards bitterly execrated his own

A POEM upon Mr. TYTUS OATES,
The first Discoverer of the late Popish Plot.

TITUS OATES
Anagramatis
TESTIS OVAT

*This is the true Originall taken from the Life,
done for Hen. Browne and Ric. Chiswell, All others are Counterfeit.*

Behold the Chief and Happy Instrument,
Whom Providence for Britain's Safety sent.
Westminster taught him, Cambridge bred him, then
Left him instead of Books, to study Men.
d those he studied with so true an Art,
deeply div'd into the very Heart
Foul Conspiracy. He smil'd the while
see the busie Jesuit vainly toil,
ntrive, design, and pamper his lewd Hate
Prince condemn'd for Excommunicate,
hopes of his Cajol'd Assassinate.

But here the far fam'd OATES, for far his Fame
Is spread ere this, (to Odescalchi's shame)
By Acts that seem'd Illegal, ventur'd on,
To make that Legal which himself had done.
Crimes cease to be so, where the main Intent
Shews the whole Act religiously meant.
No more than what brave Cassius did long since,
'Gainst Rebel Son to Father and to Prince:
And in the Noble Persian well approv'd,
That farr beyond himself his Sovereign lov'd.
The Wise Director shew'd his prudent art,
On such a Stage so well to act his part,
That cunning Loyola's more cunning Sect
Could not his true and lawful aims detect.
Submissive Constancy no less appear'd,
And no less Courage that so little fear'd

The fatal Consequence of smart Revenge,
(Wherein the Jesuits are no Sons of Change)
With Bloudy Hands and Minds prepared still,
If Kings themselves, the meaner OATES to kill.
For had they known his aim, be you secure,
Th'had more Cravats than one t'have made him sure.
Fools to deny the Fact) His very Name
Speaks the whole Truth in one short Anagram:
While TESTIS OVAT in an easie sense
Yields him the Triumph of his Evidence.
And lest that he should fail, Themselves provide
By raising Proofs in Crimson Murder dy'd,
While the red Streams of Honour'd Godfrey's Bloud
So mournfully convince, and cry so loud:
Who, had they their own Campanella read,
Would sure have weigh'd th'Imprudence of the Deed,
And nere have been so sillily unholy
To stain their vile Impiety with Folly.
But when the Fact was done, more fondly vain,
Not onely to deny the Fact, but Man)
Makes their Foes smile, their Favourets despair,
While TESTIS OVAT sounds in every Ear.
But wonder not the Plot should be maintain'd,
An Act of Truth, where Jesuits have a hand:
They whose curs'd Principles are such, that all
Mankind disputes their first Original;
Whether by savage Beasts or Men begot,
Since all Mankind abhors the Bloudy Knot,

And where soe'r they come, exterminates,
Their fury from their Kingdoms and their States;
More Cannibals than Samoïdes, that quaff
Whole Streams of Bloud, and owl at Ruine laugh.
'Tis not the first Attempt, so boldly made
Against the Hearts of Kings, by them betray'd:
Two Henry's (both of France) but lately fell
Deplored Victimes to this Brood of Hell:
But this t'attempt against the Sacred Brest
Of Him that nere disturb'd their Hornets Nest,
The Prince of Piety, who governs so,
That his large Charity to all may flow !
And his black Scroll of all their Impious Deeds,
But He that sav'd him in the Royal Oke,
Sav'd him again from this more dismal stroke ;
While this Triumphing Witness brings to light
Their dark Contrivances and Deeds of Night.
May this Triumphing Witness then go on,
Till the deep Bottom of the Plot be known ;
And while he onely the bold Truth declares,
Enjoy the Honour of his Loyal Cares.

FINIS.

London, Printed for Hen. Browne and Rich. Chiswell, in St. Pauls Church-yard. 1679.

A POEM ON TITUS OATES

Number 1073 in the British Museum Catalogue of Satirical Prints

wickedness and folly. The capital and the whole nation went mad with hatred and fear. The penal laws, which had begun to lose something of their edge, were sharpened anew. Everywhere justices were busied in searching houses and seizing papers. All the gaols were filled with Papists. London had the aspect of a city in a state of siege. The trainbands were under arms all night. Preparations were made for barricading the great thoroughfares. Patrols marched up and down the streets. Cannon were planted round Whitehall. No citizen thought himself safe unless he carried under his coat a small flail loaded with lead to brain the Popish assassins. The corpse of the murdered magistrate was exhibited during several days to the gaze of great multitudes, and was then committed to the grave with strange and terrible ceremonies, which indicated rather fear and the thirst of vengeance than sorrow or religious hope. The Houses insisted that a guard should be placed in the vaults over which they sate, in order to secure them against a second Gunpowder Plot. All their proceedings were of a piece with this demand. Ever since the reign of Elizabeth the oath of supremacy had been exacted from members of the House of Commons. Some Roman Catholics, however, had contrived so to interpret this oath that they could take it without scruple. A more stringent test was now added : every member of Parliament was required to make the Declaration against Transubstantiation ; and thus the Roman Catholic Lords were for the first time excluded from their seats. Strong resolutions were adopted against the Queen. The Commons threw one of the Secretaries of State into prison for having counter-signed commissions directed to gentlemen who were not good Protestants. They impeached the Lord Treasurer of high treason. Nay, they so far forgot the doctrine which, while the memory of the civil war was still recent, they had loudly professed, that they even attempted to wrest the command of the militia out of the King's hands. To such a temper had eighteen years of misgovernment brought the most loyal Parliament that had ever met in England.

Yet it may seem strange that, even in that extremity, the King should have ventured to appeal to the people ; for the people were more excited than their representatives. The Lower House, discontented as it was, contained a larger number of Cavaliers than were likely to find seats again. But it was thought that a dissolution would put a stop to the prosecution of the Lord Treasurer, a prosecution which might probably bring to light all the guilty mysteries of the French alliance, and might thus cause extreme personal annoyance and embarrassment to Charles. Accordingly, in January 1679, the Parliament, which had been in existence ever since the beginning of the year 1661, was dissolved ; and writs were issued for a general election.

VERITAS EX CINERIBVS REVIVISCIT

ÆTATIS SVÆ 57

P. Vandrebanc Sculp

Are to be Sold at Thomas Cherets in James Street Couent Garden

The true Effigies of that worthy and never to be forgotten
Sʳ. EDMONDBURY GODFREY Knight and Iustice of the Peace who
was MURTHERED by Papists the 12ᵗʰ day of October An. Dom. 1678.
Had he not dy'd wee had not liv'd, soe ill. They for themselves contriv'd for vs so well.

SIR EDMUND BERRY GODFREY

From an engraving by P. Vandrebanc

During some weeks the contention over the whole country was fierce and obstinate beyond example.   Unprecedented sums were **First** expended.   New tactics were employed.   It was remarked **general** by the pamphleteers of that time as something extraordinary **election of** **1679** that horses were hired at a great charge for the conveyance of electors.   The practice of splitting freeholds for the purpose of multiplying votes dates from this memorable struggle.   Dissenting preachers, who had long hidden themselves in quiet nooks from persecution, now emerged from their retreats, and rode from village to village, for the purpose of rekindling the zeal of the scattered people of God. The tide ran strong against the government.   Most of the new members came up to Westminster in a mood little differing from that of their predecessors who had sent Strafford and Laud to the Tower.

Meanwhile the courts of justice, which ought to be, in the midst of political commotions, sure places of refuge for the innocent of every party, were disgraced by wilder passions and fouler corruptions than were to be found even on the hustings.   The tale of Oates, though it had sufficed to convulse the whole realm, would not, unless confirmed by other evidence, suffice to destroy the humblest of those whom he had accused.   For, by the old law of England, two witnesses are necessary to establish a charge of treason.   But the success of the first impostor produced its natural consequences.   In a few weeks he had been raised from penury and obscurity to opulence, to power which made him the dread of princes and nobles, and to notoriety such as has for low and bad minds all the attractions of glory.   He was not long without coadjutors and rivals.   A wretch named Carstairs, who had earned a livelihood in Scotland by going disguised to conventicles and then informing against the preachers, led the way.   Bedloe, a noted swindler, followed ; and soon, from all the brothels, gambling houses, and spunging houses of London, false witnesses poured forth to swear away the lives of Roman Catholics.   One came with a story about an army of thirty thousand men who were to muster in the disguise of pilgrims at Corunna, and to sail thence to Wales.   Another had been promised canonisation and five hundred pounds to murder the King.   A third had stepped into an eating house in Covent Garden, and had there heard a great Roman Catholic banker vow, in the hearing of all the guests and drawers, to kill the heretical tyrant.   Oates, that he might not be eclipsed by his imitators, soon added a large supplement to his original narrative.   He had the portentous impudence to affirm, among other things, that he had once stood behind a door which was ajar, and had there overheard the Queen declare that she had resolved to give her consent to the assassination of her husband.   The vulgar believed, and the highest magistrates pretended to believe, even such

A PROPHECY of ENGLAND's future Happiness, after the time that the Contrivers of this Popish PLOT are cut off.

The Second Impression of

Dr. OTES his VINDICATION:

SHEWING,

His EVIDENCE is not yet to be baffled by the PAPISTS;

And the Power that instructed him to discover this damnable, Popish PLOT. Where observe, None that had a hand in it, or but consented to it, without Repentance, shall ever thrive.

OTES.

WISDOM, the Fruitful Mother of all things,
The Virgin Bride of the great KING of Kings,
This Heavenly Lady, first instructed Me,
To free my Country from Rome's Tyranny.
The World is Blind, and they that Headlong run,
Without this Guid, are utterly undone.
Whilst I was galloping a full Career,
A Glorious Angel did to me appear,
Great Britain's Genius, in a mourning weed.
Clanck in my Eye, which made my Heart to bleed.

ANGEL.

Canst thou, quoth she, behold thy Country's fall,
Into the Hands of ev'ry Cannibal
Devouring Dogs, who not content with Pieces,
Do gape to grind both Fleſh and Bones to pieces!
Who, under colour of faint Holineſs,
Would make poor Albion a meer Wilderneſs.

TITUS OTES D.D.
Wisdom instructing him to discover this Hellish Popish Plot
See it in a sheet called Dr. Otes's Vindication &c.
Printed By T. Dawks

Armies of Angels, stood in battel array,
Their Generall did fight for their thin ray,
Let not the name of Otes live, let it dye,
And in the Grave of dark Oblivion lye:
Let Bedloe, Otes and Dugdale be forgot,
For they were not Discoverers of this Plot,
These were but Harps in Great Jehovah's hand,
On whom he plaid to save a Sinful Land:

The PROPHECY

Of ENGLAND'S future Happineſs,
Notwithstanding the Rage and Malice of Papists.

Henceforth, Great Britain, shew thy smiling Face,
In thee is Born a Child of Heavenly Race,
Sprung from the Loyns of the Immortal Dove,
Wisdom his Mother, and his Sire is Love:
Riding Tryumphant on his Milk white Steed,
This Prince shall Cure the Nations that now bleed.

These words did pierce my Soul, like a keen Arrow,
They glided through my Bones, and all my Marrow.
I'le follow thy Advice, thus I reply,
Though Snakes and Adders in the way do ly:
The Dye is cast, I want no farther Wooing,

The Fire of Love so flamed in my Breast,
For England's safety I could take no rest:
The Dove did shine like a bright morning Sun,
And not the Murdering Dragon to the run:
The Lamb he was my Counsellor, who said,

In all those Countrys which foul Treason breeds,
I sucks sweet Hony from most poys'nous weeds;
Of which an Antidote I did compound,
To Cure fair England of her secret Wound.

Printed. 1680. Aprill 8.

LONDON, Printed by Tb. Dawks, in Black Fryers: where you may have Mr. Bedloe's and Mr. Dugdale's Pictures, severally, thus with Verses, declaring each of their Reasons why they discovered this Damnable, Hellish, Popish PLOT: also you may have Sir Edmund B. Godfrey Murder, most of the Papists Cruelties in it, made visible, in a large Copper Plate, with a Discourse thereon, to which is added Sir Edmund's Character. Also a Chronology of the Rise and Growth of Popery, when and who brought in their Superstitious Devices: which may be had in a broad sheets joyn'd with 52 Figures, in Copper Plates (or in a Pack of Cards representing the Rise, Demonstration and Discovery of the PLOT, with a Book to explain each Figure, &c. Also there you may have Salmon's Dispensatory; and his Hor. Mathematic, or Soul of Astrology, &c. Any person may have quantities of each, tho 'tis reported, by ill condition'd persons, to many ingenious persons, Lovers of Art, both in City and Country, that none, sho all of them may there be had.

DR. OATES HIS VINDICATION

Number 1078 in the British Museum Catalogue of Satirical Prints

See here the Dauils Darling, plotting still
With Blood & Treasons all y.ᵉ world to fill,
His Romish stratagems, Loe, Non can tell
Who cañot fathom to y.ᵉ Depth of Hell.
Nothing but Murder'd Kings can him suffice
And flaming Citys as a Sacrifice

Pops.}

Yet see behind his chaire Whom Heav'n ſent
Whom God hath made a timely Instrument
Englands intended ruine to prevent
That which, y.ᵉ Devil & y.ᵉ Pops combin'd
Against our King and Proteſtants deſign'd
Diſclos'd and fruſtrated by him wee find.

Oates}

The Emblem Explayn'd

A A   the Popes Cabbinett.
B   {the Pope writing to the Jeſuits to
     {be diligent in the careing on the Plott.
C   {m.ʳ Oats who vnſeene lokes ouer his
     {sholder & ſees all his Contriuances.
D   {the Popes Crone who cries friend
     {Oates is behind you.
E   {the Popes title of Supremacie falling
     {downe occaſioned by his ſudaine Motion.
F   {a Blott which his Surpriſe made him
     {fall vpon y.ᵉ word Roman in his Letter
G   {a crowne m.ʳ Oates giues him more fitt
     {for his Head then the former.

DR. OATES, THE POPE AND THE DEVIL

Number 1068 in the British Museum Catalogue of Satirical Prints

THE HAPPY INSTRUMENTS OF ENGLAND'S PRESERVATION

Number 1114 in the British Museum Catalogue of Satirical Prints

fictions as these. The chief judges of the realm were corrupt, cruel, and timid. The leaders of the Country Party encouraged the prevailing delusion. The most respectable among them, indeed, were themselves so far deluded as to believe the greater part of the evidence of the plot to be true. Such men as Shaftesbury and Buckingham doubtless perceived that the whole was a romance. But it was a romance which served their turn; and to their seared consciences the death of an innocent man gave no more uneasiness than the death of a partridge. The juries partook of the feelings then common throughout the nation, and were encouraged by the bench to indulge those feelings without restraint. The multitude applauded Oates and his confederates, hooted and pelted the witnesses who appeared on behalf of the accused, and shouted with joy when the verdict of Guilty was pronounced. It was in vain that the sufferers appealed to the respectability of their past lives: for the public mind was possessed with a belief that the more conscientious a Papist was, the more likely he must be to plot against a Protestant government. It was in vain that, just before the cart passed from under their feet, they resolutely affirmed their innocence: for the general opinion was that a good Papist considered all lies which were serviceable to his Church as not only excusable but meritorious.

While innocent blood was shedding under the forms of justice, the new Parliament met; and such was the violence of the predominant **Violence of the new House of Commons** party that even men whose youth had been passed amidst revolutions, men who remembered the attainder of Strafford, the attempt on the five members, the abolition of the House of Lords, the execution of the King, stood aghast at the aspect of public affairs. The impeachment of Danby was resumed. He pleaded the royal pardon. But the Commons treated the plea with contempt, and insisted that the trial should proceed. Danby, however, was not their chief object. They were convinced that the only effectual way of securing the liberties and religion of the nation was to exclude the Duke of York from the throne.

The King was in great perplexity. He had insisted that his brother, the sight of whom inflamed the populace to madness, should retire for a time to Brussels: but this concession did not seem to have produced any favourable effect. The Roundhead party was now decidedly preponderant. Towards that party leaned millions who had, at the time of the Restoration, leaned towards the side of prerogative. Of the old Cavaliers many participated in the prevailing fear of Popery, and many, bitterly resenting the ingratitude of the prince for whom they had sacrificed so much, looked on his distress as carelessly as he had looked on theirs. Even the Anglican clergy, mortified and alarmed by the apostasy of the Duke

MR. EDWARD COLEMAN AS HE WAS DRAWN TO EXECUTION

From an engraving in the Sutherland Collection

of York, so far countenanced the opposition as to join cordially in the outcry against the Roman Catholics.

The King in this extremity had recourse to Sir William Temple. Of all the official men of that age Temple had preserved the fairest **Temple's** character. The Triple Alliance had been his work. He had **plan of** refused to take any part in the politics of the Cabal, and **government** had, while that administration directed affairs, lived in strict privacy. He had quitted his retreat at the call of Danby, had made peace between England and Holland, and had borne a chief part in bringing about the marriage of the Lady Mary to her cousin the Prince of Orange. Thus he had the credit of every one of the few good things which had been done by the government since the Restoration. Of the numerous crimes and blunders of the last eighteen years none could be imputed to him. His private life, though not austere, was decorous : his manners were popular ; and he was not to be corrupted either by titles or by money. Something, however, was wanting to the character of this respectable statesman. The temperature of his patriotism was lukewarm. He prized his ease and his personal dignity too much, and shrank from responsibility with a pusillanimous fear. Nor indeed had his habits fitted him to bear a part in the conflicts of our domestic factions. He had reached his fiftieth year without having sate in the English Parliament ; and his official experience had been almost entirely acquired at foreign courts. He was justly esteemed one of the first diplomatists in Europe : but the talents and accomplishments of a diplomatist are widely different from those which qualify a politician to lead the House of Commons in agitated times.

The scheme which he proposed showed considerable ingenuity. Though not a profound philosopher, he had thought more than most busy men of the world on the general principles of government ; and his mind had been enlarged by historical studies and foreign travel. He seems to have discerned more clearly than most of his contemporaries one cause of the difficulties by which the government was beset. The character of the English polity was gradually changing. The Parliament was slowly, but constantly, gaining ground on the prerogative. The line between the legislative and executive powers was in theory as strongly marked as ever, but in practice was daily becoming fainter and fainter. The theory of the constitution was that the King might name his own ministers. But the House of Commons had driven Clarendon, the Cabal, and Danby successively from the direction of affairs. The theory of the constitution was that the King alone had the power of making peace and war. But the House of Commons had forced him to make peace with Holland, and had all but forced him to make war with France. The theory of the constitution was that the King was the sole judge of the cases in which it might be proper to pardon offenders. Yet he was so much in dread of the House of Commons that, at that moment, he could not venture to rescue from the gallows men whom he well knew to be the innocent victims of perjury.

Temple, it should seem, was desirous to secure to the legislature its undoubted constitutional powers, and yet to prevent it, if possible, from encroaching further on the province of the executive administration. With this view he determined to interpose between the sovereign and the Parliament a body which might break the shock of their collision. There was a body, ancient, highly honourable, and recognised by the law, which, he thought, might be so remodelled as to serve this purpose. He determined to give to the Privy Council a new character and office in the government. The number of Councillors he fixed at thirty. Fifteen of them were to be the chief ministers of state, of law, and of religion. The other fifteen were to be unplaced noblemen and gentlemen of ample fortune and high character. There was to be no interior cabinet. All the thirty were to be entrusted with every political secret, and summoned to every meeting ; and the King was to declare that he would, on every occasion, be guided by their advice.

Temple seems to have thought that, by this contrivance, he could at once secure the nation against the tyranny of the Crown, and the Crown against the encroachments of the Parliament. It was, on one hand, highly improbable that schemes such as had been formed by the Cabal would be even propounded for discussion in an assembly consisting of thirty eminent men, fifteen of whom were bound by no tie of interest to the court. On the other hand, it might be hoped that the Commons, content with the guarantee against misgovernment which such a Privy Council furnished, would confine themselves more than they had of late done to their strictly legislative functions, and would no longer think it necessary to pry into every part of the executive administration.

This plan, though in some respects not unworthy of the abilities of its author, was in principle vicious. The new board was half a cabinet and half a Parliament, and, like almost every other contrivance, whether mechanical or political, which is meant to serve two purposes altogether different, failed of accomplishing either. It was too large and too divided to be a good administrative body. It was too closely connected with the Crown to be a good checking body. It contained just enough of popular ingredients to make it a bad council of state, unfit for the keeping of secrets, for the conducting of delicate negotiations, and for the administration of war. Yet were these popular ingredients by no means sufficient to secure the nation against misgovernment. The plan, therefore, even if it had been fairly tried, could scarcely have succeeded ;

and it was not fairly tried. The King was fickle and perfidious : the Parliament was excited and unreasonable ; and the materials out of which the new Council was made, though perhaps the best which that age afforded, were still bad.

The commencement of the new system was, however, hailed with general delight ; for the people were in a temper to think any change an improvement. They were also pleased by some of the new nominations. Shaftesbury, now their favourite, was appointed Lord President. Russell and some other distinguished members of the Country Party were sworn of the Council. But a few days later all was again in confusion. The inconveniences of having so numerous a cabinet were such that Temple himself consented to infringe one of the fundamental rules which he had laid down, and to become one of a small knot which really directed everything. With him were joined three other ministers, Arthur Capel, Earl of Essex, George Savile, Viscount Halifax, and Robert Spencer, Earl of Sunderland.

Of the Earl of Essex, then First Commissioner of the Treasury, it is sufficient to say that he was a man of solid, though not brilliant parts, and of grave and melancholy character, that he had been connected with the Country Party, and that he was at this time honestly desirous to effect, on terms beneficial to the state, a reconciliation between that party and the throne.

Among the statesmen of those times Halifax was, in genius, the first. His intellect was fertile, subtle, and capacious. His polished, luminous, and animated eloquence, set off by the silver tones of his voice, was the delight of the House of Lords. His conversation overflowed with thought, fancy, and wit. His political tracts well deserve to be studied for their literary merit, and fully entitle him to a place among English classics. To the weight derived from talents so great and various he united all the influence which belongs to rank and ample possessions. Yet he was less successful in politics than many who enjoyed smaller advantages. Indeed, those intellectual peculiarities which make his writings valuable frequently impeded him in the contests of active life. For he always saw passing events, not in the point of view in which they commonly appear to one who bears a part in them, but in the point of view in which, after the lapse of many years, they appear to the philosophic historian. With such a turn of mind, he could not long continue to act cordially with any body of men. All the prejudices, all the exaggerations, of both the great parties in the state moved his scorn. He despised the mean arts and unreasonable clamours of demagogues. He despised still more the doctrines of divine right and passive obedience. He sneered impartially at the bigotry of the Churchman and at the bigotry of the Puritan. He was equally

Character of Halifax

Arthur Earle of Essex.

P. Lely pinx.   E. Luttrell fe.   I. Smith excud.

ARTHUR CAPEL, EARL OF ESSEX

From a mezzotint by J. Smith, after the painting by Sir P. Lely unable to comprehend how any man should object to Saints' days and surplices, and how any man should persecute any other man for objecting to them.   In temper he was what, in our time, is called a Conservative : in theory he was a Republican.   Even when his dread of anarchy and his disdain for vulgar delusions led him to side for a time with the defenders of arbitrary power, his intellect was always with Locke and Milton.   Indeed, his jests upon hereditary monarchy were sometimes such as would have better become a member of the Calf's Head Club than a Privy Councillor of the Stuarts.   In religion he was so far from being a zealot that he was called by the uncharitable an atheist : but this imputation he vehemently repelled ; and in truth, though he sometimes gave scandal by the way in which he exerted his rare powers both of reasoning and of ridicule on serious subjects, he seems to have been by no means unsusceptible of religious impressions.

He was the chief of those politicians whom the two great parties contemptuously called Trimmers.   Instead of quarrelling with this nickname, he assumed it as a title of honour, and vindicated, with great vivacity, the dignity of the appellation.   Everything good, he said, trims between extremes.   The temperate zone trims between the climate in which men are roasted and the climate in which they are frozen.   The English Church trims between the Anabaptist madness and the Papist lethargy.   The English constitution trims between Turkish despotism and Polish anarchy.   Virtue is nothing but a just temper between propensities any one of which, if indulged to excess, becomes vice. Nay, the perfection of the Supreme Being himself consists in the exact equilibrium of attributes, none of which could preponderate without disturbing the whole moral and physical order of the world.[1]   Thus Halifax was a Trimmer on principle.   He was also a Trimmer by the constitution both of his head and of his heart.   His understanding was keen, sceptical, inexhaustibly fertile in distinctions and objections ; his taste refined ; his sense of the ludicrous exquisite ; his temper placid and forgiving, but fastidious, and by no means prone either to malevolence or to enthusiastic admiration.   Such a man could not long be constant to any band of political allies.   He must not, however, be confounded with the vulgar crowd of renegades.   For though, like them, he passed from side to side, his transition was always in the direction opposite to theirs.   He had nothing in common with those who fly from extreme to extreme, and who regard the party which they have deserted with an animosity far exceeding that of consistent enemies. His place was on the debatable ground between the hostile divisions of the community, and he never wandered far beyond the frontier of

[1] Halifax was undoubtedly the real author of the Character of a Trimmer, which, for a time, went under the name of his kinsman, Sir William Coventry.

either. The party to which he at any moment belonged was the party which, at that moment, he liked least, because it was the party of which at that moment he had the nearest view. He was therefore always severe upon his violent associates, and was always in friendly relations with his moderate opponents. Every faction in the day of its insolent and vindictive triumph incurred his censure ; and every faction, when vanquished and persecuted, found in him a protector. To his lasting honour it must be mentioned that he attempted to save those victims whose fate has left the deepest stain both on the Whig and on the Tory name.

He had greatly distinguished himself in opposition, and had thus drawn on himself the royal displeasure, which was indeed so strong that he was not admitted into the Council of Thirty without much difficulty and long altercation. As soon, however, as he had obtained a footing at court, the charms of his manner and of his conversation made him a favourite. He was seriously alarmed by the violence of the public discontent. He thought that liberty was for the present safe, and that order and legitimate authority were in danger. He therefore, as was his fashion, joined himself to the weaker side. Perhaps his conversion was not wholly disinterested. For study and reflection, though they had emancipated him from many vulgar prejudices, had left him a slave to vulgar desires. Money he did not want ; and there is no evidence that he ever obtained it by any means which, in that age, even severe censors considered as dishonourable ; but rank and power had strong attractions for him. He pretended, indeed, that he considered titles and great offices as baits which could allure none but fools, that he hated business, pomp, and pageantry, and that his dearest wish was to escape from the bustle and glitter of Whitehall to the quiet woods which surrounded his ancient mansion in Nottinghamshire : but his conduct was not a little at variance with his professions. In truth he wished to command the respect at once of courtiers and of philosophers, to be admired for attaining high dignities, and to be at the same time admired for despising them.

Sunderland was Secretary of State. In this man the political immorality of his age was personified in the most lively manner. Nature had given him a keen understanding, a restless and mischievous temper, a cold heart, and an abject spirit. His mind had undergone a training by which all his vices had been nursed up to the rankest maturity. At his entrance into public life, he had passed several years in diplomatic posts abroad, and had been, during some time, minister in France. Every calling has its peculiar temptations. There is no injustice in saying that diplomatists, as a class, have always been more distinguished by their address, by the art with which

Character of Sunderland

they win the confidence of those with whom they have to deal, and by
the ease with which they catch the tone of every society into which they
are admitted, than by generous enthusiasm or austere rectitude ; and the
relations between Charles and Lewis were such that no English nobleman could long reside in France as envoy, and retain any patriotic or
honourable sentiment.　Sunderland came forth from the bad school in
which he had been brought up, cunning, supple, shameless, free from
all prejudices, and destitute of all principles.　He was, by hereditary
connection, a Cavalier : but with the Cavaliers he had nothing in
common.　They were zealous for monarchy, and condemned in theory
all resistance.　Yet they had sturdy English hearts which would never
have endured real despotism.　He, on the contrary, had a languid
speculative liking for republican institutions, which was compatible with
perfect readiness to be in practice the most servile instrument of arbitrary
power.　Like many other accomplished flatterers and negotiators, he
was far more skilful in the art of reading the characters and practising
on the weaknesses of individuals, than in the art of discerning the feelings
of great masses, and of foreseeing the approach of great revolutions.
He was adroit in intrigue ; and it was difficult even for shrewd and
experienced men who had been amply forewarned of his perfidy to
withstand the fascination of his manner, and to refuse credit to his
professions of attachment.　But he was so intent on observing and
courting particular persons, that he often forgot to study the temper of
the nation.　He therefore miscalculated grossly with respect to some
of the most momentous events of his time.　More than one important
movement and rebound of the public mind took him by surprise ; and
the world, unable to understand how so clever a man could be blind to
what was clearly discerned by the politicians of the coffee houses, sometimes attributed to deep design what were in truth mere blunders.

It was only in private conference that his eminent abilities displayed
themselves.　In the royal closet, or in a very small circle, he exercised
great influence.　But at the Council board he was taciturn ; and in the
House of Lords he never opened his lips.

The four confidential advisers of the crown soon found that their
position was embarrassing and invidious.　The other members of the
Council murmured at a distinction inconsistent with the King's promises ;
and some of them, with Shaftesbury at their head, again betook themselves to strenuous opposition in Parliament.　The agitation, which had
been suspended by the late changes, speedily became more violent than
ever.　It was in vain that Charles offered to grant to the Commons any
security for the Protestant religion which they could devise, provided
only that they would not touch the order of succession.　They would
hear of no compromise.　They would have the Exclusion Bill, and

nothing but the Exclusion Bill. The King, therefore, a few weeks after he had publicly promised to take no step without the advice of his new Council, went down to the House of Lords without mentioning his intention in Council, and prorogued the Parliament.

The day of that prorogation, the twenty-sixth of May 1679, is a great era in our history. For on that day the Habeas Corpus Act received the royal assent. From the time of the Great Charter, the substantive law respecting the personal liberty of English- Prorogation of the Parliament men had been nearly the same as at present : but it had been inefficacious for want of a stringent system of procedure. What was needed was not a new right, but a prompt and searching remedy ; and such a remedy the Habeas Corpus Act supplied. The King Habeas Corpus Act would gladly have refused his consent to that measure : but he was about to appeal from his Parliament to his people on the question of the succession, and he could not venture, at so critical a moment, to reject a bill which was in the highest degree popular.

On the same day, the press of England became for a short time free. In old times printers had been strictly controlled by the Court of Star Chamber. The Long Parliament had abolished the Star Chamber, but had, in spite of the philosophical and eloquent expostulation of Milton, established and maintained a censorship. Soon after the Restoration, an Act had been passed which prohibited the printing of unlicensed books ; and it had been provided that this Act should continue in force till the end of the first session of the next Parliament. That moment had now arrived ; and the King, in the very act of dismissing the Houses, emancipated the Press.

Shortly after the prorogation came a dissolution and another general election. The zeal and strength of the opposition were at the height. The cry for the Exclusion Bill was louder than ever ; and Second general election of 1679 with this cry was mingled another cry, which fired the blood of the multitude, but which was heard with regret and alarm by all judicious friends of freedom. Not only the rights of the Duke of York, an avowed Papist, but those of his two daughters, sincere and zealous Protestants, were assailed. It was confidently affirmed that the eldest natural son of the King had been born in wedlock, and was lawful heir to the crown.

Charles, while a wanderer on the Continent, had fallen in at the Hague with Lucy Walters, a Welsh girl of great beauty, but of weak understanding and dissolute manners. She became his mis- Popularity of Monmouth tress, and presented him with a son. A suspicious lover might have had his doubts ; for the lady had several admirers, and was not supposed to be cruel to any. Charles, however, readily took her word, and poured forth on little James Crofts, as the boy was then called, an overflowing fondness, such as seemed hardly to belong to that cool and careless nature. Soon after the Restoration, the young favourite, who had learned in France the exercises then considered necessary to a fine gentleman, made his appearance at Whitehall. He was lodged in the palace, attended by pages, and permitted to enjoy several distinctions which had till then been confined to princes of the blood royal. He was married, while still in tender youth, to Anne Scott, heiress of the noble house of Buccleuch. He took her name, and received with her hand possession of her ample domains. The estate which he had acquired by this match was popularly estimated at not less than ten thousand pounds a year. Titles, and favours more substantial than titles, were lavished on him. He was made Duke of Monmouth in England, Duke of Buccleuch in Scotland, a Knight of the Garter, Master of the Horse, Commander of the first troop of Life Guards, Chief Justice of Eyre south of Trent, and Chancellor of the University of Cambridge. Nor did he appear to the public unworthy of his high fortunes. His countenance was eminently handsome and engaging, his temper sweet, his manners polite and affable. Though a libertine, he won the hearts of the Puritans. Though he was known to have been privy to the shameful attack on Sir John Coventry, he easily obtained the forgiveness of the Country Party. Even austere moralists owned that, in such a court, strict conjugal fidelity was scarcely to be expected from one who, while a child, had been married to another child. Even patriots were willing to excuse a headstrong boy for visiting with immoderate vengeance an insult offered to his father. And soon the stain left by loose amours and midnight brawls was effaced by honourable exploits. When Charles and Lewis united their forces against Holland, Monmouth commanded the English auxiliaries who were sent to the Continent, and approved himself a gallant soldier and a not unintelligent officer. On his return he found himself the most popular man in the kingdom. Nothing was withheld from him but the crown ; nor did even the crown seem to be absolutely beyond his reach. The distinction which had most injudiciously been made between him and the highest nobles had produced evil consequences. When a boy he had been invited to put on his hat in the presence chamber, while Howards and Seymours stood uncovered round him. When foreign princes died, he had mourned for them in the long purple cloak, which no other subject, except the Duke of York and Prince Rupert, was permitted to wear. It was natural that these things should lead him to regard himself as a legitimate prince of the House of Stuart. Charles, even at a ripe age, was devoted to his pleasures and regardless of his dignity. It could hardly be thought incredible that he should at twenty have secretly gone through the form of espousing a lady whose beauty had fascinated him. While Monmouth was still a child, and while the Duke of York still passed for a Protestant, it was rumoured throughout the country, and even in circles which ought to have been well informed, that the King had made Lucy Walters his wife, and that, if every one had his right, her son would be Prince of Wales. Much was said of a certain black box which, according to the vulgar belief, contained the contract of marriage. When Monmouth had returned

JAMES, DUKE OF MONMOUTH

From a mezzotint by W. Baillie in the Sutherland Collection

from the Low Countries with a high character for valour and conduct, and when the Duke of York was known to be a member of a church detested by the great majority of the nation, this idle story became important. For it there was not the slightest evidence. Against it there was the solemn asseveration of the King, made before his Council, and by his order communicated to his people. But the multitude, always fond of romantic adventures, drank in eagerly the tale of the secret espousals and the black box. Some chiefs of the opposition acted on this occasion as they acted with respect to the more odious fable of Oates, and countenanced a story which they must have despised. The interest which the populace took in him whom they regarded as the champion of the true religion, and the rightful heir of the British throne, was kept up by every artifice. When Monmouth arrived in London at midnight, the watchmen were ordered by the magistrates to proclaim the joyful event through the streets of the City : the people left their beds : bonfires were lighted : the windows were illuminated : the churches were opened ; and a merry peal rose from all the steeples. When he travelled, he was everywhere received with not less pomp, and with far more enthusiasm, than had been displayed when Kings had made progresses through the realm. He was escorted from mansion to mansion by long cavalcades of armed gentlemen and yeomen. Cities poured forth their whole population to receive him. Electors thronged round him, to assure him that their votes were at his disposal. To such a height were his pretensions carried, that he not only exhibited on his escutcheon the lions of England and the lilies of France without the baton sinister under which, according to the law of heraldry, they should have been debruised in token of his illegitimate birth, but ventured to touch for the king's evil. At the same time he neglected no art of condescension by which the love of the multitude could be conciliated. He stood godfather to the children of the peasantry, mingled in every rustic sport, wrestled, played at quarterstaff, and won footraces in his boots against fleet runners in shoes.

It is a curious circumstance that, at two of the greatest conjunctures in our history, the chiefs of the Protestant party should have committed the same error, and should by that error have greatly endangered their country and their religion. At the death of Edward the Sixth they set up the Lady Jane, without any show of birthright, in opposition, not only to their enemy Mary, but also to Elizabeth, the true hope of England and of the Reformation. Thus the most respectable Protestants, with Elizabeth at their head, were forced to make common cause with the Papists. In the same manner, a hundred and thirty years later, a part of the opposition, by setting up Monmouth as a claimant of the crown, attacked the rights, not only of James, whom they justly regarded as an implacable foe of their faith and their liberties, but also of the Prince and Princess of Orange, who were eminently marked out, both by situation and by personal qualities, as the defenders of all free governments and of all reformed churches.

The folly of this course speedily became manifest. At present the popularity of Monmouth constituted a great part of the strength of the opposition. The elections went against the court : the day fixed for the meeting of the Houses drew near ; and it was necessary that the

King should determine on some line of conduct. Those who advised him discerned the first faint signs of a change of public feeling, and hoped that, by merely postponing the conflict, he would be able to secure the victory. He therefore, without even asking the opinion of the Council of the Thirty, resolved to prorogue the new Parliament before it entered on business. At the same time the Duke of York, who had returned from Brussels, was ordered to retire to Scotland, and was placed at the head of the administration of that kingdom.

Temple's plan of government was now avowedly abandoned and very soon forgotten. The Privy Council again became what it had been. Shaftesbury and those who were connected with him in politics resigned their seats. Temple himself, as was his wont in unquiet times, retired to his garden and his library. Essex quitted the board of Treasury, and cast in his lot with the opposition. But Halifax, disgusted and alarmed by the violence of his old associates, and Sunderland, who never quitted place while he could hold it, remained in the King's service.

In consequence of the resignations which took place at this conjuncture, the way to greatness was left clear to a new set of aspirants. Two statesmen, who subsequently rose to the highest eminence which a British subject can reach, soon began to attract a large share of the public attention. These were Lawrence Hyde and Sidney Godolphin.

Lawrence Hyde was the second son of the Chancellor Clarendon, and was brother of the first Duchess of York. He had excellent parts, which had been improved by parliamentary and diplomatic experience; but the infirmities of his temper detracted much **Lawrence Hyde** from the effective strength of his abilities. Negotiator and courtier as he was, he never learned the art of governing or of concealing his emotions. When prosperous, he was insolent and boastful : when he sustained a check, his undisguised mortification doubled the triumph of his enemies : very slight provocations sufficed to kindle his anger ; and when he was angry he said bitter things which he forgot as soon as he was pacified, but which others remembered many years. His quickness and penetration would have made him a consummate man of business but for his selfsufficiency and impatience. His writings prove that he had many of the qualities of an orator : but his irritability prevented him from doing himself justice in debate: for nothing was easier than to goad him into a passion ; and, from the moment when he went into a passion, he was at the mercy of opponents far inferior to him in capacity.

Unlike most of the leading politicians of that generation he was a consistent, dogged, and rancorous party man, a Cavalier of the old school, a zealous champion of the Crown and of the Church, and a hater of Republicans and Nonconformists. He had consequently a great body of personal adherents.   The clergy especially looked on him as their own man, and extended to his foibles an indulgence of which, to say the truth, he stood in some need : for he drank deep ; and when he was in a rage,—and he very often was in a rage,—he swore like a porter.

He now succeeded Essex at the Treasury.   It is to be observed that the place of First Lord of the Treasury had not then the importance and dignity which now belong to it.   When there was a Lord Treasurer, that great officer was generally prime minister : but, when the white staff was in commission, the chief commissioner hardly ranked so high as a Secretary of State.   It was not till the time of Walpole that the First Lord of the Treasury became, under a humbler name, all that the Lord High Treasurer had been.

Godolphin had been bred a page at Whitehall, and had early acquired all the flexibility and the selfpossession of a veteran courtier. **Sidney Godolphin** He was laborious, clearheaded, and profoundly versed in the details of finance.   Every government, therefore, found him an useful servant ; and there was nothing in his opinions or in his character which could prevent him from serving any government. " Sidney Godolphin," said Charles, " is never in the way, and never out of the way."   This pointed remark goes far to explain Godolphin's extraordinary success in life.

He acted at different times with both the great political parties : but he never shared in the passions of either.   Like most men of cautious tempers and prosperous fortunes, he had a strong disposition to support whatever existed.   He disliked revolutions ; and, for the same reason for which he disliked revolutions, he disliked counterrevolutions.   His deportment was remarkably grave and reserved : but his personal tastes were low and frivolous ; and most of the time which he could save from public business was spent in racing, cardplaying, and cockfighting.   He now sate below Rochester at the Board of Treasury, and distinguished himself there by assiduity and intelligence.

Before the new Parliament was suffered to meet for the despatch of business a whole year elapsed, an eventful year, which has left lasting traces in our manners and language.   Never before had political controversy been carried on with so much freedom.   Never before had political clubs existed with so elaborate an organisation or so formidable an influence.   The one question of the Exclusion occupied the public mind.   All the presses and pulpits of the realm took part in the conflict. **Violence of factions on the subject of the Exclusion Bill** On one side it was maintained that the constitution and religion of the state could never be secure under a Popish King ; on the other, that the right of James to wear the crown in his turn was derived from God, and could not be annulled, even by the consent of all the branches of the legislature. . Every county, every town, every family, was in agitation. The civilities and hospitalities of neighbourhood were interrupted. The dearest ties of friendship and of blood were sundered. Even schoolboys were divided

LAWRENCE HYDE, EARL OF ROCHESTER

From a mezzotint by R. Williams, after the painting by Wissing

into angry parties ; and the Duke of York and the Earl of Shaftesbury had zealous adherents on all the forms of Westminster and Eton. The theatres shook with the roar of the contending factions. Pope Joan was brought on the stage by the zealous Protestants. Pensioned poets filled their prologues and epilogues with eulogies on the King and the Duke. The malecontents besieged the throne with petitions, demanding that Parliament might be forthwith convened. The loyalists sent up addresses, expressing the utmost abhorrence of all who presumed to dictate to the sovereign. The citizens of London assembled by tens of thousands to burn the Pope in effigy. The government posted cavalry at Temple Bar, and placed ordnance round Whitehall. In that year our tongue was enriched with two words, Mob and Sham, remarkable memorials of a season of tumult and imposture.[1] Opponents of the court were called Birminghams, Petitioners, and Exclusionists. Those who took the King's side were Antibirminghams, Abhorrers, and Tantivies. These appellations soon become obsolete: but at this time were first

Names of Whig and Tory heard two nicknames which, though originally given in insult, were soon assumed with pride, which are still in daily use, which have spread as widely as the English race, and which will last as long as the English literature. It is a curious circumstance that one of these nicknames was of Scotch, and the other of Irish, origin. Both in Scotland and in Ireland, misgovernment had called into existence bands of desperate men whose ferocity was heightened by religious enthusiasm. In Scotland some of the persecuted Covenanters, driven mad by oppression, had lately murdered the Primate, had taken arms against the government, had obtained some advantages against the King's forces, and had not been put down till Monmouth, at the head of some troops from England, had routed them at Bothwell Bridge. These zealots were most numerous among the rustics of the western lowlands, who were vulgarly called Whigs. Thus the appellation of Whig was fastened on the Presbyterian zealots of Scotland, and was transferred to those English politicians who showed a disposition to oppose the court, and to treat Protestant Nonconformists with indulgence. The bogs of Ireland, at the same time, afforded a refuge to Popish outlaws, much resembling those who were afterwards known as Whiteboys. These men were then called Tories. The name of Tory was therefore given to Englishmen who refused to concur in excluding a Roman Catholic prince from the throne.

The rage of the hostile factions would have been sufficiently violent, if it had been left to itself. But it was studiously exasperated by the common enemy of both. Lewis still continued to bribe and flatter both the court and the opposition. He exhorted Charles to be firm: he exhorted James to raise a civil war in Scotland: he exhorted the Whigs not to flinch, and to rely with confidence on the protection of France.

Through all this agitation a discerning eye might have perceived

[1] North's Examen, 231. 574.

SIDNEY, EARL OF GODOLPHIN

From an engraving by Houbraken, after the portrait of Godolphin as Lord High Treasurer
by Sir G. Kneller

that the public opinion was gradually changing. The persecution of the Roman Catholics went on ; but convictions were no longer matters of course. A new brood of false witnesses, among whom a villain named Dangerfield was the most conspicuous, infested the courts : but the stories of these men, though better constructed than that of Oates, found less credit. Juries were no longer so easy of belief as during the panic which had followed the murder of Godfrey ; and Judges, who, while the popular frenzy was at the height, had been its most obsequious instruments, now ventured to express some part of what they had from the first thought.

At length, in October 1680, the Parliament met. The Whigs had so great a majority in the Commons that the Exclusion Bill went **Meeting of Parliament ; the Exclusion Bill passes the Commons** through all its stages there without difficulty. The King scarcely knew on what members of his own cabinet he could reckon. Hyde had been true to his Tory opinions, and had steadily supported the cause of hereditary monarchy. But Godolphin, anxious for quiet, and believing that quiet could be restored only by concession, wished the bill to pass. Sunderland, ever false, and ever shortsighted, unable to discern the signs of approaching reaction, and anxious to conciliate the party which he believed to be irresistible, determined to vote against the court. The Duchess of Portsmouth implored her royal lover not to rush headlong to destruction. If there were any point on which he had a scruple of conscience or of honour, it was the question of the succession ; but during some days it seemed that he would submit. He wavered, asked what sum the Commons would give him if he yielded, and suffered a negotiation to be opened with the leading Whigs. But a deep mutual distrust which had been many years growing, and which had been carefully nursed by the arts of France, made a treaty impossible. Neither side would place confidence in the other. The whole nation now looked with breathless anxiety to the House of Lords. The assemblage of peers was large. The King himself was present. The debate was long, earnest, and occasionally furious. Some hands were laid on the pommels of swords, in a manner which revived the recollection of the stormy Parliaments of Henry the Third and Richard the Second. Shaftesbury and Essex were joined by the treacherous Sunderland. But the genius of Halifax **Exclusion Bill rejected by the Lords** bore down all opposition. Deserted by his most important colleagues, and opposed to a crowd of able antagonists, he defended the cause of the Duke of York, in a succession of speeches which, many years later, were remembered as masterpieces of reasoning, of wit, and of eloquence. It is seldom that oratory changes votes. Yet the attestation of contemporaries leaves no doubt that, on this occasion, votes were changed by the oratory of Halifax. The

Bishops, true to their doctrines, supported the principle of hereditary right, and the bill was rejected by a great majority.[1]

The party which preponderated in the House of Commons, bitterly mortified by this defeat, found some consolation in shedding the blood of Roman Catholics. William Howard, Viscount Stafford, one of the unhappy men who had been accused of a share in the plot, was impeached; and on the testimony of Oates and of two other false witnesses, Dugdale and Turberville, was found guilty of high treason, and suffered death. But the circumstances of his trial and execution ought to have given an useful warning to the Whig leaders. A large and respectable minority of the House of Lords pronounced the prisoner not guilty. The multitude, which a few months before had received the dying declarations of Oates's victims with mockery and execrations, now loudly expressed a belief that Stafford was a murdered man. When he with his last breath protested his innocence, the cry was, "God bless you, my Lord! We believe you, my Lord." A judicious observer might easily have predicted that the blood then shed would shortly have blood.

Execution of Stafford

The King determined to try once more the experiment of a dissolution. A new Parliament was summoned to meet at Oxford, in March 1681. Since the days of the Plantagenets the Houses had constantly sat at Westminster, except when the plague was raging in the capital: but so extraordinary a conjuncture seemed to require extraordinary precautions. If the Parliament were held in its usual place of assembling, the House of Commons might declare itself permanent, and might call for aid on the magistrates and citizens of London. The trainbands might rise to defend Shaftesbury as they had risen forty years before to defend Pym and Hampden. The Guards might be overpowered, the palace forced, the King a prisoner in the hands of his mutinous subjects. At Oxford there was no such danger. The University was devoted to the crown; and the gentry of

General election of 1681

---

[1] A peer who was present has described the effect of Halifax's oratory in words which I will quote, because, though they have been long in print, they are probably known to few even of the most curious and diligent readers of history.

"Of powerful eloquence and great parts were the Duke's enemies who did assert the Bill; but a noble Lord appeared against it who, that day, in all the force of speech, in reason, in arguments of what could concern the public or the private interests of men, in honour, in conscience, in estate, did outdo himself and every other man; and in fine his conduct and his parts were both victorious, and by him all the wit and malice of that party was overthrown."

This passage is taken from a memoir of Henry Earl of Peterborough, in a volume entitled "Succinct Genealogies, by Robert Halstead," fol. 1685. The name of Halstead is fictitious. The real authors were the Earl of Peterborough himself and his chaplain. The book is extremely rare. Only twenty-four copies were printed, two of which are now in the British Museum. Of these two one belonged to George the Fourth, and the other to Mr. Grenville.

the neighbourhood were generally Tories. Here, therefore, the opposition had more reason than the King to apprehend violence.

The elections were sharply contested. The Whigs still composed a majority of the House of Commons : but it was plain that the Tory spirit was fast rising throughout the country. It should seem that the sagacious and versatile Shaftesbury ought to have foreseen the coming change, and to have consented to the compromise which the court offered : but he appears to have forgotten his old tactics. Instead of making dispositions which, in the worst event, would have secured his retreat, he took up a position in which it was necessary that he should either conquer or perish. Perhaps his head, strong as it was, had been turned by popularity, by success, and by the excitement of conflict. Perhaps he had spurred his party till he could no longer curb it, and was really hurried on headlong by those whom he seemed to guide.

The eventful day arrived. The meeting at Oxford resembled rather that of a Polish Diet than that of an English Parliament. The Whig **Parliament held at Oxford, and dissolved** members were escorted by great numbers of their armed and mounted tenants and serving men, who exchanged looks of defiance with the royal Guards. The slightest provocation might, under such circumstances, have produced a civil war ; but neither side dared to strike the first blow. The King again offered to consent to anything but the Exclusion Bill. The Commons were determined to accept nothing but the Exclusion Bill. In a few days the Parliament was again dissolved.

The King had triumphed. The reaction, which had begun some months before the meeting of the Houses at Oxford, now went rapidly **Tory reaction** on. The nation, indeed, was still hostile to Popery : but, when men reviewed the whole history of the plot, they felt that their Protestant zeal had hurried them into folly and crime, and could scarcely believe that they had been induced by nursery tales to clamour for the blood of fellow subjects and fellow Christians. The most loyal, indeed, could not deny that the administration of Charles had often been highly blamable. But men who had not the full information which we possess touching his dealings with France, and who were disgusted by the violence of the Whigs, enumerated the large concessions which, during the last few years, he had made to his Parliaments, and the still larger concessions which he had declared himself willing to make. He had consented to the laws which excluded Roman Catholics from the House of Lords, from the Privy Council, and from all civil and military offices. He had passed the Habeas Corpus Act. If securities yet stronger had not been provided against the dangers to which the constitution and the Church might be exposed under a Roman Catholic sovereign, the fault lay, not with Charles who had invited the

Englands Mercy Explained in the Iust Execcution of
William (late) Viscount Stafford a Traytor to his King and Cuntry.

Repent ô Stafford ere y̆ blow be given
See yf there be found noe Rome for them Heads

Viscount Stafford.

THE EXECUTION OF VISCOUNT STAFFORD, DECEMBER 20, 1680

From a broadside in the possession of the Editor

Parliament to propose such securities, but with those Whigs who had refused to hear of any substitute for the Exclusion Bill.   One thing only had the King denied to his people.   He had refused to take away his brother's birthright.   And was there not good reason to believe that this refusal was prompted by laudable feelings?   What selfish motive could faction itself impute to the royal mind?   The Exclusion Bill did not curtail the reigning King's prerogatives, or diminish his income.   Indeed, by passing it, he might easily have obtained an ample addition to his own revenue.   And what was it to him who ruled after him?   Nay, if he had personal predilections, they were known to be rather in favour of the Duke of Monmouth than of the Duke of York.   The most natural explanation of the King's conduct seemed to be that, careless as was his temper and loose as were his morals, he had, on this occasion, acted from a sense of duty and honour.   And, if so, would the nation compel him to do what he thought criminal and disgraceful?   To apply, even by strictly constitutional means, a violent pressure to his conscience, seemed to zealous Royalists ungenerous and undutiful.   But strictly constitutional means were not the only means which the Whigs were disposed to employ.   Signs were already discernible which portended the approach of great troubles.   Men, who, in the time of the civil war and of the Commonwealth, had acquired an odious notoriety, had emerged from the obscurity in which, after the Restoration, they had hidden themselves from the general hatred, showed their confident and busy faces everywhere, and appeared to anticipate a second reign of the Saints.   Another Naseby, another High Court of Justice, another usurper on the throne, the Lords again ejected from their hall by violence, the Universities again purged, the Church again robbed and persecuted, the Puritans again dominant, to such results did the desperate policy of the opposition seem to tend.

Strongly moved by these apprehensions, the majority of the upper and middle classes hastened to rally round the throne.   The situation of the King bore, at this time, a great resemblance to that in which his father stood just after the Remonstrance had been voted.   But the reaction of 1641 had not been suffered to run its course.   Charles the First, at the very moment when his people, long estranged, were returning to him with hearts disposed to reconciliation, had, by a perfidious violation of the fundamental laws of the realm, forfeited their confidence for ever.   Had Charles the Second taken a similar course, had he arrested the Whig leaders in an irregular manner, had he impeached them of high treason before a tribunal which had no legal jurisdiction over them, it is highly probable that they would speedily have regained the ascendency which they had lost.   Fortunately for himself he was induced, at this crisis, to adopt a policy singularly judicious.   He

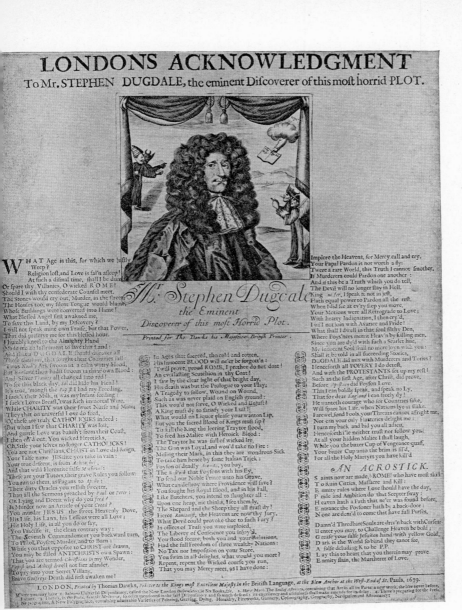

LONDON'S ACKNOWLEDGMENT TO MR. STEPHEN DUGDALE

From a broadside in the Sutherland Collection

determined to conform to the law, but at the same time to make vigorous and unsparing use of the law against his adversaries. He was not bound to convoke a Parliament till three years should have elapsed. He was not much distressed for money. The produce of the taxes which had been settled on him for life exceeded the estimate. He was at peace with all the world. He could retrench his expenses by giving up the costly and useless settlement of Tangier; and he might hope for pecuniary aid from France. He had, therefore, ample time and means for a systematic attack on the opposition under the forms of the constitution. The Judges were removable at his pleasure: the juries were nominated by the Sheriffs; and, in almost all the counties of England, the Sheriffs were nominated by himself. Witnesses, of the same class with those who had recently sworn away the lives of Papists, were ready to swear away the lives of Whigs.

The first victim was College, a noisy and violent demagogue of mean birth and education. He was by trade a joiner, and was cele-
Persecution of the Whigs brated as the inventor of the Protestant flail.[1] He had been at Oxford when the Parliament sate there, and was accused of having planned a rising and an attack on the King's guards. Evidence was given against him by Dugdale and Turberville, the same infamous men who had, a few months earlier, borne false witness against Stafford. In the sight of a jury of country squires no Exclusionist was likely to find favour. College was convicted. The crowd which filled the court house of Oxford received the verdict with a roar of exultation, as barbarous as that which he and his friends had been in the habit of raising when innocent Papists were doomed to the gallows. His execution was the beginning of a new judicial massacre, not less atrocious than that in which he had himself borne a share.

The government, emboldened by this first victory, now aimed a blow at an enemy of a very different class. It was resolved that Shaftesbury should be brought to trial for his life. Evidence was collected which, it was thought, would support a charge of treason. But the facts which it was necessary to prove were alleged to have been committed in London. The Sheriffs of London, chosen by the citizens, were zealous Whigs. They named a Whig grand jury, which threw out the bill. This defeat, far from discouraging those who advised the King, suggested
Charter of the City confiscated to them a new and daring scheme. Since the charter of the capital was in their way, that charter must be annulled. It was pretended, therefore, that the City had by some irregularities forfeited its municipal privileges; and proceedings were instituted

[1] This is mentioned in the curious work entitled " Ragguaglio della solenne Comparsa fatta in Roma gli otto di Gennaio, 1687, dall' illustrissimo et eccellentissimo signor Conte di Castlemaine."

against the corporation in the Court of King's Bench. At the same time those laws which had, soon after the Restoration, been enacted against Nonconformists, and which had remained dormant during the ascendency of the Whigs, were enforced all over the kingdom with extreme rigour.

By Irish Oaths, & wrested Law I fell,
A prey to Rome, a Sacrifice to Hell
My bleeding Innocence, for Iustice cryes
Heare, Heare, O Heaven for man my suit denyes.

Stephen College.

STEPHEN COLLEGE

From an engraving in the Sutherland Collection

Yet the spirit of the Whigs was not subdued. Though in evil plight, they were still a numerous and powerful party; and, as they mustered strong in the large towns, and especially in the capital, they made a noise and a show more than proportioned

Whig conspiracies

to their real force.   Animated by the recollection of past triumphs, and
by the sense of present oppression, they overrated both their strength
and their wrongs.   It was not in their power to make out that clear
and overwhelming case which can alone justify so violent a remedy as
resistance to an established government.   Whatever they might suspect,
they could not prove that their sovereign had entered into a treaty with
France against the religion and liberties of England.   What was
apparent was not sufficient to warrant an appeal to the sword.   If the
Lords had thrown out the Exclusion Bill, they had thrown it out in the
exercise of a right coeval with the constitution.   If the King had
dissolved the Oxford Parliament, he had done so by virtue of a prerogative which had never been questioned.   If he had, since the dissolution,
done some harsh things, still those things were in strict conformity with
the letter of the law, and with the recent practice of the malecontents
themselves.   If he had prosecuted his opponents, he had prosecuted
them according to the proper forms, and before the proper tribunals.
The evidence now produced for the crown was at least as worthy of
credit as the evidence on which the noblest blood of England had lately
been shed by the opposition.   The treatment which an accused Whig
had now to expect from judges, advocates, sheriffs, juries, and spectators,
was no worse than the treatment which had lately been thought by the
Whigs good enough for an accused Papist.   If the privileges of the
City of London were attacked, they were attacked, not by military
violence or by any disputable exercise of prerogative, but according to
the regular practice of Westminster Hall.   No tax was imposed by
royal authority.   No law was suspended.   The Habeas Corpus Act was
respected.   Even the Test Act was enforced.   The opposition therefore
could not bring home to the King that species of misgovernment which
alone could justify insurrection.   And, even had his misgovernment been
more flagrant than it was, insurrection would still have been criminal,
because it was almost certain to be unsuccessful.   The situation of the
Whigs in 1682 differed widely from that of the Roundheads forty years
before.   Those who took up arms against Charles the First acted under
the authority of a Parliament which had been legally assembled, and
which could not, without its own consent, be legally dissolved.   The
opponents of Charles the Second were private men.   Almost all the
military and naval resources of the kingdom had been at the disposal of
those who resisted Charles the First.   All the military and naval
resources of the kingdom were at the disposal of Charles the Second.
The House of Commons had been supported by at least half the nation
against Charles the First.   But those who were disposed to levy war
against Charles the Second were certainly a minority.   It could hardly
be doubted, therefore, that, if they attempted a rising, they would fail.

Still less could it be doubted that their failure would aggravate every evil of which they complained. The true policy of the Whigs was to submit with patience to adversity which was the natural consequence and the just punishment of their errors, to wait patiently for that turn of public feeling which must inevitably come, to observe the law, and to avail themselves of the protection, imperfect indeed, but by no means nugatory, which the law afforded to innocence. Unhappily they took a very different course. Unscrupulous and hotheaded chiefs of the party

MEDAL CELEBRATING THE ACQUITTAL OF THE EARL OF SHAFTESBURY

With explanatory lines from Dryden's poem entitled "The Medal"

Never did art so well with nature strive,
Nor ever idol seemed so much alive ;
So like the man, so golden to the sight,
So base within, so counterfeit and light.
One side is filled with title and with face ;
And, lest the King should want a regal place,
On the reverse a Tower the town surveys,
O'er which our mounting sun his beams displays.
The word, pronounced aloud by shrieval voice,
Laetamur, which in Polish is *rejoice*,
The day, month, year, to the great act are joined,
And a new canting holiday designed.

formed and discussed schemes of resistance, and were heard, if not with approbation, yet with the show of acquiescence, by much better men than themselves. It was proposed that there should be simultaneous insurrections in London, in Cheshire, at Bristol, and at Newcastle. Communications were opened with the discontented Presbyterians of Scotland, who were suffering under a tyranny such as England, in the worst times, had never known. While the leaders of the opposition thus revolved plans of open rebellion, but were still restrained by fears or scruples from taking any decisive step, a design of a very different kind was meditated by some of their accomplices. To fierce spirits, unrestrained by principle, or maddened by fanaticism, it seemed that to waylay and murder the King and his brother was the shortest and surest way of vindicating the Protestant religion and the liberties of England. A place and a time were named ; and the details of the butchery were frequently discussed, if not definitely arranged. This scheme was known but to few, and was concealed with especial care from the upright and humane Russell, and from Monmouth, who, though not a man of delicate conscience, would have recoiled with horror from the guilt of parricide. Thus there were two plots, one within the other. The object of the great Whig plot was to raise the nation in arms against the government. The lesser plot, commonly called the Rye House Plot, in which only a few desperate men were concerned, had for its object the assassination of the King and of the heir presumptive.

Both plots were soon discovered. Cowardly traitors hastened to save themselves, by divulging all, and more than all, that had passed in the deliberations of the party. That only a small minority of those who meditated resistance had admitted into their minds the thought of assassination is fully established : but, as the two conspiracies ran into each other, it was not difficult for the government to confound them together. The just indignation excited by the Rye House Plot was extended for a time to the whole Whig body. The King was now at liberty to exact full vengeance for years of restraint and humiliation. Shaftesbury, indeed, had escaped the fate which his manifold perfidy had well deserved. He had seen that the ruin of his party was at hand, had in vain endeavoured to make his peace with the royal brothers, had fled to Holland, and had died there, under the generous protection of a government which he had cruelly wronged. Monmouth threw himself at his father's feet and found mercy, but soon gave new offence, and thought it prudent to go into voluntary exile. Essex perished by his own hand in the Tower. Russell, who appears to have been guilty of no offence falling within the definition of high treason, and Sidney, of whose guilt no legal evidence could be produced, were beheaded in defiance of law and justice. Russell died with the fortitude of a Christian, Sidney with the fortitude of a Stoic. Some active politicians of meaner rank were sent to the gallows. Many quitted the country. Numerous prosecutions for misprision of treason, for libel, and for conspiracy were instituted. Convictions were obtained without difficulty from Tory juries, and rigorous punishments were inflicted by courtly judges. With these criminal proceedings were joined civil proceedings scarcely less formidable. Actions were brought against persons who had defamed the Duke of York ; and damages tantamount to a sentence of perpetual imprisonment were demanded by the plaintiff, and without

Detection of the Whig conspiracies

Severity of the government

difficulty obtained. The Court of King's Bench pronounced that the franchises of the City of London were forfeited to the crown. Flushed with this great victory, the government proceeded to attack **Seizure of** the constitutions of other corporations which were governed **charters** by Whig officers, and which had been in the habit of returning Whig members to Parliament. Borough after borough was compelled to surrender its privileges; and new charters were granted which gave the ascendency everywhere to the Tories.

SATIRICAL PORTRAIT OF CHARLES II

Number 1148 in the British Museum Catalogue of Satirical Prints

These proceedings, however reprehensible, had yet the semblance of legality. They were also accompanied by an act intended to quiet the uneasiness with which many loyal men looked forward to the accession of a Popish sovereign. The Lady Anne, younger daughter of the Duke of York by his first wife, was married to George, a prince of the orthodox House of Denmark. The Tory gentry and clergy might now flatter themselves that the Church of England had been effectually secured without any violation of the order of succession. The King and the heir presumptive were nearly of the same age. Both were approaching the decline of life. The King's health was good. It was therefore probable that James, if he ever came to the throne, would

ALGERNON SIDNEY

From the painting by Van Egmont in the National Portrait Gallery

BALLAD ON THE EXECUTION OF WILLIAM, LORD RUSSELL

From the Pepysian Collection of Ballads

have but a short reign.   Beyond his reign there was the gratifying prospect of a long series of Protestant sovereigns.

The liberty of unlicensed printing was of little or no use to the vanquished party ; for the temper of judges and juries was such that no writer whom the government prosecuted for a libel had any chance of escaping.   The dread of punishment therefore did all that a censorship could have done.   Meanwhile, the pulpits resounded with harangues against the sin of rebellion.   The treatises in which Filmer maintained that hereditary despotism was the form of government ordained by God, and that limited monarchy was a pernicious absurdity, had recently appeared, and had been favourably received by a large section of the Tory party.   The University of Oxford, on the very day on which Russell was put to death, adopted by a solemn public act these strange doctrines, and ordered the political works of Buchanan, Milton, and Baxter to be publicly burned in the court of the Schools.

Thus emboldened, the King at length ventured to overstep the bounds which he had during some years observed, and to violate the plain letter of the law.   The law was that not more than three years should pass between the dissolving of one Parliament and the convoking of another.   But, when three years had elapsed after the dissolution of the Parliament which sate at Oxford, no writs were issued for an election.   This infraction of the constitution was the more reprehensible, because the King had little reason to fear a meeting with a new House of Commons.   The counties were generally on his side ; and many boroughs in which the Whigs had lately held sway had been so remodelled that they were certain to return none but courtiers.

In a short time the law was again violated in order to gratify the Duke of York.   That prince was, partly on account of his religion, *Influence of the Duke of York* and partly on account of the sternness and harshness of his nature, so unpopular that it had been thought necessary to keep him out of sight while the Exclusion Bill was before Parliament, lest his appearance should give an advantage to the party which was struggling to deprive him of his birthright.   He had therefore been sent to govern Scotland, where the savage old tyrant Lauderdale was sinking into the grave.   Even Lauderdale was now outdone. The administration of James was marked by odious laws, by barbarous punishments, and by judgments to the iniquity of which even that age furnished no parallel.   The Scottish Privy Council had power to put state prisoners to the question.   But the sight was so dreadful that, as soon as the boots appeared, even the most servile and hard-hearted courtiers hastened out of the chamber.   The board was sometimes quite deserted : and it was at length found necessary to make an order that the members should keep their seats on such occasions. The Duke of York, it was remarked, seemed to take pleasure in the spectacle which some of the worst men then living were unable to contemplate without pity and horror. He not only came to Council when the torture was

JOHN, DUKE OF LAUDERDALE, IN OLD AGE

From a mezzotint by I. Beckett, after the painting by Riley

to be inflicted, but watched the agonies of the sufferers with that sort of interest and complacency with which men observe a curious experiment in science. Thus he employed himself at Edinburgh, till the event of the conflict between the court and the Whigs was no longer doubtful.

He then returned to England : but he was still excluded by the Test Act from all public employment ; nor did the King at first think it safe to violate a statute which the great majority of his most loyal subjects regarded as one of the chief securities of their religion and of their civil rights. When, however, it appeared, from a succession of trials, that the nation had patience to endure almost anything that the government had courage to do, Charles ventured to dispense with the law in his brother's favour. The Duke again took his seat in the Council, and resumed the direction of naval affairs.

These breaches of the constitution excited, it is true, some murmurs among the moderate Tories, and were not unanimously approved even by the King's ministers. Halifax in particular, now a Marquess and Lord Privy Seal, had, from the very day on which the Tories had by his help gained the ascendant, begun to turn Whig. As soon as the Exclusion Bill had been thrown out, he had pressed the House of Lords to make provision against the danger to which, in the next reign, the liberties and religion of the nation might be exposed. He now saw with alarm the violence of that reaction which was, in no small measure, his own work. He did not try to conceal the scorn which he felt for the servile doctrines of the University of Oxford. He detested the French alliance. He disapproved of the long intermission of Parliaments. He regretted the severity with which the vanquished party was treated. He who, when the Whigs were predominant, had ventured to pronounce Stafford not guilty, ventured, when they were vanquished and helpless, to intercede for Russell. At one of the last councils which Charles held a remarkable scene took place. The charter of Massachusetts had been forfeited. A question arose how, for the future, the colony should be governed. The general opinion of the board was that the whole power, legislative as well as executive, should abide in the crown. Halifax took the opposite side, and argued with great energy against absolute monarchy, and in favour of representative government. It was vain, he said, to think that a population, sprung from the English stock, and animated by English feelings, would long bear to be deprived of English institutions. Life, he exclaimed, would not be worth having in a country where liberty and property were at the mercy of one despotic master. The Duke of York was greatly incensed by this language, and represented to his brother the danger of retaining in office a man who appeared to be infected with all the worst notions of Marvell and Sidney.

Some modern writers have blamed Halifax for continuing in the ministry while he disapproved of the manner in which both domestic and foreign affairs were conducted. But this censure is unjust. Indeed it is to be remarked that the word ministry, in the sense in which we

He is opposed by Halifax

use it, was then unknown.[1]   The thing itself did not exist ; for it belongs
to an age in which parliamentary government is fully established.   At
present the chief servants of the crown form one body.   They are under-

JAMES, DUKE OF YORK, IN 1684

From a mezzotint by J. Verkolje, after a painting by Sir G. Kneller

stood to be on terms of friendly confidence with each other, and to agree
as to the main principles on which the executive administration ought

[1] North's Examen, 69.

to be conducted.   If a slight difference of opinion arises among them, it is easily compromised : but, if one of them differs from the rest on a vital point, it is his duty to resign.   While he retains his office, he is held responsible even for steps which he has tried to dissuade his colleagues from taking.   In the seventeenth century, the heads of the various branches of the administration were bound together in no such partnership.   Each of them was accountable for his own acts, for the use which he made of his own official seal, for the documents which he signed, for the counsel which he gave to the King.   No statesman was held answerable for what he had not himself done, or induced others to do.   If he took care not to be the agent in what was wrong, and if, when consulted, he recommended what was right, he was blameless.   It would have been thought strange scrupulosity in him to quit his post, because his advice as to matters not strictly within his own department was not taken by his master ; to leave the Board of Admiralty, for example, because the finances were in disorder, or the Board of Treasury because the foreign relations of the kingdom were in an unsatisfactory state. It was, therefore, by no means unusual to see in high office, at the same time, men who avowedly differed from one another as widely as ever Pulteney differed from Walpole, or Fox from Pitt.

The moderate and constitutional counsels of Halifax were timidly and feebly seconded by Francis North, Lord Guildford, who had lately **Lord** been made Keeper of the Great Seal.   The character of **Guildford** Guildford has been drawn at full length by his brother Roger North, a most intolerant Tory, a most affected and pedantic writer, but a vigilant observer of all those minute circumstances which throw light on the dispositions of men.   It is remarkable that the biographer, though he was under the influence of the strongest fraternal partiality, and though he was evidently anxious to produce a flattering likeness, was unable to portray the Lord Keeper otherwise than as the most ignoble of mankind. Yet the intellect of Guildford was clear, his industry great, his proficiency in letters and science respectable, and his legal learning more than respectable.   His faults were selfishness, cowardice, and meanness.   He was not insensible to the power of female beauty, nor averse from excess in wine.   Yet neither wine nor beauty could ever seduce the cautious and frugal libertine, even in his earliest youth, into one fit of indiscreet generosity.   Though of noble descent, he rose in his profession by paying ignominious homage to all who possessed influence in the courts.   He became Chief Justice of the Common Pleas, and as such was party to some of the foulest judicial murders recorded in our history.   He had sense enough to perceive from the first that Oates and Bedloe were impostors : but the Parliament and the country were greatly excited : the government had yielded to the pressure ; and North was not a man

FRANCIS NORTH, LORD GUILDFORD

From an engraving by D. Loggan

to risk a good place for the sake of justice and humanity.   Accordingly, while he was in secret drawing up a refutation of the whole romance of the Popish plot, he declared in public that the truth of the story was as plain as the sun in heaven, and was not ashamed to browbeat, from the seat of judgment, the unfortunate Roman Catholics who were arraigned before him for their lives.   He had at length reached the highest post in the law.   But a lawyer, who, after many years devoted to professional labour, engages in politics for the first time at an advanced period of life, seldom distinguishes himself as a statesman ; and Guildford was no exception to the general rule.   He was indeed so sensible of his deficiencies that he never attended the meetings of his colleagues on foreign affairs.   Even on questions relating to his own profession his opinion had less weight at the Council board than that of any man who has ever held the Great Seal.   Such as his influence was, however, he used it, as far as he dared, on the side of the laws.

The chief opponent of Halifax was Lawrence Hyde, who had recently been created Earl of Rochester.   Of all Tories, Rochester was the most intolerant and uncompromising.   The moderate members of his party complained that the whole patronage of the Treasury, while he was First Commissioner there, went to noisy zealots, whose only claim to promotion was that they were always drinking confusion to Whiggery, and lighting bonfires to burn the Exclusion Bill.   The Duke of York, pleased with a spirit which so much resembled his own, supported his brother in law passionately and obstinately.

The attempts of the rival ministers to surmount and supplant each other kept the court in incessant agitation.   Halifax pressed the King to summon a Parliament, to grant a general amnesty, to deprive the Duke of York of all share in the government, to recall Monmouth from banishment, to break with Lewis, and to form a close union with Holland on the principles of the Triple Alliance.   The Duke of York, on the other hand, dreaded the meeting of a Parliament, regarded the vanquished Whigs with undiminished hatred, still flattered himself that the design formed fourteen years before at Dover might be accomplished, daily represented to his brother the impropriety of suffering one who was at heart a Republican to hold the Privy Seal, and strongly recommended Rochester for the great place of Lord Treasurer.

While the two factions were struggling, Godolphin, cautious, silent, and laborious, observed a neutrality between them.   Sunderland, with his usual restless perfidy, intrigued against them both.   He had been turned out of office in disgrace for having voted in favour of the Exclusion Bill, but had made his peace by employing the good offices of the Duchess of Portsmouth and by cringing to the Duke of York, and was once more Secretary of State.

Nor was Lewis negligent or inactive. Everything at that moment favoured his designs. He had nothing to apprehend from the German empire, which was then contending against the Turks on the **Policy of** Danube. Holland could not, unsupported, venture to oppose **Lewis** him. He was therefore at liberty to indulge his ambition and insolence

MEDALS COMMEMORATING THE DUKE OF YORK'S VICTORY AT LOWESTOFT AND HIS MARRIAGE TO MARY OF MODENA

without restraint. He seized Strasburg, Courtray, Luxemburg. He exacted from the republic of Genoa the most humiliating submissions. The power of France at that time reached a higher point than it ever before or ever after attained, during the ten centuries which separated the reign of Charlemagne from the reign of Napoleon. It was not easy to say where her acquisitions would stop, if only England could be kept in a state of vassalage. The first object of the court of Versailles was therefore to prevent the calling of a Parliament and the reconciliation of English parties. For this end bribes, promises, and menaces were unsparingly employed. Charles was sometimes allured by the hope of a subsidy, and sometimes frightened by being told that, if he convoked the Houses, the secret articles of the treaty of Dover should be published. Several Privy Councillors were bought; and attempts were made to buy Halifax, but in vain. When he had been found incorruptible, all the art and influence of the French embassy were employed to drive him from office : but his polished wit and his various accomplishments had made him so agreeable to his master, that the design failed.[1]

Halifax was not content with standing on the defensive. He openly accused Rochester of malversation. An inquiry took place. It appeared that forty thousand pounds had been lost to the public by the mismanagement of the First Lord of the Treasury. In consequence of this discovery he was not only forced to relinquish his hopes of the white staff, but was removed from the direction of the finances to the more dignified but less lucrative and important post of Lord President. " I have seen people kicked down stairs," said Halifax ; " but my Lord Rochester is the first person that I ever saw kicked up stairs." Godolphin, now a peer, became First Commissioner of the Treasury.

Still, however, the contest continued. The event depended wholly on the will of Charles ; and Charles could not come to a decision. In his perplexity he promised everything to everybody. He would stand by France : he would break with France : he would never meet another Parliament : he would order writs for a Parliament to be issued without delay. He assured the Duke of York that Halifax should be dismissed from office, and Halifax that the Duke should be sent to Scotland. In public he affected implacable resentment against Monmouth, and in private conveyed to Monmouth assurances of unalterable affection. How long, if the King's life had been protracted, his hesitation would have lasted, and what would have been his resolve, can only be conjectured. Early in the year 1685, while hostile parties were anxiously awaiting his determination, he died, and a new scene opened. In a few months the

State of factions in the court of Charles at the time of his death

---

[1] Lord Preston, who was envoy at Paris, wrote thence to Halifax as follows :—" I find that your lordship lies still under the same misfortune of being no favourite to this court ; and Monsieur Barillon dare not do you the honour to shine upon you, since his master frowneth. They know very well your lordship's qualifications, which make them fear and consequently hate you ; and be assured, my lord, if all their strength can send you to Rufford, it shall be employed for that end. Two things, I hear, they particularly object against you, your secrecy, and your being incapable of being corrupted. Against these two things I know they have declared." The date of the letter is October 5. N. S. 1683.

excesses of the government obliterated the impression which had been made on the public mind by the excesses of the opposition. The violent reaction which had laid the Whig party prostrate was followed by a still more violent reaction in the opposite direction ; and signs not to be mistaken indicated that the great conflict between the prerogatives of the Crown and the privileges of the Parliament, was about to be brought to a final issue.

CHAPTER III

I INTEND, in this chapter, to give a description of the state in which England was at the time when the crown passed from Charles the Second to his brother. Such a description, composed from scanty and dispersed materials, must necessarily be very imperfect. Yet it may perhaps correct some false notions which would make the subsequent narrative unintelligible or uninstructive.

If we would study with profit the history of our ancestors, we must be constantly on our guard against that delusion which the well known names of families, places, and offices naturally produce, and must never forget that the country of which we read was a very different country from that in which we live. In every experimental science there is a tendency towards perfection. In every human being there is a wish to ameliorate his own condition. These two principles have often sufficed, even when counteracted by great public calamities and by bad institutions, to carry civilisation rapidly forward. No ordinary misfortune, no ordinary misgovernment, will do so much to make a nation wretched, as the constant progress of physical knowledge and the constant effort of every man to better himself will do to make a nation prosperous. It has often been found that profuse expenditure, heavy taxation, absurd commercial restrictions, corrupt tribunals, disastrous wars, seditions, persecutions, conflagrations, inundations, have not been able to destroy capital so fast as the exertions of private citizens have been able to create it. It can easily be proved that, in our own land, the national wealth has, during at least six centuries, been almost uninterruptedly increasing; that it was greater under the Tudors than under the Plantagenets; that it was greater under the Stuarts than under the Tudors; that, in spite of battles, sieges, and confiscations, it was greater on the day of the Restoration than on the day when the Long Parliament met; that, in spite of maladministration, of extravagance, of public bankruptcy, of two costly and unsuccessful wars, of the pestilence and of the fire, it was greater on the day of the death of Charles the Second than on the day of his Restoration. This progress, having continued during many ages, became at length, about the middle of the eighteenth century, portentously rapid, and has proceeded, during the nineteenth, with accelerated velocity.   In consequence partly of our geographical and partly of our moral position, we have, during several generations, been exempt from evils which have elsewhere impeded the efforts and

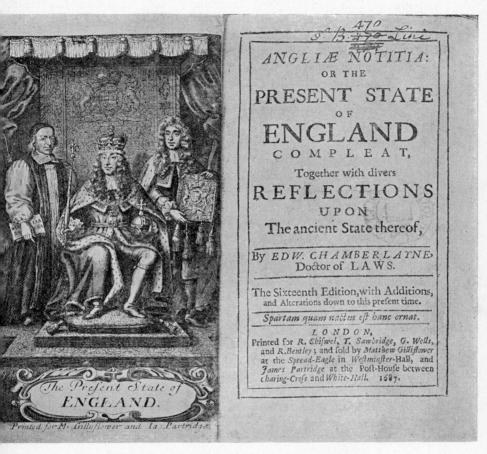

TITLE PAGE AND FRONTISPIECE OF CHAMBERLAYNE'S
PRESENT STATE OF ENGLAND, 1687

destroyed the fruits of industry.   While every part of the Continent, from Moscow to Lisbon, has been the theatre of bloody and devastating wars, no hostile standard has been seen here but as a trophy.   While revolutions have taken place all around us, our government has never once been subverted by violence.   During more than a hundred years there has been in our island no tumult of sufficient importance to be called an insurrection ; nor has the law been once borne down either by popular fury or by regal tyranny : public credit has been held sacred : the administration of justice has been pure : even in times which might by Englishmen be justly called evil times, we have enjoyed what almost every other nation in the world would have considered as an ample measure of civil and religious freedom.   Every man has felt entire confidence that the state would protect him in the possession of what had been earned by his diligence and hoarded by his selfdenial.   Under the benignant influence of peace and liberty, science has flourished, and has been applied to practical purposes on a scale never before known.

Great change in the state of England since 1685   The consequence is that a change to which the history of the old world furnishes no parallel has taken place in our country. Could the England of 1685 be, by some magical process, set before our eyes, we should not know one landscape in a hundred or one building in ten thousand.   The country gentleman would not recognise his own fields.   The inhabitant of the town would not recognise his own street.   Everything has been changed, but the great features of nature, and a few massive and durable works of human art.   We might find out Snowdon and Windermere, the Cheddar Cliffs and Beachy Head.   We might find out here and there a Norman minster, or a castle which witnessed the wars of the Roses.   But, with such rare exceptions, everything would be strange to us.   Many thousands of square miles which are now rich corn land and meadow, intersected by green hedgerows, and dotted with villages and pleasant country seats, would appear as moors overgrown with furze, or fens abandoned to wild ducks.   We should see straggling huts built of wood and covered with thatch, where we now see manufacturing towns and seaports renowned to the farthest ends of the world.   The capital itself would shrink to dimensions not much exceeding those of its present suburb on the south of the Thames.   Not less strange to us would be the garb and manners of the people, the furniture and the equipages, the interior of the shops and dwellings.   Such a change in the state of a nation seems to be at least as well entitled to the notice of a historian as any change of the dynasty or of the ministry.[1]

One of the first objects of an inquirer, who wishes to form a correct notion of the state of a community at a given time, must be to ascertain of how many persons that community then consisted.   Unfortunately the population of England in 1685 cannot be ascertained with

---

[1] During the interval which has elapsed since this chapter was written, England has continued to advance rapidly in material prosperity.   I have left my text nearly as it originally stood ; but I have added a few notes which may enable the reader to form some notion of the progress which has been made during the last nine years ; and, in general, I would desire him to remember that there is scarcely a district which is not more populous, or a source of wealth which is not more productive, at present than in 1848.   (1857.)

perfect accuracy.   For no great state had then adopted the wise course of periodically numbering the people.   All men were left to conjecture for themselves ; and, as they generally conjectured without **Population** examining facts, and under the influence of strong passions **of England** and prejudices, their guesses were often ludicrously absurd. **in 1685** Even intelligent Londoners ordinarily talked of London as containing several millions of souls.   It was confidently asserted by many that, during the thirty-five years which had elapsed between the accession of Charles the First and the Restoration, the population of the City had increased by two millions.[1]   Even while the ravages of the plague and fire were recent, it was the fashion to say that the capital still had a million and a half of inhabitants.[2]   Some persons, disgusted by these exaggerations, ran violently into the opposite extreme.   Thus Isaac Vossius, a man of undoubted parts and learning, strenuously maintained that there were only two millions of human beings in England, Scotland, and Ireland taken together.[3]

We are not, however, left without the means of correcting the wild blunders into which some minds were hurried by national vanity and others by a morbid love of paradox.   There are extant three computations which seem to be entitled to peculiar attention.   They are entirely independent of each other : they proceed on different principles ; and yet there is little difference in the results.

One of these computations was made in the year 1696 by Gregory King, Lancaster herald, a political arithmetician of great acuteness and judgment.   The basis of his calculations was the number of houses returned in 1690 by the officers who made the last collection of the hearth money.   The conclusion at which he arrived was that the population of England was nearly five millions and a half.[4]

About the same time King William the Third was desirous to ascertain the comparative strength of the religious sects into which the community was divided.   An inquiry was instituted ; and reports were laid before him from all the dioceses of the realm.   According to these reports the number of his English subjects must have been about five million two hundred thousand.[5]

---

[1] Observations on the Bills of Mortality, by Captain John Graunt (Sir William Petty), chap. xi.

[2]
"She doth comprehend
Full fifteen hundred thousand which do spend
Their days within."   Great Britain's Beauty, 1671.

[3] Isaac Vossius, De Magnitudine Urbium Sinarum, 1685.   Vossius, as we learn from Saint Evremond, talked on this subject oftener and longer than fashionable circles cared to listen.

[4] King's Natural and Political Observations, 1696.   This valuable treatise, which ought to be read as the author wrote it, and not as garbled by Davenant, will be found in some editions of Chalmers's Estimate.

[5] Dalrymple's Appendix to Part II. Book I.   The practice of reckoning the population by

Lastly, in our own days, Mr Finlaison, an actuary of eminent skill, subjected the ancient parochial registers of baptisms, marriages, and burials, to all the tests which the modern improvements in statistical science enabled him to apply. His opinion was, that, at the close of the seventeenth century, the population of England was a little under five million two hundred thousand souls.[1]

Of these three estimates, framed without concert by different persons from different sets of materials, the highest, which is that of King, does not exceed the lowest, which is that of Finlaison, by one twelfth. We may, therefore, with confidence pronounce that, when James the Second reigned, England contained between five million and five million five hundred thousand inhabitants. On the very highest supposition she then had less than one third of her present population, and less than three times the population which is now collected in her gigantic capital.

The increase of the people has been great in every part of the kingdom, but generally much greater in the northern than in the southern shires. In truth a large part of the country beyond Trent was, down to the eighteenth century, in a state of barbarism. Physical and moral causes had concurred to prevent civilisation from spreading to that region. The air was inclement; the soil was generally such as required skilful and industrious cultivation; and there could be little skill or industry in a tract which was often the theatre of war, and which, even when there was nominal peace, was constantly desolated by bands of Scottish marauders. Before the union of the two British crowns, and long after that union, there was as great a difference between Middlesex and Northumberland as there now is between Massachusetts and the settlements of those squatters who, far to the west of the Mississippi, administer a rude justice with the rifle and the dagger. In the reign of Charles the Second, the traces left by ages of slaughter and pillage were distinctly perceptible, many miles south of the Tweed, in the face of the country and in the lawless manners of the people. There was still a large class of mosstroopers, whose calling was to plunder dwellings and to drive away whole herds of cattle. It was found necessary, soon after the Restoration, to enact laws of great severity for the prevention of these outrages. The magistrates of Northumberland and Cumberland were authorised to raise bands of armed men for the defence of property and order; and provision was made for meeting the expense of these levies

Marginal note: Increase of population greater in the north than in the south

sects was long fashionable. Gulliver says of the King of Brobdingnag; " He laughed at my odd arithmetic, as he was pleased to call it, in reckoning the numbers of our people by a computation drawn from the several sects among us in religion and politics."

[1] Preface to the Population Returns of 1831.

GREAT
And Good NEWS to the
CHURCH OF ENGLAND:
Being the Exact NUMBERS of
CHURCH-MEN, DISSENTERS, And ROMANS,
In ENGLAND And WALES;

As they were given to the Late King *JAMES*, on the 3d day of *May*, 1688. From an Authentick *Calculation*; Wherein it appears, That the *Churchmen* are more in Number than *Romans* and *Diffenters* 2354727, (*Viz.*) Proteftants 179 to One *Roman*, Proteftants 23 to One *Diffenter*, Proteftants more than Both 102 to One.

Alfo is prefented to the World the 7 Bifhops SPEECH to King *JAMES*, and His *Anfwer* to the faid Speech. *With* Choice Obfervations *upon the* Bifhops Commitment *to the* Tower; *And alfo upon their* Deliverance out of *Prifon, Worthy the* Remark of all Good Chriftians.

Provinces	Proteftants,	Romans,	Diffenters.
Canterbury,	2123362.	11878.	93153.
York,	0353890.	01978.	15525.
Total of Each. ——	2477261.	13856.	108678.

Proteftants 179 to One Roman. Proteftants 23 to One Non-Con.
Proteftants more than Both Romans and Non-Cons, 2354727. which is 102 to One.

The Seven Bifhops *Speech to* King JAMES, on May 8. 1688. Concerning Reading the Declaration for Liberty of Confcience, in Churches.

May it pleafe Your Majefty, WE are not Averfe to the Reading Your MAJESTY's *Declaration* for Liberty of CONSCIENCE for fuch a Temper, as fhall be thought fit, when the Matter fhall come to be Confidered and Settled in Parliament and Convocation, The Declaration, being Founded upon fuch a Difpenfing Power, as may at Pleafure fet afide all Laws *Ecclefiaftical* and Civil, Appears to Us Illegal; and did fo in the *Parliaments* in 1662, and 72: And it is a Point of fuch Great Confequence, That We cannot fo far make Our Selves a **Party** to it as the Reading of it in the **Church** in the Time of Divine Service.

King JAMES's Anfwer. I *Have heard of This before, But could not Believe it, You look like* Trumpeters *of* Rebellion; *You aim at my* Prerogative, *But I will not lofe One Branch of it ;* Take Your Courfe, *and I will take* Mine; *My Commands fhall be Obeyed,* Deny it *at* Your Perils.

Note, Here follows Four moft Remarkable Providences, Worthy the Confideration of every True Son of the Church of England, which import that God Almighty of His infinite Wifdom and Goodnefs has frequently given his People peculiar Tokens to diftinguifh Good from Evil; more efpecially in difpofing Matters fo Agreeable to the Leffons, Epiftles, and Collects for thefe following Days which have been Attended with fuch Extraordinary Circumftances.

(four columns of small text regarding the four providences)

GOD Preferve the CHURCH of ENGLAND,
May No Sword Form'd againft It Ever Profper.

GOD fave the QUEEN.
AMEN.

Printed and Sold by the Bookfellers of *London,* and *Weftminfter.* MDCCV.

GREAT AND GOOD NEWS TO THE CHURCH OF ENGLAND

From a broadside in the Bodleian Library

by local taxation.[1] The parishes were required to keep bloodhounds for the purpose of hunting the freebooters. Many old men who were living in the middle of the eighteenth century could well remember the time when those ferocious dogs were common.[2] Yet, even with such auxiliaries, it was often found impossible to track the robbers to their retreats among the hills and morasses. For the geography of that wild country was very imperfectly known. Even after the accession of George the Third, the path over the fells from Borrowdale to Ravenglas was still a secret carefully kept by the dalesmen, some of whom had probably in their youth escaped from the pursuit of justice by that road.[3] The seats of the gentry and the larger farmhouses were fortified. Oxen were penned at night beneath the overhanging battlements of the residence, which was known by the name of the Peel. The inmates slept with arms at their sides. Huge stones and boiling water were in readiness to crush and scald the plunderer who might venture to assail the little garrison. No traveller ventured into that country without making his will. The Judges on circuit, with the whole body of barristers, attorneys, clerks, and serving men, rode on horseback from Newcastle to Carlisle, armed and escorted by a strong guard under the command of the Sheriffs. It was necessary to carry provisions ; for the country was a wilderness which afforded no supplies. The spot where the cavalcade halted to dine, under an immense oak, is not yet forgotten. The irregular vigour with which criminal justice was administered shocked observers whose lives had been passed in more tranquil districts. Juries, animated by hatred and by a sense of common danger, convicted housebreakers and cattle stealers with the promptitude of a court martial in a mutiny ; and the convicts were hurried by scores to the gallows.[4] Within the memory of some whom this generation has seen, the sportsman who wandered in pursuit of game to the sources of the Tyne found the heaths round Keeldar Castle peopled by a race scarcely less savage than the Indians of California, and heard with surprise the half naked women chaunting a wild measure, while the men with brandished dirks danced a war dance.[5]

Slowly and with difficulty peace was established on the border. In the train of peace came industry and all the arts of life. Meanwhile it was discovered that the regions north of the Trent possessed in their coal beds a source of wealth far more precious than the gold mines of Peru. It was found that, in the neighbourhood of these beds, almost

[1] Statutes 14 Car. II. c. 22. ; 18 & 19 Car. II. c. 3. ; 29 and 30 Car. II. c. 2.
[2] Nicholson and Bourne, Discourse on the Ancient State of the Border, 1777.
[3] Gray's Journal of a Tour in the Lakes, Oct. 3, 1769.
[4] North's Life of Guildford ; Hutchinson's History of Cumberland, Parish of Brampton.
[5] See Sir Walter Scott's Journal, Oct. 7, 1827, in his Life by Mr. Lockhart.

every manufacture might be most profitably carried on. A constant stream of emigrants began to roll northward. It appeared by the returns of 1841 that the ancient archiepiscopal province of York contained two sevenths of the population of England. At the time of the Revolution that province was believed to contain only one seventh of the population.[1] In Lancashire the number of inhabitants appears to have increased ninefold, while in Norfolk, Suffolk, and Northamptonshire it has hardly doubled.[2]

Of the taxation we can speak with more confidence and precision than of the population. The revenue of England, when Charles the Second died, was small, when compared with the resources **Revenue in** which she even then possessed, or with the sums which were **1685** raised by the governments of the neighbouring countries. It had, from the time of the Restoration, been almost constantly increasing: yet it was little more than three fourths of the revenue of the United Provinces, and was hardly one fifth of the revenue of France.

The most important head of receipt was the excise, which, in the last year of the reign of Charles, produced five hundred and eighty-five thousand pounds, clear of all deductions. The net proceeds of the customs amounted in the same year to five hundred and thirty thousand pounds. These burdens did not lie very heavy on the nation. The tax on chimneys, though less productive, called forth far louder murmurs. The discontent excited by direct imposts is, indeed, almost always out of proportion to the quantity of money which they bring into the Exchequer; and the tax on chimneys was, even among direct imposts, peculiarly odious: for it could be levied only by means of domiciliary visits; and of such visits the English have always been impatient to a degree which the people of other countries can but faintly conceive. The poorer householders were frequently unable to pay their hearth money to the day. When this happened, their furniture was distrained without mercy: for the tax was farmed; and a farmer of taxes is, of all creditors, proverbially the most rapacious. The collectors were loudly accused of performing their unpopular duty with harshness and insolence. It was said that, as soon as they appeared at the threshold of a cottage, the children began to wail, and the old women ran to hide their earthenware. Nay, the single bed of a poor family had sometimes been carried away and

---

[1] Dalrymple, Appendix to Part II. Book I. The returns of the hearth money lead to nearly the same conclusion. The hearths in the province of York were not a sixth of the hearths of England.

[2] I do not, of course, pretend to strict accuracy here; but I believe that whoever will take the trouble to compare the last returns of hearth money in the reign of William the Third with the census of 1841, will come to a conclusion not very different from mine.

sold. The net annual receipt from this tax was two hundred thousand pounds.[1]

When to the three great sources of income which have been mentioned we add the royal domains, then far more extensive than at present, the first fruits and tenths, which had not yet been surrendered to the Church, the Duchies of Cornwall and Lancaster, the forfeitures, and the fines, we shall find that the whole annual revenue of the crown may be fairly estimated at about fourteen hundred thousand pounds. Of this revenue part was hereditary: the rest had been granted to Charles for life ; and he was at liberty to lay out the whole exactly as he thought fit. Whatever he could save by retrenching from the expenditure of the public departments was an addition to his privy purse. Of the Post Office more will hereafter be said. The profits of that establishment had been appropriated by Parliament to the Duke of York.

The King's revenue was, or rather ought to have been, charged with the payment of about eighty thousand pounds a year, the interest of the sum fraudulently detained in the Exchequer by the Cabal. While Danby was at the head of the finances, the creditors had received dividends, though not with the strict punctuality of modern times : but those who had succeeded him at the Treasury had been less expert, or less solicitous to maintain public faith. Since the victory won by the court over the Whigs, not a farthing had been paid ; and no redress was granted to the sufferers, till a new dynasty had been many years on the throne. There can be no greater error than to imagine that the device

---

[1] There are in the Pepysian Library, some ballads of that age on the chimney money. I will give a specimen or two :—

> " The good old dames, whenever they the chimney man espied,
> Unto their nooks they haste away, their pots and pipkins hide.
> There is not one old dame in ten, and search the nation through,
> But, if you talk of chimney men, will spare a curse or two."

Again :

> " Like plundering soldiers they'd enter the door,
> And make a distress on the goods of the poor,
> While frighted poor children distractedly cried ;
> This nothing abated their insolent pride."

In the British Museum there are doggrel verses composed on the same subject and in the same spirit :

> " Or, if through poverty it be not paid,
> For cruelty to tear away the single bed,
> On which the poor man rests his weary head,
> At once deprives him of his rest and bread."

I take this opportunity, the first which occurs, of acknowledging most gratefully the kind and liberal manner in which the Master and Vicemaster of Magdalene College, Cambridge, gave me access to the valuable collections of Pepys.

Charles R.

MOst Reverend Father in God, We Greet you well: Whereas by an Act made by this present Parliament, in the fourteenth year of Our Reign, for Granting unto Us the Duty of two shillings upon every Fire-Hearth, Stove, &c. Entituled, *An Act for establishing an additional Revenue upon His Majesty, His Heirs, and Successors, for the better Support of His, and their Crown and Dignity.* It is provided and enacted, That if the Church-wardens and Overseers of the poor of any Parish, together with the Minister of the same, or any two of them (whereof the Minister to be one) shall in Writing under their Hands, yearly certifie their belief, that the House wherein any person doth inhabit, is not of greater value than twenty shillings *per annum*, upon the full improved Rent. And that neither the person so inhabiting, nor any other using the same Messuage, hath, useth, or occupieth any Lands or Tenements of their own, or others, of the yearly value of twenty shillings *per annum*, nor hath any Lands, Tenements, Goods, or Chattels of the value of ten pounds in their own possession, or in the possession of any other in trust for them; That then upon such Certificate made in such case to the two next Justices of the Peace, and allowed by them (for which Certificate and Allowance, no Fee shall be paid) the person in whose behalf such Certificate is made, shall not be returned by the Constable or other Officer. And the said House is thereby discharged of, and from all the Duties by the said Act imposed.

And whereas We are informed, That either through the ignorance of some persons in the Law in this behalf, or by partiality and favour, great number of undue Certificates are from time to time signed in all places of the Kingdom, by the respective Ministers, Vicars, and Curates of the places, and the Church-wardens and Overseers of the poor of the same, for persons not qualified, as the Law above recited doth require, to the great diminishing and detriment of Our said Revenue. Now to the end that some better care may be taken for the future in this matter; Our Will and Pleasure is, And We have thought fit hereby, to require you forthwith to write to the Right Reverend Fathers in God the Bishops of the several Dioceses within your Province of *Canterbury*, and by them and Me to be put in speedy Execution, to take effectual Order strictly to charge all Ministers, Parsons, Vicars, Curates, and Church-wardens within their respective Dioceses, to use all possible circumspection in the signing of any Certificates, and that they be well assured, that the persons for whom they do certifie, are in all respects qualified as the Law directs. And that they do not certifie for any other persons whatsoever: And you are also to take care, That the same charge be given to all Ministers, Parsons, Vicars, and Curates within your immediate Diocese of *Canterbury*. Given at our Court at *Whitehall* this fourth day of *November*, in the six and twentieth Year of our Reign, 1674.

To Our Right Trusty and Right Entirely Beloved
Cousin and Counsellor, the most Reverend Father
in God, G......r Archbishop of *Canterbury*, Primate
and Me..., ...n of all *England*.

By His Majesties Command,

Danby.

The Archbishop of CANTERBURY His Letter to each Bishop in His Province.

My very Good Lord,

THe inclosed contains a true Copy of His Majestie's Commands directed unto Me, to be Communicated to the Rest of my Brethren my Lords the Bishops of this Province of *Canterbury*, and by them and Me to be put in speedy Execution within Our Respective Jurisdictions. Upon Perusal thereof Your Lordship will be sufficiently informed of the Nature of the Business therein intended: And I doubt not but accordingly You will take Care that all Means possible be used to give punctual Satisfaction to His Majestie's Desire and Commands in each Particular: At least that your Lordship by your Chancellor, Arch-Deacon, Commissary, and other Inferiour Officers, will give such Intimation to the Clergy, and other Persons within your Diocess therein concerned, as is thereby required; To the End that all Occasion of Complaint in such Cases may cease, And that they may proceed therein with such Circumspection and Integrity, as by Law they ought; And by this Notice prevent that Trouble to themselves which will unavoidably ensue if they proceed in the contrary Practice for the future. I bid your Lordship heartily farewel, And am

My Lord,

Your Lordships Affectionate Friend and Brother,

GILBERT *Cant.*

Lambeth-House
Novemb. 12. 1674.

November 17. 1674.

FOr the more speedy Notice and Execution of His Majestie's Pleasure; Order and leave is given by the Archbishop of *Canterbury*, That these Letters be Printed.

LONDON, Printed *Anno Dom.* 1674.

PROCLAMATION CONCERNING THE PAYMENT OF CHIMNEY MONEY, 1674

From a broadside in the Bodleian Library

of meeting the exigencies of the state by loans was imported into our island by William the Third.   What really dates from his reign is not the system of borrowing, but the system of funding.   From a period of immemorial antiquity it had been the practice of every English government to contract debts.   What the Revolution introduced was the practice of honestly paying them.[1]

By plundering the public creditor, it was possible to make an income of about fourteen hundred thousand pounds, with some occasional help from Versailles, support the necessary charges of the government and the wasteful expenditure of the court.   For that load which pressed most heavily on the finances of the great continental states was here scarcely felt.   In France, Germany, and the Netherlands, armies, such as Henry the Fourth and Philip the Second had never employed in time of war, were kept up in the midst of peace.   Bastions and ravelins were everywhere rising, constructed on principles unknown to Parma and Spinola.   Stores of artillery and ammunition were accumulated, such as even Richelieu, whom the preceding generation had regarded as a worker of prodigies, would have pronounced fabulous.   No man could journey many leagues in those countries without hearing the drums of a regiment on march, or being challenged by the sentinels on the draw-

Military
system
bridge of a fortress.   In our island, on the contrary, it was possible to live long and to travel far, without being once reminded, by any martial sight or sound, that the defence of nations had become a science and a calling.   The majority of Englishmen who were under twenty-five years of age had probably never seen a company of regular soldiers.   Of the cities which, in the civil war, had valiantly repelled hostile armies, scarcely one was now capable of sustaining a siege.   The gates stood open night and day.   The ditches were dry. The ramparts had been suffered to fall into decay, or were repaired only that the townsfolk might have a pleasant walk on summer evenings. Of the old baronial keeps many had been shattered by the cannon of Fairfax and Cromwell, and lay in heaps of ruin, overgrown with ivy. Those which remained had lost their martial character, and were now rural palaces of the aristocracy.   The moats were turned into preserves of carp and pike.   The mounds were planted with fragrant shrubs, through which spiral walks ran up to summer houses adorned with mirrors and paintings.[2]   On the capes of the sea coast, and on many inland hills, were still seen tall posts, surmounted by barrels.   Once those barrels had been filled with pitch.   Watchmen had been set round

---

[1] My chief authorities for this financial statement will be found in the Commons' Journal, March 1. and March 20. 168⅞.

[2] See for example the picture of the mound at Marlborough, in Stukeley's Itinerarium Curiosum.

THE MOUNT AT MARLBOROUGH AND THE CASCADE AT WILTON

From Stukeley's Itinerarium Curiosum

them in seasons of danger ; and, within a few hours after a Spanish sail had been discovered in the Channel, or after a thousand Scottish moss-troopers had crossed the Tweed, the signal fires were blazing fifty miles off, and whole counties were rising in arms.   But many years had now elapsed since the beacons had been lighted ; and they were regarded rather as curious relics of ancient manners than as parts of a machinery necessary to the safety of the state.[1]

The only army which the law recognised was the militia.   That force had been remodelled by two Acts of Parliament passed shortly after the Restoration.   Every man who possessed five hundred pounds a year derived from land, or six thousand pounds of personal estate, was bound to provide, equip, and pay, at his own charge, one horseman. Every man who had fifty pounds a year derived from land, or six hundred pounds of personal estate, was charged in like manner with one pikeman or musketeer.   Smaller proprietors were joined together in a kind of society, for which our language does not afford a special name, but which an Athenian would have called a Synteleia ; and each society was required to furnish, according to its means, a horse soldier or a foot soldier.   The whole number of cavalry and infantry thus maintained was popularly estimated at a hundred and thirty thousand men.[2]

The King was, by the ancient constitution of the realm, and by the recent and solemn acknowledgment of both Houses of Parliament, the sole Captain General of this large force.   The Lords Lieutenants and their Deputies held the command under him, and appointed meetings for drilling and inspection.   The time occupied by such meetings, how-ever, was not to exceed fourteen days in one year.   The Justices of the Peace were authorised to inflict slight penalties for breaches of discipline. Of the ordinary cost no part was paid by the crown : but, when the trainbands were called out against an enemy, their subsistence became a charge on the general revenue of the state, and they were subject to the utmost rigour of martial law.

There were those who looked on the militia with no friendly eye. Men who had travelled much on the Continent, who had marvelled at the stern precision with which every sentinel moved and spoke in the citadels built by Vauban, who had seen the mighty armies which poured along all the roads of Germany to chase the Ottoman from the gates of Vienna, and who had been dazzled by the well ordered pomp of the household troops of Lewis, sneered much at the way in which the peasants of Devonshire and Yorkshire marched and wheeled, shouldered muskets and ported pikes.   The enemies of the liberties and religion

---

[1] Chamberlayne's State of England, 1684.
[2] 13 & 14 Car. II. c. 3 ; 15 Car. II. c. 4.   Chamberlayne's State of England, 1684.

of England looked with aversion on a force which could not, without extreme risk, be employed against those liberties and that religion, and missed no opportunity of throwing ridicule on the rustic soldiery.[1] Enlightened patriots, when they contrasted these rude levies with the battalions which, in time of war, a few hours might bring to the coast of Kent or Sussex, were forced to acknowledge that, dangerous as it might be to keep up a permanent military establishment, it might be more dangerous still to stake the honour and independence of the country on the result of a contest between ploughmen officered by Justices of the Peace, and veteran warriors led by Marshals of France. In Parliament, however, it was necessary to express such opinions with some reserve; for the militia was an institution eminently popular. Every reflection thrown on it excited the indignation of both the great parties in the state, and especially of that party which was distinguished by peculiar zeal for monarchy and for the Anglican Church. The array of the counties was commanded almost exclusively by Tory noblemen and gentlemen. They were proud of their military rank, and considered an insult offered to the service to which they belonged as offered to themselves. They were also perfectly aware that whatever was said against a militia was said in favour of a standing army; and the name of standing army was hateful to them. One such army had held dominion in England; and under that dominion the King had been murdered, the nobility degraded, the landed gentry plundered, the Church persecuted. There was scarcely a rural grandee who could not tell a story of wrongs and insults suffered by himself, or by his father, at the hands of the parliamentary soldiers. One old Cavalier had seen half his manor house blown up. The hereditary elms of another had been hewn down. A third could never go into his parish church without being reminded by the defaced scutcheons and headless statues of his ancestry, that Oliver's redcoats had once stabled their horses there. The consequence was that those very Royalists, who were most ready to fight for the King themselves, were the last persons whom he could venture to ask for the means of hiring regular troops.

---

[1] Dryden, in his Cymon and Iphigenia, expressed, with his usual keenness and energy, the sentiments which had been fashionable among the sycophants of James the Second :—

> " The country rings around with loud alarms,
> And raw in fields the rude militia swarms ;
> Mouths without hands, maintained at vast expense,
> In peace a charge, in war a weak defence.
> Stout once a month they march, a blustering band,
> And ever, but in time of need, at hand.
> This was the morn when, issuing on the guard,
> Drawn up in rank and file, they stood prepared
> Of seeming arms to make a short essay,
> Then hasten to be drunk, the business of the day."

Charles, however, had, a few months after his restoration, begun to form a small standing army. He felt that, without some better protection than that of the trainbands and beefeaters, his palace and person would hardly be secure, in the vicinity of a great city swarming with warlike Fifth Monarchy men who had just been disbanded. He therefore, careless and profuse as he was, contrived to spare from his pleasures a sum sufficient to keep up a body of guards. With the increase of trade and of public wealth his revenues increased; and he was thus enabled, in spite of the occasional murmurs of the Commons, to make gradual additions to his regular forces. One considerable addition was made a few months before the close of his reign. The costly, useless, and pestilential settlement of Tangier was abandoned to the barbarians who dwelt around it; and the garrison, consisting of one regiment of horse and two regiments of foot, was brought to England.

The little army formed by Charles the Second was the germ of that great and renowned army which has, in the present century, marched triumphant into Madrid and Paris, into Canton and Candahar. The Life Guards, who now form two regiments, were then distributed into three troops, each of which consisted of two hundred carabineers, exclusive of officers. This corps, to which the safety of the King and royal family was confided, had a very peculiar character. Even the privates were designated as gentlemen of the Guard. Many of them were of good families, and had held commissions in the civil war. Their pay was far higher than that of the most favoured regiment of our time, and would in that age have been thought a respectable provision for the younger son of a country squire. Their fine horses, their rich housings, their cuirasses, and their buff coats adorned with ribands, velvet, and gold lace, made a splendid appearance in Saint James's Park. A small body of grenadier dragoons, who came from a lower class and received lower pay, was attached to each troop. Another body of household cavalry distinguished by blue coats and cloaks, and still called the Blues, was generally quartered in the neighbourhood of the capital. Near the capital lay also the corps which is now designated as the first regiment of dragoons, but which was then the only regiment of dragoons on the English establishment. It had recently been formed out of the cavalry which had returned from Tangier. A single troop of dragoons, which did not form part of any regiment, was stationed near Berwick, for the purpose of keeping the peace among the mosstroopers of the border. For this species of service the dragoon was then thought to be peculiarly qualified. He has since become a mere horse soldier. But in the seventeenth century he was accurately described by Montecuculi as a foot soldier who used a horse only in order to arrive with more speed at the place where military service was to be performed.

1 The Governour House Prospect of ye Innerpart of Tangier, with the upper Castle. from South East. 6 + The Market place,
2 Peterborow Tower,   W. Hollar delineavit et fecit.
3 Head Court, ye Gate. 1.

VIEW OF TANGIERS

From an engraving by W. Hollar

The household infantry consisted of two regiments, which were then, as now, called the first regiment of Foot Guards, and the Coldstream Guards. They generally did duty near Whitehall and Saint James's Palace. As there were then no barracks, and as, by the Petition of Right, it had been declared unlawful to quarter soldiers on private families, the redcoats filled all the alehouses of Westminster and the Strand.

There were five other regiments of foot. One of these, called the Admiral's Regiment, was especially destined to service on board of the fleet. The remaining four still rank as the first four regiments of the line. Two of these represented two brigades which had long sustained on the Continent the fame of British valour. The first, or Royal regiment, had, under the great Gustavus, borne a conspicuous part in the deliverance of Germany. The third regiment, distinguished by fleshcoloured facings, from which it had derived the well known name of the Buffs, had, under Maurice of Nassau, fought not less bravely for the deliverance of the Netherlands. Both these gallant bands had at length, after many vicissitudes, been recalled from foreign service by Charles the Second, and had been placed on the English establishment.

The regiments which now rank as the second and fourth of the line had, in 1685, just returned from Tangier, bringing with them cruel and licentious habits contracted in a long course of warfare with the Moors. A few companies of infantry which had not been regimented lay in garrison at Tilbury Fort, at Portsmouth, at Plymouth, and at some other important stations on or near the coast.

Since the beginning of the seventeenth century a great change had taken place in the arms of the infantry. The pike had been gradually giving place to the musket; and, at the close of the reign of Charles the Second, most of his foot were musketeers. Still, however, there was a large intermixture of pikemen. Each class of troops was occasionally instructed in the use of the weapon which peculiarly belonged to the other class. Every foot soldier had at his side a sword for close fight. The musketeer was generally provided with a weapon which had, during many years, been gradually coming into use, and which the English then called a dagger, but which, from the time of William the Third, has been known among us by the French name of bayonet. The bayonet seems not to have been then so formidable an instrument of destruction as it has since become; for it was inserted in the muzzle of the gun; and in action much time was lost while the soldier unfixed his bayonet in order to fire, and fixed it again in order to charge. The dragoon, when dismounted, fought as a musketeer.

The regular army which was kept up in England at the beginning of the year 1685 consisted, all ranks included, of about seven thousand foot, and about seventeen hundred cavalry and dragoons. The whole

THE LIFE GUARDS

From Ogilby's Coronation of Charles II

charge amounted to about two hundred and ninety thousand pounds a year, less than a tenth part of what the military establishment of France then cost in time of peace. The daily pay of a private in the Life Guards was four shillings, in the Blues two shillings and sixpence, in the Dragoons eighteenpence, in the Foot Guards tenpence, and in the line eightpence. The discipline was lax, and indeed could not be otherwise. The common law of England knew nothing of courts martial, and made no distinction, in time of peace, between a soldier and any other subject ; nor could the government then venture to ask even the most loyal Parliament for a Mutiny Bill. A soldier, therefore, by knocking down his colonel, incurred only the ordinary penalties of assault and battery, and by refusing to obey orders, by sleeping on guard, or by deserting his colours, incurred no legal penalty at all. Military punishments were doubtless inflicted during the reign of Charles the Second; but they were inflicted very sparingly, and in such a manner as not to attract public notice, or to produce an appeal to the courts of Westminster Hall.

Such an army as has been described was not very likely to enslave five millions of Englishmen. It would indeed have been unable to suppress an insurrection in London, if the trainbands of the City had joined the insurgents. Nor could the King expect that, if a rising took place in England, he would obtain effectual help from his other dominions. For, though both Scotland and Ireland supported separate military establishments, those establishments were not more than sufficient to keep down the Puritan malecontents of the former kingdom, and the Popish malecontents of the latter. The government had, however, an important military resource which must not be left unnoticed. There were in the pay of the United Provinces six fine regiments, of which three had been raised in England and three in Scotland. Their native prince had reserved to himself the power of recalling them, if he needed their help against a foreign or domestic enemy. In the meantime they were maintained without any charge to him, and were kept under an excellent discipline, to which he could not have ventured to subject them.[1]

If the jealousy of the Parliament and of the nation made it impossible for the King to maintain a formidable standing army, no similar impediment prevented him from making England the first of maritime powers. Both Whigs and Tories were ready to applaud every step tending to increase the efficiency of that force which, while it was the best protection of the island against foreign

The navy

---

[1] Most of the materials which I have used for this account of the regular army will be found in the Historical Records of Regiments, published by command of King William the Fourth, and under the direction of the Adjutant General. See also Chamberlayne's State of England, 1684 ; Abridgment of the English Military Discipline, printed by especial command, 1685 ; Exercise of Foot, by their Majesties' command, 1690.

enemies, was powerless against civil liberty. All the greatest exploits achieved within the memory of that generation by English soldiers had been achieved in war against English princes. The victories of our sailors had been won over foreign foes, and had averted havoc and rapine from our own soil. By at least half the nation the battle of Naseby was remembered with horror, and the battle of Dunbar with pride chequered by many painful feelings: but the defeat of the Armada, and the encounters of Blake with the Hollanders and Spaniards, were recollected with unmixed exultation by all parties. Ever since the Restoration, the Commons, even when most discontented and most parsimonious, had always been bountiful to profusion where the interest of the navy was concerned. It had been represented to them, while Danby was minister, that many of the vessels in the royal fleet were old and unfit for sea; and, although the House was, at that time, in no giving mood, an aid of near six hundred thousand pounds had been granted for the building of thirty new men of war.

But the liberality of the nation had been made fruitless by the vices of the government. The list of the King's ships, it is true, looked well. There were nine first rates, fourteen second rates, thirty-nine third rates, and many smaller vessels. The first rates, indeed, were less than the third rates of our time; and the third rates would not now rank as very large frigates. This force, however, if it had been efficient, would in those days have been regarded by the greatest potentate as formidable. But it existed only on paper. When the reign of Charles terminated, his navy had sunk into degradation and decay, such as would be almost incredible if it were not certified to us by the independent and concurring evidence of witnesses whose authority is beyond exception. Pepys, the ablest man in the English Admiralty, drew up, in the year 1684, a memorial on the state of his department, for the information of Charles. A few months later Bonrepaux, the ablest man in the French Admiralty, having visited England for the especial purpose of ascertaining her maritime strength, laid the result of his inquiries before Lewis. The two reports are to the same effect. Bonrepaux declared that he found everything in disorder and in miserable condition, that the superiority of the French marine was acknowledged with shame and envy at Whitehall, and that the state of our shipping and dockyards was of itself a sufficient guarantee that we should not meddle in the disputes of Europe.[1] Pepys informed his master that the

---

[1] I refer to a despatch of Bonrepaux to Seignelay, dated Feb. $\frac{8}{18}$. 1686. It was transcribed for Mr. Fox from the French archives, during the peace of Amiens, and, with the other materials brought together by that great man, was entrusted to me by the kindness of the late Lady Holland, and of the present Lord Holland. I ought to add that, even in the midst of the troubles which have lately agitated Paris, I found no difficulty in obtaining, from the liberality of the functionaries there, extracts supplying some chasms in Mr. Fox's collection. (1848.)

naval administration was a prodigy of wastefulness, corruption, ignorance, and indolence, that no estimate could be trusted, that no contract was performed, that no check was enforced. The vessels which the recent liberality of Parliament had enabled the government to build, and which had never been out of harbour, had been made of such wretched timber that they were more unfit to go to sea than the old hulls which had been battered thirty years before by Dutch and Spanish broadsides. Some of the new men of war, indeed, were so rotten that, unless speedily repaired, they would go down at their moorings. The sailors were paid with so little punctuality that they were glad to find some usurer who would purchase their tickets at forty per cent discount. The commanders who had not powerful friends at court were even worse treated. Some officers, to whom large arrears were due, after vainly importuning the government during many years, had died for want of a morsel of bread.

Most of the ships which were afloat were commanded by men who had not been bred to the sea. This, it is true, was not an abuse introduced by the government of Charles. No state, ancient or modern, had, before that time, made a complete separation between the naval and military services. In the great civilised nations of antiquity, Cimon and Lysander, Pompey and Agrippa, had fought battles by sea as well as by land. Nor had the impulse which nautical science received at the close of the fifteenth century produced any new division of labour. At Flodden the right wing of the victorious army was led by the Admiral of England. At Jarnac and Moncontour the Huguenot ranks were marshalled by the Admiral of France. Neither John of Austria, the conqueror of Lepanto, nor Lord Howard of Effingham, to whose direction the marine of England was confided when the Spanish invaders were approaching our shores, had received the education of a sailor. Raleigh, highly celebrated as a naval commander, had served during many years as a soldier in France, the Netherlands, and Ireland. Blake had distinguished himself by his skilful and valiant defence of an inland town before he humbled the pride of Holland and of Castile on the ocean. Since the Restoration the same system had been followed. Great fleets had been entrusted to the direction of Rupert and Monk; Rupert, who was renowned chiefly as a hot and daring cavalry officer, and Monk, who, when he wished his ship to change her course, moved the mirth of his crew by calling out, " Wheel to the left ! "

But about this time wise men began to perceive that the rapid improvement, both of the art of war and of the art of navigation, made it necessary to draw a line between two professions which had hitherto been confounded. Either the command of a regiment or the command of a ship was now a matter quite sufficient to occupy the attention of a

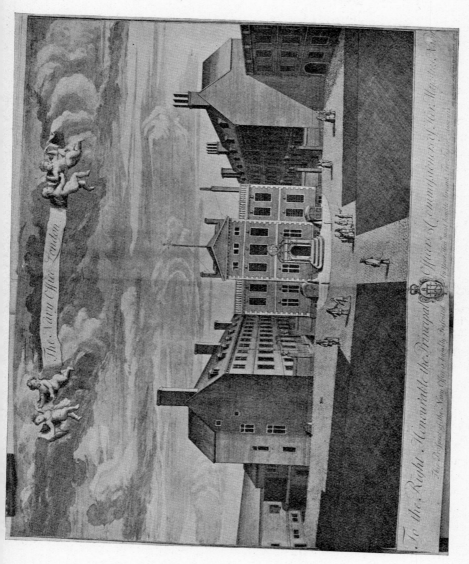

THE NAVY OFFICE IN 1714

From an engraving by Thomas Taylor

single mind. In the year 1672 the French government determined to educate young men of good family from a very early age specially for the sea service. But the English government, instead of following this excellent example, not only continued to distribute high naval commands among landsmen, but selected for such commands landsmen who, even on land, could not safely have been put in any important trust. Any lad of noble birth, any dissolute courtier for whom one of the King's mistresses would speak a word, might hope that a ship of the line, and with it the honour of the country and the lives of hundreds of brave men, would be committed to his care. It mattered not that he had never in his life taken a voyage except on the Thames, that he could not keep his feet in a breeze, that he did not know the difference between latitude and longitude. No previous training was thought necessary ; or, at most, he was sent to make a short trip in a man of war, where he was subjected to no discipline, where he was treated with marked respect, and where he lived in a round of revels and amusements. If, in the intervals of feasting, drinking, and gambling, he succeeded in learning the meaning of a few technical phrases and the names of the points of the compass, he was thought fully qualified to take charge of a three-decker. This is no imaginary description. In 1666, John Sheffield, Earl of Mulgrave, at seventeen years of age, volunteered to serve at sea against the Dutch. He passed six weeks on board, diverting himself, as well as he could, in the society of some young libertines of rank, and then returned home to take the command of a troop of horse. After this he was never on the water till the year 1672, when he again joined the fleet, and was almost immediately appointed Captain of a ship of eighty-four guns, reputed the finest in the navy. He was then twenty-three years old, and had not, in the whole course of his life, been three months afloat. As soon as he came back from sea he was made Colonel of a regiment of foot. This is a specimen of the manner in which naval commands of the highest importance were then given ; and a very favourable specimen ; for Mulgrave, though he wanted experience, wanted neither parts nor courage. Others were promoted in the same way who not only were not good officers, but who were intellectually and morally incapable of ever becoming good officers, and whose only recommendation was that they had been ruined by folly and vice. The chief bait which allured these men into the service was the profit of conveying bullion and other valuable commodities from port to port ; for both the Atlantic and the Mediterranean were then so much infested by pirates from Barbary that merchants were not willing to trust precious cargoes to any custody but that of a man of war. A Captain might thus clear several thousands of pounds by a short voyage ; and for this lucrative business he too often neglected the interests of his country and the honour of his flag, made mean submissions to foreign powers, disobeyed the most direct injunctions of his superiors, lay in port when he was ordered to chase a Sallee rover, or ran with dollars to Leghorn when his instructions directed him to repair to Lisbon. And all this he did with impunity. The same interest which had placed him in a post for which he was unfit maintained him there. No Admiral, bearded by these corrupt and dissolute minions of the palace, dared to do more than mutter something about a court martial. If any officer showed a higher sense of duty than his fellows, he soon found that he lost money without acquiring honour. One Captain, who, by strictly obeying the orders of the Admiralty, missed a cargo which would have been worth four thousand pounds to him, was told by Charles, with ignoble levity, that he was a great fool for his pains.

The discipline of the navy was of a piece throughout. As the courtly Captain despised the Admiralty, he was in turn despised by his crew. It could not be concealed that he was inferior in seamanship to every foremast man on board. It was idle to expect that old sailors, familiar with the hurricanes of the tropics and with the icebergs of the Arctic Circle, would pay prompt and respectful obedience to a chief who knew no more of winds and waves than could be learned in a gilded barge between Whitehall Stairs and Hampton Court. To trust such a novice with the working of a ship was evidently impossible. The direction of the navigation was therefore taken from the Captain and given to the Master : but this partition of authority produced innumerable inconveniences. The line of demarcation was not, and perhaps could not be, drawn with precision. There was therefore constant wrangling. The Captain, confident in proportion to his ignorance, treated the Master with lordly contempt. The Master, well aware of the danger of disobliging the powerful, too often, after a struggle, yielded against his better judgment ; and it was well if the loss of ship and crew was not the consequence. In general the least mischievous of the aristocratical Captains were those who completely abandoned to others the direction of the vessels, and thought only of making money and spending it. The way in which these men lived was so ostentatious and voluptuous that, greedy as they were of gain, they seldom became rich. They dressed as if for a gala at Versailles, ate off plate, drank the richest wines, and kept harams on board, while hunger and scurvy raged among the crews, and while corpses were daily flung out of the portholes.

Such was the ordinary character of those who were then called gentlemen Captains. Mingled with them were to be found, happily for our country, naval commanders of a very different description, men whose whole life had been passed on the deep, and who had worked and fought their way from the lowest offices of the forecastle to rank and distinction. One of the most eminent of these officers was Sir Christopher Mings, who entered the service as a cabin boy, who fell fighting bravely against the Dutch, and whom his crew, weeping and vowing vengeance, carried to the grave. From him sprang, by a singular kind of descent, a line of valiant and expert sailors. His cabin boy was Sir John Narborough; and the cabin boy of Sir John Narborough was Sir Cloudesley Shovel. To the strong natural sense and dauntless courage of this class of men England owes a debt never to be forgotten. It was by such resolute hearts that, in spite of much maladministration, and in spite of the blunders and treasons of more courtly admirals, our coasts were protected and the reputation of our flag upheld during many gloomy and perilous years. But to a landsman these tarpaulins, as they were called, seemed a strange and half savage race. All their knowledge was professional; and their professional knowledge was practical rather than scientific. Off their own element they were as simple as children. Their deportment was uncouth. There was roughness in their very good nature; and their talk, where it was not made up of nautical phrases, was too commonly made up of oaths and curses. Such were the chiefs in whose rude school were formed those sturdy warriors from whom Smollet, in the next age, drew Lieutenant Bowling and Commodore Trunnion. But it does not appear that there was in the service of any of the Stuarts a single naval officer such as, according to the notions of our times, a naval officer ought to be, that is to say, a man versed in the theory and practice of his calling, and steeled against all the dangers of battle and tempest, yet of cultivated mind and polished manners. There were gentlemen and there were seamen in the navy of Charles the Second. But the seamen were not gentlemen; and the gentlemen were not seamen.

The English navy at that time might, according to the most exact estimates which have come down to us, have been kept in an efficient state for three hundred and eighty thousand pounds a year. Four hundred thousand pounds a year was the sum actually expended, but expended, as we have seen, to very little purpose. The cost of the French marine was nearly the same; the cost of the Dutch marine considerably more.[1]

---

[1] My information respecting the condition of the navy, at this time, is chiefly derived from Pepys. His report, presented to Charles the Second in May 1684, has never, I believe, been printed. The manuscript is at Magdalene College, Cambridge. At Magdalene College is also a valuable manuscript containing a detailed account of the maritime establishments of the country in December 1684. Pepys's "Memoirs relating to the State of the Royal Navy for Ten Years, determined December 1688," and his diary and correspondence during his mission to Tangier, are in print. I have made large use of them. See also Sheffield's memoirs, Teonge's Diary, Aubrey's Life of Monk, the Life of Sir Cloudesley Shovel, 1708, Commons' Journals, March 1. and March 20. 168⅞.

CAPTAIN JOHN KEMPTHORNE'S ENGAGEMENT WITH SIX SHIPS OF ALGIERS IN 1669

From an engraving by W. Hollar

The charge of the English ordnance in the seventeenth century was, as compared with other military and naval charges, much smaller than at present. At most of the garrisons there were gunners; and here and there, at an important post, an engineer was to be found. But there was no regiment of artillery, no brigade of sappers and miners, no college in which young soldiers could learn the scientific part of the art of war. The difficulty of moving field pieces was extreme. When, a few years later, William marched from Devonshire to London, the apparatus which he brought with him, though such as had long been in constant use on the Continent, and such as would now be regarded at Woolwich as rude and cumbrous, excited in our ancestors an admiration resembling that which the Indians of America felt for the Castilian harquebusses. The stock of gunpowder kept in the English forts and arsenals was boastfully mentioned by patriotic writers as something which might well impress neighbouring nations with awe. It amounted to fourteen or fifteen thousand barrels, about a twelfth of the quantity which it is now thought necessary to have in store. The expenditure under the head of ordnance was on an average a little above sixty thousand pounds a year.[1]

The whole effective charge of the army, navy, and ordnance, was about seven hundred and fifty thousand pounds. The noneffective charge, which is now a heavy part of our public burdens, can hardly be said to have existed. A very small number of naval officers, who were not employed in the public service, drew half pay. No Lieutenant was on the list, nor any Captain who had not commanded a ship of the first or second rate. As the country then possessed only seventeen ships of the first and second rate that had ever been at sea, and as a large proportion of the persons who had commanded such ships had good posts on shore, the expenditure under this head must have been small indeed.[2] In the army, half pay was given merely as a special and temporary allowance to a small number of officers belonging to two regiments, which were peculiarly situated.[3] Greenwich Hospital had not been founded. Chelsea Hospital was building: but the cost of that institution was defrayed partly by a deduction from the pay of the troops, and partly by private subscription. The King promised to contribute only twenty thousand pounds for architectural expenses, and five thousand a year for the maintenance of

The ordnance

Noneffective charge

---

[1] Chamberlayne's State of England, 1684; Commons' Journals, March 1. and March 20. 168⅞. In 1833, it was determined, after full enquiry, that a hundred and seventy thousand barrels of gunpowder should constantly be kept in store.

[2] It appears from the records of the Admiralty, that Flag officers were allowed half pay in 1668, Captains of first and second rates not till 1674.

[3] Warrant in the War Office Records, dated March 26. 1678.

CHELSEA HOSPITAL IN 1690

From an engraving by J. Kip

the invalids.[1]   It was no part of the plan that there should be out-pensioners.   The whole noneffective charge, military and naval, can scarcely have exceeded ten thousand pounds a year.   It now exceeds ten thousand pounds a day.

Of the expense of civil government only a small portion was defrayed by the crown.   The great majority of the functionaries whose business

Charge of civil government
was to administer justice and preserve order either gave their services to the public gratuitously, or were remunerated in a manner which caused no drain on the revenue of the state. The sheriffs, mayors, and aldermen of the towns, the country gentlemen who were in the commission of the peace, the headboroughs, bailiffs, and petty constables, cost the King nothing.   The superior courts of law were chiefly supported by fees.

Our relations with foreign courts had been put on the most econo-mical footing.   The only diplomatic agent who had the title of Ambas-sador resided at Constantinople, and was partly supported by the Turkey Company.   Even at the court of Versailles England had only an Envoy; and she had not even an Envoy at the Spanish, Swedish, and Danish courts.   The whole expense under this head cannot, in the last year of the reign of Charles the Second, have much exceeded twenty thousand pounds.[2]

In this frugality there was nothing laudable.   Charles was, as usual, niggardly in the wrong place, and munificent in the wrong place.   The

Great gains of ministers and courtiers
public service was starved that courtiers might be pampered. The expense of the navy, of the ordnance, of pensions to needy old officers, of missions to foreign courts, must seem small indeed to the present generation.   But the personal favourites of the sovereign, his ministers, and the creatures of those ministers, were gorged with public money.   Their salaries and pensions, when com-pared with the incomes of the nobility, the gentry, the commercial and professional men of that age, will appear enormous.   The greatest estates in the kingdom then very little exceeded twenty thousand a year.   The Duke of Ormond had twenty-two thousand a year.[3]   The Duke of Buckingham, before his extravagance had impaired his great property, had nineteen thousand six hundred a year.[4]   George Monk, Duke of Albemarle, who had been rewarded for his eminent services with immense grants of crown land, and who had been notorious both

---

[1] Evelyn's Diary, Jan. 27. 1682.   I have seen a privy seal, dated May 17. 1683, which con-firms Evelyn's testimony.

[2] James the Second sent Envoys to Spain, Sweden, and Denmark ; yet in his reign the diplomatic expenditure was little more than 30,000*l.* a year.   See the Commons' Journals, March 20. 168⅔.   Chamberlayne's State of England, 1684, 1687.

[3] Carte's Life of Ormond.   [4] Pepys's Diary, Feb. 14. 166⅔.

for covetousness and for parsimony, left fifteen thousand a year of real estate, and sixty thousand pounds in money which probably yielded seven per cent.[1] These three Dukes were supposed to be three of the very richest subjects in England. The Archbishop of Canterbury can hardly have had five thousand a year.[2] The average income of a temporal peer was estimated, by the best informed persons, at about three thousand a year, the average income of a baronet at nine hundred a year, the average income of a member of the House of Commons at less than eight hundred a year.[3] A thousand a year was thought a large revenue for a barrister. Two thousand a year was hardly to be made in the Court of King's Bench, except by the crown lawyers.[4] It is evident, therefore, that an official man would have been well paid if he had received a fourth or fifth part of what would now be an adequate stipend. In fact, however, the stipends of the higher class of official men were as large as at present, and not seldom larger. The Lord Treasurer, for example, had eight thousand a year, and, when the Treasury was in commission, the junior Lords had sixteen hundred a year each. The Paymaster of the Forces had a poundage, amounting, in time of peace, to about five thousand a year, on all the money which passed through his hands. The Groom of the Stole had five thousand a year, the Commissioners of the Customs twelve hundred a year each, the Lords of the Bedchamber a thousand a year each.[5] The regular salary, however, was the smallest part of the gains of an official man of that age. From the noblemen who held the white staff and the great seal, down to the humblest tidewaiter and gauger, what would now be called gross corruption was practised without disguise and without reproach. Titles, places, commissions, pardons, were daily sold in market overt by the great dignitaries of the realm ; and every clerk in every department imitated, to the best of his power, the evil example.

During the last century no prime minister, however powerful, has become rich in office ; and several prime ministers have impaired their

[1] See the Report of the Bath and Montague case, which was decided by Lord Keeper Somers, in December 1693.

[2] During three quarters of a year, beginning from Christmas 1689, the revenues of the see of Canterbury were received by an officer appointed by the crown. That officer's accounts are now in the British Museum. (Lansdowne MSS. 885.) The gross revenue for the three quarters was not quite four thousand pounds ; and the difference between the gross and the net revenue was evidently something considerable.

[3] King's Natural and Political Conclusions. Davenant on the Balance of Trade. Sir W. Temple says, " The revenues of a House of Commons have seldom exceeded four hundred thousand pounds." Memoirs, Third Part.

[4] Langton's Conversations with Chief Justice Hale, 1672.

[5] Commons' Journals, April 27. 1689 ; Chamberlayne's State of England, 1684.

private fortune in sustaining their public character.   In the seventeenth century, a statesman who was at the head of affairs might easily, and without giving scandal, accumulate in no long time an estate amply sufficient to support a dukedom.   It is probable that the income of the prime minister, during his tenure of power, far exceeded that of any other subject.   The place of Lord Lieutenant of Ireland was popularly reported to be worth forty thousand pounds a year.[1]   The gains of the Chancellor Clarendon, of Arlington, of Lauderdale, and of Danby, were certainly enormous.   The sumptuous palace to which the populace of London gave the name of Dunkirk House, the stately pavilions, the fish-ponds, the deer park and the orangery of Euston, the more than Italian luxury of Ham, with its busts, fountains, and aviaries, were among the many signs which indicated what was the shortest road to boundless wealth.   This is the true explanation of the unscrupulous violence with which the statesmen of that day struggled for office, of the tenacity with which, in spite of vexations, humiliations and dangers, they clung to it, and of the scandalous compliances to which they stooped in order to retain it.   Even in our own age, formidable as is the power of opinion, and high as is the standard of integrity, there would be great risk of a lament-able change in the character of our public men, if the place of First Lord of the Treasury or Secretary of State were worth a hundred thousand pounds a year.   Happily for our country the emoluments of the highest class of functionaries have not only not grown in pro-portion to the general growth of our opulence, but have positively diminished.

The fact that the sum raised in England by taxation has, in a time not exceeding two long lives, been multiplied fortyfold, is strange, and **State of** may at first sight seem appalling.   But those who are **agriculture** alarmed by the increase of the public burdens may perhaps be reassured when they have considered the increase of the public resources.   In the year 1685, the value of the produce of the soil far exceeded the value of all the other fruits of human industry.   Yet agri-culture was in what would now be considered as a very rude and im-perfect state.   The arable land and pasture land were not supposed by the best political arithmeticians of that age to amount to much more than half the area of the kingdom.[2]   The remainder was believed to consist of moor, forest, and fen.   These computations are strongly con-firmed by the road books and maps of the seventeenth century.   From those books and maps it is clear that many routes which now pass through an endless succession of orchards, cornfields, hayfields, and bean-

[1] See the Travels of the Grand Duke Cosmo.
[2] King's Natural and Political Conclusions.   Davenant on the Balance of Trade.

A PAGE FROM OGILBY'S ITINERARIUM ANGLIÆ, 1675

fields, then ran through nothing but heath, swamp, and warren.[1] In the drawings of English landscapes made in that age for the Grand Duke Cosmo, scarce a hedgerow is to be seen, and numerous tracts, now rich with cultivation, appear as bare as Salisbury Plain.[2] At Enfield, hardly out of sight of the smoke of the capital, was a region of five and twenty miles in circumference, which contained only three houses and scarcely any enclosed fields.   Deer, as free as in an American forest, wandered there by thousands.[3]   It is to be remarked, that wild animals of large size were then far more numerous than at present.   The last wild boars, indeed, which had been preserved for the royal diversion, and had been allowed to ravage the cultivated land with their tusks, had been slaughtered by the exasperated rustics during the license of the civil war.   The last wolf that has roamed our island had been slain in Scotland a short time before the close of the reign of Charles the Second. But many breeds, now extinct or rare, both of quadrupeds and birds, were still common.   The fox, whose life is now, in many counties, held almost as sacred as that of a human being, was then considered as a mere nuisance.   Oliver Saint John told the Long Parliament that Strafford was to be regarded, not as a stag or a hare, to whom some law was to be given, but as a fox, who was to be snared by any means, and knocked on the head without pity.   This illustration would be by no means a happy one, if addressed to country gentlemen of our time : but in Saint John's days there were not seldom great massacres of foxes to which the peasantry thronged with all the dogs that could be mustered : traps were set : nets were spread : no quarter was given ; and to shoot a female with cub was considered as a feat which merited the warmest gratitude of the neighbourhood.   The red deer were then as common in Gloucestershire and Hampshire as they now are among the Grampian Hills.   On one occasion Queen Anne, travelling to Portsmouth, saw a herd of no less than five hundred.   The wild bull with his white mane was still to be found wandering in a few of the southern forests.   The badger made his dark and tortuous hole on the side of every hill where the copsewood grew thick.   The wild cats were

[1] See the Itinerarium Angliæ, 1675, by John Ogilby, Cosmographer Royal. He describes great part of the land as wood, fen, heath on both sides, marsh on both sides. In some of his maps the roads through enclosed country are marked by lines, and the roads through unenclosed country by dots. The proportion of unenclosed country, which, if cultivated, must have been wretchedly cultivated, seems to have been very great. From Abingdon to Gloucester, for example, a distance of forty or fifty miles, there was not a single enclosure, and scarcely one enclosure between Biggleswade and Lincoln.

[1] Large copies of these highly interesting drawings are in the noble collection bequeathed by Mr. Grenville to the British Museum. See particularly the drawings of Exeter and Northampton.

[3] Evelyn's Diary, June 2. 1675.

PROSPECTS OF CAMBRIDGE FROM THE EAST AND THE WEST, SHOWING THE OPEN FIELD SYSTEM OF AGRICULTURE

From Loggan's Cantabrigia Illustrata

frequently heard by night wailing round the lodges of the rangers of Whittlebury and Needwood. The yellow-breasted martin was still pursued in Cranbourne Chase for his fur, reputed inferior only to that of the sable. Fen eagles, measuring more than nine feet between the extremities of the wings, preyed on fish along the coast of Norfolk. On all the downs, from the British Channel to Yorkshire, huge bustards strayed in troops of fifty or sixty, and were often hunted with greyhounds. The marshes of Cambridgeshire and Lincolnshire were covered during some months of every year by immense clouds of cranes. Some of these races the progress of cultivation has extirpated. Of others the numbers are so much diminished that men crowd to gaze at a specimen as at a Bengal tiger, or a Polar bear.[1]

The progress of this great change can nowhere be more clearly traced than in the Statute Book. The number of enclosure acts passed since King George the Second came to the throne exceeds four thousand. The area enclosed under the authority of those acts exceeds, on a moderate calculation, ten thousand square miles. How many square miles, which were formerly uncultivated or ill cultivated, have, during the same period, been fenced and carefully tilled by the proprietors, without any application to the legislature, can only be conjectured. But it seems highly probable that a fourth part of England has been, in the course of little more than a century, turned from a wild into a garden.

Even in those parts of the kingdom which at the close of the reign of Charles the Second were the best cultivated, the farming, though greatly improved since the civil war, was not such as would now be thought skilful. To this day no effectual steps have been taken by public authority for the purpose of obtaining accurate accounts of the produce of the English soil. The historian must therefore follow, with some misgivings, the guidance of those writers on statistics whose reputation for diligence and fidelity stands highest. At present an average crop of wheat, rye, barley, oats, and beans, is supposed considerably to exceed thirty millions of quarters. The crop of wheat would be thought wretched if it did not exceed twelve millions of quarters. According to the computation made in the year 1696 by Gregory King, the whole quantity of wheat, rye, barley, oats, and beans, then annually grown in the kingdom, was somewhat less than ten millions of quarters. The wheat, which was then cultivated only on the strongest clay, and consumed only by those who were in easy circumstances, he

---

[1] See White's Selborne ; Bell's History of British Quadrupeds ; Gentleman's Recreation, 1686 ; Aubrey's Natural History of Wiltshire, 1685 ; Morton's History of Northamptonshire, 1712 ; Willoughby's Ornithology, by Ray, 1678 ; Latham's General Synopsis of Birds ; and Sir Thomas Browne's Account of Birds found in Norfolk.

estimated at less than two millions of quarters.   Charles Davenant, an acute and well informed though most unprincipled and rancorous politician, differed from King as to some of the items of the account, but came to nearly the same general conclusions.[1]

The rotation of crops was very imperfectly understood.   It was known, indeed, that some vegetables lately introduced into our island, particularly the turnip, afforded excellent nutriment in winter to sheep and oxen : but it was not yet the practice to feed cattle in this manner. It was therefore by no means easy to keep them alive during the season when the grass is scanty.   They were killed and salted in great numbers at the beginning of the cold weather ; and, during several months, even the gentry tasted scarcely any fresh animal food, except game and river fish, which were consequently much more important articles in house-keeping than at present.   It appears from the Northumberland Household Book that, in the reign of Henry the Seventh, fresh meat was never eaten even by the gentlemen attendant on a great Earl, except during the short interval between Midsummer and Michaelmas.   But in the course of two centuries an improvement had taken place ; and under Charles the Second it was not till the beginning of November that families laid in their stock of salt provisions, then called Martinmas beef.[2]

The sheep and the ox of that time were diminutive when compared with the sheep and oxen which are now driven to our markets.[3]   Our native horses, though serviceable, were held in small esteem, and fetched low prices.   They were valued, one with another, by the ablest of those who computed the national wealth, at not more than fifty shillings each. Foreign breeds were greatly preferred.   Spanish jennets were regarded as the finest chargers, and were imported for purposes of pageantry and war.   The coaches of the aristocracy were drawn by grey Flemish mares, which trotted, as it was thought, with a peculiar grace, and endured better than any cattle reared in our island the work of drag-ging a ponderous equipage over the rugged pavement of London. Neither the modern dray horse nor the modern race horse was then known.   At a much later period the ancestors of the gigantic quadru-peds, which all foreigners now class among the chief wonders of London, were brought from the marshes of Walcheren ; the ancestors of Childers and Eclipse from the sands of Arabia.   Already, however, there was among our nobility and gentry a passion for the amusements of the turf.   The importance of improving our studs by an infusion of new blood was strongly felt ; and with this view a considerable number of barbs had lately been brought into the country.   Two men whose

---

[1] King's Natural and Political Conclusions.   Davenant on the Balance of Trade.
[2] See the Almanacks of 1684 and 1685.
[3] See Mr. M'Culloch's Statistical Account of the British Empire, Part III. chap i. sec. 6.

authority on such subjects was held in great esteem, the Duke of
Newcastle and Sir John Fenwick, pronounced that the meanest hack
ever imported from Tangier would produce a finer progeny than could
be expected from the best sire of our native breed.   They would not
readily have believed that a time would come when the princes and
nobles of neighbouring lands would be as eager to obtain horses from
England as ever the English had been to obtain horses from Barbary.[1]

The increase of vegetable and animal produce, though great, seems
small when compared with the increase of our mineral wealth.   In 1685
the tin of Cornwall, which had, more than two thousand years
before, attracted the Tyrian sails beyond the pillars of Hercules,
was still one of the most valuable subterranean productions of
the island.   The quantity annually extracted from the earth was found to
be, some years later, sixteen hundred tons, probably about a third of what
it now is.[2]   But the veins of copper which lie in the same region were, in
the time of Charles the Second, altogether neglected, nor did any land-
owner take them into the account in estimating the value of his property.
Cornwall and Wales at present yield annually near fifteen thousand
tons of copper, worth near a million and a half sterling ; that is to say,
worth about twice as much as the annual produce of all English mines
of all descriptions in the seventeenth century.[3]   The first bed of rock
salt had been discovered in Cheshire not long after the Restoration, but
does not appear to have been worked till much later.   The salt which
was obtained by a rude process from brine pits was held in no high
estimation.   The pans in which the manufacture was carried on exhaled
a sulphurous stench ; and, when the evaporation was complete, the substance which was left was scarcely fit to be used with food.   Physicians
attributed the scorbutic and pulmonary complaints which were common
among the English to this unwholesome condiment.   It was therefore
seldom used by the upper and middle classes; and there was a regular and
considerable importation from France.   At present our springs and mines
not only supply our own immense demand, but send annually more than
seven hundred millions of pounds of excellent salt to foreign countries.[4]

Mineral wealth of the country.

[1] King and Davenant as before ; The Duke of Newcastle on Horsemanship ; Gentleman's
Recreation, 1686.   The "dappled Flanders mares" were marks of greatness in the time of
Pope, and even later.
   The vulgar proverb, that the grey mare is the better horse, originated, I suspect, in the
preference generally given to the grey mares of Flanders over the finest coach horses of England

[2] See a curious note by Tonkin, in Lord De Dunstanville's edition of Carew's Survey of
Cornwall.

[3] Borlase's Natural History of Cornwall, 1758.   The quantity of copper now produced, I have
taken from parliamentary returns.   Davenant, in 1700, estimated the annual produce of all the
mines of England at between seven and eight hundred thousand pounds.

[4] Philosophical Transactions, No. 53. Nov. 1669, No. 66. Dec. 1670, No. 103. May 1674,
No. 156. Feb. 168$\frac{3}{4}$.

Systema
Agriculturæ.
Being
The Mystery Of Husbandry
Discovered and
layd Open
by
J W

H Van Houe scul.

Printed for Tho. Dring at ꝯ Corner of Chancery lane in Fleetstreet. 1675.

THE FRONTISPIECE TO JOHN WORLIDGE'S SYSTEMA AGRICULTURAE, 1675

Far more important has been the improvement of our iron works. Such works had long existed in our island, but had not prospered, and had been regarded with no favourable eye by the government and by the public. It was not then the practice to employ coal for smelting the ore ; and the rapid consumption of wood excited the alarm of politicians. As early as the reign of Elizabeth there had been loud complaints that whole forests were cut down for the purpose of feeding the furnaces ; and the Parliament had interfered to prohibit the manufacturers from burning timber. The manufacture consequently languished. At the close of the reign of Charles the Second, great part of the iron which was used in this country was imported from abroad ; and the whole quantity cast here annually seems not to have exceeded ten thousand tons. At present the trade is thought to be in a depressed state if less than a million of tons are produced in a year.[1]

One mineral, perhaps more important than iron itself, remains to be mentioned. Coal, though very little used in any species of manufacture, was already the ordinary fuel in some districts which were fortunate enough to possess large beds, and in the capital, which could easily be supplied by water carriage. It seems reasonable to believe that at least one half of the quantity then extracted from the pits was consumed in London. The consumption of London seemed to the writers of that age enormous, and was often mentioned by them as a proof of the greatness of the imperial city. They scarcely hoped to be believed when they affirmed that two hundred and eighty thousand chaldrons, that is to say, about three hundred and fifty thousand tons, were, in the last year of the reign of Charles the Second, brought to the Thames. At present three millions and a half of tons are required yearly by the metropolis; and the whole annual produce cannot, on the most moderate computation, be estimated at less than thirty millions of tons.[2]

While these great changes have been in progress, the rent of land has, as might be expected, been almost constantly rising. In
Increase
of rent
some districts it has multiplied more than tenfold. In some it has not more than doubled. It has probably, on the average, quadrupled.

Of the rent, a large proportion was divided among the country

---

[1] Yarranton, England's Improvement by Sea and Land, 1677 ; Porter's Progress of the Nation. See also a remarkably perspicuous history, in small compass, of the English iron works, in Mr. M'Culloch's Statistical Account of the British Empire.

[2] See Chamberlayne's State of England, 1684, 1687 ; Angliæ Metropolis, 1691 ; M'Culloch's Statistical Account of the British Empire, Part III. chap. ii. (edition of 1847). In 1845 the quantity of coal brought into London appeared, by the parliamentary returns, to be 3,460,000 tons. (1848.) In 1854 the quantity of coal brought into London amounted to 4,378,000 tons. (1857.)

gentlemen, a class of persons whose position and character it is most important that we should clearly understand; for by their influence and

Small Coale
Qui veut du Charbon

THE SMALL-COAL SELLER

From Tempest's Cries of London, 1711

by their passions the fate of the nation was, at several important conjunctures, determined.

We should be much mistaken if we pictured to ourselves the squires of the seventeenth century as men bearing a close resemblance to their **The country gentlemen** descendants, the county members and chairmen of quarter sessions with whom we are familiar. The modern country gentleman generally receives a liberal education, passes from a distinguished school to a distinguished college, and has ample opportunity to become an excellent scholar. He has generally seen something of foreign countries. A considerable part of his life has generally been passed in the capital; and the refinements of the capital follow him into the country. There is perhaps no class of dwellings so pleasing as the rural seats of the English gentry. In the parks and pleasure grounds, nature, dressed yet not disguised by art, wears her most alluring form. In the buildings, good sense and good taste combine to produce a happy union of the comfortable and the graceful. The pictures, the musical instruments, the library, would in any other country be considered as proving the owner to be an eminently polished and accomplished man. A country gentleman who witnessed the Revolution was probably in receipt of about a fourth part of the rent which his acres now yield to his posterity. He was, therefore, as compared with his posterity, a poor man, and was generally under the necessity of residing, with little interruption, on his estate. To travel on the Continent, to maintain an establishment in London, or even to visit London frequently, were pleasures in which only the great proprietors could indulge. It may be confidently affirmed that of the squires whose names were then in the Commissions of Peace and Lieutenancy not one in twenty went to town once in five years, or had ever in his life wandered so far as Paris. Many lords of manors had received an education differing little from that of their menial servants. The heir of an estate often passed his boyhood and youth at the seat of his family with no better tutors than grooms and gamekeepers, and scarce attained learning enough to sign his name to a Mittimus. If he went to school and to college, he generally returned before he was twenty to the seclusion of the old hall, and there, unless his mind were very happily constituted by nature, soon forgot his academical pursuits in rural business and pleasures. His chief serious employment was the care of his property. He examined samples of grain, handled pigs, and, on market days, made bargains over a tankard with drovers and hop merchants. His chief pleasures were commonly derived from field sports and from an unrefined sensuality. His language and pronunciation were such as we should now expect to hear only from the most ignorant clowns. His oaths, coarse jests, and scurrilous terms of abuse, were uttered with the broadest accent of his province. It was easy to discern, from the first words which he spoke, whether he came from Somersetshire or Yorkshire. He troubled himself little about decorating his abode, and, if he attempted decoration, seldom produced anything but deformity. The litter of a farmyard gathered under the windows of his bedchamber, and the cabbages and gooseberry bushes grew close to his hall door. His table was loaded with coarse plenty; and guests were cordially welcomed to it. But, as the habit of drinking to excess was general in the class to which he belonged, and as his fortune did not enable him to intoxicate large assemblies daily with claret or canary, strong beer was the ordinary beverage. The quantity of beer consumed in those days was indeed enormous. For beer then was to the middle and lower classes, not only all that beer now is, but all that wine, tea, and ardent spirits now are. It was only at great houses, or on great occasions, that foreign drink was placed on the board. The ladies of the house, whose business it had commonly been to cook the repast, retired as soon as the dishes had been devoured, and left the gentlemen to their ale and tobacco. The coarse jollity of the afternoon was often prolonged till the revellers were laid under the table.

It was very seldom that the country gentleman caught glimpses of the great world; and what he saw of it tended rather to confuse than to enlighten his understanding. His opinions respecting religion, government, foreign countries and former times, having been derived, not from study, from observation, or from conversation with enlightened companions, but from such traditions as were current in his own small circle, were the opinions of a child. He adhered to them, however, with the obstinacy which is generally found in ignorant men accustomed to be fed with flattery. His animosities were numerous and bitter. He hated Frenchmen and Italians, Scotchmen and Irishmen, Papists and Presbyterians, Independents and Baptists, Quakers and Jews. Towards London and Londoners he felt an aversion which more than once produced important political effects. His wife and daughter were in tastes and acquirements below a housekeeper or a stillroom maid of the present day. They stitched and spun, brewed gooseberry wine, cured marigolds, and made the crust for the venison pasty.

From this description it might be supposed that the English esquire of the seventeenth century did not materially differ from a rustic miller or alehouse keeper of our time. There are, however, some important parts of his character still to be noted, which will greatly modify this estimate. Unlettered as he was and unpolished, he was still in some most important points a gentleman. He was a member of a proud and powerful aristocracy, and was distinguished by many both of the good and of the bad qualities which belong to aristocrats. His family pride was beyond that of a Talbot or a Howard. He knew the genealogies and coats of arms of all his neighbours, and could tell which of them had assumed supporters without any right, and which of them were so unfortunate as to be greatgrandsons of aldermen. He was a magistrate, and, as such, administered gratuitously to those who dwelt around him a rude patriarchal justice, which, in spite of innumerable blunders and of occasional acts of tyranny, was yet better than no justice at all. He was an officer of the trainbands ; and his military dignity, though it might move the mirth of gallants who had served a campaign in Flanders, raised his character in his own eyes and in the eyes of his neighbours. Nor indeed was his soldiership justly a subject of derision. In every county there were elderly gentlemen who had seen service which was no child's play. One had been knighted by Charles the First, after the battle of Edgehill. Another still wore a patch over the scar which he had received at Naseby. A third had defended his old house till Fairfax had blown in the door with a petard. The presence of these old Cavaliers, with their old swords and holsters, and with their old stories about Goring and Lunsford, gave to the musters of militia an earnest and warlike aspect which would otherwise have been wanting. Even those country gentlemen who were too young to have themselves exchanged blows with the cuirassiers of the Parliament had, from child-hood, been surrounded by the traces of recent war, and fed with stories of the martial exploits of their fathers and uncles. Thus the character of the English esquire of the seventeenth century was compounded of two elements which we seldom or never find united. His ignorance and uncouthness, his low tastes and gross phrases, would, in our time, be considered as indicating a nature and a breeding thoroughly plebeian. Yet he was essentially a patrician, and had, in large measure, both the virtues and the vices which flourish among men set from their birth in high place, and used to respect themselves and to be respected by others. It is not easy for a generation accustomed to find chivalrous sentiments only in company with liberal studies and polished manners to image to itself a man with the deportment, the vocabulary, and the accent of a carter, yet punctilious on matters of genealogy and precedence, and ready to risk his life rather than see a stain cast on the honour of his house. It is however only by thus joining together things seldom or never found together in our own experience, that we can form a just idea of that rustic aristocracy which constituted the main strength of the armies of Charles the First, and which long supported, with strange fidelity, the interest of his descendants.

The gross, uneducated, untravelled country gentleman was commonly a Tory : but, though devotedly attached to hereditary monarchy, he had no partiality for courtiers and ministers. He thought, not without reason, that Whitehall was filled with the most corrupt of mankind, and that of the great sums which the House of Commons had voted to the crown since the Restoration part had been embezzled by cunning politicians, and part squandered on buffoons and foreign courtesans. His stout English heart swelled with indignation at the thought that the government of his country should be subject to French dictation. Being himself generally an old Cavalier, or the son of an old Cavalier, he reflected with bitter resentment on the ingratitude with which the Stuarts had requited their best friends. Those who heard him grumble at the neglect with which he was treated, and at the profusion with which wealth was lavished on the bastards of Nell Gwynn and Madam Carwell, would have supposed him ripe for rebellion. But all this ill humour lasted only till the throne was really in danger. It was precisely when those whom the sovereign had loaded with wealth and honours shrank from his side that the country gentlemen, so surly and mutinous in the season of his prosperity, rallied round him in a body. Thus, after murmuring twenty years at the misgovernment of Charles the Second, they came to his rescue in his extremity, when his own Secretaries of State and the Lords of his own Treasury had deserted him, and enabled him to gain a complete victory over the opposition ; nor can there be any doubt that they would have shown equal loyalty to his brother James, if James would, even at the last moment, have refrained from outraging their strongest feeling. For there was one institution, and one only, which they prized even more than hereditary monarchy ; and that institution was the Church of England. Their love of the Church was not, indeed, the effect of study or meditation. Few among them could have given any reason, drawn from Scripture or ecclesiastical history, for adhering to her doctrines, her ritual, and her polity ; nor were they, as a class, by any means strict observers of that code of morality which is common to all Christian sects. But the experience of many ages proves that men may be ready to fight to the death, and to persecute without pity, for a religion whose creed they do not understand, and whose precepts they habitually disobey.[1]

The rural clergy were even more vehement in Toryism than the rural gentry, and were a class scarcely less important. It is to be observed, however, that the individual clergyman, as com-pared with the individual gentleman, then ranked much lower **The clergy** than in our days. The main support of the Church was derived from the tithe ; and the tithe bore to the rent a much smaller ratio than at present. King estimated the whole income of the parochial and collegiate clergy at only four hundred and eighty thousand pounds a year ; Davenant at only five hundred and forty-four thousand a year.

---

[1] My notion of the country gentleman of the seventeenth century has been derived from sources too numerous to be recapitulated. I must leave my description to the judgment of those who have studied the history and the lighter literature of that age.

It is certainly now more than seven times as great as the larger of these two sums. The average rent of the land has not, according to any estimate, increased proportionally. It follows that the rectors and vicars must have been, as compared with the neighbouring knights and squires, much poorer in the seventeenth than in the nineteenth century.

The place of the clergyman in society had been completely changed by the Reformation. Before that event, ecclesiastics had formed the majority of the House of Lords, had, in wealth and splendour, equalled, and sometimes outshone, the greatest of the temporal barons, and had generally held the highest civil offices. Many of the Treasurers, and almost all the Chancellors of the Plantagenets were Bishops. The Lord Keeper of the Privy Seal and the Master of the Rolls were ordinarily churchmen. Churchmen transacted the most important diplomatic business. Indeed, all that large portion of the administration which rude and warlike nobles were incompetent to conduct was considered as especially belonging to divines. Men, therefore, who were averse to the life of camps, and who were, at the same time, desirous to rise in the state, commonly received the tonsure. Among them were sons of all the most illustrious families, and near kinsmen of the throne, Scroops and Nevilles, Bourchiers, Staffords, and Poles. To the religious houses belonged the rents of immense domains, and all that large portion of the tithe which is now in the hands of laymen. Down to the middle of the reign of Henry the Eighth, therefore, no line of life was so attractive to ambitious and covetous natures as the priesthood. Then came a violent revolution. The abolition of the monasteries deprived the Church at once of the greater part of her wealth, and of her predominance in the Upper House of Parliament. There was no longer an Abbot of Glastonbury or an Abbot of Reading seated among the peers, and possessed of revenues equal to those of a powerful Earl. The princely splendour of William of Wykeham and of William of Waynflete had disappeared. The scarlet hat of the Cardinal, the silver cross of the Legate, were no more. The clergy had also lost the ascendency which is the natural reward of superior mental cultivation. Once the circumstance that a man could read had raised a presumption that he was in orders. But, in an age which produced such laymen as William Cecil and Nicholas Bacon, Roger Ascham and Thomas Smith, Walter Mildmay and Francis Walsingham, there was no reason for calling away prelates from their dioceses to negotiate treaties, to superintend the finances, or to administer justice. The spiritual character not only ceased to be a qualification for high civil office, but began to be regarded as a disqualification. Those worldly motives, therefore, which had formerly induced so many able, aspiring, and high born youths to assume the ecclesiastical habit, ceased to operate. Not one parish in two hundred then afforded what a man of family considered as a maintenance. There were still indeed prizes in the Church : but they were few ; and even the highest were mean, when compared with the glory which had once surrounded the princes of the hierarchy. The state kept by Parker and Grindal seemed beggarly to those who remembered the imperial pomp of Wolsey, his palaces, which had become the favourite abodes of royalty, Whitehall and Hampton Court, the three sumptuous tables daily spread in his refectory, the forty-four gorgeous copes in his chapel, his running footmen in rich liveries, and his body guards with gilded poleaxes. Thus the sacerdotal office lost its attraction for the higher classes. During the century which followed the accession of Elizabeth, scarce a single person of noble descent took orders. At the close of the reign of Charles the Second, two sons of peers were Bishops ; four or five sons of peers were priests, and held valuable preferment : but these rare exceptions did not take away the reproach which lay on the body. The clergy were regarded as, on the whole, a plebeian class.[1] And, indeed, for one who made the figure of a gentleman, ten were mere menial servants. A large proportion of those divines who had no benefices, or whose benefices were too small to afford a comfortable revenue, lived in the houses of laymen. It had long been evident that this practice tended to degrade the priestly character. Laud had exerted himself to effect a change ; and Charles the First had repeatedly issued positive orders that none but men of high rank should presume to keep domestic chaplains.[2] But these injunctions had become obsolete. Indeed, during the domination of the Puritans, many of the ejected ministers of the Church of England could obtain bread and shelter only by attaching themselves to the households of royalist gentlemen ; and the habits which had been formed in those times of trouble continued long after the reestablishment of monarchy and episcopacy. In the mansions of men of liberal sentiments and cultivated understandings, the chaplain was doubtless treated with urbanity and kindness. His conversation, his literary assistance, his spiritual advice, were considered as an ample return for his food, his lodging, and his stipend. But this was not the general feeling of the country gentlemen. The coarse and ignorant squire, who thought that it belonged to his dignity to have grace said every day at his table by an ecclesiastic in full canonicals, found means to reconcile dignity with

[1] In the eighteenth century the great increase in the value of benefices produced a change. The younger sons of the nobility were allured back to the clerical profession. Warburton in a letter to Hurd, dated the 5th of July 1752, mentions this change, which was then recent. "Our grandees have at last found their way back into the Church. I only wonder they have been so long about it. But be assured that nothing but a new religious revolution, to sweep away the fragments that Henry the Eighth left after banqueting his courtiers, will drive them out again."

[2] See Heylin's Cyprianus Anglicus.

economy.   A young Levite—such was the phrase then in use—might
be had for his board, a small garret, and ten pounds a year, and might
not only perform his own professional functions, might not only be the
most patient of butts and of listeners, might not only be always ready
in fine weather for bowls, and in rainy weather for shovelboard, but
might also save the expense of a gardener, or of a groom.   Sometimes
the reverend man nailed up the apricots ; and sometimes he curried the
coach horses.   He cast up the farrier's bills.   He walked ten miles with
a message or a parcel.   He was permitted to dine with the family ; but
he was expected to content himself with the plainest fare.   He might
fill himself with the corned beef and the carrots : but, as soon as the
tarts and cheesecakes made their appearance, he quitted his seat, and
stood aloof till he was summoned to return thanks for the repast, from
a great part of which he had been excluded.[1]

Perhaps, after some years of service, he was presented to a living
sufficient to support him : but he often found it necessary to purchase
his preferment by a species of Simony, which furnished an inexhaustible
subject of pleasantry to three or four generations of scoffers.   With his
cure he was expected to take a wife.   The wife had ordinarily been in
the patron's service ; and it was well if she was not suspected of standing
too high in the patron's favour.   Indeed, the nature of the matrimonial
connections which the clergymen of that age were in the habit of forming
is the most certain indication of the place which the order held in the
social system.   An Oxonian, writing a few months after the death of
Charles the Second, complained bitterly, not only that the country
attorney and the country apothecary looked down with disdain on the
country clergyman, but that one of the lessons most earnestly inculcated
on every girl of honourable family was to give no encouragement to a
lover in orders, and that, if any young lady forgot this precept, she was
almost as much disgraced as by an illicit amour.[2]   Clarendon, who
assuredly bore no ill will to the priesthood, mentions it as a sign of the
confusion of ranks which the great rebellion had produced, that some
damsels of noble families had bestowed themselves on divines.[3]   A
waiting woman was generally considered as the most suitable helpmate
for a parson.   Queen Elizabeth, as head of the Church, had given what

---

[1] Eachard, Causes of the Contempt of the Clergy ; Oldham, Satire addressed to a Friend
about to leave the University ; Tatler, 255. 258.   That the English clergy were a lowborn class,
is remarked in the Travels of the Grand Duke Cosmo, Appendix A.

[2] "A causidico, medicastro, ipsaque artificum farragine, ecclesiæ rector aut vicarius contemnitur
et fit ludibrio.   Gentis et familiæ nitor sacris ordinibus pollutus censetur : fœminisque natalitio
insignibus unicum inculcatur sæpius præceptum, ne modestiæ naufragium faciant, aut, (quod idem
auribus tam delicatulis sonat,) ne clerico se nuptas dari patiantur."—Angliæ Notitia, by T. Wood,
of New College, Oxford, 1686.

[3] Clarendon's Life, ii. 21.

The Careful RESIDENT.

The Carelefs NON~RESIDENT.

The Proteſtant Mirrour, in proper Poſtures and Principles :

O R,

The Careful Reſident, and the Carelefs Non-Reſident.

CARICATURE AGAINST THE CLERGY. THE RESIDENT AND THE PLURALIST

From a broadside in the possession of the Editor

seemed to be a formal sanction to this prejudice, by issuing special orders that no clergyman should presume to espouse a servant girl, without the consent of the master or mistress.[1] During several generations accordingly the relation between divines and handmaidens was a theme for endless jest ; nor would it be easy to find, in the comedy of the seventeenth century, a single instance of a clergyman who wins a spouse above the rank of a cook.[2] Even so late as the time of George the Second, the keenest of all observers of life and manners, himself a priest, remarked that, in a great household, the chaplain was the resource of a lady's maid whose character had been blown upon, and who was therefore forced to give up hopes of catching the steward.[3]

In general the divine who quitted his chaplainship for a benefice and a wife found that he had only exchanged one class of vexations for another. Hardly one living in fifty enabled the incumbent to bring up a family comfortably. As children multiplied and grew, the household of the priest became more and more beggarly. Holes appeared more and more plainly in the thatch of his parsonage and in his single cassock. Often it was only by toiling on his glebe, by feeding swine, and by loading dungcarts, that he could obtain daily bread ; nor did his utmost exertions always prevent the bailiffs from taking his concordance and his inkstand in execution. It was a white day on which he was admitted into the kitchen of a great house, and regaled by the servants with cold meat and ale. His children were brought up like the children of the neighbouring peasantry. His boys followed the plough ; and his girls went out to service.[4] Study he found impossible : for the advowson of his living would hardly have sold for a sum sufficient to purchase a good theological library ; and he might be considered as unusually lucky if he had ten or twelve dogeared volumes among the pots and pans on his shelves. Even a keen and strong intellect might be expected to rust in so unfavourable a situation.

Assuredly there was at that time no lack in the English Church of ministers distinguished by abilities and learning. But it is to be observed

[1] See the injunctions of 1559, in Bishop Sparrow's Collection. Jeremy Collier, in his Essay on Pride, speaks of this injunction with a bitterness which proves that his own pride had not been effectually tamed.

[2] Roger and Abigail in Fletcher's Scornful Lady, Bull and the Nurse in Vanbrugh's Relapse, Smirk and Susan in Shadwell's Lancashire Witches, are instances.

[3] Swift's Directions to Servants. In Swift's Remarks on the Clerical Residence Bill, he describes the family of an English vicar thus :—"His wife is little better than a Goody, in her birth, education, or dress. . . . His daughters shall go to service, or be sent apprentice to the sempstress of the next town."

[4] Even in Tom Jones, published two generations later, Mrs. Seagrim, the wife of a gamekeeper, and Mrs. Honour, a waitingwoman, boast of their descent from clergymen. "It is to be hoped," says Fielding, "such instances will in future ages, when some provision is made for the families of the inferior clergy, appear stranger than they can be thought at present."

that these ministers were not scattered among the rural population. They were brought together at a few places where the means of acquiring knowledge were abundant, and where the opportunities of vigorous intellectual exercise were frequent.[1] At such places were to be found divines qualified by parts, by eloquence, by wide knowledge of literature, of science, and of life, to defend their Church victoriously against heretics and sceptics, to command the attention of frivolous and worldly congregations, to guide the deliberations of senates, and to make religion respectable, even in the most dissolute of courts. Some laboured to fathom the abysses of metaphysical theology : some were deeply versed in biblical criticism ; and some threw light on the darkest parts of ecclesiastical history. Some proved themselves consummate masters of logic. Some cultivated rhetoric with such assiduity and success that their discourses are still justly valued as models of style. These eminent men were to be found, with scarcely a single exception, at the Universities, at the great Cathedrals, or in the capital. Barrow had lately died at Cambridge ; and Pearson had gone thence to the episcopal bench. Cudworth and Henry More were still living there. South and Pococke, Jane and Aldrich, were at Oxford. Prideaux was in the close of Norwich, and Whitby in the close of Salisbury. But it was chiefly by the London clergy, who were always spoken of as a class apart, that the fame of their profession for learning and eloquence was upheld. The principal pulpits of the metropolis were occupied about this time by a crowd of distinguished men, from among whom was selected a large proportion of the rulers of the Church. Sherlock preached at the Temple, Tillotson at Lincoln's Inn, Wake and Jeremy Collier at Gray's Inn, Burnet at the Rolls, Stillingfleet at Saint Paul's Cathedral, Patrick at Saint Paul's in Covent Garden, Fowler at Saint Giles's, Cripplegate, Sharp at Saint Giles's in the Fields, Tenison at Saint Martin's, Sprat at Saint Margaret's, Beveridge at Saint Peter's in Cornhill. Of these twelve men, all of high note in ecclesiastical history, ten became Bishops, and four Archbishops. Meanwhile almost the only important theological works which came forth from a rural parsonage were those of George Bull, afterwards Bishop of Saint David's ; and Bull never would have produced those works, had he not inherited an estate, by the sale of which he was enabled to collect a library, such as probably no other country clergyman in England possessed.[2]

Thus the Anglican priesthood was divided into two sections, which, in acquirements, in manners, and in social position, differed widely from

[1] This distinction between country clergy and town clergy is strongly marked by Eachard, and cannot but be observed by every person who has studied the ecclesiastical history of that age.

[2] Nelson's Life of Bull. As to the extreme difficulty which the country clergy found in procuring books, see the Life of Thomas Bray, the founder of the Society for the Propagation of the Gospel.

each other. One section, trained for cities and courts, comprised men familiar with all ancient and modern learning ; men able to encounter Hobbes or Bossuet at all the weapons of controversy ; men who could, in their sermons, set forth the majesty and beauty of Christianity with such justness of thought, and such energy of language, that the indolent Charles roused himself to listen, and the fastidious Buckingham forgot to sneer ; men whose address, politeness, and knowledge of the world qualified them to manage the consciences of the wealthy and noble ; men with whom Halifax loved to discuss the interests of empires, and from whom Dryden was not ashamed to own that he had learned to write.[1] The other section was destined to ruder and humbler service. It was dispersed over the country, and consisted chiefly of persons not at all wealthier, and not much more refined, than small farmers or upper servants. Yet it was in these rustic priests, who derived but a scanty subsistence from their tithe sheaves and tithe pigs, and who had not the smallest chance of ever attaining high professional honours, that the professional spirit was strongest. Among those divines who were the boast of the Universities and the delight of the capital, and who had attained, or might reasonably expect to attain, opulence and lordly rank, a party, respectable in numbers, and more respectable in character, leaned towards constitutional principles of government, lived on friendly terms with Presbyterians, Independents, and Baptists, would gladly have seen a full toleration granted to all Protestant sects, and would even have consented to make alterations in the Liturgy, for the purpose of conciliating honest and candid Nonconformists. But such latitudinarianism was held in horror by the country parson. He took, indeed, more pride in his ragged gown than his superiors in their lawn and their scarlet hoods. The very consciousness that there was little in his worldly circumstances to distinguish him from the villagers to whom he preached led him to hold immoderately high the dignity of that sacerdotal office which was his single title to reverence. Having lived in seclusion, and having had little opportunity of correcting his opinions by reading or conversation, he held and taught the doctrines of indefeasible hereditary right, of passive obedience, and of non-resistance, in all their crude absurdity. Having been long engaged in a petty war against the neighbouring dissenters, he too often hated them for the wrong which he had done them, and found no fault with the Five Mile Act and the Conventicle Act, except that those odious laws had not a sharper edge. Whatever influence his office gave him was exerted with passionate zeal on the Tory side ; and that influence was immense. It

[1] "I have frequently heard him (Dryden) own with pleasure, that if he had any talent for English prose it was owing to his having often read the writings of the great Archbishop Tillotson."—Congreve's Dedication of Dryden's Plays

The Character of a Good *Clergy-Man*.

A Worthy OBSERVATION, but Scarce EXAMPLE, in This Degenerate AGE.

YOUR Saviour came not with a gawdy Show,
Nor was his Kingdom of the World below:
Patience in Want, and Poverty of Mind,
These Marks of Council and Churchmen he design'd,
And Living Taught, and Dying left behind.
The Grown he wore was of the pointed Thorn,
In Purple he was Crucify'd, not Born:
They who contend for Place and high Degree,
Are not his Sons, but those of Zebedee.

Is not the Care of Souls a Load sufficient?
Were you not bred apart from Worldly Noise,
To study Souls, their Cures, and their Diseases?
The Province of the Soul is large enough
To fill up ev'ry Cranny of your Time,
And leave you much to answer, if one Wretch
Be Damn'd by your Neglect.

The CHARACTER.

HAPPIEST of all, O LORD, are they whose very Business is thy sacred Service: Who not only bestow an interrupted Glance, but steadily fix their Eyes on Thee: Who are devoted to the happy service of the sanctuary, and Night and Day dwell in thy Presence: Who not engag'd in the Cares and Tumults of the World, spend their Time in Retirement and Devotion: If the Sun rise, it finds them at their Master's Work; and when it sets, leaves them at the same sweet Task. Every Place is a Church to such consecrated Souls, and every Day a holy Sabbath: Every Object is an Occasion of Piety, and every Accident an Exercise of Virtue. Do they behold the Beauteous Stars, they presently adore their great Creator: Do they look down on the fruitful Earth, they instantly begin to praise his Bounty: Let War or Peace do what they will, and the inconstant World reel up and down, they pass through all with a serene Mind, and smoothly go on their regular Course; looking still up to that glorious Life above, and entertaining this present in Hope, and labour to attain it: When they depart sometimes from their proper Center, and forsake a while their belov'd Retirement; 'tis to approach and give Light to others, and enflame some cold and luke-warm Hearts: While they are Abroad they are still with Thee, and nothing can divide them from thy dear Presence: When they return, still Devout and Innocent, thou receivest them as familiar Friends, and freely admit'st them to thy secret sweetness: Thou givest them a Taste from thine own full Board, and overflowest their Hearts with the Wine of Gladness. Often they feel a little Beam from Heaven strike gently, and fill their Breasts with Light; often that gentle Light is kindled into a Flame, and Chastly burns with pure Desires: Desires that still mount up and aim at Thee, the super-natural Centre of all their Hopes. Oh happy State of the Reverend Clergy, who empty of the World, are full of God! Such shall seldom fall, and quickly rise, and make swift Advances in the Way to Heaven: They shall live in Purity, and die with Confidence, and go to sing with the Choirs of Angels.

THE CHARACTER OF A GOOD CLERGYMAN (WITH A PORTRAIT OF DR. BULL)

From a broadside in the possession of the Editor

would be a great error to imagine, because the country rector was in general not regarded as a gentleman, because he could not dare to aspire to the hand of one of the young ladies at the manor house, because he was not asked into the parlours of the great, but was left to drink and smoke with grooms and butlers, that the power of the clerical body was smaller than at present.   The influence of a class is by no means proportioned to the consideration which the members of that class enjoy in their individual capacity.   A Cardinal is a much more exalted personage than a begging friar : but it would be a grievous mistake to suppose that the College of Cardinals has exercised a greater dominion over the public mind of Europe than the Order of Saint Francis. In Ireland, at present, a peer holds a far higher station in society than a Roman Catholic priest : yet there are in Munster and Connaught few counties where a combination of priests would not carry an election against a combination of peers.   In the seventeenth century the pulpit was to a large portion of the population what the periodical press now is.   Scarce any of the clowns who came to the parish church ever saw a Gazette or a political pamphlet.   Ill informed as their spiritual pastor might be, he was yet better informed than themselves : he had every week an opportunity of haranguing them; and his harangues were never answered.   At every important conjuncture, invectives against the Whigs and exhortations to obey the Lord's anointed resounded at once from many thousands of pulpits ; and the effect was formidable indeed.   Of all the causes which, after the dissolution of the Oxford Parliament, produced the violent reaction against the Exclusionists, the most potent seems to have been the oratory of the country clergy.

The power which the country gentlemen and the country clergymen exercised in the rural districts was in some measure counterbalanced **The yeomanry** by the power of the yeomanry, an eminently manly and true-hearted race.   The petty proprietors who cultivated their own fields with their own hands, and enjoyed a modest competence, without affecting to have scutcheons and crests, or aspiring to sit on the bench of justice, then formed a much more important part of the nation than at present.   If we may trust the best statistical writers of that age, not less than a hundred and sixty thousand proprietors, who with their families must have made up more than a seventh of the whole population, derived their subsistence from little freehold estates.   The average income of these small landholders, an income made up of rent, profit, and wages, was estimated at between sixty and seventy pounds a year. It was computed that the number of persons who tilled their own land was greater than the number of those who farmed the land of others.[1] A large portion of the yeomanry had, from the time of the Reformation,

[1] I have taken Davenant's estimate, which is a little lower than King's.

leaned towards Puritanism, had, in the civil war, taken the side of the Parliament, had, after the Restoration, persisted in hearing Presbyterian and Independent preachers, had, at elections, strenuously supported the Exclusionists, and had continued, even after the discovery of the Rye House plot and the proscription of the Whig leaders, to regard Popery and arbitrary power with unmitigated hostility.

Great as has been the change in the rural life of England since the Revolution, the change which has come to pass in the cities is still more amazing. At present above a sixth part of the nation is **Growth of** crowded into provincial towns of more than thirty thousand **the towns** inhabitants. In the reign of Charles the Second no provincial town in the kingdom contained thirty thousand inhabitants ; and only four provincial towns contained so many as ten thousand inhabitants.

Next to the capital, but next at an immense distance, stood Bristol, then the first English seaport, and Norwich, then the first English manufacturing town. Both have since that time been far outstripped by younger rivals ; yet both have made great **Bristol** positive advances. The population of Bristol has quadrupled. The population of Norwich has more than doubled.

Pepys, who visited Bristol eight years after the Restoration, was struck by the splendour of the city. But his standard was not high ; for he noted down as a wonder the circumstance that, in Bristol, a man might look round him and see nothing but houses. It seems that, in no other place with which he was acquainted, except London, did the buildings completely shut out the woods and fields. Large as Bristol might then appear, it occupied but a very small portion of the area on which it now stands. A few churches of eminent beauty rose out of a labyrinth of narrow lanes built upon vaults of no great solidity. If a coach or a cart entered those alleys, there was danger that it would be wedged between the houses, and danger also that it would break in the cellars. Goods were therefore conveyed about the town almost exclusively in trucks drawn by dogs ; and the richest inhabitants exhibited their wealth, not by riding in gilded carriages, but by walking the streets with trains of servants in rich liveries, and by keeping tables loaded with good cheer. The pomp of the christenings and burials far exceeded what was seen at any other place in England. The hospitality of the city was widely renowned, and especially the collations with which the sugar refiners regaled their visitors. The repast was dressed in the furnace, and was accompanied by a rich beverage made of the best Spanish wine, and celebrated over the whole kingdom as Bristol milk. This luxury was supported by a thriving trade with the North American plantations and with the West Indies. The passion for colonial traffic was so strong that there was scarcely a small shopkeeper in Bristol who had not a venture on board of some ship bound for Virginia or the Antilles. Some of these ventures indeed were not of the most honourable kind. There was, in the Transatlantic possessions of the crown, a great demand for labour; and this demand was partly supplied by a system of crimping and kidnapping at the principal English seaports. Nowhere was this system in such active and extensive operation as at Bristol. Even the first magistrates of that city were not ashamed to enrich themselves by so odious a commerce. The number of houses appears, from the returns of the hearth money, to have been, in the year 1685, just five thousand three hundred. We can hardly suppose the number of persons in a house to have been greater than in the city of London; and in the city of London we learn from the best authority that there were then fifty-five persons to ten houses. The population of Bristol must therefore have been about twenty-nine thousand souls.[1]

Norwich was the capital of a large and fruitful province. It was the residence of a Bishop and of a Chapter. It was the chief seat of the chief manufacture of the realm. Some men distinguished

Norwich by learning and science had recently dwelt there; and no place in the kingdom, except the capital and the Universities, had more attractions for the curious. The library, the museum, the aviary, and the botanical garden of Sir Thomas Browne, were thought by Fellows of the Royal Society well worthy of a long pilgrimage. Norwich had also a court in miniature. In the heart of the city stood an old palace of the Dukes of Norfolk, said to be the largest town house in the kingdom out of London. In this mansion, to which were annexed a tennis court, a bowling green, and a wilderness stretching along the banks of the Wansum, the noble family of Howard frequently resided, and kept a state resembling that of petty sovereigns. Drink was served to guests in goblets of pure gold. The very tongs and shovels were of silver. Pictures by Italian masters adorned the walls. The cabinets were filled with a fine collection of gems purchased by that Earl of Arundel whose marbles are now among the ornaments of Oxford. Here, in the year 1671, Charles and his court were sumptuously entertained. Here, too, all comers were annually welcomed, from Christmas to Twelfth Night. Ale flowed in oceans for the populace. Three coaches, one of which had been built at a cost of five hundred pounds

---

[1] Evelyn's Diary, June 27. 1654; Pepys's Diary, June 13. 1668, Roger North's Lives of Lord Keeper Guildford, and of Sir Dudley North, Petty's Political Arithmetic. I have taken Petty's facts, but, in drawing inferences from them, I have been guided by King and Davenant, who, though not abler men than he, had the advantage of coming after him. As to the kidnapping for which Bristol was infamous, see North's Life of Guildford, 121. 216., and the harangue of Jeffreys on the subject, in the Impartial History of his Life and Death, printed with the Bloody Assizes. His style was, as usual, coarse; but I cannot reckon the reprimand which he gave to the magistrates of Bristol among his crimes.

to contain fourteen persons, were sent every afternoon round the city to
bring ladies to the festivities ; and the dances were always followed by
a luxurious banquet.   When the Duke of Norfolk came to Norwich, he
was greeted like a King returning to his capital.   The bells of the
Cathedral and of St. Peter Mancroft were rung : the guns of the castle
were fired ; and the Mayor and Aldermen waited on their illustrious

PLAN OF BRISTOL IN 1671

By James Millerd

fellow citizen with complimentary addresses.   In the year 1693 the
population of Norwich was found, by actual enumeration, to be between
twenty-eight and twenty-nine thousand souls.[1]

Far below Norwich, but still high in dignity and importance, were

[1] Fuller's Worthies ; Evelyn's Diary, Oct. 17. 1671 ; Journal of E. Browne, son of Sir
Thomas Browne, Jan. 166¾ ; Blomefield's History of Norfolk ; History of the City and County
of Norwich, 2 vols. 1768.

some other ancient capitals of shires.   In that age it was seldom that a country gentleman went up with his family to London.   The county town was his metropolis.   He sometimes made it his residence during part of the year.   At all events, he was often attracted thither by business and pleasure, by assizes, quarter sessions, elections, musters of militia, festivals, and races.   There were the halls where the judges, robed in scarlet and escorted by javelins and trumpets, opened the King's commission twice a year.   There were the markets at which the corn, the cattle, the wool, and the hops of the surrounding country were exposed to sale.   There were the great fairs to which merchants came down from London, and where the rural dealer laid in his annual stores of sugar, stationery, cutlery, and muslin.   There were the shops at which the best families of the neighbourhood bought grocery and millinery. Some of these places derived dignity from interesting historical recollections, from cathedrals decorated by all the art and magnificence of the middle ages, from palaces where a long succession of prelates had dwelt, from closes surrounded by the venerable abodes of deans and canons, and from castles which had in the old time repelled the Nevilles or De Veres, and which bore more recent traces of the vengeance of Rupert or of Cromwell.

Conspicuous amongst these interesting cities, were York, the capital of the north, and Exeter, the capital of the west.   Neither can have contained much more than ten thousand inhabitants.   Wor-

Other country towns

cester, the queen of the cider land, had but eight thousand ; Nottingham probably as many.   Gloucester, renowned for that resolute defence which had been fatal to Charles the First, had certainly between four and five thousand ; Derby not quite four thousand.   Shrewsbury was the chief place of an extensive and fertile district.   The Court of the Marches of Wales was held there.   In the language of the gentry many miles round the Wrekin, to go to Shrewsbury was to go to town.   The provincial wits and beauties imitated, as well as they could, the fashions of Saint James's Park, in the walks along the side of the Severn.   The inhabitants were about seven thousand.[1]

[1] The population of York appears, from the return of baptisms and burials, in Drake's History, to have been about 13,000 in 1730.   Exeter had only 17,000 inhabitants in 1801.   The population of Worcester was numbered just before the siege in 1646.   See Nash's History of Worcestershire.   I have made allowance for the increase which must be supposed to have taken place in forty years.   In 1740, the population of Nottingham was found, by enumeration, to be just 10,000.   See Dering's History.   The population of Gloucester may readily be inferred from the number of houses which King found in the returns of hearth money, and from the number of births and burials which is given in Atkyns's History.   The population of Derby was 4000 in 1712.   See Wolley's MS. History, quoted in Lyson's Magna Britannia.   The population of Shrewsbury was ascertained, in 1695, by actual enumeration.   As to the gaieties of Shrewsbury, see Farquhar's Recruiting Officer.   Farquhar's description is borne out by a ballad in the Pepysian Library, of which the burden is " Shrewsbury for me."

PART OF A VIEW OF NORWICH ABOUT 1738

From Buck's Antiquities of England

The population of every one of these places has, since the Revolution, much more than doubled. The population of some has multiplied sevenfold. The streets have been almost entirely rebuilt. Slate has succeeded to thatch, and brick to timber. The pavements and the lamps, the display of wealth in the principal shops, and the luxurious neatness of the dwellings occupied by the gentry would, in the seventeenth century, have seemed miraculous. Yet is the relative importance of the old capitals of counties by no means what it was. Younger towns, towns which are rarely or never mentioned in our early history and which sent no representatives to our early Parliaments, have, within the memory of persons still living, grown to a greatness which this generation contemplates with wonder and pride, not unaccompanied by awe and anxiety.

The most eminent of these towns were indeed known in the seventeenth century as respectable seats of industry. Nay, their rapid progress and their vast opulence were then sometimes described in language which seems ludicrous to a man who has seen their present grandeur.

Manchester

One of the most populous and prosperous among them was Manchester. Manchester had been required by the Protector to send one representative to his Parliament, and was mentioned by writers of the time of Charles the Second as a busy and opulent place. Cotton had, during half a century, been brought thither from Cyprus and Smyrna ; but the manufacture was in its infancy. Whitney had not yet taught how the raw material might be furnished in quantities almost fabulous. Arkwright had yet not taught how it might be worked up with a speed and precision which seem magical. The whole annual import did not, at the end of the seventeenth century, amount to two millions of pounds, a quantity which would now hardly supply the demand of forty-eight hours. That wonderful emporium, which in population and wealth far surpasses capitals so much renowned as Berlin, Madrid, and Lisbon, was then a mean and ill built market town, containing under six thousand people. It then had not a single press. It now supports a hundred printing establishments. It then had not a single coach. It now supports twenty coachmakers.[1]

Leeds was already the chief seat of the woollen manufactures of Yorkshire : but the elderly inhabitants could still remember the time

Leeds

when the first brick house, then and long after called the Red House, was built. They boasted loudly of their increasing wealth, and of the immense sales of cloth which took place in

[1] Blome's Britannia, 1673 ; Aikin's Country round Manchester ; Manchester Directory, 1845; Baines, History of the Cotton Manufacture. The best information which I have been able to find, touching the population of Manchester in the seventeenth century, is contained in a paper drawn up by the Reverend R. Parkinson, and published in the Journal of the Statistical Society for October 1842.

PART OF A VIEW OF LEEDS ABOUT 1720

From Buck's Antiquities of England

the open air on the bridge.　Hundreds, nay thousands of pounds, had been paid down in the course of one busy market day.　The rising importance of Leeds had attracted the notice of successive governments. Charles the First had granted municipal privileges to the town.　Oliver had invited it to send one member to the House of Commons.　But from the returns of the hearth money it seems certain that the whole population of the borough, an extensive district which contains many hamlets, did not, in the reign of Charles the Second, exceed seven thousand souls.　In 1841 there were more than a hundred and fifty thousand.[1]

About a day's journey south of Leeds, on the verge of a wild moorland tract, lay an ancient manor, now rich with cultivation, then barren **Sheffield** and unenclosed, which was known by the name of Hallamshire.　Iron abounded there ; and, from a very early period, the rude whittles fabricated there had been sold all over the kingdom. They had indeed been mentioned by Geoffrey Chaucer in one of his Canterbury Tales.　But the manufacture appears to have made little progress during the three centuries which followed his time.　This languor may perhaps be explained by the fact that the trade was, during almost the whole of this long period, subject to such regulations as the lord and his court leet thought fit to impose.　The more delicate kinds of cutlery were either made in the capital, or brought from the Continent.　Indeed it was not till the reign of George the First that the English surgeons ceased to import from France those exquisitely fine blades which are required for operations on the human frame.　Most of the Hallamshire forges were collected in a market town which had sprung up near the castle of the proprietor, and which, in the reign of James the First, had been a singularly miserable place, containing about two thousand inhabitants, of whom a third were half starved and half naked beggars.　It seems certain from the parochial registers that the population did not amount to four thousand at the end of the reign of Charles the Second.　The effects of a species of toil singularly unfavourable to the health and vigour of the human frame were at once discerned by every traveller.　A large proportion of the people had distorted limbs.　This is that Sheffield which now, with its dependencies, contains a hundred and twenty thousand souls, and which sends forth its admirable knives, razors, and lancets to the farthest ends of the world.[2]

Birmingham had not been thought of sufficient importance to return a member to Oliver's Parliament.　Yet the manufacturers of Birmingham

---

[1] Thoresby's Ducatus Leodensis ; Whitaker's Loidis and Elmete ; Wardell's Municipal History of the Borough of Leeds. (1848.)　In 1851 Leeds had 172,000 inhabitants. (1857.)

[2] Hunter's History of Hallamshire. (1848.)　In 1851 the population of Sheffield had increased to 135,000. (1857.)

PART OF A VIEW OF SHEFFIELD ABOUT 1720

From Buck's Antiquities of England

were already a busy and thriving race. They boasted that their hardware was highly esteemed, not indeed as now, at Pekin and Lima, at Bokhara and Timbuctoo, but in London, and even as far off **Birmingham** as Ireland. They had acquired a less honourable renown as coiners of bad money. In allusion to their spurious groats, some Tory wit had fixed on demagogues, who hypocritically affected zeal against Popery, the nickname of Birminghams. Yet in 1685 the population, which is now little less than two hundred thousand, did not amount to four thousand. Birmingham buttons were just beginning to be known : of Birmingham guns nobody had yet heard ; and the place whence, two generations later, the magnificent editions of Baskerville went forth to astonish all the librarians of Europe, did not contain a single regular shop where a Bible or an almanack could be bought. On market days a bookseller named Michael Johnson, the father of the great Samuel Johnson, came over from Lichfield, and opened a stall during a few hours. This supply of literature was long found equal to the demand.[1]

These four chief seats of our great manufactures deserve especial mention. It would be tedious to enumerate all the populous and opulent hives of industry which, a hundred and fifty years ago, were hamlets without parish churches, or desolate moors, inhabited only by grouse and wild deer. Nor has the change been less signal in those outlets by which the products of the English looms and forges are poured forth over the whole world. At present Liverpool contains more than three hundred thousand inhabitants. The shipping registered at her port amounts to between four and five hundred thousand **Liverpool** tons. Into her custom house has been repeatedly paid in one year a sum more than thrice as great as the whole income of the English crown in 1685. The receipts of her post office, even since the great reduction of the duty, exceed the sum which the postage of the whole kingdom yielded to the Duke of York. Her endless docks, quays, and warehouses are among the wonders of the world. Yet even those docks and quays and warehouses seem hardly to suffice for the gigantic trade of the Mersey ; and already a rival city is growing fast on the opposite shore. In the days of Charles the Second Liverpool was described as a rising town which had recently made great advances, and which maintained a profitable intercourse with Ireland and with the sugar colonies. The customs had multiplied eight-fold within sixteen

---

[1] Blome's Britannia, 1673; Dugdale's Warwickshire; North's Examen, 321.; Preface to Absalom and Achitophel; Hutton's History of Birmingham; Boswell's Life of Johnson. In 1690 the burials at Birmingham were 150, the baptisms 125. I think it probable that the annual mortality was little less than one in twenty-five. In London it was considerably greater. A historian of Nottingham, half a century later, boasted of the extraordinary salubrity of his town, where the annual mortality was one in thirty. See Dering's History of Nottingham. (1848.) In 1851 the population of Birmingham had increased to 232,000. (1857.)

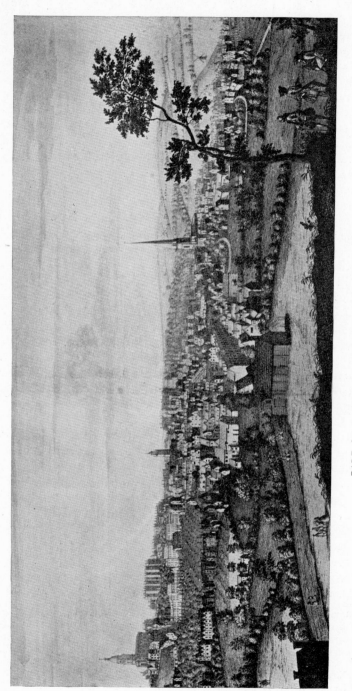

PART OF A VIEW OF BIRMINGHAM ABOUT 1729

From Buck's Antiquities of England

years, and amounted to what was then considered as the immense sum of fifteen thousand pounds annually. But the population can hardly have exceeded four thousand : the shipping was about fourteen hundred tons, less than the tonnage of a single modern Indiaman of the first class; and the whole number of seamen belonging to the port cannot be estimated at more than two hundred.[1]

Such has been the progress of those towns where wealth is created and accumulated. Not less rapid has been the progress of towns of a

Watering places very different kind, towns in which wealth, created and accumulated elsewhere, is expended for purposes of health and recreation. Some of the most remarkable of these gay places have sprung into existence since the time of the Stuarts. Cheltenham is now

Cheltenham a greater city than any which the kingdom contained in the seventeenth century, London alone excepted. But in the seventeenth century, and at the beginning of the eighteenth, Cheltenham was mentioned by local historians merely as a rural parish lying under the Cotswold Hills, and affording good ground, both for tillage and pasture. Corn grew and cattle browsed over the space now covered by that long succession of streets and villas.[2] Brighton was described as a

Brighton place which had once been thriving, which had possessed many small fishing barks, and which had, when at the height of prosperity, contained above two thousand inhabitants, but which was sinking fast into decay. The sea was gradually gaining on the buildings, which at length almost entirely disappeared. Ninety years ago the ruins of an old fort were to be seen lying among the pebbles and seaweed on the beach; and ancient men could still point out the traces of foundations on a spot where a street of more than a hundred huts had been swallowed up by the waves. So desolate was the place after this calamity, that the vicarage was thought scarcely worth having. A few poor fishermen, however, still continued to dry their nets on those cliffs, on which now a town, more than twice as large and populous as the Bristol of the Stuarts, presents, mile after mile, its gay and fantastic front to the sea.[3]

England, however, was not, in the seventeenth century, destitute of watering places. The gentry of Derbyshire and of the neighbouring

Buxton counties repaired to Buxton, where they were lodged in low rooms under bare rafters, and regaled with oatcake, and with a viand which the hosts called mutton, but which the guests suspected

---

[1] Blome's Britannia; Gregson's Antiquities of the County Palatine and Duchy of Lancaster, Part II.; Petition from Liverpool in the Privy Council Book, May 10. 1686. In 1690 the burials at Liverpool were 151, the baptisms 120. In 1844 the net receipt of the customs at Liverpool was 4,365,526l. 1s. 8d. (1848.) In 1851 Liverpool contained 375,000 inhabitants. (1857.)

[2] Atkyns's Gloucestershire.

[3] Magna Britannia; Grose's Antiquities; New Brighthelmstone Directory, 1770.

VIEW OF TUNBRIDGE WELLS

From an engraving by John Kip

to be dog.   A single good house stood near the spring.[1]   Tunbridge

Tunbridge Wells   Wells, lying within a day's journey of the capital, and in one of the richest and most highly civilised parts of the kingdom, had much greater attractions.   At present we see there a town which would, a hundred and sixty years ago, have ranked, in population, fourth or fifth among the towns of England.   The brilliancy of the shops and the luxury of the private dwellings far surpasses anything that England could then show.   When the court, soon after the Restoration, visited Tunbridge Wells, there was no town : but, within a mile of the spring, rustic cottages, somewhat cleaner and neater than the ordinary cottages of that time, were scattered over the heath.   Some of these cabins were movable, and were carried on sledges from one part of the common to another.   To these huts men of fashion, wearied with the din and smoke of London, sometimes came in the summer to breathe fresh air, and to catch a glimpse of rural life.   During the season a kind of fair was daily held near the fountain.   The wives and daughters of the Kentish farmers came from the neighbouring villages with cream, cherries, wheatears, and quails.   To chaffer with them, to flirt with them, to praise their straw hats and tight heels, was a refreshing pastime to voluptuaries sick of the airs of actresses and maids of honour.   Milliners, toymen, and jewellers came down from London, and opened a bazaar under the trees.   In one booth the politician might find his coffee and the London Gazette ; in another were gamblers playing deep at basset ; and, on fine evenings, the fiddles were in attendance, and there were morris dances on the elastic turf of the bowling green.   In 1685 a subscription had just been raised among those who frequented the wells for building a church, which the Tories, who then domineered everywhere, insisted on dedicating to Saint Charles the Martyr.[2]

But at the head of the English watering places, without a rival, was Bath.   The springs of that city had been renowned from the days of

Bath   the Romans.   It had been, during many centuries, the seat of a Bishop.   The sick repaired thither from every part of the realm.   The King sometimes held his court there.   Nevertheless, Bath was then a maze of only four or five hundred houses, crowded within an old wall in the vicinity of the Avon.   Pictures of what were considered as the finest of those houses are still extant, and greatly resemble the lowest rag shops and pothouses of Ratcliffe Highway.   Travellers indeed complained loudly of the narrowness and meanness of the streets.   That beautiful city which charms even eyes familiar with the masterpieces of Bramante and Palladio, and which the genius of Anstey and of Smollett,

---

[1] Tour in Derbyshire, by Thomas Browne, son of Sir Thomas.

[2] Mémoires de Grammont ; Hasted's History of Kent ; Tunbridge Wells, a Comedy, 1678 ; Causton's Tunbridgialia, 1688 ; Metellus, a poem on Tunbridge Wells, 1693.

of Frances Burney and of Jane Austen, has made classic ground, had not begun to exist.   Milsom Street itself was an open field lying far beyond the walls ; and hedgerows intersected the space which is now covered by the Crescent and the Circus.   The poor patients to whom the waters had been recommended lay on straw in a place which, to use the language of a contemporary physician, was a covert rather than a lodging.   As to the comforts and luxuries which were to be found in the interior of the houses of Bath by the fashionable visitors who resorted thither in search of health or amusement, we possess information more complete and minute than can generally be obtained on such subjects. A writer who published an account of that city about sixty years after the Revolution has accurately described the changes which had taken place within his own recollection.   He assures us that, in his younger days, the gentlemen who visited the springs slept in rooms hardly as good as the garrets which he lived to see occupied by footmen.   The floors of the dining rooms were uncarpeted, and were coloured brown with a wash made of soot and small beer, in order to hide the dirt. Not a wainscot was painted.   Not a hearth or a chimneypiece was of marble.   A slab of common freestone and fire irons which had cost from three to four shillings were thought sufficient for any fireplace. The best apartments were hung with coarse woollen stuff, and were furnished with rushbottomed chairs.   Readers who take an interest in the progress of civilisation and of the useful arts will be grateful to the humble topographer who has recorded these facts, and will perhaps wish that historians of far higher pretensions had sometimes spared a few pages from military evolutions and political intrigues, for the purpose of letting us know how the parlours and bedchambers of our ancestors looked.[1]

The position of London, relatively to the other towns of the empire, was, in the time of Charles the Second, far higher than at present.   For at present the population of London is little more than six times the population of Manchester or of Liverpool.   In the   London days of Charles the Second the population of London was more than seventeen times the population of Bristol or of Norwich.   It may be doubted whether any other instance can be mentioned of a great kingdom in which the first city was more than seventeen times as large as the second.   There is reason to believe that, in 1685, London had been, during about half a century, the most populous capital in Europe.   The inhabitants, who are now at least nineteen hundred thousand, were then

[1] See Wood's History of Bath, 1749 ; Evelyn's Diary, June 27. 1654 ; Pepys's Diary, June 12. 1668 ; Stukeley's Itinerarium Curiosum ; Collinson's Somersetshire ; Dr. Peirce's History and Memoirs of the Bath, 1713, Book I. chap. viii. obs. 2. 1684.   I have consulted several old maps and pictures of Bath, particularly one curious map which is surrounded by views of the principal buildings.   It bears the date of 1717.

H.E. I   Y

probably little more than half a million.[1]   London had in the world only one commercial rival, now long ago outstripped, the mighty and opulent Amsterdam.   English writers boasted of the forest of masts and yardarms which covered the river from the Bridge to the Tower, and of the stupendous sums which were collected at the Custom House in Thames Street.   There is, indeed, no doubt that the trade of the metropolis then bore a far greater proportion than at present to the whole trade of the country ; yet to our generation the honest vaunting of our ancestors must appear almost ludicrous.   The shipping which they thought incredibly great appears not to have exceeded seventy thousand tons.   This was, indeed, then more than a third of the whole tonnage of the kingdom, but is now less than a fourth of the tonnage of Newcastle, and is nearly equalled by the tonnage of the steam vessels of the Thames.   The customs of London amounted, in 1685, to about three hundred and thirty thousand pounds a year.   In our time the net duty paid annually, at the same place, exceeds ten millions.[2]

Whoever examines the maps of London which were published towards the close of the reign of Charles the Second will see that only the nucleus of the present capital then existed.   The town did not, as now, fade by imperceptible degrees into the country.   No long avenues of villas, embowered in lilacs and laburnums, extended from the great centre of wealth and civilisation almost to the boundaries of Middlesex and far into the heart of Kent and Surrey.   In the east, no part of the immense line of warehouses and artificial lakes which now stretches from the Tower to Blackwall had even been projected.   On the west, scarcely one of those stately piles of building which are inhabited by the noble and wealthy was in existence ; and Chelsea, which is now peopled by more than forty thousand human beings, was a quiet country village with about a thousand inhabitants.[3]   On the north, cattle fed, and sportsmen wandered with dogs and guns, over the site of the borough of Marylebone, and over far the greater part of the space now covered by the boroughs of Finsbury and of the Tower Hamlets.   Islington was almost a solitude ; and poets loved to contrast its silence and repose with the din and turmoil of the monster London.[4]   On the south the capital is now connected with

[1] According to King 530,000. (1848.)   In 1851 the population of London exceeded 2,300,000. (1857.)

[2] Macpherson's History of Commerce ; Chalmers's Estimate ; Chamberlayne's State of England, 1684.   The tonnage of the steamers belonging to the port of London was, at the end of 1847, about 60,000 tons.   The customs of the port, from 1842 to 1845, very nearly averaged 11,000,000l. (1848.)   In 1854 the tonnage of the steamers of the port of London amounted to 138,000 tons, without reckoning vessels of less than fifty tons. (1857.)

[3] Lyson's Environs of London.   The baptisms at Chelsea, between 1680 and 1690, were only 42 a year.

[4] Cowley, Discourse of Solitude.

its suburb by several bridges, not inferior in magnificence and solidity to the noblest works of the Cæsars. In 1685, a single line of irregular arches, overhung by piles of mean and crazy houses, and garnished, after a fashion worthy of the naked barbarians of Dahomy, with scores of mouldering heads, impeded the navigation of the river.

Of the metropolis, the City, properly so called, was the most important division. At the time of the Restoration it had been built, for the most part, of wood and plaster; the few bricks that were used were ill

THE CUSTOM HOUSE, LONDON

From an engraving by John Dunstall

baked; the booths where goods were exposed to sale projected far into the streets, and were overhung by the upper stories. A few specimens of this architecture may still be seen in those districts which were not reached by the great fire. That fire had, in a few days, **The City** covered a space of little less than a square mile with the ruins of eighty-nine churches and of thirteen thousand houses. But the City had risen again with a celerity which had excited the admiration of neighbouring countries. Unfortunately, the old lines of the streets had been to a great extent preserved; and those lines, originally traced in an age when even princesses performed their journeys on horseback, were often too narrow to allow wheeled carriages to pass each other with ease, and were therefore ill adapted for the residence of wealthy persons in an age when a coach and six was a fashionable luxury. The style of building was, however, far superior to that of the City which had perished. The ordinary material was brick, of much better quality than had formerly been used. On the sites of the ancient parish churches had arisen a multitude of new domes, towers, and spires which bore the mark of the fertile genius of Wren. In every place save one the traces of the great devastation had been completely effaced. But the crowds of workmen, the scaffolds, and the masses of hewn stone were still to be seen where the noblest of Protestant temples was slowly rising on the ruins of the old Cathedral of Saint Paul.[1]

The whole character of the City has, since that time, undergone a complete change. At present the bankers, the merchants, and the chief shopkeepers repair thither on six mornings of every week for the transaction of business : but they reside in other quarters of the metropolis, or at suburban country seats surrounded by shrubberies and flower gardens. This revolution in private habits has produced a political revolution of no small importance. The City is no longer regarded by the wealthiest traders with that attachment which every man naturally feels for his home. It is no longer associated in their minds with domestic affections and endearments. The fireside, the nursery, the social table, the quiet bed are not there. Lombard Street and Threadneedle Street are merely places where men toil and accumulate. They go elsewhere to enjoy and to expend. On a Sunday, or in an evening after the hours of business, some courts and alleys, which a few hours before had been alive with hurrying feet and anxious faces, are as silent as the glades of a forest. The chiefs of the mercantile interest are no longer citizens. They avoid, they almost contemn, municipal honours and duties. Those honours and duties are abandoned to men who, though useful and highly respectable, seldom belong to the princely commercial houses of which the names are renowned throughout the world.

In the seventeenth century the City was the merchant's residence. Those mansions of the great old burghers which still exist have been turned into counting houses and warehouses : but it is evident that they were originally not inferior in magnificence to the dwellings which were then inhabited by the nobility. They sometimes stand in retired and gloomy courts, and are accessible only by inconvenient passages : but their dimensions are ample, and their aspect stately. The entrances are decorated with richly carved pillars and canopies. The staircases and landing places are not wanting in grandeur. The floors are sometimes

---

[1] The fullest and most trustworthy information about the state of the buildings of London at this time is to be derived from the maps and drawings in the British Museum and in the Pepysian Library. The badness of the bricks in the old buildings of London is particularly mentioned in the Travels of the Grand Duke Cosmo. There is an account of the works at Saint Paul's in Ward's London Spy. I am almost ashamed to quote such nauseous balderdash ; but I have been forced to descend even lower, if possible, in search of materials.

LONDON BRIDGE AT THE END OF THE SEVENTEENTH CENTURY

From an engraving by Ogilby

of wood, tessellated after the fashion of France. The palace of Sir
Robert Clayton, in the Old Jewry, contained a superb banqueting room
wainscoted with cedar, and adorned with battles of gods and giants in
fresco.[1] Sir Dudley North expended four thousand pounds, a sum
which would then have been important to a Duke, on the rich furniture
of his reception rooms in Basinghall Street.[2] In such abodes, under the
last Stuarts, the heads of the great firms lived splendidly and hospitably.
To their dwelling place they were bound by the strongest ties of interest
and affection. There they had passed their youth, had made their friendships, had courted their wives, had seen their children grow up, had laid
the remains of their parents in the earth, and expected that their own
remains would be laid. That intense patriotism which is peculiar to the
members of societies congregated within a narrow space was, in such
circumstances, strongly developed. London was, to the Londoner, what
Athens was to the Athenian of the age of Pericles, what Florence was to
the Florentine of the fifteenth century. The citizen was proud of the
grandeur of his city, punctilious about her claims to respect, ambitious
of her offices, and zealous for her franchises.

At the close of the reign of Charles the Second the pride of the
Londoners was smarting from a cruel mortification. The old charter
had been taken away ; and the magistracy had been remodelled. All
the civic functionaries were Tories : and the Whigs, though in numbers
and in wealth superior to their opponents, found themselves excluded
from every local dignity. Nevertheless, the external splendour of the
municipal government was not diminished, nay, was rather increased by
this change. For, under the administration of some Puritans who had
lately borne rule, the ancient fame of the City for good cheer had
declined : but under the new magistrates, who belonged to a more
festive party, and at whose boards guests of rank and fashion from
beyond Temple Bar were often seen, the Guildhall and the halls of the
great companies were enlivened by many sumptuous banquets. During
these repasts, odes, composed by the poet laureate of the corporation, in
praise of the King, the Duke, and the Mayor, were sung to music. The
drinking was deep, the shouting loud. An observant Tory, who had
often shared in these revels, has remarked that the practice of huzzaing
after drinking healths dates from this joyous period.[3]

The magnificence displayed by the first civic magistrate was almost
regal. The gilded coach, indeed, which is now annually admired by the
crowd, was not yet a part of his state. On great occasions he appeared

---

[1] Evelyn's Diary, Sept. 20. 1672.   [2] Roger North's Life of Sir Dudley North.
[3] North's Examen. This amusing writer has preserved a specimen of the sublime raptures in
which the Pindar of the City indulged :—
        " The worshipful Sir John Moor !
        After age that name adore !"

OLD ST. PAUL'S FROM THE NORTH

From an engraving by W. Hollar, 1656

on horseback, attended by a long cavalcade inferior in magnificence only to that which, before a coronation, escorted the sovereign from the Tower to Westminster. The Lord Mayor was never seen in public without his rich robe, his hood of black velvet, his gold chain, his jewel, and a great attendance of harbingers and guards.[1] Nor did the world find anything ludicrous in the pomp which constantly surrounded him. For it was not more than became the place which, as wielding the strength and representing the dignity of the City of London, he was entitled to occupy in the state. That City, being then not only without equal in the country, but without second, had, during five and forty years, exercised almost as great an influence on the politics of England as Paris has, in our own time, exercised on the politics of France. In intelligence London was greatly in advance of every other part of the kingdom. A government, supported and trusted by London, could in a day obtain such pecuniary means as it would have taken months to collect from the rest of the island. Nor were the military resources of the capital to be despised. The power which the Lord Lieutenants exercised in other parts of the kingdom was in London entrusted to a Commission of eminent citizens. Under the orders of this Commission were twelve regiments of foot and two regiments of horse. An army of drapers' apprentices and journeymen tailors, with common councilmen for captains and aldermen for colonels, might not indeed have been able to stand its ground against regular troops; but there were then very few regular troops in the kingdom. A town, therefore, which could send forth, at an hour's notice, thousands of men, abounding in natural courage, provided with tolerable weapons, and not altogether untinctured with martial discipline, could not but be a valuable ally and a formidable enemy. It was not forgotten that Hampden and Pym had been protected from lawless tyranny by the London trainbands; that, in the great crisis of the civil war, the London trainbands had marched to raise the siege of Gloucester; or that, in the movement against the military tyrants which followed the downfall of Richard Cromwell, the London trainbands had borne a signal part. In truth, it is no exaggeration to say that, but for the hostility of the City, Charles the First would never have been vanquished, and that, without the help of the City, Charles the Second could scarcely have been restored.

These considerations may serve to explain why, in spite of that attraction which had, during a long course of years, gradually drawn the aristocracy westward, a few men of high rank had continued, till a very recent period, to dwell in the vicinity of the Exchange and of the Guildhall. Shaftesbury and Buckingham, while engaged in bitter and unscrupulous opposition to the government, had thought that they could

[1] Chamberlayne's State of England, 1684; Angliæ Metropolis, 1690; Seymour's London, 1734.

SIR JOHN MOORE, LORD MAYOR OF LONDON IN 1682

From a mezzotint by McArdell in the Sutherland Collection

nowhere carry on their intrigues so conveniently or so securely as under the protection of the City magistrates and the City militia. Shaftesbury had therefore lived in Aldersgate Street, at a house which may still be easily known by pilasters and wreaths, the graceful work of Inigo. Buckingham had ordered his mansion near Charing Cross, once the abode of the Archbishops of York, to be pulled down ; and, while streets and alleys which are still named after him were rising on that site, chose to reside in Dowgate.[1]

These, however, were rare exceptions. Almost all the noble families of England had long migrated beyond the walls. The district where most of their town houses stood lies between the City and the regions which are now considered as fashionable. A few great men still retained their hereditary hotels in the Strand. The stately dwellings on the south and west of Lincoln's Inn Fields, the Piazza of Covent Garden, Southampton Square, which is now called Bloomsbury Square, and King's Square in Soho Fields, which is now called Soho Square, were among the favourite spots. Foreign princes were carried to see Bloomsbury Square, as one of the wonders of England.[2] Soho Square, which had just been built, was to our ancestors a subject of pride with which their posterity will hardly sympathise. Monmouth Square had been the name while the fortunes of the Duke of Monmouth flourished ; and on the southern side towered his mansion. The front, though ungraceful, was lofty and richly adorned. The walls of the principal apartments were finely sculptured with fruit, foliage, and armorial bearings, and were hung with embroidered satin.[3] Every trace of this magnificence has long disappeared ; and no aristocratical mansion is to be found in that once aristocratical quarter. A little way north from Holborn, and on the verge of the pastures and cornfields, rose two celebrated palaces, each with an ample garden. One of them, then called Southampton House, and subsequently Bedford House, was removed about fifty years ago to make room for a new city, which now covers, with its squares, streets, and churches, a vast area, renowned in the seventeenth century for peaches and snipes. The other, Montague House, celebrated for its frescoes and furniture, was, a few months after the death of Charles the Second, burned to the ground, and was speedily succeeded by a more magnificent Montague House, which, having been long the repository of such various and precious treasures of art, science, and learning as were scarcely ever before assembled under a single roof, has now given place to an edifice more magnificent still.[4]

Fashionable part of the capital

[1] North's Examen, 116 ; Wood, Ath. Ox. Shaftesbury ; The Duke of B.'s Litany.

[2] Travels of the Grand Duke Cosmo.

[3] Chamberlayne's State of England, 1684 ; Pennant's London ; Smith's Life of Nollekens.

[4] Evelyn's Diary, Oct. 10. 1683, Jan. 19. 168$\frac{4}{5}$.

SOUTHAMPTON OR BLOOMSBURY SQUARE ABOUT 1720

By Sutton Nicholls

Nearer to the Court, on a space called Saint James's Fields, had just been built Saint James's Square and Jermyn Street. Saint James's Church had recently been opened for the accommodation of the inhabitants of this new quarter.[1] Golden Square, which was in the next generation inhabited by lords and ministers of state, had not yet been begun. Indeed the only dwellings to be seen on the north of Piccadilly were three or four isolated and almost rural mansions, of which the most celebrated was the costly pile erected by Clarendon, and nicknamed Dunkirk House. It had been purchased after its founder's downfall by the Duke of Albemarle. The Clarendon Hotel and Albemarle Street still preserve the memory of the site.

He who then rambled to what is now the gayest and most crowded part of Regent Street found himself in a solitude, and was sometimes so fortunate as to have a shot at a woodcock.[2] On the north the Oxford road ran between hedges. Three or four hundred yards to the south were the garden walls of a few great houses which were considered as quite out of town. On the west was a meadow renowned for a spring from which, long afterwards, Conduit Street was named. On the east was a field not to be passed without a shudder by any Londoner of that age. There, as in a place far from the haunts of men, had been dug, twenty years before, when the great plague was raging, a pit into which the dead carts had nightly shot corpses by scores. It was popularly believed that the earth was deeply tainted with infection, and could not be disturbed without imminent risk to human life. No foundations were laid there till two generations had passed without any return of the pestilence, and till the ghastly spot had long been surrounded by buildings.[3]

We should greatly err if we were to suppose that any of the streets and squares then bore the same aspect as at present. The great majority of the houses, indeed, have, since that time, been wholly, or in great part, rebuilt. If the most fashionable parts of the capital could be placed before us, such as they then were, we should be disgusted by their squalid appearance, and poisoned by their noisome atmosphere.

In Covent Garden a filthy and noisy market was held close to the dwellings of the great. Fruit women screamed, carters fought, cabbage stalks and rotten apples accumulated in heaps at the thresholds of the Countess of Berkshire and of the Bishop of Durham.[4]

[1] Stat. 1 Jac. II. c. 22. ; Evelyn's Diary, Dec. 7. 1684.

[2] Old General Oglethorpe, who died in 1785, used to boast that he had shot birds here in Anne's reign. See Pennant's London, and the Gentleman's Magazine for July 1785.

[3] The pest field will be seen in maps of London as late as the end of George the First's reign.

[4] See a very curious plan of Covent Garden made about 1690, and engraved for Smith's History of Westminster. See also Hogarth's Morning, painted while some of the houses in the Piazza were still occupied by people of fashion.

PLAN OF BEDFORD HOUSE AND COVENT GARDEN ABOUT 1690

From J. T. Smith's History of Westminster

The centre of Lincoln's Inn Fields was an open space where the rabble congregated every evening, within a few yards of Cardigan House and Winchester House, to hear mountebanks harangue, to see bears dance, and to set dogs at oxen. Rubbish was shot in every part of the area. Horses were exercised there. The beggars were as noisy and importunate as in the worst governed cities of the Continent. A Lincoln's Inn mumper was a proverb. The whole fraternity knew the arms and liveries of every charitably disposed grandee in the neighbour-hood, and, as soon as his lordship's coach and six appeared, came hopping and crawling in crowds to persecute him. These disorders lasted, in spite of many accidents, and of some legal proceedings, till, in the reign of George the Second, Sir Joseph Jekyll, Master of the Rolls, was knocked down and nearly killed in the middle of the square. Then at length palisades were set up, and a pleasant garden laid out.[1]

Saint James's Square was a receptacle for all the offal and cinders, for all the dead cats and dead dogs of Westminster. At one time a cudgel player kept the ring there. At another time an impudent squatter settled himself there, and built a shed for rubbish under the windows of the gilded saloons in which the first magnates of the realm, Norfolk, Ormond, Kent, and Pembroke, gave banquets and balls. It was not till these nuisances had lasted through a whole generation, and till much had been written about them, that the inhabitants applied to Parliament for permission to put up rails, and to plant trees.[2]

When such was the state of the region inhabited by the most luxurious portion of society, we may easily believe that the great body of the population suffered what would now be considered as insupportable grievances. The pavement was detestable : all foreigners cried shame upon it. The drainage was so bad that in rainy weather the gutters soon became torrents. Several facetious poets have commemorated the fury with which these black rivulets roared down Snow Hill and Ludgate Hill, bearing to Fleet Ditch a vast tribute of animal and vegetable filth from the stalls of butchers and greengrocers. This flood was profusely thrown to right and left by coaches and carts. To

---

[1] London Spy ; Tom Brown's Comical View of London and Westminster ; Turner's Propositions for the employing of the Poor, 1678 ; Daily Courant and Daily Journal of June 7. 1733 ; Case of Michael v. Allestree, in 1676, 2 Levinz, p. 172. Michael had been run over by two horses which Allestree was breaking in Lincoln's Inn Fields. The declaration set forth that the defendant "porta deux chivals ungovernable en un coach, et improvide, incaute, et absque debita consideratione ineptitudinis loci la eux drive pur eux faire tractable et apt pur un coach, quels chivals, pur ceo que, per leur ferocite, ne poient estre rule, curre sur le plaintiff et le noie."

[2] Stat. 12 Geo. I. c. 25. ; Commons' Journals, Feb. 25. March 2. 172⅚ ; London Gardener, 1712 ; Evening Post, March 23. 1731. I have not been able to find this number of the Evening Post ; I therefore quote it on the faith of Mr. Malcolm, who mentions it in his History of London.

THE TEMPLE ABOUT 1671

keep as far from the carriage road as possible was therefore the wish of every pedestrian. The mild and timid gave the wall. The bold and athletic took it. If two roisterers met, they cocked their hats in each other's faces, and pushed each other about till the weaker was shoved towards the kennel. If he was a mere bully he sneaked off, muttering that he should find a time. If he was pugnacious, the encounter probably ended in a duel behind Montague House.[1]

The houses were not numbered. There would indeed have been little advantage in numbering them ; for of the coachmen, chairmen, porters, and errand boys of London, a very small proportion could read. It was necessary to use marks which the most ignorant could understand. The shops were therefore distinguished by painted or sculptured signs, which gave a gay and grotesque aspect to the streets. The walk from Charing Cross to Whitechapel lay through an endless succession of Saracens' Heads, Royal Oaks, Blue Bears, and Golden Lambs, which disappeared when they were no longer required for the direction of the common people.

When the evening closed in, the difficulty and danger of walking about London became serious indeed. The garret windows were opened, and pails were emptied, with little regard to those who were passing below. Falls, bruises, and broken bones were of constant occurrence. For, till the last year of the reign of Charles the Second, most of the streets were left in profound darkness. Thieves and robbers plied their trade with impunity : yet they were hardly so terrible to peaceable citizens as another class of ruffians. It was a favourite amusement of dissolute young gentlemen to swagger by night about the town, breaking windows, upsetting sedans, beating quiet men, and offering rude caresses to pretty women. Several dynasties of these tyrants had, since the Restoration, domineered over the streets. The Muns and Tityre Tus

Police of London had given place to the Hectors, and the Hectors had been recently succeeded by the Scourers. At a later period arose the Nicker, the Hawcubite, and the yet more dreaded name of Mohawk.[2]

---

[1] Lettres sur les Anglois, written early in the reign of William the Third ; Swift's City Shower ; Gay's Trivia. Johnson used to relate a curious conversation which he had with his mother about giving and taking the wall.

[2] Oldham's Imitation of the 3d Satire of Juvenal, 1682 ; Shadwell's Scourers, 1690. Many other authorities will readily occur to all who are acquainted with the popular literature of that and the succeeding generation. It may be suspected that some of the Tityre Tus, like good Cavaliers, broke Milton's windows shortly after the Restoration. I am confident that he was thinking of those pests of London when he dictated the noble lines :—

> "And in luxurious cities, when the noise
> Of riot ascends above their loftiest towers,
> And injury and outrage, and when night
> Darkens the streets, then wander forth the sons
> Of Belial, flown with insolence and wine."

The machinery for keeping the peace was utterly contemptible   There was an Act of Common Council which provided that more than a

The Squire of Alfatia
Badaux de Londres

THE SQUIRE OF ALSATIA

From Tempest's Cries of London

thousand watchmen should be constantly on the alert in the city, from sunset to sunrise, and that every inhabitant should take his turn of duty. But this Act was negligently executed. Few of those who were summoned left their homes ; and those few generally found it more agreeable to tipple in alehouses than to pace the streets.[1]

It ought to be noticed that, in the last year of the reign of Charles the Second, began a great change in the police of London, a change **Lighting of London** which has perhaps added as much to the happiness of the body of the people as revolutions of much greater fame. An ingenious projector, named Edward Heming, obtained letters patent conveying to him, for a term of years, the exclusive right of lighting up London. He undertook, for a moderate consideration, to place a light before every tenth door, on moonless nights, from Michaelmas to Lady Day, and from six to twelve of the clock. Those who now see the capital all the year round, from dusk to dawn, blazing with a splendour beside which the illuminations for La Hogue and Blenheim would have looked pale, may perhaps smile to think of Heming's lanterns, which glimmered feebly before one house in ten during a small part of one night in three. But such was not the feeling of his contemporaries. His scheme was enthusiastically applauded, and furiously attacked. The friends of improvement extolled him as the greatest of all the benefactors of his city. What, they asked, were the boasted inventions of Archimedes, when compared with the achievement of the man who had turned the nocturnal shades into noon day ? In spite of these eloquent eulogies the cause of darkness was not left undefended. There were fools in that age who opposed the introduction of what was called the new light as strenuously as fools in our age have opposed the introduction of vaccination and railroads, as strenuously as the fools of an age anterior to the dawn of history doubtless opposed the introduction of the plough and of alphabetical writing. Many years after the date of Heming's patent there were extensive districts in which no lamp was seen.[2]

We may easily imagine what, in such times, must have been the state of the quarters of London which were peopled by the outcasts of **Whitefriars** society. Among those quarters one had attained a scandalous preeminence. On the confines of the City and the Temple had been founded, in the thirteenth century, a House of Carmelite Friars, distinguished by their white hoods. The precinct of this house had, before the Reformation, been a sanctuary for criminals, and still retained the privilege of protecting debtors from arrest. Insolvents consequently were to be found in every dwelling, from cellar to garret. Of these a large proportion were knaves and libertines, and were followed to their asylum by women more abandoned than themselves. The civil power was unable to keep order in a district swarming with such inhabitants ;

[1] Seymour's London.
[2] Angliæ Metropolis, 1690, Sect. 17. entitled, " Of the new lights " ; Seymour's London.

THE ROYAL EXCHANGE IN 1671

and thus Whitefriars became the favourite resort of all who wished to be emancipated from the restraints of the law. Though the immunities legally belonging to the place extended only to cases of debt, cheats, false witnesses, forgers, and highwaymen found refuge there. For amidst a rabble so desperate no peace officer's life was in safety. At the cry of " Rescue," bullies with swords and cudgels, and termagant hags with spits and broomsticks, poured forth by hundreds ; and the intruder was fortunate if he escaped back into Fleet Street, hustled, stripped, and pumped upon. Even the warrant of the Chief Justice of England could not be executed without the help of a company of musketeers. Such relics of the barbarism of the darkest ages were to be found within a short walk of the chambers where Somers was studying history and law, of the chapel where Tillotson was preaching, of the coffee house where Dryden was passing judgment on poems and plays, and of the hall where the Royal Society was examining the astronomical system of Isaac Newton.[1]

Each of the two cities which made up the capital of England had its own centre of attraction. In the metropolis of commerce the point of convergence was the Exchange; in the metropolis of fashion the Palace. But the Palace did not retain its influence so long as the Exchange. The Revolution completely altered the relations between the Court and the higher classes of society. It was by degrees discovered that the King, in his individual capacity, had very little to give ; that coronets and garters, bishoprics and embassies, lordships of the Treasury and tellerships of the Exchequer, nay, even charges in the royal stud and bedchamber, were really bestowed, not by him, but by his advisers. Every ambitious and covetous man perceived that he would consult his own interest far better by acquiring the dominion of a Cornish borough, and by rendering good service to the ministry during a critical session, than by becoming the companion, or even the minion, of his prince. It was therefore in the antechambers, not of George the First and of George the Second, but of Walpole and of Pelham, that the daily crowd of courtiers was to be found. It is also to be remarked that the same Revolution, which made it impossible that our Kings should use the patronage of the state merely for the purpose of gratifying their personal predilections, gave us several Kings unfitted by their education and habits to be gracious and affable hosts. They had been born and bred on the Continent. They never felt themselves at home in our island. If they spoke our language, they spoke it inelegantly and with effort. Our national character they never fully understood. Our national manners they hardly attempted to acquire. The most

The Court

---

[1] Stowe's Survey of London ; Shadwell's Squire of Alsatia ; Ward's London Spy ; Stat. 8 & 9 Gul. III. cap. 27.

WHITEHALL FROM THE THAMES

From Ogilby's plan of London in 1677

important part of their duty they performed better than any ruler who had preceded them : for they governed strictly according to law : but they could not be the first gentlemen of the realm, the heads of polite society. If ever they unbent, it was in a very small circle where hardly an English face was to be seen ; and they were never so happy as when they could escape for a summer to their native land. They had indeed their days of reception for our nobility and gentry ; but the reception was mere matter of form, and became at last as solemn a ceremony as a funeral.

Not such was the court of Charles the Second. Whitehall, when he dwelt there, was the focus of political intrigue and of fashionable gaiety. Half the jobbing and half the flirting of the metropolis went on under his roof. Whoever could make himself agreeable to the prince, or could secure the good offices of the mistress, might hope to rise in the world without rendering any service to the government, without being even known by sight to any minister of state. This courtier got a frigate, and that a company ; a third, the pardon of a rich offender ; a fourth, a lease of crown land on easy terms. If the King notified his pleasure that a briefless lawyer should be made a judge, or that a libertine baronet should be made a peer, the gravest counsellors, after a little murmuring, submitted.[1] Interest, therefore, drew a constant press of suitors to the gates of the palace ; and those gates always stood wide. The King kept open house every day, and all day long, for the good society of London, the extreme Whigs only excepted. Hardly any gentleman had any difficulty in making his way to the royal presence. The levee was exactly what the word imports. Some men of quality came every morning to stand round their master, to chat with him while his wig was combed and his cravat tied, and to accompany him in his early walk through the Park. All persons who had been properly introduced might, without any special invitation, go to see him dine, sup, dance, and play at hazard, and might have the pleasure of hearing him tell stories, which indeed he told remarkably well, about his flight from Worcester, and about the misery which he had endured when he was a state prisoner in the hands of the canting meddling preachers of Scotland. Bystanders whom His Majesty recognised often came in for a courteous word. This proved a far more successful kingcraft than any that his father or grandfather had practised. It was not easy for the most austere republican of the school of Marvel to resist the fascination of so much goodhumour and affability : and many a veteran Cavalier, in whose heart the remembrance of unrequited sacrifices and services had been festering during twenty years, was compensated in one moment

---

[1] See Sir Roger North's account of the way in which Wright was made a judge, and Clarendon's account of the way in which Sir George Savile was made a peer.

GENERAL VIEW OF WHITEHALL IN 1714

From a drawing by Kip in the British Museum

for wounds and sequestrations by his sovereign's kind nod, and " God bless you, my old friend ! "

Whitehall naturally became the chief staple of news. Whenever there was a rumour that anything important had happened or was about to happen, people hastened thither to obtain intelligence from the fountain head. The galleries presented the appearance of a modern club room at an anxious time. They were full of people enquiring whether the Dutch mail was in, what tidings the express from France had brought, whether John Sobiesky had beaten the Turks, whether the Doge of Genoa was really at Paris. These were matters about which it was safe to talk aloud. But there were subjects concerning which information was asked and given in whispers. Had Halifax got the better of Rochester? Was there to be a Parliament? Was the Duke of York really going to Scotland? Had Monmouth really been summoned from the Hague? Men tried to read the countenance of every minister as he went through the throng to and from the royal closet. All sorts of auguries were drawn from the tone in which His Majesty spoke to the Lord President, or from the laugh with which His Majesty honoured a jest of the Lord Privy Seal ; and in a few hours the hopes and fears inspired by such slight indications had spread to all the coffee houses from Saint James's to the Tower.[1]

The coffee house must not be dismissed with a cursory mention. It might indeed at that time have been not improperly called a most **The coffee houses.** important political institution. No Parliament had sat for years. The municipal council of the City had ceased to speak the sense of the citizens. Public meetings, harangues, resolutions, and the rest of the modern machinery of agitation had not yet come into fashion. Nothing resembling the modern newspaper existed. In such circumstances the coffee houses were the chief organs through which the public opinion of the metropolis vented itself.

The first of these establishments had been set up, in the time of the Commonwealth, by a Turkey merchant, who had acquired among the Mahometans a taste for their favourite beverage. The convenience of being able to make appointments in any part of the town, and of being able to pass evenings socially at a very small charge, was so great that the fashion spread fast. Every man of the upper or middle class went daily to his coffee house to learn the news and to discuss it. Every coffee house had one or more orators to whose eloquence the crowd listened with admiration, and who soon became, what the journalists of

---

[1] The sources from which I have drawn my information about the state of the Court are too numerous to recapitulate. Among them are the Despatches of Barillon, Van Citters, Ronquillo, and Adda, the Travels of the Grand Duke Cosmo, the works of Roger North, the Diaries of Pepys, Evelyn, and Teonge, and the Memoirs of Grammont and Reresby.

our time have been called, a fourth Estate of the realm. The Court had long seen with uneasiness the growth of this new power in the state. An attempt had been made, during Danby's administration, to close the coffee houses. But men of all parties missed their usual places of resort so much that there was an universal outcry. The government did not venture, in opposition to a feeling so strong and general, to enforce a regulation of which the legality might well be questioned. Since that time ten years had elapsed, and during those years the number and influence of the coffee houses had been constantly increasing. Foreigners remarked that the coffee house was that which especially distinguished London from all other cities ; that the coffee house was the Londoner's home, and that those who wished to find a gentleman commonly asked, not whether he lived in Fleet Street or Chancery Lane, but whether he frequented the Grecian or the Rainbow. Nobody was excluded from these places who laid down his penny at the bar. Yet every rank and profession, and every shade of religious and political opinion, had its own head quarters. There were houses near Saint James's Park where fops congregated, their heads and shoulders covered with black or flaxen wigs, not less ample than those which are now worn by the Chancellor and by the Speaker of the House of Commons. The wig came from Paris ; and so did the rest of the fine gentleman's ornaments, his embroidered coat, his fringed gloves, and the tassel which upheld his pantaloons. The conversation was in that dialect which, long after it had ceased to be spoken in fashionable circles, continued, in the mouth of Lord Foppington, to excite the mirth of theatres.[1] The atmosphere was like that of a perfumer's shop. Tobacco in any other form than that of richly scented snuff was held in abomination. If any clown, ignorant of the usages of the house, called for a pipe, the sneers of the whole assembly and the short answers of the waiters soon convinced him that he had better go somewhere else. Nor, indeed, would he have had far to go. For, in general, the coffee rooms reeked with tobacco like a guardroom ; and strangers sometimes expressed their surprise that so many people should leave their own firesides to sit in the midst of eternal fog and stench. Nowhere was the smoking more constant than at Will's. That celebrated house, situated between Covent Garden and Bow Street, was sacred to polite letters. There the talk was about poetical justice and the unities of place and time. There was a faction for Perrault and the moderns, a faction for Boileau and the ancients. One group debated whether Paradise Lost ought not to have been in

---

[1] The chief peculiarity of this dialect was that, in a large class of words, the O was pronounced like A. Thus Lord was pronounced Lard. See Vanbrugh's Relapse. Lord Sunderland was a great master of this court tune, as Roger North calls it ; and Titus Oates affected it in the hope of passing for a fine gentleman. Examen, 77. 254.

rhyme. To another an envious poetaster demonstrated that Venice Preserved ought to have been hooted from the stage. Under no roof was a greater variety of figures to be seen. There were Earls in stars and garters, clergymen in cassocks and bands, pert Templars, sheepish lads from the Universities, translators and indexmakers in ragged coats of frieze. The great press was to get near the chair where John Dryden sate. In winter that chair was always in the warmest nook by the fire; in summer it stood in the balcony. To bow to the Laureate, and to hear his opinion of Racine's last tragedy or of Bossu's treatise on epic poetry, was thought a privilege. A pinch from his snuff box was an honour sufficient to turn the head of a young enthusiast. There were coffee houses where the first medical men might be consulted. Doctor John Radcliffe, who, in the year 1685, rose to the largest practice in London, came daily, at the hour when the Exchange was full, from his house in Bow Street, then a fashionable part of the capital, to Garraway's, and was to be found, surrounded by surgeons and apothecaries, at a particular table. There were Puritan coffee houses where no oath was heard, and where lankhaired men discussed election and reprobation through their noses; Jew coffee houses where darkeyed money changers from Venice and from Amsterdam greeted each other; and Popish coffee houses where, as good Protestants believed, Jesuits planned, over their cups, another great fire, and cast silver bullets to shoot the King.[1]

These gregarious habits had no small share in forming the character of the Londoner of that age. He was, indeed, a different being from the rustic Englishman. There was not then the intercourse which now exists between the two classes. Only very great men were in the habit of dividing the year between town and country. Few esquires came to the capital thrice in their lives. Nor was it yet the practice of all citizens in easy circumstances to breathe the fresh air of the fields and woods during some weeks of every summer. A cockney, in a rural village, was stared at as much as if he had intruded into a Kraal of Hottentots. On the other hand, when the lord of a Lincolnshire or Shropshire manor appeared in Fleet Street, he was as easily distinguished from the resident population as a Turk or a Lascar. His dress, his gait, his accent, the manner in which he gazed at the shops, stumbled into the gutters, ran against the porters, and stood under the waterspouts, marked him out as an excellent subject for the operations of swindlers and banterers. Bullies jostled him into the kennel. Hackney coach-

[1] Lettres sur les Anglois; Tom Brown's Tour; Ward's London Spy; The Character of a Coffee House, 1673; Rules and Orders of the Coffee House, 1674; Coffee Houses vindicated, 1675; A Satyr against Coffee; North's Examen, 138.; Life of Guildford, 152.; Life of Sir Dudley North, 149.; Life of Dr. Radcliffe, published by Curll in 1715. The liveliest description of Will's is in the City and Country Mouse. There is a remarkable passage about the influence of the coffee house orators in Halstead's Succinct Genealogies, printed in 1685.

men splashed him from head to foot. Thieves explored with perfect security the huge pockets of his horseman's coat, while he stood en-

London Curtezan
la Putain de Londres
Cortegiana di Londra

M. Laureon delin.   I. Tempest excud.
                                     cum Privilegio

THE LONDON COURTEZAN

From Tempest's Cries of London

tranced by the splendour of the Lord Mayor's show. Moneydroppers, sore from the cart's tail, introduced themselves to him, and appeared to

him the most honest friendly gentlemen that he had ever seen.   Painted
women, the refuse of Lewkner Lane and Whetstone Park, passed themselves on him for countesses and maids of honour.   If he asked his
way to Saint James's, his informants sent him to Mile End.   If he went
into a shop, he was instantly discerned to be a fit purchaser of everything that nobody else would buy, of secondhand embroidery, copper
rings, and watches that would not go.   If he rambled into any fashionable coffee house, he became a mark for the insolent derision of fops
and the grave waggery of Templars.   Enraged and mortified, he soon
returned to his mansion, and there, in the homage of his tenants and
the conversation of his boon companions, found consolation for the vexations and humiliations which he had undergone.   There he was once
more a great man, and saw nothing above himself except when at the
assizes he took his seat on the bench near the Judge, or when at the
muster of the militia he saluted the Lord Lieutenant.

The chief cause which made the fusion of the different elements of
society so imperfect was the extreme difficulty which our ancestors
Difficulty of found in passing from place to place.   Of all inventions,
travelling the alphabet and the printing press alone excepted, those
inventions which abridge distance have done most for the civilisation of
our species.   Every improvement of the means of locomotion benefits
mankind morally and intellectually as well as materially, and not only
facilitates the interchange of the various productions of nature and art,
but tends to remove national and provincial antipathies, and to bind
together all the branches of the great human family.   In the seventeenth century the inhabitants of London were, for almost every practical
purpose, farther from Reading than they now are from Edinburgh, and
farther from Edinburgh than they now are from Vienna.

The subjects of Charles the Second were not, it is true, quite un-
acquainted with that principle which has, in our own time, produced an
unprecedented revolution in human affairs, which has enabled navies to
advance in face of wind and tide, and brigades of troops, attended by all
their baggage and artillery, to traverse kingdoms at a pace equal to that
of the fleetest race horse.   The Marquess of Worcester had recently
observed the expansive power of moisture rarefied by heat.   After
many experiments he had succeeded in constructing a rude steam
engine, which he called a fire water work, and which he pronounced to
be an admirable and most forcible instrument of propulsion.[1]   But the
Marquess was suspected to be a madman, and known to be a Papist.
His inventions, therefore, found no favourable reception.   His fire water
work might, perhaps, furnish matter for conversation at a meeting of the
Royal Society, but was not applied to any practical purpose.   There

[1] Century of Inventions, 1663, No. 68.

were no railways, except a few made of timber, on which coals were carried from the mouths of the Northumbrian pits to the banks of the Tyne.[1] There was very little internal communication by water. A few attempts had been made to deepen and embank the natural streams, but with slender success. Hardly a single navigable canal had been even projected. The English of that day were in the habit of talking with mingled admiration and despair of the immense trench by which Lewis the Fourteenth had made a junction between the Atlantic and the Mediterranean. They little thought that their country would, in the course of a few generations, be intersected, at the cost of private adventurers, by artificial rivers making up more than four times the length of the Thames, the Severn, and the Trent together.

It was by the highways that both travellers and goods generally passed from place to place ; and those highways appear to have been far worse than might have been expected from the degree of Badness of wealth and civilisation which the nation had even then the roads attained. On the best lines of communication the ruts were deep, the descents precipitous, and the way often such as it was hardly possible to distinguish, in the dusk, from the unenclosed heath and fen which lay on both sides. Ralph Thoresby, the antiquary, was in danger of losing his way on the great North road, between Barnby Moor and Tuxford, and actually lost his way between Doncaster and York.[2] Pepys and his wife, travelling in their own coach, lost their way between Newbury and Reading. In the course of the same tour they lost their way near Salisbury, and were in danger of having to pass the night on the plain.[3] It was only in fine weather that the whole breadth of the road was available for wheeled vehicles. Often the mud lay deep on the right and the left ; and only a narrow track of firm ground rose above the quagmire.[4] At such times obstructions and quarrels were frequent, and the path was sometimes blocked up during a long time by carriers, neither of whom would break the way. It happened, almost every day, that coaches stuck fast, until a team of cattle could be procured from some neighbouring farm, to tug them out of the slough. But in bad seasons the traveller had to encounter inconveniences still more serious. Thoresby, who was in the habit of travelling between Leeds and the capital, has recorded, in his Diary, such a series of perils and disasters as might suffice for a journey to the Frozen Ocean or to the Desert of Sahara. On one occasion he learned that the floods were out between Ware and London, that passengers had to swim for their lives, and that a higgler had perished in the attempt to cross. In consequence of these tidings he turned out of the high road, and was

[1] North's Life of Guildford, 136.   [2] Thoresby's Diary, Oct. 21. 1680, Aug. 3. 1712.
[3] Pepys's Diary, June 12. and 16. 1668.   [4] Ibid. Feb. 28. 1660.

conducted across some meadows, where it was necessary for him to ride to the saddle skirts in water.[1] In the course of another journey he narrowly escaped being swept away by an inundation of the Trent. He was afterwards detained at Stamford four days, on account of the state of the roads, and then ventured to proceed only because fourteen members of the House of Commons, who were going up in a body to Parliament with guides and numerous attendants, took him into their company.[2] On the roads of Derbyshire, travellers were in constant fear for their necks, and were frequently compelled to alight and lead their beasts.[3] The great route through Wales to Holyhead was in such a state that, in 1685, a viceroy, going to Ireland, was five hours in travelling fourteen miles, from Saint Asaph to Conway. Between Conway and Beaumaris he was forced to walk great part of the way ; and his lady was carried in a litter. His coach was, with much difficulty, and by the help of many hands, brought after him entire. In general, carriages were taken to pieces at Conway, and borne, on the shoulders of stout Welsh peasants, to the Menai Straits.[4] In some parts of Kent and Sussex, none but the strongest horses could, in winter, get through the bog, in which, at every step, they sank deep. The markets were often inaccessible during several months. It is said that the fruits of the earth were sometimes suffered to rot in one place, while in another place, distant only a few miles, the supply fell far short of the demand. The wheeled carriages were, in this district, generally pulled by oxen.[5] When Prince George of Denmark visited the stately mansion of Petworth in wet weather, he was six hours in going nine miles ; and it was necessary that a body of sturdy hinds should be on each side of his coach, in order to prop it. Of the carriages which conveyed his retinue several were upset and injured. A letter from one of the party has been preserved, in which the unfortunate courtier complains that, during fourteen hours, he never once alighted, except when his coach was overturned or stuck fast in the mud.[6]

One chief cause of the badness of the roads seems to have been the defective state of the law. Every parish was bound to repair the highways which passed through it. The peasantry were forced to give their gratuitous labour six days in the year. If this was not sufficient, hired labour was employed, and the expense was met by a parochial rate. That a route connecting two great towns, which have a large and

[1] Thoresby's Diary, May 17. 1695.　　　　　[2] Ibid. Dec. 27. 1708.

[3] Tour in Derbyshire, by J. Browne, son of Sir Thomas Browne, 1662 ; Cotton's Angler, 1676.

[4] Correspondence of Henry Earl of Clarendon, Dec. 30. 1685, Jan. 1. 1686.

[5] Postlethwaite's Dictionary, Roads ; History of Hawkhurst, in the Bibliotheca Topographica Britannica.

[6] Annals of Queen Anne, 1703, Appendix, No. 3.

thriving trade with each other, should be maintained at the cost of the rural population scattered between them is obviously unjust ; and this injustice was peculiarly glaring in the case of the great North road, which traversed very poor and thinly inhabited districts, and joined very rich and populous districts. Indeed it was not in the power of the parishes of Huntingdonshire to mend a highway worn by the constant traffic between the West Riding of Yorkshire and London. Soon after

TRAVELLING COACH AND PACKHORSES

From Loggan's Oxonia Illustrata, 1675

the Restoration this grievance attracted the notice of Parliament ; and an act, the first of our many turnpike acts, was passed, imposing a small toll on travellers and goods, for the purpose of keeping some parts of this important line of communication in good repair.[1] This innovation, however, excited many murmurs ; and the other great avenues to the capital were long left under the old system. A change was at length effected, but not without much difficulty. For unjust and absurd taxation to which men are accustomed is often borne far more willingly

[1] 15 Car. II. c. 1.

than the most reasonable impost which is new.   It was not till many
toll bars had been violently pulled down, till the troops had in many
districts been forced to act against the people, and till much blood had
been shed, that a good system was introduced.[1]   By slow degrees
reason triumphed over prejudice ; and our island is now crossed in
every direction by near thirty thousand miles of turnpike road.

On the best highways heavy articles were, in the time of Charles
the Second, generally conveyed from place to place by stage waggons.
In the straw of these vehicles nestled a crowd of passengers, who could
not afford to travel by coach or on horseback, and who were prevented
by infirmity, or by the weight of their luggage, from going on foot.
The expense of transmitting heavy goods in this way was enormous.
From London to Birmingham the charge was seven pounds a ton; from
London to Exeter twelve pounds a ton.[2]   This was about fifteen pence
a ton for every mile, more by a third than was afterwards charged on
turnpike roads, and fifteen times what is now demanded by railway
companies.   The cost of conveyance amounted to a prohibitory tax on
many useful articles.   Coal in particular was never seen except in the
districts where it was produced, or in the districts to which it could be
carried by sea, and was indeed always known in the south of England
by the name of sea coal.

On byroads, and generally throughout the country north of York
and west of Exeter, goods were carried by long trains of packhorses.
These strong and patient beasts, the breed of which is now extinct,
were attended by a class of men who seem to have borne much resemblance to the Spanish muleteers.   A traveller of humble condition often
found it convenient to perform a journey mounted on a pack-saddle
between two baskets, under the care of these hardy guides.   The expense
of this mode of conveyance was small.   But the caravan moved at a
foot's pace ; and in winter the cold was often insupportable.[3]

The rich commonly travelled in their own carriages, with at least
four horses.   Cotton, the facetious poet, attempted to go from London
to the Peak with a single pair, but found at Saint Albans that the
journey would be insupportably tedious, and altered his plan.[4]   A coach
and six is in our time never seen, except as part of some pageant.   The
frequent mention therefore of such equipages in old books is likely to

[1] The evils of the old system are strikingly set forth in many petitions which appear in the
Commons' Journal of 172⅚.   How fierce an opposition was offered to the new system may be
learned from the Gentleman's Magazine of 1749.

[2] Postlethwaite's Dict., Roads.

[3] Loidis and Elmete; Marshall's Rural Economy of England.   In 1739 Roderic Random
came from Scotland to Newcastle on a packhorse.

[4] Cotton's Epistle to J. Bradshaw.

mislead us. We attribute to magnificence what was really the effect of a very disagreeable necessity. People, in the time of Charles the Second, travelled with six horses, because with a smaller number there was great danger of sticking fast in the mire. Nor were even six horses always sufficient. Vanbrugh, in the succeeding generation, described with great humour the way in which a country gentleman, newly chosen a member of Parliament, went up to London. On that occasion all the exertions

CARTS

From Loggan's Oxonia Illustrata, 1675

of six beasts, two of which had been taken from the plough, could not save the family coach from being embedded in a quagmire.

Public carriages had recently been much improved. During the years which immediately followed the Restoration, a diligence ran between London and Oxford in two days. The passengers slept at Beaconsfield. At length, in the spring of 1669, a great and daring innovation was attempted. It was announced that a vehicle, described as the Flying Coach, would perform the whole journey between sunrise and sunset. This spirited undertaking was solemnly

Stage Coaches

considered and sanctioned by the Heads of the University, and appears to have excited the same sort of interest which is excited in our own time by the opening of a new railway. The Vicechancellor, by a notice affixed in all public places, prescribed the hour and place of departure. The success of the experiment was complete. At six in the morning the carriage began to move from before the ancient front of All Souls College; and at seven in the evening the adventurous gentlemen who had run the first risk were safely deposited at their inn in London.[1] The emulation of the sister University was moved; and soon a diligence was set up which in one day carried passengers from Cambridge to the capital. At the close of the reign of Charles the Second, flying carriages ran thrice a week from London to the chief towns. But no stage coach, indeed no stage waggon, appears to have proceeded further north than York, or further west than Exeter. The ordinary day's journey of a flying coach was about fifty miles in the summer; but in winter, when the ways were bad and the nights long, little more than thirty. The Chester coach, the York coach, and the Exeter coach generally reached London in four days during the fine season, but at Christmas not till the sixth day. The passengers, six in number, were all seated in the carriage. For accidents were so frequent that it would have been most perilous to mount the roof. The ordinary fare was about twopence halfpenny a mile in summer, and somewhat more in winter.[2]

This mode of travelling, which by Englishmen of the present day would be regarded as insufferably slow, seemed to our ancestors wonderfully and indeed alarmingly rapid. In a work published a few months before the death of Charles the Second, the flying coaches are extolled as far superior to any similar vehicles ever known in the world. Their velocity is the subject of special commendation, and is triumphantly contrasted with the sluggish pace of the continental posts. But with boasts like these was mingled the sound of complaint and invective. The interests of large classes had been unfavourably affected by the establishment of the new diligences; and, as usual, many persons were, from mere stupidity and obstinacy, disposed to clamour against the innovation, simply because it was an innovation. It was vehemently argued that this mode of conveyance would be fatal to the breed of horses and to the noble art of horsemanship; that the Thames, which had long been an important nursery of seamen, would cease to be the chief thoroughfare from London up to Windsor and down to Gravesend; that saddlers and spurriers would be ruined by hundreds; that numerous inns, at which mounted travellers had been in the habit of stopping,

[1] Anthony à Wood's Life of himself.

[2] Chamberlayne's State of England, 1684. See also the list of stage coaches and waggons at the end of the book, entitled Angliæ Metropolis, 1690.

WHEREAS the Appointment, Ordering, and Government of all Carriers of what kind soever, Trading to or with the University and Citty of *Oxford*, does of Right belong and appertain to the Chancellor, Masters, and Scholars of the said University, by their Charters, Priviledges, and Customes : the said Carriers to be Ordered and Governed by such Rules as shall be limited and prescribed by the Chancellor of the said University, or his deputy for the time being. AND whereas *Thomas Moore* and *Robert Stonehill* Licensed Carriers of the said University, have undertaken to provide sufficient Coaches and Horses for the Conveiance of Passengers between the said University and the Citty of *London*, which shall in one day Commodiously perform the whole Journey during the Summer half year, (that is to say) from the Twenty sixth day of *April*, being the Munday next before *Easter Terme*, to *Michaelmas* ensuing; for the better regulating of the said Carriers, and Securing the Convenience of all Passengers who shall happen to go with them, It is Ordered by the *Vice-Chancellor* of the University aforesaid, as followeth.

1. That the Carriers aforesaid shall not demand above Twelve shillings for the conveiance of each Passenger.

2. That they, the said Carriers, shall carry without expectation of farther reward, the necessaries of each Passenger, their severall fardles not being incommodious in their Bulk, and not exceeding six pound in weight.

3. That they, the said Carriers, shall not upon pretence of expectation of Passengers, or any other suggestion, delay the time of their setting out; But before six of the clock in the Morning, be ready over against *Alsouls Colledge* in *Oxford*, and the signe of the Greyhound in *Holborne* in *London*; and Immediatly upon the striking of the Clock of St *Maries* in *Oxford*, and St *Andrews Holborn London* begin their Journey.

4. That the said Carriers shall both at *Oxford* & *London* keep a Book for the Entry of Names of the Passengers, and the receipt of the twelve shillings which shall be laid down upon the entry of their names, and shall be responsible for the fraud or negligence which shall happen either by themselves or Servants in the aforesaid particulars.

5. That the said Carriers shall constantly keep their weekely stages, that is to say, every Munday, Wednesday, and Friday depart from *Oxford*, and Tuesday, Thursday and Saturday returne homeward from *London*.

6. That the said Carriers shall not take upon them to dispose of places in their coach, but shall permit all persons to be seated according to their priority, in taking of their seats, & their respective condition.

7. That the aforesaid Orders and Rules shall not be interpreted to limit or concern those coaches, which shall as formerly perform their Journey in part of two days.

Ap: 5.1669.   *JOHN FELL Vicechancellor.*

ADVERTISEMENT OF THE FLYING COACH FROM OXFORD TO LONDON, 1669

From a broadside in the Bodleian Library

would be deserted, and would no longer pay any rent; that the new carriages were too hot in summer and too cold in winter; that the passengers were grievously annoyed by invalids and crying children; that the coach sometimes reached the inn so late that it was impossible to get supper, and sometimes started so early that it was impossible to get breakfast. On these grounds it was gravely recommended that no public coach should be permitted to have more than four horses, to start oftener than once a week, or to go more than thirty miles a day. It was hoped that, if this regulation were adopted, all except the sick and the lame would return to the old mode of travelling. Petitions embodying such opinions as these were presented to the King in council from several companies of the City of London, from several provincial towns, and from the justices of several counties. We smile at these things. It is not impossible that our descendants, when they read the history of the opposition offered by cupidity and prejudice to the improvements of the nineteenth century, may smile in their turn.[1]

In spite of the attractions of the flying coaches, it was still usual for men who enjoyed health and vigour, and who were not encumbered by much baggage, to perform long journeys on horseback. If the traveller wished to move expeditiously he rode post. Fresh saddle horses and guides were to be procured at convenient distances along all the great lines of road. The charge was threepence a mile for each horse, and fourpence a stage for the guide. In this manner, when the ways were good, it was possible to travel, for a considerable time, as rapidly as by any conveyance known in England, till vehicles were propelled by steam. There were as yet no post chaises; nor could those who rode in their own coaches ordinarily procure a change of horses. The King, however, and the great officers of state were able to command relays. Thus Charles commonly went in one day from Whitehall to Newmarket, a distance of about fifty-five miles through a level country; and this was thought by his subjects a proof of great activity. Evelyn performed the same journey in company with the Lord Treasurer Clifford. The coach was drawn by six horses, which were changed at Bishop Stortford and again at Chesterford. The travellers reached Newmarket at night. Such a mode of conveyance seems to have been considered as a rare luxury confined to princes and ministers.[2]

Whatever might be the way in which a journey was performed, the travellers, unless they were numerous and well armed, ran considerable

[1] John Cresset's Reasons for suppressing Stage Coaches, 1672. These reasons were afterwards inserted in a tract, entitled "The Grand Concern of England explained, 1673." Cresset's attack on stage coaches called forth some answers which I have consulted.

[2] Chamberlayne's State of England, 1684. North's Examen, 105. ; Evelyn's Diary, Oct. 9, 10. 1671.

risk of being stopped and plundered.   The mounted highwayman, a marauder known to our generation only from books, was to be found on every main road.   The waste tracts which lay on the great **Highway-**
routes near London were especially haunted by plunderers of **men**
this class.   Hounslow Heath, on the great Western Road, and Finchley Common, on the great Northern Road, were perhaps the most cele-brated of these spots.   The Cambridge scholars trembled when they approached Epping Forest, even in broad daylight.   Seamen who had just been paid off at Chatham were often compelled to deliver their purses on Gadshill, celebrated near a hundred years earlier by the greatest of poets as the scene of the depredations of Falstaff.   The public authorities seem to have been often at a loss how to deal with the plunderers.   At one time it was announced in the Gazette, that several persons, who were strongly suspected of being highwaymen, but against whom there was not sufficient evidence, would be paraded at Newgate in riding dresses : their horses would also be shown ; and all gentlemen who had been robbed were invited to inspect this singular exhibition.   On another occasion a pardon was publicly offered to a robber if he would give up some rough diamonds, of immense value, which he had taken when he stopped the Harwich mail.   A short time after appeared another proclamation, warning the innkeepers that the eye of the government was upon them.   Their criminal connivance, it was affirmed, enabled banditti to infest the roads with impunity.   That these suspicions were not without foundation, is proved by the dying speeches of some penitent robbers of that age, who appear to have received from the innkeepers services much resembling those which Farquhar's Boniface rendered to Gibbet.[1]

It was necessary to the success and even to the safety of the highwayman that he should be a bold and skilful rider, and that his manners and appearance should be such as suited the master of a fine horse.   He therefore held an aristocratical position in the community of thieves, appeared at fashionable coffee houses and gaming houses, and betted with men of quality on the race ground.[2]   Sometimes, indeed, he was a man of good family and education.   A romantic interest therefore attached, and perhaps still attaches, to the names of freebooters of this class.   The vulgar eagerly drank in tales of their ferocity and audacity, of their occasional acts of generosity and good nature, of their amours, of their miraculous escapes, of their desperate

---

[1] See the London Gazette, May 14. 1677, August 4. 1687, Dec. 5. 1687.   The last confession of Augustin King, who was the son of an eminent divine, and had been educated at Cambridge, but was hanged at Colchester in March 1688, is highly curious.

[2] *Aimwell.* Pray sir, han't I seen your face at Will's coffeehouse ?
Gibbet. Yes, sir, and at White's too.—Beaux' Stratagem.

struggles, and of their manly bearing at the bar and in the cart.   Thus it was related of William Nevison, the great robber of Yorkshire, that he levied a quarterly tribute on all the northern drovers, and, in return, not only spared them himself, but protected them against all other thieves ; that he demanded purses in the most courteous manner ; that he gave largely to the poor what he had taken from the rich ; that his life was once spared by the royal clemency, but that he again tempted his fate, and at length died, in 1685, on the gallows of York.[1]   It was related how Claude Duval, the French page of the Duke of Richmond, took to the road, became captain of a formidable gang, and had the honour to be named first in a royal proclamation against notorious offenders ; how at the head of his troop he stopped a lady's coach, in which there was a booty of four hundred pounds ; how he took only one hundred, and suffered the fair owner to ransom the rest by dancing a coranto with him on the heath ; how his vivacious gallantry stole away the hearts of all women ; how his dexterity at sword and pistol made him a terror to all men ; how, at length, in the year 1670, he was seized when overcome by wine ; how dames of high rank visited him in prison, and with tears interceded for his life ; how the King would have granted a pardon, but for the interference of Judge Morton, the terror of highwaymen, who threatened to resign his office unless the law were carried into full effect ; and how, after the execution, the corpse lay in state with all the pomp of scutcheons, wax lights, black hangings and mutes, till the same cruel Judge, who had intercepted the mercy of the crown, sent officers to disturb the obsequies.[2]   In these anecdotes there is doubtless a large mixture of fable ; but they are not on that account unworthy of being recorded; for it is both an authentic and an important fact that such tales, whether false or true, were heard by our ancestors with eagerness and faith.

All the various dangers by which the traveller was beset were greatly increased by darkness.   He was therefore commonly desirous of having the shelter of a roof during the night ; and such

Inns

shelter it was not difficult to obtain.   From a very early period the inns of England had been renowned.   Our first great poet had described the excellent accommodation which they afforded to the

---

[1] Gent's History of York.   Another marauder of the same description, named Biss, was hanged at Salisbury in 1695.   In a ballad which is in the Pepysian Library, he is represented as defending himself thus before the Judge :

> " What say you now, my honoured Lord,
> What harm was there in this ?
> Rich, wealthy misers were abhorred
> By brave, freehearted Biss."

[2] Pope's Memoirs of Duval, published immediately after the execution.   Oates's Εἰκὼν βασιλική, Part I.

THE

Penitent Highway-man:

OR,

The Last Farewel of Mr. Biss.

Who was Born at *Shaftsbury*, in *Wiltshire*, and was arrain'd and found guilty, and accordingly received Sentence of Death, and was Executed at *Salisbury*, on the 12th of *March*, 1695. To the Tune of, *Russel's Farewel*, &c.

GOod People all I pray attend,
　and listen now to me,
A sad Relation here I send
　of Biss in Shaftsbury:
A noted Highway-man he was
　Into on the Road and rise,
And at the length it came to pass,
　He was so damn'd and by'd.

When he was to his Tryal brought,
　and at the Bar did stand,
Before no Sum of Labour fought,
　but there brib'd its Gain,
Declaring to the antient Judge,
　who hang to try him there,
He should not bear him any grudge,
　he wan't the word of Fear.

Be kind, The Scriptures I assirm,
　though I this Life did lead,
So lub in the Naked I beheld,
　I cloyed them with spreen:
Sometimes in Cloath and Winter-tide,
　sometimes in skissegray,
The Poor Fick, the Rich likewise
　I helpt fast away.

What say you now my honour'd Lord,
　what harm was there in this?
My wealthy Sisters was assford
　by brave free-hearted Biss.
I never robb'd no wamong'd the Poor,
　as well it both appear;
Be pleas'd to favour me therefore,
　and be not too severe.

Upon the Road a Man I met,
　was going to a Fair,
Because by Christ not pay his Debt,
　nor no sufficient Bail;
A kind and loving Friend to found,
　that very hap of me,
Who pay'd the Officer forty Pound,
　and so the Prisoner free.

Tho' he had got the Guinneys bright,
　and put them in his Purse,
I follow'd him that very night,
　I could not leave him thus;
Bowing my Pistol once again,
　I cros'd a point of Land,
Deering the Water a-fane,
　Deliver'd I do him stand:

You borrow'd forty Pound, you know,
　of me this very Day,
I cannot trust, before you go
　I must have present pay:
Without the O—— I'll search't all round,
　and r—— all else sore,
Where straight I got my forty Pound,
　with twenty Guinneys more.

The Judge he made him this reply,
　Your Joaks are all in vain,
By Law you are condemn'd to Die,
　nor will no Pardon gain,
Therefore, Repent, repent with speed,
　while it is God and past,
Tho' you the Poor did cloathe and feed,
　you suffer must at last.

That word was like a fatal sword,
　it pierc'd unto the heart;
The Lord for Mercy be implor'd,
　as knowing he must part
With all his Friends and Pleasures too,
　to be as I have said,
At Salsbury to Peoples view,
　a sad Example made.

His melting Eyes did over-flow
　with penitential tears,
To see his dismal Overthrow,
　just in the strength of Years.
O Sinners, take warning now by me,
　and mind the pains of Death also,
this day in Salsbury.

In grief and sorrow now I pass
　out of the World this day,
Like a letter untimely in the grass,
　that soon doth fade away,
That as this sinful Life I leave,
　the Lord may pity it:
And in his arms my Soul receive,
　even for his Species sake.

Lic. according to Order.

LONDON:

Printed for P. Brooksby, at the Golden-Ball, in Pye-corner, near West-Smithfield.

pilgrims of the fourteenth century.   Nine and twenty persons, with
their horses, found room in the wide chambers and stables of the
Tabard in Southwark.   The food was of the best, and the wines such
as drew the company on to drink largely.   Two hundred years later,
under the reign of Elizabeth, William Harrison gave a lively description
of the plenty and comfort of the great hostelries.   The Continent of
Europe, he said, could show nothing like them.   There were some in
which two or three hundred people, with their horses, could without
difficulty be lodged and fed.   The bedding, the tapestry, above all, the
abundance of clean and fine linen was matter of wonder.   Valuable
plate was often set on the tables.   Nay, there were signs which had cost
thirty or forty pounds.   In the seventeenth century England abounded
with excellent inns of every rank.   The traveller sometimes, in a small
village, lighted on a public house such as Walton has described,
where the brick floor was swept clean, where the walls were stuck
round with ballads, where the sheets smelt of lavender, and where
a blazing fire, a cup of good ale, and a dish of trouts fresh from the
neighbouring brook, were to be procured at small charge.   At the
larger houses of entertainment were to be found beds hung with silk,
choice cookery, and claret equal to the best which was drunk in
London.[1]   The innkeepers too, it was said, were not like other
innkeepers.   On the Continent the landlord was the tyrant of those
who crossed the threshold.   In England he was a servant.   Never was
an Englishman more at home than when he took his ease in his inn.
Even men of fortune, who might in their own mansions have enjoyed
every luxury, were often in the habit of passing their evenings in the
parlour of some neighbouring house of public entertainment.   They
seem to have thought that comfort and freedom could in no other place
be enjoyed in equal perfection.   This feeling continued during many
generations to be a national peculiarity.   The liberty and jollity of inns
long furnished matter to our novelists and dramatists.   Johnson
declared that a tavern chair was the throne of human felicity ; and
Shenstone gently complained that no private roof, however friendly,
gave the wanderer so warm a welcome as that which was to be found
at an inn.

Many conveniences which were unknown at Hampton Court and
Whitehall in the seventeenth century, are in all modern hotels.   Yet on
the whole it is certain that the improvement of our houses of public
entertainment has by no means kept pace with the improvement of our
roads and of our conveyances.   Nor is this strange ; for it is evident

[1] See the prologue to the Canterbury Tales, Harrison's Historical Description of the Island of
Great Britain, and Pepys's account of his tour in the summer of 1668.   The excellence of the
English inns is noticed in the Travels of the Grand Duke Cosmo.

that, all other circumstances being supposed equal, the inns will be best where the means of locomotion are worst. The quicker the rate of travelling, the less important is it that there should be numerous agreeable resting places for the traveller. A hundred and sixty years ago a person who came up to the capital from a remote county generally required, by the way, twelve or fifteen meals, and lodging for five or six nights. If he were a great man, he expected the meals and lodging to be comfortable, and even luxurious. At present we fly from York or Exeter to London by the light of a single winter's day. At present, therefore, a traveller seldom interrupts his journey merely for the sake of rest and refreshment. The consequence is that hundreds of excellent inns have fallen into utter decay. In a short time no good houses of that description will be found, except at places where strangers are likely to be detained by business or pleasure.

The mode in which correspondence was carried on between distant places may excite the scorn of the present generation; yet it was such as might have moved the admiration and envy of the polished nations of antiquity, or of the contemporaries of Raleigh and Cecil. A rude and imperfect establishment of posts for the conveyance of letters had been set up by Charles the First, and had been swept away by the civil war. Under the Commonwealth the design was resumed. At the Restoration the proceeds of the Post Office, after all expenses had been paid, were settled on the Duke of York. On most lines of road the mails went out and came in only on the alternate days. In Cornwall, in the fens of Lincolnshire, and among the hills and lakes of Cumberland, letters were received only once a week. During a royal progress a daily post was despatched from the capital to the place where the court sojourned. There was also daily communication between London and the Downs; and the same privilege was sometimes extended to Tunbridge Wells and Bath at the seasons when those places were crowded by the great. The bags were carried on horseback day and night at the rate of about five miles an hour.[1]

Post office

The revenue of this establishment was not derived solely from the charge for the transmission of letters. The Post Office alone was entitled to furnish post horses; and, from the care with which this monopoly was guarded, we may infer that it was found profitable.[2] If, indeed, a traveller had waited half an hour without being supplied, he might hire a horse wherever he could.

To facilitate correspondence between one part of London and another was not originally one of the objects of the Post Office. But,

[1] Stat. 12 Car. II. c. 35.; Chamberlayne's State of England, 1684; Angliæ Metropolis, 1690; London Gazette, June 22. 1685, August 15. 1687.

[2] London Gazette, Sept. 14. 1685.

in the reign of Charles the Second, an enterprising citizen of London, William Dockwray, set up, at great expense, a penny post, which delivered letters and parcels six or eight times a day in the busy and crowded streets near the Exchange, and four times a day in the outskirts of the capital. This improvement was, as usual, strenuously resisted. The porters complained that their interests were attacked, and tore down the placards in which the scheme was announced to the public. The excitement caused by Godfrey's death, and by the discovery of Coleman's papers, was then at the height. A cry was therefore raised that the penny post was a Popish contrivance. The great Doctor Oates, it was affirmed, had hinted a suspicion that the Jesuits were at the bottom of the scheme, and that the bags, if examined, would be found full of treason.[1] The utility of the enterprise was, however, so great and obvious that all opposition proved fruitless. As soon as it became clear that the speculation would be lucrative, the Duke of York complained of it as an infraction of his monopoly ; and the courts of law decided in his favour.[2]

The revenue of the Post Office was from the first constantly increasing. In the year of the Restoration a committee of the House of Commons, after strict enquiry, had estimated the net receipt at about twenty thousand pounds. At the close of the reign of Charles the Second, the net receipt was little short of fifty thousand pounds ; and this was then thought a stupendous sum. The gross receipt was about seventy thousand pounds. The charge for conveying a single letter was twopence for eighty miles, and threepence for a longer distance. The postage increased in proportion to the weight of the packet.[3] At present a single letter is carried to the extremity of Scotland or of Ireland for a penny ; and the monopoly of post horses has long ceased to exist. Yet the gross annual receipts of the department amount to more than eighteen hundred thousand pounds, and the net receipts to more than seven hundred thousand pounds. It is, therefore, scarcely possible to doubt that the number of letters now conveyed by mail is seventy times the number which was so conveyed at the time of the accession of James the Second.[4]

No part of the load which the old mails carried out was more important than the newsletters. In 1685 nothing like the London daily paper of our time existed, or could exist. Neither the necessary

---

[1] Smith's Current Intelligence, March 30. and April 3. 1680.   [2] Angliæ Metropolis, 1690.

[3] Commons' Journals, Sept. 4. 1660, March 1. 168⅝ ; Chamberlayne, 1684 ; Davenant on the Public Revenue, Discourse IV.

[4] I have left the text as it stood in 1848. In the year 1856 the gross receipt of the Post Office was more than 2,800,000*l.* ; and the net receipt was about 1,200,000*l.* The number of letters conveyed by post was 478,000,000. (1857.)

London, From Friday *Septemb.* 22. *to* Tuesday *Septemb.* 26. 1682.

London, September 25.

LEtters from *Vienna,* of the 14th. Instant, say, That the *Turks* and Malecontents still continue the Siege of *Villeck,* which defends it self very vigorously, insomuch that upon opening the Trenches, more than 2000 Janizaries had been slain; That the Besieged had made two Sallies, and dismounted a Battery against it, and brought some of their Cannon into the Fortress; whereupon Count *Teckley* had writ to the Baron *Cohary,* Commander of the Place, to persuade him to surrender, and take part with the *Hungarians;* but he returned Answer, That he would defend the same to the last Man. This instant is arrived a Courrier from General *Caprara,* That he had joyned his Forces to those of Count *Strasoldo,* and that they were on the March towards *Villeck,* and had sent out their Scouts to learn the Number of the Assailants, with the Situation of their Camp, that they might take their Measures accordingly; and they had sent to all their Troops in those Parts to advance with all possible expedition, which, when joyned, will consist of 17000 *German* Foot, and 15000 Curassiers; upon which a Battel is daily expected; but there comes News, That the Prince of *Transylvania* is arrived before *Villeck,* in the Camp of the Vizier of *Buda,* with 10000 fresh Men. The Imperial Court is still at *Ebersdorf,* where the Council of State, and that of War, continue to sit, to consider on the present Juncture of Affairs. The Duke of *Lorain* is now in a much better State of Health, insomuch that he was four hours on Horseback hunting a Stag.

His Majesty having received an Account of His Grace the Duke of *Monmouth's* Journey into *Cheshire,* together with some Informations tending to the Breach of His Peace, was pleased to order a Warrant forthwith to be issued out, to bring the Duke to Town; and to satisfie the Curious, I shall insert a Copy thereof, *viz.*

Sir *Leoline Jenkins* Knight, one of His Majesties Most Honourable Privy-Council, and Principal Secretary of State.

WHEREAS His Majesty hath received Informations, That James Duke of Monmouth hath lately appeared in several Parts of this Kingdom, with great Numbers of People, in a Riotous and an Unlawful Manner, to the disturbance of the Publick Peace, and to the terrour of His Majesties good Subjects: THESE are therefore in His Majesties Name, and by Special Command, to Will and Require you forthwith to repair to any Place where you shall understand the said Duke of Monmouth to be, and him forthwith to apprehend, and bring in safe Custody before me, or any of the Lords of His Majesties Most Honourable Privy Council, to answer to such things as on His Majesties behalf shall be objected to him the said James Duke of Monmouth: And for so doing, this shall be your Warrant. AND all Mayors, Bailiffs, Constables, and other His Majesties Officers, are hereby required to be herein aiding and assisting to you, as they will answer the contrary at their peril. Given at His Majesties Court of Whitehall, the 16 day of September, 1682.

To John Ramsey *Esq;* one of
His Majesties Serjeants at   L. Jenkins.
Arms.

Which said Warrant being delivered to Serjeant *Ramsey,* he went forthwith into the Country, and we are told that he met with the Duke on *Wednesday* last, at Dinner with divers Persons of Quality, in the Town of *Stafford;* who signifying to the Duke the Subject of his Message, his Grace very readily dispatched his Business, and repaired for *London:* but some of his Friends demanding a Copy of the Warrant, rode speedily to Town, and went to Mr. Justice *Raymond* for a *Habeas Corpus,* the same being moved by an Eminent Lawyer. The Judge at first seemed to scruple the Affair, the Duke not being in Prison; and questioned whether in the Custody of Serjeant *Ramsey* they mentioned; but the latter being by Affidavit made appear, the Judge thereupon granted one, which was speedily prepared and sent after the Duke, who arriving on *Saturday,* his Grace was brought before Mr. Justice *Dolben,* by his *Habeas Corpus,* and tendered sufficient Bail; but we are told that the Judge remanded him, taking the Liberty of two days, which the *Habeas Corpus* Act allows in those Cases.

After which, Mr. Serjant *Ramsey* acquainted the Duke, That he must have him
to

capital nor the necessary skill was to be found. Freedom too was
wanting, a want as fatal as that of either capital or skill. The press was
Newspapers not indeed at that moment under a general censorship. The
licensing act, which had been passed soon after the Restoration, had expired in 1679. Any person might therefore print, at his
own risk, a history, a sermon, or a poem, without the previous approbation of any officer; but the Judges were unanimously of opinion that
this liberty did not extend to Gazettes, and that, by the common law of
England, no man, not authorised by the crown, had a right to publish
political news.[1] While the Whig party was still formidable, the government thought it expedient occasionally to connive at the violation of
this rule. During the great battle of the Exclusion Bill, many newspapers were suffered to appear, the Protestant Intelligence, the Current
Intelligence, the Domestic Intelligence, the True News, the London
Mercury.[2] None of these was published oftener than twice a week.
None exceeded in size a single small leaf. The quantity of matter
which one of them contained in a year was not more than is often
found in two numbers of the Times. After the defeat of the Whigs it
was no longer necessary for the King to be sparing in the use of that
which all his Judges had pronounced to be his undoubted prerogative.
At the close of his reign no newspaper was suffered to appear without
his allowance: and his allowance was given exclusively to the London
Gazette. The London Gazette came out only on Mondays and Thurs-
days. The contents generally were a royal proclamation, two or three
Tory addresses, notices of two or three promotions, an account of a
skirmish between the imperial troops and the Janissaries on the Danube,
a description of a highwayman, an announcement of a grand cockfight
between two persons of honour, and an advertisement offering a reward
for a strayed dog. The whole made up two pages of moderate size.
Whatever was communicated respecting matters of the highest moment
was communicated in the most meagre and formal style. Sometimes,
indeed, when the government was disposed to gratify the public curiosity
respecting an important transaction, a broadside was put forth giving
fuller details than could be found in the Gazette: but neither the
Gazette nor any supplementary broadside printed by authority ever
contained any intelligence which it did not suit the purposes of the Court to
publish. The most important parliamentary debates, the most important
state trials, recorded in our history, were passed over in profound silence.[3]

[1] London Gazette, May 5. and 17. 1680.

[2] There is a very curious, and, I should think, unique collection of these papers in the British
Museum.

[3] For example, there is not a word in the Gazette about the important parliamentary proceedings of November 1685, or about the trial and acquittal of the seven Bishops.

In the capital the coffee houses supplied in some measure the place of a journal. Thither the Londoners flocked, as the Athenians of old flocked to the market place, to hear whether there was any news. There men might learn how brutally a Whig had been treated the day before in Westminster Hall, what horrible accounts the letters from Edinburgh gave of the torturing of Covenanters, how grossly the Navy Board had cheated the crown in the victualling of the fleet, and what grave charges the Lord Privy Seal had brought against the Treasury in the matter of the hearth money. But people **Newsletters** who lived at a distance from the great theatre of political contention could be kept regularly informed of what was passing there only by means of newsletters. To prepare such letters became a calling in London, as it now is among the natives of India. The newswriter rambled from coffee room to coffee room, collecting reports, squeezed himself into the Sessions House at the Old Bailey if there was an interesting trial, nay, perhaps obtained admission to the gallery of Whitehall, and noticed how the King and Duke looked. In this way he gathered materials for weekly epistles destined to enlighten some county town or some bench of rustic magistrates. Such were the sources from which the inhabitants of the largest provincial cities, and the great body of the gentry and clergy, learned almost all that they knew of the history of their own time. We must suppose that at Cambridge there were as many persons curious to know what was passing in the world as at almost any place in the kingdom, out of London. Yet at Cambridge, during a great part of the reign of Charles the Second, the Doctors of Laws and the Masters of Arts had no regular supply of news except through the London Gazette. At length the services of one of the collectors of intelligence in the capital were employed. That was a memorable day on which the first newsletter from London was laid on the table of the only coffee room in Cambridge.[1] At the seat of a man of fortune in the country the newsletter was impatiently expected. Within a week after it had arrived it had been thumbed by twenty families. It furnished the neighbouring squires with matter for talk over their October, and the neighbouring rectors with topics for sharp sermons against Whiggery or Popery. Many of these curious journals might doubtless still be detected by a diligent search in the archives of old families. Some are to be found in our public libraries ; and one series, which is not the least valuable part of the literary treasures collected by Sir James Mackintosh, will be occasionally quoted in the course of this work.[2]

[1] Roger North's Life of Dr. John North. On the subject of newsletters, see the Examen, 133.

[2] I take this opportunity of expressing my warm gratitude to the family of my dear and honoured friend Sir James Mackintosh for confiding to me the materials collected by him at a

It is scarcely necessary to say that there were then no provincial newspapers. Indeed, except in the capital and at the two Universities, there was scarcely a printer in the kingdom. The only press in England north of Trent appears to have been at York.[1]

It was not only by means of the London Gazette that the government undertook to furnish political instruction to the people. That
**The
Observator** journal contained a scanty supply of news without comment. Another journal, published under the patronage of the court, consisted of comment without news. This paper, called the Observator, was edited by an old Tory pamphleteer named Roger Lestrange. Lestrange was by no means deficient in readiness and shrewdness ; and his diction, though coarse, and disfigured by a mean and flippant jargon which then passed for wit in the green room and the tavern, was not without keenness and vigour. But his nature, at once ferocious and ignoble, showed itself in every line that he penned. When the first Observators appeared there was some excuse for his acrimony. For the Whigs were then powerful ; and he had to contend against numerous adversaries, whose unscrupulous violence might seem to justify unsparing retaliation. But in 1685 all opposition had been crushed. A generous spirit would have disdained to insult a party which could not reply, and to aggravate the misery of prisoners, of exiles, of bereaved families : but from the malice of Lestrange the grave was no hiding place, and the house of mourning no sanctuary. In the last month of the reign of Charles the Second, William Jenkyn, an aged dissenting pastor of great note, who had been cruelly persecuted for no crime but that of worshipping God according to the fashion generally followed throughout Protestant Europe, died of hardships and privations in Newgate. The outbreak of popular sympathy could not be repressed. The corpse was followed to the grave by a train of a hundred and fifty coaches. Even courtiers looked sad. Even the unthinking King showed some signs of concern. Lestrange alone set up a howl of savage exultation, laughed at the weak compassion of the Trimmers, proclaimed that the blasphemous old impostor had met with a most righteous punishment, and vowed to wage war, not only to the death, but after death, with all

---

time when he meditated a work similar to that which I have undertaken. I have never seen, and I do not believe that there anywhere exists, within the same compass, so noble a collection of extracts from public and private archives. The judgment with which Sir James, in great masses of the rudest ore of history, selected what was valuable, and rejected what was worthless, can be fully appreciated only by one who has toiled after him in the same mine.

[1] Life of Thomas Gent. A complete list of all printing houses in 1724 will be found in Nichols's Literary Anecdotes of the eighteenth century. There had then been a great increase within a few years in the number of presses ; and yet there were thirty four counties in which there was no printer, one of those counties being Lancashire.

VOS NON VOBIS

G. Kneller pinxit.   R. White sculpsit.

Roger L'Estrange Esq. Ætatis Suæ 68
1684.

SIR ROGER L'ESTRANGE

From an engraving by Robert White after a portrait by Sir G. Kneller the mock saints and martyrs.[1]   Such was the spirit of the paper which was at this time the oracle of the Tory party, and especially of the parochial clergy.

Literature which could be carried by the post bag then formed the greater part of the intellectual nutriment ruminated by the country divines and country justices.   The difficulty and expense of conveying large packets from place to place was so great, that an extensive work was longer in making its way from Paternoster Row to Devonshire or Lancashire than it now is in reaching Kentucky.   How scantily a rural parsonage was then furnished, even with books the most necessary to a theologian, has already been remarked.   The houses of the gentry were not more plentifully supplied.   Few knights of the shire had libraries so good as may now perpetually be found in a servants' hall, or in the back parlour of a small shopkeeper.   An esquire passed among his neighbours for a great scholar, if Hudibras and Baker's Chronicle, Tarlton's Jests and the Seven Champions of Christendom, lay in his hall window among the fishing rods and fowling pieces.   No circulating library, no book society, then existed even in the capital : but in the capital those students who could not afford to purchase largely had a resource.   The shops of the great booksellers, near Saint Paul's Churchyard, were crowded every day and all day long with readers ; and a known customer was often permitted to carry a volume home.   In the country there was no such accommodation ; and every man was under the necessity of buying whatever he wished to read.[2]

As to the lady of the manor and her daughters, their literary stores generally consisted of a prayer book and a receipt book.   But in truth they lost little by living in rural seclusion.   For, even in the highest ranks, and in those situations which afforded the greatest facilities for mental improvement, the English women of that generation were decidedly worse educated than they have been at any other time since the revival of learning.   At an earlier period they had studied the masterpieces of ancient genius.   In the present day they seldom bestow much attention on the dead languages ; but they are familiar with the tongue of Pascal and Moliere, with the tongue of Dante and Tasso, with the tongue of Goethe and Schiller ; nor is there any purer or more graceful English than that which accomplished women now speak and write.   But, during the latter part of the seven-

Scarcity of books in country places

Female education

[1] Observator, Jan. 29. and 31. 1685 ; Calamy's Life of Baxter ; Nonconformist Memorial.

[2] Cotton seems, from his Angler, to have found room for his whole library in his hall window; and Cotton was a man of letters.   Even when Franklin first visited London in 1724, circulating libraries were unknown there.   The crowd at the booksellers' shops in Little Britain is mentioned by Roger North in his life of his brother John.

teenth century, the culture of the female mind seems to have been almost entirely neglected. If a damsel had the least smattering of literature she was regarded as a prodigy. Ladies highly born, highly bred, and naturally quick witted, were unable to write a line in their mother tongue without solecisms and faults of spelling such as a charity girl would now be ashamed to commit.[1]

The explanation may easily be found. Extravagant licentiousness, the natural effect of extravagant austerity, was now the mode ; and licentiousness had produced its ordinary effect, the moral and intellectual degradation of women. To their personal beauty, it was the fashion to pay rude and impudent homage. But the admiration and desire which they inspired were seldom mingled with respect, with affection, or with any chivalrous sentiment. The qualities which fit them to be companions, advisers, confidential friends, rather repelled than attracted the libertines of Whitehall. In that court a maid of honour, who dressed in such a manner as to do full justice to a white bosom, who ogled significantly, who danced voluptuously, who excelled in pert repartee, who was not ashamed to romp with Lords of the Bedchamber and Captains of the Guards, to sing sly verses with sly expression, or to put on a page's dress for a frolic, was more likely to be followed and admired, more likely to be honoured with royal attentions, more likely to win a rich and noble husband than Jane Grey or Lucy Hutchinson would have been. In such circumstances the standard of female attainments was necessarily low; and it was more dangerous to be above that standard than to be beneath it. Extreme ignorance and frivolity were thought less unbecoming in a lady than the slightest tincture of pedantry. Of the too celebrated women whose faces we still admire on the walls of Hampton Court, few indeed were in the habit of reading anything more valuable than acrostics, lampoons, and translations of the Clelia and the Grand Cyrus.

The literary acquirements, even of the accomplished gentlemen of that generation, seem to have been somewhat less solid and profound than at an earlier or a later period. Greek learning, at least, *Literary* did not flourish among us in the days of Charles the Second, *attainments of* as it had flourished before the civil war, or as it again *gentlemen* flourished long after the Revolution. There were undoubtedly scholars to whom the whole Greek literature, from Homer to Photius, was

---

[1] One instance will suffice. Queen Mary, the daughter of James, had excellent natural abilities, had been educated by a Bishop, was fond of history and poetry, and was regarded by very eminent men as a superior woman. There is, in the library at the Hague, a superb English Bible which was delivered to her when she was crowned in Westminster Abbey. In the titlepage are these words in her own hand, " This book was given the King and I, at our crownation. Marie R."

familiar : but such scholars were to be found almost exclusively among the clergy resident at the Universities, and even at the Universities were few, and were not fully appreciated. At Cambridge it was not thought by any means necessary that a divine should be able to read the Gospels in the original.[1] Nor was the standard at Oxford higher. When, in the reign of William the Third, Christ Church rose up as one man to defend the genuineness of the Epistles of Phalaris, that great college, then considered as the first seat of philology in the kingdom, could not muster such a stock of Attic learning as is now possessed by several youths at every great public school. It may easily be supposed that a dead language, neglected at the Universities, was not much studied by men of the world. In a former age the poetry and eloquence of Greece had been the delight of Raleigh and Falkland. In a later age the poetry and eloquence of Greece were the delight of Pitt and Fox, of Windham and Grenville. But during the latter part of the seventeenth century there was in England scarcely one eminent statesman who could read with enjoyment a page of Sophocles or Plato.

Good Latin scholars were numerous. The language of Rome, indeed, had not altogether lost its imperial prerogatives, and was still, in many parts of Europe, almost indispensable to a traveller or a negotiator. To speak it well was therefore a much more common accomplishment than in our time ; and neither Oxford nor Cambridge wanted poets who, on a great occasion, could lay at the foot of the throne happy imitations of the verses in which Virgil and Ovid had celebrated the greatness of Augustus.

Yet even the Latin was giving way to a younger rival. France united at that time almost every species of ascendency. Her military glory was at the height. She had vanquished mighty coalitions. She had dictated treaties. She had subjugated great cities and provinces. She had forced the Castilian pride to yield her the precedence. She had summoned Italian princes to prostrate themselves at her footstool. Her authority was supreme in all matters of good breeding, from a duel to a minuet. She determined how a gentleman's coat must be cut, how long his peruke must be, whether his heels must be high or low, and whether the lace on his hat must be broad or narrow. In literature she gave law to the world. The fame of her great writers filled Europe. No other country could produce a tragic poet equal to Racine, a comic poet equal to Moliere, a trifler so agreeable as La Fontaine, a rhetorician so skilful as Bossuet. The literary glory of Italy and of Spain had set ; that of Germany had not yet dawned. The genius, therefore, of the eminent men who

Influence of French literature

---

[1] Roger North tells us that his brother John, who was Greek professor at Cambridge, complained bitterly of the general neglect of the Greek tongue among the academical clergy.

adorned Paris shone forth with a splendour which was set off to full advantage by contrast. France, indeed, had at that time an empire over mankind, such as even the Roman Republic never attained. For, when Rome was politically dominant, she was in arts and letters the humble pupil of Greece. France had, over the surrounding countries, at once the ascendency which Rome had over Greece, and the ascendency which Greece had over Rome. French was fast becoming the universal language, the language of fashionable society, the language of diplomacy. At several courts princes and nobles spoke it more accurately and politely than their mother tongue. In our island there was less of this servility than on the Continent. Neither our good nor our bad qualities were those of imitators. Yet even here homage was paid, awkwardly indeed and sullenly, to the literary supremacy of our neighbours. The melodious Tuscan, so familiar to the gallants and ladies of the court of Elizabeth, sank into contempt. A gentleman who quoted Horace or Terence was considered in good company as a pompous pedant. But to garnish his conversation with scraps of French was the best proof which he could give of his parts and attainments.[1] New canons of criticism, new models of style came into fashion. The quaint ingenuity which had deformed the verses of Donne, and had been a blemish on those of Cowley, disappeared from our poetry. Our prose became less majestic, less artfully involved, less variously musical than that of an earlier age, but more lucid, more easy, and better fitted for controversy and narrative. In these changes it is impossible not to recognise the influence of French precept and of French example. Great masters of our language, in their most dignified compositions, affected to use French words, when English words, quite as expressive and sonorous, were at hand :[2] and from France was imported the tragedy in rhyme, an exotic which, in our soil, drooped, and speedily died.

It would have been well if our writers had also copied the decorum which their great French contemporaries, with few exceptions, preserved; for the profligacy of the English plays, satires, songs, and novels of that age is a deep blot on our national fame. The evil may easily be traced to its source. The wits and the Puritans had never been on friendly terms. There was no sympathy

Immorality of the polite literature of England

---

[1] Butler, in a satire of great asperity, says,

> " For, though to smatter words of Greek
> And Latin be the rhetorique
> Of pedants counted, and vainglorious,
> To smatter French is meritorious."

[2] The most offensive instance which I remember is in a poem on the coronation of Charles the Second by Dryden, who certainly could not plead poverty as an excuse for borrowing words from any foreign tongue :—

> " Hither in summer evenings you repair
> To taste the fraicheur of the cooler air."

between the two classes.   They looked on the whole system of human
life from different points and in different lights.   The earnest of each
was the jest of the other.   The pleasures of each were the torments of
the other.   To the stern precisian even the innocent sport of the fancy
seemed a crime.   To light and festive natures the solemnity of the
zealous brethren furnished copious matter of ridicule.   From the Reformation to the civil war, almost every writer, gifted with a fine sense of
the ludicrous, had taken some opportunity of assailing the straighthaired,
snuffling, whining saints, who christened their children out of the Book
of Nehemiah, who groaned in spirit at the sight of Jack in the Green,
and who thought it impious to taste plum porridge on Christmas day.
At length a time came when the laughers began to look grave in their
turn.   The rigid, ungainly zealots, after having furnished much good
sport during two generations, rose up in arms, conquered, ruled, and,
grimly smiling, trod down under their feet the whole crowd of mockers.
The wounds inflicted by gay and petulant malice were retaliated with
the gloomy and implacable malice peculiar to bigots who mistake their
own rancour for virtue.   The theatres were closed.   The players were
flogged.   The press was put under the guardianship of austere licensers.
The Muses were banished from their own favourite haunts, Cambridge
and Oxford.   Cowley, Crashaw, and Cleveland were ejected from their
fellowships.   The young candidate for academical honours was no longer
required to write Ovidian epistles or Virgilian pastorals, but was strictly
interrogated by a synod of lowering Supralapsarians as to the day and
hour when he experienced the new birth.   Such a system was of course
fruitful of hypocrites.   Under sober clothing and under visages composed to the expression of austerity lay hid during several years the
intense desire of license and of revenge.   At length that desire was
gratified.   The Restoration emancipated thousands of minds from a yoke
which had become insupportable.   The old fight recommenced, but with
an animosity altogether new.   It was now not a sportive combat, but a
war to the death.   The Roundhead had no better quarter to expect from
those whom he had persecuted than a cruel slavedriver can expect from
insurgent slaves still bearing the marks of his collars and his scourges.

The war between wit and Puritanism soon became a war between
wit and morality.   The hostility excited by a grotesque caricature of
virtue did not spare virtue herself.   Whatever the canting Roundhead
had regarded with reverence was insulted.   Whatever he had proscribed
was favoured.   Because he had been scrupulous about trifles, all scruples
were treated with derision.   Because he had covered his failings with
the mask of devotion, men were encouraged to obtrude with Cynic
impudence all their most scandalous vices on the public eye.   Because
he had punished illicit love with barbarous severity, virgin purity and

EDMUND WALLER

From the painting by J. Riley in the National Portrait Gallery conjugal fidelity were made a jest. To that sanctimonious jargon which was his Shibboleth, was opposed another jargon not less absurd and much more odious. As he never opened his mouth except in scriptural phrase, the new breed of wits and fine gentlemen never opened their mouths without uttering ribaldry of which a porter would now be ashamed, and without calling on their Maker to curse them, sink them, confound them, blast them, and damn them.

It is not strange, therefore, that our polite literature, when it revived with the revival of the old civil and ecclesiastical polity, should have been profoundly immoral. A few eminent men, who belonged to an earlier and better age, were exempt from the general contagion. The verse of Waller still breathed the sentiments which had animated a more chivalrous generation. Cowley, distinguished as a loyalist and as a man of letters, raised his voice courageously against the immorality which disgraced both letters and loyalty. A mightier poet, tried at once by pain, danger, poverty, obloquy, and blindness, meditated, undisturbed by the obscene tumult which raged all around him, a song so sublime and so holy that it would not have misbecome the lips of those ethereal Virtues whom he saw, with that inner eye which no calamity could darken, flinging down on the jasper pavement their crowns of amaranth and gold. The vigorous and fertile genius of Butler, if it did not altogether escape the prevailing infection, took the disease in a mild form. But these were men whose minds had been trained in a world which had passed away. They gave place in no long time to a younger generation of wits ; and of that generation, from Dryden down to Durfey, the common characteristic was hardhearted, shameless, swaggering licentiousness, at once inelegant and inhuman. The influence of these writers was doubtless noxious, yet less noxious than it would have been had they been less depraved. The poison which they administered was so strong that it was, in no long time, rejected with nausea. None of them understood the dangerous art of associating images of unlawful pleasure with all that is endearing and ennobling. None of them was aware that a certain decorum is essential even to voluptuousness, that drapery may be more alluring than exposure, and that the imagination may be far more powerfully moved by delicate hints which impel it to exert itself, than by gross descriptions which it takes in passively.

The spirit of the Antipuritan reaction pervades almost the whole polite literature of the reign of Charles the Second. But the very quintessence of that spirit will be found in the comic drama. The playhouses, shut by the meddling fanatic in the day of his power, were again crowded. To their old attractions new and more powerful attractions had been added. Scenery, dresses, and decorations, such as would now be thought mean or absurd, but such as would have been esteemed

Gul. Faithorne ad Virum.   Delin. et sculpsit.

Joannis Miltoni Effigies Ætat: 62.
1670.

JOHN MILTON

From the engraved portrait by William Faithorne

incredibly magnificent by those who, early in the seventeenth century, sate on the filthy benches of the Hope, or under the thatched roof of the Rose, dazzled the eyes of the multitude. The fascination of sex was called in to aid the fascination of art : and the young spectator saw, with emotions unknown to the contemporaries of Shakspeare and Jonson, tender and sprightly heroines personated by lovely women. From the day on which the theatres were reopened they became seminaries of vice ; and the evil propagated itself. The profligacy of the representations soon drove away sober people. The frivolous and dissolute who remained required every year stronger and stronger stimulants. Thus the artists corrupted the spectators, and the spectators the artists, till the turpitude of the drama became such as must astonish all who are not aware that extreme relaxation is the natural effect of extreme restraint, and that an age of hypocrisy is, in the regular course of things, followed by an age of impudence.

Nothing is more characteristic of the times than the care with which the poets contrived to put all their loosest verses into the mouths of women. The compositions in which the greatest license was taken were the epilogues. They were almost always recited by favourite actresses ; and nothing charmed the depraved audience so much as to hear lines grossly indecent repeated by a beautiful girl, who was supposed to have not yet lost her innocence.[1]

Our theatre was indebted in that age for many plots and characters to Spain, to France, and to the old English masters : but whatever our dramatists touched they tainted. In their imitations the houses of Calderon's stately and highspirited Castilian gentlemen became sties of vice, Shakspeare's Viola a procuress, Moliere's Misanthrope a ravisher, Moliere's Agnes an adulteress. Nothing could be so pure or so heroic but that it became foul and ignoble by transfusion through those foul and ignoble minds.

Such was the state of the drama ; and the drama was the department of polite literature in which a poet had the best chance of obtaining a subsistence by his pen. The sale of books was so small that a man of the greatest name could hardly expect more than a pittance for the copyright of the best performance. There cannot be a stronger instance than the fate of Dryden's last production, the Fables. That volume was published when he was universally admitted to be the chief of living English poets. It contains about twelve thousand lines. The versification is admirable, the narratives and descriptions full of life. To this day Palamon and Arcite, Cymon and Iphigenia, Theodore and Honoria, are the delight both of critics and of schoolboys. The collection includes Alexander's Feast, the noblest ode in our language. For

---

[1] Jeremy Collier has censured this odious practice with his usual force and keenness.

the copyright Dryden received two hundred and fifty pounds, less than in our days has sometimes been paid for two articles in a review.[1] Nor

SCENE FROM E. SETTLE'S EMPRESS OF MOROCCO
Showing the Stage and Scenery

does the bargain seem to have been a hard one. For the book went off slowly; and the second edition was not required till the author had been

[1] The contract will be found in Sir Walter Scott's edition of Dryden.

ten years in his grave. By writing for the theatre it was possible to earn a much larger sum with much less trouble. Southern made seven hundred pounds by one play.[1] Otway was raised from beggary to temporary affluence by the success of his Don Carlos.[2] Shadwell cleared a hundred and thirty pounds by a single representation of the Squire of Alsatia.[3] The consequence was that every man who had to live by his wit wrote plays, whether he had any internal vocation to write plays or not. It was thus with Dryden. As a satirist he has rivalled Juvenal. As a didactic poet he perhaps might, with care and meditation, have rivalled Lucretius. Of lyric poets he is, if not the most sublime, the most brilliant and spiritstirring. But nature, profuse to him of many rare gifts, had withheld from him the dramatic faculty. Nevertheless all the energies of his best years were wasted on dramatic composition. He had too much judgment not to be aware that in the power of exhibiting character by means of dialogue he was deficient. That deficiency he did his best to conceal, sometimes by surprising and amusing incidents, sometimes by stately declamation, sometimes by harmonious numbers, sometimes by ribaldry but too well suited to the taste of a profane and licentious pit. Yet he never obtained any theatrical success equal to that which rewarded the exertions of some men far inferior to him in general powers. He thought himself fortunate if he cleared a hundred guineas by a play ; a scanty remuneration, yet apparently larger than he could have earned in any other way by the same quantity of labour.[4]

The recompense which the wits of that age could obtain from the public was so small, that they were under the necessity of eking out their incomes by levying contributions on the great. Every rich and goodnatured lord was pestered by authors with a mendicancy so importunate, and a flattery so abject, as may in our time seem incredible. The patron to whom a work was inscribed was expected to reward the writer with a purse of gold. The fee paid for the dedication of a book was often much larger than the sum which any publisher would give for the copyright. Books were therefore frequently printed merely that they might be dedicated. This traffic in praise produced the effect which might have been expected. Adulation pushed to the verge, sometimes of nonsense, and sometimes of impiety, was not thought to disgrace a poet. Independence, veracity, selfrespect, were things not required by the world from him. In truth, he was in morals something between a pandar and a beggar.

To the other vices which degraded the literary character was added, towards the close of the reign of Charles the Second, the most savage intemperance of party spirit. The wits, as a class, had been impelled

---

[1] See the Life of Southern, by Shiels.　　[2] See Rochester's Trial of the Poets.
[3] Some Account of the English stage.　　[4] Life of Southern, by Shiels.

FRANCISCI
DE VERULAMIO,
Summi Angliæ
CANCELLARII,
Instauratio
magna.

Multi pertransibunt & augebitur scientia.

Anno

LONDINI
Apud Joannem Billium
Typographum
Regium.

1620.

THE TITLE PAGE TO BACON'S NOVUM ORGANUM 1620

by their old hatred of Puritanism to take the side of the court, and had been found useful allies.   Dryden, in particular, had done good service to the government.   His Absalom and Achitophel, the greatest satire of modern times, had amazed the town, had made its way with unprecedented rapidity even into rural districts, and had, wherever it appeared, bitterly annoyed the Exclusionists, and raised the courage of the Tories. But we must not, in the admiration which we naturally feel for noble diction and versification, forget the great distinctions of good and evil. The spirit by which Dryden and several of his compeers were at this time animated against the Whigs deserves to be called fiendish.   The servile Judges and Sheriffs of those evil days could not shed blood so fast as the poets cried out for it.   Calls for more victims, hideous jests on hanging, bitter taunts on those who, having stood by the King in the hour of danger, now advised him to deal mercifully and generously by his vanquished enemies, were publicly recited on the stage, and, that nothing might be wanting to the guilt and the shame, were recited by women, who, having long been taught to discard all modesty, were now taught to discard all compassion.[1]

It is a remarkable fact that, while the lighter literature of England was thus becoming a nuisance and a national disgrace, the English genius was effecting in science a revolution which will, to the

State of
science in
England

end of time, be reckoned among the highest achievements of the human intellect.   Bacon had sown the good seed in a sluggish soil and an ungenial season.   He had not expected an early crop, and in his last testament had solemnly bequeathed his fame to the next age.   During a whole generation his philosophy had, amidst tumults, wars, and proscriptions, been slowly ripening in a few well constituted minds.   While factions were struggling for dominion over each other, a small body of sages had turned away with benevolent disdain from the conflict, and had devoted themselves to the nobler work of extending the dominion of man over matter.   As soon as tranquillity was restored, these teachers easily found attentive audience. For the discipline through which the nation had passed had brought the public mind to a temper well fitted for the reception of the Verulamian doctrine.   The civil troubles had stimulated the faculties of the educated classes, and had called forth a restless activity and an insatiable curiosity, such as had not before been known among us.   Yet the effect of those troubles was that schemes of political and religious reform were generally regarded with suspicion and contempt.   During twenty years the chief employment of busy and ingenious men had been to frame constitutions with first magistrates, without first magistrates, with hereditary senates,

---

[1] If any reader thinks my expressions too severe, I would advise him to read Dryden's Epilogue to the Duke of Guise, and to observe that it was spoken by a woman.

CHARLES II CROWNED AS PATRON OF THE ROYAL SOCIETY

From the engraving by W. Hollar after a design by John Evelyn

with senates appointed by lot, with annual senates, with perpetual
senates.   In these plans nothing was omitted.   All the detail, all the
nomenclature, all the ceremonial of the imaginary government was fully
set forth, Polemarchs and Phylarchs, Tribes and Galaxies, the Lord
Archon and the Lord Strategus.   Which ballot boxes were to be green
and which red, which balls were to be of gold and which of silver, which
magistrates were to wear hats and which black velvet caps with peaks,
how the mace was to be carried and when the heralds were to uncover,
these, and a hundred more such trifles, were gravely considered and
arranged by men of no common capacity and learning.[1]   But the time
for these visions had gone by ; and, if any steadfast republican still
continued to amuse himself with them, fear of public derision and of a
criminal information generally induced him to keep his fancies to himself.
It was now unpopular and unsafe to mutter a word against the fundamental laws of the monarchy : but daring and ingenious men might
indemnify themselves by treating with disdain what had lately been
considered as the fundamental laws of nature.   The torrent which had
been dammed up in one channel rushed violently into another.   The
revolutionary spirit, ceasing to operate in politics, began to exert itself
with unprecedented vigour and hardihood in every department of
physics.   The year 1660, the era of the restoration of the old constitution, is also the era from which dates the ascendency of the new
philosophy.   In that year the Royal Society, destined to be a chief
agent in a long series of glorious and salutary reforms, began to exist.[2]
In a few months experimental science became all the mode.   The
transfusion of blood, the ponderation of air, the fixation of mercury,
succeeded to that place in the public mind which had been lately
occupied by the controversies of the Rota.   Dreams of perfect forms of
government made way for dreams of wings with which men were to fly
from the Tower to the Abbey, and of doublekeeled ships which were
never to founder in the fiercest storm.   All classes were hurried along
by the prevailing sentiment.   Cavalier and Roundhead, Churchman and
Puritan, were for once allied.   Divines, jurists, statesmen, nobles, princes,
swelled the triumph of the Baconian philosophy.   Poets sang with
emulous fervour the approach of the golden age.   Cowley, in lines
weighty with thought and resplendent with wit, urged the chosen seed
to take possession of the promised land flowing with milk and honey,
that land which their great deliverer and lawgiver had seen, as from the
summit of Pisgah, but had not been permitted to enter.[3]   Dryden, with
more zeal than knowledge, joined his voice to the general acclamation,
and foretold things which neither he nor anybody else understood.   The

[1] See particularly Harrington's Oceana.   [2] See Sprat's History of the Royal Society.
[3] Cowley's Ode to the Royal Society.

ROBERT BOYLE

From the portrait by F. Kerseboom in the National Portrait Gallery

Royal Society, he predicted, would soon lead us to the extreme verge of the globe, and there delight us with a better view of the moon.[1]   Two able and aspiring prelates, Ward, Bishop of Salisbury, and Wilkins, Bishop of Chester, were conspicuous among the leaders of the movement.   Its history was eloquently written by a younger divine, who was rising to high distinction in his profession, Thomas Sprat, afterwards Bishop of Rochester.   Both Chief Justice Hale and Lord Keeper Guildford stole some hours from the business of their courts to write on hydrostatics.   Indeed it was under the immediate direction of Guildford that the first barometers ever exposed to sale in London were constructed.[2]   Chemistry divided, for a time, with wine and love, with the stage and the gaming table, with the intrigues of a courtier and the intrigues of a demagogue, the attention of the fickle Buckingham. Rupert has the credit of having invented mezzotinto ; and from him is named that curious bubble of glass which has long amused children and puzzled philosophers.   Charles himself had a laboratory at Whitehall, and was far more active and attentive there than at the council board. It was almost necessary to the character of a fine gentleman to have something to say about airpumps and telescopes ; and even fine ladies, now and then, thought it becoming to affect a taste for science, went in coaches and six to visit the Gresham curiosities, and broke forth into cries of delight at finding that a magnet really attracted a needle, and that a microscope really made a fly look as large as a sparrow.[3]

In this, as in every great stir of the human mind, there was doubtless something which might well move a smile.   It is the universal law that whatever pursuit, whatever doctrine, becomes fashionable, shall lose a portion of that dignity which it had possessed while it was confined to a small but earnest minority, and was loved for its own sake alone.   It is true that the follies of some persons who, without any real aptitude for science, professed a passion for it, furnished matter of contemptuous mirth to a few malignant satirists who belonged to the preceding generation, and were not disposed to unlearn the lore of their youth.[4]   But it is not less true that the great work of interpreting nature was performed by the English of that age as it had never before been performed in any age by any nation.   The spirit of Francis Bacon was abroad, a spirit

[1]   " Then we upon the globe's last verge shall go,
                    And view the ocean leaning on the sky ;
              From thence our rolling neighbours we shall know,
                    And on the lunar world securely pry."—Annus Mirabilis, 164.

[2] North's Life of Guildford.   [3] Pepys's Diary, May 30. 1667.

[4] Butler was, I think, the only man of real genius who, between the Restoration and the Revolution, showed a bitter enmity to the new philosophy, as it was then called.   See the Satire on the Royal Society, and the Elephant in the Moon.

G. Kneller Bar.t pinx. 1716   J. Faber fecit 1729.

Dⁿᵘˢ Hans Sloane Baronettus

Collegÿ Regÿ. Medicorum Londinensiũ & Regiæ Societatis Præses &c.

Printed for Bowles & Carver, N.º 69 in S.t Paul's Church Yard, London.

SIR HANS SLOANE

From a mezzotint by Faber after a portrait by Sir G. Kneller

H. E. I   2C

admirably compounded of audacity and sobriety.   There was a strong
persuasion that the whole world was full of secrets of high moment to
the happiness of man, and that man had, by his Maker, been entrusted
with the key which, rightly used, would give access to them.   There
was at the same time a conviction that in physics it was impossible to
arrive at the knowledge of general laws except by the careful observation of particular facts.   Deeply impressed with these great truths, the
professors of the new philosophy applied themselves to their task, and,
before a quarter of a century had expired, they had given ample earnest
of what has since been achieved.   Already a reform of agriculture had
been commenced.   New vegetables were cultivated.   New implements
of husbandry were employed.   New manures were applied to the soil.[1]
Evelyn had, under the formal sanction of the Royal Society, given
instruction to his countrymen in planting.   Temple, in his intervals of
leisure, had tried many experiments in horticulture, and had proved that
many delicate fruits, the natives of more favoured climates, might, with
the help of art, be grown on English ground.   Medicine, which in
France was still in abject bondage, and afforded an inexhaustible subject
of just ridicule to Moliere, had in England become an experimental and
progressive science, and every day made some new advance, in defiance
of Hippocrates and Galen.   The attention of speculative men had been,
for the first time, directed to the important subject of sanitary police.
The great plague of 1665 induced them to consider with care the
defective architecture, draining, and ventilation of the capital.   The
great fire of 1666 afforded an opportunity for effecting extensive improvements.   The whole matter was diligently examined by the Royal
Society ; and to the suggestions of that body must be partly attributed
the changes which, though far short of what the public welfare required,
yet made a wide difference between the new and the old London, and
probably put a final close to the ravages of pestilence in our country.[2]
At the same time one of the founders of the Society, Sir William Petty,
created the science of political arithmetic, the humble but indispensable
handmaid of political philosophy.   No kingdom of nature was left un-
explored.   To that period belong the chemical discoveries of Boyle, and
the earliest botanical researches of Sloane.   It was then that Ray made
a new classification of birds and fishes, and that the attention of Wood-
ward was first drawn towards fossils and shells.   One after another
phantoms which had haunted the world through ages of darkness fled
before the light.   Astrology and alchymy became jests.   Soon there
was scarcely a county in which some of the Quorum did not smile

[1] The eagerness with which the agriculturists of that age tried experiments and introduced improvements is well described by Aubrey.   See the Natural History of Wiltshire, 1685.

[2] Sprat's History of the Royal Society.

contemptuously when an old woman was brought before them for riding on broomsticks or giving cattle the murrain. But it was in those noblest and most arduous departments of knowledge in which induction and mathematical demonstration cooperate for the discovery of truth, that the English genius won in that age the most memorable triumphs. John Wallis placed the whole system of statics on a new foundation. Edmund Halley investigated the properties of the atmosphere, the ebb and flow of the sea, the laws of magnetism, and the course of the comets; nor did he shrink from toil, peril, and exile in the cause of science. While he, on the rock of Saint Helena, mapped the constellations of the southern hemisphere, our national observatory was rising at Greenwich ; and John Flamsteed, the first Astronomer Royal, was commencing that long series of observations which is never mentioned without respect and gratitude in any part of the globe. But the glory of these men, eminent as they were, is cast into the shade by the transcendent lustre of one immortal name. In Isaac Newton two kinds of intellectual power, which have little in common, and which are not often found together in a very high degree of vigour, but which nevertheless are equally necessary in the most sublime departments of physics, were united as they have never been united before or since. There may have been minds as happily constituted as his for the cultivation of pure mathematical science: there may have been minds as happily constituted for the cultivation of science purely experimental: but in no other mind have the demonstrative faculty and the inductive faculty coexisted in such supreme excellence and perfect harmony. Perhaps in the days of Scotists and Thomists even his intellect might have run to waste, as many intellects ran to waste which were inferior only to his. Happily the spirit of the age on which his lot was cast, gave the right direction to his mind ; and his mind reacted with tenfold force on the spirit of the age. In the year 1685 his fame, though splendid, was only dawning ; but his genius was in the meridian. His great work, that work which effected a revolution in the most important provinces of natural philosophy, had been completed, but was not yet published, and was just about to be submitted to the consideration of the Royal Society.

It is not very easy to explain why the nation which was so far before its neighbours in science should in art have been far behind them. Yet such was the fact. It is true that in architecture, an art **State of the** which is half a science, an art in which none but a geome- **fine arts** trician can excel, an art which has no standard of grace but what is directly or indirectly dependent on utility, an art of which the creations derive a part, at least, of their majesty from mere bulk, our country could boast of one truly great man, Christopher Wren ; and the fire which laid London in ruins had given him an opportunity, unprecedented in modern history, of displaying his powers. The austere beauty of the Athenian portico, the gloomy sublimity of the Gothic arcade, he was, like almost all his contemporaries, incapable of emulating, and perhaps incapable of appreciating : but no man, born on our side of the Alps, has imitated with so much success the magnificence of the palacelike churches of Italy. Even the superb Lewis has left to posterity no work which can bear a comparison with Saint Paul's. But at the close of the reign of Charles the Second there was not a single English painter or statuary whose name is now remembered. This sterility is somewhat mysterious ; for painters and statuaries were by no means a despised or an ill paid class. Their social position was at least as high as at present. Their gains, when compared with the wealth of the nation and with the remuneration of other descriptions of intellectual labour, were even larger than at present. Indeed the munificent patronage which was extended to artists drew them to our shores in multitudes. Lely, who has preserved to us the rich curls, the full lips, and the languishing eyes of the frail beauties celebrated by Hamilton, was a Westphalian. He had died in 1680, having long lived splendidly, having received the honour of knighthood, and having accumulated a good estate out of the fruits of his skill. His noble collection of drawings and pictures was, after his decease, exhibited by the royal permission in the Banqueting House at Whitehall, and was sold by auction for the almost incredible sum of twenty six thousand pounds, a sum which bore a greater proportion to the fortunes of the rich men of that day than a hundred thousand pounds would bear to the fortunes of the rich men of our time.[1] Lely was succeeded by his countryman Godfrey Kneller, who was made first a knight and then a baronet, and who, after keeping up a sumptuous establishment, and after losing much money by unlucky speculations, was still able to bequeath a large fortune to his family. The two Vandeveldes, natives of Holland, had been tempted by English liberality to settle here, and had produced for the King and his nobles some of the finest sea pieces in the world. Another Dutchman, Simon Varelst, painted glorious sunflowers and tulips for prices such as had never before been known. Verrio, a Neapolitan, covered ceilings and staircases with Gorgons and Muses, Nymphs and Satyrs, Virtues and Vices, Gods quaffing nectar, and laurelled princes riding in triumph. The income which he derived from his performances enabled him to keep one of the most expensive tables in England. For his pieces at Windsor alone he received seven thousand pounds, a sum then sufficient to make a gentleman of moderate wishes perfectly easy for life, a sum greatly exceeding all that Dryden, during a literary life of forty years, obtained from the

[1] Walpole's Anecdotes of Painting; London Gazette, May 31. 1683; North's Life of Guildford.

booksellers.[1]   Verrio's assistant and successor, Lewis Laguerre, came from France.   The two most celebrated sculptors of that day were also

SIR PETER LELY

From a mezzotint by I. Beckett after a painting by Sir P. Lely

foreigners.   Cibber, whose pathetic emblems of Fury and Melancholy still adorn Bedlam, was a Dane.   Gibbons, to whose graceful fancy and

[1] The great prices paid to Varelst and Verrio are mentioned in Walpole's Anecdotes of Painting.

delicate touch many of our palaces, colleges, and churches owe their finest decorations, was a Dutchman.   Even the designs for the coin were made by French artists.   Indeed, it was not till the reign of George the Second that our country could glory in a great painter ; and George the Third was on the throne before she had reason to be proud of any of her sculptors.

It is time that this description of the England which Charles the Second governed should draw to a close.   Yet one subject of the highest moment still remains untouched.   Nothing has yet been said of the great body of the people, of those who held the ploughs, who tended the oxen, who toiled at the looms of Norwich, and squared the Portland stone for Saint Paul's.   Nor can very much be said.   The most numerous class is precisely the class respecting which we have the most meagre information.   In those times philanthropists did not yet regard it as a sacred duty, nor had demagogues yet found it a lucrative trade, to talk and write about the distress of the labourer. History was too much occupied with courts and camps to spare a line for the hut of the peasant or the garret of the mechanic.   The press now often sends forth in a day a greater quantity of discussion and declamation about the condition of the working man than was published during the twenty eight years which elapsed between the Restoration and the Revolution.   But it would be a great error to infer from the increase of complaint that there has been any increase of misery.

The great criterion of the state of the common people is the amount of their wages ; and as four fifths of the common people were, in the **State of the common people** seventeenth century, employed in agriculture, it is especially important to ascertain what were then the wages of agricultural industry.   On this subject we have the means of arriving at conclusions sufficiently exact for our purpose.

Sir William Petty, whose mere assertion carries great weight, informs us that a labourer was by no means in the lowest state who received **Agricultural wages** for a day's work fourpence with food, or eightpence without food.   Four shillings a week therefore were, according to Petty's calculation, fair agricultural wages.[1]

That this calculation was not remote from the truth we have abundant proof.   About the beginning of the year 1685 the justices of Warwickshire, in the exercise of a power entrusted to them by an Act of Elizabeth, fixed, at their quarter sessions, a scale of wages for the county, and notified that every employer who gave more than the authorised sum, and every working man who received more, would be liable to punishment.   The wages of the common agricultural labourer,

[1] Petty's Political Arithmetic.

from March to September, were fixed at the precise amount mentioned by Petty, namely four shillings a week without food. From

SIR GODFREY KNELLER

From a mezzotint by J. Smith after a painting by Sir G. Kneller

September to March the wages were to be only three and sixpence a week.[1]

[1] Stat. 5 Eliz. c. 4.; Archæologia, vol. xi.

But in that age, as in ours, the earnings of the peasant were very different in different parts of the kingdom. The wages of Warwickshire were probably about the average, and those of the counties near the Scottish border below it : but there were more favoured districts. In the same year, 1685, a gentleman of Devonshire, named Richard Dunning, published a small tract, in which he described the condition of the poor of that county. That he understood his subject well it is impossible to doubt ; for a few months later his work was reprinted, and was, by the magistrates assembled in quarter sessions at Exeter, strongly recommended to the attention of all parochial officers. According to him, the wages of the Devonshire peasant were, without food, about five shillings a week.[1]

Still better was the condition of the labourer in the neighbourhood of Bury Saint Edmund's. The magistrates of Suffolk met there in the spring of 1682 to fix a rate of wages, and resolved that, where the labourer was not boarded, he should have five shillings a week in winter, and six in summer.[2]

In 1661 the justices at Chelmsford had fixed the wages of the Essex labourer, who was not boarded, at six shillings in winter and seven in summer. This seems to have been the highest remuneration given in the kingdom for agricultural labour between the Restoration and the Revolution ; and it is to be observed that, in the year in which this order was made, the necessaries of life were immoderately dear. Wheat was at seventy shillings the quarter, which would even now be considered as almost a famine price.[3]

These facts are in perfect accordance with another fact which seems to deserve consideration. It is evident that, in a country where no man can be compelled to become a soldier, the ranks of an army cannot be filled if the government offers much less than the wages of common rustic labour. At present the pay and beer money of a private in a regiment of the line amount to seven shillings and sevenpence a week. This stipend, coupled with the hope of a pension, does not attract the English youth in sufficient numbers ; and it is found necessary to supply the deficiency by enlisting largely from among the poorer population of Munster and Connaught. The pay of the private foot soldier in 1685 was only four shillings and eightpence a week ; yet it is certain that the government in that year found no difficulty in obtaining many thousands of English recruits at very short notice. The pay of the private foot soldier in the army of the Commonwealth had been seven shillings

---

[1] Plain and easy Method showing how the office of Overseer of the Poor may be managed, by Richard Dunning ; 1st edition, 1685 ; 2d edition, 1686.

[2] Cullum's History of Hawsted.　　　　　　　　[3] Ruggles on the Poor.

WILLIAM DOBSON

From a mezzotint by G. White in the British Museum

a week, that is to say, as much as a corporal received under Charles the Second ;[1] and seven shillings a week had been found sufficient to fill the ranks with men decidedly superior to the generality of the people. On the whole, therefore, it seems reasonable to conclude that, in the reign of Charles the Second, the ordinary wages of the peasant did not exceed four shillings a week ; but that, in some parts of the kingdom, five shillings, six shillings, and, during the summer months, even seven shillings were paid.   At present a district where a labouring man earns only seven shillings a week is thought to be in a state shocking to humanity.   The average is very much higher ; and, in prosperous counties, the weekly wages of husbandmen amount to twelve, fourteen, and even sixteen shillings.

The remuneration of workmen employed in manufactures has always been higher than that of the tillers of the soil.   In the year 1680, a member of the House of Commons remarked that the high wages paid in this country made it impossible for our textures to maintain a competition with the produce of the Indian looms.   An English mechanic, he said, instead of slaving like a native of Bengal for a piece of copper, exacted a shilling a day.[2]   Other evidence is extant, which proves that a shilling a day was the pay to which the English manufacturer then thought himself entitled, but that he was often forced to work for less.   The common people of that age were not in the habit of meeting for public discussion, of haranguing, or of petitioning Parliament.   No newspaper pleaded their cause.   It was in rude rhyme that their love and hatred, their exultation and their distress found utterance.   A great part of their history is to be learned only from their ballads.   One of the most remarkable of the popular lays chaunted about the streets of Norwich and Leeds in the time of Charles the Second may still be read on the original broadside.   It is the vehement and bitter cry of labour against capital.   It describes the good old times when every artisan employed in the woollen manufacture lived as well as a farmer.   But those times were past.   Sixpence a day was now all that could be earned by hard labour at the loom.   If the poor complained that they could not live on such a pittance, they were told that they were free to take it or leave it.   For so miserable a recompense were the producers of wealth compelled to toil, rising early and lying down late, while the master clothier, eating, sleeping, and idling, became rich by their exertions.   A shilling a day, the poet declares, is what the weaver would have, if justice were

Wages of manufacturers

---

[1] See, in Thurloe's State Papers, the Memorandum of the Dutch Deputies, dated August $\frac{2}{12}$. 1653.

[2] The orator was Mr. John Basset, member for Barnstaple.   See Smith's Memoirs of Wool. chapter lxviii.

The Clothiers Delight:

OR, The Rich Mens Joy, and the Poor Mens Sorrow.

Wherein is exprest the craftineſs and ſubtilty of many Clothiers in England, by beating down their Work-mens wages, Combers, Weavers, and Spinners, for little gains, Doth Earn their money by taking of hard pains.

To the Tune of, *Jenny come tye me*, &c. *Packington's Pound*, Or, *Monk hath confounded*, &c.

With Allowance, Ro. L'Eſtrange.

By T. Lanfiere.

OF all ſorts of callings that in England be,
There is none that liveth ſo gallant as we;
We live at our pleaſure, and taketh delight;
We hoard up our riches and treaſure great ſtore,
Which we get by grinding the poor,
And this is a way for to fill up our purſe,
Although we do get it with many a Curſe.

Throughout the whole Kingdom in Country and Town,
There is no danger of our Trade going down,
So long as the Comber can work with his Comb,
And alſo the Weaver weave in his Loom;
The Tucker and Spinner that ſpins all the year,
We will make them to earn their wages full dear,
And this is the way, &c.

In former ages we us'd to give,
So that our Work-folks like Farmers did live;
But the times are alter'd, we will make them know
All we can for to bring them all under our Low;
We will make them to work hard for Sixpence a day,
Though a ſhilling they deſerve if they had their juſt pay;
And this is the way, &c.

And firſt for the Combers we will bring them down,
From Eight-groats a-ſcore unto Half a Crown:
If at all they murmur, and ſay 'tis too ſmall,
We bid them chooſe whether they will take it at all:
We'll make them believe that trading is bad,
We care not a pin, though they are ne'r ſo ſad,
And this is the way, &c.

We'll make the poor Weavers work at a low rate,
We'll find fault where's no fault, and ſo we will bate:
If trading grows dead we will preſently ſhew it,
But if it grows good they ſhall never know it:
We'll tell them that Cloath beyond Sea will not go,
We care not whether we keep ſloathing or no;
And this is the way, &c.

Then next for the Spinners we ſhall enſue,
We'll make them ſpin three pound inſtead of two;
When they bring home their work then unto us, they complain,
And ſay that their wages will not them maintain:
But if that an Ounce of weight it do lack,
Then for to bate threepence we will not be ſlack;
And this is the way, &c.

But if it fall too light, then their wages they bate,
We have put no money, and what's that you'd have;
We have Bread and Bacon, and Butter that's good,
With Oatmeal and Salt that is wholeſome for food,
And yet we may toyſt by them ſo long as you have ſight,
And this is the way, &c.

We will make the Market and Shearman underſtand,
Though with their wages ſhall never buy Land;
Yet now we will make them ſubmit humbly,
We will keep them under in every degree:
And this is the way, &c.

When we go to Market our work-men are glad,
But when we come home then we do look ſad,
We ſit in the corner as if our hearts did ake,
We tell them 'tis not a penny we can take:
And plead poverty before we have need,
And thus we do cooks them moſt bravely indeed;
And this is the way, &c.

But if to an Ale-houſe they Cuſtomers be,
Then preſently with the Ale-wiſe we agree,
When we count to a reckoning, then we do crave
Two-pence on a Shilling, and that we will have;
By ſuch cunning ways for our treaſure we get,
For it is all fiſh that both come to our Net;
And this is the way, &c.

And thus we do gain all our Wealth and Eſtate,
By many poor men that work early and late:
If it were not for thoſe that do labour full hard,
We might go and hang our ſelves without regard:
The Combers, and Weavers, and Tuckers alſo,
With the Spinners that work for ſmall Wages full low:
By theſe peoples labours we fill up our purſe, &c.

Then hey for the Cloathing-trade, it goes on brave,
We ſcorn for to toyl and moyl, no yet to ſlave;
Our Work-men do work hard, but we live at eaſe,
We go when we will, and come when we pleaſe,
We hoard up our bags of ſilver and Gold,
But conſcience and charity with us is cold:
By poor peoples labour we fill up our purſe,
Although we do get it with many a curſe.

FINIS.

Printed for F. Coles, T. Vere, I. Wright, and I. Clarke.

THE CLOTHIER'S DELIGHT

From the Roxburghe Ballads in the British Museum

done.[1] We may therefore conclude that, in the generation which preceded the Revolution, a workman employed in the great staple manufacture of England thought himself fairly paid if he gained six shillings a week.

It may here be noticed that the practice of setting children prematurely to work, a practice which the state, the legitimate protector of **Labour of children in factories** those who cannot protect themselves, has, in our time, wisely and humanely interdicted, prevailed in the seventeenth century to an extent which, when compared with the extent of the manufacturing system, seems almost incredible. At Norwich, the chief seat of the clothing trade, a little creature of six years old was thought fit for labour. Several writers of that time, and among them some who were considered as eminently benevolent, mention, with exultation, the fact that, in that single city, boys and girls of very tender age created wealth exceeding what was necessary for their own subsistence by twelve thousand pounds a year.[2] The more carefully we examine the history of the past, the more reason shall we find to dissent from those who imagine that our age has been fruitful of new social evils. The truth is that the evils are, with scarcely an exception, old. That which is new is the intelligence which discerns and the humanity which remedies them.

When we pass from the weavers of cloth to a different class of artisans, our enquiries will still lead us to nearly the same conclusions. **Wages of different classes of artisans** During several generations, the Commissioners of Greenwich Hospital have kept a register of the wages paid to different classes of workmen who have been employed in the repairs of the building. From this valuable record it appears that, in the course

---

[1] This ballad is in the British Museum. The precise year is not given ; but the Imprimatur of Roger Lestrange fixes the date sufficiently for my purpose. I will quote some of the lines. The master clothier is introduced speaking as follows :—

> "In former ages we used to give,
> So that our workfolks like farmers did live ;
> But the times are changed, we will make them know.
> *　　*　　*　　*　　*　　*　　*
> "We will make them to work hard for sixpence a day,
> Though a shilling they deserve if they had their just pay ;
> If at all they murmur and say 'tis too small,
> We bid them choose whether they'll work at all.
> And thus we do gain all our wealth and estate,
> By many poor men that work early and late.
> Then hey for the clothing trade ! It goes on brave ;
> We scorn for to toyl and moyl, nor yet to slave.
> Our workmen do work hard, but we live at ease,
> We go when we will, and we come when we please."

[2] Chamberlayne's State of England ; Petty's Political Arithmetic, chapter viii. ; Dunning's Plain and Easy Method ; Firmin's Proposition for the Employing of the Poor. It ought to be observed that Firmin was an eminent philanthropist.

ENGLAND'S GREAT JOY AND GRATITUDE

Broadside illustrating the history of the woollen trade, in the possession of the Editor of a hundred and twenty years, the daily earnings of the bricklayer have risen from half a crown to four and tenpence, those of the mason from half a crown to five and threepence, those of the carpenter from half a crown to five and fivepence, and those of the plumber from three shillings to five and sixpence.

It seems clear, therefore, that the wages of labour, estimated in money, were, in 1685, not more than half of what they now are ; and there were few articles important to the working man of which the price was not, in 1685, more than half of what it now is. Beer was undoubtedly much cheaper in that age than at present. Meat was also cheaper, but was still so dear that hundreds of thousands of families scarcely knew the taste of it.[1] In the cost of wheat there has been very little change. The average price of the quarter, during the last twelve years of Charles the Second, was fifty shillings. Bread, therefore, such as is now given to the inmates of a workhouse, was then seldom seen, even on the trencher of a yeoman or of a shopkeeper. The great majority of the nation lived almost entirely on rye, barley, and oats.

The produce of tropical countries, the produce of the mines, the produce of machinery, was positively dearer than at present. Among the commodities for which the labourer would have had to pay higher in 1685 than his posterity now pay were sugar, salt, coals, candles, soap, shoes, stockings, and generally all articles of clothing and all articles of bedding. It may be added, that the old coats and blankets would have been, not only more costly, but less serviceable than the modern fabrics.

It must be remembered that those labourers who were able to maintain themselves and their families by means of wages were not the

Number of paupers most necessitous members of the community. Beneath them lay a large class which could not subsist without some aid from the parish. There can hardly be a more important test of the condition of the common people than the ratio which this class bears to the whole society. At present the men, women, and children who receive relief appear from the official returns to be, in bad years, one tenth of the inhabitants of England, and, in good years, one thirteenth. Gregory King estimated them in his time at about a fourth ; and this estimate, which all our respect for his authority will scarcely prevent us from calling extravagant, was pronounced by Davenant eminently judicious.

We are not quite without the means of forming an estimate for ourselves. The poor rate was undoubtedly the heaviest tax borne by our ancestors in those days. It was computed, in the reign of Charles

[1] King in his Natural and Political Conclusions roughly estimated the common people of England at 880,000 families. Of these families 440,000, according to him, ate animal food twice a week. The remaining 440,000 ate it not at all, or at most not oftener than once a week.

The IDLE 'PRENTICE Executed at Tyburn.

THE IDLE APPRENTICE EXECUTED AT TYBURN

From Hogarth's Industry and Idleness

the Second, at near seven hundred thousand pounds a year, much more than the produce either of the excise or of the customs, and little less than half the entire revenue of the crown. The poor rate went on increasing rapidly, and appears to have risen in a short time to between eight and nine hundred thousand a year, that is to say, to one sixth of what it now is. The population was then less than a third of what it now is. The minimum of wages, estimated in money, was half of what it now is; and we can therefore hardly suppose that the average allowance made to a pauper can have been more than half of what it now is. It seems to follow that the proportion of the English people which received parochial relief then must have been larger than the proportion which receives relief now. It is good to speak on such questions with diffidence: but it has certainly never yet been proved that pauperism was a less heavy burden or a less serious social evil during the last quarter of the seventeenth century than it is in our own time.[1]

In one respect it must be admitted that the progress of civilisation has diminished the physical comforts of a portion of the poorest class. It has already been mentioned that, before the Revolution, many thousands of square miles, now enclosed and cultivated, were marsh, forest, and heath. Of this wild land much was, by law, common, and much of what was not common by law was worth so little that the proprietors suffered it to be common in fact. In such a tract, squatters and trespassers were tolerated to an extent now unknown. The peasant who dwelt there could, at little or no charge, procure occasionally some palatable addition to his hard fare, and provide himself with fuel for the winter. He kept a flock of geese on what is now an orchard rich with apple blossoms. He snared wild fowl on the fen which has long since been drained and divided into corn fields and turnip fields. He cut turf among the furze bushes on the moor which is now a meadow bright with clover and renowned for butter and cheese. The progress of agriculture and the increase of population necessarily deprived him of these privileges. But against this disadvantage a long list of advantages

[1] Fourteenth Report of the Poor Law Commissioners, Appendix B. No. 2. Appendix C. No. 1. 1848. Of the two estimates of the poor rate mentioned in the text one was formed by Arthur Moore, the other, some years later, by Richard Dunning. Moore's estimate will be found in Davenant's Essay on Ways and Means; Dunning's in Sir Frederic Eden's valuable work on the poor. King and Davenant estimate the paupers and beggars in 1696, at the incredible number of 1,330,000 out of a population of 5,500,000. In 1846 the number of persons who received relief appears from the official returns to have been only 1,332,089 out of a population of about 17,000,000. It ought also to be observed that, in those returns, a pauper must very often be reckoned more than once.

I would advise the reader to consult De Foe's pamphlet entitled "Giving Alms no Charity," and the Greenwich tables which will be found in Mr. M'Culloch's Commercial Dictionary under the head Prices.

is to be set off.   Of the blessings which civilisation and philosophy bring with them a large proportion is common to all ranks, and would, if withdrawn, be missed as painfully by the labourer as by the peer.   The market-place which the rustic can now reach with his cart in an hour was, a hundred and sixty years ago, a day's journey from him.   The street which now affords to the artisan, during the whole night, a secure, a convenient, **Benefits derived by the common people from the progress of civilisation** and a brilliantly lighted walk was, a hundred and sixty years ago, so dark after sunset that he would not have been able to see his hand, so ill paved that he would have run constant risk of breaking his neck, and so ill watched that he would have been in imminent danger of being knocked down and plundered of his small earnings.   Every bricklayer who falls from a scaffold, every sweeper of a crossing who is run over by a carriage, may now have his wounds dressed and his limbs set with a skill such as, a hundred and sixty years ago, all the wealth of a great lord like Ormond, or of a merchant prince like Clayton, could not have purchased.   Some frightful diseases have been extirpated by science ; and some have been banished by police.   The term of human life has been lengthened over the whole kingdom, and especially in the towns. The year 1685 was not accounted sickly ; yet in the year 1685 more than one in twenty three of the inhabitants of the capital died.[1]   At present only one inhabitant of the capital in forty dies annually.   The difference in salubrity between the London of the nineteenth century and the London of the seventeenth century is very far greater than the difference between London in an ordinary year and London in a year of cholera.

Still more important is the benefit which all orders of society, and especially the lower orders, have derived from the mollifying influence of civilisation on the national character.   The groundwork of that character has indeed been the same through many generations, in the sense in which the groundwork of the character of an individual may be said to be the same when he is a rude and thoughtless schoolboy and when he is a refined and accomplished man.   It is pleasing to reflect that the public mind of England has softened while it has ripened, and that we have, in the course of ages, become, not only a wiser, but also a kinder people.   There is scarcely a page of the history or lighter literature of the seventeenth century which does not contain some proof that our ancestors were less humane than their posterity.   The discipline of workshops, of schools, of private families, though not more efficient than at present, was infinitely harsher.   Masters, well born and bred, were in the habit of beating their servants.   Pedagogues knew no way of imparting knowledge but by beating their pupils.   Husbands, of decent station, were not ashamed to beat their wives.   The implacability of

[1] The deaths were 23,222.   Petty's Political Arithmetic.

hostile factions was such as we can scarcely conceive. Whigs were disposed to murmur because Stafford was suffered to die without seeing his bowels burned before his face. Tories reviled and insulted Russell as his coach passed from the Tower to the scaffold in Lincoln's Inn Fields.[1] As little mercy was shown by the populace to sufferers of a humbler rank. If an offender was put into the pillory, it was well if he escaped with life from the shower of brickbats and paving stones.[2] If he was tied to the cart's tail, the crowd pressed round him, imploring the hangman to give it the fellow well, and make him howl.[3] Gentlemen arranged parties of pleasure to Bridewell on court days, for the purpose of seeing the wretched women who beat hemp there whipped.[4] A man pressed to death for refusing to plead, a woman burned for coining, excited less sympathy than is now felt for a galled horse or an overdriven ox. Fights compared with which a boxing match is a refined and humane spectacle were among the favourite diversions of a large part of the town. Multitudes assembled to see gladiators hack each other to pieces with deadly weapons, and shouted with delight when one of the combatants lost a finger or an eye. The prisons were hells on earth, seminaries of every crime and of every disease. At the assizes the lean and yellow culprits brought with them from their cells to the dock an atmosphere of stench and pestilence which sometimes avenged them signally on bench, bar, and jury. But on all this misery society looked with profound indifference. Nowhere could be found that sensitive and restless compassion which has, in our time, extended a powerful protection to the factory child, to the Hindoo widow, to the negro slave, which pries into the stores and watercasks of every emigrant ship, which winces at every lash laid on the back of a drunken soldier, which will not suffer the thief in the hulks to be ill fed or overworked, and which has repeatedly endeavoured to save the life even of the murderer. It is true that compassion ought, like all other feelings, to be under the government of reason, and has, for want of such government, produced some ridiculous and some deplorable effects. But the more we study the annals of the past the more shall we rejoice that we live in a merciful age, in an age in which cruelty is abhorred, and in which pain, even when deserved, is inflicted reluctantly and from a sense of duty. Every class doubtless has gained largely by this great moral change : but the class which has gained most is the poorest, the most dependent, and the most defenceless.

The general effect of the evidence which has been submitted to the reader seems hardly to admit of doubt. Yet, in spite of evidence, many

---

[1] Burnet, i. 560.   [2] Muggleton's Acts of the Witnesses of the Spirit.

[3] Tom Brown describes such a scene in lines which I do not venture to quote.

[4] Ward's London Spy.

WOMEN BEATING HEMP IN BRIDEWELL

From Hogarth's Harlot's Progress

will still imagine to themselves the England of the Stuarts as a more pleasant country than the England in which we live.   It may at first sight seem strange that society, while constantly moving forward with eager speed, should be constantly looking backward with tender regret.   But these two propensities, inconsistent as they may appear, can easily be resolved into the same principle.   Both spring from our impatience of the state in which we actually are.   That impatience, while it stimulates us to surpass preceding generations, disposes us to overrate their happiness.   It is, in some sense, unreasonable and ungrateful in us to be constantly discontented with a condition which is constantly improving.   But, in truth, there is constant improvement precisely because there is constant discontent.   If we were perfectly satisfied with the present, we should cease to contrive, to labour, and to save with a view to the future.   And it is natural that, being dissatisfied with the present, we should form a too favourable estimate of the past.

Delusion which leads men to overrate the happiness of preceding generations

In truth we are under a deception similar to that which misleads the traveller in the Arabian desert.   Beneath the caravan all is dry and bare: but far in advance, and far in the rear, is the semblance of refreshing waters.   The pilgrims hasten forward and find nothing but sand where, an hour before, they had seen a lake.   They turn their eyes and see a lake where, an hour before, they were toiling through sand.   A similar illusion seems to haunt nations through every stage of the long progress from poverty and barbarism to the highest degrees of opulence and civilisation.   But, if we resolutely chase the mirage backward, we shall find it recede before us into the regions of fabulous antiquity.   It is now the fashion to place the golden age of England in times when noblemen were destitute of comforts the want of which would be intolerable to a modern footman, when farmers and shopkeepers breakfasted on loaves the very sight of which would raise a riot in a modern workhouse, when to have a clean shirt once a week was a privilege reserved for the higher class of gentry, when men died faster in the purest country air than they now die in the most pestilential lanes of our towns, and when men died faster in the lanes of our towns than they now die on the coast of Guiana.   We too shall, in our turn, be outstripped, and in our turn be envied.   It may well be, in the twentieth century, that the peasant of Dorsetshire may think himself miserably paid with twenty shillings a week; that the carpenter at Greenwich may receive ten shillings a day; that labouring men may be as little used to dine without meat as they now are to eat rye bread; that sanitary police and medical discoveries may have added several more years to the average length of human life ; that numerous comforts and luxuries which are now unknown, or confined to a few, may be within the reach of every diligent and thrifty working man. And yet it may then be the mode to assert that the increase of wealth and the progress of science have benefited the few at the expense of the many, and to talk of the

A DEBTOR'S PRISON

Frontispiece to the Cry of the Oppressed, by Moses Pitts, 1692

reign of Queen Victoria as the time when England was truly merry England, when all classes were bound together by brotherly sympathy, when the rich did not grind the faces of the poor, and when the poor did not envy the splendour of the rich.

CHAPTER IV

THE death of King Charles the Second took the nation by surprise. His frame was naturally strong, and did not appear to have suffered from excess. He had always been mindful of his health even in his pleasures; and his habits were such as promise a long life and a robust old age. Indolent as he was on all occasions which required tension of the mind, he was active and persevering in bodily exercise. He had, when young, been renowned as a tennis player,[1] and was, even in the decline of life, an indefatigable walker. His ordinary pace was such that those who were admitted to the honour of his society found it difficult to keep up with him. He rose early, and generally passed three or four hours a day in the open air. He might be seen, before the dew was off the grass in Saint James's Park, striding among the trees, playing with his spaniels, and flinging corn to his ducks; and these exhibitions endeared him to the common people, who always love to see the great unbend.[2]

1685
Death of
Charles II

At length, towards the close of the year 1684, he was prevented, by a slight attack of what was supposed to be gout, from rambling as usual. He now spent his mornings in his laboratory, where he amused himself with experiments on the properties of mercury. His temper seemed to have suffered from confinement. He had no apparent cause for disquiet. His kingdom was tranquil: he was not in pressing want of money: his power was greater than it had ever been: the party which had long thwarted him had been beaten down; but the cheerfulness which had supported him against adverse fortune had vanished in this season of prosperity. A trifle now sufficed to depress those elastic spirits which had borne up against defeat, exile, and penury. His irritation frequently showed itself by looks and words such as could hardly have been expected from a man so eminently distinguished by good humour and good breeding. It was not supposed however that his constitution was seriously impaired.[3]

[1] Pepys's Diary, Dec. 28. 1663, Sept. 2. 1667.
[2] Burnet, i. 606.; Spectator No. 462.; Lords' Journals, October 28. 1678.; Cibber's Apology.
[3] Burnet, i. 605, 606.; Welwood; North's Life of Guildford, 251.

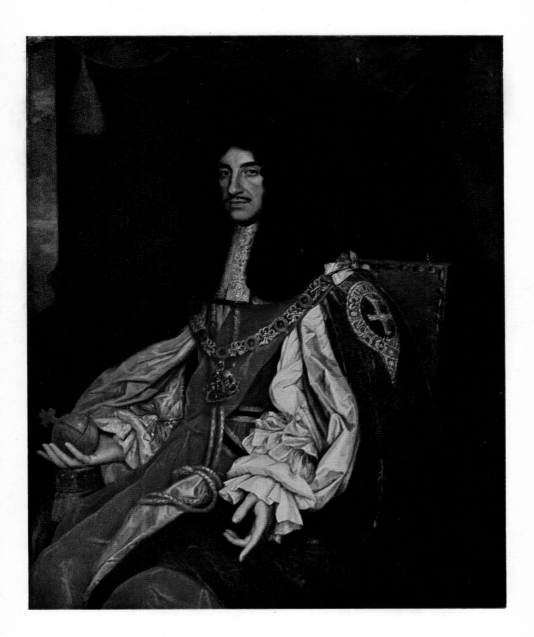

CHARLES II., 1630-1685.

From the painting by John Michael Wright, in the National Portrait Gallery.

His palace had seldom presented a gayer or a more scandalous appearance than on the evening of Sunday the first of February 1685.[1] Some grave persons who had gone thither, after the fashion of that age, to pay their duty to their sovereign, and who had expected that, on such a day, his court would wear a decent aspect, were struck with astonishment and horror. The great gallery of Whitehall, an admirable relic of the magnificence of the Tudors, was crowded with revellers and gamblers. The King sate there chatting and toying with three women, whose charms were the boast, and whose vices were the disgrace, of three nations. Barbara Palmer, Duchess of Cleveland, was there, no longer young, but still retaining some traces of that superb and voluptuous loveliness which twenty years before overcame the hearts of all men. There too was the Duchess of Portsmouth, whose soft and infantine features were lighted up with the vivacity of France. Hortensia Mancini, Duchess of Mazarin, and niece of the great Cardinal, completed the group. She had been early removed from her native Italy to the court where her uncle was supreme. His power and her own attractions had drawn a crowd of illustrious suitors round her. Charles himself, during his exile, had sought her hand in vain. No gift of nature or of fortune seemed to be wanting to her. Her face was beautiful with the rich beauty of the South, her understanding quick, her manners graceful, her rank exalted, her possessions immense; but her ungovernable passions had turned all these blessings into curses. She had found the misery of an ill assorted marriage intolerable, had fled from her husband, had abandoned her vast wealth, and, after having astonished Rome and Piedmont by her adventures, had fixed her abode in England. Her house was the favourite resort of men of wit and pleasure, who, for the sake of her smiles and her table, endured her frequent fits of insolence and ill humour. Rochester and Godolphin sometimes forgot the cares of state in her company. Barillon and Saint Evremond found in her drawing room consolation for their long banishment from Paris. The learning of Vossius, the wit of Waller, were daily employed to flatter and amuse her. But her diseased mind required stronger stimulants, and sought them in gallantry, in basset, and in usquebaugh.[2] While Charles flirted with his three sultanas, Hortensia's French page, a handsome boy, whose vocal performances were the delight of Whitehall, and were rewarded by numerous presents of rich clothes, ponies, and

---

[1] I may take this opportunity of mentioning that whenever I give only one date, I follow the old style, which was, in the seventeenth century, the style of England; but I reckon the year from the first of January.

[2] Saint Evremond, *passim*; Saint Réal, Mémoires de la Duchesse de Mazarin; Rochester's Farewell; Evelyn's Diary, Sept. 6. 1676, June 11. 1699.

guineas, warbled some amorous verses.[1]   A party of twenty courtiers
was seated at cards round a large table on which gold was heaped in
mountains.[2]   Even then the King had complained that he did not feel
quite well.   He had no appetite for his supper : his rest that night was
broken ; but on the following morning he rose, as usual, early.

To that morning the contending factions in his council had, during
some days, looked forward with anxiety.   The struggle between Halifax
and Rochester seemed to be approaching a decisive crisis.   Halifax,
not content with having already driven his rival from the Board of
Treasury, had undertaken to prove him guilty of such dishonesty or
neglect in the conduct of the finances as ought to be punished by
dismission from the public service.   It was even whispered that the
Lord President would probably be sent to the Tower.   The King had
promised to enquire into the matter.   The second of February had been
fixed for the investigation ; and several officers of the revenue had been
ordered to attend with their books on that day.[3]   But a great turn of
fortune was at hand.

Scarcely had Charles risen from his bed when his attendants perceived that his utterance was indistinct, and that his thoughts seemed
to be wandering.   Several men of rank had, as usual, assembled to see
their sovereign shaved and dressed.   He made an effort to converse
with them in his usual gay style ; but his ghastly look surprised and
alarmed them.   Soon his face grew black ; his eyes turned in his head ;
he uttered a cry, staggered, and fell into the arms of one of his lords.
A physician who had charge of the royal retorts and crucibles happened
to be present.   He had no lancet ; but he opened a vein with a pen-
knife.   The blood flowed freely ; but the King was still insensible.

He was laid on his bed, where, during a short time, the Duchess of
Portsmouth hung over him with the familiarity of a wife.   But the
alarm had been given.   The Queen and the Duchess of York were
hastening to the room.   The favourite concubine was forced to retire to
her own apartments.   Those apartments had been thrice pulled down
and thrice rebuilt by her lover to gratify her caprice.   The very furniture of the chimney was massy silver.   Several fine paintings, which
properly belonged to the Queen, had been transferred to the dwelling of
the mistress.   The sideboards were piled with richly wrought plate.   In
the niches stood cabinets, the masterpieces of Japanese art.   On the
hangings, fresh from the looms of Paris, were depicted, in tints which no

[1] Evelyn's Diary, Jan. 28. 168⅘ ; Saint Evremond's Letter to Déry.

[2] Evelyn's Diary, February 4. 168⅘.

[3] Roger North's Life of Sir Dudley North, 170. ; The True Patriot vindicated, or a Justifica-
tion of his Excellency the E—— of R—— ; Burnet, i. 605.   The Treasury Books prove that
Burnet had good intelligence.

HORTENSE MANCINI, DUCHESS OF MAZARIN

From the painting by Pierre Mignard, in the possession of the Earl of Sandwich

English tapestry could rival, birds of gorgeous plumage, landscapes, hunting matches, the lordly terrace of Saint Germains, the statues and fountains of Versailles.[1] In the midst of this splendour, purchased by guilt and shame, the unhappy woman gave herself up to an agony of grief, which, to do her justice, was not wholly selfish.

And now the gates of Whitehall, which ordinarily stood open to all comers, were closed. But persons whose faces were known were still permitted to enter. The antechambers and galleries were soon filled to overflowing ; and even the sick room was crowded with peers, privy councillors, and foreign ministers. All the medical men of note in London were summoned. So high did political animosities run that the presence of some Whig physicians was regarded as an extraordinary circumstance.[2] One Roman Catholic whose skill was then widely renowned, Doctor Thomas Short, was in attendance. Several of the prescriptions have been preserved. One of them is signed by fourteen Doctors. The patient was bled largely. Hot iron was applied to his head. A loathsome volatile salt, extracted from human skulls, was forced into his mouth. He recovered his senses ; but he was evidently in a situation of extreme danger.

The Queen was for a time assiduous in her attendance. The Duke of York scarcely left his brother's bedside. The Primate and four other Bishops were then in London. They remained at Whitehall all day, and took it by turns to sit up at night in the King's room. The news of his illness filled the capital with sorrow and dismay. For his easy temper and affable manners had won the affection of a large part of the nation ; and those who most disliked him preferred his unprincipled levity to the stern and earnest bigotry of his brother.

On the morning of Thursday the fifth of February, the London Gazette announced that His Majesty was going on well, and was thought by the physicians to be out of danger. The bells of all the churches rang merrily ; and preparations for bonfires were made in the streets. But in the evening it was known that a relapse had taken place, and that the medical attendants had given up all hope. The public mind was greatly disturbed ; but there was no disposition to tumult. The Duke of York, who had already taken on himself to give orders, ascertained that the City was perfectly quiet, and that he might without difficulty be proclaimed as soon as his brother should expire.

The King was in great pain, and complained that he felt as if a fire was burning within him. Yet he bore up against his sufferings with a fortitude which did not seem to belong to his soft and luxurious nature. The sight of his misery affected his wife so much that she fainted, and

---

[1] Evelyn's Diary, Jan. 24. 168½, Oct. 4. 1683.   [2] Dugdale's Correspondence.

SIR EDMUND KING

From an engraving by R. White, after a painting by Sir G. Kneller was carried senseless to her chamber. The prelates who were in waiting had from the first exhorted him to prepare for his end. They now thought it their duty to address him in a still more urgent manner. William Sancroft, Archbishop of Canterbury, an honest and pious, though narrowminded, man, used great freedom. "It is time," he said, "to speak out; for, Sir, you are about to appear before a Judge who is no respecter of persons." The King answered not a word.

Thomas Ken, Bishop of Bath and Wells, then tried his powers of persuasion. He was a man of parts and learning, of quick sensibility and stainless virtue. His elaborate works have long been forgotten; but his morning and evening hymns are still repeated daily in thousands of dwellings. Though, like most of his order, zealous for monarchy, he was no sycophant. Before he became a Bishop, he had maintained the honour of his gown by refusing, when the court was at Winchester, to let Eleanor Gwynn lodge in the house which he occupied there as a prebendary.[1] The King had sense enough to respect so manly a spirit. Of all the prelates he liked Ken the best. It was to no purpose, however, that the good Bishop now put forth all his eloquence. His solemn and pathetic exhortation awed and melted the bystanders to such a degree that some among them believed him to be filled with the same spirit which, in the old time, had, by the mouths of Nathan and Elias, called sinful princes to repentance. Charles however was unmoved. He made no objection indeed when the service for the Visitation of the Sick was read. In reply to the pressing questions of the divines, he said that he was sorry for what he had done amiss; and he suffered the absolution to be pronounced over him according to the forms of the Church of England: but, when he was urged to declare that he died in the communion of that Church, he seemed not to hear what was said; and nothing could induce him to take the Eucharist from the hands of the Bishops. A table with bread and wine was brought to his bedside, but in vain. Sometimes he said that there was no hurry, and sometimes that he was too weak.

Many attributed this apathy to contempt for divine things, and many to the stupor which often precedes death. But there were in the palace a few persons who knew better. Charles had never been a sincere member of the Established Church. His mind had long oscillated between Hobbism and Popery. When his health was good and his spirits high, he was a scoffer. In his few serious moments he was a Roman Catholic. The Duke of York was aware of this, but was entirely occupied with the care of his own interests. He had ordered the outports to be closed. He had posted detachments of the Guards in different parts of the City. He had also procured the feeble signature

[1] Hawkins's Life of Ken, 1713.

of the dying King to an instrument by which some duties, granted only till the demise of the Crown, were let to farm for a term of three years. These things occupied the attention of James to such a degree that, though, on ordinary occasions, he was indiscreetly and unseasonably eager to bring over proselytes to his Church, he never reflected that his brother was in danger of dying without the last sacraments. This neglect was the more extraordinary because the Duchess of York had, at the request of the Queen, suggested, on the morning on which the King was taken ill, the propriety of procuring spiritual assistance. For such assistance Charles was at last indebted to an agency very different from that of his pious wife and sister in law. A life of frivolity and vice had not extinguished in the Duchess of Portsmouth all sentiments of religion, or all that kindness which is the glory of her sex. The French ambassador Barillon, who had come to the palace to enquire after the King, paid her a visit. He found her in an agony of sorrow. She took him into a secret room, and poured out her whole heart to him. " I have," she said, " a thing of great moment to tell you. If it were known, my head would be in danger. The King is really and truly a Catholic ; but he will die without being reconciled to the Church. His bed-chamber is full of Protestant clergymen. I cannot enter it without giving scandal. The Duke is thinking only of himself. Speak to him. Remind him that there is a soul at stake. He is master now. He can clear the room. Go this instant, ·or it will be too late."

Barillon hastened to the bedchamber, took the Duke aside, and delivered the message of the mistress. The conscience of James smote him. He started as if roused from sleep, and declared that nothing should prevent him from discharging the sacred duty which had been too long delayed. Several schemes were discussed and rejected. At last the Duke commanded the crowd to stand aloof, went to the bed, stooped down, and whispered something which none of the spectators could hear, but which they supposed to be some question about affairs of state. Charles answered in an audible voice, " Yes, yes, with all my heart." None of the bystanders, except the French Ambassador, guessed that the King was declaring his wish to be admitted into the bosom of the Church of Rome.

" Shall I bring a priest ? " said the Duke. " Do, brother," replied the sick man. " For God's sake do, and lose no time. But no ; you will get into trouble." " If it costs me my life," said the Duke, " I will fetch a priest."

To find a priest, however, for such a purpose, at a moment's notice, was not easy. For, as the law then stood, the person who admitted a proselyte into the Roman Catholic Church was guilty of a capital crime. The Count of Castel Melhor, a Portuguese nobleman, who, driven by political troubles from his native land, had been hospitably received at the English court, undertook to procure a confessor. He had recourse to his countrymen who belonged to the Queen's household ; but he found that none of her chaplains knew English or French enough to shrive the King. The Duke and Barillon were about to send to the Venetian minister for a clergyman, when they heard that a Benedictine monk, named John Huddleston, happened to be at Whitehall. This man had, with great risk to himself, saved the King's life after the battle of Worcester, and had, on that account, been, ever since the Restoration, a privileged person. In the sharpest proclamations which had been put forth against Popish priests, when false witnesses had inflamed the nation to fury, Huddleston had been excepted by name.[1] He readily consented to put his life a second time in peril for his prince; but there was still a difficulty. The honest monk was so illiterate that he did not know what he ought to say on an occasion of such importance. He however obtained some hints, through the intervention of Castel Melhor, from a Portuguese ecclesiastic, and, thus instructed, was brought up the back stairs by Chiffinch, a confidential servant, who, if the satires of that age are to be credited, had often introduced visitors of a very different description by the same entrance. The Duke then, in the King's name, commanded all who were present to quit the room, except Lewis Duras, Earl of Feversham, and John Granville, Earl of Bath. Both these Lords professed the Protestant religion ; but James conceived that he could count on their fidelity. Feversham, a Frenchman of noble birth, and nephew of the great Turenne, held high rank in the English army, and was Chamberlain to the Queen. Bath was Groom of the Stole.

The Duke's orders were obeyed ; and even the physicians withdrew. The back door was then opened ; and Father Huddleston entered. A cloak had been thrown over his sacred vestments; and his shaven crown was concealed by a flowing wig. " Sir," said the Duke, " this good man once saved your life. He now comes to save your soul." Charles faintly answered, " He is welcome." Huddleston went through his part better than had been expected. He knelt by the bed, listened to the confession, pronounced the absolution, and administered extreme unction. He asked if the King wished to receive the Lord's supper. " Surely," said Charles, " if I am not unworthy." The host was brought in. Charles feebly strove to rise and kneel before it. The priest bade him lie still, and assured him that God would accept the humiliation of the soul, and would not require the humiliation of the body. The King found so much difficulty in swallowing the bread that it was necessary to open the door and to procure a glass of water. This rite ended, the

[1] See the London Gazette of Nov. 21. 1678. Barillon and Burnet say that Huddleston was excepted out of all the Acts of Parliament made against priests ; but this is a mistake.

monk held up a crucifix before the penitent, charged him to fix his last thoughts on the sufferings of the Redeemer, and withdrew. The whole ceremony had occupied about three quarters of an hour ; and, during that time, the courtiers who filled the outer room had communicated their suspicions to each other by whispers and significant glances. The door was at length thrown open, and the crowd again filled the chamber of death.

It was now late in the evening. The King seemed much relieved

THE REV. JOHN HUDDLESTON, O.S.B.

From an engraving in the Sutherland Collection

by what had passed. His natural children were brought to his bedside, the Dukes of Grafton, Southampton, and Northumberland, sons of the Duchess of Cleveland, the Duke of Saint Albans, son of Eleanor Gwynn, and the Duke of Richmond, son of the Duchess of Portsmouth. Charles blessed them all, but spoke with peculiar tenderness to Richmond. One face which should have been there was wanting. The eldest and best beloved child was an exile and a wanderer. His name was not once mentioned by his father.

During the night Charles earnestly recommended the Duchess of

Portsmouth and her boy to the care of James ; " And do not," he good-naturedly added, " let poor Nelly starve." The Queen sent excuses for her absence by Halifax. She said that she was too much disordered to resume her post by the couch, and implored pardon for any offence which she might unwittingly have given. " She ask my pardon, poor woman ! " cried Charles ; " I ask hers with all my heart."

The morning light began to peep through the windows of Whitehall; and Charles desired the attendants to pull aside the curtains, that he might have one more look at the day. He remarked that it was time to wind up a clock which stood near his bed. These little circumstances were long remembered, because they proved beyond dispute that, when he declared himself a Roman Catholic, he was in full possession of his faculties. He apologised to those who had stood round him all night for the trouble which he had caused. He had been, he said, a most unconscionable time dying ; but he hoped that they would excuse it. This was the last glimpse of that exquisite urbanity, so often found potent to charm away the resentment of a justly incensed nation. Soon after dawn the speech of the dying man failed. Before ten his senses were gone. Great numbers had repaired to the churches at the hour of morning service. When the prayer for the King was read, loud groans and sobs showed how deeply his people felt for him. At noon on Friday, the sixth of February, he passed away without a struggle.[1]

[1] Clarke's Life of James the Second, i. 746. Orig. Mem. ; Barillon's Despatch of Feb. $\frac{8}{13}$. 1685 ; Van Citters's Despatches of Feb. $\frac{8}{13}$. and Feb. $\frac{6}{10}$. ; Huddleston's Narrative ; Letters of Philip, second Earl of Chesterfield, 277. ; Sir H. Ellis's Original Letters, First Series, iii. 333. ; Second Series, iv. 74. ; Chaillot MS. ; Burnet, i. 606. ; Evelyn's Diary, Feb. 4. 168$\frac{4}{5}$; Welwood's Memoirs, 140. ; North's Life of Guildford, 252. ; Examen, 648. ; Hawkins's Life of Ken ; Dryden's Threnodia Augustalis ; Sir H. Halford's Essay on Deaths of Eminent Persons. See also a fragment of a letter written by the Earl of Ailesbury, which is printed in the European Magazine for April 1795. Ailesbury calls Burnet an impostor. Yet his own narrative and Burnet's will not, to any candid and sensible reader, appear to contradict each other. I have seen in the British Museum, and also in the Library of the Royal Institution, a curious broadside containing an account of the death of Charles. It will be found in the Somers Collection. The author was evidently a zealous Roman Catholic, and must have had access to good sources of information. I strongly suspect that he had been in communication, directly or indirectly, with James himself. No name is given at length ; but the initials are perfectly intelligible, except in one place. It is said that the D. of Y. was reminded of the duty which he owed to his brother by P. M. A. C. F. I must own myself quite unable to decipher the last five letters. It is some consolation that Sir Walter Scott was equally unsuccessful. (1848.) Since the first edition of this work was published, several very ingenious conjectures touching these mysterious letters have been communicated to me ; but I am convinced that the true solution has not yet been suggested. (1850.) I still greatly doubt whether the riddle has been solved. But the most plausible interpretation is one which, with some variations, occurred, almost at the same time, to myself and to several other persons ; I am inclined to read " Père Mansuete A Cordelier Friar." Mansuete, a Cordelier, was then James's confessor. To Mansuete therefore it peculiarly belonged to remind James of a sacred duty which had been culpably neglected. The writer of the broad-side must have been unwilling to inform the world that a soul which many devout Roman Catholics had left to perish had been snatched from destruction by the courageous charity of a

ELEANOR GWYN, 1650-1687.

From the painting by Sir Peter Lely, in the National Portrait Gallery.

A
TRUE RELATION
OF THE
Late Kings Death.

ON Monday, *being the 2d. of February, the King rose early, saying, that he had not slept well the last Night : And about seven of the Clock, coming from his private Devotions, out of his Closet, fell down, (and scarce any sign of of Life remaining in him for the space of four Houres) of a Fit of an Apoplexy, but with the loss of sixteen Ounces of Blood, and other Aplications, came again to his Sences, and great Hopes were of his Recovery, till* Thursday *one of the Clock; so that at* five, *the* Doctors *being come before the* Council, *declared that the* K--- *was in great* Danger *; and on* Friday, *a quarter before twelve, he departed this Life.* God have Mercy on his Soul.

P. M. *A. C. F.* came to the D. upon the Doctors telling him of the State of the K. and tould him *that now was the time for him to take care of his Br. Soul,* and that it was his Duty to tell him so : The D. with this Admonishment went to the K. and after some private Discourse, the K. uttered these Expressions, *Oh B. how long have I wished—— but now help me* ; withal declaring that he would have Mr. *H.* who had preserved him in the Tree, and now hoped would preserve his Soul. Mr. *Hud.* was accordingly sent for, and desired to bring all Nessisaries for a dying Man, but he not having the blessed Sacrament by him, went to one of the Q. P. and telling him the Occasion, desired his Assistance to procure it, and to bring it to the back Stairs. The K. having notice that Mr. *H.* waited at the Door, desired to be in private, whereupon the Bps. and all the Nobles withdrew, the D. catching fast the Door, the Lords *P. E.* and *F.* were going out also, but the D. told them that they might stay. The K. seeing Mr. *H.* cryed out, *Almighty God, what good Planet governs me, that all my Life is Wonders and Miracles ? When, O Lord, I consider my Infancy, my Exile, my Escape at* Worcester, *my Preservation in the Tree, with the Assistance of this good Father ; and now to have him again to preserve my Soul : O Lord, my wonderful Restoration, my great Danger in the late Conspiracy ; and last of all, to be raised from Death to Life, and to have my Soul preserved by the Assistance of this Father, whom I see, O good Lord, that thou hast created for my Good.* The D. and Lords withdrew into the Closset for the space of an houre and half, then entring again the Room, the F. asked the K. whether he would be pleased to receive ; he answered, *If I were worthy of it* — *Amen, Amen.* The F. remaining comforting and praying with him, he said, *Father if I am worthy of it, I pray let me have it?* The F. said it would be brought to him imediately, and asked his Leave to proceed with extream Unction, the K. reply'd, *with all my Heart,* the D. and Lords assisting at the time. Mr. *H.* was called to the Door, where he received the blessed Sacrament, and desiring the K. to compose himself to receive, he would fain have arose (but was perswaded to the contrary) saying, *Let me meet my heavenly Father in a better manner than lying on my back.* But being overruled, they continue in Prayer: Amongst others, the Father repeats an Act of Contrition, desiring the K. to repeat it word by word after him : Having made an end, the K. received with the greatest Expressions of Devotion imaginable : This being ended, they go on with the Prayers *de Anima* ; that being done, the K. desired the Act of Contrition to be again repeated, saying, *O Lord, good God, when my Lips fail, let my Heart speak these Words Eternally, Amen.* The Bishops and Lords enter again the Room, and desire the K. to remember his last End, and to endeavour to make a good End ; he said he had thought of it, and hoped he had made his Peace with God ; they asked him whether he would receive, he said he would not ; so persisting in Extolling the Q. and D. saying he was not sorry to leave the World, leaving so good a Brother to Rule behind him.

F I N I S.

A TRUE RELATION OF THE LATE KING'S DEATH

From a broadside in the British Museum

At that time the common people throughout Europe, and nowhere more than in England, were in the habit of attributing the deaths of Suspicions of poison princes, especially when the prince was popular and the death unexpected, to the foulest and darkest kind of assassination. Thus James the First had been accused of poisoning Prince Henry. Thus Charles the First had been accused of poisoning James the First. Thus when, in the time of the Commonwealth, the Princess Elizabeth died at Carisbrook, it was loudly asserted that Cromwell had stooped to the senseless and dastardly wickedness of mixing noxious drugs with the food of a young girl whom he had no conceivable motive to injure.[1] A few years later, the rapid decomposition of Cromwell's own corpse was ascribed by many to a deadly potion administered in his medicine. The death of Charles the Second could scarcely fail to occasion similar rumours. The public ear had been repeatedly abused by stories of Popish plots against his life. There was, therefore, in many minds, a strong predisposition to suspicion; and there were some unlucky circumstances which, to minds so predisposed, might seem to indicate that a crime had been perpetrated. The fourteen Doctors who deliberated on the King's case contradicted each other and themselves. Some of them

woman of loose character. It is therefore not unlikely that he would prefer a fiction, at once probable and edifying, to a truth which could not fail to give scandal. (1856.)

It should seem that no transactions in history ought to be more accurately known to us than those which took place round the deathbed of Charles the Second. We have several relations written by persons who were actually in his room. We have several relations written by persons who, though not themselves eyewitnesses, had the best opportunity of obtaining information from eyewitnesses. Yet whoever attempts to digest this vast mass of materials into a consistent narrative will find the task a difficult one. Indeed James and his wife, when they told the story to the nuns of Chaillot, could not agree as to some circumstances. The Queen said that, after Charles had received the last sacraments, the Protestant Bishops renewed their exhortations. The King said that nothing of the kind took place. " Surely," said the Queen, " you told me so yourself." " It is impossible that I could have told you so," said the King ; " for nothing of the sort happened."

It is much to be regretted that Sir Henry Halford should have taken so little trouble to ascertain the facts on which he pronounced judgment. He does not seem to have been aware of the existence of the narratives of James, Barillon, and Huddleston.

As this is the first occasion on which I cite the correspondence of the Dutch ministers at the English court, I ought here to mention that a series of their despatches, from the accession of James the Second to his flight, forms one of the most valuable parts of the Mackintosh collection. The subsequent despatches, down to the settlement of the government in February 1689, I procured from the Hague. The Dutch archives have been far too little explored. They abound with information interesting in the highest degree to every Englishman. They are admirably arranged ; and they are in the charge of gentlemen whose courtesy, liberality, and zeal for the interests of literature, cannot be too highly praised. I wish to acknowledge, in the strongest manner, my own obligations to Mr. De Jonge and to Mr. Van Zwanne.

[1] Clarendon mentions this calumny with just scorn. " According to the charity of the time towards Cromwell, very many would have it believed to be by poison, of which there was no appearance, nor any proof ever after made."—Book xiv.

thought that his fit was epileptic, and that he should be suffered to have his doze out. The majority pronounced him apoplectic, and tortured him during some hours like an Indian at a stake. Then it was determined to call his complaint a fever, and to administer doses of bark. One physician, however, protested against this course, and assured the Queen that his brethren would kill the King among them. Nothing better than dissension and vacillation could be expected from such a multitude of advisers. But many of the vulgar not unnaturally concluded, from the perplexity of the great masters of the healing art, that the malady had some extraordinary origin. There is reason to believe that a horrible suspicion did actually cross the mind of Short, who, though skilful in his profession, seems to have been a nervous and fanciful man, and whose perceptions were probably confused by dread of the odious imputations to which he, as a Roman Catholic, was peculiarly exposed. We cannot, therefore, wonder that wild stories without number were repeated and believed by the common people. His Majesty's tongue had swelled to the size of a neat's tongue. A cake of deleterious powder had been found in his brain. There were blue spots on his breast. There were black spots on his shoulder. Something had been put into his snuffbox. Something had been put into his broth. Something had been put into his favourite dish of eggs and ambergrease. The Duchess of Portsmouth had poisoned him in a cup of chocolate. The Queen had poisoned him in a jar of dried pears. Such tales ought to be preserved ; for they furnish us with a measure of the intelligence and virtue of the generation which eagerly devoured them. That no rumour of the same kind has ever, in the present age, found credit among us, even when lives on which great interests depended have been terminated by unforeseen attacks of disease, is to be attributed partly to the progress of medical and chemical science, but partly also, it may be hoped, to the progress which the nation has made in good sense, justice, and humanity.[1]

When all was over, James retired from the bedside to his closet, where, during a quarter of an hour, he remained alone. Meanwhile the Privy Councillors who were in the palace assembled. The new King came forth, and took his place at the head of the board. He commenced his administration, according to usage, by a speech to the Council. He expressed his regret for the loss

Speech of James II. to the Privy Council

[1] Welwood, 139. ; Burnet, i. 609. ; Sheffield's Character of Charles the Second ; North's Life of Guildford, 252. ; Examen, 648. ; Revolution Politics ; Higgons on Burnet. What North says of the embarrassment and vacillation of the physicians is confirmed by the despatches of Van Citters. I have been much perplexed by the strange story about Short's suspicions. I was, at one time, inclined to adopt North's solution. But, though I attach little weight to the authority of Welwood and Burnet in such a case, I cannot reject the testimony of so well informed and so unwilling a witness as Sheffield.

which he had just sustained, and he promised to imitate the singular lenity which had distinguished the late reign.   He was aware, he said, that he had been accused of a fondness for arbitrary power.   But that was not the only falsehood which had been told of him.   He was resolved to maintain the established government both in Church and State.   The Church of England he knew to be eminently loyal.   It should therefore always be his care to support and defend her.   The laws of England, he also knew, were sufficient to make him as great a King as he could wish to be.   He would not relinquish his own rights ; but he would respect the rights of others.   He had formerly risked his life in defence of his country ; and he would still go as far as any man in support of her just liberties.

This speech was not, like modern speeches on similar occasions, carefully prepared by the advisers of the sovereign.   It was the extemporaneous expression of the new King's feelings at a moment of great excitement.   The members of the Council broke forth into clamours of delight and gratitude.   The Lord President, Rochester, in the name of his brethren, expressed a hope that His Majesty's most welcome declaration would be made public.   The Solicitor General, Heneage Finch, offered to act as clerk.   He was a zealous churchman, and, as such, was naturally desirous that there should be some permanent record of the gracious promises which had just been uttered.   "Those promises," he said, "have made so deep an impression on me that I can repeat them word for word."   He soon produced his report.   James read it, approved of it, and ordered it to be published.   At a later period he said that he had taken this step without due consideration, that his unpremeditated expressions touching the Church of England were too strong, and that Finch had, with a dexterity which at the time escaped notice, made them still stronger.[1]

The King had been exhausted by long watching and by many violent emotions.   He now retired to rest.   The Privy Councillors, **James proclaimed** having respectfully accompanied him to his bedchamber, returned to their seats, and issued orders for the ceremony of proclamation.   The Guards were under arms ; the heralds appeared in their gorgeous coats ; and the pageant proceeded without any obstruction.   Casks of wine were broken up in the streets, and all who passed were invited to drink to the health of the new sovereign.   But, though an occasional shout was raised, the people were not in a joyous mood.   Tears were seen in many eyes ; and it was remarked that there was scarcely a housemaid in London who had not

[1] London Gazette, Feb. 9. 168⅘ ; Clarke's Life of James the Second, ii. 3. ; Barillon, Feb. ⁹⁄₁₉. ; Evelyn's Diary, Feb. 6.

contrived to procure some fragment of black crape in honour of King Charles.[1]

An Account of what His Majeſty ſaid at His firſt coming to Council.

His Majeſty at His firſt Sitting in His Privy Council, was Graciouſly Pleaſed to Expreſs Himſelf in this manner.

MY LORDS,

Efore I enter upon any other Buſineſs, I think fit to ſay ſomething to you; Since it hath pleaſed Almighty God to place Me in this Station, and I am now to Succeed ſo Good and Gracious a King, as well as ſo very Kind a Brother; I think it fit to Declare to you, That I will endeavour to follow His Example, and moſt eſpecially in that of His Great Clemency and Tenderneſs to His People : I have been Reported to be a Man for Arbitrary Power, but that is not the onely Story has been made of Me; And I ſhall make it my Endeavours to Preſerve this Government both in Church and State as it is now by Law Eſtabliſh'd : I know the Principles of the Church of *England* are for Monarchy, and the Members of it have ſhewed themſelves Good and Loyal Subjects, therefore I ſhall always take Care to Defend and Support it : I know too, That the Laws of *England* are ſufficient to make the King as Great a Monarch as I can wiſh; And as I ſhall never Depart from the Juſt Rights and Prerogative of the Crown, ſo I ſhall never Invade any mans Property; I have often heretofore ventured my Life in Defence of this Nation, and I ſhall ſtill go as far as any man in Preſerving it in all its Juſt Rights and Liberties.

Whereupon the Lords of the Council were humble Suiters to His Majeſty, That theſe His Gracious Expreſſions might be made Publick, which His Majeſty did Order accordingly.

Printed by the Aſſigns of *John Bill* deceas'd: And by *Henry Hills*, and *Thomas Newcomb*, Printers to the Kings moſt Excellent Majeſty. 1685.

AN ACCOUNT OF WHAT HIS MAJESTY SAID AT HIS FIRST COMING TO COUNCIL

The funeral called forth much censure. It would, indeed, hardly have been accounted worthy of a noble and opulent subject. The Tories gently blamed the new King's parsimony : the Whigs sneered at his want of natural affection ; and the fiery Covenanters of Scotland

[1] See the authorities cited in the last note. See also the Examen, 647. ; Burnet, i. 620. ; Higgons on Burnet.

exultingly proclaimed that the curse denounced of old against wicked princes had been signally fulfilled, and that the departed tyrant had been buried with the burial of an ass.[1] Yet James commenced his administration with a large measure of public good will. His speech to the Council appeared in print, and the impression which it produced was highly favourable to him. This, then, was the prince whom a faction had driven into exile and had tried to rob of his birthright, on the ground that he was a deadly enemy to the religion and laws of England. He had triumphed : he was on the throne ; and his first act was to declare that he would defend the Church, and would strictly respect the rights of his people. The estimate which all parties had formed of his character, added weight to every word that fell from him. The Whigs called him haughty, implacable, obstinate, regardless of public opinion. The Tories, while they extolled his princely virtues, had often lamented his neglect of the arts which conciliate popularity. Satire itself had never represented him as a man likely to court public favour by professing what he did not feel, and by promising what he had no intention of performing. On the Sunday which followed his accession, his speech was quoted in many pulpits. " We have now for our Church," cried one loyal preacher, " the word of a King, and of a King who was never worse than his word." This pointed sentence was fast circulated through town and country, and was soon the watchword of the whole Tory party.[2]

The great offices of state had become vacant by the demise of the crown ; and it was necessary for James to determine how they should be filled. Few of the members of the late cabinet had any reason to expect his favour. Sunderland, who was Secretary of State, and Godolphin, who was First Lord of the Treasury, had supported the Exclusion Bill. Halifax, who held the Privy Seal, had opposed that bill with unrivalled powers of argument and eloquence. But Halifax was the mortal enemy of despotism and of Popery. He saw with dread the progress of the French arms on the Continent, and the influence of French gold in the counsels of England. Had his advice been followed, the laws would have been strictly observed : clemency would have been extended to the vanquished Whigs : the Parliament would have been convoked in due season : an attempt would have been made to reconcile our domestic factions ; and the principles of the Triple Alliance would again have guided our foreign policy. He had therefore incurred the bitter animosity of James. The Lord Keeper Guildford could hardly be said to belong to either of the parties into

State of the administration

---

[1] London Gazette, Feb. 14. 168⅘ ; Evelyn's Diary of the same day ; Burnet, i. 610. ; The Hind let loose.

[2] Burnet, i. 628. ; Lestrange, Observator, Feb. 11. 168⅘.

THE MOURNFUL SUBJECTS

From the Roxburghe Ballads

which the court was divided.   He could by no means be called a friend of liberty ; and yet he had so great a reverence for the letter of the law that he was not a serviceable tool of arbitrary power.   He was accordingly designated by the vehement Tories as a Trimmer, and was to James an object of aversion with which contempt was largely mingled. Ormond, who was Lord Steward of the Household and Viceroy of Ireland, then resided at Dublin.   His claims on the royal gratitude were superior to those of any other subject.   He had fought bravely for Charles the First : he had shared the exile of Charles the Second ; and, since the Restoration, he had, in spite of many provocations, kept his loyalty unstained.   Though he had been disgraced during the predominance of the Cabal, he had never gone into factious opposition, and had, in the days of the Popish Plot and the Exclusion Bill, been foremost among the supporters of the throne.   He was now old, and had been recently tried by the most cruel of all calamities.   He had followed to the grave a son who should have been his own chief mourner, the gallant Ossory.   The eminent services, the venerable age, and the domestic misfortunes of Ormond made him an object of general interest to the nation.   The Cavaliers regarded him as, both by right of seniority and by right of merit, their head ; and the Whigs knew that, faithful as he had always been to the cause of monarchy, he was no friend either to Popery or to arbitrary power.   But, high as he stood in the public estimation, he had little favour to expect from his new master. James, indeed, while still a subject, had urged his brother to make a complete change in the Irish administration.   Charles had assented ; and it had been arranged that, in a few months, there should be a new Lord Lieutenant.[1]

Rochester was the only member of the cabinet who stood high in the favour of the King.   The general expectation was that he would **New arrangements** be immediately placed at the head of affairs, and that all the other great officers of state would be changed.   This expectation proved to be well founded in part only.   Rochester was declared Lord Treasurer, and thus became prime minister.   Neither a Lord High Admiral nor a Board of Admiralty was appointed.   The new King, who loved the details of naval business, and would have made a respectable clerk in the dockyard at Chatham, determined to be his own minister of marine.   Under him the management of that important department was confided to Samuel Pepys, whose library and diary have kept his name fresh to our time.   No servant of the late sovereign was publicly disgraced.   Sunderland exerted so much art and address, employed so many intercessors, and was in possession

[1] The letters which passed between Rochester and Ormond on this subject will be found in the Clarendon Correspondence.

THOMAS BUTLER, EARL OF OSSORY

From the painting by Sir P. Lely in the National Portrait Gallery of so many secrets, that he was suffered to retain his seals.　Godolphin's obsequiousness, industry, experience, and taciturnity, could ill be spared. As he was no longer wanted at the Treasury, he was made Chamberlain to the Queen.　With these three Lords the King took counsel on all important questions.　As to Halifax, Ormond, and Guildford, he determined not yet to dismiss them, but merely to humble and annoy them.

Halifax was told that he must give up the Privy Seal and accept the Presidency of the Council.　He submitted with extreme reluctance. For, though the President of the Council had always taken precedence of the Lord Privy Seal, the Lord Privy Seal was, in that age, a much more important officer than the Lord President.　Rochester had not forgotten the jest which had been made a few months before on his own removal from the Treasury, and enjoyed in his turn the pleasure of kicking his rival up stairs.　The Privy Seal was delivered to Rochester's elder brother, Henry Earl of Clarendon.

To Barillon James expressed the strongest dislike of Halifax.　" I know him well, I never can trust him.　He shall have no share in the management of public business.　As to the place which I have given him, it will just serve to show how little influence he has."　But to Halifax it was thought convenient to hold a very different language. " All the past is forgotten," said the King, " except the service which you did me in the debate on the Exclusion Bill."　This speech has often been cited to prove that James was not so vindictive as he had been called by his enemies.　It seems rather to prove that he by no means deserved the praises which have been bestowed on his sincerity by his friends.[1]

Ormond was politely informed that his services were no longer needed in Ireland, and was invited to repair to Whitehall, and to perform the functions of Lord Steward.　He dutifully submitted, but did not affect to deny that the new arrangement wounded his feelings deeply.　On the eve of his departure he gave a magnificent banquet at Kilmainham Hospital, then just completed, to the officers of the garrison of Dublin.　After dinner he rose, filled a goblet to the brim with wine, and, holding it up, asked whether he had spilt one drop.　" No, gentlemen : whatever the courtiers may say, I am not yet sunk into dotage. My hand does not fail me yet ; and my hand is not steadier than my heart.　To the health of King James ! "　Such was the last farewell of Ormond to Ireland.　He left the administration in the hands of Lords Justices, and repaired to London, where he was received with unusual marks of public respect.　Many persons of rank went forth to meet him

---

[1] The ministerial changes are announced in the London Gazette, Feb. 19. 168⅘.　See Burnet, i. 621. ; Barillon, Feb. $\frac{9}{19}$. $\frac{16}{26}$. ; and $\frac{\text{Feb. 19.}}{\text{Mar. 1.}}$

SAMUEL PEPYS AT THE AGE OF 34

From the painting by John Hayls in the National Portrait Gallery on the road.　A long train of equipages followed him into Saint James's Square, where his mansion stood ; and the Square was thronged by a multitude which greeted him with loud acclamations.[1]

The Great Seal was left in Guildford's custody : but a marked indignity was at the same time offered to him.　It was determined that **Sir George Jeffreys** another lawyer of more vigour and audacity should be called to assist in the administration.　The person selected was Sir George Jeffreys, Chief Justice of the Court of King's Bench.　The depravity of this man has passed into a proverb.　Both the great English parties have attacked his memory with emulous violence : for the Whigs considered him as their most barbarous enemy ; and the Tories found it convenient to throw on him the blame of all the crimes which had sullied their triumph.　A diligent and candid enquiry will show that some frightful stories which have been told concerning him are false or exaggerated.　Yet the dispassionate historian will be able to make very little deduction from the vast mass of infamy with which the memory of the wicked judge has been loaded.

He was a man of quick and vigorous parts, but constitutionally prone to insolence and to the angry passions.　When just emerging from boyhood he had risen into practice at the Old Bailey bar, a bar where advocates have always used a license of tongue unknown in Westminster Hall.　Here, during many years, his chief business was to examine and cross-examine the most hardened miscreants of a great capital.　Daily conflicts with prostitutes and thieves called out and exercised his powers so effectually that he became the most consummate bully ever known in his profession.　Tenderness for others and respect for himself were feelings alike unknown to him.　He acquired a boundless command of the rhetoric in which the vulgar express hatred and contempt.　The profusion of maledictions and vituperative epithets which composed his vocabulary could hardly have been rivalled in the fishmarket or the beargarden.　His countenance and his voice must always have been unamiable.　But these natural advantages,—for such he seems to have thought them,—he had improved to such a degree that there were few who, in his paroxysms of rage, could see or hear him without emotion.　Impudence and ferocity sate upon his brow.　The glare of his eyes had a fascination for the unhappy victim on whom they were fixed.　Yet his brow and his eye were less terrible than the savage lines of his mouth.　His yell of fury, as was said by one who had often heard it, sounded like the thunder of the judgment day.　These qualifications he carried, while still a young man, from the bar to the bench.　He early became Common Serjeant, and then

[1] Carte's Life of Ormond ; Secret Consults of the Romish Party in Ireland, 1690 ; Memoirs of Ireland, 1716.

Recorder of London. As a judge at the City sessions he exhibited the same propensities which afterwards, in a higher post, gained for him an unenviable immortality. Already might be remarked in him the most odious vice which is incident to human nature, a delight in misery

JAMES BUTLER, FIRST DUKE OF ORMOND

From a mezzotint by R. Williams, after a painting by W. Wissing

merely as misery. There was a fiendish exultation in the way in which he pronounced sentence on offenders. Their weeping and imploring seemed to titillate him voluptuously; and he loved to scare them into fits by dilating with luxuriant amplification on all the details of what they were to suffer. Thus, when he had an opportunity of ordering an

unlucky adventuress to be whipped at the cart's tail, "Hangman," he
would exclaim, "I charge you to pay particular attention to this lady!
Scourge her soundly, man! Scourge her till the blood runs down! It
is Christmas, a cold time for Madam to strip in! See that you warm
her shoulders thoroughly!"[1] He was hardly less facetious when he
passed judgment on poor Lodowick Muggleton, the drunken tailor who
fancied himself a prophet. "Impudent rogue!" roared Jeffreys, "thou
shalt have an easy, easy, easy punishment!" One part of this easy
punishment was the pillory, in which the wretched fanatic was almost
killed with brickbats.[2]

By this time the heart of Jeffreys had been hardened to that
temper which tyrants require in their worst implements. He had
hitherto looked for professional advancement to the corporation of
London. He had therefore professed himself a Roundhead, and had
always appeared to be in a higher state of exhilaration when he
explained to Popish priests that they were to be cut down alive, and
were to see their own bowels burned, than when he passed ordinary
sentences of death. But, as soon as he had got all that the City could
give, he made haste to sell his forehead of brass and his tongue of
venom to the Court. Chiffinch, who was accustomed to act as broker
in infamous contracts of more than one kind, lent his aid. He had
conducted many amorous and many political intrigues; but he assuredly
never rendered a more scandalous service to his masters than when he
introduced Jeffreys to Whitehall. The renegade soon found a patron in
the obdurate and revengeful James, but was always regarded with scorn
and disgust by Charles, whose faults, great as they were, had no affinity
with insolence and cruelty. "That man," said the King, "has no
learning, no sense, no manners, and more impudence than ten carted
street-walkers."[3] Work was to be done, however, which could be
trusted to no man who reverenced law or was sensible of shame; and
thus Jeffreys, at an age at which a barrister thinks himself fortunate if
he is employed to conduct an important cause, was made Chief Justice
of the King's Bench.

His enemies could not deny that he possessed some of the qualities
of a great judge. His legal knowledge, indeed, was merely such as he
had picked up in practice of no very high kind. But he had one of
those happily constituted intellects which, across labyrinths of sophistry,

[1] Christmas Sessions Paper of 1678.

[2] The Acts of the Witnesses of the Spirit, part v. chapter v. In this work, Lodowick, after
his fashion, revenges himself on the "bawling devil," as he calls Jeffreys, by a string of curses
which Ernulphus, or Jeffreys himself, might have envied. The trial was in January 1677.

[3] This saying is to be found in many contemporary pamphlets. Titus Oates was never tired
of quoting it. See his Εἰκὼν Βασιλική.

WILLIAM CHIFFINCH
From the painting by John Riley in the National Portrait Gallery

and through masses of immaterial facts, go straight to the true point. Of his intellect, however, he seldom had the full use. Even in civil causes his malevolent and despotic temper perpetually disordered his judgment. To enter his court was to enter the den of a wild beast, which none could tame, and which was as likely to be roused to rage by caresses as by attacks. He frequently poured forth on plaintiffs and defendants, barristers and attorneys, witnesses and jurymen, torrents of frantic abuse, intermixed with oaths and curses. His looks and tones had inspired terror when he was merely a young advocate struggling into practice. Now that he was at the head of the most formidable tribunal in the realm, there were few indeed who did not tremble before him. Even when he was sober, his violence was sufficiently frightful. But in general his reason was overclouded and his evil passions stimulated by the fumes of intoxication. His evenings were ordinarily given to revelry. People who saw him only over his bottle would have supposed him to be a man gross indeed, sottish, and addicted to low company and low merriment, but social and goodhumoured. He was constantly surrounded on such occasions by buffoons selected, for the most part, from among the vilest pettifoggers who practised before him. These men bantered and abused each other for his entertainment. He joined in their ribald talk, sang catches with them, and, when his head grew hot, hugged and kissed them in an ecstasy of drunken fondness. But though wine at first seemed to soften his heart, the effect a few hours later was very different. He often came to the judgment seat, having kept the court waiting long, and yet having but half slept off his debauch, his cheeks on fire, his eyes staring like those of a maniac. When he was in this state, his boon companions of the preceding night, if they were wise, kept out of his way : for the recollection of the familiarity to which he had admitted them inflamed his malignity ; and he was sure to take every opportunity of overwhelming them with execration and invective. Not the least odious of his many odious peculiarities was the pleasure which he took in publicly browbeating and mortifying those whom, in his fits of maudlin tenderness, he had encouraged to presume on his favour.

The services which the government had expected from him were performed, not merely without flinching, but eagerly and triumphantly. His first exploit was the judicial murder of Algernon Sidney. What followed was in perfect harmony with this beginning. Respectable Tories lamented the disgrace which the barbarity and indecency of so great a functionary brought upon the administration of justice. But the excesses which filled such men with horror were titles to the esteem of James. Jeffreys, therefore, very soon after the death of Charles, obtained a seat in the cabinet and a peerage. This last honour was a signal

GEORGE, 1st LORD JEFFREYS, P.C., 1648-1689.

From the painting (artist unknown) in the National Portrait Gallery.

mark of royal approbation. For, since the judicial system of the realm had been remodelled in the thirteenth century, no Chief Justice had been a Lord of Parliament.[1]

Guildford now found himself superseded in all his political functions, and restricted to his business as a judge in equity. At Council he was treated by Jeffreys with marked incivility. The whole legal patronage was in the hands of the Chief Justice; and it was well known by the bar that the surest way to propitiate the Chief Justice was to treat the Lord Keeper with disrespect.

James had not been many hours King when a dispute arose between the two heads of the law. The customs had been settled on Charles for life only, and could not therefore be legally exacted by the new sovereign. Some weeks must elapse before a House of Commons could be chosen. If, in the meantime, the duties were suspended, the revenue would suffer; the regular course of trade would be interrupted; the consumer would derive no benefit; and the only gainers would be those fortunate speculators whose cargoes might happen to arrive during the interval between the demise of the crown and the meeting of the Parliament. The Treasury was besieged by merchants whose warehouses were filled with goods on which duty had been paid, and who were in grievous apprehension of being undersold and ruined. Impartial men must admit that this was one of those cases in which a government may be justified in deviating from the strictly constitutional course. But when it is necessary to deviate from the strictly constitutional course, the deviation clearly ought to be no greater than the necessity requires. Guildford felt this, and gave advice which did him honour. He proposed that the duties should be levied, but should be kept in the Exchequer apart from other sums till the Parliament should meet. In this way the King, while violating the letter of the laws, would show that he wished to conform to their spirit. Jeffreys gave very different counsel. He advised James to put forth an edict declaring it to be His Majesty's will and pleasure that the customs should continue to be paid. This advice was well suited to the King's temper. The judicious proposition of the Lord Keeper was rejected as worthy only of a Whig, or of what was still worse, a Trimmer. A proclamation, such as the Chief Justice had suggested, appeared. Some people expected that a violent outbreak of public indignation would be the consequence: but they

The revenue collected without an Act of Parliament

[1] The chief sources of information concerning Jeffreys are the State Trials and North's Life of Lord Guildford. Some touches of minor importance I owe to contemporary pamphlets in verse and prose. Such are the Bloody Assizes, the Life and Death of George Lord Jeffreys, the Panegyric on the late Lord Jeffreys, the Letter to the Lord Chancellor, Jeffreys's Elegy. See also Evelyn's Diary, Dec. 5. 1683, Oct. 31. 1685. I scarcely need advise every reader to consult Lord Campbell's excellent Life of Jeffreys.

were deceived.   The spirit of opposition had not yet revived ; and the court might safely venture to take steps which, five years before, would have produced a rebellion.   In the City of London, lately so turbulent, scarcely a murmur was heard.[1]

The proclamation, which announced that the customs would still be levied, announced also that a Parliament would shortly meet.   It was A Parlia- not without many misgivings that James had determined to ment called call the Estates of his realm together.   The moment was, indeed, most auspicious for a general election.   Never since the accession of the House of Stuart had the constituent bodies been so favourably disposed towards the Court.   But the new sovereign's mind was haunted by an apprehension not to be mentioned, even at this distance of time, without shame and indignation.   He was afraid that by summoning his Parliament he might incur the displeasure of the King of France.

To the King of France it mattered little which of the two English factions triumphed at the elections : for all the Parliaments which had Transactions met since the Restoration, whatever might have been their between temper as to domestic politics, had been jealous of the grow-James and the French ing power of the House of Bourbon.   On this subject there King was little difference between the Whigs and the sturdy country gentlemen who formed the main strength of the Tory party. Lewis had therefore spared neither bribes nor menaces to prevent Charles from convoking the Houses; and James, who had from the first been in the secret of his brother's foreign politics, had, in becoming King of England, become also a hireling and vassal of France.

Rochester, Godolphin, and Sunderland, who now formed the interior cabinet, were perfectly aware that their late master had been in the habit of receiving money from the court of Versailles.   They were consulted by James as to the expediency of convoking the legislature. They acknowledged the importance of keeping Lewis in good humour : but it seemed to them that the calling of a Parliament was not a matter of choice.   Patient as the nation appeared to be, there were limits to its patience.   The principle, that the money of the subject could not be lawfully taken by the King without the assent of the Commons, was firmly rooted in the public mind ; and though, on an extraordinary emergency, even Whigs might be willing to pay, during a few weeks, duties not imposed by statute, it was certain that even Tories would become refractory if such irregular taxation should continue longer than the special circumstances which alone justified it.   The Houses then must meet ; and, since it was so, the sooner they were summoned the better.   Even the short delay which would be occasioned by a reference to Versailles might produce irreparable mischief.   Discontent and sus-

[1] London Gazette, Feb. 12. 168⅘.   North's Life of Guildford, 254.

picion would spread fast through society. Halifax would complain that the fundamental principles of the constitution were violated. The Lord Keeper, like a cowardly pedantic special pleader as he was, would take the same side. What might have been done with a good grace would at last be done with a bad grace. Those very ministers whom His Majesty most wished to lower in the public estimation would gain popularity at his expense. The ill temper of the nation might seriously affect the result of the elections. These arguments were unanswerable. The King therefore notified to the country his intention of holding a Parliament. But he was painfully anxious to exculpate himself from the guilt of having acted undutifully and disrespectfully towards France. He led Barillon into a private room, and there apologised for having dared to take so important a step without the previous sanction of Lewis. "Assure your master," said James, "of my gratitude and attachment. I know that without his protection I can do nothing. I know what troubles my brother brought on himself by not adhering steadily to France. I will take good care not to let the Houses meddle with foreign affairs. If I see in them any disposition to make mischief, I will send them about their business. Explain this to my good brother. I hope that he will not take it amiss that I have acted without consulting him. He has a right to be consulted; and it is my wish to consult him about everything. But in this case the delay even of a week might have produced serious consequences."

These ignominious excuses were, on the following morning, repeated by Rochester. Barillon received them civilly. Rochester, grown bolder, proceeded to ask for money. "It will be well laid out," he said: "your master cannot employ his revenues better. Represent to him strongly how important it is that the King of England should be dependent, not on his own people, but on the friendship of France alone."[1]

Barillon hastened to communicate to Lewis the wishes of the English government; but Lewis had already anticipated them. His first act, after he was apprised of the death of Charles, was to collect bills of exchange on England to the amount of five hundred thousand livres, a sum equivalent to about thirty-seven thousand five hundred pounds sterling. Such bills were not then to be easily procured in Paris at a day's notice. In a few hours, however, the purchase was effected, and a courier started for London.[2] As soon as Barillon received the remittance, he flew to Whitehall, and communicated the welcome news. James was not ashamed to shed, or pretend to shed, tears of delight and

---

[1] The chief authority for these transactions is Barillon's despatch of February $\frac{9}{19}$. 1685. It will be found in the Appendix to Mr. Fox's History. See also Preston's letter to James, dated April $\frac{18}{28}$. 1685, in Dalrymple.

[2] Lewis to Barillon, Feb. $\frac{16}{26}$. 1685.

gratitude. "Nobody but your King," he said, "does such kind, such noble things. I never can be grateful enough. Assure him that my attachment will last to the end of my days." Rochester, Sunderland, and Godolphin came, one after another, to embrace the ambassador, and to whisper to him that he had given new life to their royal master.[1]

But though James and his three advisers were pleased with the promptitude which Lewis had shown, they were by no means satisfied with the amount of the donation. As they were afraid, however, that they might give offence by importunate mendicancy, they merely hinted their wishes. They declared that they had no intention of haggling with so generous a benefactor as the French King, and that they were willing to trust entirely to his munificence. They, at the same time, attempted to propitiate him by a large sacrifice of national honour. It was well known that one chief end of his politics was to add the Belgian provinces to his dominions. England was bound by a treaty, which had been concluded with Spain when Danby was Lord Treasurer, to resist any attempt which France might make on those provinces. The three ministers informed Barillon that their master considered that treaty as no longer obligatory. It had been made, they said, by Charles : it might, perhaps, have been binding on him ; but his brother did not think himself bound by it. The most Christian King might, therefore, without any fear of opposition from England, proceed to annex Brabant and Hainault to his empire.[2]

It was at the same time resolved that an extraordinary embassy should be sent to assure Lewis of the gratitude and affection of

Churchill sent ambassador to France James. For this mission was selected a man who did not as yet occupy a very eminent position, but whose renown, strangely made up of infamy and glory, filled at a later period the whole civilised world.

Soon after the Restoration, in the gay and dissolute times which have been celebrated by the lively pen of Hamilton, James, young and

His history ardent in the pursuit of pleasure, had been attracted by Arabella Churchill, one of the maids of honour who waited on his first wife. The young lady was plain : but the taste of James was not nice : and she became his avowed mistress. She was the daughter of a poor Cavalier knight who haunted Whitehall, and made himself ridiculous by publishing a dull and affected folio, long forgotten, in praise of monarchy and monarchs. The necessities of the Churchills were pressing : their loyalty was ardent ; and their only feeling about Arabella's seduction seems to have been joyful surprise that so homely a girl should have attained such high preferment.

[1] Barillon, Feb. $\frac{16}{26}$. 1685.   [2] Barillon, Feb. $\frac{18}{28}$. 1685.

ARABELLA CHURCHILL.

From a Picture at Strawberry Hill.

ARABELLA CHURCHILL

From an engraving in the Sutherland Collection

Her interest was indeed of great use to her relations : but none of them was so fortunate as her eldest brother John, a fine youth, who carried a pair of colours in the foot guards. He rose fast in the court and in the army, and was early distinguished as a man of fashion and of pleasure. His stature was commanding, his face handsome, his address singularly winning, yet of such dignity that the most impertinent fops never ventured to take any liberty with him ; his temper, even in the most vexatious and irritating circumstances, always under perfect command. His education had been so much neglected that he could not spell the most common words of his own language : but his acute and vigorous understanding amply supplied the place of book learning. He was not talkative : but, when he was forced to speak in public, his natural eloquence moved the envy of practised rhetoricians.[1] His courage was singularly cool and imperturbable. During many years of anxiety and peril, he never, in any emergency, lost, even for a moment, the perfect use of his admirable judgment.

In his twenty-third year he was sent with his regiment to join the French forces, then engaged in operations against Holland. His serene intrepidity distinguished him among thousands of brave soldiers. His professional skill commanded the respect of veteran officers. He was publicly thanked at the head of the army, and received many marks of esteem and confidence from Turenne, who was then at the height of military glory.

Unhappily the splendid qualities of John Churchill were mingled with alloy of the most sordid kind. Some propensities, which in youth are singularly ungraceful, began very early to show themselves in him. He was thrifty in his very vices, and levied ample contributions on ladies enriched by the spoils of more liberal lovers. He was, during a short time, the object of the violent but fickle fondness of the Duchess of Cleveland. On one occasion he was caught with her by the King, and was forced to leap out of the window. She rewarded this hazardous feat of gallantry with a present of five thousand pounds. With this sum the prudent young hero instantly bought an annuity of five hundred a year, well secured on landed property.[2] Already his private drawer contained a hoard of broad pieces which, fifty years later, when he was

---

[1] Swift who hated Marlborough, and who was little disposed to allow any merit to those whom he hated, says, in the famous letter to Crassus, " You are no ill orator in the Senate."

[2] Dartmouth's note on Burnet, i. 264. Chesterfield's Letters, Nov. 18. 1748. Chesterfield is an unexceptionable witness ; for the annuity was a charge on the estate of his grandfather, Halifax. I believe that there is no foundation for a disgraceful addition to the story which may be found in Pope :

> " The gallant, too, to whom she paid it down,
> Lived to refuse his mistress half a crown."

Curl calls this a piece of travelling scandal.

a Duke, a Prince of the Empire, and the richest subject in Europe, remained untouched.[1]

After the close of the war he was attached to the household of the Duke of York, accompanied his patron to the Low Countries and to Edinburgh, and was rewarded for his services with a Scotch peerage

JOHN CHURCHILL, AFTERWARDS DUKE OF MARLBOROUGH

From a miniature in the possession of His Grace the Duke of Buccleugh

and with the command of the only regiment of dragoons which was then on the English establishment.[2]   His wife had a post in the family of James's younger daughter, the Princess of Denmark.

[1] Pope in Spence's Anecdotes.

[2] See the Historical Records of the First or Royal Dragoons. The appointment of Churchill to the command of this regiment was ridiculed as an instance of absurd partiality. One lampoon

Lord Churchill was now sent as ambassador extraordinary to Versailles.   He had it in charge to express the warm gratitude of the English government for the money which had been so generously bestowed. It had been originally intended that he should, at the same time, ask Lewis for a much larger sum ; but, on full consideration, it was apprehended that such indelicate greediness might disgust the benefactor whose spontaneous liberality had been so signally displayed.   Churchill was therefore directed to confine himself to thanks for what was past, and to say nothing about the future.[1]

But James and his ministers, even while protesting that they did not mean to be importunate, contrived to hint, very intelligibly, what they wished and expected.   In the French ambassador they had a dexterous, a zealous, and, perhaps, not a disinterested intercessor.   Lewis made some difficulties, probably with the design of enhancing the value of his gifts.   In a very few weeks, however, Barillon received from Versailles fifteen hundred thousand livres more.   This sum, equivalent to about a hundred and twelve thousand pounds sterling, he was instructed to dole out cautiously.   He was authorised to furnish the English government with thirty thousand pounds, for the purpose of corrupting members of the new House of Commons.   The rest he was directed to keep in reserve for some extraordinary emergency, such as a dissolution or an insurrection.[2]

The turpitude of these transactions is universally acknowledged : but their real nature seems to be often misunderstood : for, though the foreign policy of the last two Kings of the House of Stuart has never, since the correspondence of Barillon was exposed to the public eye, found an apologist among us, there is still a party which labours to excuse their domestic policy.   Yet it is certain that between their domestic policy and their foreign policy there was a necessary and indissoluble connection.   If they had upheld, during a single year, the honour of the country abroad, they would have been compelled to change the whole system of their administration at home.   To praise them for refusing to govern in conformity with the sense of Parliament, and yet to blame them for submitting to the dictation of Lewis, is inconsistent. For they had only one choice, to be dependent on Lewis, or to be dependent on Parliament.

James, to do him justice, would gladly have found out a third way :

of that time, which I do not remember to have seen in print, but of which a manuscript copy is in the British Museum, contains these lines :

> " Let's cut our meat with spoons :
> The sense is as good
> As that Churchill should
> Be put to command the dragoons."

[1] Barillon, Feb. $\frac{16}{26}$. 1685.   [2] Barillon, April $\frac{6}{16}$. ; Lewis to Barillon, April $\frac{14}{24}$.

Louis XIIII. Roy de France.

J. Gole fec. et Exc.   Cum Privilegio Amsteledami

LEWIS XIV

From a mezzotint by Gole in the Sutherland Collection

but there was none.   He became the slave of France : but it would be incorrect to represent him as a contented slave.   He had spirit enough to be at times angry with himself for submitting to such thraldom, and impatient to break loose from it ; and this disposition was studiously encouraged by the agents of many foreign powers.

His accession had excited hopes and fears in every Continental court : and the commencement of his administration was watched by **Feelings of** strangers with interest scarcely less deep than that which was **the Con-** **tinental** felt by his own subjects.   One government alone wished **governments** that the troubles which had, during three generations, dis- **towards** **England** tracted England, might be eternal.   All other governments, whether republican or monarchical, whether Protestant or Roman Catholic, wished to see those troubles happily terminated.

The nature of the long contest between the Stuarts and their Parliaments was indeed very imperfectly apprehended by foreign statesmen : but no statesman could fail to perceive the effect which that contest had produced on the balance of power in Europe.   In ordinary circumstances, the sympathies of the courts of Vienna and Madrid would doubtless have been with a prince struggling against subjects, and especially with a Roman Catholic prince struggling against heretical subjects : but all such sympathies were now overpowered by a stronger feeling.   The fear and hatred inspired by the greatness, the injustice, and the arrogance of the French King were at the height.   His neighbours might well doubt whether it were more dangerous to be at war or at peace with him.   For in peace he continued to plunder and to outrage them ; and they had tried the chances of war against him in vain. In this perplexity they looked with intense anxiety towards England. Would she act on the principles of the Triple Alliance or on the principles of the treaty of Dover ?   On that issue depended the fate of all her neighbours.   With her help Lewis might yet be withstood : but no help could be expected from her till she was at unity with herself. Before the strife between the throne and the Parliament began, she had been a power of the first rank : on the day on which that strife terminated she became a power of the first rank again : but while the dispute remained undecided, she was condemned to inaction and to vassalage.   She had been great under the Plantagenets and Tudors : she was again great under the princes who reigned after the Revolution : but, under the Kings of the House of Stuart, she was a blank in the map of Europe.   She had lost one class of energies, and had not yet acquired another.   That species of force, which, in the fourteenth century, had enabled her to humble France and Spain, had ceased to exist. That species of force, which, in the eighteenth century, humbled France and Spain once more, had not yet been called into action.   The government was no longer a limited monarchy after the fashion of the middle ages. It had not yet become a limited monarchy after the modern fashion. With the vices of two different systems it had the strength of

POPE INNOCENT XI

From an engraving by A. Clonnet in the Sutherland Collection

neither. The elements of our polity, instead of combining in harmony, counteracted and neutralised each other. All was transition, conflict, and disorder. The chief business of the sovereign was to infringe the

privileges of the legislature. The chief business of the legislature was
to encroach on the prerogatives of the sovereign. The King readily
accepted foreign aid, which relieved him from the misery of being
dependent on a mutinous Parliament. The Parliament refused to the
King the means of supporting the national honour abroad, from an
apprehension, too well founded, that those means might be employed in
order to establish despotism at home. The effect of these jealousies
was that our country, with all her vast resources, was of as little weight
in Christendom as the duchy of Savoy or the duchy of Lorraine, and
certainly of far less weight than the small province of Holland.

France was deeply interested in prolonging this state of things.[1]
All other powers were deeply interested in bringing it to a close. The
general wish of Europe was that James would govern in conformity
with law and with public opinion. From the Escurial itself
came letters, expressing an earnest hope that the new King
of England would be on good terms with his Parliament and
his people.[2] From the Vatican itself came cautions against immoderate
zeal for the Roman Catholic faith. Benedict Odescalchi, who filled the
papal chair under the name of Innocent the Eleventh, felt, in his character of temporal sovereign, all those apprehensions with which other
princes watched the progress of the French power. He had also grounds
of uneasiness which were peculiar to himself. It was a happy circumstance for the Protestant religion that, at the moment when the last
Roman Catholic King of England mounted the throne, the Roman
Catholic Church was torn by dissension, and threatened with a new
schism. A quarrel similar to that which had raged in the eleventh
century between the Emperors and the Supreme Pontiffs had arisen
between Lewis and Innocent. Lewis, zealous even to bigotry for the
doctrines of the Church of Rome, but tenacious of his regal authority,

Policy of the court of Rome

---

[1] I might transcribe half Barillon's correspondence in proof of this proposition : but I will quote
only one passage, in which the policy of the French government towards England is exhibited
concisely and with perfect clearness.

" On peut tenir pour un maxime indubitable que l'accord du Roy d'Angleterre avec son parle-
ment, en quelque manière qu'il se fasse, n'est pas conforme aux intérêts de V. M. Je me con-
tente de penser cela sans m'en ouvrir à personne, et je cache avec soin mes sentimens à cet
égard."—Barillon to Lewis, $\frac{\text{Feb. 28.}}{\text{Mar. 10.}}$ 1687. That this was the real secret of the whole policy of
Lewis towards our country was perfectly understood at Vienna. The Emperor Leopold wrote
thus to James, $\frac{\text{March 30.}}{\text{April 9.}}$ 1689 : " Galli id unum agebant, ut, perpetuas inter Serenitatem vestram
et ejusdem populos fovendo simultates, reliquæ Christianæ Europæ tanto securius insultarent."

[2] " Que sea unido con su reyno, y en todo buena intelligencia con el parlamento."—Despatch
from the King of Spain to Don Pedro Ronquillo, March $\frac{16}{26}$. 1685. This despatch is in the
archives of Simancas, which contain a great mass of papers relating to English affairs. Copies of
the most interesting of those papers are in the possession of M. Guizot, and were by him lent to
me. It is with peculiar pleasure that, at this time, I acknowledge this mark of the friendship of
so great a man. (1848.)

accused the Pope of encroaching on the secular rights of the French Crown, and was in turn accused by the Pope of encroaching on the spiritual power of the keys. The King, haughty as he was, encountered a spirit even more determined than his own. Innocent was, in all private relations, the meekest and gentlest of men : but, when he spoke officially from the chair of Saint Peter, he spoke in the tones of Gregory the Seventh and of Sixtus the Fifth. The dispute became serious. Agents of the King were excommunicated. Adherents of the Pope were banished. The King made the champions of his authority Bishops. The Pope refused them institution. They took possession of the episcopal palaces and revenues : but they were incompetent to perform the episcopal functions. Before the struggle terminated, there were in France thirty prelates who could not confirm or ordain.[1]

Had any prince then living, except Lewis, been engaged in such a dispute with the Vatican, he would have had all Protestant governments on his side. But the fear and resentment which the ambition and insolence of the French King had inspired were such that whoever had the courage manfully to oppose him was sure of public sympathy. Even Lutherans and Calvinists, who had always detested the Pope, could not refrain from wishing him success against a tyrant who aimed at universal monarchy. It was thus that, in the present century, many who regarded Pius the Seventh as Antichrist were well pleased to see Antichrist confront the gigantic power of Napoleon.

The resentment which Innocent felt towards France disposed him to take a mild and liberal view of the affairs of England. The return of the English people to the fold of which he was the shepherd would undoubtedly have rejoiced his soul. But he was too wise a man to believe that a nation, so bold and stubborn, could be brought back to the Church of Rome by the violent and unconstitutional exercise of royal authority. It was not difficult to foresee that, if James attempted to promote the interests of his religion by illegal and unpopular means, the attempt would fail ; the hatred with which the heretical islanders regarded the true faith would become fiercer and stronger than ever ; and an indissoluble association would be created in their minds between Protestantism and civil freedom, between Popery and arbitrary power. In the meantime the King would be an object of aversion and suspicion to his people. England would still be, as she had been under James the First, under Charles the First, and under Charles the Second, a power of the third rank ; and France would domineer unchecked beyond the Alps and the Rhine. On the other hand, it was probable that James, by acting with prudence and moderation, by strictly observing the laws,

---

[1] Few English readers will be desirous to go deep into the history of this quarrel. Summaries will be found in Cardinal Bausset's Life of Bossuet, and in Voltaire's Age of Lewis XIV.

and by exerting himself to win the confidence of his Parliament, might be able to obtain, for the professors of his religion, a large measure of relief. Penal statutes would go first. Statutes imposing civil incapacities would soon follow. In the meantime, the English King and the English nation united might head the European coalition, and might oppose an insuperable barrier to the cupidity of Lewis.

Innocent was confirmed in his judgment by the principal Englishmen who resided at his court. Of these the most illustrious was Philip Howard, sprung from the noblest houses of Britain, grandson, on one side, of an Earl of Arundel, on the other, of a Duke of Lennox. Philip had long been a member of the sacred college: he was commonly designated as the Cardinal of England; and he was the chief counsellor of the Holy See in matters relating to his country. He had been driven into exile by the outcry of Protestant bigots; and a member of his family, the unfortunate Stafford, had fallen a victim to their rage. But neither the Cardinal's own wrongs, nor those of his house, had so heated his mind as to make him a rash adviser. Every letter, therefore, which went from the Vatican to Whitehall, recommended patience, moderation, and respect for the prejudices of the English people.[1]

In the mind of James there was a great conflict. We should do him injustice if we supposed that a state of vassalage was agreeable to

Struggle in the mind of James his temper. He loved authority and business. He had a high sense of his own personal dignity. Nay, he was not altogether destitute of a sentiment which bore some affinity to patriotism. It galled his soul to think that the kingdom which he ruled was of far less account in the world than many states which possessed smaller natural advantages; and he listened eagerly to foreign ministers when they urged him to assert the dignity of his rank, to place himself at the head of a great confederacy, to become the protector of injured nations, and to tame the pride of that power which held the Continent in awe. Such exhortations made his heart swell with emotions unknown to his careless and effeminate brother. But those emotions were soon subdued by a stronger feeling. A vigorous foreign policy necessarily implied a conciliatory domestic policy. It was impossible at once to confront the might of France and to trample on the liberties of England. The executive government could undertake nothing great without the support of the Commons, and could obtain their support only by acting in conformity with their opinion. Thus

Fluctuations of his policy James found that the two things which he most desired could not be enjoyed together. His second wish was to be feared and respected abroad. But his first wish was to be absolute master at home. Between the incompatible objects on which his heart was set,

[1] Burnet, i. 661., and Letter from Rome; Dodd's Church History, part viii. book i. art. 1.

CARDINAL HOWARD

From an engraving by J. van der Bruggen after a painting by du Chatel he, for a time, went irresolutely to and fro. The conflict in his own breast gave to his public acts a strange appearance of indecision and insincerity. Those who, without the clue, attempted to explore the maze of his politics were unable to understand how the same man could be, in the same week, so haughty and so mean. Even Lewis was perplexed by the vagaries of an ally who passed, in a few hours, from homage to defiance, and from defiance to homage. Yet, now that the whole conduct of James is before us, this inconsistency seems to admit of a simple explanation.

At the moment of his accession he was in doubt whether the kingdom would peaceably submit to his authority. The Exclusionists, lately so powerful, might rise in arms against him. He might be in great need of French money and French troops. He was therefore, during some days, content to be a sycophant and a mendicant. He humbly apologised for daring to call his Parliament together without the consent of the French government. He begged hard for a French subsidy. He wept with joy over the French bills of exchange. He sent to Versailles a special embassy charged with assurances of his gratitude, attachment, and submission. But scarcely had the embassy departed when his feelings underwent a change. He had been everywhere proclaimed without one riot, without one seditious outcry. From all corners of the island he received intelligence that his subjects were tranquil and obedient. His spirit rose. The degrading relation in which he stood to a foreign power seemed intolerable. He became proud, punctilious, boastful, quarrelsome. He held such high language about the dignity of his crown and the balance of power that his whole court fully expected a complete revolution in the foreign politics of the realm. He commanded Churchill to send home a minute report of the ceremonial of Versailles, in order that the honours with which the English embassy was received there might be repaid, and not more than repaid, to the representative of France at Whitehall. The news of this change was received with delight at Madrid, Vienna, and the Hague.[1] Lewis was at first merely diverted. " My good ally talks big," he said ; " but he is as fond of my pistoles as ever his brother was." Soon, however, the altered demeanour of James, and the hopes with which that demeanour inspired both the branches of the House of Austria, began to call for more serious notice. A remarkable letter is still extant, in which the French King intimated a strong suspicion that he had been duped, and that the very money which he had sent to Westminster would be employed against him.[2]

[1] Consultations of the Spanish Council of State on April $\frac{2}{12}$. and April $\frac{16}{26}$. 1685, in the Archives of Simancas.

[2] Lewis to Barillon, $\frac{\text{May 22}}{\text{June 1.}}$ 1685 ; Burnet, i. 622.

By this time England had recovered from the sadness and anxiety caused by the death of the good-natured Charles. The Tories were loud in professions of attachment to their new master. The hatred of the Whigs was kept down by fear. That great mass which is not steadily Whig or Tory, but which inclines alternately to Whiggism and to Toryism, was still on the Tory side. The reaction which had followed the dissolution of the Oxford parliament had not yet spent its force.

The King early put the loyalty of his Protestant friends to the proof. While he was a subject, he had been in the habit of hearing mass with closed doors in a small oratory which had been fitted up for his wife. He now ordered the doors to be thrown open, in order that all who came to pay their duty to him might see the ceremony. When the host was elevated there was a strange confusion in the antechamber. The Roman Catholics fell on their knees: the Protestants hurried out of the room. Soon a new pulpit was erected in the palace; and, during Lent, a series of sermons was preached there by Popish divines, to the great discomposure of zealous churchmen.[1]

Public celebration of the Roman Catholic rites in the palace

A more serious innovation followed. Passion week came; and the King determined to hear mass with the same pomp with which his predecessors had been surrounded when they repaired to the temples of the established religion. He announced his intention to the three members of the interior cabinet, and requested them to attend him. Sunderland, to whom all religions were the same, readily consented. Godolphin, as Chamberlain of the Queen, had already been in the habit of giving her his hand when she repaired to her oratory, and felt no scruple about bowing himself officially in the house of Rimmon. But Rochester was greatly disturbed. His influence in the country arose chiefly from the opinion entertained by the clergy and by the Tory gentry, that he was a zealous and uncompromising friend of the Church. His orthodoxy had been considered as fully atoning for faults which would otherwise have made him the most unpopular man in the kingdom, for boundless arrogance, for extreme violence of temper, and for manners almost brutal.[2] He feared that, by complying with the royal wishes, he should greatly lower himself in the estimation of his party. After some altercation he obtained permission to pass the holidays out of town. All the other great civil dignitaries were ordered to be at their posts on Easter

---

[1] Life of James the Second, ii. 5.; Barillon, $\frac{\text{Feb. 19}}{\text{Mar. 1.}}$ 1685; Evelyn's Diary, March 5. 168⅘.

[2]
       "To those that ask boons
       He swears by God's oons,
And chides them as if they came there to steal spoons."
           Lamentable Lory, a ballad, 1684.

CORONATION OF JAMES II—THE KING

From Sandford's History of the Coronation of James II, 1687

1. The Orb, borne by the Duke of Somerset
2. The Crown, borne by ye Duke of Ormond
3. The Scepter with ye Dove, borne by ye Duke of Albemarle

A. The Kings Majestie
B. The Bishop of Durham
C. The Bishop of Bath and Wells
D. Four Earls Eldest Sons
E. The Master of the Robes

F. Sixteen Barons of the Cinque ports
G. The Earl of Huntingdon, Captain of the Band of Gt. Pensioners
H. The Duke of Northumberland, Captain of the Guard in Waiting
I. The Viscount Grandison, Captain of the Yeomen of the Guard
K. Gentlemen Pensioners

CORONATION OF JAMES II—THE QUEEN

From Sandford's History of the Coronation of James II, 1687

A. The Queens Majestie
B. The Bishop of London
C. The Bishop of Winchester
D. The Dutchess of Norfolk
E. Four Earls Daughters

F. Sixteen Barons of the Cinque ports
G. A Lady of the Bedchamber
H. Two of her Majesties Women
I. Gentlemen Pensioners

Sunday. The rites of the Church of Rome were once more, after an interval of a hundred and twenty seven years, performed at Westminster with regal splendour. The Guards were drawn out. The Knights of the Garter wore their collars. The Duke of Somerset, second in rank among the temporal nobles of the realm, carried the sword of state. A long train of great lords accompanied the King to his seat. But it was remarked that Ormond and Halifax remained in the antechamber. A few years before they had gallantly defended the cause of James against some of those who now pressed past them. Ormond had borne no share in the slaughter of Roman Catholics. Halifax had courageously pronounced Stafford not guilty. As the timeservers who had pretended to shudder at the thought of a Popish king, and who had shed without pity the innocent blood of a Popish peer, now elbowed each other to get near a Popish altar, the accomplished Trimmer might, with some justice, indulge his solitary pride in that unpopular nickname.[1]

Within a week after this ceremony James made a far greater sacrifice of his own religious prejudices than he had yet called on any

His corona- of his Protestant subjects to make. He was crowned on the
tion   twenty-third of April, the feast of the patron saint of the
realm. The Abbey and the Hall were splendidly decorated. The presence of the Queen and of the peeresses gave to the solemnity a charm which had been wanting to the magnificent inauguration of the late King. Yet those who remembered that inauguration pronounced that there was a great falling off. The ancient usage was that, before a coronation, the sovereign, with all his heralds, judges, councillors, lords, and great dignitaries, should ride in state from the Tower to Westminster. Of these cavalcades the last and the most glorious was that which passed through the capital while the feelings excited by the Restoration were still in full vigour. Arches of triumph overhung the road. All Cornhill, Cheapside, Saint Paul's Church Yard, Fleet Street, and the Strand, were lined with scaffolding. The whole city had thus been admitted to gaze on royalty in the most splendid and solemn form that royalty could wear. James ordered an estimate to be made of the cost of such a procession, and found that it would amount to about half as much as he proposed to expend in covering his wife with trinkets. He accordingly determined to be profuse where he ought to have been frugal, and niggardly where he might pardonably have been profuse. More than a hundred thousand pounds were laid out in dressing the Queen, and the procession from the Tower was omitted. The folly of this course is obvious. If pageantry be of any use in politics, it is of use as a means of striking the imagination of the multitude. It is surely the height of absurdity to shut out the populace from a show of

[1] Barillon, April $\frac{20}{30}$. 1685.

which the main object is to make an impression on the populace. James would have shown a more judicious munificence and a more judicious parsimony, if he had traversed London from east to west with the accustomed pomp, and had ordered the robes of his wife to be somewhat less thickly set with pearls and diamonds. His example was, however, long followed by his successors ; and sums, which, well employed, would have afforded exquisite gratification to a large part of the nation, were squandered on an exhibition to which only three or four thousand privileged persons were admitted. At length the old practice was partially revived. On the day of the coronation of Queen Victoria there was a procession in which many deficiencies might be noted, but which was seen with interest and delight by half a million of her subjects, and which undoubtedly gave far greater pleasure, and called forth far greater enthusiasm, than the more costly display which was witnessed by a select circle within the Abbey.

James had ordered Sancroft to abridge the ritual. The reason publicly assigned was that the day was too short for all that was to be done. But whoever examines the changes which were made will see that the real object was to remove some things highly offensive to the religious feelings of a zealous Roman Catholic. The Communion Service was not read. The ceremony of presenting the sovereign with a richly bound copy of the English Bible, and of exhorting him to prize above all earthly treasures a volume which he had been taught to regard as adulterated with false doctrine, was omitted. What remained, however, after all this curtailment, might well have raised scruples in the mind of a man who sincerely believed the Church of England to be a heretical society, within the pale of which salvation was not to be found. The King made an oblation on the altar. He appeared to join in the petitions of the Litany which was chaunted by the Bishops. He received from those false prophets the unction typical of a divine influence, and knelt with the semblance of devotion while they called down upon him that Holy Spirit of which they were, in his estimation, the malignant and obdurate foes. Such are the inconsistencies of human nature that this man, who, from a fanatical zeal for his religion, threw away three kingdoms, yet chose to commit what was little short of an act of apostasy, rather than forego the childish pleasure of being invested with the gewgaws symbolical of kingly power.[1]

Francis Turner, Bishop of Ely, preached. He was one of those writers who still affected the obsolete style of Archbishop Williams and Bishop Andrews. The sermon was made up of quaint conceits, such as

---

[1] From Adda's despatch of $\frac{\text{Jan. 22.}}{\text{Feb. 1.}}$ 1686, and from the expressions of the Père d'Orléans (Histoire des Révolutions d'Angleterre, liv. xi.), it is clear that rigid Catholics thought the King's conduct indefensible.

seventy years earlier might have been admired, but such as moved the scorn of a generation accustomed to the purer eloquence of Sprat, of South, and of Tillotson. King Solomon was King James. Adonijah was Monmouth. Joab was a Rye House conspirator; Shimei, a Whig libeller; Abiathar, an honest but misguided old Cavalier. One phrase in the Book of Chronicles was construed to mean that the King was above the Parliament; and another was cited to prove that he alone ought to command the militia. Towards the close of the discourse the orator very timidly alluded to the new and embarrassing position in which the Church stood with reference to the sovereign, and reminded his hearers that the Emperor Constantius Chlorus, though not himself a Christian, had held in honour those Christians who remained true to their religion, and had treated with scorn those who sought to earn his favour by apostasy. The service in the Abbey was followed by a stately banquet in the Hall, the banquet by brilliant fireworks, and the fireworks by much bad poetry.[1]

This may be fixed upon as the moment at which the enthusiasm of the Tory party reached the zenith. Ever since the accession of the new King, addresses had been pouring in which expressed profound veneration for his person and office, and bitter detestation of the vanquished Whigs. The magistrates of Middlesex thanked God for having confounded the designs of those regicides and exclusionists who, not content with having murdered one blessed monarch, were bent on destroying the foundations of monarchy. The city of Gloucester execrated the bloodthirsty villains who had tried to deprive His Majesty of his just inheritance. The burgesses of Wigan assured their sovereign that they would defend him against all plotting Achitophels and rebellious Absaloms. The grand jury of Suffolk expressed a hope that the Parliament would proscribe all the exclusionists. Many corporations pledged themselves never to return to the House of Commons any person who had voted for taking away the birthright of James. Even the capital was profoundly obsequious. The lawyers and the traders vied with each other in servility. Inns of Court and Inns of Chancery sent up fervent professions of attachment and submission. All the great commercial societies, the East India Company, the African Company, the Turkey Company, the Muscovy Company, the Hudson's

Enthusiasm of the Tories

Addresses

---

[1] London Gazette; Gazette de France; Life of James the Second, ii. 10.; History of the Coronation of King James the Second and Queen Mary, by Francis Sandford, Lancaster Herald, fol. 1687; Evelyn's Diary, May 21. 1685; Despatch of the Dutch Ambassadors, April $\frac{1}{5}\frac{0}{1}$. 1685; Burnet, i. 628.; Eachard, iii. 734.; A sermon preached before their Majesties King James the Second and Queen Mary at their Coronation in Westminster Abbey, April 23. 1685, by Francis, Lord Bishop of Ely, and Lord Almoner. I have seen an Italian account of the Coronation, which was published at Modena, and which is chiefly remarkable for the skill with which the writer sinks the fact that the prayers and psalms were in English, and that the Bishops were heretics.

FRANCIS TURNER, BISHOP OF ELY

From a painting in the National Portrait Gallery attributed to Mary Beale

Bay Company, the Maryland Merchants, the Jamaica Merchants, the Merchant Adventurers, declared that they most cheerfully complied with the royal edict which required them still to pay custom.   Bristol, the second city of the island, echoed the voice of London.   But nowhere was the spirit of loyalty stronger than in the two Universities.   Oxford declared that she would never swerve from those religious principles which bound her to obey the King without any restrictions or limitations.   Cambridge condemned, in severe terms, the violence and treachery of those turbulent men who had maliciously endeavoured to turn the stream of succession out of the ancient channel.[1]

Such addresses as these filled, during a considerable time, every number of the London Gazette.   But it was not only by addressing **The elections** that the Tories showed their zeal.   The writs for the new Parliament had gone forth, and the country was agitated by the tumult of a general election.   No election had ever taken place under circumstances so favourable to the Court.   Hundreds of thousands whom the Popish plot had scared into Whiggism had been scared back by the Rye House plot into Toryism.   In the counties the government could depend on an overwhelming majority of the gentlemen of three hundred a year and upwards, and on the clergy almost to a man. Those boroughs which had once been the citadels of Whiggism had recently been deprived of their charters by legal sentence, or had prevented the sentence by voluntary surrender.   They had now been reconstituted in such a manner that they were certain to return members devoted to the crown.   Where the townsmen could not be trusted, the freedom had been bestowed on the neighbouring squires.   In some of the small western corporations, the constituent bodies were in great part composed of Captains and Lieutenants of the Guards.   The returning officers were almost everywhere in the interest of the court.   In every shire the Lord Lieutenant and his deputies formed a powerful, active, and vigilant committee, for the purpose of cajoling and intimidating the freeholders.   The people were solemnly warned from thousands of pulpits not to vote for any Whig candidate, as they should answer it to Him who had ordained the powers that be, and who had pronounced rebellion a sin not less deadly than witchcraft.   All these advantages the predominant party not only used to the utmost, but abused in so shameless a manner that grave and reflecting men, who had been true to the monarchy in peril, and who bore no love to republicans and schismatics, stood aghast, and augured from such beginnings the approach of evil times.[2]

[1] See the London Gazette during the months of February, March, and April, 1685.

[2] It would be easy to fill a volume with what Whig historians and pamphleteers have written on this subject.   I will cite only one witness, a churchman and a Tory.   " Elections," says

Yet the Whigs, though suffering the just punishment of their errors, though defeated, disheartened, and disorganised, did not yield without an effort. They were still numerous among the traders and artisans of the towns, and among the yeomanry and peasantry of the open country. In some districts, in Dorsetshire for example, and in Somersetshire, they were the great majority of the population. In the remodelled boroughs they could do nothing : but, in every county where they had a chance, they struggled desperately. In Bedfordshire, which had lately been represented by the virtuous and unfortunate Russell, they were victorious on the show of hands, but were beaten at the poll.[1] In Essex they polled thirteen hundred votes to eighteen hundred.[2] At the election for Northamptonshire the common people were so violent in their hostility to the court candidate that a body of troops was drawn out in the marketplace of the county town, and was ordered to load with ball.[3] The history of the contest for Buckinghamshire is still more remarkable. The Whig candidate, Thomas Wharton, eldest son of Philip Lord Wharton, was a man distinguished alike by dexterity and by audacity, and destined to play a conspicuous, though not always a respectable, part in the politics of several reigns. He had been one of those members of the House of Commons who had carried up the Exclusion Bill to the bar of the Lords. The court was therefore bent on throwing him out by fair or foul means. The Lord Chief Justice Jeffreys himself came down into Buckinghamshire, for the purpose of assisting a gentleman named Hacket, who stood on the high Tory interest. A stratagem was devised which, it was thought, could not fail of success. It was given out that the polling would take place at Ailesbury ; and Wharton, whose skill in all the arts of electioneering was unrivalled, made his arrangements on that supposition. At a moment's warning the Sheriff adjourned the poll to Newport Pagnell. Wharton and his friends hurried thither, and found that Hacket, who was in the secret, had already secured every inn and lodging. The Whig freeholders were compelled to tie their horses to the hedges, and to sleep under the open sky in the meadows which surround the little town. It was with the greatest difficulty that refreshments could be procured at such short notice for so large a number of men and beasts,

Evelyn, " were thought to be very indecently carried on in most places. God give a better issue of it than some expect ! " May 10. 1685. Again he says, " The truth is there were many of the new members whose elections and returns were universally condemned." May 22.

[1] This fact I learned from a newsletter in the library of the Royal Institution. Van Citters mentions the strength of the Whig party in Bedfordshire.

[2] Bramston's Memoirs.

[3] Reflections on a Remonstrance and Protestation of all the good Protestants of this Kingdom, 1689 ; Dialogue between Two Friends, 1689.

though Wharton, who was utterly regardless of money when his ambition and party spirit were roused, disbursed fifteen hundred pounds in one day, an immense outlay for those times. Injustice seems, however, to have animated the courage of the stouthearted yeomen of Bucks, the sons of the constituents of John Hampden. Not only was Wharton at the head of the poll; but he was able to spare his second votes to a man of moderate opinions, and to throw out the Chief Justice's candidate.[1]

In Cheshire the contest lasted six days. The Whigs polled about seventeen hundred votes, the Tories about two thousand. The common people were vehement on the Whig side, raised the cry of "Down with the Bishops," insulted the clergy in the streets of Chester, knocked down one gentleman of the Tory party, broke the windows and beat the constables. The militia was called out to quell the riot, and was kept assembled, in order to protect the festivities of the conquerors. When the poll closed, a salute of five great guns from the castle, proclaimed the triumph of the Church and the Crown to the surrounding country. The bells rang. The newly elected members went in state to the City Cross, accompanied by a band of music, and by a long train of knights and squires. The procession, as it marched, sang "Joy to Great Cæsar," a loyal ode, which had lately been written by Durfey, and which, though, like all Durfey's writings, utterly contemptible, was, at that time, almost as popular as Lillibullero became a few years later.[2] Round the Cross the trainbands were drawn up in order: a bonfire was lighted: the Exclusion Bill was burned: and the health of King James was drunk with loud acclamations. The following day was Sunday. In the morning the militia lined the streets leading to the Cathedral. The two knights of the shire were escorted with great pomp to their choir by the magistracy of the city, heard the Dean preach a sermon, probably on the duty of passive obedience, and were afterwards feasted by the Mayor.[3]

In Northumberland the triumph of Sir John Fenwick, a courtier whose name afterwards obtained a melancholy celebrity, was attended by circumstances which excited interest in London, and which were thought not unworthy of being mentioned in the despatches of foreign ministers. Newcastle was lighted up with great piles of coal. The steeples sent forth a joyous peal. A copy of the Exclusion Bill, and a black box, resembling that which, according to the popular fable, con-

---

[1] Memoirs of the Life of Thomas Marquess of Wharton, 1715.

[2] See the Guardian, No. 67.; an exquisite specimen of Addison's peculiar manner. It would be difficult to find in the works of any other writer such an instance of benevolence delicately flavoured with contempt.

[3] The Observator, April 4. 1685.

THE SOUTH-WEST PROSPECT OF THE CITY OF CHESTER

From Buck's Antiquities of England

tained the contract between Charles the Second and Lucy Walters, were publicly committed to the flames, with loud acclamations.[1]

The general result of the elections exceeded the most sanguine expectations of the court. James found with delight that it would be unnecessary for him to expend a farthing in buying votes. He said that, with the exception of about forty members, the House of Commons was just such as he should himself have named.[2] And this House of Commons it was in his power, as the law then stood, to keep to the end of his reign.

Secure of parliamentary support, he might now indulge in the luxury of revenge. His nature was not placable ; and, while still a subject, he had suffered some injuries and indignities which might move even a placable nature to fierce and lasting resentment. One set of men in particular had, with a baseness and cruelty beyond all example and all description, attacked his honour and his life, the witnesses of the plot. He may well be excused for hating them ; since, even at this day, the mention of their names excites the disgust and horror of all sects and parties.

Some of these wretches were already beyond the reach of human justice. Bedloe had died in his wickedness, without one sign of remorse or shame.[3] Dugdale had followed, driven mad, men said, by the Furies of an evil conscience, and with loud shrieks imploring those who stood round his bed to take away Lord Stafford.[4] Carstairs, too, was gone. His end had been all horror and despair ; and, with his last breath, he had told his attendants to throw him into a ditch like a dog, for that he was not fit to sleep in a Christian burial ground.[5] But Oates and Dangerfield were still within the reach of the stern prince whom they **Proceedings** had wronged. James, a short time before his accession, had **against** instituted a civil suit against Oates for defamatory words ; **Oates** and a jury had given damages to the enormous amount of a hundred thousand pounds.[6] The defendant had been taken in execution, and was lying in prison as a debtor, without hope of release. Two bills of indictment against him for perjury had been found by the grand jury of Middlesex, a few weeks before the death of Charles. Soon after the close of the elections the trial came on.

Among the upper and middle classes Oates had few friends left. The most respectable Whigs were now convinced that, even if his narrative had some foundation in fact, he had erected on that foundation a

---

[1] Despatch of the Dutch Ambassadors, April ⁱ⁰⁄₂₀. 1685.   [2] Burnet, i. 626.

[3] A faithful account of the Sickness, Death, and Burial of Captain Bedlow, 1680 ; Narrative of Lord Chief Justice North.

[4] Smith's Intrigues of the Popish Plot, 1685.   [5] Burnet, i. 439.

[6] See the proceedings in the Collection of State Trials.

vast superstructure of romance. A considerable number of low fanatics, however, still regarded him as a public benefactor. These people well knew that, if he were convicted, his sentence would be one of extreme severity, and were therefore indefatigable in their endeavours to manage an escape. Though he was as yet in confinement only for debt, he was put into irons by the authorities of the King's Bench prison; and even so he was with difficulty kept in safe custody. The mastiff that guarded his door was poisoned; and, on the very night preceding the trial, a ladder of ropes was introduced into the cell.

On the day in which Titus was brought to the bar, Westminster Hall was crowded with spectators, among whom were many Roman Catholics, eager to see the misery and humiliation of their persecutor.[1] A few years earlier his short neck, his legs uneven, the vulgar said, as those of a badger, his forehead low as that of a baboon, his purple cheeks, and his monstrous length of chin, had been familiar to all who frequented the courts of law. He had then been the idol of the nation. Wherever he had appeared, men had uncovered their heads to him. The lives and estates of the magnates of the realm had been at his mercy. Times had now changed; and many, who had formerly regarded him as the deliverer of his country, shuddered at the sight of those hideous features on which villany seemed to be written by the hand of God.[2]

It was proved, beyond all possibility of doubt, that this man had, by false testimony, deliberately murdered several guiltless persons. He called in vain on the most eminent members of the Parliaments which had rewarded and extolled him to give evidence in his favour. Some of those whom he had summoned absented themselves. None of them said anything tending to his vindication. One of them, the Earl of Huntingdon, bitterly reproached him with having deceived the Houses and drawn on them the guilt of shedding innocent blood. The Judges browbeat and reviled the prisoner with an intemperance which, even in the most atrocious cases, ill becomes the judicial character. He betrayed, however, no sign of fear or of shame, and faced the storm of invective which burst upon him from bar, bench, and witness box, with the insolence of despair. He was convicted on both indictments. His offence, though, in a moral light, murder of the most aggravated kind, was, in the eye of the law, merely a misdemeanour. The tribunal, how-ever, was desirous to make his punishment more severe than that of felons or traitors, and not merely to put him to death, but to put him to

---

[1] Evelyn's Diary, May 7. 1685.

[2] There remain many pictures of Oates. The most striking descriptions of his person are in North's Examen, 225., in Dryden's Absalom and Achitophel, and in a broadside entitled, A Hue and Cry after T. O.

death by frightful torments. He was sentenced to be stripped of his clerical habit, to be pilloried in Palace Yard, to be led round Westminster Hall with an inscription declaring his infamy over his head, to be pilloried again in front of the Royal Exchange, to be whipped from Aldgate to Newgate, and, after an interval of two days, to be whipped from Newgate to Tyburn. If, against all probability, he should happen to survive this horrible infliction, he was to be kept close prisoner during life. Five times every year he was to be brought forth from his dungeon and exposed on the pillory in different parts of the capital.[1] This rigorous sentence was rigorously executed. On the day on which Oates was pilloried in Palace Yard, he was mercilessly pelted and ran some risk of being pulled in pieces.[2] But in the City his partisans mustered in great force, raised a riot, and upset the pillory.[3] They were, however, unable to rescue their favourite. It was supposed that he would try to escape the horrible doom which awaited him by swallowing poison. All that he ate and drank was therefore carefully inspected. On the following morning he was brought forth to undergo his first flogging. At an early hour an innumerable multitude filled all the streets from Aldgate to the Old Bailey. The hangman laid on the lash with such unusual severity as showed that he had received special instructions. The blood ran down in rivulets. For a time the criminal showed a strange constancy : but at last his stubborn fortitude gave way. His bellowings were frightful to hear. He swooned several times ; but the scourge still continued to descend. When he was unbound, it seemed that he had borne as much as the human frame can bear without dissolution. James was entreated to remit the second flogging. His answer was short and clear : " He shall go through with it, if he has breath in his body." An attempt was made to obtain the Queen's intercession ; but she indignantly refused to say a word in favour of such a wretch. After an interval of only forty eight hours, Oates was again brought out of his dungeon. He was unable to stand, and it was necessary to drag him to Tyburn on a sledge. He seemed quite insensible ; and the Tories reported that he had stupified himself with strong drink. A person who counted the stripes on the second day said that they were seventeen hundred. The bad man escaped with life, but so narrowly that his ignorant and bigoted admirers thought his recovery miraculous, and appealed to it as a proof of his innocence. The doors of the prison closed upon him. During many months he remained ironed in the darkest hole of Newgate. It was said that in his cell he gave himself up to melancholy, and sate whole days uttering deep groans, his arms folded, and his hat pulled over his eyes. It was

---

[1] The proceedings will be found at length in the Collection of State Trials.

[2] Gazette de France, $\frac{May 29.}{June 9.}$ 1685. 　　[3] Despatch of the Dutch Ambassadors, May $\frac{19}{29}$. 1685.

TITUS OATES IN THE PILLORY

From a Dutch engraving in the Sutherland Collection

not in England alone that these events excited strong interest. Millions of Roman Catholics, who knew nothing of our institutions or of our factions, had heard that a persecution of singular barbarity had raged in our island against the professors of the true faith, that many pious men had suffered martyrdom, and that Titus Oates had been the chief murderer. There was, therefore, great joy in distant countries when it was known that the divine justice had overtaken him. Engravings of him, looking out from the pillory, and writhing at the cart's tail, were circulated all over Europe; and epigrammatists, in many languages, made merry with the doctoral title which he pretended to have received from the University of Salamanca, and remarked that, since his forehead could not be made to blush, it was but reasonable that his back should do so.[1]

Horrible as were the sufferings of Oates, they did not equal his crimes. The old law of England, which had been suffered to become obsolete, treated the false witness, who had caused death by means of perjury, as a murderer.[2] This was wise and righteous; for such a witness is, in truth, the worst of murderers. To the guilt of shedding innocent blood he has added the guilt of violating the most solemn engagement into which man can enter with his fellow men, and of making institutions, to which it is desirable that the public should look with respect and confidence, instruments of frightful wrong and objects of general distrust. The pain produced by ordinary murder bears no proportion to the pain produced by murder of which the courts of justice are made the agents. The mere extinction of life is a very small part of what makes an execution horrible. The prolonged mental agony of the sufferer, the shame and misery of all connected with him, the stain abiding even to the third and fourth generation, are things far more dreadful than death itself. In general it may be safely affirmed that

---

[1] Evelyn's Diary, May 22. 1685; Eachard, iii. 741.; Burnet, i. 637.; Observator, May 27. 1685; Oates's Εἰκών, 89.; Εἰκὼν βροτολοιγοῦ, 1697; Commons' Journals of May, June, and July, 1689; Tom Brown's Advice to Dr. Oates. Some interesting circumstances are mentioned in a broadside, printed for A. Brooks, Charing Cross, 1685. I have seen contemporary French and Italian pamphlets containing the history of the trial and execution. A print of Titus in the pillory was published at Milan, with the following curious inscription: "Questo è il naturale ritratto di Tito Otez, o vero Oatz, Inglese, posto in berlina, uno de' principali professori della religion protestante, acerrimo persecutore de' Cattolici, e gran spergiuro." I have also seen a Dutch engraving of his punishment, with some Latin verses, of which the following are a specimen:

"At Doctor fictus non fictos pertulit ictus,
A tortore datos haud molli in corpore gratos,
Disceret ut vere scelera ob commissa rubere."

The anagram of his name, "Testis Ovat," may be found on many prints published in different countries.

[2] Blackstone's Commentaries, Chapter of Homicide.

DANGERFIELDs Dance.

Giving an Account of several Notorious Crimes by him Committed; *VIZ.*

He pretended to be a DUKE,

And feigned Himself to be MONMOUTH.

With several other PRANKS: For which he was Sentenced

To Stand in the *Pillory*, to be VVhip'd at the *Carts Arse*, and to be sent back to Prison.

This may be Printed, *July* 2. 1685. *R. L. S.*   *Entred according to Order*

It is no Wonder in this *Crittick Age*,
To see Offenders mounted on the Stage,
And Shameful Punishment on them attend,
Who on their Shamming Wits so much depend;
Scourging and *Pillorys* fall to their share,
But all too little to make them beware:
And *Impudence* to such a heighth is grown,
As I believe the like was never known.
Here you may see how *Dangerfeld*'s Afpir'd!
Who needs would be a *Duke!* by all admir'd!
His subtile *Crotchets*, and his cunning Pate,
Hath brought his Person to a dreadful State.
How he did Scamper, if you did but mind,
When on his Back he did the Torment find
Of Scourging Justice, it would make you Smile,
To see how Fortune did his hopes beguile;
And brought his feigned *Highness* to the Lash,
Till brinish Tears his Brazen-Face did Wash.
O hapless *Dangerfeld!* thou art mistook,
That did for *Honour* and *Obedience* look.
Thy great Ambition all Men do Rebuke,
Could nothing serve, but thou must be a DUKE?
Fie, fie, it was too great and high a Scile,
Tho' Fortune for a moment feem'd to Smile;
Yet from thy Honour thou cam'st tumbling down,
When she once fac'd about on thee to Frown:
Old *Newgate* was the place to Entertain
The *Shamming* DUKE, where thou didst long remain;
Till thou wert *Whipt* and *Scourg'd* along the Streets,
Which seem'd so *Sowre Sauce* after so many *Sweets*;

Yet 'twas but Just thou should'st it undergo,
Because that you such *Shirking Tricks* did shew;
And brought thee unto Condign Punishment,
Ift please Your Highness, what was your intent?
Poor VVomen to deceive, and get their Coyn,
It is no better then for to *Purloyn*;
And make the VVorld believe thou wert some Spark
VVho had such Honour from thy Servant *Mark*,
Like *Oats*, thy hopes are now in pieces crash'd,
The Brains of thy Ambition out are dash'd.
Whipping, instead of *Cringing* unto thee,
Thou may'st expect will now thy Portion be.
Thy Name for ever will be on Record,
Thou must not be a *Duke*, nor yet a *Lord*;
A *Newgate-Bird* thou may'st accounted be,
Highly deserving of the *PILLORY*.
And since so Arch and Cunning thou art grown,
To play such Pranks as ne'r before was known;
Tis pitty thou should'st want of thy Desert,
Tho' now thy Title is not worth a *Fart*.
And so *Duke Dangerfeld* I bid adieu,
A thousand *Lashes* I bequeath to you;
And hope you may to others warning be,
Never to practice such base Villany.
Your Suffering, you cannot well deny,
Is the Reward of your Audacity;
To this your Reason cannot chuse but yield,
And now look to your Hits, *Duke Dangerfeld.*
FINIS.

London, Printed by *J. M.* in the Year MDCLXXXV.

DANGERFIELD'S DANCE

From the Bagford Ballads

the father of a large family would rather be bereaved of all his children by accident or by disease than lose one of them by the hands of the hangman.   Murder by false testimony is therefore the most aggravated species of murder ; and Oates had been guilty of many such murders. Nevertheless the punishment which was inflicted upon him cannot be justified.   In sentencing him to be stripped of his ecclesiastical habit and imprisoned for life, the judges exceeded their legal power.   They were undoubtedly competent to inflict whipping ; nor had the law assigned a limit to the number of stripes.   But the spirit of the law clearly was that no misdemeanour should be punished more severely than the most atrocious felonies.   The worst felon could only be hanged. The judges, as they believed, sentenced Oates to be scourged to death. That the law was defective is not a sufficient excuse : for defective laws should be altered by the legislature, and not strained by the tribunals ; and least of all should the law be strained for the purpose of inflicting torture and destroying life.   That Oates was a bad man is not a sufficient excuse ; for the guilty are almost always the first to suffer those hardships which are afterwards used as precedents against the innocent. Thus it was in the present case.   Merciless flogging soon became an ordinary punishment for political misdemeanours of no very aggravated kind.   Men were sentenced, for words spoken against the government, to pain so excruciating that they, with unfeigned earnestness, begged to be brought to trial on capital charges, and sent to the gallows.   Happily the progress of this great evil was speedily stopped by the Revolution, and by that article of the Bill of Rights which condemns all cruel and unusual punishments.

The villany of Dangerfield had not, like that of Oates, destroyed many innocent victims ; for Dangerfield had not taken up the trade of a witness till the plot had been blown upon and till juries had become incredulous.[1]   He was brought to trial, not for perjury, but for the less heinous offence of libel.   He had, during the agitation caused by the Exclusion Bill, put forth a narrative containing some false and odious imputations on the late and on the present King. For this publication he was now, after the lapse of five years, suddenly taken up, brought before the Privy Council, committed, tried, convicted, and sentenced to be whipped from Aldgate to Newgate and from Newgate to Tyburn.   The wretched man behaved with great effrontery during the trial ; but, when he heard his doom, he went into agonies of

Proceedings against Dangerfield

---

[1] According to Roger North the judges decided that Dangerfield, having been previously convicted of perjury, was incompetent to be a witness of the plot.   But this is one among many instances of Roger's inaccuracy.   It appears, from the report of the trial of Lord Castlemaine in June 1680, that, after much altercation between counsel, and much consultation among the judges of the different courts in Westminster Hall, Dangerfield was sworn and suffered to tell his story : but the jury very properly gave no credit to his testimony.

A True Relation of the SENTENCE and CONDEMNATION of Thomas Dangerfield, at the King's Bench Bar, for his horrid Crimes and Perjuries.

THE Great Myſtery of Iniquity being now in a great meaſure laid open, and the long Phanatical Vizor to ſhrowd their own Helliſh Deſigns, under the pretended Danger of *Popery* and Arbitrary Power, that old Stale *cheat*, that ſo lately brought the beſt of Monarchs to a Scaffold, and Three flouriſhing Kingdoms to Confuſion, being now taken off; it has pleaſed Heaven to bring the Blackeſt of *Villains*, and Vileſt of *Impoſtors*, the late infamouſly memorable *Titus Otes*, to ſome part of a Puniſhment for his moſt egregious and unexampled Deluſions and Perjuries. And *Truth* and *Reaſon* beginning to run in their right Channel again, one of the junior Imps of this ſenior *Belzebub, viz. Thomas Dangerfield*, has been alſo brought to taſte the ſame *laſh* with him.

Now as there's a certain way of Eternizing a Man's Name, as well by the *blackeſt* of Impieties, as the *brighteſt* of *Vertues*; and one ſingle *Judas* ſhall be as long remembred, and recorded, as the whole *Twelve Apoſtles*; or whether one Devil or all of them (which is moſt likely) had a hand in hardening the Fronts, and ſeering the Conſciences of our late Saviours of the Nation (the Diſcoverers of the Pretended *Popiſh Plot*) to bring them to the *Kiſſing* of *Bibles, Swallowing* of *Oaths* and *Sacraments*, the barbarous ſhedding of *Innocent Blood*, and the renouncing of *Heaven* and *Eternity*; and all to miſlead a Jealous unthinking Kingdom to Lunacy and Madneſs, and conſequently, to *Treaſon* and *Rebellion*, and ſo in a fair way to *Hell* and *Damnation*, it matters not.

But in ſhort our Grand *Beukblawer, Titus*, that truly Original of the kind, came upon our Blind ſide with his Popiſh Diſcovery, a little (as a Man may ſay) like a Jugler of Skill. For though Inviſible Commiſſions, to raiſe Inviſible Armies; whole Thouſands of Arm'd Papiſts, Muſter'd and Diſciplined under-ground; Black Bills, and Pilgrims innumerable at the very Throats of us; and yet the Devil a Mortal Eye, or indeed a Rational Imagination capable ſo much as of conceiving the *when, where*, and *how*, all theſe *Popiſh Engines* were a working: yet, to the credit of little *England* be it ſpoken, all this was *Sworn* to ſo ſolemnly, and believed ſo heartily, and truly almoſt ſo univerſally by the multitude, That really Garlick and Onions, amongſt the old *Egyptians*, were not more eaſily made Gods of, than *Titus* his Narrative made Goſpel.

But though I ſay all this wonderful Diſcovery was rendred almoſt no leſs than Evangelical, yet the Narrative of our True Proteſtant, *Thomas Dangerfield*, ſo far out-does him, That nothing certainly can be more ſtupendiouſly miraculous: For how wide ſoever was the large *Engliſh* ſwallow, and how Romantick ſoever was *Titus's* Diſcovery, the Gorgon was ſtill of a piece: and *Otes*, with the ſofter Front of Braſs, was graciouſly pleaſed to give us a plain and manifeſt Compurgation of his preſent Majeſty, from ſo much as a *Thought* of Conſpiring againſt his Brother; inſtancing the careful conduct of the Jeſuits, in concealing the whole Plot from him, as conſcious of the untaintable Integrity, and immoveable Loyalty of ſo Faithful a Friend and Dear a Brother. Nay, he was ſo far from being ſuſpected even the leaſt plyable to their Popiſh Deſigns, That the ſame Death that was intended his Brother, was threatned Him alſo; and no leſs than the whole *Race* of the *Stuarts*, expreſly in his Narrative, *Root* and *Branch* to be extirpated by the Popiſh Conſpirators.

But to confront all this, up ſtarts *Dangerfield*, and ſince Swearing was grown ſo beneficial, and every new Projector ought to out-ſhoot the firſt Bolt; very briskly, with an Impudence even beyond *Otes* himſelf, Forges ſuch a Maſs of Villany, not to be named without Execration and Horror.

The hidious Contexture of his whole Libelous Narrative, to confirm this Diabolical piece of *Perjury*, is all ſo much of the ſame *Infernal Hew*; That, in ſhort, it has long ſince anſwered it ſelf. Nay, in the very height of the late True Proteſtant *Implicite* Faith, the higheſt ferment of the then Reigning *Phanaticiſm*, and when almoſt every thing went down, our *Dangerfield* ſo far over-acted the true Proteſtant *Plot Evidence* in his whole Narrative, that the very Faction that ſet up the Tool, and who at that time of day had Inſolence enough, even to Depoſe Princes, were, neverthelesſ ſo modeſt, and indeed, ſo aſhamed of our Captain *Willoughby's*, alias *Dangerfield's* Diſcovery, That they laid it aſide as Waſte Paper, and never ſo much as indeavoured to ſtart up his Teſtimony, though for their deareſt darling Idol the *Excluſion* Bill, and the Propagation of the moſt ſacred *Good Old Cauſe*. This was the *Diſcoverer*, and this the *Monſter*, that now-Juſtice has brought to his too much merited Publick Shame and Infamy.

See here the Minor *Undergraduate Tool*,	March, honeſt Ketch, devoutly his by ſide,
Takes his Degree i'th' *Doctor's* Flogging School:	And Diſcipline, dear Jack, his Perjured Hide.
Whilſt the brisk Captain does in ſtate advance,	The outward Man of Sin's within thy Power;
To Titus his Old Jigg, the Tyburn Dance.	But the foul inſide let the Devil ſcowr.

This may be Printed. July 2. 1685. R. L. S.

LONDON: Printed, and are to be Sold by *Walter Davis* in *Amen-Corner*. 1685.

A TRUE RELATION OF THE SENTENCE AND CONDEMNATION OF
THOMAS DANGERFIELD

despair, gave himself up for dead, and chose a text for his funeral
sermon.   His forebodings were just.   He was not, indeed, scourged
quite so severely as Oates had been ; but he had not Oates's iron
strength of body and mind.   After the execution Dangerfield was put
into a hackney coach and was taken back to prison.   As he passed the
corner of Hatton Garden, a Tory gentleman of Gray's Inn, named
Francis, stopped the carriage, and cried out with brutal levity, " Well,
friend, have you had your heat this morning ? "   The bleeding prisoner,
maddened by this insult, answered with a curse.   Francis instantly
struck him in the face with a cane which injured the eye.   Dangerfield
was carried dying into Newgate.   This dastardly outrage roused the
indignation of the bystanders.   They seized Francis, and were with
difficulty restrained from tearing him to pieces.   The appearance of
Dangerfield's body, which had been frightfully lacerated by the whip,
inclined many to believe that his death was chiefly, if not wholly, caused
by the stripes which he had received.   The government and the Chief
Justice thought it convenient to lay the whole blame on Francis, who,
though he seems to have been at worst guilty only of aggravated man-
slaughter, was tried and executed for murder.   His dying speech is one
of the most curious monuments of that age.   The savage spirit which
had brought him to the gallows remained with him to the last.   Boasts
of his loyalty and abuse of the Whigs were mingled with the parting
ejaculations in which he commended his soul to the divine mercy.   An
idle rumour had been circulated that his wife was in love with Dangerfield, who was eminently handsome and renowned for gallantry.   The
fatal blow, it was said, had been prompted by jealousy.   The dying
husband, with an earnestness, half ridiculous, half pathetic, vindicated
the lady's character.   She was, he said, a virtuous woman : she came of
a loyal stock, and, if she had been inclined to break her marriage vow,
would at least have selected a Tory and a churchman for her paramour.[1]

About the same time a culprit, who bore very little resemblance to
Oates or Dangerfield, appeared on the floor of the Court of King's
Proceedings   Bench.   No eminent chief of a party has ever passed through
against   many years of civil and religious dissension with more
Baxter   innocence than Richard Baxter.   He belonged to the mildest
and most temperate section of the Puritan body.   He was a young man

---

[1] Dangerfield's trial was not reported ; but I have seen a concise account of it in a contemporary broadside.   An abstract of the evidence against Francis, and his dying speech, will be
found in the Collection of State Trials.   See Eachard, iii. 741.   Burnet's narrative contains more
mistakes than lines.   See also North's Examen, 256., the sketch of Dangerfield's life in the
Bloody Assizes, the Observator of July 29. 1685, and the poem entitled " Dangerfield's Ghost to
Jeffreys."   In the very rare volume entitled " Succinct Genealogies, by Robert Halstead," Lord
Peterborough says that Dangerfield, with whom he had had some intercourse, was "a young
man who appeared under a decent figure, a serious behaviour, and with words that did not seem
to proceed from a common understanding."

RICHARD BAXTER

From the painting in the National Portrait Gallery. Artist unknown

when the civil war broke out. He thought that the right was on the side of the Houses ; and he had no scruple about acting as chaplain to a regiment in the parliamentary army : but his clear and somewhat sceptical understanding, and his strong sense of justice, preserved him from all excesses. He exerted himself to check the fanatical violence of the soldiery. He condemned the proceedings of the High Court of Justice. In the days of the Commonwealth he had the boldness to express, on many occasions, and once even in Cromwell's presence, love and reverence for the ancient institutions of the country. While the royal family was in exile, Baxter's life was chiefly passed at Kidderminster in the assiduous discharge of parochial duties. He heartily concurred in the Restoration, and was sincerely desirous to bring about an union between Episcopalians and Presbyterians. For, with a liberality rare in his time, he considered questions of ecclesiastical polity as of small account when compared with the great principles of Christianity, and had never, even when prelacy was most odious to the ruling powers, joined in the outcry against Bishops. The attempt to reconcile the contending factions failed. Baxter cast in his lot with his proscribed friends, refused the mitre of Hereford, quitted the parsonage of Kidderminster, and gave himself up almost wholly to study. His theological writings, though too moderate to be pleasing to the bigots of any party, had an immense reputation. Zealous Churchmen called him a Roundhead ; and many Nonconformists accused him of Erastianism and Arminianism. But the integrity of his heart, the purity of his life, the vigour of his faculties, and the extent of his attainments were acknowledged by the best and wisest men of every persuasion. His political opinions, in spite of the oppression which he and his brethren had suffered, were moderate. He was friendly to that small party which was hated by both Whigs and Tories. He could not, he said, join in cursing the Trimmers, when he remembered who it was that had blessed the peacemakers.[1]

In a Commentary on the New Testament he had complained, with some bitterness, of the persecution which the Dissenters suffered. That men who, for not using the Prayer Book, had been driven from their homes, stripped of their property, and locked up in dungeons, should dare to utter a murmur, was then thought a high crime against the State and the Church. Roger Lestrange, the champion of the government and the oracle of the clergy, sounded the note of war in the Observator. An information was filed. Baxter begged that he might be allowed some time to prepare for his defence. It was on the day on which Oates was pilloried in Palace Yard that the illustrious chief of the Puritans, oppressed by age and infirmities, came to Westminster

[1] Baxter's preface to Sir Matthew Hale's Judgment of the Nature of True Religion, 1684.

Hall to make this request. Jeffreys burst into a storm of rage. "Not a minute," he cried, "to save his life. I can deal with saints as well as with sinners. There stands Oates on one side of the pillory; and, if Baxter stood on the other, the two greatest rogues in the kingdom would stand together."

When the trial came on at Guildhall, a crowd of those who loved and honoured Baxter filled the court. At his side stood Doctor William Bates, one of the most eminent of the Nonconformist divines. Two Whig barristers of great note, Pollexfen and Wallop, appeared for the defendant. Pollexfen had scarcely begun his address to the jury, when the Chief Justice broke forth: "Pollexfen, I know you well. I will set a mark on you. You are the patron of the faction. This is an old rogue, a schismatical knave, a hypocritical villain. He hates the Liturgy. He would have nothing but longwinded cant without book:" and then his Lordship turned up his eyes, clasped his hands, and began to sing through his nose, in imitation of what he supposed to be Baxter's style of praying, "Lord, we are thy people, thy peculiar people, thy dear people." Pollexfen gently reminded the court that his late Majesty had thought Baxter deserving of a bishopric. "And what ailed the old block-head then," cried Jeffreys, "that he did not take it?" His fury now rose almost to madness. He called Baxter a dog, and swore that it would be no more than justice to whip such a villain through the whole City.

Wallop interposed, but fared no better than his leader. "You are in all these dirty causes, Mr Wallop," said the Judge. "Gentlemen of the long robe ought to be ashamed to assist such factious knaves." The advocate made another attempt to obtain a hearing, but to no purpose. "If you do not know your duty," said Jeffreys, "I will teach it you."

Wallop sate down; and Baxter himself attempted to put in a word. But the Chief Justice drowned all expostulation in a torrent of ribaldry and invective, mingled with scraps of Hudibras. "My Lord," said the old man, "I have been much blamed by Dissenters for speaking respectfully of Bishops." "Baxter for Bishops!" cried the Judge, "that's a merry conceit indeed. I know what you mean by Bishops, rascals like yourself, Kidderminster Bishops, factious snivelling Presbyterians!" Again Baxter essayed to speak, and again Jeffreys bellowed, "Richard, Richard, dost thou think we will let thee poison the court? Richard, thou art an old knave. Thou hast written books enough to load a cart, and every book as full of sedition as an egg is full of meat. By the grace of God, I'll look after thee. I see a great many of your brotherhood waiting to know what will befall their mighty Don. And there," he continued, fixing his savage eye on Bates, "there is a Doctor of the party at your elbow. But, by the grace of God Almighty, I will crush you all."

Baxter held his peace. But one of the junior counsel for the defence made a last effort, and undertook to show that the words of which complaint was made would not bear the construction put on them by the information. With this view he began to read the context. In a moment he was roared down. " You sha'n't turn the court into a conventicle." The noise of weeping was heard from some of those who surrounded Baxter. " Snivelling calves ! " said the Judge.

Witnesses to character were in attendance, and among them were several clergymen of the Established Church. But the Chief Justice would hear nothing. " Does your Lordship think," said Baxter, " that any jury will convict a man on such a trial as this ? " " I warrant you, Mr Baxter," said Jeffreys : " don't trouble yourself about that." Jeffreys was right. The Sheriffs were the tools of the government. The jurymen, selected by the Sheriffs from among the fiercest zealots of the Tory party, conferred for a moment, and returned a verdict of Guilty. " My Lord," said Baxter, as he left the court, " there was once a Chief Justice who would have treated me very differently." He alluded to his learned and virtuous friend Sir Matthew Hale. " There is not an honest man in England," answered Jeffreys, " but looks on thee as a knave." [1]

The sentence was, for those times, a lenient one. What passed in conference among the judges cannot be certainly known. It was believed among the Nonconformists, and is highly probable, that the Chief Justice was overruled by his three brethren. He proposed, it is said, that Baxter should be whipped through London at the cart's tail. The majority thought that an eminent divine, who, a quarter of a century before, had been offered a mitre, and who was now in his seventieth year, would be sufficiently punished for a few sharp words by fine and imprisonment. [2]

The manner in which Baxter was treated by a judge, who was a member of the cabinet and a favourite of the Sovereign, indicated, in

Meeting of the Parliament of Scotland

a manner not to be mistaken, the feeling with which the government at this time regarded the Protestant Nonconformists. But already that feeling had been indicated by still stronger and more terrible signs. The Parliament of Scotland had met. James had purposely hastened the session of this body, and had postponed the session of the English Houses, in the hope that the example set at Edinburgh would produce a good effect at Westminster. For the legislature of his northern kingdom was as obsequious as those provincial Estates which Lewis the Fourteenth still suffered to play at

[1] See the Observator of February 25. 1685, the information in the Collection of State Trials, the account of what passed in court given by Calamy, Life of Baxter, chap. xiv., and the very curious extracts from the Baxter MSS. in the Life, by Orme, published in 1830.

[2] Baxter MS. cited by Orme.

The Reverend & Learned
WILLIAM BATES D.D.
Obyt 14. Iuly 1699. Ætat. 74.

WILLIAM BATES

From an engraving by White after a portrait by Sir G. Kneller some of their ancient functions in Britanny and Burgundy. None but an Episcopalian could sit in the Scottish Parliament, or could even vote for a member, and in Scotland an Episcopalian was always a Tory or a timeserver. From an assembly thus constituted little opposition to the royal wishes was to be apprehended ; and even the assembly thus constituted could pass no law which had not been previously approved by a committee of courtiers.

All that the government asked was readily granted. In a financial point of view, indeed, the liberality of the Scottish Estates was of little consequence. They gave, however, what their scanty means permitted. They annexed in perpetuity to the crown the duties which had been granted to the late King, and which in his time had been estimated at forty thousand pounds sterling a year. They also settled on James for life an additional annual income of two hundred and sixteen thousand pounds Scots, equivalent to eighteen thousand pounds sterling. The whole sum which they were able to bestow was about sixty thousand a year, little more than what was poured into the English Exchequer every fortnight.[1]

Having little money to give, the Estates supplied the defect by loyal professions and barbarous statutes. The King, in a letter which was read to them at the opening of their session, called on them in vehement language to provide new penal laws against the refractory Presbyterians, and expressed his regret that business made it impossible for him to propose such laws in person from the throne. His commands were obeyed. A statute framed by his ministers was promptly passed, a statute which stands forth, even among the statutes of that unhappy country at that unhappy period, preeminent in atrocity. It was enacted, in few but emphatic words, that whoever should preach in a conventicle under a roof, or should attend, either as preacher or as hearer, a conventicle in the open air, should be punished with death and confiscation of property.[2]

This law, passed at the King's instance by an assembly devoted to his will, deserves especial notice. For he has been frequently repre-

Feeling of James towards the Puritans sented by ignorant writers as a prince rash, indeed, and injudicious in his choice of means, but intent on one of the noblest ends which a ruler can pursue, the establishment of entire religious liberty. Nor can it be denied that some portions of his life, when detached from the rest and superficially considered, seem to warrant this favourable view of his character.

While a subject he had been, during many years, a persecuted man ;

[1] Act. Parl. Car. II. March 29. 1661 ; Jac. VII. April 28. 1685, and May 13. 1685.

[2] Act. Parl. Jac. VII. May 8. 1685 ; Observator, June 20. 1685. Lestrange evidently wished to see the precedent followed in England.

and persecution had produced its usual effect on him. His mind, dull and narrow as it was, had profited under that sharp discipline. While he was excluded from the Court, from the Admiralty, and from the Council, and was in danger of being also excluded from the throne, only because he could not help believing in transubstantiation and in the authority of the see of Rome, he made such rapid progress in the doctrines of toleration that he left Milton and Locke behind. What, he often said, could be more unjust, than to visit speculations with penalties which ought to be reserved for acts? What more impolitic than to reject the services of good soldiers, seamen, lawyers, diplomatists, financiers, because they hold unsound opinions about the number of the sacraments or the pluripresence of saints? He learned by rote those commonplaces which all sects repeat so fluently when they are enduring oppression, and forget so easily when they are able to retaliate it. Indeed he rehearsed his lesson so well, that those who chanced to hear him on this subject gave him credit for much more sense and much readier elocution than he really possessed. His professions imposed on some charitable persons, and perhaps imposed on himself. But his zeal for the rights of conscience ended with the predominance of the Whig party. When fortune changed, when he was no longer afraid that others would persecute him, when he had it in his power to persecute others, his real propensities began to show themselves. He hated the Puritan sects with a manifold hatred, theological and political, hereditary and personal. He regarded them as the foes of Heaven, as the foes of all legitimate authority in Church and State, as his greatgrandmother's foes and his grandfather's, his father's and his mother's, his brother's and his own. He, who had complained so loudly of the laws against Papists, now declared himself unable to conceive how men could have the impudence to propose the repeal of the laws against Puritans.[1] He, whose favourite theme had been the injustice of requiring civil functionaries to take religious tests, established in Scotland, when he resided there as Viceroy, the most rigorous religious test that has ever been known in the empire.[2] He, who had expressed just indignation when the priests of his own faith were hanged and quartered, amused himself with hearing Covenanters shriek and seeing them writhe while their knees were beaten flat in the boots.[3] In this mood he became King; and he im-

[1] His own words reported by himself. Life of James the Second, i. 656. Orig. Mem.

[2] Act. Parl. Car. II. August 31. 1681.

[3] Burnet, i. 583 ; Wodrow, III. v. 2. Unfortunately the Acta of the Scottish Privy Council during almost the whole administration of the Duke of York are wanting. (1848.) This assertion has been met by a direct contradiction. But the fact is exactly as I have stated it. There is in the Acta of the Scottish Privy Council a hiatus extending from August 1678 to August 1682. The Duke of York began to reside in Scotland in December 1679. He left Scotland, never to return, in May 1682. (1857.)

mediately demanded and obtained from the obsequious Estates of Scotland, as the surest pledge of their loyalty, the most sanguinary law that has ever in our island been enacted against Protestant Nonconformists.

With this law the whole spirit of his administration was in perfect harmony.   The fiery persecution, which had raged when he ruled **Cruel treatment of the Scotch Covenanters** Scotland as vicegerent, waxed hotter than ever from the day on which he became sovereign.   Those shires in which the Covenanters were most numerous were given up to the license of the army.   With the army was mingled a militia, composed of the most violent and profligate of those who called themselves Episcopalians.   Preeminent among the bands which oppressed and wasted these unhappy districts were the dragoons commanded by John Graham of Claverhouse.   The story ran that these wicked men used in their revels to play at the torments of hell, and to call each other by the names of devils and damned souls.[1]   The chief of this Tophet, a soldier of distinguished courage and professional skill, but rapacious and profane, of violent temper and of obdurate heart, has left a name which, wherever the Scottish race is settled on the face of the globe, is mentioned with a peculiar energy of hatred.   To recapitulate all the crimes, by which this man, and men like him, goaded the peasantry of the Western Lowlands into madness, would be an endless task.   A few instances must suffice ; and all those instances shall be taken from the history of a single fortnight, that very fortnight in which the Scottish Parliament, at the urgent request of James, enacted a new law of unprecedented severity against Dissenters.

John Brown, a poor carrier of Lanarkshire, was, for his singular piety, commonly called the Christian carrier.   Many years later, when Scotland enjoyed rest, prosperity, and religious freedom, old men who remembered the evil days described him as one versed in divine things, blameless in life, and so peaceable that the tyrants could find no offence in him except that he absented himself from the public worship of the Episcopalians.   On the first of May he was cutting turf, when he was seized by Claverhouse's dragoons, rapidly examined, convicted of nonconformity, and sentenced to death.   It is said that, even among the soldiers, it was not easy to find an executioner.   For the wife of the poor man was present : she led one little child by the hand : it was easy to see that she was about to give birth to another ; and even those wild and hardhearted men, who nicknamed one another Beelzebub and Apollyon, shrank from the great wickedness of butchering her husband before her face.   The prisoner, meanwhile, raised above himself by the near prospect of eternity, prayed loud and fervently as one inspired, till

[1] Wodrow, III. ix. 6.

Claverhouse, in a fury, shot him dead. It was reported by credible witnesses that the widow cried out in her agony, " Well, sir, well ; the day of reckoning will come ; " and that the murderer replied, " To man I can answer for what I have done ; and as for God, I will take him into mine own hand." Yet it was rumoured that even on his seared conscience and adamantine heart the dying ejaculations of his victim made an impression which was never effaced.[1]

On the fifth of May two artisans, Peter Gillies and John Bryce, were tried in Ayrshire by a military tribunal consisting of fifteen soldiers. The indictment is still extant. The prisoners were charged, not with any act of rebellion, but with holding the same pernicious doctrines which had impelled others to rebel, and with wanting only opportunity to act upon those doctrines. The proceeding was summary. In a few hours the two culprits were convicted, hanged, and flung together into a hole under the gallows.[2]

The eleventh of May was made remarkable by more than one great crime. Some rigid Calvinists had from the doctrine of reprobation drawn the consequence that to pray for any person who had been pre-destined to perdition was an act of mutiny against the eternal decrees of the Supreme Being. Three poor labouring men, deeply imbued with this unamiable divinity, were stopped by an officer in the neighbour-hood of Glasgow. They were asked whether they would pray for King James the Seventh. They refused to do so except under the condition that he was one of the elect. A file of musketeers was drawn out. The prisoners knelt down : they were blindfolded ; and, within an hour after they had been arrested, their blood was lapped up by the dogs.[3]

---

[1] Wodrow, III. ix. 6. The editor of the Oxford edition of Burnet attempts to excuse this act by alleging that Claverhouse was then employed to intercept all communication between Argyle and Monmouth, and by supposing that John Brown may have been detected in conveying intel-ligence between the rebel camps. Unfortunately for this hypothesis John Brown was shot on the first of May, when both Argyle and Monmouth were in Holland, and when there was no insur-rection in any part of our island.

[2] Wodrow, III. ix. 6.

[3] Ibid. It has been confidently asserted, by persons who have not taken the trouble to look at the authority to which I have referred, that I have grossly calumniated these unfortunate men ; that I do not understand the Calvinistic theology ; and that it is impossible that members of the Church of Scotland can have refused to pray for any man, on the ground that he was not one of the elect.

I can only refer to the narrative which Wodrow has inserted in his History, and which he justly calls plain and natural. That narrative is signed by two eyewitnesses, and Wodrow, before he published it, submitted it to a third eyewitness who pronounced it strictly accurate. From that narrative I will extract the only words which bear on the point in question : " When all the three were taken, the officers consulted among themselves, and, withdrawing to the west side of the town, questioned the prisoners, particularly if they would pray for King James VII. They answered, they would pray for all within the election of grace. Balfour said, Do you

My Lord

Upon saturdays night when my lord
Ross came in to this place I marched out and
becaus of the insolency that was don
tuu nights befor at Ruglen I went thither
and inquyred for their names. so soon as I got
them I sent out partys to seas on them
and found not only three of those rogues
but also ane intercomend minister called King
we had them at Strevin about sex in
the morning yesterday. and resolving
to conboy them to this I thoght that we
might maka litle tour to see if we could
fall upon a conventicle which did lie
to our advantadge. for when we came
in sight of them we found them drawen
up in batell upon a most advantagious
ground to which there was no coming
but through mosses and lakes. they were
not preaching and had got away all their
women and shildreng. they consisted of
four battallons of foot all well armed with
fuses and pitchforks and three squadrons
off horse. we sent both partys to skirmish
they off foot and we of dragoons they ran
for it and sent down a battallon off foot
against them we sent threescor of dragoons
who mad them run again shamfully but in

FACSIMILE OF A LETTER FROM CLAVERHOUSE TO LORD

From the Stowe Mss.

end. they perceaving that we had the better of them in skirmish they resolved a generall ingadgement. and imidiatly advanced with there foot the horse folowing they came through the loche and the greatest body of all made up against my troup we keeped our fyr till they ware within ten pace of us they receaved our fyr and advanced to the shok they first they gave us brok doun the coronet mr crafford and captain bleith befords that with a schot they made such an opening in my sorder forces fell that his guts hung out half an elle and yet he caryed me af a can myt which so discoraged our men that they sustined not the shok but fell into disorder there horse took the occasion of this and persewd us so hotly that we got no tym to raly. I saved the standarts but lost on the place about aught or ten men besids wounded but the dragoons lost many mor they ar not com affly af on the other place for I saw ga several of them fall befor we cam to the shok. I mad the best retrait the confusion of our people would suffer and am now laying with my Lord Roff. the toun of strotten dron up as now was making our retrait and thoght of a pas to cut us of but we took couradge and fell to them made them run leaving a dousain on the place what thoses rogues will dou next I know not but the contry was floking to them from all hands this may counted the beginning of the rebellion in my openion. I am my Lord

my lord I am so. your lordships most woaried and so sleapy humble sarbant that I shall wryten tas very confusedly

Grahame

While this was done in Clydesdale, an act not less horrible was perpetrated in Eskdale. One of the proscribed Covenanters, overcome by sickness, had found shelter in the house of a respectable widow, and had died there. The corpse was discovered by the Laird of Westerhall, a petty tyrant who had, in the days of the Covenant, professed inordinate zeal for the Presbyterian Church, who had, since the Restoration, purchased the favour of the government by apostasy, and who felt towards the party which he had deserted the implacable hatred of an apostate. This man pulled down the house of the poor woman, carried away her furniture, and, leaving her and her younger children to wander in the fields, dragged her son Andrew, who was still a lad, before Claverhouse, who happened to be marching through that part of the country. Claverhouse was just then strangely lenient. Some thought that he had not been quite himself since the death of the Christian carrier, ten days before. But Westerhall was eager to signalise his loyalty, and extorted a sullen consent. The guns were loaded, and the youth was told to pull his bonnet over his face. He refused, and stood confronting his murderers with the Bible in his hand. " I can look you in the face," he said ; " I have done nothing of which I need be ashamed. But how will you look in that day when you shall be judged by what is written in this book ? " He fell dead, and was buried in the moor.[1]

On the same day two women, Margaret Maclachlan and Margaret Wilson, the former an aged widow, the latter a maiden of eighteen, suffered death for their religion in Wigtonshire. They were offered their lives if they would consent to abjure the cause of the insurgent Covenanters, and to attend the Episcopal worship. They refused ; and they were sentenced to be drowned. They were carried to a spot which the Solway overflows twice a day, and were fastened to stakes fixed in the sand, between high and low water mark. The elder sufferer was placed near to the advancing flood, in the hope that her last agonies might terrify the younger into submission. The sight was dreadful. But the courage of the survivor was sustained by an enthusiasm as lofty as any that is recorded in martyrology. She saw the sea draw nearer and nearer, but gave no sign of alarm. She prayed and sang verses of psalms till the waves choked her voice. After she had tasted the

question the King's election? They answered, sometimes they questioned their own. Upon which he swore dreadfully, and said they should die presently, because they would not pray for Christ's vicegerent, and so, without one word more, commanded Thomas Cook to go to his prayers, for he should die."

In this narrative Wodrow saw nothing improbable ; and I shall not easily be convinced that any writer now living understands the feelings and opinions of the Covenanters better than Wodrow did. (1857.)

[1] Wodrow, III. ix. 6.   Cloud of Witnesses.

THE PERSECUTION OF THE COVENANTERS

From the frontispiece to A Cloud of Witnesses, 1720

bitterness of death, she was, by a cruel mercy, unbound and restored to life. When she came to herself, pitying friends and neighbours implored her to yield. " Dear Margaret, only say, God save the King ! " The poor girl, true to her stern theology, gasped out, " May God save him, if it be God's will ! " Her friends crowded round the presiding officer. " She has said it ; indeed, sir, she has said it." " Will she take the abjuration ? " he demanded. " Never ! " she exclaimed. " I am Christ's : let me go ! " And the waters closed over her for the last time.[1]

Thus was Scotland governed by that prince whom ignorant men have represented as a friend of religious liberty, whose misfortune it was to be too wise and too good for the age in which he lived. Nay, even those laws which authorised him to govern thus were in his judgment reprehensibly lenient. While his officers were committing the murders which have just been related, he was urging the Scottish Parliament to pass a new Act compared with which all former Acts might be called merciful.

In England his authority, though great, was circumscribed by ancient and noble laws which even the Tories would not patiently have seen him infringe. Here he could not hurry Dissenters before military tribunals, or enjoy at Council the luxury of seeing them swoon in the boots. Here he could not drown young girls for refusing to take the abjuration, or shoot poor countrymen for doubting whether he was one of the elect. Yet even in England he continued to persecute the Puritans as far as his power extended, till events which will hereafter be related induced him to form the design of uniting Puritans and Papists in a coalition for the humiliation and spoliation of the Established Church.

One sect of Protestant Dissenters indeed he, even at this early period of his reign, regarded with some tenderness, the Society of **Feeling** Friends. His partiality for that singular fraternity cannot be **of James** **towards the** attributed to religious sympathy ; for, of all who acknowledge **Quakers** the divine mission of Jesus, the Roman Catholic and the Quaker differ most widely. It may seem paradoxical to say that this very circumstance constituted a tie between the Roman Catholic and the Quaker ; yet such was really the case. For they deviated in opposite directions so far from what the great body of the nation

---

[1] Wodrow, III. ix. 6. The epitaph of Margaret Wilson, in the churchyard at Wigton, is printed in the Appendix to the Cloud of Witnesses :

> " Murdered for owning Christ supreme
> Head of his Church, and no more crime,
> But her not owning Prelacy,
> And not abjuring Presbytery,
> Within the sea, tied to a stake,
> She suffered for Christ Jesus' sake."

regarded as right, that even liberal men generally considered them both as lying beyond the pale of the largest toleration. Thus the two extreme sects, precisely because they were extreme sects, had a common interest distinct from the interest of the intermediate sects. The Quakers were also guiltless of all offence against James and his House. They had not been in existence as a community till the war between his father and the Long Parliament was drawing towards a close. They had been cruelly persecuted by some of the revolutionary governments. They had, since the Restoration, in spite of much ill usage, submitted themselves meekly to the royal authority. For they had, though reasoning on premises which the Anglican divines regarded as heterodox, arrived, like the Anglican divines, at the conclusion, that no excess of tyranny on the part of a prince can justify active resistance on the part of a subject. No libel on the government had ever been traced to a Quaker.[1] In no conspiracy against the government had a Quaker been implicated. The society had not joined in the clamour for the Exclusion Bill, and had solemnly condemned the Rye House plot as a hellish design and a work of the devil.[2] Indeed, the Friends then took very little part in civil contentions; for they were not, as now, congregated in large towns, but were generally engaged in agriculture, a pursuit from which they have been gradually driven by the vexations consequent on their strange scruple about paying tithe. They were, therefore, far removed from the scene of political strife. They also, even in domestic privacy, avoided on principle all political conversation. For such conversation was, in their opinion, unfavourable to their spirituality of mind, and tended to disturb the austere composure of their deportment. The yearly meetings of that age repeatedly admonished the brethren not to hold discourse touching affairs of state.[3] Even within the memory of persons now living those grave elders who retained the habits of an earlier generation systematically discouraged such worldly talk.[4] It was natural that James should make a wide distinction between these harmless people and those fierce and restless sects which considered resistance to tyranny as a Christian duty, which had, in Germany, France, and Holland, made war on legitimate princes, and which had, during four generations, borne peculiar enmity to the House of Stuart.

It happened, moreover, that it was possible to grant large relief to the Roman Catholic and to the Quaker without mitigating the sufferings of the Puritan sects. A law was in force which imposed severe penalties

---

[1] See the letter to King Charles II. prefixed to Barclay's Apology.

[2] Sewel's History of the Quakers, book x.

[3] Minutes of Yearly Meetings, 1689, 1690.

[4] Clarkson on Quakerism; Peculiar Customs, chapter v.

on every person who refused to take the oath of supremacy when required to do so. This law did not affect Presbyterians, Independents,

John the Quaker
Le Trembleur de Londre
Bachetone di Londra

Maurion delin   P Tempest exc
Cum Privilegio

A QUAKER

From Tempest's Cries of London

or Baptists; for they were all ready to call God to witness that they renounced all spiritual connection with foreign prelates and potentates.

But the Roman Catholic would not swear that the Pope had no jurisdiction in England, and the Quaker would not swear to anything. On
the other hand, neither the Roman Catholic nor the Quaker was touched

The London Quaker

M.auron delin.
I.Savage sculp

P.Tempest ex:
Cum privilegio

A FEMALE QUAKER

From Tempest's Cries of London

by the Five Mile Act, which, of all the laws in the Statute Book, was
perhaps the most annoying to the Puritan Nonconformists.[1]

[1] After this passage was written, I found, in the British Museum, a manuscript (Harl. MS.
7506.) entitled, "An Account of the Seizures, Sequestrations, great Spoil and Havock made

The Quakers had a powerful and zealous advocate at court.　Though, as a class, they mixed little with the world, and shunned politics as a pursuit dangerous to their spiritual interests, one of them,

William Penn

widely distinguished from the rest by station and fortune, lived in the highest circles, and had constant access to the royal ear. This was the celebrated William Penn.　His father had held great naval commands, had been a Commissioner of the Admiralty, had sate in Parliament, had received the honour of knighthood, and had been encouraged to expect a peerage.　The son had been liberally educated, and had been designed for the profession of arms, but had, while still young, injured his prospects and disgusted his friends by joining what was then generally considered as a gang of crazy heretics.　He had been sent sometimes to the Tower, and sometimes to Newgate.　He had been tried at the Old Bailey for preaching in defiance of the law. After a time, however, he had been reconciled to his family, and had succeeded in obtaining such powerful protection that, while all the gaols of England were filled with his brethren, he was permitted, during many years, to profess his opinions without molestation.　Towards the close of the late reign he had obtained, in satisfaction of an old debt due to him from the crown, the grant of an immense region in North America. In this tract, then peopled only by Indian hunters, he had invited his persecuted friends to settle.　His colony was still in its infancy when James mounted the throne.

Between James and Penn there had long been a familiar acquaintance.　The Quaker now became a courtier, and almost a favourite. He was every day summoned from the gallery into the closet, and sometimes had long audiences while peers were kept waiting in the antechambers.　It was noised abroad that he had more real power to help and hurt than many nobles who filled high offices.　He was soon surrounded by flatterers and suppliants.　His house at Kensington was sometimes thronged, at his hour of rising, by more than two hundred suitors.[1]　He paid dear, however, for this seeming prosperity.　Even

upon the Estates of the several Protestant Dissenters called Quakers, upon Prosecution of old Statutes made against Papist and Popish Recusants." The manuscript is marked as having belonged to James, and appears to have been given by his confidential servant, Colonel Graham, to Lord Oxford. This circumstance appears to me to confirm the view which I have taken of the King's conduct towards the Quakers.

[1] Penn's visits to Whitehall, and levees at Kensington, are described with great vivacity, though in very bad Latin, by Gerard Croese.　" Sumebat," he says, " rex sæpe secretum, non horarium, vero horarum plurium, in quo de variis rebus cum Penno serio sermonem conferebat, et interim differebat audire præcipuorum nobilium ordinem, qui hoc interim spatio in procœtone, in proximo, regem conventum præsto erant."　Of the crowd of suitors at Penn's house, Croese says, " Visi quandoque de hoc genere hominum non minus bis centum."—Historia Quakeriana, lib. ii. 1695.

his own sect looked coldly on him, and requited his services with obloquy.   He was loudly accused of being a Papist, nay, a Jesuit. Some affirmed that he had been educated at St. Omers, and others that he had been ordained at Rome.   These calumnies, indeed, could find credit only with the undiscerning multitude : but with these calumnies were mingled accusations much better founded.

To speak the whole truth concerning Penn is a task which requires some courage ; for he is rather a mythical than a historical person. Rival nations and hostile sects have agreed in canonising him.   England is proud of his name.   A great commonwealth beyond the Atlantic regards him with a reverence similar to that which the Athenians felt for Theseus, and the Romans for Quirinus.   The respectable society of which he was a member honours him as an apostle. By pious men of other persuasions he is generally regarded as a bright pattern of Christian virtue.   Meanwhile admirers of a very different sort have sounded his praises.   The French philosophers of the eighteenth century pardoned what they regarded as his superstitious fancies in consideration of his contempt for priests, and of his cosmopolitan benevolence, impartially extended to all races and to all creeds.   His name has thus become, throughout all civilised countries, a synonyme for probity and philanthropy.

Nor is this high reputation altogether unmerited.   Penn was without doubt a man of eminent virtues.   He had a strong sense of religious duty and a fervent desire to promote the happiness of mankind.   On one or two points of high importance he had notions more correct than were, in his day, common even among men of enlarged minds ; and, as the proprietor and legislator of a province which, being almost uninhabited when it came into his possession, afforded a clear field for moral experiments, he had the rare good fortune of being able to carry his theories into practice without any compromise, and yet without any shock to existing institutions.   He will always be mentioned with honour as a founder of a colony, who did not, in his dealings with a savage people, abuse the strength derived from civilisation, and as a lawgiver who, in an age of persecution, made religious liberty the corner stone of a polity.   But his writings and his life furnish abundant proofs that he was not a man of strong sense.   He had no skill in reading the characters of others.   His confidence in persons less virtuous than himself led him into great errors and misfortunes.   His enthusiasm for one great principle sometimes impelled him to violate other great principles which he ought to have held sacred.   Nor was his rectitude altogether proof against the temptations to which it was exposed in that splendid and polite, but deeply corrupted society, with which he now mingled. The whole court was in a ferment with intrigues of gallantry and intrigues of ambition.　The traffic in honours, places, and pardons was incessant.　It was natural that a man who was daily seen at the palace, and who was known to have free access to majesty, should be frequently importuned to use his influence for purposes which a rigid morality must condemn.　The integrity of Penn had stood firm against obloquy and persecution.　But now, attacked by royal smiles, by female blandishments, by the insinuating eloquence and delicate flattery of veteran diplomatists and courtiers, his resolution began to give way.　Titles and phrases against which he had often borne his testimony dropped occasionally from his lips and his pen.　It would be well if he had been guilty of nothing worse than such compliances with the fashions of the world.　Unhappily it cannot be concealed that he bore a chief part in some transactions condemned, not merely by the rigid code of the society to which he belonged, but by the general sense of all honest men.　He afterwards solemnly protested that his hands were pure from illicit gain, and that he had never received any gratuity from those whom he had obliged, though he might easily, while his influence at court lasted, have made a hundred and twenty thousand pounds.[1]　To this assertion full credit is due.　But bribes may be offered to vanity as well as to cupidity; and it is impossible to deny that Penn was cajoled into bearing a part in some unjustifiable transactions of which others enjoyed the profits.

The first use which he made of his credit was highly commendable. He strongly represented the sufferings of his brethren to the new King, who saw with pleasure that it was possible to grant indulgence to these quiet sectaries and to the Roman Catholics, without showing similar favour to other classes which were then under persecution.　A list was framed of prisoners against whom proceedings had been instituted for not taking the oaths, or for not going to church, and of whose loyalty certificates had been produced to the government.　These persons were discharged, and orders were given that no similar proceeding should be instituted till the royal pleasure should be further signified.　In this way about fifteen hundred Quakers, and a still greater number of Roman Catholics, regained their liberty.[2]

Peculiar favour shown to Roman Catholics and Quakers

And now the time had arrived when the English Parliament was to meet.　The members of the House of Commons who had repaired to

---

[1] "Twenty thousand into my pocket; and a hundred thousand into my province."—Penn's Letter to Popple.

[2] These orders, signed by Sunderland, will be found in Sewel's History.　They bear date April 18. 1685.　They are written in a style singularly obscure and intricate; but I think that I have exhibited the meaning correctly.　I have not been able to find any proof that any person, not a Roman Catholic or a Quaker, regained his freedom under these orders.　See Neal's History of the Puritans, vol. ii. chap. ii.; Gerard Croese, lib. ii.　Croese estimates the number of Quakers liberated at fourteen hundred and sixty.

the capital were so numerous that there was much doubt whether their chamber, as it was then fitted up, would afford sufficient accommodation for them. They employed the days which immediately preceded the opening of the session in talking over public affairs with each other and with the agents of the government. A great meeting of the loyal party was held at the Fountain Tavern in the Strand ; and Roger Lestrange, who had recently been knighted by the King, and returned to Parliament by the city of Winchester, took a leading part in their consultations.[1]

It soon appeared that a large portion of the Commons had views which did not altogether agree with those of the Court. The Tory country gentlemen were, with scarcely one exception, desirous to maintain the Test Act and the Habeas Corpus Act ; and some among them talked of voting the revenue only for a term of years. But they were perfectly ready to enact severe laws against the Whigs, and would gladly have seen all the supporters of the Exclusion Bill made incapable of holding office. The King, on the other hand, desired to obtain from the Parliament a revenue for life, the admission of Roman Catholics to office, and the repeal of the Habeas Corpus Act. On these three objects his heart was set ; and he was by no means disposed to accept as a substitute for them a penal law against Exclusionists. Such a law, indeed, would have been positively unpleasing to him ; for one class of Exclusionists stood high in his favour, that class of which Sunderland was the representative, that class which had joined the Whigs in the days of the plot, merely because the Whigs were predominant, and which had changed with the change of fortune. James justly regarded these renegades as the most serviceable tools that he could employ. It was not from the stouthearted Cavaliers, who had been true to him in his adversity, that he could expect abject and unscrupulous obedience in his prosperity. The men who, impelled, not by zeal for liberty or for religion, but merely by selfish cupidity and selfish fear, had assisted to oppress him when he was weak, were the very men who, impelled by the same cupidity and the same fear, would assist him to oppress his people now that he was strong.[2] Though vindictive, he was not indiscriminately vindictive. Not a single instance can be mentioned in which he showed a generous compassion to those who had opposed him honestly and on public grounds. But he frequently spared and promoted those whom some vile motive had induced to injure him.

---

[1] Barillon, $\frac{\text{May 28.}}{\text{June 7.}}$ 1685. Observator, May 27. 1685 ; Sir J. Reresby's Memoirs.

[2] Lewis wrote to Barillon about this class of Exclusionists as follows : " L'intérêt qu'ils auront à effacer cette tâche par des services considérables les portera, selon toutes les apparences, à le servir plus utilement que ne pourroient faire ceux qui ont toujours été les plus attachés à sa personne." May $\frac{15}{25}$. 1685.

For that meanness which marked them out as fit implements of tyranny was so precious in his estimation that he regarded it with some indulgence even when it was exhibited at his own expense.

The King's wishes were communicated through several channels to the Tory members of the Lower House. The majority was easily persuaded to forego all thoughts of a penal law against the Exclusionists, and to consent that His Majesty should have the revenue for life. But about the Test Act and the Habeas Corpus Act the emissaries of the Court could obtain no satisfactory assurances.[1]

On the nineteenth of May the session was opened. The benches of the Commons presented a singular spectacle. That great party, **Meeting of the English Parliament** which, in the last three Parliaments, had been predominant, had now dwindled to a pitiable minority, and was indeed little more than a fifteenth part of the House. Of the five hundred and thirteen knights and burgesses only a hundred and thirty five had ever sate in that place before. It is evident that a body of men so raw and inexperienced must have been, in some important qualities, far below the average of our representative assemblies.[2]

The management of the House was confided by James to two peers of the kingdom of Scotland. One of them, Charles Middleton, Earl of Middleton, after holding high office at Edinburgh, had, shortly before the death of the late King, been sworn of the English Privy Council, and appointed one of the Secretaries of State. With him was joined Richard Graham, Viscount Preston, who had long held the post of Envoy at Versailles.

The first business of the Commons was to elect a Speaker. Who should be the man, was a question which had been much debated in the **Trevor chosen speaker** cabinet. Guildford had recommended Sir Thomas Meres, who, like himself, ranked among the Trimmers. Jeffreys, who missed no opportunity of crossing the Lord Keeper, had pressed the claims of Sir John Trevor. Trevor had been bred half a pettifogger and half a gambler, had brought to political life sentiments and principles worthy of both his callings, had become a parasite of the Chief Justice, and could, on occasion, imitate, not unsuccessfully, the vituperative style of his patron. The minion of Jeffreys was, as might have been expected, preferred by James, was proposed by Middleton, and was chosen without opposition.[3]

Thus far all went smoothly. But an adversary of no common prowess was watching his time. This was Edward Seymour of Berry Pomeroy Castle, member for the city of Exeter. Seymour's birth put

---

[1] Barillon, May $\frac{4}{14}$. 1685 ; Sir John Reresby's Memoirs.

[2] Burnet, i. 626 ; Evelyn's Diary, May 22. 1685.

[3] Roger North's Life of Guildford, 218. ; Bramston's Memoirs.

him on a level with the noblest subjects in Europe.   He was the right heir male of the body of that Duke of Somerset who had been brother in law of King Henry the Eighth, and Protector of the realm   Character of of England.   In the limitation of the dukedom of Somerset,   Seymour the elder son of the Protector had been postponed to the younger son. From the younger son the Dukes of Somerset were descended.   From the elder son was descended the family which dwelt at Berry Pomeroy. Seymour's fortune was large, and his influence in the west of England extensive.   Nor was the importance derived from descent and wealth the only importance which belonged to him.   He was one of the most skilful debaters and men of business in the kingdom.   He had sate many years in the House of Commons, had studied all its rules and usages, and thoroughly understood its peculiar temper.   He had been elected Speaker in the late reign under circumstances which made that distinction peculiarly honourable.   During several generations none but lawyers had been called to the chair ; and he was the first country gentleman whose abilities and acquirements enabled him to break that long prescription.   He had subsequently held high political office, and had sate in the cabinet.   But his haughty and unaccommodating temper had given so much disgust that he had been forced to retire.   He was a Tory and a Churchman : he had strenuously opposed the Exclusion Bill : he had been persecuted by the Whigs in the day of their prosperity ; and he could therefore safely venture to hold language for which any person suspected of republicanism would have been sent to the Tower.   He had long been at the head of a strong parliamentary connection, which was called the Western Alliance, and which included many gentlemen of Devonshire, Somersetshire, and Cornwall.[1]

In every House of Commons, a member who unites eloquence, knowledge, and habits of business, to opulence and illustrious descent, must be highly considered.   But in a House of Commons from which many of the most eminent orators and parliamentary tacticians of the age were excluded, and which was crowded with people who had never heard a debate, the influence of such a man was peculiarly formidable. Weight of moral character was indeed wanting to Edward Seymour. He was licentious, profane, corrupt, too proud to behave with common politeness, yet not too proud to pocket illicit gain.   But he was so useful an ally, and so mischievous an enemy, that he was frequently courted even by those who most detested him.[2]

He was now in bad humour with the government.   His interest had been weakened in some places by the remodelling of the western

[1] North's Life of Guildford, 228. ; News from Westminster.

[2] Burnet, i. 382. ; Letter from Lord Conway to Sir George Rawdon, Dec. 28. 1677, in the Rawdon Papers.

boroughs : his pride had been wounded by the elevation of Trevor to the chair ; and he took an early opportunity of revenging himself.

On the twenty-second of May the Commons were summoned to the bar of the Lords ; and the King, seated on his throne, made a **The King's** speech to both Houses. He declared himself resolved to **speech to the Parlia-** maintain the established government in Church and State. **ment** But he weakened the effect of this declaration by addressing an extraordinary admonition to the Commons. He was apprehensive, he said, that they might be inclined to dole out money to him, from time to time, in the hope that they should thus force him to call them frequently together. But he must warn them that he was not to be so dealt with, and that, if they wished him to meet them often, they must use him well. As it was evident that without money the government could not be carried on, these expressions plainly implied that, if they did not give him as much money as he wished, he would take it. Strange to say, this harangue was received with loud cheers by the Tory gentlemen at the bar. Such acclamations were then usual. It has now been, during many years, the grave and decorous usage of Parliaments to hear, in respectful silence, all expressions, acceptable or unacceptable, which are uttered from the throne.[1]

It was then the custom that, after the King had concisely explained his reasons for calling Parliament together, the minister who held the Great Seal should, at more length, explain to the Houses the state of public affairs. Guildford, in imitation of his predecessors, Clarendon, Bridgeman, Shaftesbury, and Nottingham, had prepared an elaborate oration, but found, to his great mortification, that his services were not wanted.[2]

Debate in the Com- As soon as the Commons had returned to their own **mons** chamber, it was proposed that they should resolve themselves into a Committee, for the purpose of settling a revenue on the King.

Then Seymour stood up. How he stood, looking like what he was, the chief of a dissolute and high spirited gentry, with the artificial ring- **Speech of** lets clustering in fashionable profusion round his shoulders, **Seymour** and a mingled expression of voluptuousness and disdain in his eye and on his lip, the likenesses of him which still remain enable us to imagine. It was not, the haughty Cavalier said, his wish that the Parliament should withhold from the Crown the means of carrying on the government. But was there indeed a Parliament ? Were there not on the benches many men who had, as all the world knew, no right to sit there, many men whose elections were tainted by corruption, many

[1] London Gazette, May 25. 1685 ; Evelyn's Diary, May 22. 1685.
[2] North's Life of Guildford, 256.

SIR EDWARD SEYMOUR'S MONUMENT IN THE CHURCH OF MAIDEN BRADLEY

From a drawing in the Sutherland Collection

men forced by intimidation on reluctant voters, and many men returned by corporations which had no legal existence? Had not constituent bodies been remodelled, in defiance of royal charters and of immemorial prescription? Had not returning officers been everywhere the unscrupulous agents of the Court? Seeing that the very principle of representation had been thus systematically attacked, he knew not how to call the throng of gentlemen which he saw around him by the honourable name of a House of Commons. Yet never was there a time when it more concerned the public weal that the character of Parliament should stand high. Great dangers impended over the ecclesiastical and civil constitution of the realm. It was matter of vulgar notoriety, it was matter which required no proof, that the Test Act, the rampart of religion, and the Habeas Corpus Act, the rampart of liberty, were marked out for destruction. " Before we proceed to legislate on questions so momentous, let us at least ascertain whether we really are a legislature. Let our first proceeding be to enquire into the manner in which the elections have been conducted. And let us look to it that the enquiry be impartial. For, if the nation shall find that no redress is to be obtained by peaceful methods, we may perhaps ere long suffer the justice which we refuse to do." He concluded by moving that, before any supply was granted, the House would take into consideration petitions against returns, and that no member whose right to sit was disputed should be allowed to vote.

Not a cheer was heard. Not a member ventured to second the motion. Indeed, Seymour had said much that no other man could have said with impunity. The proposition fell to the ground, and was not even entered on the journals. But a mighty effect had been produced. Barillon informed his master that many who had not dared to applaud that remarkable speech had cordially approved of it, that it was the universal subject of conversation throughout London, and that the impression made on the public mind seemed likely to be durable.[1]

The Revenue voted   The Commons went into committee without delay, and voted to the King, for life, the whole revenue enjoyed by his brother.[2]

The zealous churchmen who formed the majority of the House seem to have been of opinion that the promptitude with which they had met the wish of James, touching the revenue, entitled them to expect some concession on his part. They said that much had been done to gratify him, and that they must now do something to gratify the nation.

---

[1] Burnet, i. 639. ; Evelyn's Diary, May 22. 1685 ; Barillon, $\frac{May\ 23}{June\ 2.}$ and $\frac{May\ 25.}{June\ 4.}$ 1685. The silence of the journals perplexed Mr. Fox : but it is explained by the circumstance that Seymour's motion was not seconded.

[2] Journals, May 22. Stat. Jac. II. i. 1.

The House, therefore, resolved itself into a Grand Committee of Religion, in order to consider the best means of providing for the security of the ecclesiastical establishment. In that Committee two resolutions were unanimously adopted. The first expressed fervent attachment to the Church of England. The second called on the King to put in execution the penal laws against all persons who were not members of that Church.[1]

Proceedings of the Commons concerning religion

The Whigs would doubtless have wished to see the Protestant dissenters tolerated, and the Roman Catholics alone persecuted. But the Whigs were a small and a disheartened minority. They therefore kept themselves as much as possible out of sight, dropped their party name, abstained from obtruding their peculiar opinions on a hostile audience, and steadily supported every proposition tending to disturb the harmony which as yet subsisted between the Parliament and the Court.

When the proceedings of the Committee of Religion were known at Whitehall, the King's anger was great. Nor can we justly blame him for resenting the conduct of the Tories. If they were disposed to require the rigorous execution of the penal code, they clearly ought to have supported the Exclusion Bill. For to place a Papist on the throne, and then to insist on his persecuting to the death the teachers of that faith in which alone, on his principles, salvation could be found, was monstrous. In mitigating by a lenient administration the severity of the bloody laws of Elizabeth, the King violated no constitutional principle. He only exerted a power which has always belonged to the crown. Nay, he only did what was afterwards done by a succession of sovereigns zealous for Protestantism, by William, by Anne, and by the princes of the House of Brunswick. Had he suffered Roman Catholic priests, whose lives he could save without infringing any law, to be hanged, drawn, and quartered, for discharging what he considered as their first duty, he would have drawn on himself the hatred and contempt even of those to whose prejudices he had made so shameful a concession; and, had he contented himself with granting to the members of his own Church a practical toleration by a large exercise of his unquestioned prerogative of mercy, posterity would have unanimously applauded him.

The Commons probably felt on reflection that they had acted absurdly. They were also disturbed by learning that the King, to whom they looked up with superstitious reverence, was greatly provoked. They made haste, therefore, to atone for their offence. In the House, they unanimously reversed the decision which, in the Committee, they had unanimously adopted, and passed a resolution importing that they

[1] Journals, May 26, 27. Sir J. Reresby's Memoirs.

relied with entire confidence on His Majesty's gracious promise to protect that religion which was dearer to them than life itself.[1]

Three days later the King informed the House that his brother had left some debts, and that the stores of the navy and ordnance were **Additional taxes voted** nearly exhausted. It was promptly resolved that new taxes should be imposed. The person on whom devolved the task of devising ways and means was Sir Dudley North, younger brother of the Lord Keeper. Dudley North was one of the ablest men of his **Sir Dudley North** time. He had early in life been sent to the Levant, and had there been long engaged in mercantile pursuits. Most men would, in such a situation, have allowed their faculties to rust. For at Smyrna and Constantinople there were few books and few intelligent companions. But the young factor had one of those vigorous understandings which are independent of external aids. In his solitude he meditated deeply on the philosophy of trade, and thought out by degrees a complete and admirable theory, substantially the same with that which, a century later, was expounded by Adam Smith. After an exile of many years, Dudley North returned to England with a large fortune, and commenced business as a Turkey merchant in the City of London. His profound knowledge, both speculative and practical, of commercial matters, and the perspicuity and liveliness with which he explained his views, speedily introduced him to the notice of statesmen. The government found in him at once an enlightened adviser and an unscrupulous slave. For with his rare mental endowments were joined lax principles and an unfeeling heart. When the Tory reaction was in full progress, he had consented to be made Sheriff for the express purpose of assisting the vengeance of the court. His juries had never failed to find verdicts of Guilty; and, on a day of judicial butchery, carts, loaded with the legs and arms of quartered Whigs, were, to the great discomposure of his lady, driven to his fine house in Basinghall Street for orders. His services had been rewarded with the honour of knighthood, with an Alderman's gown, and with the office of Commissioner of the Customs. He had been brought into Parliament for Banbury, and, though a new member, was the person on whom the Lord Treasurer chiefly relied for the conduct of financial business in the Lower House.[2]

Though the Commons were unanimous in their resolution to grant a further supply to the crown, they were by no means agreed as to the sources from which that supply should be drawn. It was speedily determined that part of the sum which was required should be raised

[1] Commons' Journals, May 27. 1685.

[2] Roger North's Life of Sir Dudley North ; Life of Lord Guildford, 166.; Mr. M'Culloch's Literature of Political Economy.

The Honble Sr DUDLEY NORTH K.^t
Commissioner of the Treasury
to King Charles the Second.

G. Vertue Sculp 1743.

SIR DUDLEY NORTH

From an engraving by Vertue in Roger North's Life of his brother by laying an additional impost, for a term of eight years, on wine and vinegar : but something more than this was needed. Several absurd schemes were suggested. Many country gentlemen were disposed to put a heavy tax on all new buildings in the capital. Such a tax, it was hoped, would check the growth of a city which had long been regarded with jealousy and aversion by the rural aristocracy. Dudley North's plan was that additional duties should be imposed, for a term of eight years, on sugar and tobacco. A great clamour was raised. Colonial merchants, grocers, sugar bakers and tobacconists, petitioned the House and besieged the public offices. The people of Bristol, who were deeply interested in the trade with Virginia and Jamaica, sent up a deputation which was heard at the bar of the Commons. Rochester was for a moment staggered ; but North's ready wit and perfect knowledge of trade prevailed, both in the Treasury and in the Parliament, against all opposition. The old members were amazed at seeing a man who had not been a fortnight in the House, and whose life had been chiefly passed in foreign countries, assume with confidence, and discharge with ability, all the functions of a Chancellor of the Exchequer.[1]

His plan was adopted ; and thus the Crown was in possession of a clear income of about nineteen hundred thousand pounds, derived from England alone. Such an income was then more than sufficient for the support of the government in time of peace.[2]

The Lords had, in the meantime, discussed several important questions. The Tory party had always been strong among the peers. Proceedings of the Lords It included the whole bench of Bishops, and had been reinforced, during the four years which had elapsed since the last dissolution, by several fresh creations. Of the new nobles, the most conspicuous were the Lord Treasurer Rochester, the Lord Keeper Guildford, the Lord Chief Justice Jeffreys, the Lord Godolphin, and the Lord Churchill, who, after his return from Versailles, had been made a baron of England.

The peers early took into consideration the case of four members of their body who had been impeached in the late reign, but had never been brought to trial, and had, after a long confinement, been admitted to bail by the Court of King's Bench. Three of the noblemen who were thus under recognisances were Roman Catholics. The fourth was a Protestant of great note and influence, the Earl of Danby. Since he had fallen from power and had been accused of treason by the Commons, four Parliaments had been dissolved ; but he had been neither acquitted nor condemned. In 1679 the Lords had considered, with reference to his situation, the question whether an impeachment was or was not

---

[1] Life of Dudley North, 176. ; Lonsdale's Memoirs ; Van Citters, June $\frac{12}{22}$. 1685.
[2] Commons' Journals, March 1. 1689.

terminated by a dissolution. They had resolved, after long debate and full examination of precedents, that the impeachment was still pending. That resolution they now rescinded. A few Whig nobles protested against this step, but to little purpose. The Commons silently acquiesced in the decision of the Upper House. Danby again took his seat among his peers, and became an active and powerful member of the Tory party.[1]

The constitutional question on which the Lords thus, in the short space of six years, pronounced two diametrically opposite decisions, slept during more than a century, and was at length revived by the dissolution which took place during the long trial of Warren Hastings. It was then necessary to determine whether the rule laid down in 1679, or the opposite rule laid down in 1685, was to be accounted the law of the land. The point was long debated in both Houses ; and the best legal and parliamentary abilities which an age preeminently fertile both in legal and in parliamentary ability could supply were employed in the discussion. The lawyers were not unequally divided. Thurlow, Kenyon, Scott, and Erskine maintained that the dissolution had put an end to the impeachment. The contrary doctrine was held by Mansfield, Camden, Loughborough, and Grant. But among those statesmen who grounded their arguments, not on precedents and technical analogies, but on deep and broad constitutional principles, there was little difference of opinion. Pitt and Grenville, as well as Burke and Fox, held that the impeachment was still pending. Both Houses by great majorities set aside the decision of 1685, and pronounced the decision of 1679 to be in conformity with the law of Parliament.

Of the national crimes which had been committed during the panic excited by the fictions of Oates, the most signal had been the judicial murder of Stafford. The sentence of that unhappy nobleman **Bill for re-** was now regarded by all impartial persons as unjust. The **versing the** **attainder of** principal witness for the prosecution had been convicted of a **Stafford** series of foul perjuries. It was the duty of the legislature, in such circumstances, to do justice to the memory of a guiltless sufferer, and to efface an unmerited stain from a name long illustrious in our annals. A bill for reversing the attainder of Stafford was passed by the Upper House, in spite of the murmurs of a few peers who were unwilling to admit that they had shed innocent blood. The Commons read the bill twice without a division, and ordered it to be committed. But, on the day appointed for the committee, arrived news that a formidable rebellion had broken out in the West of England. It was consequently necessary to postpone much important business. The amends due to the memory of Stafford were deferred, as was supposed, only for a short time. But

[1] Lords' Journals, March 18, 19. 1679, May 22. 1685.

the misgovernment of James in a few months completely turned the tide of public feeling. During several generations the Roman Catholics were in no condition to demand reparation for injustice, and accounted themselves happy if they were permitted to live unmolested in obscurity and silence. At length, in the reign of King George the Fourth, more than a hundred and forty years after the day on which the blood of Stafford was shed on Tower Hill, the tardy expiation was accomplished. A law annulling the attainder and restoring the injured family to its ancient dignities was presented to Parliament by the ministers of the crown, was eagerly welcomed by public men of all parties, and was passed without one dissentient voice.[1]

It is now necessary that I should trace the origin and progress of that rebellion by which the deliberations of the Houses were suddenly interrupted.

[1] Stat. 5 Geo. IV. c. 46.

END OF VOLUME I

GLASGOW: PRINTED AT THE UNIVERSITY PRESS BY ROBERT MACLEHOSE AND CO. LTD.